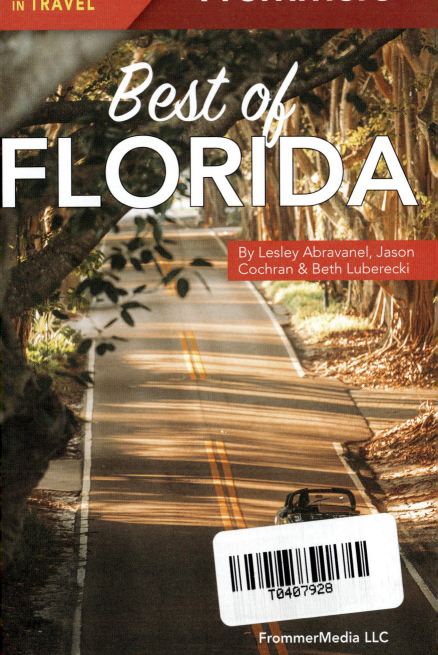

Frommer's®

THE MOST TRUSTED NAME IN TRAVEL

Best of FLORIDA

By Lesley Abravanel, Jason Cochran & Beth Luberecki

FrommerMedia LLC

Frommer's Best of Florida, 1st Edition

Published by:
Frommer Media LLC

Copyright © 2025 by Frommer Media LLC. All rights reserved. No part of this publication may be reproduced, stored in a retrieval system, or transmitted in any form or by any means, electronic, mechanical, photocopying, recording, scanning or otherwise, except as permitted under Sections 107 or 108 of the 1976 United States Copyright Act, without the prior written permission of the Publisher. Requests to the Publisher for permission should be addressed to the support@frommermedia.com.

Frommer's is a registered trademark of Arthur Frommer. Frommer Media LLC is not associated with any product or vendor mentioned in this book.

ISBN 978-1-62887-627-7 (paper), 978-1-62887-628-4 (e-book)

Editorial Director: Pauline Frommer
Editor: Pauline Frommer
Production Editor: Cheryl Lenser
Cartographer: Andrew Dolan

Photo Editor: Liza Schoenfein
Indexer: Cheryl Lenser
Compositor: Lissa Auciello-Brogan
Cover Design: Dave Riedy

Front cover: White sand beach.
Title page: Martin Grade Scenic Highway.

For information on our other products or services, see www.frommers.com.

Frommer Media LLC also publishes its books in a variety of electronic formats. Some content that appears in print may not be available in electronic formats.

Manufactured in Malaysia

5 4 3 2 1

HOW TO CONTACT US

In researching this book, we discovered many wonderful places—hotels, restaurants, shops, and more. We're sure you'll find others. Please tell us about them, so we can share the information with your fellow travelers in upcoming editions. If you were disappointed with a recommendation, we'd love to know that, too. Please write to: Support@FrommerMedia.com

FROMMER'S STAR RATINGS SYSTEM

Every hotel, restaurant and attraction listed in this guide has been ranked for quality and value. Here's what the stars mean:

★ Recommended
★★ Highly Recommended
★★★ A must! Don't miss!

AN IMPORTANT NOTE

The world is a dynamic place. Hotels change ownership, restaurants hike their prices, museums alter their opening hours, and buses and trains change their routings. And all of this can occur in the several months after our authors have visited, inspected, and written about these hotels, restaurants, museums, and transportation services. Though we have made valiant efforts to keep all our information fresh and up-to-date, some few changes can inevitably occur in the periods before a revised edition of this guidebook is published. So please bear with us if a tiny number of the details in this book have changed. Please also note that we have no responsibility or liability for any inaccuracy or errors or omissions, or for inconvenience, loss, damage, or expenses suffered by anyone as a result of assertions in this guide.

CONTENTS

LIST OF MAPS v

1 THE BEST OF FLORIDA 1

2 FLORIDA IN DEPTH 15
Florida Today 16
Florida History 17
Florida in Pop Culture 22
When to Go 24
Calendar of Events 25
Responsible Travel 27
Special-Interest Trips 28

3 SUGGESTED FLORIDA ITINERARIES 34
South Florida in 2 Weeks 35
A Week in Historic Northern Florida 42
Orlando's Theme Parks in 1, 2 & 3 Days 43
A Week in South Florida, Family-Style 46
The Regions in Brief 48

4 MIAMI ESSENTIALS 51
Orientation 52
Getting Around 58
Fast Facts: Miami 61
Where to Stay in Miami 62
Where to Eat in Miami 79

5 EXPLORING MIAMI 110
Miami's Beaches 111
South Beach: Art Deco District 114
North Miami 121
Key Biscayne 122
Downtown 123
Midtown Miami 125
Coral Gables 126
Coconut Grove 128
Wynwood 129
South Miami-Dade County 130
Homestead 132
Organized Tours 133
Watersports 135
More Ways to Play, Indoors & Out 137
Spectator Sports 140
Shopping 141
Miami After Dark 144

6 THE KEYS & THE DRY TORTUGAS 154
The Upper & Middle Keys 158
The Lower Keys 178
Key West 185
The Dry Tortugas 212

7 THE EVERGLADES & BISCAYNE NATIONAL PARK 215
Everglades National Park 216
Biscayne National Park 230

8 THE GOLD COAST: HALLANDALE TO THE PALM BEACHES 234
Fort Lauderdale 237
Boca Raton & Delray Beach 260
Palm Beach & West Palm Beach 275

9 THE TAMPA BAY AREA 295
Tampa 296
St. Petersburg 319
St. Pete & Clearwater Beaches 330
Sarasota 342

10 WALT DISNEY WORLD, UNIVERSAL & ORLANDO 359

Essentials 360

Getting Around 364

Fast Facts: Walt Disney World & Orlando 366

Exploring Walt Disney World 367

Magic Kingdom 370

EPCOT 375

Disney's Hollywood Studios 379

Disney's Animal Kingdom 382

Other WDW Attractions 385

Beyond Disney: Universal Orlando & SeaWorld 386

Worthy Area Attractions 396

Where to Stay 398

Where to Dine 414

11 NORTHEAST FLORIDA 427

The Space Coast 428

Daytona Beach 439

St. Augustine: America's First City 454

Jacksonville 476

Amelia Island 490

12 PLANNING YOUR TRIP TO FLORIDA 501

Getting There 502

Getting Around 504

Tips on Accommodations 505

Fast Facts: Florida 506

INDEX 510

LIST OF MAPS

Florida 4
Suggested Florida Itineraries 37
South Beach Hotels & Restaurants 65
Miami Area Hotels & Restaurants 71
Downtown Miami, Midtown, Wynwood & Little Havana 73
Coral Gables & Coconut Grove 77
South Beach Attractions & Entertainment 113
Miami Attractions & Entertainment 115
The Florida Keys 156
Key West 186
The Everglades 217
The Gold Coast 236
Fort Lauderdale, Hollywood & Pompano Beach 239

Boca Raton & Delray Beach 261
Palm Beach & West Palm Beach 277
Tampa Bay Area 299
Downtown Tampa, Hyde Park & Ybor City 301
Busch Gardens Area, St. Petersburg & the Beaches 308
Sarasota 343
Orlando Area 361
Northeast Florida 429
Daytona Beach 441
St. Augustine 456
Jacksonville 479
Amelia Island 493

ABOUT THE AUTHORS

New York raised and Florida bronzed, **Lesley Abravanel** has covered the amusingly vapid celeb scene in South Florida for the *Miami Herald* and several illustrious supermarket mags since the Kardashians were fetuses. She has also chronicled the evolution of Florida's culinary scene, nightlife, celebrity culture, suburbia, and travel for such outlets as Miami.com, *Maxim, The Forward*, TripAdvisor, and the *Daily Mail* for, gasp, nearly 3 decades. In addition to penning several Frommer's books on Florida, she is also the author of the not-so-cheekily titled *Florida for Dummies*. On the sly, she is a ghostwriter for various organizations, personalities, and businesses. When she's not writing, she collects hot sauces, raises twin teens, and attempts to learn Swedish from her Stockholm-born husband. You can find her at @lesleyabravanel on various social media channels, where she has no qualms speaking her mind on everything from reality television to (mostly) politics.

Jason Cochran is also the author of *Frommer's London, Frommer's Disney World, Universal & Orlando*, and *Here Lies America*. He was twice awarded Guide Book of the Year by the Lowell Thomas Awards (Society of American Travel Writers) and once by the North American Travel Journalists Association for his books on London and Orlando. His voice has reached millions of travelers, from the mid-'90s, when as a long-term backpacker he wrote one of the world's first travel blogs, to his long-running WABC radio show co-hosted with Pauline Frommer, to appearances as a commentator on CBS and for AOL, and to his work at Frommers.com, which under his editorship won Silver for Travel Journalism Website in the 2021 Lowell Thomas Awards.

Beth Luberecki is a Florida-based freelance writer who writes about travel, business, and lifestyle topics for a variety of regional and national publications and websites. A resident of Florida's Gulf Coast for 2 decades, she serves as a senior editor for FamilyVacationist.com, and her travel writing has appeared in publications and on websites including *USA Today*, Forbes Vetted, TourScoop.com, *Times of the Islands*, and SmarterTravel.com. Learn more about her at BethLuberecki.com or find her on Instagram at @bethlubereckiwrites.

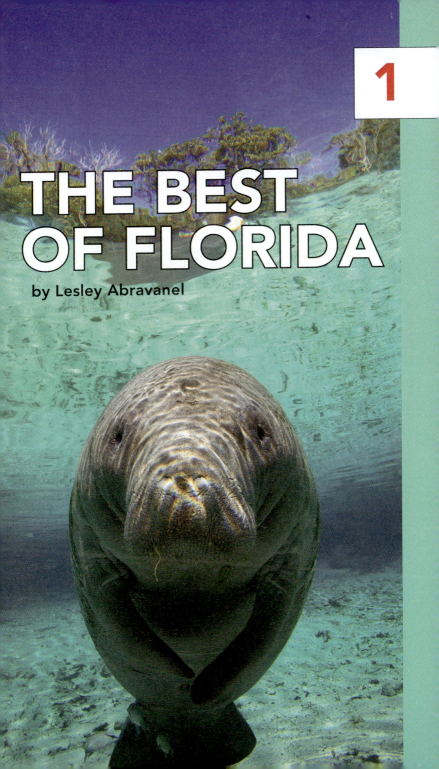

THE BEST OF FLORIDA

by Lesley Abravanel

1

1

Florida has everything: sun, fun, nature, history, heat, humidity, Mickey, Minnie, and even its own hashtag: #BecauseFlorida. Hey, it's the only state in the country that borders both the Atlantic Ocean *and* the Gulf of Mexico. But the best of Florida is what *you* make of it. For some, it's theme parks, for others, it's getting out into nature, for still others it's art fairs and museums, golf courses, fishing trips, space travel, and historic cities. And for many (most?) it's just bumming on a beach doing absolutely nothing.

Yes, Florida is so much more than animatronic rodents and sunshine. And America's third largest state is in the throes of so many cultural, economic, and environmental changes it makes puberty and menopause look like a day on a pre-eroded beach. Not all changes are bad, but not all are great either. What's unchanged, however, is the landscape, a peninsula with the third-largest water area of any state. Sure, scientists are bracing for too much water in Florida's future, but for now, it's a tropical fever dream, infused like a masterful cocktail with a dash of urban, suburban, and Southern flair. Here, you can visit fishing towns still steeped in old Florida culture, or walk along miles of golden-sand beaches. Acres of citrus groves still can be found in the center of the state, and Alligator Alley crosses southern Florida with its landscape of sawgrass, cypress, gumbo-limbo trees and the slow-moving river that is the Everglades.

The cities are unique entities, too. St. Augustine, the oldest city in the U.S., is a well-preserved look back at history from roughly the 17th century to today. Orlando draws families with its theme parks. Tampa Bay is booming, and at Florida's southern tip, Miami has morphed into a billionaire's playground, and year-round destination for celebrity sightings, and yes, a few remnants of Miami days of yore.

The selections in this chapter are just some of the highlights of the highlights of the state. With an open mind and a sense of adventure, you'll come up with your own "bests."

THE best AUTHENTIC TRAVEL EXPERIENCES

- **Swimming with the Manatees** (Crystal River, north of Clearwater): Some 360 manatees spend the winter in the Crystal River, and you can swim, snorkel, or scuba with them in the natural springs of Kings Bay, about 7 miles north of Homosassa Springs. It's not uncommon to be surrounded in the 72°F (22°C) water by 30 to 40 "sea cows" that nudge and caress you as you swim with them. See p. 325.
- **People-Watching in Miami's Wynwood Arts District and on Palm Beach's Worth Avenue** (Miami and Palm Beach): In Miami's booming arts district, colorful locals and luminaries walk amidst Insta-worthy backdrops of street art as if every day were the Easter parade. In Palm Beach, titled

PREVIOUS PAGE: **A manatee at Crystal River Hot Springs.**

nobility, bejeweled socialites, and an assortment of upper-crusters put on the Ritz along the city's version of Rodeo Drive. See p. 129 and p. 283.

o **Alabama Jack's** (Key Largo): En route to the Keys, veer off onto Card Sound Road, once the only way to get down there, and follow the Harley-Davidsons to Alabama Jack's. A waterfront biker bar, restaurant, and live-music joint on two barges, Alabama Jack's is the place to be for country line dancers, especially on Sundays, when many show up in full *Hee Haw* regalia. See p. 158.

o **Learning to Surf the Big Curls at Ron Jon Surf School** (Cocoa Beach): Even if you don't know how to hang ten, this school will get you riding the waves with the best of them. It provides equipment and lessons for all skill levels—beginner to pro—at the best surf beaches in Florida. See p. 437.

Art is a part of daily life in Miami's Wynwood neighborhood.

THE best **BEACHES**

o **Siesta Key Beach** (Siesta Key, Sarasota): A public beach with 8 magnificent miles of fine white, quartz-crystal sand, Siesta Key is not just a former MTV reality show. It's just ¾ mile long but has a huge reputation as one of the state's—and country's—best spots for sand and surf. See p. 344.

o **Bill Baggs Cape Florida State Park** (Key Biscayne): A mile-long undeveloped beach on the southern tip of Key Biscayne is an ultra-secluded, picturesque beach with biking and walking trails, where people purposely go to not be found. For those craving a jolt of city, Bill Baggs reminds you that you're not alone with stellar city skyline views, too. See p. 122.

o **Lummus Park** (South Beach): This beach, between 5th and 15th streets, buttressed by walking and biking paths along Art Deco landmark Ocean Drive, is world renowned, and better known as **South Beach.** Here seeing, being seen, and partying, goes hand in hand with sunscreen and beach towels. The 12th Street section is the beach of choice for LGBTQ+ residents and travelers. See p. 111.

o **Bahia Honda State Park** (Bahia Honda Key): This is one of the nicest and most peaceful beaches in Florida. It's located off the Overseas Highway amid 524 acres of nature trails and a portion of Henry Flagler's railroad, a fascinating remnant of how the Gilded Age headed south for the winter. See p. 179.

o **Dr. Von D. Mizell-Eula Johnson State Park** (Dania Beach): Named for Civil Rights Movement leaders who led "wade-in" protests to desegregate South Florida beaches in the 1950s and '60s, this beach, the last of Broward County's undeveloped coastal ecosystems, remains free of high-rises, T-shirt shops, and hotels, with an untouched shoreline surrounded by a canopy of Australian pine. See p. 242.

THE BEST OF FLORIDA

The Best Offbeat Travel Experiences

Beachgoers stroll barefoot on the white sands of Caladesi Island State Park.

- **Caladesi Island State Park** (Dunedin/Clearwater Beach): Even though 3½-mile-long Caladesi Island is in the Tampa Bay area, it has a relatively secluded beach with soft white sand edged in seagrass and palmettos. In the park, there's a nature trail where you might see one of the black racers, raccoons, armadillos, or rabbits that live here. The park is accessible only by ferry from Honeymoon Island State Recreation Area, off Dunedin. See p. 332.

- **Fort DeSoto Park** (St. Petersburg): Where else can you get a good tan *and* a history lesson? At Fort DeSoto Park, established circa the Spanish-American War, you have not only 1,136 acres of five interconnected islands and 3 miles of beaches, but also a fort that's listed on the National Register of Historic Places. There are also nature trails, fishing piers, a 2.25-mile canoe trail, a leash-free dog beach, snack bar, and spectacular views of Tampa Bay and the Gulf. See p. 333.

THE best OFFBEAT TRAVEL EXPERIENCES

- **Toilet Seat Cut:** Once upon a time, a man named Vernon Lamp so loved going to a now-defunct yacht club near Tavernier in the Florida Keys he decided to dredge a shortcut to get there faster. When a hurricane blew through the area in 1960, a lone toilet seat was hanging on a marker. People found it so amusing, they kept adding toilet seats along the shortcut. They're still there and we're not sh*tting you. It's a must see (by boat) and so very Florida.

- **Underwater Stay at Jules Undersea Lodge** (Key Largo): We give this a vote as one of Florida's most romantic retreats, but this underwater hotel is also, hands down, the most unusual. Where else can you have a pizza delivered via scuba diver? See p. 170.

Dancers from Bahama Village during a Key West Fantasy Fest parade.

- **Fantasy Fest** (Key West): Mardi Gras takes a Floridian vacation as the streets of Key West are overtaken by wildly costumed revelers who have no shame and no parental guidance. This weeklong, hedonistic, X-rated Halloween party is *not* for children 17 and under. See p. 26.
- **Columbus Day Regatta** (Biscayne Bay): This unique observation of Columbus Day revolves around a so-called regatta in Biscayne Bay but always ends with participants stripping down to their bare, ahem, necessities and partying at the sandbar in the middle of the bay. There is a boat race at some point of the day, but most people are too preoccupied to notice.
- **See Who's on the Other Side in Cassadaga** (near Daytona): Billing itself as the Psychic Capital of the World, this 115-year-old spiritualist camp composed of psychic mediums, healers, and metaphysical mavens is as offbeat as it comes. See p. 452.

THE most overrated FLORIDA EXPERIENCES

- **Shell Shops:** Global warming has led to beach erosion, which has led to the disappearance of the shells many people love to collect. So many visitors are turning to the ubiquitous shell shops in seaside towns but it's important to know: Their seashells usually are imported, and have less to do with Florida's beaches than snow. You want shells? Head to Venice Beach an hour north of shell-haven Sanibel Island, which is known as the Shark Tooth Capital of the World. You find it, you keep it.
- **Alligator Farms:** You'll see them advertised all over the roads down here—even gas stations will promise you can pet a baby alligator. Just don't.

These "attractions" are cheesy, overpriced, and dangerous—not necessarily for you, but for the animals. You want to see scores of alligators in their own habitat instead of at the Exxon? Head to the Everglades instead. Not feeling so adventurous? Google "Florida Man" to really see what goes on in the wild. See p. 216.

An alligator is baited with raw chicken.

o **South Beach:** Yup, you read right. What was once the crown jewel of the South Florida scene, the Kim Kardashian to her other siblings, is now passe. It's overdeveloped with zillion-dollar condos, full of overpriced, mediocre restaurants and shops. Yes, there are decent beaches, but meh. All that action, glitz and glam has done what was once unheard of: crossed the causeway to the mainland. See p. 114.

o **Florida Orange Juice:** Yes, it's good for you, yes it's delicious, but that free glass of juice they're offering you at those tourist-trappy rest stops and whatnot is probably not even from Florida. A citrus greening disease has caused a nearly 80% drop in Florida's citrus production since 2005. Scientists are working on that with citrus breeding, but for now you can pass on the free juice.

o **Weeki Wachee Springs State Park:** It may have been a titillating attraction back in 1947, but today the "City of Live Mermaids" feels like the colorization of a black-and-white movie gone wrong. It's cheesy but not in a kitschy, fun, old Florida way. Save your money and watch a Disney flick instead. See p. 324.

o **Swimming with Dolphins:** Dolphins are wild animals. They do not enjoy swimming with humans, and they need a larger area to roam than most parks can provide. An exception is the Dolphin Research Center (p. 162) where dolphins are rehabbed, and the only ones visitors swim with are those that cannot be released into the wild for medical reasons.

THE best FAMILY ATTRACTIONS

o **Walt Disney World and Universal Orlando** (Orlando): Central Florida was expressly built to cater to family vacations. Magic Kingdom alone is the single-most popular family theme park on the planet, attracting 17 million visits a year. When kids get old enough for more intense thrills, they can graduate to the aggressive steel coasters and movie monsters at Universal Orlando, which, as of 2025, operates three full theme parks of its own. Orlando is simply a family memory-making mecca. See chapter 10.

o **Kennedy Space Center Visitor Complex** (Cape Canaveral): As the space race between bored billionaires heats up, the Kennedy Space Center keeps things a bit more grounded with its exceptional exhibitions dedicated to the astronomically brilliant people and innovations that got us off this planet in the first place. See p. 431.

- **Miami Children's Museum** (Miami): This museum takes children's imaginations for a ride. Dozens of other interactive exhibits are related to arts, culture, community, and communication. See p. 120.
- **Seagrass Adventure** (Miami): This is not your typical nature tour. With Seagrass Adventure, you will wade into the water on Key Biscayne with your guide and catch (and release) an assortment of sea life in the provided nets. See p. 123.
- **Busch Gardens Tampa Bay** (Tampa): Although the thrill rides, live entertainment, shops, restaurants, and games get most of the ink at this 335-acre family theme park, Busch Gardens also ranks among the top zoos in the country, with several thousand animals living in naturalistic environments. Seasonal water park Adventure Island is ideal during the oppressively hot summer months. See p. 298.
- **Frost Science** (Miami): A high-tech highlight of downtown Miami's waterfront Maurice A. Ferré Park, Frost Science is divided into four buildings: the

Kennedy Space Center, Cape Canaveral.

The breathtaking aquarium at Frost Science.

Frost Planetarium, Aquarium, and North and West wings where a multitude of hands-on exhibits captivate the curious with the core science behind living systems, the solar system and known universe, the physics of flight, light and lasers, and the biology of the human body and mind. See p. 123.

- **MOSI (Museum of Science and Industry)** (Tampa): MOSI aptly calls itself a scientific playground. It has over 100 hands-on activities including a life-size game of Operation, a 90-foot "Dinovations Lab: a Jurassic Themed Exhibit," an Ideazone in which you can build your own robot, plus a ropes course, planetarium, and virtual reality simulator not for the faint of vertigo. See p. 304.

- **The Ringling Circus Museum** (Sarasota): Kids will go for the circus memorabilia here (the museum features everything from parade wagons and calliopes to costumes and colorful posters), adults will want to stick around even longer to tour the entire **John and Mable Ringling Museum of Art,** which has one of the finest and most varied art collections in the United States. See p. 348.

- **Daytona International Speedway** (Daytona Beach): Behind-the-scenes tours take speed fans into the garages, the drivers' meeting room, the press box, and even Victory Lane. Or experience a 200-mph ride on a simulator at **The NASCAR Racing Experience.** See p. 442.

THE best MUSEUMS

- **Miami's Contemporary Art Museums** (Miami): It wasn't by chance that the most important art fair on the planet, Art Basel, decided to make Miami its first non-European satellite fair in 2002. The city has long been passionate about art. Today, it's an international contemporary and street art hub, thanks to its largely new, extraordinarily rich collection of cutting edge institutions: **The Bass Museum of Art** (p. 117), **Museum of Contemporary Art** (MOCA, p. 122), **Patricia and Phillip Frost Art Museum** (p. 130), **Pérez Art Museum Miami** (p. 125), **Rubell Museum** (p. 125), **Superblue Miami** (p. 129), and **Wynwood Walls** (p. 130).

- **The Wolfsonian** (Miami): How does design both mirror and shape reality? That's the provocative question asked by the Wolfsonian and it's a heckuva lot of fun traipsing through its wildly varied exhibits in search of an answer. See p. 120.

- **The Dalí** (St. Petersburg): Arguably the most important museum dedicated to artist Salvador Dalí (it has such masterworks as *Eggs on the Plate without the Plate* and *The Hallucinogenic Toreador*), this geodesic dome–topped museum has architecture as surreal as its holdings. See p. 321.

- **John and Mable Ringling Museum of Art** (Sarasota): As you might expect, this museum has an array of joyous circus memorabilia. But the Ringlings were also serious art collectors, and knew something about high style, so visiting what is today the official art museum of Florida is an enthralling experience for art and design lovers. See p. 348.

- **Museum of Arts and Sciences** (Daytona Beach): With the world's largest collection of Floridian art, and an upgraded-in-2024 planetarium with dazzling shows, this proud institution belies the notion that Daytona Beach is only about fast cars and tiny bikinis. See p. 447.

An elegant statue of horses pulling a chariot stands outside the John and Mable Ringling Museum of Art.

- **Mel Fisher Maritime Heritage Museum** (Key West): Surprisingly moving, and totally engrossing, this museum not only brings to the surface tales of underwater exploration, pirate booty, and shipwrecks, it also looks at the slave ships that once swarmed the Keys. See p. 193.

THE best DINING EXPERIENCES

- **Maty's** (Miami): In 2024, chef Valerie Chang won the "Oscar" of the culinary world when she was named Best Chef in the South for this inventive Peruvian restaurant. See p. 94.
- **Miami Culinary Tours** (Miami): These expertly led tours introduce visitors to the foods and history of Little Havana, South Beach, the Design District, and Wynwood. See p. 93.
- **El Palacio de los Jugos** (Miami): For the true, cacophonous Miami Cuban experience, this is the place to go, where heaps of gloriously greasy fare and sort-of-healthy fresh-squeezed juices have people coming in packs. See p. 108.
- **Café La Trova** (Miami): Dinner and a show! This supper club harkens back to pre-Castro Cuba with its decor, live music, and flashy cocktails. It's a fun time, even for vegans (they get their own menu). See p. 98.
- **Pierre's** (Islamorada): This is your date-night-in-the-Keys pick, an elegant, plantation-style converted home with accomplished French-with-a-lot-of-Floridian-influences fare. Dine outside. See p. 174.

Blue Heaven Restaurant in Key West.

- **Blue Heaven** (Key West): What was once a well-kept secret in Bahama Village is now a popular eatery known for fresh food (it's some of the best in town) and a motley, bohemian crowd. See p. 207.
- **Singleton's Seafood Shack** (Mayport/Jacksonville): This rustic Old Florida joint has kept up with the times by offering fresh fish in more ways than just battered and fried, yet it has still managed to retain the charming casualness of a riverside fish camp. See p. 489.
- **Bern's Steak House** (Tampa): Travel back to the 1950s at this old-timey, mahogany-paneled temple to beef, where every cut gets several delish sides gratis, and desserts are served in semi-private booths, with live music. A real experience. See p. 313.
- **Columbia Restaurant** (Tampa): Florida's oldest restaurant is still going strong! Eat at the original, under the chandeliers, and consider taking in the flamenco show here. A classic. See p. 316.
- **The Floridian** (St. Augustine): Celebrating the cuisine and products of Florida, everything served here was grown or caught in state, and all the recipes are classic, well, Floridian ones. See p. 473.

THE best SNORKELING & DIVING

Florida's coral reefs in recent years have experienced severe declines due to a combination of factors including coral disease, coral bleaching, high ocean temperatures, and human impacts and pollution. As a result, some reefs are so damaged scientists are planting nursery corals and even trying to move entire coral shelves to spare them. Please be sure to check in advance at www.coris.noaa.gov before you head to a specific dive spot.

- **Dry Tortugas National Park** (Dry Tortugas): Snorkelers of all levels bubble over when talking about the carpet of white sand that's illuminated by Technicolor tropical fish and living coral at this coral island off Key West. See p. 212.

- **John Pennekamp Coral Reef State Park** (Key Largo): This is the country's first undersea preserve, with 188 nautical square miles of protected coral reefs, 25 miles long and extending 3 miles into the Atlantic Ocean. The water throughout much of the park is shallow, so it's a great place for snorkelers to see a vibrant array of coral, including tree-size elkhorn coral and giant brain coral. See p. 165.

- **Looe Key National Marine Sanctuary** (Bahia Honda State Park): With 5⅓ square miles of gorgeous coral reef, rock ledges up to 35 feet tall, and a colorful and motley marine community, it's like snorkeling or diving in a massive aquarium. See p. 179.

- **Florida Keys Shipwreck Trail:** The Keys Shipwreck Heritage Trail features nine historic sites from Key Largo to Key West. For each of the nine Shipwreck Trail sites there is an underwater site guide available, who provides the shipwreck and mooring buoy positions, history, and a site map, and identifies marine life you can expect to see. See p. 198.

Shipwrecks and boats purposefully sunk to create new reefs give variety to the underwater sights off the coast of Florida.

1 | THE best LODGINGS

- **Faena Hotel Miami Beach** (Miami): Faena transformed an entire neighborhood, taking over 6 blocks and turning them into an artsy district of culture and comfort. The hotel's look comes directly from the film *Moulin Rouge,* which is no surprise: The set designer for that also did the Faena. See p. 69.

- **Simonton Court Historic Inn & Cottages** (Key West): People book years in advance to stay at this romantic former cigar factory, where many of the guest cottages are from the 1880s. Each room is individually designed, with flawless amenities and service. See p. 201.

- **The Moorings Village** (Islamorada): A former coconut plantation, the Moorings features 18 different cottages on 18 stunning acres of beachfront, and lush gardens studded with bougainvillea and coconut palms. See p. 170.

- **The Gardens Hotel** (Key West): A serene and sultry escape from the frat-boy madness that ensues on nearby Duval Street. See p. 200.

- **Little Palm Island Resort & Spa** (Little Torch Key): Accessible only by boat, this private 5-acre island is not only remote but also romantic—there are no TVs or telephones in the luxurious thatched cottages. See p. 182.

- **The Breakers Palm Beach** (Palm Beach): This stately, historic hotel epitomizes *la dolce vita,* Palm Beach–style, with an elegant lobby, impeccable service, expansive manicured lawns, and a scenic golf course, the state's oldest. See p. 285.

- **Turtle Beach Resort & Inn** (Siesta Key, off Sarasota): Sitting beside the bay, this intimate charmer began life as a traditional Old Florida fishing camp, but today it's one of the state's most romantic retreats. High wooden fences surround each unit's private outdoor hot tub, and one-way-mirror walls let you lounge in bed while passersby see only reflections of themselves. See p. 354.

An elegant lamp at The Breakers.

- **Lost Inn Paradise** (Cape Canaveral): Another affordable winner, it's the extraordinary hospitality that puts this re-furbbed beachfront motel on our list. Not only are all guests treated like family, the Inn provides all kinds of beach gear gratis to guests (even kayaks). You'll often see dolphins dancing in the waves from the property's deck. See p. 437.

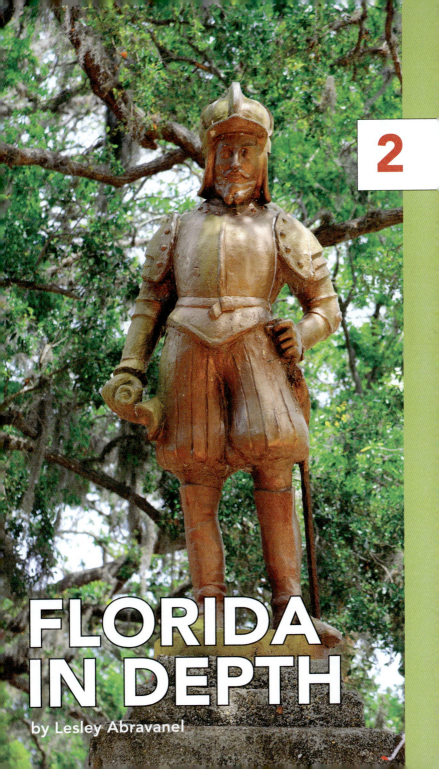

FLORIDA IN DEPTH

by Lesley Abravanel

2

Florida's history is a lot richer than its reputation as a haven for retirees, celebrities, bored billionaires, and people in dire need of a thaw and a deep, dark tan. From its emergence as a prehistoric swamp, a nexus of Native American culture and civilization, and a 16th-century hot spot for treasure-hunting Spanish explorers to a 21st-century destination of development, politics, and pop culture, Florida has experienced more reinventions than Bravo's Real Housewives.

FLORIDA TODAY

The ubiquitous meme and hashtag "Because Florida" isn't just being cheeky, it's an apt explanation for so many things, but in 2024, many of those things weren't very funny. Though Florida remained a tourism hot spot—in 2022, it had 137.6 million visitors, the most in its history, according to the state tourism organization, with Orlando winning the prize as the most-visited city in the United States—there may have been even more had politics not gotten in the way. Tourism did see a drop in 2023 and 2024, due to the state's divisive politics.

With its controversial governor, whose policies led to the NAACP and various LGBTQ+ organizations issuing travel warnings and bans, and to the cancellation of some very popular business and entertainment conventions, Florida took a bit of a hit because, well, because Florida.

Members of Florida's Black and LGBTQ+ communities have banded together to make sure their voices are heard, their histories are told, and their members are welcome. In January 2024, several Florida cities—St. Augustine, Opa Locka, Panama City, St. Petersburg, and Eatonville, the hometown of acclaimed Black novelist Zora Neale Hurston—made their cases to become the future home of the Florida African American History Museum. In Fort Lauderdale's gay mecca Wilton Manors, the Stonewall National Museum, Archives & Library hosts events to educate people about Florida's LGBTQ+ history and communities.

Then there was that whole dustup between the governor and Disney. But Disney die-hards—and there are millions—didn't let the governor get between them and Mickey. In 2022, over 47 million people visited the "Happiest Place on Earth" despite rising costs and despite the politics.

Politics aside, the state is booming. Miami has matured from a burgeoning metropolis to what some may consider a megalopolis, completely unrecognizable from even a decade ago. Some worry the city may sink into the ocean fairly soon. In the meantime, no one seems overly concerned. Tampa is also booming.

Natural disasters and hurricanes have also been a shaping force in recent years, damaging infrastructure, historic sights, and ecosystems in Fort Myers, Sanibel Island, and Apalachicola, among other places. But thanks to industrious locals, much effort is going into bringing those areas back to normal as the state continues to forge into the future.

PREVIOUS PAGE: Juan Ponce de León was one of the first European explorers to come to Florida, though he never did find the Fountain of Youth.

FLORIDA HISTORY

PREHISTORIC FLORIDA Fourteen thousand years ago, the Florida peninsula was underwater and did not exist as a landmass. After the land developed, **Paleo-Indians** arrived in about 13,000 B.C., crossing over to North America from Asia. Most of their activity was around the watering holes, sinkholes, and basins in the beds of modern rivers.

Paleo-Indian culture was replaced by, or evolved into, the **Early Archaic** culture around 7900 B.C. There were now more people in Florida, and as they were no longer tied to a few water holes in an arid land, they left their artifacts in many more locations.

The Early Archaic period evolved into the **Middle Archaic** period around 5000 B.C. People started living in villages near wetlands, and favored sites may have been occupied for multiple generations. The **Late Archaic** period started around 3000 B.C., when Florida's climate had reached current conditions and the sea had risen close to its present level. People now lived everywhere fresh- or saltwater wetlands were found. Many people lived in large villages with purpose-built mounds. Fired pottery appeared in Florida by 2000 B.C. By about 500 B.C., the Archaic culture that had been fairly uniform across Florida began to fragment into regional cultures.

The post-Archaic cultures of eastern and southern Florida developed in isolation, and it is likely that the peoples living in those areas at the time of first European contact were descendants of the inhabitants of the areas in late Archaic times. The cultures of the Florida Panhandle and the north and central Gulf coast of the Florida peninsula were strongly influenced by the Mississippian culture, although there is continuity in cultural history, suggesting that the peoples of those cultures were also descended from the inhabitants of the Archaic period. Cultivation of maize was adopted in the Panhandle and the northern part of the peninsula, but was absent or very restricted in the tribes that lived south of the Timucuan-speaking people (that is, south of a line approximately from present-day Daytona Beach to a point on or north of Tampa Bay).

NATIVE AMERICANS Spanish explorers of the early 16th century were likely the first Europeans to interact with the native population of Florida. The first documented encounter of Europeans with Native Americans of the United States came with the first expedition of **Juan Ponce de León** to Florida in 1513, although he encountered at least one native who spoke Spanish. In 1521, he encountered the **Calusa Indians,** who established 30 villages in the Everglades, during a failed colonization attempt in which they drove off the Europeans.

The Spanish recorded nearly 100 names of groups they encountered, ranging from organized political entities, such as the **Apalachee,** with a population of around 50,000, to villages with no known political affiliation. There were an estimated 150,000 speakers of dialects of the Timucua language, but the **Timucua** were organized only as groups of villages, and did not share a common culture. Other tribes in Florida at the time of first contact included the Ais; Calusa; Jaega; Mayaimi; Tequesta, who lived on the southeast coast of the Everglades; and Tocobaga. All these tribes diminished in numbers during the period of Spanish control of Florida.

At the beginning of the 18th century, tribes from areas to the north of Florida, supplied, encouraged, and occasionally accompanied by white colonists from the Province of Carolina, raided throughout Florida, burning villages, killing many of the inhabitants, and carrying captives back to Charles Towne to be sold as slaves.

Most of the villages in Florida were abandoned, and the survivors sought refuge at St. Augustine or in isolated spots around the state. Some of the Apalachee eventually reached Louisiana, where they survived as a distinct group for at least another century.

The few surviving members of these tribes were evacuated to Cuba when Spain transferred Florida to the British Empire in 1763. The **Seminole,** originally an offshoot of the Creek people who absorbed other groups, developed as a distinct tribe in Florida during the 18th century, and are now represented in the Seminole Nation of Oklahoma, the Seminole Tribe of Florida, and the Miccosukee Tribe of Indians of Florida.

SPANISH RULE Once Ponce de León laid his eyes on Florida in 1513, a slew of competitive conquistadors made futile efforts to find gold there and colonize the region. The first to establish a fort in Florida were the French, actually, but it was ultimately destroyed by the Spanish, who introduced Christianity, horses, and cattle to the region. Unfortunately, they also introduced diseases and conquistador brutality, which ultimately decimated Indian populations. Eager to expand its own American colony collection, Britain led several raids into Florida in the 1700s to overthrow Spanish rule. Among the most notable Spaniards in Florida were the aforementioned Ponce de León; **Hernando de Soto,** the most ruthless of the explorers, whose thirst for gold led to the massacre of many Indians; **Panfilo de Narvaez,** whose quest for El Dorado—the land of gold—landed him in Tampa Bay; and **Pedro Menéndez de Avilés,** who founded St. Augustine after defeating the French.

BRITISH RULE The Brits weren't interested in gold: They were all about Florida's bounty of hides and furs. After taking control in 1763, the Brits divided Florida into two. Because Florida was subsidized by the English, Floridians remained loyal to Mother England during the American Revolution—that is, until the Spanish returned and regained West Florida in 1781 and, 2 years later, East Florida. During the Spanish reconquest, American slaves fled to Florida, causing major turmoil between Spain and the U.S. Combined with Indian raids in the north and an Indian alliance with runaway slaves, Florida was, well, a mess, until **General Andrew Jackson** invaded Spanish Florida, captured Pensacola, and occupied West Florida. Then it was a disaster. Jackson's invasion kicked off the First Seminole War in 1817. Finally, to settle Spain's $5-million debt to the U.S., all Spanish lands east of the Mississippi, including Florida, were ceded to the U.S. in 1819.

AMERICAN RULE Florida became an organized territory of the United States on March 30, 1822. The Americans merged East Florida and West Florida (although the majority of West Florida was annexed to Orleans Territory and Mississippi Territory), and established a new capital in **Tallahassee,** located halfway between the East Florida capital of St. Augustine and the West Florida capital of Pensacola. The boundaries of Florida's first two counties, Escambia and St. Johns, approximately coincided with the boundaries of West and East Florida.

At this time, the plantation system was adopted by north Florida and because the settlers wanted the best possible land, the federal government tried moving all Indians west of the Mississippi, resulting in the Second and Third Seminole Wars. When Abraham Lincoln was elected president in 1860, Florida became the third state to secede from the Union. Florida saw little action during the Civil War—its main role was to supply beef and salt to the Confederates.

After meeting the requirements of Reconstruction, including writing a new state constitution, Florida was readmitted to the United States on July 25, 1868.

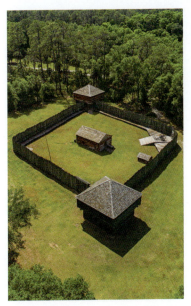

Fort Foster was built in 1836, during the Second Seminole War.

THE SEMINOLE WARS Wartime ravaged Florida during the Seminole Wars, a trio of wars between the United States Army and the Seminole Indians and their African-American allies, also known as the Florida Wars. The **First Seminole War** (ca. 1817 or thereabouts—different history books give different dates) was sparked by American slave owners looking for runaway slaves of African and Native American descent who traded weapons with the Brits during the War of 1812. Andrew Jackson led the American response in Florida, commanding an army of 3,000. Jackson divided Florida into two counties, Escambia and St. Johns, and, after establishing county courts and mayors in St. Augustine and Pensacola, left William Pope DuVal as governor.

On March 30, 1822, Florida became an official territory. The **Second Seminole War** (1835–42) erupted as Northern settlers had their eyes on Tallahassee, a Seminole settlement, and in a futile effort to calm the tension, DuVal asked the Seminoles to move south to a 4-million-acre reservation south of present-day Ocala. While their former home became the territory's capital, Jackson became president and again asked the Indians to move, this time west of the Mississippi. They refused and what ensued lasted longer than any war in the U.S. between the American Revolution and the Vietnam War.

The **Third Seminole War** (1855–58) was a sporadic one following Florida's entry into the union and laws sending Indians into reservations in the west. After this final confrontation, many Seminoles retreated to the Everglades, where some of their descendants still live today.

THE CIVIL WAR Following Lincoln's election in 1860, Florida became the third of the original seven states to secede from the Union. But because Florida was so sparsely populated, it contributed more in goods than manpower. The large coastline served as a barrier to the Union navy, who had a hard time curbing runners from bringing in supplies and materials from foreign suppliers. Union troops occupied major ports like Cedar Key, Jacksonville, Key West, and Pensacola. With the exception of Fort Zachary Taylor and Fort Pickens, Confederate forces seized control of every U.S. Army fort in the state.

The Confederates put more than 61,000 Florida slaves to work transporting supplies and as laborers in salt mines and fisheries. Many escaped and served the Union, providing them with intelligence on Confederate activity. In 1862, the Union military encouraged slaves in plantation areas to flee their owners.

Increasingly dissatisfied by oppressive drafting policies, Confederate soldiers began to desert to some Florida counties that served as havens for deserters from all Confederate states. These bands of deserters began attacking Confederates and, though many skirmishes did happen in Florida, the only major one to take place during the war's duration was the **Battle of Olustee** near Lake City, in which Union forces eventually retreated, causing the North to question the further Union involvement in what was deemed a "militarily insignificant" Florida.

In January 1865, Union General William Tecumseh Sherman set aside a part of Florida as a home for runaway and freed former slaves, but the order was never enforced and was eventually repealed by President Andrew Johnson. On May 13, 1865, Colonel George Washington Scott surrendered what was left of the Florida Confederate troops. On May 20, slavery was officially ended in the state as troopers raised the U.S. flag over the state capitol building. Tallahassee was the last Confederate state capital to fall to the Union army.

Confederate General Joe Wheeler with members of a volunteer regiment in Tampa.

BOOMTOWN, FLORIDA After the Civil War, Florida met its best friend: tourism. Although the state's economy was in the dumps, its warm climate and smallish population called out to investors and developers. Railroad barons Henry Flagler and Henry Plant laid their tracks down the east and west coasts of Florida during the late 1880s, offering tourists a not-so-quick escape to paradise, or something close to it. The influx of vacationers stimulated the economy and Florida's new railroads opened up large areas to development, spurring the Florida land boom of the 1920s. Investors of all kinds, mostly from outside Florida, raced to buy and sell rapidly appreciating land in newly platted communities such as Miami and Palm Beach. A majority of the people who bought land in Florida were able to do so without stepping foot in the state, by hiring people to speculate and buy the land for them.

By 1925, the market ran out of buyers to pay the high prices and the boom became a bust. The 1926 Miami hurricane further depressed the real estate market. The Great Depression arrived in 1929; however, by that time, economic decay already consumed much of Florida from the land boom that collapsed 4 years earlier.

THE EVERGLADES FINALLY GRANTED NATIONAL PARK STATUS Thanks to the work of the Everglades' foremost supporter, Ernest F. Coe, Congress passed a park bill in 1934. Dubbed by opponents as the "alligator and snake swamp bill," the legislation stalled during the Great Depression and World War II. Finally, on December 6, 1947, President Harry S Truman dedicated the Everglades National Park.

In that same year, Marjory Stoneman Douglas first published *The Everglades: River of Grass*. She understood its importance as the major watershed for South Florida and as a unique ecosystem.

VARIATIONS ON A THEME (PARK) Florida's first theme parks emerged in the 1930s and included **Cypress Gardens** (1936), near Winter Haven, and **Marineland** (1938), near St. Augustine. Walt Disney chose Central Florida as the site of his planned Walt Disney World Resort in the 1960s and began purchasing land. In 1971, the first component of the resort, the **Magic Kingdom,** opened and began the dramatic transformation of the Orlando area into a major resort destination.

ROAD-TRIPPING THROUGH FLORIDA'S FABULOUS '50S Despite the fact that in 1950 frozen concentrate of citrus juice became a major industry in the state, things were motoring toward a different trend beginning in 1954 with the completion of the Sunshine Skyway stretching 15 miles across Lower Tampa Bay. In 1955, the state legislature authorized plans for a state-long turnpike. And in what sealed the deal for the '50s being the decade of Florida transportation, in 1958 a second major federal agency, the National Aeronautics and Space Administration (NASA), began operations at Cape Canaveral.

THE SPACE RACE & CUBAN INFLUX With the **space race** in full blast, Cape Canaveral brought even more of a boom to Florida in the '60s—especially when Buzz Aldrin and Neil Armstrong blasted off from the so-called Florida Space Coast and onto the moon. Sixties Florida also saw another kind of race, as more than 300,000 **Cubans** fled to Florida when Fidel Castro took over Cuba in 1959. Early arrivals landed in Florida via Freedom Flights, but later, refugees risked—and often lost—their lives as they made the dangerous 90-mile trip from Cuba to Key West on flimsy rafts. Florida was again in the spotlight in 1962 as the world was on edge during the Cuban Missile Crisis. The large wave of Cubans into South Florida transformed Miami into a major center of commerce, finance, and transportation for all of Latin America. Immigration from Haiti and other Caribbean states continues to the present day.

THE SO-SO '70S After being over the moon about the space race, the '70s had Florida in a bit of a depression beginning in 1971, when Richard M. Nixon ordered a halt to the Cross Florida Barge Canal after $50 million had been spent on the 107-mile structure. On a positive note, Amtrak began operation of service into Orlando as **Walt Disney World** opened its gates on October 1. Things were looking up in '73 when, despite fuel shortages, Florida set an all-time record for influx of visitors, as 26 million people visited the Sunshine State. And after 7½ years and nearly 260,000 refugees, the Freedom Flights from Cuba came to an end on April 7, 1973. The airlifts, bringing refugees into Miami at the rate of 48,000 a year, transformed the ethnic makeup of Dade County by adding at least 100,000 Cubans to the 150,000 already there.

THE GO-GO '80S The plight of Cubans fleeing their native island was highlighted again in 1980 during the **Mariel Boatlift,** a mass movement of Cubans who departed from Cuba's Mariel Harbor for the U.S. between April 15 and October 31, 1980. The exodus was ended by mutual agreement between the U.S. and Cuba in October 1980. By that time, up to 125,000 Cubans had made the journey to Florida. Also in 1980, race riots tore Miami apart, Disney opened its $800-million EPCOT center, and the next phase of the space program saw the first manned space shuttle launches from Kennedy Space Center (KSC). In 1986, the program was dealt a tragic blow when the space shuttle *Challenger* exploded after takeoff. All seven astronauts aboard were killed. By 1987, the U.S. Census Bureau estimate indicated that Florida had surpassed Pennsylvania to become the fourth-most-populous state in the nation.

END OF THE CENTURY The decade started with the arrival of Panama's governor, Manuel Noriega, who was being brought to Miami for trial on drug charges. In 1992, Homestead and adjacent South Florida were devastated on August 24 by the costliest natural disaster in American history, Hurricane Andrew, demanding billions in aid.

THIS MILLENNIUM & BEYOND Florida became the battleground of the controversial 2000 U.S. presidential election when a count of the popular votes from Election Day was extremely close and became mired in accusations of fraud and manipulation. Ultimately, the United States Supreme Court let stand the official count, and George W. Bush was declared winner of the election. Through the first half of the decade, Florida continued to be one of the fastest-growing states in the country, with the economy still depending greatly on tourism, but with expanding industries in business and manufacturing, until the economy imploded in 2008. Things got better and in 2010, Florida's census revealed that Spanish speakers in Miami outnumbered English speakers, and in 2014, Florida officially became the nation's third most populous state. In 2016, the Pulse nightclub shooting in an Orlando LGBTQ+ club became one of the nation's deadliest. In 2018, a sleepy suburb of Fort Lauderdale became a global headline with the deadliest school shooting in history at Parkland's Marjorie Stoneman Douglas High School. In 2023, the governor signed into law permitless carry, allowing gun owners to carry concealed weapons without permits. He also signed various bans on books, drag shows, and more while touting Florida as the "Freedom State."

FLORIDA IN POP CULTURE
Recommended Books

Florida is an author's dream come true. A state of much diversity (read: bizarre characters, to say the least), Florida practically hangs inspiration from the palm trees. Where to begin? Here's a short list of some of the books that tell the story of Florida, in its many personas. Happy reading!

- ***Miami, the Magic City*** (Centennial Press), by Arva Moore Parks: An authoritative history of the city.
- ***The Everglades: River of Grass*** (Pineapple Press), by Marjory Stoneman Douglas: A personal account of the treasures of Florida's most famous natural resource.
- ***Celebration USA: Living in Disney's Brave New Town*** (Holt Paperbacks), by Douglas Frantz and Catherine Collins: An eye-opening true story about living in Disney's "model town."
- ***The Yearling*** (Collier MacMillan Publishers), by Marjorie Kinnan Rawlings: A classic novel about life in the Florida backwoods.
- ***The Perez Family*** (W. W. Norton & Co. Inc.), by Christine Bell: A work of historic fiction about the lives of Cuban immigrants from the Mariel Boat Lift.

Notable Movies Filmed in Florida

- John Huston's ***Key Largo*** (1948), based on the novel by Hemingway (gangsters, hurricanes, and Bogey and Bacall)
- Harry Levin's ***Where the Boys Are*** (1960; spring break in Fort Lauderdale)
- Lawrence Kasdan's ***Body Heat*** (1981; crime)
- Ron Howard's ***Cocoon*** (1985), based on a novel by David Saperstein (retirees)

FLORIDA literary tour

Key West: A literary lover's mecca, Key West was home to Ernest Hemingway, Tennessee Williams, and currently, Judy Blume, who owns a bookstore in town, so you may even run into her. See p. 185.

Pompano Beach and Miami: Author Elmore Leonard took his mother to a small motel on Pompano Beach, which some say was his inspiration for the Coconut Palms Resort Apartments, featured in Leonard's 1982 book, *Cat Chaser*. Elmore Leonard's favorite backdrop—as seen in *Get Shorty*, *La Brava*, and *Rum Punch*—was the Cardozo Hotel at 1300 Ocean Dr., Miami Beach.

Bahia Mar Fort Lauderdale Beach Resort: Travis McGee, the protagonist in John D. MacDonald's 21 novels (including *The Deep Blue Goodbye*), lived at this resort, 801 Seabreeze Blvd. (© **954/764-2233**).

Little Haiti: The place where a no-good former oil-burner repairman wanders, in Russell Banks's *Continental Drift*.

Lilian Place Heritage Center: The oldest house beachside in Daytona Beach is the place where *Red Badge of Courage* author Stephen Crane recuperated after his boat sank off the Daytona shoreline. Rumor has it, his ghost still visits. See p. 446.

Eatonville: Just outside of Orlando is the hometown of Zora Neale Hurston, who wrote *Their Eyes Were Watching God*. **The Hurston Museum,** 344 E. Kennedy Blvd. (hurstonmuseum.org; © **407/647-3307**), celebrates her legacy.

- Tim Burton's ***Edward Scissorhands*** (1990; modern fairy tale filmed in Dade City and Lakeland)
- Mike Nichols's ***The Birdcage*** (1996; South Beach comedy)
- John Singleton's ***Rosewood*** (1997; African-American culture), based on the historic Rosewood massacre
- Spike Jonze's ***Adaptation*** (2002), loosely based on Susan Orleans's *The Orchid Thief*
- Dave Barry's ***Best. State. Ever.: A Florida Man Defends His Homeland*** (2016)
- Craig Pittman's ***Oh, Florida! How America's Weirdest State Influences the Rest of the Country*** (2016)
- Barry Jenkin's Academy Award–winning film ***Moonlight*** (2016; a young Black man coming of age in Miami)

Music of Florida

The Miami recording industry did not begin with Gloria Estefan's Miami Sound Machine, contrary to popular belief. In fact, some major rock albums were recorded in Miami's Criteria Studios. Among them: *Rumours* by Fleetwood Mac and *Hotel California* by the Eagles. Longtime local music entrepreneur Henry Stone and his label, TK Records, created the local indie scene in the 1970s. TK Records produced the R&B group KC and the Sunshine Band, along with soul singers Betty Wright, George McCrae, and Jimmy "Bo" Horne, as well as a number of minor soul and disco hits, many influenced by Caribbean music.

In the 1970s and early 1980s, Jacksonville saw a very active music recording scene with Southern rock bands such as Molly Hatchet, the Allman Brothers Band, 38 Special, the Outlaws, and Lynyrd Skynyrd. Tom Petty was from Gainesville, Florida, while boy band *NSYNC, Britney Spears, Christina Aguilera, and Justin Timberlake were graduates of Orlando's Mickey Mouse Club.

In the 2000s, Miami saw an enormous rap boom in the form of Daddy Yankee, Pitbull, Rick Ross, and more. In 2017, Miami-cultivated Latin artists from Luis Fonsi to Bad Bunny and J Balvin climbed the charts into the mainstream. In the 2020s, the state became host to a number of major music festivals, in a number of different Floridian cities.

WHEN TO GO

To a large extent, the timing of your visit will determine how much you'll spend—and how much company you'll have—once you get to Florida. That's because room rates can more than double during so-called high seasons, when countless visitors flock to Florida.

The weather determines the high seasons (see "Weather," below). In subtropical South Florida, **high season** is in the winter, from **mid-December to mid-April.** In North Florida the reverse is true: Tourists flock here during the summer, from Memorial Day to Labor Day.

Hurricane season runs from **June to November,** and during that period you never know what will happen. Pay close attention to weather forecasts during this season and always be prepared.

Presidents' Day weekend in February, Easter week, Memorial Day weekend, the Fourth of July, Labor Day weekend, Thanksgiving, Christmas, and New Year's are busy throughout the state, especially at the Orlando-area attractions, which can be packed any time school is out (see chapter 12, "Walt Disney World, Universal & Orlando," for more information on those areas).

Northern and southern Florida share the same **shoulder seasons: April through May,** and **September through November,** when the weather is pleasant throughout Florida and the hotel rates are considerably lower than during the high season. If price is a consideration, these months of moderate temperatures and fewer tourists are the best times to visit.

Weather

Northern Florida has a temperate climate, and even in the warmer southern third of the state, it's subtropical, not tropical. Accordingly, Florida sees more extremes of temperatures than, say, the Caribbean islands, especially with climate change in play.

Spring, which runs from **late March to May,** sees warm temperatures throughout Florida, but it also brings tropical showers.

Summer in Florida extends from **May to September,** when it's hot and very humid throughout the state. Severe afternoon thunderstorms are prevalent during the summer heat (there aren't professional sports teams here named Lightning and Thunder for nothing), so schedule your activities for earlier in the day, and take precautions to avoid being hit by lightning during the storms.

Autumn—about **September through November**—is a great time to visit, as the hottest days are gone and the crowds have thinned out. But it is a risky time to visit, as it's the peak of hurricane season.

Winter can get a bit nippy throughout the state and, in recent years, downright freezing, especially in northern Florida. The "cold snaps" usually last only a few days in the southern half of the state, however, and daytime temperatures should quickly return to the 70s (20s Celsius). That said, whenever you travel to Florida, bring a jacket. Even in summertime you may need it indoors, when air-conditioning reaches freezing temperatures.

For up-to-the-minute weather info, tune in to cable TV's Weather Channel or check out its website at **www.weather.com**.

Holidays

Banks, government offices, post offices, and many stores, restaurants, and museums are closed on the following legal national holidays: January 1 (New Year's Day), the third Monday in January (Martin Luther King, Jr., Day), the third Monday in February (Presidents' Day), the last Monday in May (Memorial Day), July 4 (Independence Day), the first Monday in September (Labor Day), the second Monday in October (Columbus Day), November 11 (Veterans Day/Armistice Day), the fourth Thursday in November (Thanksgiving Day), and December 25 (Christmas). The Tuesday after the first Monday in November is Election Day, a federal government holiday in presidential-election years (held every 4 years, and next in 2028).

Calendar of Events

JANUARY

Key West Literary Seminar (kwls.org; ✆ **888/293-9291**), Key West. This 3-day event features a different theme every year, along with a roster of world-renowned authors, writers, and other literary types. The event is so popular it sells out well in advance, so call early for tickets. Second week of January.

ROLEX 24 at Daytona (daytonainternationalspeedway.com; ✆ **800/748-7467**), Daytona. A 24-hour endurance car race. This is another very popular event so get hotel reservations and tickets early. Last week of January.

FEBRUARY

Everglades City Seafood Festival (evergladesseafoodfestival.com; ✆ **239/695-2561**), Everglades City. A 2-day feeding frenzy centered around Floridian specialties like stone crab and gator tails. Free admission, but you pay for the food you eat, booth by booth. First full weekend in February.

Speedweeks (daytonaintlspeedway.com; ✆ **386/254-2700**), Daytona. Nineteen days of events, with a series of races that draw the top names in NASCAR stock car racing, culminating in the Daytona 500. Especially for the Daytona 500, tickets must be purchased as far as a year in advance; they go on sale January 1 of the prior year. First 3 weeks of February.

Miami International Boat Show (miamiboatshow.com; ✆ **954/463-6762**), Miami Beach. A quarter of a million boat enthusiasts head to the Miami Beach Convention Center, and five other locations around town, to view some of the planet's priciest and most cutting edge megayachts, speedboats, sailboats, and schooners. Mid-February.

Food Network South Beach Wine & Food Festival (sobewineandfoodfest.com; ✆ **866/271-8540**), South Beach. A 3-day celebration featuring some of the Food Network's best chefs, with tastings, lectures, seminars, and parties. Last weekend in February.

MARCH

Bike Week (officialbikeweek.com; ✆ **800/748-7467**), Daytona Beach. This 10-day gathering of motorcycle enthusiasts draws a crowd of more than 500,000. Major races are held at Daytona International Speedway, plus motorcycle shows, beach parties, and the Annual Motorcycle Parade, with thousands of riders. First week in March.

Winter Party (winterparty.com; ✆ **305/571-1924**), Miami Beach. LGBTQ+ folks from around the world book trips to Miami far in advance to attend this weekend-long series of parties and events benefiting the Dade Human Rights Foundation. Early March.

Calle Ocho Festival (carnavalmiami.com; ✆ **305/644-8888**), Little Havana. What Carnaval is to Rio, the Calle Ocho Festival is to Miami. This 10-day extravaganza, also called Carnival Miami, features a block party spanning 15 blocks, with live salsa music, parades, and tons of savory Cuban delicacies. Mid-March.

APRIL
Conch Republic Independence Celebration (conchrepublic.com; ✆ **305/304-2400**), Key West. A 10-day party celebrating the day the Conch Republic seceded from the Union. Events include a kooky bed race, a drag queen race, minigolf tournaments, cruiser car shows, and more. Mid-April.

JULY
Lower Keys Underwater Music Fest (destinationfloridakeys.com; ✆ **800/872-2411**), Looe Key. This aural aquatic event involves boaters heading out to the underwater reef at the Looe Key Marine Sanctuary, dropping speakers into the water, and piping in all sorts of music, creating a disco-diving spectacular. Mid-July.

SEPTEMBER
Womenfest (gaykeywestfl.com/womenfest; ✆ **800/535-7797**), Key West. A 5-day fest for women who love women, with comedy shows, concerts, parties, boating, and more. Early September.

OCTOBER
NKF Labor Day Pro-Am Surfing Festival (nkfsurf.com; ✆ **407/894-7325**), Cocoa Beach. One of the largest surfing events on the East Coast. Mid-October.

Biketoberfest (biketoberfest.org; ✆ **386/255-0415**), Daytona Beach. A 4-day rally of rides, races, and raucousness for chopper fans. Mid-October.

Clearwater Jazz Holiday (clearwaterjazz.com; ✆ **727/461-5200**), Clearwater. Top jazz musicians play for 4 days and nights at bayfront Coachman Park in this free musical extravaganza. Mid-October.

Halloween Horror Nights (universalorlando.com; ✆ **800/837-2273** or 407/363-8000), Orlando. **Universal Studios** spookifies its grounds for 19 nights. That means live bands, a psychopath's maze, special shows, and hundreds of ghouls and goblins roaming the streets. The studio closes at dusk, reopening in macabre form at 7pm. Full admission is charged for the event, which is geared toward adults. Mid-October to Halloween.

Mickey's Not-So-Scary Halloween Party (disneyworld.com; ✆ **407/934-7639**), Orlando. At Walt Disney World, guests are invited to trick-or-treat in the Magic Kingdom, starting at 7pm. The party includes parades, storytelling, live music, and fireworks display. End of October.

Fantasy Fest (fantasyfest.net; ✆ **305/296-1817**), Key West. This

Revelers at Key West's Fantasy Fest.

weeklong, hedonistic, X-rated Halloween party is not for children. Make reservations in Key West early, as hotels tend to book up quickly during this event. Last week of October.

NOVEMBER

American Sandsculpting Festival (facebook.com/AmericanSandSculpting; ✆ **239/454-7500**), Fort Myers Beach. Thousands of fans gather to sculpt and to see the world's finest sandcastles. First weekend in November.

Miami Book Fair International (miamibookfair.com; ✆ **305/237-3258**), Miami. This weeklong homage to the written word is the largest book fair in the United States. The weekend street fair is the best attended event. Many lectures are free but fill up quickly, so get there early. Mid-November.

Blue Angels Homecoming Air Show (visitpensacola.com or blueangels.navy.mil; ✆ **800/874-1234** or 850/434-1234), Pensacola. World-famous Navy pilots do their aerial acrobatics just 33 feet off the beach. Second weekend in November.

DECEMBER

Capital One Orange Bowl (orangebowl.org; ✆ **305/341-4700**), Miami. The big Orange Bowl football game (held at Hard Rock Stadium), usually on New Year's Day, featuring two of the year's best college football teams. Tickets sell out quickly. Last week of December/first week of January.

Art Basel Miami Beach (artbasel.com/miami-beach), Miami. The world's most prominent art galleries set up shop on South Beach, and in the Design District, Wynwood, and beyond, with thousands of exhibitions, not to mention cocktail parties, concerts, and containers—as in shipping—that are set up on the beach and transformed into makeshift galleries. First or second weekend in December.

Nights of Lights (visitstaugustine.com/event/nights-lights; ✆ **904/829-1711**), St. Augustine. Three million lights hail the holiday season here, adorning every corner and crevice of the historic district. November–January.

Christmas at Walt Disney World (www.disneyworld.com), Orlando. In the Magic Kingdom, Main Street is lavishly decked out with lights and holly and an 80-foot glistening tree. Other "Worlds" have their own holiday theming. Throughout December.

Seminole-Hard Rock Winterfest Boat Parade (winterfestparade.com; ✆ **954/767-0686**), Fort Lauderdale. A spectacular boat parade along the Intracoastal Waterway. Mid-December.

RESPONSIBLE TRAVEL

Florida's biggest attraction isn't a theme park, but rather its natural resources. Thanks to some of the state's initiatives, keeping Florida green is becoming second nature. The **Florida Green Lodging** program, for instance, is a voluntary initiative of the Florida Department of Environmental Protection that recognizes lodging facilities making a commitment to conserving and protecting Florida's natural resources. As of November 13, 2023, there were 322 designated Florida Green Lodging properties. In order to be considered for membership, lodgings must educate customers, employees, and the public on conservation; participate in waste reduction, reuse, recycling, water conservation, and energy efficiency; and provide eco-friendly transportation. The designation is valid for 3 years, and all properties are required to submit environmental performance data every year. So that you can stay at these properties (we list many in the book), go to https://floridadep.gov/osi/green-lodging to see the full list.

The Everglades is an eco-tourism hot spot where responsible tourism isn't an option but a requirement for anyone visiting or working there. The Biden Administration's $1.5-billion investment in Everglades restoration, including $1.1 billion through the **Bipartisan Infrastructure Law,** was allocated to, among other things, protect the critical ecosystem and water supplies of the Everglades. Similar efforts can be seen throughout the state, such as in North Florida, where the new Northwest Florida Beaches International Airport in Panama Beach is the nation's first Leadership in Energy and Design (LEED)–certified passenger terminal.

SPECIAL-INTEREST TRIPS

Bird-watching, boating and sailing, camping, canoeing and kayaking, fishing, golfing, tennis, pickleball—you can be very active in Florida. These and other activities are described in the outdoor activities sections of every destination chapter, but here's a brief overview of some of the best places to get outdoors, with tips on how to get more detailed information.

BIKING, SCOOTERING & SKATING Florida's relatively flat terrain makes it ideal for bicycling and in-line skating. You can bike right into **Everglades National Park** along the 38-mile-long Main Park Road, and bike or skate from **St. Petersburg** to **Tarpon Springs** on the 47-mile-long converted railroad bed known as the **Pinellas Trail.** Many towns and cities have designated routes for cyclists, skaters, joggers, and walkers, such as scenic **Bayshore Boulevard** in **Tampa, Ocean Drive** on South Beach, and the bike lanes from downtown **Sarasota** out to St. Armands, Lido, and Longboat keys.

BIRD-WATCHING With hundreds of both land- and sea-based species, Florida is one of America's best places for bird-watching—if you're not careful, pelicans will steal your picnic lunch on **Naples Pier.**

The **Great Florida Birding and Wildlife Trail** is a network of over 500 viewing sites throughout the state. Fort Clinch State Park, on Amelia Island, and Merritt Island National Wildlife Refuge, in Cape Canaveral, are gateways to the northeast trail. Info and maps are available from the Florida Fish & Wildlife Conservation Commission (floridabirdingtrail.com; © **850/922-0664**).

For an up-to-date guide of some of the state's best wildlife viewing, go to visitflorida.com/things-to-do/outdoors-and-adventure/wildlife.

BOATING & SAILING With some 1,350 miles of shoreline, it's not surprising that Florida is a boating and sailing mecca.

The **Moorings** (moorings.com; © **888/952-8420** or 727/530-5651), the worldwide sailboat charter company, has its headquarters in Clearwater, and its Florida yacht base nearby in St. Petersburg. From St. Pete, experienced sailors can take bareboats as far as the Keys and the Dry Tortugas, out in the Gulf of Mexico.

Key West keeps gaining prominence as a world sailing capital. The Southernmost Regatta is a 5-day race that returned to Key West in January 2024, bringing fleets of fantastic sailing vessels to the Southernmost Point, and smaller events take place regularly.

Even if you've never hauled on a halyard, you can learn the art of sailing at **Steve and Doris Colgate's Offshore Sailing School** (www.offshoresailing.com) in Key West and St. Petersburg. **The American Sailing Association** (asa.com) has schools and classes throughout the state.

And if you know how to boat, or want to hire a boat with a captain, such marketplace sites as **Boatsetting.com** and **GetMyBoat.com** can help you find rental vessels of every type, and in every price range. In fact, some individual owners rent out their boats when they're not using them, meaning that experienced sailors can get deals at these websites that they may not find by simply working with an agency or marina.

Finally, *The Florida Fish and Wildlife Conservation Commission* (myfwc.com/research/gis/boating-guides) is a treasure trove of tips on safe boating; state regulations and info on licenses; county-by-county marina locations; marine products and services; and more. *Note:* You need a license issued in Florida to rent a boat in the state. You'll find out more about the education needed to get that license at the link above.

CAMPING Florida is dotted with RV parks (if you own such a vehicle, it's the least expensive way to spend your winters here). But for the best tent camping, look to Florida's national preserves and at least 52 state parks that offer RV camping and recreation areas. Options range from luxury sites with hot-water showers and cable TV hookups, to primitive island and beach camping with no facilities whatsoever.

Regular and primitive camping in **Dr. Julian G. Bruce St. George Island State Park,** near Apalachicola, is a bird-watcher's dream—plus you'll be on one of the nation's most magnificent beaches. The nearly 2,000-acre barrier island park has nearly 60 campsites with electricity and water hookups. Equally swell are the sands at **St. Andrews State Park,** in Panama City Beach, where most campsites have lagoon views. Other top spots are **Ocala National Forest,** north of Orlando, featuring 14 developed camp grounds; **Fort DeSoto Park,** in St. Pete Beach (more gorgeous bayside sites plus modern, clean bathrooms); **Canaveral National Seashore,** near the Kennedy Space Center; **Anastasia State Park,** in St. Augustine, which offers the Bedtime Story Camper Lending Library of picture books for campers ages 4 to 9; **Fort Clinch State Park,** on Amelia Island, which has a campground just steps from the beach or, our fave, 42 campsites amidst Spanish moss-laden oak trees and breathtaking views of the Amelia River; and **Bill Baggs Cape Florida State Park,** on Key Biscayne in Miami. Down in the Keys, **Bahia Honda State Park** is the most popular and soon it will have a brand new, remodeled bath house, which is a bonus; the oceanside sites in **Long Key State Park** are about as nice as they get, and while **John Pennekamp Coral Reef State Park** is best known for its underwater sites, some enjoy the camp sites here, though others consider it like camping in a parking lot.

In each of these popular campgrounds, reservations are essential, especially during the high season. Florida's state parks take bookings up to 11 months in advance.

For a list of tent and RV sites in Florida's state parks and recreation areas, go to floridastateparks.org/rv-camping.

Pet owners, note: Pets are permitted at some—but not all—state park beaches, campgrounds, and food service areas. Before bringing your animal, check with the individual park to see if your pet will be allowed. And bring your pet's rabies certificate, which is required.

For private campgrounds, **Camp Florida** (campflorida.com; © **850/562-7151**) has locator maps and details about its member establishments. The website **Outdoorsy.com** is another good resource.

CANOEING & KAYAKING Canoers and kayakers have almost limitless options for discovery here: picturesque rivers, sandy coastlines, marshes, mangroves, and gigantic Lake Okeechobee. Exceptional trails run through several parks and wildlife preserves, including **Everglades National Park** and **Briggs Nature Center,** on the edge of the Everglades near Marco Island.

According to the Florida State Legislature, however, the state's official "Canoe Capital" is the Panhandle town of **Milton,** on U.S. 90 near Pensacola. Up here, Blackwater River, Coldwater River, Sweetwater Creek, and Juniper Creek are perfect for tubing, rafting, and paddleboating, as well as canoeing and kayaking.

Another good venue is the waterways winding through the marshes between **Amelia Island** and the mainland.

Based during the winter at Everglades City, on the park's western border, **Everglades Adventures Kayak & Eco Tours** (evergladesadventures.com; ✆ **239/294-8456**) offers guided kayak expeditions through the Everglades.

There are 60 designated Florida paddling trails covering 4,100 miles altogether; they can be found at floridadep.gov/PaddlingTrails.

ECO-ADVENTURES If you don't want to do it yourself, you can observe Florida's flora and fauna on guided field expeditions—and contribute to conservation efforts while you're at it.

The **Sierra Club,** the oldest and largest grass-roots environmental organization in the U.S., offers eco-adventures through its Florida chapter (sierraclub.org/florida). The club's outings include canoeing or kayaking through the Everglades, hiking the Florida Trail in America's southernmost national forest, camping on a barrier island, and exploring the sinkhole phenomenon in North-Central Florida. You do have to be a Sierra Club member, but you can join at the time of the trip.

The Florida chapter of the **Nature Conservancy** (nature.org; ✆ **407/682-3664**) has protected 578,000 acres of natural lands in Florida and presently owns and manages 40,000 acres including four preserves. For a small fee, you can join one of the field trips or work parties that take place periodically; fees vary from year to year and event to event, so see the website for more info. Participants get a chance to learn about and even participate in the preservation of the ecosystem.

A nonprofit organization dedicated to environmental research, the **Earthwatch Institute** (earthwatch.org; ✆ **800/776-0188**) has volunteer vacations that pair travelers with marine scientists in Sarasota. Together you'll track sharks and sea rays.

FISHING In addition to the amberjack, bonito, grouper, mackerel, mahimahi, marlin, pompano, redfish, sailfish, snapper, snook, tarpon, tuna, and wahoo running offshore and in inlets, Florida has countless miles of rivers and streams, plus about 30,000 lakes and springs stocked with about 222 species of freshwater fish. Indeed, Floridians seem to fish everywhere: off canal banks and old bridges, from fishing piers and fishing fleets. You'll even see them standing alongside the Tamiami Trail (U.S. 41) that cuts across the Everglades—one eye on their line, the other watching for alligators.

Anglers 16 and older need a license for any kind of saltwater or freshwater fishing, including lobstering and spearfishing. Licenses are sold at bait-and-tackle shops around the state.

GOLF Florida is the unofficial golf capital of the United States—some say the world. It has more golf courses than any other U.S. state: more than 1,250 at last count, and growing. We picked the best for chapter 1, but suffice it to say that you can tee off almost anywhere, anytime there's daylight, and sometimes at night. The highest concentrations of excellent courses are in Southwest Florida, around Naples and Fort Myers (more than 1,700 holes!); in the Orlando area (Disney alone has 99 holes open to the public); and in the Panhandle, around Destin and Panama City Beach. It's a rare town in Florida that doesn't have a municipal golf course—even Key West has 18 great holes.

Greens fees are usually much lower at the municipal courses than at privately owned clubs. Whether public or private, greens fees tend to vary greatly, depending on the time of year. You could pay $300 or more at a private course during the high season, but less than half that when the tourists are gone. And half of that lower fee if you'll accept an unpopular tee time.

You can learn the game or hone your strokes at one of several excellent golf schools in the state. **David Leadbetter** has teaching facilities in Orlando and an academy at the PGA National Resort in Palm Beach Gardens. *Golf Magazine* 100 teacher **Fred Griffin** also teaches in Orlando, and you'll find the guy who some foreplayers call the most underrated golf instructor **Jimmy Ballard**'s school in Stuart. The golf academy at the **Innisbrook** resort in Palm Harbor near Tampa is led by Class A PGA instructor Dawn Mercer. The **Sawgrass Marriott Golf Resort & Spa** in Ponte Vedra Beach features a TPC Performance Center with expert instructors.

You can get information about most Florida courses, including current greens fees, and reserve tee times through **Tee Times USA** (teetimesusa.com; *©* **800/374-8633**).

You can get more info on courses and coaches from the **Professional Golfers' Association** (**PGA;** pga.com; *©* **800/477-6465**); or from the **Ladies Professional Golf Association** (**LPGA;** lpga.com; *©* **386/274-5742**).

HIKING Although you won't be climbing any mountains in this relatively flat state, there are thousands of beautiful hiking trails in Florida. The ideal hiking months are October through April, when the weather is cool(ish) and dry and mosquitoes are less prominent. Like anywhere else, you'll find trails that are gentle and short, and others that are challenging—some trails in the Everglades require you to wade waist-deep in water!

Most Florida snakes are harmless, but a few have deadly bites, so it's a good idea to avoid them all. If you're venturing into the backcountry, watch out for gators, and don't ever try to feed them (or any wild animal). You risk getting bitten. (They can't tell the difference between the food and your hand.) You're also upsetting the balance of nature; animals fed by humans lose their ability to find their own food.

The **Florida Trail Association** (florida-trail.org; *©* **352/378-8823**) maintains a large percentage of the public trails in the state and has good info on its website. The app **AllTrails** is another fine resource, as is the interactive map of the **Florida National Scenic Trail,** from the USDA Forest Service at fs.usda.gov/fnst.

SCUBA DIVING & SNORKELING Divers *love* the Keys for their magnificent formations of tree-size elkhorn coral and giant brain coral, as well as colorful sea fans and dozens of other varieties, sharing space with 300 or more species of rainbow-hued fish. Reef diving is good all the way from Key Largo to Key West, with plenty of tour operators, outfitters, and dive shops. Particularly worthy are **John Pennekamp Coral Reef State Park** in Key Largo, and **Looe Key National**

Scuba diver with Christ of the Abyss statue at John Pennekamp Coral Reef State Park.

Marine Sanctuary off Big Pine Key. Also, the clearest waters in which to view some of the 4,000 sunken ships along Florida's coast are in the Middle Keys and the waters between Key West and the Dry Tortugas. Snorkeling in the Keys is particularly fine between Islamorada and Marathon.

In Northwest Florida, the 100-fathom curve draws closer to the white, sandy Panhandle beaches than to any other spot on the Gulf of Mexico. It's too far north here for coral, but you can see brilliantly colored sponges and fish and, in Timber Hole, discover an undersea "petrified forest" of sunken planes, ships, and even a railroad car. The battleship USS *Massachusetts* lies in 30 feet of water just 3 miles off Pensacola, also where *Scuba Diving* magazine's 10th best dive spot in 2023, the USS *Oriskany,* is located. Every beach town in Northwest Florida has dive shops to outfit, tour, or certify visitors.

In the Crystal River area, north of the St. Petersburg and Clearwater beaches, you can snorkel with the manatees in the warm spring waters of Kings Bay.

The Professional Association of Diving Instructors (PADI) has a fantastic website covering the best dive spots in Florida at padi.com/diving-in/florida.

TENNIS & PICKLEBALL The weather in Florida is usually ideal for tennis and pickleball, though in sweltering summer months, you may want to play indoors. There are plenty of courts throughout the state, from municipal courts to exclusive resorts. The **United States Tennis Association** has a comprehensive list of all the best places where you can make—and swing—a racquet at ustaflorida.com/places-to-play.

If you can afford it, you can learn from the best in Florida. The **Frank Veltri Tennis Center** in Fort Lauderdale features a **Rafa Nadal Tennis Academy** (rafanadalacademycampusa.com), usually in December. The USTA has both tennis and pickleball academies at its campus in Orlando. Amateurs can hobnob with the superstars at **ATP Tour International Headquarters** in Ponte Vedra Beach. And **Chris Evert** has her own tennis academy in Boca Raton.

In Miami, the 21 hard courts and 6 Har-Tru clay courts at the **Crandon Park Tennis Center** (see p. 139 for full info) get crowded on weekends because they're some of the city's most beautiful. There's also a Cliff Drysdale Tennis Program for novices and experts alike. You'll play on the same courts as all the greats—Lendl, Graf, Evert, McEnroe, Federer, Djokovic, Medvedev, Venus, Serena, and more. There's a full-service pro shop, plus many good pros.

Famous as the spot where Chris Evert (and Jennifer Capriati, among others) got in her early serves with her dad trainer, who taught here up until his death in 2015, the **Jimmy Evert Tennis Center,** in Holiday Park, 701 NE 12th Ave. (off Sunrise Blvd.), Fort Lauderdale (parks.fortlauderdale.gov; ✆ **954/828-5378**), has 18 clay and 3 hard courts (15 lighted).

Other top places at which to learn and play include the **Delray Beach Tennis Center,** 201 W. Atlantic Ave. (delraytennis.com; ✆ **561/243-7360**), where champ Coco Gauff honed her skills at this full-service public tennis facility with 14 clay courts, 4 hard courts, 8 pickleball courts, and an 8,200-seat stadium located in the heart of Delray Beach. Resorts including the Saddlebrook near Tampa, Omni Amelia Island, PGA National in Palm Beach Gardens, and Sandestin Golf & Beach Resort in the Panhandle are among tennis players' tops.

With pickleball's popularity exploding, Florida has nearly 300 public pickleball courts and counting. In addition to the aforementioned tennis spots that also have p'ball facilities, the best paddle places are listed on the website pickleheads.com.

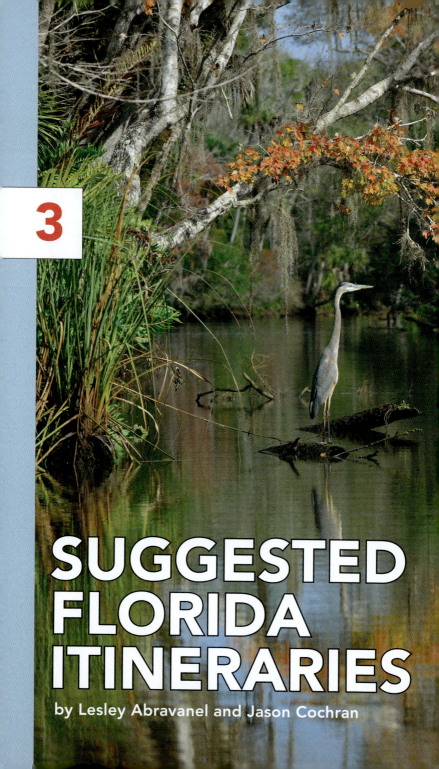

3

SUGGESTED FLORIDA ITINERARIES

by Lesley Abravanel and Jason Cochran

Ask anyone who lives here, and they'll tell you: Florida is a *long* state. If you drive from Jacksonville to the southernmost point in Key West, it'll take 10 hours at least—without traffic. Same goes for the tedious drive from Miami to the Panhandle.

Thankfully, there are flights—and even trains—throughout the state that make exploration much easier. Don't tear your hair out if you can't get from Disney to the Everglades in the same trip. Set your sights on what you want to do and see the most, and simply unwind—this is, after all, a holiday.

The range of possible itineraries is endless; what we've suggested below is a very full program covering South Florida over a 2-week period. We've also given you plans for 1, 2 and 3 days in Orlando; another family-friendly itinerary for South Florida; and a final itinerary for the historic northern reaches of the state. We've done our best to keep these itineraries geographically viable and logical. And the great thing about Florida is: If an attraction is closed, in many areas a beach day can be a wonderful, and affordable, substitute. So don't be shy about hitting the sands if you get tired of touring around.

SOUTH FLORIDA IN 2 WEEKS

Consider this tour to be a South Florida sampler. There's not enough time in 2 weeks to see and do everything, but our custom-built itinerary will provide you with a taste of South Florida's most iconic sights and experiences.

DAY 1: Miami

Since round-trip flights are the best way to go cost-wise, fly into and out of either Miami or Fort Lauderdale (the latter is usually less expensive for domestic flights) and make your way to Miami via Uber, taxi, or some form of public transportation (see your options on p. 52). Miami parking rates are outrageous, so we won't saddle you with a car until you start the road trip portion of this itinerary. After checking into your hotel, grab lunch or a snack and then head to **Wynwood Walls** (p. 130), an 80,000-square-foot outdoor street art museum that is world renowned (and can serve as a backdrop for some very fun "I'm in Miami!" social media posts). Nearby, **Superblue Miami** (p. 129) is a very contemporary immersive art museum that's a worthy add-on. Or you could engage in some retail therapy at Wynwood's artsy **boutiques** (p. 141). Stay in this neighborhood for dinner (you have a lot of options; see p. 93).

DAY 2: South Beach Miami

Sleep in or take an early morning dip in the ocean, and then head to South Beach for the daily 10:30am Art Deco **walking tour** with the Miami Design Preservation league (it's terrific; see p. 116). After lunch in the area, spend the afternoon exploring the sights of South Beach, taking in contemporary art

FACING PAGE: A pristine waterway with a great blue heron near Daytona Beach.

powerhouse **The Bass Museum** (p. 117) and the very moving **Holocaust Memorial** (p. 117). If you're not "museumed out," two others in South Beach are worthwhile: the fascinating **Jewish Museum of Florida** (p. 118) or **The Wolfsonian** (p. 120), which takes a deep and sometimes eccentric look at the intersection of design and culture. You'll have many choices in South Beach for dinner, and maybe for drinks and dancing afterwards (see p. 80 and p. 144). *Note:* If you're here on a Monday, sub in the equally extraordinary **Pérez Art Museum** (p. 125) for the Bass, which will be closed.

DAY 3: More Miami

You'll start day 3 with a trip back to Gilded Age Florida at the **Vizcaya Museum and Gardens** (p. 128), one of the most dazzling historic mansions in the United States. When you're done touring it, zip over to **Little Havana** to experience the international side of Miami. Have lunch at one of the classic Latin American joints here (p. 98) and then explore the neighborhood, either on your own or with the daily 2pm **walking tour** (p. 134). Enjoy one last dinner in Miami somewhere special and go to bed early to get up early.

DAY 4: Miami to Little Torch Key or Big Pine Key

Zip back to the airport first thing in the morning so you can pick up your rental car, then start your drive to the Keys before Miami traffic gets too hairy (7–9am Mon–Fri is peak traffic). You'll want to get an early start, as well, so you can experience some of the sights and adventures of the Middle Keys before bedding down in the Lower Keys (you'll get a chance to explore the

Groups of men playing dominoes are a common sight on the streets of Little Havana.

Upper Keys on the way back). First stop today, either before or after lunch (depending on traffic and timing—it should take roughly 2 hr. to drive from the airport here), will be **Robbie's Pier** (p. 164) in Islamorada, where steely tarpon circle the waters by the hundreds waiting to be fed. Robbie's is also an excellent place to join tours, and rent watercraft of all sorts, so, again, depending on timing, consider booking some sort of expedition here. You want to put aside enough time, however, for the most moving attraction in these parts: **The Turtle Hospital** (p. 165), which has a 90-minute tour offered every half-hour until 4pm. Also read up on **Seven Mile Bridge,** an engineering marvel (p. 162) which you'll be on for part of your journey today. After dinner nearby, check into a hotel in Big Pine Key or Little Torch Key.

DAY 5: Key West

Today you have two choices: sleep in, or wake near dawn so you can check out of your hotel and head to **National Key Deer Refuge** (p. 180) to see its eponymous wonder. Key deer are an endangered species of tiny mammals, usually the size of small dogs. They're most active early and late in the day, so taking a morning hike here gives you a good chance of seeing them. The refuge opens 30 minutes before dawn. After your hike (or when you wake), drive to Key West for brunch or early lunch. Then board the **Conch Tour Train** (p. 194) near the Pier House Hotel in Old Town. The tour will fill you in on the surprising story, soup-to-nuts (yes, there are a lot of the latter in Key West), of this storied town. You should have time for two classic visitor experiences before (or right after) dinner: a pilgrimage to the home of the great American novelist **Ernest Hemingway** (p. 190) and the sunset festivities that happen each night on **Mallory Square** (p. 185). After dinner, throw back a daiquiri, Hemingway's favorite cocktail, at his favorite bar, **Sloppy Joe's** (p. 210).

Day drinking in Key West.

DAY 6: More Key West

One of the most thought-provoking attractions in Florida is your first stop of the day: the **Mel Fisher Maritime Museum** (p. 193). You'll learn about the most lucrative sunken treasure find ever (half a billion dollars!), as well as the disturbing story of the *Henrietta Marie,* a merchant slave ship marine archeologists salvaged. A short stroll from the museum is the place where the decision to drop the atomic bomb on Japan was made: the **Harry S. Truman**

Because the Dolphin Research Center only houses dolphins that cannot be released into the wild, this is an ethical place to see and interact with them.

Little White House (p. 191). Tours start every 15 minutes, and last for roughly 45 minutes. Afterwards grab lunch, and then head to the home of Key West's other literary lion (besides Ernest Hemingway): **Tennessee Williams** (p. 194). Spend the rest of the afternoon, evening, and perhaps even the small hours of the morning, on and around **Duval Street,** Key West's raucous version of New Orleans' Bourbon Street. There's shopping (head to **Books & Books @ The Studios,** co-owned by legendary author Judy Blume, who often works the cash register), people-watching, dining, drinking, and more drinking here.

DAY 7: Middle & Upper Keys to the Everglades

Check out of your hotel, and start your drive back east to the mainland, stopping along the way at the **Dolphin Research Center** (p. 162) in Marathon, a facility that only works with dolphins that have been rescued or have come here from other facilities, and have been deemed unreleasable for medical reasons. It's an ethical place to interact with dolphins (get advance reservations for an encounter). Then, grab lunch and continue on to **John Pennekamp Coral Reef State Park,** the U.S.'s first undersea reserve. You can't really say you've been to the Keys until you've been out on or *in* the water, and you can see this park by kayak, glass-bottom boat, snorkeling, scuba diving, and more. For all the options, see p. 165. Afterwards grab dinner in Key Largo, and then drive 1½ hours to your hotel near Everglades National Park.

DAYS 8 & 9: Everglades National Park

How you see this spectacular park, and the surrounding Everglades, will depend on your fitness level. Kayaking and canoeing gets you up-close-and-personal with the sounds and sights here, but if that's too strenuous, there are a number of airboat tours outside the park (but within the same ecosystem), electric boats for people with noise sensitivities, an enjoyable guided tram tour, boardwalks, cycling and walking paths, and more. Two full days will be enough time to give you a taste of the park (many stay longer). The decommissioned **Nikes Hercules Nuclear Missile Base** (p. 222) is a fascinating non-nature site in these parts to add in if you're here at the right time (it's only open Dec–Mar).

DAYS 10 & 11: Delray Beach & the Palm Beaches

After the Everglades, drive east and north to Delray Beach, where the only alligators you'll likely see are the purses of the ladies who lunch there. After you join them for that meal, take in a perfect simulacrum of Japan at the **Morikami Museum and Japanese Gardens** (p. 265) before moving on to West Palm Beach where you'll base yourself for two nights. There you can do some retail therapy and light sociological research at the boutiques, antique stores, galleries, bars, and restaurants downtown, and in Pineapple Grove. On **DAY 11**, you could take in the outside of **Mar-a-Lago** (p. 280; no matter what your political convictions are, it counts as a historic site) in nearby Jupiter, and then divide your time between sunbathing and museum-going at the over-the-top mansion that was Standard Oil tycoon Henry

Cycling in Everglades National Park can get you very close to nature.

A water taxi chugs through one of Fort Lauderdale's many canals.

Flagler's wedding present to his third wife (**The Flagler Museum,** p. 281) and the Impressionism-rich **Norton Museum of Art** (p. 282).

DAYS 12 & 13: Fort Lauderdale

No longer spring break central, Fort Lauderdale's sands are still mighty appealing, meaning you could ditch everything that follows and just spend two days tanning on these wide, pleasant beaches. But if you want to explore the city, hop a **water taxi** (p. 240) to see the mansions on its canal systems and the New River, and discover why the city is known as the "Venice of America." Then head to the absorbing attraction too many visitors miss: the **International Swimming Hall of Fame** (p. 247). More history, this time of a bohemian bent, can be experienced at the truly spectacular **Bonnet House Museum & Gardens** (p. 245); if you prefer art, head to the **NSU Art Museum** (p. 248), which has a surprisingly rich collection. In the evening, head west to the **Seminole Hard Rock Hotel & Casino** (p. 252) where you can catch a concert by a chart-topping artist, snap a selfie by the now landmark Guitar Hotel, and hit the slots. On your last night, embrace the kitsch and visit the mermaids at the **Wreck Bar.**

DAY 14: Heading Home

Florida's mid-afternoon summer storms notoriously disrupt flight schedules, so it's wise to fly out first thing in the morning. But if you have time to explore more, consider heading back to Miami, which has a good dozen excellent museums we weren't able to hit in this itinerary.

A WEEK IN HISTORIC NORTHERN FLORIDA

Many history-driven tourists pair St. Augustine with Savannah, Georgia, and Charleston, South Carolina. But it's possible to stay in state and explore history, if you're willing to expand the definition of that to plastic pink flamingos, cracker-style homes, and small, quaint towns. Old Florida begins in St. Augustine but doesn't end there. Plus, the region is primo for getting out into nature. Here's a sample that promises to take you back to the Florida of your grandparents' day, as well as one that would seem ancient even to them.

DAYS 1, 2 & 3: St. Augustine

Everything in St. Augustine claims to be the oldest—and, in most cases, it's true: In this 17th-century-founded city you'll find America's Oldest Store, its Oldest Wooden Schoolhouse, Oldest House, and more. The Colonial Quarter St. Augustine is Florida's version of Colonial Williamsburg. To do it all justice, and also see the worthwhile attractions outside the Colonial Quarter (like Anastasia State Park, which looks like what other Florida beaches would look like if they were unfettered by modernization), we're suggesting you give the city 3 nights. That will allow you to fly into Jacksonville in the morning and start touring in the afternoon. On one of your three evenings here take a ghost tour through the old city (it'll be fun, we promise). See more on p. 454.

DAY 4: Timucuan Ecological & Historic Preserve

Drive north toward the Jacksonville area and the **Timucuan Ecological & Historic Preserve** (p. 480). It's an unusual "park," one which is made up of non-contiguous historic and natural sights. Among the most intriguing are **Fort Caroline National Memorial** (p. 481), a former 16th-century French Huguenot settlement that was wiped out by the Spanish but preserved in the form of archaeological relics; and **Kingsley Plantation** (p. 482), or at least the remains of what was once a 19th-century plantation, complete with clapboard homes and the sobering cabins used by enslaved people. Also in the park area: adorable small towns, pristine wilderness areas, and of course, beaches.

DAYS 5 & 6: Amelia Island

With 13 miles of beachfront and restored Victorian homes, Amelia Island is another world and out of this world. Steeped in history, Amelia Island is the location of **American Beach,** the only beach in the 1930s reserved for African Americans—a worthwhile tour visits Black history sites here (p. 495). Nearby is **Fernandina Beach,** which has homes dating back to the post–Civil War period. Many of the Victorian, Queen Anne, and Italianate homes are listed on the National Register. Nearby, the **Palace Saloon** claims to be Florida's oldest watering hole, challenging St. Augustine to an ongoing drinking contest. See p. 490 for full details.

An early morning shot of pedestrian-only St. George Street in St. Augustine.

DAY 7: Jacksonville

Despite its modern skyline, Jacksonville actually has some serious history. Here you'll see the Civil War–era Confederate stronghold **Camp Milton** (p. 477); the **Ritz Theatre and LaVilla Museum** (p. 480), which shines a spotlight on Black life in Jacksonville from 1921 through 1971; and the historic neighborhood of **Riverside Avondale.** The Jacksonville Zoo is home to the **Manatee Critical Care Center,** a non-historic but still compelling attraction, and the second oldest contemporary art museum in the United States (**MOCA Jacksonville;** see p. 478).

ORLANDO'S THEME PARKS IN 1, 2 & 3 DAYS

And we'll start with 1 day, but if that's your actual plan . . . well, we're sorry for you. Just as it's impossible to eat an entire box of Velveeta in one sitting (please don't try), you can't get the full breadth of Orlando in a single day. *Note:* If Epic Universe, Universal Orlando's newest theme park, has opened in time for your visit, you may want to include it in your plans.

DAY 1: Magic Kingdom

One Orlando attraction is quintessential: **Walt Disney World's Magic Kingdom** (p. 370). No matter your age or inclination, don't miss the great Disney

Audio-Animatronic odysseys **Pirates of the Caribbean, Haunted Mansion,** and **"it's a small world,"** and be sure to brave the drops of **Space Mountain, Seven Dwarfs Mine Train,** and **Tron Lightcycle / Run.** While you're there, take a free spin on the monorail through the iconic Contemporary Resort before you connect for the free round-trip ride to EPCOT (p. 375), where you'll at least see the other top Disney park from above. Stay until closing, through the fireworks, or, if you've had enough, head to the kitschy dinner banquet hoe-down, the **Hoop-Dee-Doo Musical Revue** (reservations required; p. 414). Hope you're not hungry for subtlety!

DAY 2: Universal Orlando or EPCOT

Today, arrive when the gates open at **Universal Orlando** (p. 386), one of the most attractive theme park complexes in the country. At its **Islands of Adventure** park, coaster fans should hasten to the superlative **VelociCoaster** (p. 390). From there, head to the **Hogsmeade** section of **Wizarding World of Harry Potter.** Explore the shops, full of bespoke souvenirs and snacks you can only buy here, and give your system a dose of Butterbeer, but above all, don't miss the splendid **Hagrid's Magical Creatures Motorbike Adventure.** After lunch at the **Leaky Cauldron,** you have a decision to make: Either take the **Hogwarts Express train** to the **Universal Studios** park (you'll need a park-to-park ticket) to visit the second Potter land of **Diagon Alley** and the indoor speed of the **Mummy coaster,** or stay in Islands of Adventure to take a spin on the now-iconic **Amazing Adventures of Spider-Man** and jolt yourself on **The Incredible Hulk Coaster.**

Hagrid's Magical Creatures Motorbike Adventure at the Wizarding World of Harry Potter.

Sesame Street is a big part of the SeaWorld experience, as is meeting the characters there.

Or, instead of all that, you could spend a full day at **EPCOT** (p. 375). Be sure to visit **Guardians of the Galaxy—Cosmic Rewind, Soarin',** and the traditional Disney experience, **Spaceship Earth.** Then make your way around **World Showcase** by dinnertime to select the ethnic eatery that catches your fancy, be it in Mexico, Japan, Germany, or another nation's pavilion, or queue up for the mild newcomer ride **Remy's Ratatouille Adventure.** At 9pm, you'll be in the right place for the evening's spectacular show over the lagoon. With a Park Hopper pass, you could also leave EPCOT later in the afternoon to check out **Pandora—The World of Avatar** area at **Disney's Animal Kingdom,** seeing it both in the light and after dark (if opening hours permit), when its glowing features are in full effect, or catch the **Fantasmic!** evening spectacular at **Disney's Hollywood Studios.**

If you really want to see a lot and have cash and energy to burn, do Harry Potter in the morning and then schlep back down I-4 to visit EPCOT or Pandora in the late afternoon and evening—but eat your Wheaties!

ORLANDO IN 3 DAYS

DAYS 1 & 2: Magic Kingdom, as above. But on **DAY 2,** slam through the highlights of the Universal parks with a 1-day, 2-park pass. In the morning, see Islands of Adventure, including **VelociCoaster** and **Hagrid's Magical Creatures Motorbike Adventure,** as in "Orlando in 2 Days" above, then fill the afternoon with Universal Studios. Don't neglect some of its popular rides—**Transformers: The Ride—3D** and **Harry Potter and the Escape from Gringotts** in Wizarding World of Harry Potter—Diagon Alley. Exploring that area will more than complete your day, but if you still have time, fill up on the sarcastically named dishes at **Fast Food Boulevard** in the daringly whimsical Springfield addition.

DAY 3: If you have small kids or need something more subdued today, then **SeaWorld Orlando** (p. 392), with its many (but diminishing) marine animal habitats, a terrific Sesame Street–themed land for little ones, and a passel of intense roller coasters for teens, isn't as crowded or as exhausting as most theme parks. SeaWorld could take a whole day if you stop to smell the flowers (and fish), but you can see the highlights in 4 hours, and you only have 3 days, after all. So, cram a secondary Disney park into your afternoon and evening. **EPCOT** is a fine choice for drinking and strolling (see **DAY 2** of "Orlando in 2 Days," above), but **Disney's Hollywood Studios** has some banner rides including Star Wars—Rise of the Resistance and Slinky Dog Dash. If that plan is too high-octane, spend the night at the sprawling lakeside shopping-and-dining zone of **Disney Springs** (p. 420), which has the best food at Disney.

A WEEK IN SOUTH FLORIDA, FAMILY-STYLE

The most popular Florida family vacation is to Orlando, so we've devoted an entire chapter to planning your time there, as well as including a 3-day itinerary above. But there's also that huge theme park known as nature. They'll have a ball on this beach-, critter-, and swamp-focused itinerary. (Just don't let them know Disney World is in the same state.)

DAY 1: Key Biscayne

Fly into either Fort Lauderdale or Miami, rent a car (more convenient when traveling with kids), drop your stuff at your Miami hotel, and then spend the rest of the day at the **Marjory Stoneman Douglas Biscayne Nature Center** (p. 122), where the entire family can explore an ancient fossil tidal pool or sift through seagrass beds to visit with the creatures living there. If there's time left, check out **Bill Baggs Cape Florida State Park** (p. 122, also on Key Biscayne) and take a tour of the historic lighthouse. Head back for dinner in **Little Havana** (p. 98; most kids enjoy Cuban food, and the restaurants in this area are very family-friendly).

DAY 2: Outlying Miami & Coral Gables

Get an early start and head south to Homestead's wacky **Coral Castle** (p. 132). When the kids have had their fill, head to what

The historic Venetian Pool in Coral Gables.

we'd consider a living plant museum, **Fruit and Spice Park** (p. 132). Hidden perk: You're allowed to eat anything that's naturally fallen off the branch, and what kid doesn't love scavenging? Next, hit the excellent **Zoo Miami** (you can grab lunch there) and spend several hours exploring. When you're done, clean off that stinky animal scent with a splash in Coral Gables's historic **Venetian Pool** (p. 127). Then, either dine in Coral Gables (p. 105) or head to **Julia & Henry's** (p. 90), a fun downtown food hall.

DAY 3: More Miami

Give the morning to the beguiling **Frost Science Museum** (p. 123). Its aquarium, eye-opening interactive exhibits, and planetarium will engage even the most museum-phobic kid (and adult, for that matter). You can grab lunch there before getting some much-deserved free time on the sands of **Matheson Hammock Park Beach.** Then dine in Coconut Grove at the largely outdoor **Glass & Vine** (p. 104).

DAY 4: A Safari & Fort Lauderdale Beach

Head early in the morning to **Lion Country Safari** (p. 281), which is just what it sounds like: a car safari through grounds populated by African animals. The animals are most active early and late in the day, so plan to get there just as it opens. After a morning exploring, head to your Fort Lauderdale hotel to check in. It's probably best to simply spend some time on the beautiful beaches here before grabbing dinner.

DAY 5: More Fort Lauderdale

Butterfly World (p. 246), a spectacular insectarium, is a morning activity most wee ones love. After lunch, you can either go to the **Museum of Discovery & Science** (p. 248; it has very different attractions from Miami's Frost Museum) or take another beach day. In the evening, hop on the **Jungle Queen Riverboat** (p. 247) for a watery tour, a show, and dinner. It's a classic family attraction.

DAY 6: A Forest & a Garden

The **Gumbo Limbo Nature Center** (p. 265) has a robust array of daily programs throughout the year that will teach your family about the unusual ecosystem here

The Jungle Queen Riverboat.

(the center holds one of the only subtropical hardwood forests in South Florida). Check to see what's going on before heading over, but even if you just hike and visit the nature center, with its baby turtles and other critters, you should have a good time. If you have the energy for more sightseeing, take a detour across the Pacific, and visit the **Morikami Museum & Gardens** (p. 265) before returning to your Fort Lauderdale hotel for the night.

DAY 7: Heading Home

South Florida's notorious afternoon thunderstorms are a good reason to book an early flight home. If you do decide to linger longer, consider spending some time at Fort Lauderdale's wonderful beaches, or cruising around the canals of "The Venice of the United States" in a water taxi.

THE REGIONS IN BRIEF

Contrary to popular belief, Florida is not all sun, sea, sand, and Mickey. Here's a brief rundown of the regions we cover in this guide, to help you plan your own itinerary.

MIAMI & MIAMI BEACH Sprawling across the southeastern corner of the state, metropolitan Miami is a city that prides itself on its no-passport-necessary international flair. Here you will hear a cacophony of Spanish and many other languages, not to mention accents, spoken all around you, for this area is a melting pot of immigrants from Latin America, the Caribbean, and, undeniably, the northeastern United States in particular. Cross the causeways and you'll come to the sands of Miami Beach, long a resort mecca and home to the now landmark South Beach, famous for its Art Deco architecture. The city has a number of world class museums and restaurants, and the nightlife scene is arguably the hottest in the United States. See chapters 4 and 5 for more information on the Miami area; see p. 54 for descriptions of the different districts within Miami.

THE KEYS From the southern tip of the Florida mainland, U.S. 1 travels through a 100-mile-long string of islands stretching from Key Largo to the famous, funky, and laid-back "Conch Republic" of Key West, only 90 miles from Cuba and the southernmost point in the continental United States (it's always warm down here). While some of the islands are crammed with strip malls and tourist traps, most are dense with nature, including unusual species of tropical flora and fauna. The Keys don't have the best beaches in Florida, but the waters here—all in a vast marine preserve—offer the state's best scuba diving and snorkeling, and some of its best deep-sea fishing. See chapter 6.

EVERGLADES NATIONAL PARK This is not your B-movie swamp. In fact, no Hollywood studio could afford to replicate the stunning beauty found in this national landmark. Encompassing more than 2,000 square miles and 1.5 million acres, Everglades National Park covers the entire southern tip of Florida. The park, along with nearby Big Cypress National Preserve, protects a unique and fragile "River of

Miami Mountain, a massive outdoor sculpture in South Beach.

The Lilly Pulitzer flagship store is in Palm Beach, naturally, as it epitomizes the area's aesthetics.

Grass" ecosystem teeming with wildlife that is best seen by canoe, by boat, or on long or short hikes. To the east of the Everglades is Biscayne National Park, which preserves the northernmost living-coral reefs in the continental United States. Though climate change and pollution have also set their sights on the Everglades, there is still plenty to see. See chapter 7 for more information.

THE GOLD COAST North of Miami, the Gold Coast is aptly named. Here are booming Hollywood and Fort Lauderdale, retirement-haven Boca Raton, beachy Delray Beach, West Palm Beach, and billionaire's playground Palm Beach. Beyond its dozens of gorgeous beaches, the area offers heady shopping, entertainment, dining, boating, golfing, and tennis, and many places to relax in beautiful settings. With some of the country's most famous golf courses and even more tennis—and pickleball—courts, this area also attracts big-name tournaments. See chapter 8 for more information.

THE TAMPA BAY AREA Halfway down the west coast of Florida lies Tampa Bay, one of the state's most densely populated areas and *Travel + Leisure*'s anointed Florida "it" city in 2024. A busy seaport and commercial center, the city of Tampa is home to Busch Gardens Tampa Bay, which is both a major theme park and one of the country's largest zoos. But Tampa has evolved from being a theme park destination into a savvy, sophisticated city. It's hip and happening without the hype of Miami. Boasting a unique pier and fine museums, St. Petersburg's waterfront downtown is one of Florida's most picturesque. Most visitors elect to stay near the beaches skirting the narrow barrier islands that run some 25 miles between St. Pete Beach and Clearwater Beach. Across the bay to the south lies Sarasota, one of Florida's prime performing-arts venues, another string of barrier islands with kid-friendly beaches (the surf along the Gulf Coast is far tamer than it is on the Atlantic side of Florida). See chapter 9.

Motorcycle racing at Daytona International Speedway.

WALT DISNEY WORLD & ORLANDO Central Florida attracts some 74 million visits a year, a colossal number that exceeds many nations' populations. Walt and Roy Disney were the catalysts who helped transform a swampy southern backwater into the undisputed vacation kingdom for families that includes Walt Disney World's four theme parks, two water parks, shopping districts, and dozens of hotels and restaurants; Universal Orlando's rapidly expanding empire comprising three theme parks, a waterslide park, 11 hotels, and an entertainment zone plus more room to grow; Legoland Florida's collection of attractions built for little ones; SeaWorld Orlando and its own growing arsenal of new roller coasters; and a wide landscape of campy, thrilling, and welcoming family attractions. To laugh and play in Orlando is to take a ride on the most fantastic elements of American culture and leisure. See chapter 10.

NORTHEAST FLORIDA The northeast section of the state contains the oldest permanent settlement in America—St. Augustine, where Spanish colonists settled more than 4 centuries ago. Today its history comes to life in a vibrant historic district. St. Augustine is bordered to the north by Jacksonville, a still up-and-coming Sunbelt metropolis with miles of oceanfront beach and beautiful marine views along the St. Johns River. Up on the Georgia border, Amelia Island has two of Florida's finest resorts and its own historic town of Fernandina Beach. To the south of St. Augustine is Daytona Beach, home of Daytona International Speedway and a five o'clock somewhere vibe. Another brand of excitement is offered down at Cape Canaveral, where the Kennedy Space Center continues its exploration of space, the final frontier thanks to the modern marvels of technology. See chapter 11.

MIAMI ESSENTIALS

by Lesley Abravanel

4

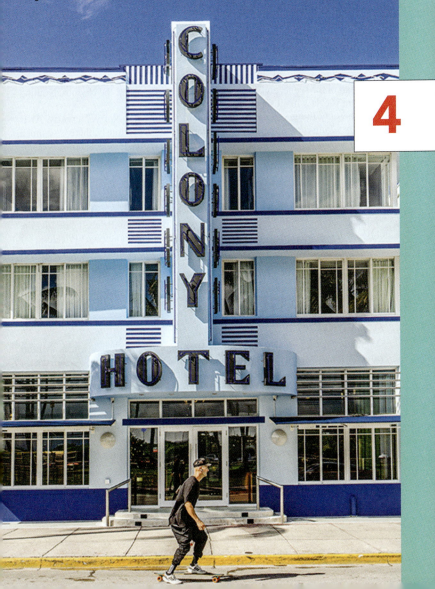

Like Cher, you'd never know that Miami was over 130 years old and yep, both beauties have had some major work done. The Magic City has stayed magical all these years thanks to money—lots of it. As another ageless beauty, Dolly Parton, once said, "It costs a lot to look this cheap."

But neither Dolly nor Miami looks or *is* cheap, and it's not just money keeping them in the headlines. Like that classic song that you can't get out of your head, Miami's beauty is beyond compare, an unforgettable, sexy seaside megalopolis of magnificent architecture, arts, culture, couture, and controversy. It's also a magnet for billionaires and people with backgrounds shadier than the ground under a palm tree canopy, but one thing it's not? Boring. The surreal, Fellini-esque world that exists way down here at the bottom of the map is a colorful cocktail of seeing, being part of the scene, and, at times, the obscene. But never the obvious. Nothing in Miami is ever what it seems.

The only thing you can't do in Miami is snow ski. Not yet anyway. AI is probably taking care of that as you are reading this, but seriously, there is so much to do in Miami if you're up for it—beaches, water sports, biking, skating, scootering, Olympic-level people-watching, shopping, fab dining, boating, celeb spotting, and art gallery and museum hopping.

Bargain hunting, now that's a toughie, but it is do-able. Pretty much anything is doable in Miami, even, yes, on a budget. Then again, Miami is also an ideal place in which to do absolutely nothing, which is the best free activity we can recommend. Doing nothing on a beach, at a pool, in a bustling Brickell cafe (ok, the coffee will cost you), with the backdrop of this bustling boomtown? Priceless.

This chapter will give you the basics of a Miami vacation: where to stay and eat and how to get around. The next chapter is all about the adventures you'll have in this dynamic city. Read on.

ORIENTATION

Arriving

Originally carved out of scrubland in 1928 by Pan American Airlines, **Miami International Airport** (**MIA;** miami-airport.com) is a hot mess—the fastest growing airport in the country with over 80 airlines and 150 destinations, through which 52 million travelers passed in 2023. In that same year, MIA was named the fifth worst airport in the country by Family Destinations Guide, for its many flight delays and cancellations. Because of these problems, travelers should consider flying into the less crowded **Fort Lauderdale Hollywood International Airport** (**FLL;** fort-lauderdale-airport.com), which is closer to north Miami than MIA, or the **Palm Beach International Airport** (**PBI;** pbia.org), which is about 1½ hours from Miami.

previous page: **Though the Colony Hotel didn't make this guide as a hotel recommendation, we think its facade is a very fine example of Art Deco architecture.**

GETTING INTO TOWN

Miami International Airport is about 6 miles west of downtown and about 10 miles from the beaches, so it's likely you can get from the plane to your hotel room in less than half an hour. Of course, if you're arriving from an international destination, it will take more time to go through Customs and Immigration.

BY CAR All the major **car-rental firms** operate off-site branches reached via shuttles from the airline terminals. If you're arriving late at night, you might want to take a taxi to your hotel and have the car delivered to you the next day.

BY TAXI Taxis line up in front of a dispatcher's desk outside the airport's arrivals terminals. Most cabs are metered, though some have flat rates to popular destinations. The fare should be about $17–$45 to Coral Gables, $20–$30 to downtown, and $35–$55 to various parts of Miami Beach, plus tip, which should be 15% to 20% (add more for each bag the driver handles). Depending on traffic, the ride to Coral Gables or downtown takes about 15 to 20 minutes, and to South Beach, 20 to 25 minutes, but prepare for the traffic, because it's almost as ubiquitous as the palm trees.

BY VAN, LIMO, OR UBER/LYFT Group limousines (multi-passenger vans) circle the arrivals area looking for fares. Destinations are posted on the front of each van, and a flat rate is charged for door-to-door service to the area marked. **SuperShuttle** (supershuttle.com; ✆ **305/871-2000**) is one of the largest airport operators, charging between $11 and $60 per person for a ride within the county or into Fort Lauderdale. Its vans operate 24 hours a day and accept credit cards. This is a cheaper alternative to a cab (if you are traveling alone or with one other person), but be prepared to be in the van for quite some time, as you may have to make several stops to drop off passengers before you reach your own destination. If you have patience, great, if not, you may want to consider **Uber, Lyft,** or another ride-sharing service, which may end up being cheaper and faster. If surge pricing is not in effect, Uber or Lyft will set you back approximately $20 from MIA to the Port of Miami in downtown, versus $27 in a cab. Conveniently, you can track the prices on the apps before deciding whether or not to hail a cab.

Private limousine arrangements can be made in advance. A one-way meet-and-greet service can cost as low as $69 to astronomically higher depending on car and destination. Recommended limo services include **Aventura Limo** (aventuralimo.com; ✆ **305/306-5466**), **Miami Prestige Limos** (miamiprestigelimos.com; ✆ **888/978-2532**), and **Miami Airport Limo** (limoinmiami.com; ✆ **305/517-1177**).

BY PUBLIC TRANSPORTATION Public transportation in South Florida is a major hassle bordering on a nightmare. Painfully slow and unreliable, buses heading downtown leave the airport only once per hour (from the arrivals level), and connections are spotty, at best. It could take about 1½ hours to get to South Beach via public transportation. Journeys to downtown and Coral Gables, however, are more direct. The fare is $2.25. For those heading to South Beach from the airport, the 150 Airport Flyer provides direct express service from MIA to Miami Beach and costs $2.65. With only one minor stop en route, the trip to the beach takes about a half-hour. Not bad.

Visitor Information

Up-to-date info is provided by the **Greater Miami Convention and Visitor's Bureau** (miamiandbeaches.com). If you arrive at Miami International Airport, you can pick up visitor info at the airport's main visitor counter on the second floor of Terminal E 24 hours a day.

Always check local newspapers for special events during your visit. The city's only daily, the *Miami Herald* (miamiherald.com), is a so-so source for current-events listings. Better is the free weekly alternative paper, the *Miami New Times* (miaminewtimes.com), available online and in bright red boxes throughout the city. Miami.com is another good source of information.

City Layout

Miami seems confusing at first, but quickly becomes easy to navigate. The small cluster of buildings that make up the downtown area is at the geographical heart of the city. In relation to downtown, the airport is northwest, the beaches are east, Coconut Grove is south, Coral Gables is west, and the rest of the city is north.

FINDING AN ADDRESS Miami is divided into dozens of areas with official and unofficial boundaries. Street numbering in the city of Miami is fairly straightforward, but you must first be familiar with the numbering system. The mainland is divided into four sections (NE, NW, SE, and SW) by the intersection of Flagler Street and Miami Avenue. Flagler Street divides Miami from north to south, and Miami Avenue divides the city from east to west. It's helpful to remember that avenues generally run north-south, while streets go east-west. Street numbers (1st St., 2nd St., and so forth) start from here and increase as you go farther out from this intersection, as do numbers of avenues, places, courts, terraces, and lanes. Streets in Hialeah are the exceptions to this pattern; they are listed separately in map indexes.

Getting around the barrier islands that make up Miami Beach is easier than moving around the mainland. Street numbering starts with 1st Street, near Miami Beach's southern tip, and goes up to 192nd Street, in the northern part of Sunny Isles. As in the city of Miami, some streets in Miami Beach have numbers as well as names. When those are listed in this book, both name and number are given.

The numbered streets in Miami Beach are not the geographical equivalents of those on the mainland, but they are close. For example, the 79th Street Causeway runs into 71st Street on Miami Beach.

The Neighborhoods in Brief

SOUTH BEACH—THE ART DECO DISTRICT Long known as a Caribbean-chic cafe society with a raging nightlife, people-watching on South Beach (1st St.–23rd St., roughly 10 miles of beach) remains an amusing pastime, but the crowds have changed. Gone are the supermodels and A-list stars. In their place are a motley crew of characters, from eccentric locals, seniors, and snowbirds, to college students and curiosity seekers. On the plus side, individuality is still as widely accepted on South Beach as Visa, MasterCard, and Apple Pay. But the crowds these days are into gigantic, sugary-sweet cocktails and no longer wear Milan-caliber clothing on Ocean Drive (today the dress code is more OnlyFans).

Of course, the reason why South Beach exists at all is its stunning buildings, the largest concentration of Art Deco architecture in the world (in 1979, much of South Beach was listed in the National Register of Historic Places). The pastel-hued structures are stalwart supermodels in their own right.

MIAMI BEACH In the fabulous '50s, Miami Beach was America's *true* Riviera, the stomping ground of choice for the Rat Pack and notorious mobsters such as Al

Lifeguard station on Miami Beach.

Capone. Then in the 1960s and '70s, people who fell in love with Miami began to buy apartments rather than rent hotel rooms. Tourism declined, and many area hotels fell into disrepair.

However, since the late 1980s, Miami Beach proper has experienced a tide of revitalization. Huge beach hotels, such as the Vegas-esque Fontainebleau, and Eden Roc, are attracting large convention crowds and international visitors. New generations of Americans are quickly rediscovering the qualities that originally made Miami Beach so popular, and they are finding out that the sand and surf now come with a thriving, technologically savvy, international city—a city with free Wi-Fi with 95% coverage outside, which means on the sand, and 70% indoors up to the second floor of any building.

Before Miami Beach turns into Surfside, there's North Beach, where there are uncrowded beaches, some restaurants, lots of locals who were priced off South Beach, and examples of Miami modernism architecture.

Surfside, Bal Harbour, and **Sunny Isles** make up the north part of the beach (island). Hotels, motels, restaurants, and beaches line Collins Avenue and, with some exceptions, the farther north one goes, the cheaper lodging becomes before you hit haute Bal Harbour. Keep in mind that beachfront properties, especially in Sunny Isles, are at a premium, so many of that area's moderately priced hotels have been converted to condos, leaving fewer affordable places to stay.

Exclusive and ritzy Bal Harbour is mostly beachfront condominium towers and fancy homes, tucked away in gated communities on the bay. The Rodeo Drive of Miami (known as the Bal Harbour Shops) attracts shoppers who don't flinch at four-, five-, and six-figure price tags.

Note that **North Miami Beach,** a residential area near the Dade-Broward County line (north of 163rd St.; part of North Dade County), is a misnomer. It is actually northwest of Miami Beach, on the mainland, and has no beaches, though it does have some of Miami's better restaurants and shops. Located within North Miami Beach is the posh residential community of **Aventura,** best known for the Aventura Mall.

KEY BISCAYNE Miami's forested and secluded Key Biscayne is technically a barrier island and is not part of the Florida Keys. This island is nothing like its southern neighbors. Located south of Miami Beach, off the shores of Coconut Grove, Key Biscayne is protected from the troubles of the mainland by the long Rickenbacker Causeway and its $3 toll.

Largely an exclusive residential community with million-dollar homes and sweeping water views, Key Biscayne also offers visitors great public beaches, world-class tennis facilities, and mediocre restaurants. Hobie Beach, adjacent to

With the Miami skyline as a backdrop, dogs and their owners frolic at Hobie Beach.

the causeway, is the city's premier spot for windsurfing, sailboarding, and jet-skiing (see "Watersports," in chapter 5). On the island's southern tip, Bill Baggs State Park has great beaches, bike paths, and dense forests.

DOWNTOWN Miami's downtown boasts one of the world's most beautiful cityscapes and, over the last decade, it has finally emerged as an actual "downtown" of a major city with daylife—and nightlife. The after dark scene is especially vibrant on Brickell Avenue and NE 11th Street. Sure, the downtown area still has the somewhat schlocky, touristy outdoor mall, Bayside Marketplace, where many cruise passengers come to browse. But there's also much better shopping in the Brickell business district. As for the culture—wow, has Miami evolved with the emergence of the sprawling bayfront Perez Art Museum and Frost Science Museum. It also has a few great restaurants, as well as the arena (whose name is constantly changing) that's home to concerts and the Miami Heat. The **Downtown Miami Partnership** offers guided historic walking tours daily at 10:30am (© **305/379-7070**). For more info, go to **downtownmiami.com**.

DESIGN DISTRICT With restaurants and luxury shopping springing up between galleries and furniture stores galore, this once sleepy, seedy district, like downtown Miami, has finally come into its own. Still a hotbed for furniture-import companies, interior designers, and architects, it has also become a player in Miami's ever-changing fashion and dining landscapes. The shopping here, however, is more glossy magazine luxe—the kind of place Jennifer Lopez comes with her security to shut down Gucci. But browsing is free, and it's always fabulous. There are often very arty events and concerts at night here, many free. An up-to-date website, **miamidesigndistrict.com**, includes a calendar of events, such as the internationally lauded Art Basel, which attracts the who's who of the art world. The district is loosely defined as the area bounded by NE 2nd Avenue, NE 5th Avenue East and West, and NW 36th Street to the south.

MIDTOWN/WYNWOOD What used to be called El Barrio is now one of Miami's trendiest areas or, as the kids say, the 'hood with the most rizz. But again, not for long. As the area is still burgeoning, what's going up are pricey condos, pushing out the arty folk once again. It's a vicious cycle of gentrification Miami can't seem to avoid. But hurry while that, uh, rizz is still rising.

Just north of downtown and roughly divided by I-395 to the south, I-195 to the north, I-95 to the west, and Biscayne Boulevard to the east, Wynwood actually includes the Miami Design District, but has developed an identity of its own thanks to an exploding, albeit still very rough and gritty, arts scene made popular by cheap rents and major exposure during Art Basel Miami Beach. It has a painfully hip collection of bars and restaurants alongside Midtown Miami, a mall-like town-center complex of apartment buildings surrounded by shops and restaurants.

BISCAYNE CORRIDOR From downtown, near Bayside, to the 70s (affectionately known as the Upper East Side), where funky curio shops and upscale restaurants close as fast as they open, Biscayne Boulevard is aspiring to reclaim itself as a safe thoroughfare where tourists can wine, dine, and shop. Once known for sketchy, dilapidated 1950s- and 1960s-era hotels, this boulevard is getting a boost from residents fleeing the high prices of the beaches. They're renovating Biscayne block by block, trying to make this famous boulevard worthy of a Sunday drive. It's still a work in progress, one which many locals are pleased about because it has yet to be fully commercialized.

LITTLE HAVANA If you've never been to Cuba, just visit this small section of Miami and you'll come pretty close. The sounds, tastes, and rhythms are very

Buckminster Fuller's Fly's Eye Dome is the centerpiece at a shopping center in the Design District.

57

reminiscent of Cuba's capital city, and you don't have to speak a word of English to live an independent life here—even street signs are in Spanish and English.

Cuban coffee shops, tailor and furniture stores, and inexpensive restaurants line Calle Ocho (pronounced *Ka*-yey *O*-choh), SW 8th Street, the region's main thoroughfare. In Little Havana, salsa and merengue beats ring loudly from old record stores while old men in *guayaberas* (loose-fitting cotton short-sleeved shirts) smoke cigars over their daily game of dominoes. The area is also noted for the artists and nocturnal types who have their galleries and performance spaces here, sparking a culturally charged neo-bohemian nightlife.

CORAL GABLES "The City Beautiful," created by George Merrick in the early 1920s, is one of Miami's first planned developments. Houses here were built in a Mediterranean style along lush, tree-lined streets that open onto beautifully carved plazas, many with centerpiece fountains. The best architectural examples of the era have Spanish-style tiled roofs and are built from Miami oolite, native limestone commonly called "coral rock." The Gables's European-flaired shopping and commerce center is home to many thriving corporations. The University of Miami is also here. Coral Gables also has landmark hotels, great golfing, upscale shopping to rival Bal Harbour, and some of the city's best restaurants.

COCONUT GROVE An arty, hippie hangout in the psychedelic '60s, Coconut Grove once had residents who dressed in swirling tie-dyed garb. Nowadays, they prefer the uniform color schemes of Lululemon. Chain stores, seriously pricey restaurants and hotels, a movie theater, and bars galore make Coconut Grove a commercial success, but this gentrification has pushed most alternative types out. The intersection of Grand Avenue, Main Highway, and McFarlane Road pierces the area's heart. Right in the center of it all is CocoWalk, once sad and empty and now re-filled with boutiques, eateries, and bars. Sidewalks here are often crowded, especially at night, when University of Miami students come out.

SOUTHERN MIAMI-DADE COUNTY To locals, South Miami is both a specific area, southwest of Coral Gables, and a general region that encompasses all of southern Miami-Dade County, including Kendall, Perrine, Cutler Ridge, and Homestead. For the purposes of clarity, this book has grouped all these southern suburbs under the rubric "Southern Miami-Dade County." The area is heavily residential and packed with strip malls amid a few remaining plots of farmland. Tourists don't usually stay in these parts, unless they are on their way to the Everglades or the Keys. However, Southern Miami-Dade County contains many of the city's top attractions (see chapter 5), meaning that you're likely to spend at least some of your time in Miami here.

GETTING AROUND

Officially, Miami-Dade County has opted for a "unified, multimodal transportation network," which basically means you can get around the city by train and bus. However, in practice, the network doesn't work very well. Things have improved somewhat thanks to Brightline, the privately owned and operated high-speed rail system that opened a station in downtown Miami and goes all the way to Orlando now, but unless you are going from downtown Miami to a not-too-distant spot, you are better off in a rental car, ride-share, or taxi.

Miami is not really a walker's city. It's more of an Uber/Lyft city, frankly. Because it is so spread out, most attractions are too far apart to make walking between them feasible. In fact, most Miamians are so used to driving that they do so even when going just a few blocks.

By Public Transportation

BY RAIL Two rail lines, operated by the **Metro-Dade Transit Agency** (www.co.miami-dade.fl.us/mdta), run in concert with each other. **Metrorail,** the city's aging, not-very-high-speed commuter train, is a 25-mile elevated line that travels north-south, between downtown Miami and the southern suburbs. Locals refer to it as Metro*fail,* but, it isn't an epic fail anymore, as it's been upgraded a bit and its coverage area is wider than it used to be, providing service to Miami International Airport, and running from Kendall through South Miami, Coral Gables, and downtown Miami; to the Civic Center/Jackson Memorial Hospital area; and to Brownsville, Liberty City, Hialeah, and Medley in northwest Miami-Dade, with connections to Broward and Palm Beach counties at three locations. There's also a transfer to the Brightline station.

If you are staying in Coral Gables or Coconut Grove, you can park your car at a nearby station and ride the rails downtown. Metrorail operates daily from about 6am to midnight. The fare is $2.25.

Metromover, a 4½-mile elevated line people mover, circles the downtown area and connects with Metrorail at the Government Center stop. Riding on rubber tires, the single-car train is like an old school Weebles toy, an amusing contrast to the rest of the ultra-modern city, and winding past many of the area's most important attractions. But give them a minute or ten. The city is working to upgrade it. Currently it runs 7 days a week in the downtown Miami and Brickell areas. Major destinations include the arena where the Heat play, Bayside Marketplace, Miami Dade College, and the Miami-Dade County School Board. That's about it.

You may not go very far on the Metromover, but it's free and you will get a beautiful perspective from the towering height of the suspended rails. System hours are daily from about 6am to midnight, and did we mention the ride is free?

Brightline, an inter-city rail route that runs between Miami and Orlando, is a $5-billion high-speed train that's a convenient way to travel if you have the cash. The brand-spanking new system features clean, comfy seats with phone chargers and leg room. With a premium ticket you get beer, wine, and cocktails on your journey. Each station—downtown Miami, Aventura, Fort Lauderdale, Boca Raton, West Palm Beach, and Orlando—has different amenities for passengers, but the best stations are by far the Miami and Orlando ones because of their sheer size and restaurants. While the trip from Miami to Orlando is pretty much the same 3½ hours it takes to drive, the other stops are obviously shorter and less expensive, making it a fun way to explore another city for a day or night. Rates range from $10 to $150 each way, and there are often specials on the website. *Tip:* It's often cheaper to buy tickets on the website (gobrightline.com) than in person.

Before Brightline, there was **Tri-Rail,** a commuter rail line linking Miami, Fort Lauderdale, and West Palm Beach—hence the word "tri." With 18 stations throughout South Florida, it connects directly to Amtrak, Metrorail, and the Miami International Airport Intermodal Center. Fares range from $2.50 to $8.75. While a far cry from the fancy Brightline, it's a favored mode of transport for students, commuters, and those not on expense accounts. It's certainly reliable. Complimentary shuttles from the major airports to Tri-Rail stations are conveniences, but there are no bathrooms or major amenities at the stations. That being said, it's a lot better being on here than sitting in I-95 traffic. For more info, go to tri-rail.com.

BY BUS Ack, no. Just no. A bus ride in Miami is grueling. Miami's suburban layout is not conducive to getting around by bus; instead of getting to know the city, relying on bus transportation will acquaint you only with how it feels to wait at bus stops. The fare is $2.25, or $2.65 for an allegedly "express" bus, which may save you 2 minutes. When on South Beach, however, consider the free **Miami Beach Trolley,** operating 15 hours a day, from 8am to 11pm 7 days a week at approximately 20-minute average service frequency along each route. For specifics on where and when, go to miamibeachfl.gov/city-hall/transportation/trolley.

By Car

Tales circulate about vacationers who have visited Miami without a car or at least without access to a car, but they are very few indeed. If you are counting on exploring the city, even to a modest degree, a car is essential. Thank goodness for Uber and Lyft, though the fare surges during popular times are oftentimes astronomical and offensive. Miami's restaurants, hotels, and attractions are far from one another, so any other form of transportation is relatively impractical. You won't need a car, however, if you are spending your entire vacation at a resort, are traveling directly to the Port of Miami for a cruise, or are here for a short stay centered on one area of the city, such as South Beach or Brickell, where everything is within walking distance and parking is a costly nightmare.

When driving across a causeway or through downtown, allow extra time to reach your destination because of frequent drawbridge openings. Some bridges open about every half-hour for large sailing vessels to make their way through the wide bays and canals that crisscross the city, stalling traffic.

RENTALS Expect to pay about $205 per week in Miami for economy cars. A minimum age, generally 25, is usually required of renters; some rental agencies have also set maximum ages!

All the national rental companies are here. Comparison shop before you make any decisions: car-rental prices can fluctuate more than airfares.

Finally, think about splurging on a convertible. Not only are convertibles one of the best ways to see the beautiful surroundings, but they're also an ideal way to perfect a tan!

PARKING Every once in a while, you'll need to pay meters with quarters, but most have been removed either in favor of credit card–operated parking payment stations (you get a printed receipt to display on your dashboard) or app-based payments. Carefully read the signs.

Parking garages are another option, as is valet parking (usually $40–$60). Because parking is at such a premium in bustling South Beach, downtown, and Coconut Grove, prices tend to be jacked up—especially at night and when there are special events (day or night). In these cases it might be smarter to rely on Uber or Lyft.

LOCAL DRIVING RULES Florida law allows drivers to make a right turn on a red light after a complete stop, unless otherwise indicated. In addition, all passengers are required to wear seat belts, and children 3 and under must be securely fastened in government-approved car seats.

By Taxi, Uber, or Lyft

If you're not planning on traveling much within the city (and especially if you plan on spending your vacation within the confines of South Beach's Art Deco District), an occasional taxi or ride-sharing service is a good alternative to renting a car and dealing with parking hassles. Taxi meters start at about $2.95 at flag-fall. For specifics on rate increases and surcharges, go to www.taxifarefinder.com.

Major cab companies include **Yellow Taxi** (℡ 786/830-6253) and, on Miami Beach, **Central** (℡ 305/532-5555).

Ride-sharing services a la **Uber** and **Lyft** *can* be less expensive than taxis depending on the time you are requesting them. For instance, during hot ticket events like Art Basel Miami Beach, the price surging on the ride-sharing services can be downright offensive, often triple the price of a cab. During quieter times, ride-shares can cost 25% less than a taxi.

By Bike

Miami is a biker's paradise, especially on Miami Beach, where the hard-packed sand and boardwalks make it an easy and scenic route. However, unless you are a former New York City bike messenger, you won't want to use a bicycle as your main means of transportation. Miami's **citibike** (citibikemiami.com), a public bike-sharing program, has 1,000 custom bikes at solar-powered, automated rental stations located at all major attractions, shops, hotels, condos, beaches, and civic centers throughout the city with rates beginning at $7.49 for an hourly pass to $24 for a day pass.

For more information on bicycles, including where to rent the best ones, see "More Ways to Play, Indoors & Out," in chapter 5.

[FastFACTS] MIAMI

Area Code The original area code for Miami and all of Miami-Dade County is 305. That is still the code for older phone numbers, but all phone numbers assigned since July 1998 have the area code 786 (SUN), and as of 2023, 645. For all local calls, even if you're just calling across the street, you must dial the area code (305, 645, or 786) first. Even though the Keys share the Miami-Dade County area code of 305, calls to there from Miami are considered long distance and must be preceded by 1-305. (Within the Keys, simply dial the seven-digit number.) The area codes for Fort Lauderdale are 954 and 754; for Palm Beach, Boca Raton, Vero Beach, and Port St. Lucie, it's 561 and the new 728.

Business Hours Most banks are open weekdays from 9am to 3pm. Several stay open until 5pm or so at least 1 day during the week, and most feature automated teller machines (ATMs) for 24-hour banking. Most stores are open daily from 10am to 6pm; however, there are *many* exceptions (noted in "Shopping," in chapter 5, beginning on p. 141). As far as business offices are concerned, Miami is generally a 9-to-5ish town.

Dentists If you're in absolute need of a dentist, go to 1800dentist.com. A lot of strip-mall chain dentists like Aspen Dental offer emergency walk-in visits, too.

Doctors In a medical emergency, call an ambulance by dialing ℡ **911**. If it's not an emergency, you can usually find an urgent care service nearby. **MD Now** (mymdnow.com) is the city's most ubiquitous and reliable.

Emergencies To reach the police, an ambulance, or the fire department, dial ℡ **911** from any phone. For a list of crisis hotlines in Miami, go to lovediscovery.org/crisis-hotlines.

Internet Access Internet access is available via free Wi-Fi in many parts of the city including downtown and Miami Beach.

Liquor Laws Only adults 21 or older may legally purchase or consume alcohol in Florida. Minors are usually permitted in bars, as long as the bars also serve food. Liquor laws are strictly enforced; if you look young, carry ID. Beer and wine are sold in most supermarkets and convenience stores.

Lost Property If you lose something at the airport, call the **Airport Lost and Found** office (© **305/876-7377**). If you lose something on the bus, Metrorail, or Metromover, call **Metro-Dade Transit Agency** (© **305/770-3131**). If you lose something anywhere else, phone the **Miami-Dade Police** (© **305/603-6640**). You may also want to fill out a police report for insurance purposes.

Newspapers The *Miami Herald* is the city's only English-language daily. The most respected alternative weekly is the giveaway tabloid, **New Times**, which contains up-to-date listings and reviews of food, films, theater, music, and whatever else is happening in town.

Police For emergencies, dial © **911** from any phone. The Miami-Dade Police Department can be reached at © **305/603-6640**.

Post Office The **Main Post Office**, 2200 NW 72nd Ave. (© **800/275-8777**), is located west of Miami International Airport. Conveniently located post offices include 20 Miracle Mile in Coral Gables, 1101 Brickell Ave. downtown, 1300 Washington Ave. in South Beach, and 3191 Grand Ave. in Coconut Grove.

Restrooms Stores rarely let customers use their restrooms, and many restaurants offer their facilities only for their patrons. However, most malls have restrooms, as do many fast-food restaurants. Public beaches and large parks often provide toilets, though in some places you have to pay or tip an attendant. Most large hotels have clean restrooms in their lobbies.

Safety As always, use your common sense and be aware of your surroundings at all times. Don't walk alone at night, and be extra wary when walking or driving though certain desolate parts of downtown Miami and surrounding areas. For some good visitor safety tips, visit www.miamidade.gov/global/police/visitor-safety.page.

Taxes A 6% state sales tax (plus 1% local tax, for a total of 7% in Miami-Dade County [from Homestead to North Miami Beach]) is added on at the register for all goods and services purchased in Florida. In addition, most municipalities levy special taxes on restaurants and hotels. In 2023, Miami was named the country's 5th city with the highest tourist tax. In Miami Beach, the resort tax is 6%. For properties off Miami Beach the resort tax is 3%.

Time Zone Miami is in the Eastern Standard Time (EST) zone. Between the second Sunday of March and the first Sunday of November, daylight saving time is adopted, and clocks are set 1 hour ahead.

Transit Information For Metrorail or Metromover schedule information, phone © **305/770-3131** or download the Miami-Dade Transit app. For bus schedules, consult the app mentioned above.

Weather Hurricane season in Miami runs June through November. For an up-to-date recording of current weather conditions and forecast reports, head to weather.gov. Also see the "When to Go" section in chapter 2.

WHERE TO STAY IN MIAMI

As much a part of the landscape as the palm trees, Miami's hotels are on display as if they were contestants in a beauty pageant. Many are from the 1930s, 1940s, and 1950s, but have been totally renovated into (mostly) independently owned "boutique" hotels.

Finding affordable hotels is the challenge, leading many visitors to seek out accommodations via Airbnb or Vrbo. Happily, it's still possible to get centrally located digs on those sharing services for less than hotels, though it's important to filter for fees as those can sometimes double the nightly rate. (*Tip:* To avoid these platforms' fees, figure out what management company is overseeing the rental you're interested in and then go to that company directly. That's easier to do on Vrbo than Airbnb.) Also, vet the properties you find on these services carefully via the most recent online reviews, because a lot of Miami condos prohibit short-term rentals and owners try to get around that at your expense.

You should also find out how near your room will be to the city's rowdy nightlife; trying to sleep directly on Ocean Drive or Brickell Avenue, especially on weekends, is next to impossible, unless your lullaby of choice happens to include throbbing salsa and bass beats.

Though it may no longer be the "it" girl of the city, the clear advantage to staying on South Beach as opposed to, say, Coral Gables or Coconut Grove, is that the beaches are within walking distance, there are bars and restaurants aplenty, and, basically, everything you need is right there. However, staying there is definitely not for everyone—especially those seeking peace and quiet. For a somewhat less expensive stay that's only a 10-minute cab or Uber ride from South Beach, Miami Beach proper (the area north of 23rd St. and Collins Ave. all the way up to 163rd St. and Collins Ave.) offers a slew of options right on the beach, many of which will be more cost effective.

What *will* cost you a small fortune are the luxury hotels in the city's financial Brickell Avenue district, the area of choice for expense-account business travelers and camera-shy celebrities trying to avoid the South Beach spotlight.

For Miami with an old-world European flair, Coral Gables and its charming hotels and exquisite restaurants are the pick. And then there's Wynwood, where grit is an amenity for the inked-up crowd too cool for the rest of the city.

SEASONS & RATES

South Florida's tourist season was once well-defined, beginning in mid-November and lasting until Easter, but with the growing popularity of the state, and the increasing number of special events, that's changing. Generally, hotel prices escalate from the beginning of the year until about March, after which they dip a tiny bit. The cheapest rates (down by 20% from winter highs) can be found in the oppressively hot months of August and September.

But timing isn't *everything*. Rates also depend on your hotel's proximity to local hot spots and to the beach, specifically how much ocean you can see from your window. Small motels or condos a block or two from the water can be considerably cheaper than similar properties right on the sand.

> **Price Categories**
>
> We're listing double room rates only. Please assume that suites will be pricier. Also note that some hotels fall into one price range in high season and a different one in low, hence the hybrid categories below.
> **Inexpensive:** $199 and under
> **Moderate:** $200–$325
> **Expensive:** $326 and up

The rates listed below are broken down into two broad categories: winter (generally, Thanksgiving through Easter) and off season (about mid-May through Aug). The months in between, the shoulder season, should fall somewhere in between the highs and lows, while rates always go up on holidays. Remember, too, that **state and city taxes** can add as much as 13% to your bill in some parts of Miami. Many hotels, especially those in South Beach, also tack on **resort fees,** and don't forget that parking is pricey. See p. 505 for our advice on always saving money on lodgings.

South Beach

The times have certainly been a-changin': many of the once A-list celeb hot spots are now part of multinational chains, and service and decor have suffered. Plus, a number of the stars from South Beach's halcyon days as the "American Riviera" have shuttered, possibly permanently (some may be coming back).

And while South Beach used to be a mecca for the LGBTQ+ community, that crowd has also moved to gayer pastures, including Wilton Manors in Fort Lauderdale. That said, South Beach is still welcoming to every kind of visitor.

Detail of an Art Deco building in South Beach.

I also have to add a small warning: Art Deco hotels, while pleasing to the eye, may be a bit run-down inside. It's par for the course on South Beach, where appearances are, at times, deceiving.

EXPENSIVE

1 Hotel South Beach ★★   1 Hotel South Beach is an eco-conscious homage to nature. Its lush greenery and natural woods are straight out of a Malibu beach house, but not Barbie's—you won't find hot pink in this place. Instead, rooms are awash in soothing, sandy, upscale beachy decor, with uber comfy Keetsa—organic, natch—mattresses, and soft bedding, rain showers, and filtered water taps. A Leed Silver-certified hotel, the 426-room property has enviable green practices, like zero-waste kitchens that source from sustainable food and beverage vendors exclusively. Staff here are not only friendly (a rarity in these parts) but go above and beyond to make sure guests feel cared for, and that goes for pets, too. There's no fee to bring them. On-site are four pools, including an adults-only rooftop pool; 600 feet of beachfront; a lobby farm stand; and a beachside food truck, plus three excellent restaurants, all of which are either vegan-friendly or fully vegan. The hotel also hosts wellness programs, spoken-word poetry nights, pottery and mixology classes, and a great kids program (ages 4–10). The house car, a fully electric Audi e-tron, is available for rides and test drives.

2341 Collins Ave. 1hotels.com/south-beach. **833/625-3111** or 305/604-1000. 426 units. $468–$2,599 double. Valet parking $55. **Amenities:** 3 restaurants; 5 bars/lounges; babysitting; kids program; concierge; 4 pools; beach; room service; spa; free Wi-Fi.

The Betsy Hotel ★★
The Betsy is the lone surviving example of Florida Georgian architecture on the famous byway, Ocean Drive. Behind its plantation-style shutters and columned façade are rooms that nod to the stately colonial rooms of yesteryear, *and* the modern aesthetic of South Beach (so yes, TVs are embedded in the mirrors of the marble bathrooms). Interestingly, this is also a bookworm's idyll: Guestrooms all have mini-libraries in them and the salon-style lobby bar evokes the days of Dorothy Parker and her Algonquin pals with unabashedly intellectual programming, from book readings to art talks and nightly live jazz. The Betsy is steps from the beach and home to two restaurants and two pools, including a rooftop one with a cafe and Zen garden for sunrise yoga. *Nice move:* Half of the pet fee goes to Miami-Dade Animal Rescue and the SPCA in Zimbabwe, the childhood home of one of the hotel's owners.

1440 Ocean Dr. thebetsyhotel.com. **844/539-2840.** 130 units. $326–$1,344 double. Valet parking $49. Pet fee $150. **Amenities:** 2 restaurants; 2 bars; coffee shop; babysitting; concierge; gym; 2 pools; room service; free Wi-Fi.

The Setai ★★★
The Setai is more tai chi than chichi, a very Zen place. All of the suites—some are actually condos participating in the condo-hotel program—are actual apartments with floor-to-ceiling windows, full kitchens, and Jacuzzi bathtubs bigger than a small swimming pool. Even the 85 regular hotel rooms are capacious, at an average of 600 square feet (suites are 1,300–3,500 sq. ft.). All are adorned in sleek Asian decor with over-the-top comforts, including hand-crafted Swedish Duxiana mattresses, Frette linens, Samsung sound bars, Nest digital thermostats, Acqua di Parma bathroom amenities, and washer/dryers. The luxe **Valmont Spa** does free yoga on the beach Friday through Sunday. Service is superlative here.

2001 Collins Ave. thesetaihotel.com. **305/520-6000.** 152 units. $608–$2,000 double. Valet parking $49. **Amenities:** 3 restaurants; 2 bars; concierge; fitness center; 3 pools; room service; spa; free Wi-Fi.

W South Beach ★★
A work of art itself, this oceanfront property features a Bali–meets–Miami Beach sensibility, with breathtaking landscape design by conceptual design garden artist Paula Hayes, and a dark, clubby lobby decked out in artwork by Basquiat, Warhol, and other modern masters. A $30-million post-pandemic reno gave the place a refreshed look, meaning bright guest rooms and suites decked out in beach house decor (natural oak, soft corals, and teal-and-white lacquered walls decorated in surfer scapes). Rooms are the largest in South Beach, and have expansive glass balconies with unobstructed views of the beach and ocean, plus the W signature bed with plush pillow-top mattress and feather bed overlay. Huge marble bathrooms have rain head showers; some have soaking tubs. Of the suites, a number are actual apartments with full kitchens. Perhaps the most unique amenities are **Swish** and **Swing,** the full-size rooftop tennis and basketball courts with city views.

2201 Collins Ave. wsouthbeach.com. **305/938-3000.** 408 units. $500–$2,600 double. Valet parking $55. Pet fee $250. **Amenities:** 2 restaurants; 3 bars; nightclub; state-of-the-art fitness center; 2 pools; spa; tennis and basketball courts; free Wi-Fi.

MODERATE/EXPENSIVE
Life House South of Fifth ★★
This 26-room cottage, a former hostel, in the still-hot South of Fifth neighborhood of South Beach, is an adorable stay… if you can snag a room. The usually well-priced guest rooms are bright and airy,

with whitewashed shiplap wood walls and ceilings. Bathrooms (one per room now) are tiny but spiffy. A lovely lobby bar features food and cocktails with locally sourced ingredients served to a crowd of locals and (mostly millennial) travelers. The staff are super friendly and while there's no pool, the beach is just a block away. Another Life House is located in Little Havana.

321 Collins Ave. lifehousehotels.com. © **305/460-4595.** 26 units. $140–$433 double. Valet parking $50. **Amenities:** Restaurant; bar; concierge; room service; free Wi-Fi.

National Hotel Miami Beach ★★ Although its once more popular, more fabulous neighbors (Delano, Raleigh, Shore Club) are now shuttered or in various states of disrepair and/or renovation, this adults-only, Art Deco landmark remains a solid stay. That's especially true for those seeking location, location, location (directly on the beach and in the heart of South Beach)—and a fabulous pool—the beach's longest infinity pool, in fact. Back in the day, 2005, specifically, Mariah Carey performed live there for the MTV VMAs. Today the hotel is much quieter, with 137 revamped rooms with exotic hardwood furniture, chrome-accented consoles, and thoroughly modern bathrooms with terrazzo floor showers, paying homage to that Deco-design. The only drawback to a visit here is that they sell pool day passes to non-hotel guests. But because it is adults-only, they're usually well behaved.

1677 Collins Ave. nationalhotel.com. © **305/532-2311.** 137 units. $225–$405. Valet parking $47. Pet fee $150. **Amenities:** 2 restaurants; 2 bars; concierge; 2 outdoor pools (one tiny one right off the beach); fitness center; spa; room service; free Wi-Fi.

INEXPENSIVE/MODERATE

The Balfour Hotel ★★ Designed in 1940 by Art Deco OG architect Anton Skislewicz, the Balfour is a charming, historic property, with 82 guest rooms and suites spread out over two buildings connected by a pretty courtyard, and located on a quieter stretch of Ocean Drive. Rooms are comfortable, clean, and have excellent lighting, pillowtop mattresses, Frette linens, and rainfall showers. For families traveling with kids there are quads with bunk beds. An elevated plunge pool with an underwater window provides an ideal Instagram shot of swimmers behind a glass wall. Bikes are free on a first come, first served basis.

350 Ocean Dr. thebalfourmiamibeach.com. © **305/538-1055.** 82 units. $136–$305 double. Valet parking $45. Pet fee $150. **Amenities:** Restaurant; bar; concierge; room service; free Wi-Fi.

Mondrian ★ A former "it" girl all grown up, Mondrian, on the western, residential bay side of South Beach, is an ideal spot for those looking for some of the South Beach sizzle, without the noise or crowds. Rooms get panoramic views of the bay and skyline and are comfy enough, as they should be, considering someone's grandma used to live there (yep, it's a renovated apartment building). Decor is by Dutch design star Marcel Wanders, who envisioned the property as Sleeping Beauty's castle, with whimsical adult-playground-style environs. The highlights of the property, however, are the waterfront restaurant and the newly renovated spa.

1100 West Ave. mondrianhotels.com/south-beach. © **305/514-1500.** 250 units. $168–$280 double. Valet parking $46. Pet fee $100. **Amenities:** Restaurant; 2 bars; babysitting; concierge; gym; pool; room service; spa; watersports equipment/rentals; free Wi-Fi.

Pelican Hotel ★★ Owned by the creative folks behind Italy's Diesel Jeans company, the recently renovated, playful Pelican features guest rooms meant to look like surrealistic movie sets inspired by classic cinema, with kitschy themes like "Lust in Space" and "Going Bananas." For fashion fans, "Old Glory" pays homage to the owners' roots: it's decked out completely in denim! Rooms all have organic mattresses (made in Italy, of course) and vintage Art Deco antiques, art, and furniture. Rates include complimentary minibar and two cocktails daily. While there's no pool here, the ocean is literally across the street.

826 Ocean Dr. pelicanhotel.com. **305/673-3373.** 32 units. $158–$249 double. Valet parking $49. Pet fee $100, plus $25/day. **Amenities:** Restaurant; bar; access to area gyms; room service; free Wi-Fi.

The Tony ★★
Way back when, during the original South Beach renaissance of the late '90s, fashion designer Todd Oldham updated this 1939 gem (formerly the Tiffany Hotel) as he would have restored a vintage piece of couture. He laced it with lush, cool colors, hand-cut mirrors, and glass mosaics from his studio, while preserving the terrazzo floors and porthole windows. In 2022, the hotel was renamed after visionary Tony Goldman, the man largely responsible for that original South Beach renaissance. The small, soundproof rooms are very comfortable and awash in blues, yellows, and browns evocative of sea, sun, and sand, though the bathrooms are a bit cramped. A cool perk here: free VIP access to Wynwood Walls (p. 130), one of the Goldman family's contributions to Miami.

801 Collins Ave. thetonyhotel.com. **877/514-4717** or 305/531-2222. 74 units. $136–$248 double. Valet parking $45/day. **Amenities:** Restaurant; bar; pool bar; concierge; gym; pool; room service; free Wi-Fi.

INEXPENSIVE

Dream South Beach ★
Formerly an independently owned NYC hipster import, Dream South Beach—comprised of two landmark Art Deco hotels, the Tudor and the Palmer House—is now part of Hyatt. It features the requisite rooftop pool lounge and mood lighting. The age is showing here, however. Decor of the hotel is something out of a sound sleep: Modern Moroccan meets late-'70s, Studio 54 style. And that's the only thing getting a sound sleep: THIS PLACE IS EXTREMELY LOUD and not family-friendly at all. But prices are good for the location (the beach is just around the corner).

1111 Collins Ave. dreamhotels.com/south-beach. **888/376-7623.** 107 units. $114–$195 double. Valet parking $47. Pet fee $50. **Amenities:** Restaurant; bar; babysitting; concierge; rooftop lounge and pool; room service; free Wi-Fi.

the goodtime hotel, Miami Beach, A Tribute Portfolio Hotel ★★
Don't be fooled by the lowercase letters in this hotel's name—everything about it screams ALL CAPS, from its founders—style and music mogul Pharrell Williams and Miami Beach nightlife and restaurant honcho David Grutman—to its renowned designer-to-the-stars, Ken Fulk. What doesn't scream the aforementioned is Marriott, which runs the place, but hey, these guys are busy. At least they partnered with people who know what they're doing: Service is great. As for the name, yep, it's appropriate. This hotel, which takes up an entire block, is party central (raging bar scene) and just a 3-minute walk to the beach. Standard rooms are cute in pinks and pastels, but tiny and, in a way, meant to push you outside so you can have that good time they promise you.

601 Washington Ave. marriott.com. **786/687-0234.** 266 units. $111–$195 double. Valet parking $50. Pet fee $150. **Amenities:** Restaurant; bar; coffee shop; gym; pool; spa; room service; free Wi-Fi.

Miami Beach: Surfside, North Beach, Bal Harbour & Sunny Isles Beach

The area just north of South Beach, known as Miami Beach, encompasses Surfside, Bal Harbour, North Beach, and Sunny Isles. Unrestricted by zoning codes throughout the 1950s, 1960s, and especially 1970s, area developers went crazy, building ever bigger and more brazen structures, especially north of 41st Street, known as "Condo Canyon." Consequently, there's now a glut of medium-to-high-end condos, with a few scattered holdouts of older hotels and motels casting shadows over the newer, swankier stays emerging on the beachfront. Many of these can be used as vacation rentals so certainly look at the usual online sources for those if you want to stay in this area but can't stomach the typical hotel costs here.

EXPENSIVE

Acqualina Resort & Residences ★★★   Though the Denny's across the street is long gone, there are still Walgreens and various strip malls in this bustling, beachfront area, a favorite among visiting Russians (which gives it its nickname, "Little Moscow"). But once you step inside, you forget that you're even in Miami and feel as if you're on the Italian Riviera. Constantly on every "best of" hotel list, this is luxe on steroids. On 4½ beachfront acres, with more than 400 feet of Atlantic coastline, Acqualina is a Mediterranean-style resort with baroque fountains, ultra cushy standard rooms so big they'd be called junior suites elsewhere, and apartment-like one-, two-, and three-bedroom suites with fully-stocked Sub-Zero fridges. Three chichi restaurants are on property, and the spa is one of Miami's poshest (which is saying a lot). The hotel has three pools just steps away from the beach. The hotel's **AcquaMarine Program** has a splashy array of marine-biology activities for kids and adults. Best of all, the chance of some teeny-bopper tabloid figure partying here is unlikely. In fact, there's really no scene here at all, which, for some, is bliss.

17875 Collins Ave. acqualina.com. **305/918-8000**. 98 units. $900–$1,950 double. Valet parking $40. Pet fee $150, but only those under 14 inches allowed. **Amenities:** 4 restaurants; 3 bars; coffee/gelato shop; babysitting; concierge; 3 pools; room service; state-of-the-art spa; free Wi-Fi.

Carillon Miami Wellness Resort ★★   Named for its original Art Deco namesake, the main draw here is a spa with up-to-the-moment treatments. These include cryotherapy, thermal hydrotherapy, a "biostation" helmed by a doctor, and, believe it or not, an on-staff sex therapist. The adjacent cutting-edge 70,000-square-foot gym has fab ocean views and a two-story rock-climbing wall. In addition to 750 feet of beach, there are four pools (some for water-therapy programs). Because the Carillon was once condos, every suite is a big one- and two-bedroom affair, starting at 720 square feet. They boast top electronics, floor-to-ceiling-windows, and high-end kitchens. *Note:* To preserve the tranquil vibe, cellphone use is prohibited in many of the hotel's public areas.

6801 Collins Ave. carillonhotel.com. **866/800-3858**. 93 units. $325–$940 one-bedroom units, 2–5 night minimum stay. Valet parking $40. Pet fee $250. **Amenities:** 3 restaurants; juice bar; babysitting; fitness center; 2 outdoor pools; room service; spa; free Wi-Fi.

Faena Hotel Miami Beach ★★★   The swankiest hotel on Miami Beach is a must-see for brilliant British artist Damien Hirst's "Gone But Not Forgotten". It's a massive, 10-foot-tall 24-karat gold sculpture of a wooly mammoth skeleton encased in glass, and it steals the scene from the seascape it shares. Also grandiose? The hotel itself, designed by movie director/producer Baz Luhrmann and his wife, Academy Award-winning production and costume designer Catherine Martin. For those who saw Lurhmann's *Moulin Rouge,* you get the idea of Faena: a French burlesque haute spot bathed in reds and golds…but with sand. That goes for the posh guest rooms, too. And the 100,000 square feet of beach and pool area is a pepper-minted paradise with red and white umbrellas catered to by butlers who will clean your sunglasses and bring you fruit-infused water. The 22,000-square-foot spa has one of the largest hammams on the East Coast as well as shaman-developed body-healing rituals.

More than just a hotel, Faena has transformed its mid-beach area into a hyped hub of arts, design, and culture called the Faena District. It plays host to everything from the Museum of Ice Cream to immersive opera experiences. Faena's sexy, intimate, cabaret-style theater has seen everyone from Billy

The pool area at the Faena Hotel Miami Beach.

Joel and Bon Jovi to Duran Duran perform. The hotel is also home to some of the city's hottest bars and restaurants (reviewed on p. 84).

For a less extravagant, less expensive (rates range from $175 to $350), but no less charming stay, **Casa Faena,** 3500 Collins Ave., is a Spanish-style boutique inn up the block featuring 38 rooms and suites, beach access, library, Mexican restaurant, and access to all Faena, the hotel and district, have to offer.

3201 Collins Ave. faena.com. © **305/534-8800.** 179 units. $630–$1,530 double. Valet parking $58. Pet fee $250 plus $25/night. **Amenities:** 3 restaurants; 3 bars; babysitting; concierge; gym; pool; room service; spa; watersports equipment/rentals; free Wi-Fi.

Four Seasons at the Surf Club ★★★

A Prohibition-era hot spot originally created for old Hollywood royalty, mobsters, and captains of industry, the Surf Club sat and rotted for many years until the Four Seasons took it over. It's been given a glow-up by architectural icon Richard Meier, and Parisian master of minimalist design, Joseph Dirand. They've blended the old with the new in the form of two new, ultra-modern 12-story residential towers a la Meier; and the 77-room historic hotel. For the latter think: tropical, seaside hideaway with coral stone steps and palms, a place that would make a perfect romantic backdrop for a film starring Bogie and Bacall. The hotel has an oceanfront spa with hammam and adults-only pool (in addition to two heated outdoor pools); a spectacular 900-foot stretch of quiet beach; and three eateries, including one from star chef Thomas Keller (p. 84). Rooms, alas, are less dramatic than the public areas, with nondescript, if cushy, Four Seasons decor. But that might suit families, who wouldn't want to live among things the kids can break; they come for the superb fully

supervised kids club. While Bal Harbour is just a few minutes to the north and South Beach to the south, the surrounding area of Surfside is a sleepy, not-that-interesting residential area.

9011 Collins Ave. fourseasons.com/surfside. © **305/381-3333.** 77 units. $1,250–$2,950 double. Valet parking $55. Pet fee: Free for ones 15 lb. and under. **Amenities:** 3 restaurants; champagne bar; concierge; gym; 3 pools; beach; room service; spa; free Wi-Fi.

MODERATE

The Palms Hotel & Spa ★★ You'll be green here, but not with envy. The Palms has been honored by a slew of green-leaning organizations for its sustainable practices. It's also a darn nice place to stay, just a stone's throw away from Miami Beach's entertainment district, right on the beach on the northern, more

71

tranquil side of Miami Beach. Lush gardens landscaped with palms and other tropical plants surround a large, heated freshwater pool, and in the evenings a tiki bar entertains guests. Immaculate, recently renovated "tropical modern" accommodations (think: dark wood beds with colorful botanical artwork) feature fabulous spa-inspired bathrooms. Service here is warm and caring, especially in the topnotch spa.

3025 Collins Ave. thepalmshotel.com. **800/550-0505** or 305/534-0505. 251 units. $199–$299 double. Valet parking $45. **Amenities:** Restaurant; lounge; poolside bar; bike rental; concierge; fitness room; heated pool; 24-hr. room service; spa; free Wi-Fi.

INEXPENSIVE

Freehand Miami ★★ A 15-minute stroll north of the main South Beach action, the Freehand is housed in a meticulously restored 1936 building with one of the first operating elevators in Miami Beach. Because of its location, which faces the Indian Creek waterway, and its lush landscaping, this place feels like an old-fashioned Key West bed-and-breakfast. Rooms come in all sorts of shapes, sizes, and costs: King Rooms for solo travelers and couples, Bungalows for group travel, and shared dorm rooms with bunk beds. There are separate dorms for women with private bathrooms, and private "premium" rooms with more storage. Decor? College dorm chic, with some modern touches. Staff here are fun, friendly, and well-informed. Just 1 block from a good stretch of sand, Freehand also has a landscaped pool area that's a focal point of the hostel's activity—towels, however, are available for a small, refundable deposit, reminding you that yep, this is a hostel. **Broken Shaker,** one of our fave bars, is on-site (p. 147). Dorm beds, by the way, sell out quickly.

2727 Indian Creek Dr. (1 block west of Collins Ave. and the ocean). freehandhotels.com. **305/531-2727.** 80 units. Private rooms $109–$140; $25–$50 shared rooms. Pet fee $75 but not available for those in dorms. **Amenities:** Restaurant; bike rentals; concierge; free Wi-Fi.

Downtown

At long last, downtown Miami has arrived. It feels like it was stuck in traffic on I-95 for decades, but finally the city has a vibrant downtown. And sure, taking a wrong turn could land you in some parts you don't want to be in, but like any major city, that's nothing new. What is new, however, is so many great options in terms of hotels, nightlife, dining, and culture.

MODERATE/EXPENSIVE

The Elser Hotel ★★ The beauty of having a glut of brand-new empty condos in a once-sleepy downtown area is, well, the Elser, a 49-story luxury hotel tower featuring 646 residential-style rooms including studios, one-bedrooms, and spectacular two- and three-bedroom suites, all with floor-to-ceiling windows, unobstructed bay views, walkout balconies, luxurious bathrooms for every bedroom, fully equipped kitchens, and washers and dryers in every unit. This luxe condo-turned-hotel has some swell amenities, including a 19,000-square-foot rooftop pool deck with 132-foot pool framed by a massive, 16-foot poolside LED screen. The rooftop also has private lounge areas and a full bar, a massive hot tub, and an impressive two-level gym. If you're looking for a scenic spot, this isn't it, but if you want to feel like you're *living* in Miami in style for a few days, the Elser is a fantastic choice with excellent service.

398 NE 5th St. marriott.com. **833/228-1576.** 646 units. $198–$630 studio. Valet parking $50. Pet fee $100. **Amenities:** Restaurant; bar; gym; pool; room service; full-service spa; free Wi-Fi.

Downtown Miami, Midtown, Wynwood & Little Havana

HOTELS
AC Wynwood **1**
Arlo Wynwood **11**
citizenM Miami Worldcenter **16**
Dua Miami Brickell, An Autograph Collection Hotel **27**
The Elser Hotel **17**
InterContinental Miami **23**
Kimpton EPIC Hotel **18**

RESTAURANTS
Bunbury **13**
Café La Trova **32**
El Rey de Las Fritas **34**
Enriquetta's Sandwich Shop **7**
Garcia's Seafood Grille & Fish Market **28**
Hiyakawa **6**
Julia & Henry's **22**
La Camaronera Seafood Joint **36**
La Mar by Gaston Acurio **26**
Lost Boy Dry Goods **21**
Lung Yai Thai Tapas **33**
MaryGold's Brasserie **11**
Maty's **2**
Miami Slice **14**
Mignonette **12**
Morgans **4**
NAOE Miami **25**
NIU Kitchen **19**
1-800-LUCKY **10**
Panther Coffee **9**
Pastis Miami **8**
Red Rooster Overtown **15**
Sanguich **35**
Sanpocho **31**
Seaspice **29**
Sugarcane Raw Bar Grill **3**
Tam Tam **20**
Terras Rooftop **30**
Versailles **37**
Zak the Baker **5**
Zuma **24**

Kimpton EPIC Hotel ★★   A number of downtown hotels are attached to condominiums, but because the EPIC has its own separate entry it doesn't make you feel like you're intruding on someone's privacy. In fact, it feels as if you are a resident as well in a posh, plush high-rise with stunning views of the Miami skyline and Biscayne Bay. The dramatic hotel lobby features 26-foot-high vaulted ceilings, a beautiful white onyx registration desk, glass walls, and shimmering pools. The guest rooms and suites are all open space and light, offering breathtaking views of the skyline and water, and a huge bathroom with open cutout into the bedroom area. Luxury services include an on-site hotel spa, an expansive outdoor 16th-floor pool deck with private cabanas, and two infinity pools. The family-friendly hotel offers free scooters and helmets for kids and an on-demand Family Fridge Program designed to help breastfeeding guests. An evening happy hour offers complimentary wine, beer, snacks, and spirits. The hotel is extremely pet-friendly, offering beds, bones, and bottled water for your furry friend at no extra cost. Furthermore, EPIC offers Kimpton's Plant Pals Program, where upon settling in, you can request a plant to brighten the room.

270 Biscayne Blvd. Way. epichotel.com. **305/424-5226.** 411 units. $188–$515 double. Valet parking $52. **Amenities:** 2 restaurants; 2 bars; fitness center; 2 outdoor pools; room service; spa; free Wi-Fi.

MODERATE

Dua Miami Brickell, An Autograph Collection Hotel ★★   For those who yearn for a taste of Miami when it was steeped in late '90s, early aughts Philippe Starck minimalism, this is the place, a (sorry!) Starck-contrast to the much bolder, in your face design and decor of the newer area hot spots. The bar here is pure, now vintage, Starck, just like the rooms, whose retro (as in 2001) mod designs—sterile, white with a splash of metals or stainless steel, maybe a splash of green, repeated use of whimsical shapes—remind of simpler times in this fast-moving city. The pool deck is quite nice, with lounge and cabanas. Beyond the design, the location can't be beat, the service is impeccable, and noted Miami chef Michael Schwartz (see our review of Michael's Genuine Food, p. 97) operates the Italian restaurant on-site.

1300 S. Miami Ave. duamiamihotel.com. **866/211-0420.** 124 units. $247–$329 double. Valet parking $61. **Amenities:** Restaurant; 2 bars; gym; pool; room service; full-service spa; free Wi-Fi.

InterContinental Miami ★★   Quiet rooms with high-quality beds, and a prime downtown waterfront location 5 minutes from the Port of Miami, makes the InterContinental a go-to for cruise passengers. But biz travelers choose it, too, for its helpful staff and rooftop pool area with requisite bar, DJ, and brand-new and quite chic poolside cabanas. Its proximity to pretty much everything—restaurants, bars, shops, and attractions—is the biggest draw. The $33/night resort fee can potentially be a wash as it gives guests a $20 spa credit and $13 allowance in the hotel's pan-Latin steakhouse.

100 Chopin Plaza. icmiamihotel.com. **305/577-1000.** 653 units. Winter $189–$299 double. Valet parking $58. Pet fee $100. **Amenities:** 3 restaurants; 2 bars; concierge; gym; pool; spa; free Wi-Fi.

INEXPENSIVE/MODERATE

citizenM Miami Worldcenter ★★   Cruise passengers, budgeteers, business travelers, and people staying overnight after an event at the arena across the street, love citizenM, with its rooftop bar and nightly DJ'd party there. Rooms are tiny, but high tech (you'll control the mood lighting from your bed), and smartly designed, meaning luggage can be stowed, despite the rooms' lilliputian dimensions. Guest rooms can hold two adults for maybe 2 nights, max (after that you'll get claustrophobic). Still, beds are very comfy, with European cotton duvets and fluffy pillows, and fabulous blackout blinds keep things sleepable. Jungle-style rain showers will wake you from your blacked-out stupor so you can hit the town, your cruise, your meeting, or the rooftop one more time.

700 NE 2nd Ave. citizenm.com. **786/744-7052.** 351 units. $110–$260 double. **Amenities:** Restaurant; bar; gym; pool; free Wi-Fi.

Design District/Wynwood

Years ago, the thought of any hotels in these areas would have been unheard of. But today the areas north of downtown and west of Miami Beach are command central for the chic elite, so a few fine sleeperies have emerged—much to the dismay of the true hipsters, who cringe at the overdevelopment of the neighborhoods they helped put on the map.

AC Wynwood ★ The AC is affordable (except in certain busy periods), and has enough artstuffs throughout, from books and well-placed graffiti to assorted tchotchkes, to fit into the neighborhood. It's conveniently located near the performing arts center and shops at Midtown Miami. Rooms are forgettable looking, but with everything you need: a good amount of space, quality beds, desks. And we're happy to report that there are guest laundry facilities. The requisite rooftop bar and pool is a nice place to have a cocktail.

3400 Biscayne Blvd. marriott.com. **786/209-0005.** 153 units. $130–$364 double. On-site parking $30. Pet fee $50/night up to $150 max. **Amenities:** Restaurant; bar; convenience store; gym; laundry; pool; room service; free Wi-Fi.

Arlo Wynwood ★★ Clean, modern and fun, Arlo is right in the middle of the Wynwood action—identifiable by the area-appropriate graffiti art on the side of the building, with vibey rooftop pool and happening third floor bar. One of Miami's best chefs, Brad Kilgore, opened **MaryGold's** here (p. 93), a restaurant as stylish (Calacatta marble bar) as it is delicious. Rooms are small and no-frills with bare-bones, Ikea-esque white oak furniture, but comfortable unless you are a business traveler and need a desk, which you won't get in standard rooms. Suites offer separate living and dining areas. Bathrooms are TINY, but the Pharmacopia amenities, hand-held steamer (you'll need it as the closet space is sparse), and great backlighting almost make up for the lack of space. Staff are exceedingly helpful, knowledgeable, and friendly.

2217 NW Miami Court. arlohotels.com/wynwood. **786/522-6600.** 217 units. $136–$417 double. Valet parking $49. Pet fee $20. **Amenities:** Restaurant; bar; complimentary bikes; gym; pool; free Wi-Fi.

Coral Gables

The Gables, as it's affectionately known, was one of Miami's original planned communities and is still among the city's prettiest, most pedestrian-friendly, and preservation-obsessed, neighborhoods. Pristine with a European flair, Coral Gables is best known for its wide array of excellent upscale restaurants of various ethnicities, as well as a hotly contested (the quiet city didn't want to welcome new traffic) shopping megacomplex.

The historic Biltmore Hotel and, behind it, its 71-par championship golf course, designed in 1925.

If you're looking for luxury, Coral Gables has a number of wonderful hotels, but if you're on a tight budget, you may be better off elsewhere.

EXPENSIVE

Biltmore Hotel ★★ The phrase "historic grande dame" can be overused, but this elegant *señora* with a 300-foot tower modeled after Seville's famous Giralda fits it to a T. The imposing neo-Spanish-colonial pile, rising regally over a 150-acre Coral Gables spread and dating back to city founder George Merrick's original plan in 1926, has seen a lot of history since, to this day regularly hosting heads of state, CEOs, and celebrities. Large Moorish-style guest rooms have European feather beds, down feather pillows, Egyptian cotton duvets, and handsome writing desks. They're decorated in plums, sages, and golds—a huge departure from the bland beiges and pastel hues of too many other Miami hotels. The landmark 23,000-square-foot winding pool once famous for Esther Williams and Johnny Weismuller sightings now has the requisite hipster accessories—the private cabana, alfresco bar, and restaurant. Always a popular destination for golfers, visiting ex-presidents, and royalty (who usually stay in a suite Al Capone once occupied), the Biltmore is situated on a lush, rolling, 18-hole Donald Ross course that is as challenging as it is beautiful. There's also a 10,000 square-foot gym. High tea and Sunday brunch are both marquee experiences: Book early.

1200 Anastasia Ave. biltmorehotel.com. ✆ **855/311-6903.** 271 units. $399–$637 double. Valet parking $42; self-parking free. Pet fee $50. **Amenities:** 4 restaurants; 4 bars; concierge; 18-hole golf course; state-of-the-art health club; outdoor pool; room service; sauna; full-service spa; 10 lit tennis courts; free Wi-Fi.

HOTELS
Biltmore Hotel 1
Hotel St. Michel 11
Loews Coral Gables 4
Mayfair House Hotel & Garden 19
Mr. C Miami 16
Shamrock Coral Gables 13

RESTAURANTS
Ariete 14
Bachour 10
Bouchon 12
Bulla Gastrobar 5
The Café at Books & Books 8
Caffe Abbracci 6
Christy's 3
Chug's Diner 15
Eating House 9
Glass & Vine 17
Havana Harrys 2
Le Bouchon du Grove 18
Omakai 20
Regatta Grove 21
Zitz Sum 7

MODERATE/EXPENSIVE

Loews Coral Gables ★★ While it's no match for the stately Biltmore, Loews is a family-friendly full resort, a bit less expensive, and, unlike the Biltmore, which is located in a residential neighborhood, it's in an excellent area for shopping, meandering, and dining. Amenities are solid, from the rooftop pool to a good spa, gym, and four restaurants and lounges. Nice rooms with big bathrooms round out the reasons to pick this one.

2950 Coconut Grove Dr. loewshotels.com/coralgables. ✆ **786/772-7600.** 242 units. $249–$549 double. Valet parking $36. Pet fee $75. **Amenities:** 2 restaurants; 2 bars; concierge; gym; pool; spa; room service; free Wi-Fi.

MODERATE/INEXPENSIVE

Hotel St. Michel ★ This European-style hotel, an ivy-covered historic landmark dating back to 1926 in the heart of Coral Gables, was long the quintessence of quaint, with just 26 B&B-style rooms. Alas, recent updates stripped them of much of their old-world charm. Yes, they still have the wooden floors and original tile work, and some still have antiques in them, but they're odd pieces now, like a too-small writing desk. Guest rooms are also smaller than the norm, and those near the elevators, and above the hotel's bustling Italian restaurant, get noisy. Amenities are nil (no pool or spa) except for a small gym with Peloton machines. We do like the brass, manual-controlled Otis elevator from the 1920s, and location here is fantastic, within walking distance of top restaurants and shopping.

162 Alcazar Ave. hotelstmichel.com. **800/848-4683**. 28 units. $131–$315 double (save 18% by booking direct). **Amenities:** Bar; lounge; concierge; fitness center; room service; free Wi-Fi.

THesis Hotel Miami ★★ Located across from the University of Miami and at the intersection of Coral Gables, Coconut Grove, and South Miami, THesis Hotel is a cute, boutique-y hotel popular with college prospects, featuring spotless, modern rooms "designed to promote creative exploration," they say, though that's pushing it a bit. Service is friendly and knowledgeable. The third-floor pool is small, but nice, overlooking Coral Gables and featuring a bar and restaurant (it's one of two on property). A complimentary shuttle service will zip you around Coral Gables every 20 minutes from 7am to 8pm, which is a great amenity. For location, see "Miami Area Hotels & Restaurants" map (p. 71).

1350 S. Dixie Highway. thesishotelmiami.com. **888/304-5055** or 305/667-5611. 245 units. $146–$315 double. Valet parking $39; self-parking $36. **Amenities:** 3 restaurants; bar; concierge; gym; spa services; room service; free Wi-Fi.

INEXPENSIVE

Shamrock Coral Gables ★★ A lucky charm for budget travelers, the Shamrock is a friendly, clean place that's affordable when other nearby digs are not. Furnishings are mass-produced and may be nicked or dented, but so what? Rooms come with cooking facilities (another savings generator), parking is free, and the staff are exceedingly helpful. The location is terrific, too, within walking distance of shops and restaurants.

2280 SW 32nd Ave; **305/598-5800**. 45 units. **Amenities:** Full kitchens; free Wi-Fi.

Coconut Grove

This waterfront village hugs the shores of Biscayne Bay, just south of U.S. 1 and about 10 minutes from the beaches. Once a haven for hippies and head shops, the Grove succumbed to the inevitable temptations of commercialism and today is home to mostly chain restaurants and shops. That could be changing (a few independent operators have moved in recently), and outside the main shopping area, you'll find remnants of Old Miami in the form of flora, fauna, and, of course, water.

EXPENSIVE/MODERATE

Mayfair House Hotel & Garden ★★ Back in the *Miami Vice* days, the Gaudi-esque, Kenneth Treister–designed Mayfair House was a premiere hotel and shopping mall for the who's who of the Colombian cartel. After several years of neglect, the place is back to its original glory, sans gangsters thankfully, with lush gardens, waterfalls, and rooftop pool complete with rambunctious rum bar and fireplace, you know, for those chilly Miami nights. Rooms are shockingly neither beige, blue, or white and instead, awash in orange and teal, with handcrafted furnishings, some with teal clawfoot tubs, and an art collection that dates back to the hotel's original halcyon days. Some rooms have working typewriters and well-stocked bar carts, and no two are exactly alike.

3000 Florida Ave. mayfairhousemiami.com. **305-441-0000**. 179 units. $249–$617 double. Valet parking $42. Pet fee $150. **Amenities:** 2 restaurants; pool grill; 2 bars; concierge; gym; pool; room service; free Wi-Fi.

Mayfair House Hotel & Garden ★★   Back in the *Miami Vice* days, the Gaudi-esque, Kenneth Treister–designed Mayfair House was a premiere hotel and shopping mall for the who's who of the Colombian cartel. After several years of neglect, the place is back to its original glory, sans gangsters thankfully, with lush gardens, waterfalls, and rooftop pool complete with rambunctious rum bar and fireplace, you know, for those chilly Miami nights. Rooms are shockingly neither beige, blue, or white and instead, awash in orange and teal, with handcrafted furnishings, some with teal clawfoot tubs, and an art collection that dates back to the hotel's original halcyon days. Some rooms have working typewriters and well-stocked bar carts, and no two are exactly alike.

3000 Florida Ave. mayfairhousemiami.com. **305-441-0000.** 179 units. $249–$617 double. Valet parking $42. Pet fee $150. **Amenities:** 2 restaurants; pool grill; 2 bars; concierge; gym; pool; room service; free Wi-Fi.

WHERE TO EAT IN MIAMI

Formerly synonymous with early-bird specials, in 2021, the Greater Miami and Miami Beach Visitor Industry Report showed a 50% increase in *food tourism.* Imagine that! Two years later, *Bon Appétit* named Miami "2023 Food City of the Year."

So, Miami delivers, dining-wise. And whatever you're craving, Miami's got it—with the exception of decent, affordable Chinese food and a New York–style slice of pizza (though everyone will claim their pizza is NY-style. Spoiler alert: It's not). In fact, there are nearly 10,000 restaurants to choose from here, including those that serve only-in-Miami-style food. Our star chefs have fused Californian-Asian with Caribbean and Latin elements to create a world-class cuisine all its own: Floribbean.

Not all Miami food is fancy and pricey. In Little Havana, you can chow down on a meal that serves about six for less than $30. And thanks to a thriving cafe society in both South Beach and Coconut Grove, you can enjoy a moderately priced meal and linger for hours without having a waiter hover over you.

> **Impressions**
>
> *Another day, another country. Miami's like that. You could eat your way across the Caribbean and through all of Latin America, and then over to Africa, if you'd like. It's all there.*
> —Anthony Bourdain

Oddly, Miami has a dearth of moderately priced restaurants, especially in South Beach and Coral Gables. Food here is either really cheap or really expensive; the in-between somehow gets lost in the culinary shuffle. But I've tried to cover a range of cuisines in a range of prices in this chapter.

HOURS   Many restaurants keep extended hours in high season (roughly Dec–Apr) and may close for lunch and/or dinner on Monday, when the traffic is slower. Like many cities in Europe and Latin America, it is fashionable to dine late, preferably after 9pm, sometimes as late as midnight.

SERVICE AND TIPPING   Always look carefully at your bill—many Miami restaurants add an 18% to 20% gratuity to your total due to the enormous influx of European tourists who are not accustomed to tipping. Keep in mind that this amount is the *suggested* amount and can be adjusted, either higher or lower, depending on your assessment of the service provided. Because of this tipping-included policy,

> **Price Categories**
>
> Meal per person, not including drinks or tip:
> **Inexpensive:** $20 and under
> **Moderate:** $21–$40
> **Expensive:** $40 and above

South Beach waitstaff especially are best known for their lax service. *Feel free to adjust it* if you feel your server deserves more or less.

DINING SAVINGS What we used to call early-bird specials for the blue-haired senior set is now happy hour. That's right: Many restaurants offer amazingly discounted deals from around 3pm, usually at the bar. And you don't need an AARP card to take advantage.

During the month of August, many Miami restaurants participate in **Miami Spice,** where three-course lunches and dinners are served at affordable prices. Check out **miamirestaurantmonth.com**.

South Beach

South Beach is home to dozens of first-rate restaurants. A few old standbys remain from the *Miami Vice* days, but newcomers dominate the scene, with places going in and out of style as quickly as the tides.

Alas, some are offensively overpriced. With very few exceptions, the places on Ocean Drive are crowded with tourists and priced accordingly. But others are worth the investment. You'll do better to venture a little farther onto the pedestrian-friendly streets just west of Ocean Drive.

To locate the restaurants in this section, see the "South Beach Hotels & Restaurants" map (p. 65).

EXPENSIVE

Joe's Stone Crab Restaurant ★ SEAFOOD From humble origins in Joe Weiss' lunch counter in 1913, this now enormous, retro-feeling classic in southernmost South Beach, run by his descendants like a well-oiled machine, may no longer be the last word in seafood hereabouts. But attention must be paid, as Mrs. Loman would say. And Joe's does deliver, for the most part. The storied stone-crab claws, served with a mustard-based dipping sauce, may or may not be your cup of brine (they're served cold, and last time I was in I detected a whiff of the ammoniac; in any case, some folks actually prefer the king crab), but on the menu there are plenty of other marine critters, along with land-based meat and fowl. Highlights to look out for include the seafood bisque; the sides of creamed spinach, slaw, and hash browns; and for dessert, one of South Florida's better Key lime pies. The vibe and certainly the decor are old-school and the service usually pretty good; just keep in mind that you'll want to budget for time as no reservations are taken. You put your name on the list and settle in for a bit of a wait (shorter at lunch than dinner). If you don't feel like waiting, try **Joe's Takeaway,** which is next door to the restaurant—it's a lot quicker and just as tasty.

11 Washington Ave. (at Biscayne St., just south of 1st St). joesstonecrab.com. ⓒ **305/673-0365** or 305/673-4611 for takeout. Reservations not accepted. Market price varies but averages $35–$65. Wed–Sun 11:30am–2:30pm; Sun–Thurs 5–10pm; Fri –Sat 5–11pm. Closed mid-May to mid-Oct.

Queen Miami Beach ★★★ JAPANESE Some $40 million dollars were poured into this jaw-droppingly stunning Art Deco landmark (the Henry Hohauser–designed Paris Theater) to turn it into this temple of fine Japanese dining. I know you can't eat the decor, but it certainly is delicious: an old Hollywood meets modern day South Beach palace of terrazzo floors, Italian mosaics, velvet banquettes, marble countertops, and Lobmeyr chandeliers. The food is as spectacular, often crafted from rare ingredients, like wagyu from Hasewaga farm, a family-owned spot north of Tokyo, from which only 400 of its cattle go to market every year. That beef might be seared in a Josper charcoal oven or over a robata grill, and preceded by exquisite sushi, or a seafood tower, or sea bass tempura. Diners (who include many a celebrity) have the choice between ordering a la carte, or taking part in an *omakase* (tasting menu) meal, which, in some cases, gets you into a glam upstairs room. A heady experience.

550 Washington Ave. queenmiamibeach.com. **786/373-2930.** Entrees $24–$425. Daily 6pm–midnight.

Stubborn Seed ★★★ AMERICAN   Chef Jeremy Ford, season 13 winner of *Top Chef* and star of TruTV's wacky *Fast Foodies,* has a whimsical TV persona, but when it comes to cuisine, he's as serious as it gets. This understatedly chic 70-seat hot spot, named for, as Ford says, "Our stubborn approach to what we do and what we purchase," features locally sourced ingredients in a diverse menu of meat, fish, and raw items, ordered in an 8- or 11-course tasting menu. (A la carte dining is available at the bar only.) Examples of Ford's savory stubbornness include sesame milk bread with cultured miso butter, Koji honey, and pickled radish; beef tartare cannelloni with winter truffle, lemon dill aioli, and crispy potato; and charred venison tenderloin with "sun choke textures." The last item is hard to describe but best I can say it's potato-y and delicious. Ford has done so well that he's opening a second location in Las Vegas.

101 Washington Ave. stubbornseed.com. **786/322-5211.** 8-course tasting menu $175, 11-course tasting menu $250. A la carte entrees $9–$31. Sun–Thurs 6–10pm; Fri–Sat 6–11pm.

MODERATE

Macchialina ★★★ ITALIAN   This 70-seat, rustic Italian spot has garnered major accolades, from James Beard to *Wine Spectator,* thanks to chef/owner Michael Pirolo's pasta precision and soulful cooking, and his sister Jacqueline's sommelier savvy. The menu starts with appetizers like a local burrata with luscious heirloom tomatoes or a beef carpaccio with shaved mushrooms and celery. But pasta dishes are the highlight, including a tagliolini with abalone mushrooms, and a gnocchi fra diavlo with lobster, Calabrese chili, and basil. For gluten-free folks (or those with larger appetites), entrees such as veal Milanese or veal parm pack powerful punches, but it's the pacific halibut with sunchokes, brown butter, delicata squash, and trumpet mushrooms that's truly magical. A four-course chef's tasting menu at $70 per person with an option for wine pairing add-on (do it—Jacqueline is an award-winning oenophile) is the way to go here. ***Note:*** As we go to press, plans to expand next door are underway, meaning more seating (they'll have an outdoor patio).

820 Alton Rd. macchialina.com. **305/534-2124.** Main courses $25–$47. Mon–Thurs 6–11pm; Fri–Sun 5–11pm.

Sweet Liberty Drinks & Supply Company ★★ AMERICAN   An off-the-beaten-path cocktail mecca that's industrial-chic-with-a-twist-of-country in looks, Sweet Liberty was put on the map by its creative boozy concoctions. But it also has a menu that impresses—and seesaws between high-end fare and reimagined comfort food faves. On the fancy side, there are oysters, oysters, and more oysters, some served with James Beard–award winner Michelle Bernstein's fennel mignonette, crème fraiche, and caviar; others baked with garlic chili butter and parmesan breadcrumbs; and our personal fave, the Aguachile Oysters with cucumber, avocado, and wasabi tobiko caviar. On the other end of the scale, there's a sensational spinach and artichoke dip (move over, Houston's), a to-die-for cauliflower nacho appetizer, fab burgers, and a Maine lobster hot pocket. Desserts? The cheesecake is the way to go or, for those who prefer to drink their desserts, the Grasshopper 2.0 with Valrhona chocolate is Sweet Liberty in a nutshell. It is IT.

237 20th St. mysweetliberty.com. © **305/763-8217**. Main courses $19–$34. Daily 4pm–5am; Sun brunch noon–4pm.

INEXPENSIVE

Sometimes all you want is a good diner, and South Beach delivers on this front. In fact, it doesn't get more authentic than the **11th Street Diner** ★ (1065 Washington Ave.; eleventhstreetdiner.com; © **305/534-6373**; dishes $9–$22; daily 7:30am–11:45pm). It was uprooted from its 1948 Wilkes-Barre, Pennsylvania, foundation, dismantled, and rebuilt on this busy and colorful corner of Washington Avenue. **Big Pink** ★ (157 Collins Ave.; mylesrestaurantgroup.com; © **305/532-4700;** main courses $13–$22; Mon–Wed 8am–midnight, Thurs–Sat 8am–5:30am, Sun 8am–2am) is a somewhat kitschy spin on a diner, but the food is solid and comes in big portions. Thirty-plus-year Ocean Drive veteran **Front Porch Café** ★ (1458 Ocean Dr.; frontporchoceandrive.com; © **305/531-8300**; main courses $15–$38; daily 8am–11pm) has the breakfast and burger chops to rival the diners above, though it identifies as a cafe. Service is a bit more attitudinal at Front Porch than at the other two. ***Note:*** Both the 11th Street Diner and Big Pink have full bars.

La Sandwicherie ★★ SANDWICHES   This gourmet sandwich bar, open until the crack of dawn, caters to ravenous club kids, biker types, and the body artists who work in the tattoo parlor next door. For many people, in fact, no night of

Step back in time at the 11th Street Diner.

clubbing is complete without capping it off with a delish sub (hoagie, sandwich, grinder, whatever you call it) from La Sandwicherie. There are four other locations in Brickell, Wynwood, North Beach, and Coral Gables, but this is the original in so many ways.

229 14th St. lasandwicherie.com. ✆ **305/532-8934.** $7–$15. Daily 7am–5am.

Lucali ★★ PIZZA   When people around here crave NY-style pizza, they head to this Sunset Harbor neighborhood mainstay, a Brooklyn import that's the closest Miami comes. Not a slice joint, it's a fancy pizza place with pies crafted from hand-thrown dough. There are not many toppings you can add, but it's hard to beat the plain with roasted garlic. The crispy dough is excellent—not classic NY, but still great. Alas, service is snippy and rushed.

1930 Bay Rd. lucali.com. ✆ **305/695-4441.** Shareable pizzas $30 plus toppings. Mon–Thurs noon–11pm; Fri–Sat noon–midnight; Sun noon–11pm.

Puerto Sagua ★★ CUBAN/SPANISH   Surrounded these days by chichi shops, this blast-from-the-past Latin dive—with wood paneling, fluorescent lighting, a drop ceiling, and stick-to-your-ribs Cuban fare—remains popular with old-timers, late-night partiers, and a motley mélange of locals and in-the-know visitors who appreciate a good feed at good prices. Among the less heavy dishes is a super chunky fish soup with pieces of whole flaky grouper. Also tasty are the shrimp dishes, especially shrimp in garlic sauce, and the roast chicken with rice, black beans, and fried plantains. Don't be intimidated by the hunched, older waiters in their white button-down shirts and black pants. If you don't speak Spanish, they're usually willing to do charades and the extensive menu is in English.

700 Collins Ave. ✆ **305/673-1115.** Main courses $10–$50. Daily 7am–11pm.

Miami Beach, Surfside, Bal Harbour & Sunny Isles

Today this area has many more residents, albeit seasonal, than visitors. The result on the culinary front is a handful of super-expensive, traditional establishments as well as a number of value-oriented spots.

To locate the restaurants in this section, see the map "Miami Area Hotels & Restaurants" (p. 71).

EXPENSIVE

Hakkasan ★★★ CHINESE   Tucked away on the fourth floor of the labyrinthine Fontainebleau, Hakkasan exudes a nightclubby, Vegas vibe with thumping music and scantily clad diners. Although we're of the hole-in-the-wall school of Chinese food, we can't deny the fact that this is some seriously good, gourmet food, created by Michelin-starred chef Alan Yau. Signature dishes include charcoal-grilled honey Chilean sea bass; roasted duck with crisped skin and a savory soy sauce; and clay pot beef tenderloin with garlic. Service is professional if sometimes aloof. Your best bet is to go with a group of people, especially for the a la carte dim sum brunch, so you can share a number of dishes. Just watch the drinks—that's where they always get you.

In the Fontainebleau, 4441 Collins Ave. hakkasan.com. ✆ **786/276-1403** or 305/538-2000. Main courses $10–$208. Sun 11:30am–3pm and 5:30–10pm; Mon–Thurs 6–10pm; Fri–Sat 6pm–midnight.

Los Fuegos by Francois Mallmann ★★★ SOUTH AMERICAN

Mallmann, Argentina's most famous chef, is known for live fire cooking, a Patagonian method of barbecue. He's bringing the heat to Miami Beach with this elegant (even with the leopard-print booths), culinarily theatrical, Michelin-anointed restaurant. So, what does live fire mean? In this case, all the entrees are cooked in a bespoke wood oven the chef invented, with hooks for hanging fish and beef over the fire, as well as *planchas* (grill plates), and an area for cooking in ashes. The latter is used to create the restaurant's most famous appetizer: beets that are buried in hot ash for 8 hours, and then plated with pistachio yogurt, shallot vinaigrette, and garlic chips, a dish so flavorful even beet loathers end up loving it. All entrees are cooked over fire, including a divine prime beef tenderloin that comes with a wood-fired stuffed onion, truffle beef jus and sourdough breadcrumbs; and for vegetarians, a magnificent roasted cauliflower that's served with an almond and caper vinaigrette, fresh herb salad, and crispy rice. For dessert? Two words: burnt cheesecake. Don't ask, just order it. Service matches the room: exceptional.

In the Faena Hotel, 3201 Collins Ave. faena.com. ✆ **786/655-5600.** Main courses $38–$310. Daily 7–11am and noon–4pm; Sun–Thurs 6:30–10:30pm; Fri–Sat 6:30–11pm.

Makoto ★★ JAPANESE

Makoto Okuwa has impressive bonafides as one of TV's Iron Chefs, and former sous to fellow Iron Chef Morimoto. He specializes in Edomae sushi, a 19th-century style that introduced vinegar to the dish to both preserve and enhance the flavor of the fish. He serves that classic cuisine alongside creative modern Japanese fare such as raw tuna pizza with anchovy aioli, and spicy tuna crispy rice. All of it is crafted from very fine imported fish. The India Mahdavi–designed dining room is made for Instagram, a cross between Mad Men and the Golden Girls if they both went on a field trip to Tokyo.

At the Bal Harbour Shops, 9700 Collins Ave. makoto-restaurant.com. ✆ **305/864-8600.** Main courses $16–$60. Daily 11:30am–4pm; Sun–Thurs 4–10pm; Fri–Sat 4–11pm.

Pao by Paul Qui ★★★ ASIAN FUSION

Paul Qui won season 9 of *Top Chef* but became a headline name, sadly, when he was accused of assaulting his girlfriend. Eventually, charges were dropped, Qui went into rehab, and moved from Texas to Florida to open this restaurant. If you believe in second chances, you owe it to yourself to try his phenomenal fusion of Filipino, Japanese, Spanish, and French cuisines. Among the many big-impact menu items is Singapore-style chili crab (jumbo lump blue crab, egg, peppers, and fermented tomato). We also stan the wagyu short rib with toasted rice cake, red curry, and crispy basil. But it's "The Unicorn" that put this place on the map: sea urchin, grilled sweet corn pudding, sake aioli, chile de arbol, and lime. There's also excellent sashimi and nigiri and an unusual "bread service" of traditional Filipino bread served with bone marrow caramel and smoked butter miso. We'd have that instead of dessert, frankly.

At the Faena, 3201 Collins Ave. faena.com. ✆ **786/655-5600.** Main courses $19–$138. Tues–Wed 7–10pm; Thurs–Sat 7–11pm. Closed Sun and Mon.

The Surf Club Restaurant ★★★ CONTINENTAL

Thomas Keller is the OG of destination dining. His Napa Valley restaurant, the French Laundry—named "Best Restaurant on the Planet" umpteen times, by umpteen different publications—draws visitors from around the world. Keller is the reason anyone comes to the Surf Club . . . even if he's never here personally. But his expert staff maintain his high, high standards and cook such signature dishes as Maine Lobster

Thermidor with aplomb. By the way, it is pure poetry: poached tail in a puff pastry shell with morels, floating on a Gruyere sauce. The Dover sole meuniere serves two and isn't like anything you'll find in Miami, especially because it was caught off the coast of Brittany and jetted in like Taylor Swift to a Chiefs game. The room is sexy, there's live jazz in the lounge, and service is masterful.

At the Four Seasons Surf Club, 9011 Collins Ave. surfclubrestaurant.com. © **305/768-9440.** Main courses $23–$230. Daily 6–10pm.

MODERATE

aba ★★ MEDITERRANEAN   A Chicago import, aba's gorgeous space is meant to evoke summer in the Med, with trees and lush greenery and a menu to match. Smoky garlic hummus, shawarma-spiced skirt steak, crispy chicken thigh with piquillo pepper, and an assortment of kebabs, meze, and raw stuff (like ahi tuna with black grapes, fried capers and shallots, and garlic aioli) are among the many menu items we recommend. Also stellar: the truffle baked orzo. This is one of the area's most popular brunch spots.

At the Bal Harbour Shops, 9700 Collins Ave. abarestaurants.com. © **305/677-2840.** Most courses $16–$39, more for steak. Mon–Fri 11:30am–4pm; Mon–Thurs 4–10pm; Sat 3–11pm; Sun 3–9pm.

Cafe Prima Pasta ★★ ITALIAN   Entering its third decade in biz—a feat in these parts—Café Prima Pasta is finally generating the kind of fanfare it should. The pasta here is homemade, and the kitchen's other ingredients are all primo (or Prima!). They include ripe, juicy tomatoes; fresh, drippy mozzarella; fish that tastes as if it has just been caught, right out back; and imported olive oil that would cost you a boatload if you bought it in a store. That zesty oil, studded with garlic, is brought out as dip for the bread and it should be kept with you during your meal, because it can double as extra seasoning for your food—not that that's usually necessary. Due to the chef's fancy for garlic, this is a three-Altoid restaurant, so be prepared to pop a few. Though tables are packed in, the atmosphere still manages to be romantic.

414 71st St. cafeprimapasta.com. © **305/867-0106.** Main courses $20–$37. Mon–Thurs 4:30–11pm; Fri–Sat 4:30–11:30pm; Sun 4–10:30pm.

INEXPENSIVE

If you're just hoping to grab a quick sandwich lunch in these parts, **Josh's Deli** ★★ (9517 Harding Ave., Surfside; © **305/397-8494;** main dishes $9.50–$17.50; daily 8:30am–3:30pm) has the goods, and that includes mighty fine pastrami and corned beef. It's a sit-down joint, but speedy. And with all meats and fish cured in house, high quality.

Taquiza Tacos ★★ MEXICAN   This off-the-beaten path Mexican taquería serves up seriously good tacos and street fare made from their signature blue masa, stone ground daily with corn from the Midwest and hand pressed into homemade tortillas and totopos. There are only about a dozen tacos to choose from—try beef tongue braised in Victoria beer, charred onion, and bay leaf if you are adventurous—but they are all excellent. The margaritas are too. This is one of the best bargains in the area and because of that—and the fact that the tacos are sooo good—it's always packed.

7450 Ocean Terrace. taquizatacos.com. © **786/588-4755.** Tacos $4–$8. Sun–Thurs noon–9pm; Fri–Sat noon–10pm.

North Miami/Aventura

Although there aren't many hotels in North Dade, the population in the winter months explodes due to the onslaught of seasonal residents from the Northeast. Many many of these folks dine out nightly, which supports a bustling culinary scene, with many of the top choices in the Aventura Mall.

To locate the restaurants in this section, see the map "Miami Area Hotels & Restaurants" (p. 71).

EXPENSIVE

Joey Aventura ★★ INTERNATIONAL   This massive Canadian import is a stunner—a two-level, indoor-outdoor space with 241 seats, floor-to-ceiling windows (a nice touch after a day of shopping in what feels like a Vegas casino), greenery, and artwork from contemporary artists Elsbeth Shaw and Valerie

---

A berry GOOD TIME

South Florida's farmland has been steadily shrinking in the face of industrial expansion, but you'll still find several spots where you can indulge in a local gastronomic tradition—picking your own produce at the "U-Pic-'Em" farms that dot south Miami-Dade's landscape. Depending on what's in season, you can get everything from fresh herbs and veggies to citrus fruits and berries. During berry season—January through April—it's not uncommon to see pickers leaving the groves with hands and faces stained a tale-telling crimson. Our faves:

The Berry Farm, 13720 SW 216th St. (visittheberryfarm.com; *786/701-8100*; Mon–Thurs 9am–6:30pm, Fri–Sun 9am–7pm), located in the Redlands, about an hour from downtown Miami, is a third-generation, family-run farm with events like berry beer fests, and even gem mining for the kids. To get there, go south on U.S. 1 and turn right on SW 216th Street; the stand is about 1 mile west.

For fresh fruit in a tasty pastry or tart, head over to **Knaus Berry Farm,** 15980 SW 248th St. (KnausBerryFarm.com; *305/247-0668*; Mon–Sat 8am–5:30pm), also in the Redlands. Some people call this an Amish farm, but it's actually run by a family from a sect of German Baptists. The stand sells items ranging from fresh flowers to homemade ice cream to its famous homemade cinnamon buns. Be prepared to wait in a long line—people flock here from as far away as Palm Beach. Head south on U.S. 1 and turn right on 248th Street. The stand is 2½ miles farther on the left.

Another area landmark, part of the historic **Redland Tropical Trail** (redlandtrail.com) between the Everglades and Homestead, is **Robert Is Here,** 19200 SW 344th St., Homestead (robertishere.com; *305/246-1592*; daily 9am–6pm), a fruit stand that Robert Moehling opened as a 6-year-old boy in 1959 and is still here, selling luscious tropical fruits—jackfruit, guanabana, dragon fruit, Key Lime shakes, and veggies.

Also part of the trail is the **Schnebly Redland's Winery,** 30205 SW 217th Ave., Homestead (schneblywinery.com; *305/242-1224*; Mon–Thurs noon–5pm, Fri–Sat 11am–midnight, Sun 11am–8pm), where the aforementioned exotic fruits are turned into wine at the southernmost winery in the U.S., featuring a 5,000-square-foot tasting room and French restaurant.

Capewell. Its menu takes you on a culinary tour as sprawling as the restaurant itself, with everything from sushi and Korean-fried cauliflower to behemoth burgers, poke bowls, pasta, and steaks, all high quality. That said, prices are exorbitant. But daily happy hours (3–6pm Mon–Fri, 9pm–closing Sun–Thurs, 10pm–closing Fri–Sat) cut the cost of many drinks, at least.

19505 Biscayne Blvd. in the Aventura Mall Esplanade. joeyrestaurants.com. 📞 **786/763-2300.** Main courses $13–$90. Daily 11am–"late."

MODERATE

Motek ★★ MEDITERRANEAN/MIDDLE EASTERN   Named for the word "sweetheart" in Hebrew, Motek has six locations in Miami—Brickell, Coral Gables, Downtown, South Beach, and Miami Beach—but the one at the Aventura mall is its flagship. While the food here is called "kosher style," it's not certified kosher because they serve dairy, are open on the Sabbath, and do not have separate kitchens, utensils, etc. Located on the ground floor of the mall near the always mobbed Apple store, it can feel a bit frenetic. On the menu? A lot! Motek serves specialties from Israel, Lebanon, Turkey, Morocco, and Yemen. Much of it is good for sharing, which cuts the cost of eating here to moderate (despite the costly entrees). Best for a group: the flat pita with artichoke, cured fish roe, goat cheese, parmesan, wilted kale, and caramelized onion; and the chicken shawarma plate, which comes with a house salad and delicious hummus. There are also excellent and large salads and hot mezzes. They serve hard-to-find Greek and Israeli beer, which are a value during their very popular happy hours (Mon–Thurs 3–7pm, Fri–Sat 3–6pm) when all beer, well spirits, and selected wines are half off, and half sandwiches, hot and cold meze are offered at a bargain rate of $5 and $7.

19505 Biscayne Blvd. in the Aventura Mall. motekcafe.com. 📞 **305/974-2626.** Main courses $9–$36. Sun–Fri 10am–10pm; Sat 10am–11pm.

Reunion Kitchn Bar ★★★ INTERNATIONAL   Even though we scream, "Vanna, we'd like to buy a vowel" every time we see this restaurant's name, we ignore the obvious because the food is really *xcellent*—heh—at this buzzy neighborhood strip-mall spot. The hip, cozy, reclaimed wood-sy vibe immediately makes you forget you're sandwiched between a dentist's office and a pizza place, but it's the food that really takes you on a trip. Small "bites," shared plates, and main courses include Truffle-shitake croquettes, Swiss cheese fondue, crispy Iberian artichokes, naan bread, Moroccan pastilla, and sushi—because everyone has sushi—make you kind of ask "where am I?" but each taste is authentically good. An adjacent lounge gives speakeasy vibes with smoking cocktails.

18167 Biscayne Blvd. reunionkb.com. 📞 **305/974-2626.** Most entrees $12–$29. Mon–Wed noon–10pm; Thurs–Fri noon–11pm; Sat 11am–11pm; Sun 11am–10pm.

INEXPENSIVE

Neverland Coffee Bar ★★★ CAFE   If you can find this place you will love it. A hideaway across the Brightline tracks and the hustle and bustle of Aventura, Neverland is a charmer, inspired by European coffeehouses where people come to work, watch people and actually—we swear—talk to other people over cups of coffee, glasses of beer and wine, or a lingering brunch or lunch. The menu has nice salads, breakfast fare, pizzas, a fabulous challah burger, and delicious sweet stuff. Dog friendly, kid friendly (fantastic kids menu actually), LGBTQ+ friendly, just people in general friendly, Neverland is a welcome respite from the pretentiousness and pace across the tracks.

17830 W. Dixie Hwy. neverlandcoffeebar.com. 📞 **305/916-3560.** $10–$19. Daily 8am–11pm.

Downtown Miami/Brickell

Downtown Miami is a large, sprawling area divided by the Brickell Bridge into two distinct areas: Brickell Avenue and the bayfront area near Biscayne Boulevard. Massive (over)development has transformed a once sleepy banking district into a bustling day and night destination, with outdoor shopping centers like the original Mary Brickell Village and the swanky Brickell City Centre. These are very walkable day or night, but you probably shouldn't walk from the Brickell area to the bayfront area at night—it's quite a distance, but there's always CitiBikes to ride during the day. Convenient Metromover stops adjoin the areas, so it's better to hop on the scenic sky tram (it's closed after midnight) or take an Uber. Also sizzling in this area is the Miami River district, a 5½-mile river flowing from the Miami Canal through the epicenter Greater Downtown Miami to Biscayne Bay. A recent spate of development has brought with it high-end condos and restaurants.

To locate the restaurants in this section, see the map "Downtown Miami, Midtown, Wynwood & Little Havana" (p. 73).

EXPENSIVE

La Mar by Gaston Acurio ★★★ ASIAN PERUVIAN FUSION The Emeril of Peru, star chef Gaston Acurio's Miami restaurant has magnificent waterfront and skyline views and an expert executive chef, Diego Oka at the helm. This chilihead uses a lot of *Aji Amarillo,* a South American hot chili pepper and staple of Peruvian cuisine. You can find it in many of the menu's made-to-order *cebiches* including one with grouper and crispy calamari, and also in the empanada and quinoa caprese. Those who prefer milder flavors have a lot of good choices, too, foremost among them the pan-seared scallops with 24-month-aged parmesan cheese foam; or the stir-fried tenderloin, served with white rice, thick-cut potato wedges, and *choclo* (Peruvian large kernel corn that's very dry and very addicting). The menu is huge but the Pisco Sours are a "must order", a luscious taste of Lima in downtown Miami.

At the Mandarin Oriental, 500 Brickell Key Dr. mandarinoriental.com. ✆ **305/913-8288.** Main courses $14–$95. Sun–Thurs 6–11pm; Fri–Sat 6pm–midnight; Sun brunch 12:30–3pm.

NAOE Miami ★★★ SUSHI This may be the closest Miami gets to Tokyo. Chef Kevin Cory is known for his exquisitely prepared, hyperfresh sushi (the restaurant's apt motto is "It's not fresh, it's alive.") Among the items you may find on your plate or in your bento box: smooth egg custard with soft bits of freshwater eel; fresh giant clam sashimi in a tangy *shiso* vinaigrette; in-shell conch; sweet, chilled corn-miso soup; and *uni* so creamy it's been known to silence even the pickiest of reviewers. Be careful about what you ask for, though, as extras add up quickly: They charge for fresh grated wasabi. You'll need 2 to 3 hours for the experience. *Warning*: NAOE only serves the chef choice menu. Those with special requests or dietary requirements must inform the restaurant 10 days in advance.

661 Brickell Key Dr. naoemiami.com. ✆ **305/947-6263.** Tasting menus $280 plus 20% service charge. Daily 5–9pm. Ages 12 and up only.

Red Rooster Overtown ★★★ SOUL FOOD Established by Black workers who built Miami's railroads and hotels, Overtown was the Harlem of the South, where, in the '50s and '60s, the likes of Ella Fitzerald and Louis Armstrong stayed when performing across the causeway on Miami Beach. Overtown was decimated when I-95 was built right through it, but thanks to star chef Marcus Samuelsson, and some other area visionaries, that is changing. Samuelsson has brought his Harlem hot spot to this historic area, where he serves his modern comfort food celebrating the roots of African-American cuisine. An all-day menu features unbelievably good starters: cornbread with jalapeno honey butter and blackberry bourbon jam; chargrilled chicken wings with Red Rooster hot sauce; and garlic crab with Old Bay garlic butter and buttermilk biscuit croutons. Mains include fab Cajun-spiced red shrimp and grits, and fried catfish sandwich with pickled onions. The mac and cheese and "glamorous greens" are stellar side dishes. Saturday and Sunday gospel brunches are very popular as is the **Pool Hall,** a separate lounge and eatery open Friday through Sunday from 9pm until 2am and inspired by the former Clyde Killens Pool Hall, where legends like Aretha Franklin partied and played during segregation. It features its own menu of late night eats including Guyanese roti, cornbread dumplings, oysters, sandwiches, and sides. Also on-site: **The Creamery,** open Saturday and Sunday from noon to 4pm and featuring Samuelsson's homemade ice cream flavors like Cornbread (honey butter caramel and blackberry jam).

920 NW 2nd Ave. redroosterovertown.com. **305/640-9880.** Main courses $18–$46. Mon–Fri noon–4pm; Sun–Thurs 5–10pm; Fri–Sat 5–11pm; Sat–Sun 10am-3pm.

Seaspice ★ SEAFOOD   Although there's an indoor dining room, the action is always in the outside dining areas here: This is a see-and-be-seen spot, and much of the fun of dining here is watching zillion-dollar yachts pull up with celebrities like Leonardo DiCaprio or Beyonce on them. They're here for good, albeit expensive, food, from seafood to slow-cooked veal osso bucco. There's also grub for those who just like to graze: pizzas, salads, ham croquettes, crab tempura, you name it. Not a quiet place ever, there's often a DJ spinning a soundtrack to match the cacophony of cocktail chatter.

422 NW N. River Dr. seaspice.com. **305/440-4200.** Main courses $17–$110. Tues–Sun noon–midnight.

Zuma ★★★ JAPANESE   The brainchild of German star chef Rainer Becker, who chose Miami as the city of choice for the restaurant's stateside debut—"We wanted our first Zuma in the USA to be located within an energetic, vibrant, multicultural, and popular city; that to me is Miami"—Zuma is constantly at the top of the "best of" lists, including the exclusive S. Pellegrino list, which rated the restaurant as one of the *world's* best. Based on the traditional Japanese school of cooking known as Izakaya with dishes cooked on a traditional, wood charcoal-fired robata grill, menu highlights include prawn and black cod dumplings; sea bass sashimi with yuzu, truffle oil, and salmon roe; yellowtail sashimi with green-chili relish, ponzu, and pickled garlic; and sliced seared wagyu striploin tataki with truffle ponzu. Weekend brunch here is an event and a marathon, with prices starting at $128 a person and including welcome champagne and caviar, a behemoth buffet, main dish of your choice, and deluxe dessert platter. Did we mention that the space is stunning?

In the EPIC Hotel, 270 Biscayne Blvd. Way. zumarestaurant.com. **305/577-0277.** Reservations necessary. Main courses $12–$83. Mon–Fri 11:30am–3pm; Sun–Thurs 6–11pm; Fri–Sat 6–11:30pm; Sat 11:30am–3pm; Sun 11:30am–3:30pm.

MODERATE

Bunbury ★★ ARGENTINIAN   Located in the edgy Edgewater area of downtown Miami, this utterly charming Argentinian wine bar is housed in a converted tire shop and has mismatched furniture, book-filled bookcases, a terrace with twinkly lights and, oh yeah, owners who happen to be sommeliers, too. It's a neighborhood hangout with some of the best baked empanadas—the ones with

Julia & Henry's is a spectacular, relatively new food hall.

prosciutto, mushrooms, and brie are beyond—you'll ever have, not to mention over 100 vintages of wine. There are also meat-and-cheese boards, salads, and all sorts of small plates to share or horde. The pan-seared duck breast with raspberry sauce is worthy of the horde. Almost as delicious as the food and wine is the soundtrack, a trippy trip around the dial of jazz and Neil Diamond.

55 NE 14th St. bunburymiami.com. **305/333-6929.** Main courses $29–$49. Tues–Wed 5–11pm; Thurs–Fri 5–11:30pm; Sat 10:30am–11pm; Sun 10:30am–4pm.

Garcia's Seafood Grille & Fish Market ★★ SEAFOOD

In 1976, the Cuban refugee García brothers added a restaurant side to the seafood market and wholesaler they'd founded a decade earlier, and today it's a cherished institution. Its location very much off the beaten path—along the Miami River west of downtown's Brickell area—lends even more authenticity, not to mention some great atmosphere as you take in the river and distant high-rise skyline from the outdoor decks both upstairs and downstairs. The simple yet tasty menu is of fresh fish cooked in a number of ways—grilled, broiled, fried, or, the best in our opinion, in garlic or green sauce. Meals are quite the good deal here, all served with two sides (definitely order the *tostones*) and a complimentary fish-spread appetizer. There's usually a wait for a table.

398 NW N. River Dr. **305/375-0765.** garciasmiami.com. Main courses $19–$34. Daily 11am–9pm.

Julia & Henry's ★★ FOOD HALL

This food hall, named after Miami pioneers Julia Tuttle and Henry Flagler, is spectacular, housed in an Art Deco landmark on the National Register of Historic Places, with a neon-lit glass elevator from which you'd almost expect Willy Wonka to emerge. It has nearly 30 food stalls—er, restaurants—including a few from some Miami faves, like chef Michelle Bernstein (Michy's Chicken Shack), and a few bars. Do lunch here; it's easier on the wallet. There are also recording studios in here in case the smell of food makes you feel like singing, a children's play area on the second floor, a basement bar, and a rooftop with a restaurant helmed by renowned Italian chef Mossimo Bottura.

200 E. Flagler St. JuliaandHenrys.com. **786/703-2126.** Prices vary. Sun–Thurs 11:30am–10pm; Fri–Sat 11:30am–11pm.

Mignonette ★★ SEAFOOD A pioneer in the now bustling Edgewater neighborhood, this seafood bistro is an ideal spot for bivalves and bubby before or after a show at the nearby performing arts center or arena. Informal, yet stylish, the diminutive spot serves some of the freshest seafood in town, from the best lobster roll you'll find south of New England, to crispy skinned snapper in a beurre blanc, to their "oyster flight" (six raw, three grilled, and three Rockefeller). An impressive range of veggie sides includes fried Roman artichokes with smoked paprika aioli that are like, to use chef Serfer's terminology, a fancy version of bar nuts. Speaking of bar, there are excellent wines by the glass, and local beers, and the staff are knowledgeable enough to tell you what goes best with what.

210 NE 18th St. mignonettemiami.com. **305/374-4635.** Main courses $25–$55. Sun–Thurs 5–10pm; Fri–Sat 5–11pm.

Herb and veggie laden fish at the River Oyster Bar.

NIU Kitchen ★★★ SPANISH   The MO in this cool, cozy (ok, fine, tiny) Catalonian tapas spot is "plates to share, glasses to clink," as Barcelona native, chef Deme Lomas, throws down some damned good eats, from charbroiled oysters and Branzino tartare with white garlic cold soup to Lomas's mom's recipe for clams made with Iberico ham. The charcuterie here is also impressive. Wines are natural and biodynamic and also available at the adjacent shop should you sip something sensational—which you will. Say *ànims* (that's "cheers" in Catalan)!

104 NE 2nd Ave. NiuKitchen.com. **786/717-6711.** Charcuterie and tapas $8–$27. Tues–Sun 6–10pm.

The River Oyster Bar ★★ SEAFOOD   Open since 2003, this remains a go-to for some of the best oysters in town, shipped in fresh daily from all over the world. Other hits on the menu include mushroom-crusted black grouper, gnocchi and jumbo lump blue crab, and for the landlubber, pasture-raised prime beef from North Carolina in three different cuts. This buzzy place is a top spot for happy hour (daily 3–7pm), when the cost of both tipples and oysters drops. Because there are so few tables, it's usually standing room only at the bar. Good thing service is swift because oftentimes people end up eating there as they wait for that elusive table.

33 SE 7th St. therivermiami.com. **305/530-1915.** Most entrees $16–$42. Mon–Thurs noon–3pm and 6–10:30pm; Fri noon–3pm and 6–11pm; Sat 11am–3pm and 6–11pm; Sun 11am–3pm and 6–10:30pm.

Tam Tam ★★★ VIETNAMESE   Inspired by "*quán nhậu*"—a Vietnamese term for "drinking places"—Tam Tam is owned by a husband-and-husband team, one of whom spent 2 years teaching in Vietnam, the other a native of Saigon. They were underwhelmed by Miami's Vietnamese options so created this friendly place, which feels like you're eating in their private home, a cozily decorated dining room with wood-paneled walls, hand-painted tables, and floral upholstery. Oh, it also has karaoke bathrooms. Yes, really. There are mics in the bathrooms for those who feel like belting out a Mariah Carey tune while on the toilet. But back to the food: It's some good "drinking food" as owner Tam Pham says. Think: sticky tamarind-glazed pork ribs with crushed peanuts, scallion, and pickled cucumber; Nhau bone marrow with grilled sourdough, garlic herb salad, and a Birdseye chili-infused fish sauce; and goat curry with egg noodle, lemongrass, coconut, and herbs. To encourage drinking, the wine (and beer) list is made of all-natural, zero-intervention wines meaning no chemical agents, enhancers, filtration, sulfur, or commercially made yeast. However, you say "cheers" in Vietnamese, we're saying it about this place. Loudly.

99 NW 1st St. tam-tam-mia.com. **305/990-8707.** Main courses $11–$40. Tues–Sat 5:30–11pm.

INEXPENSIVE

Lost Boy Dry Goods ★★ BAR FOOD   Mismatched couches, brick walls, Elvis pictures, Madonna music: There's no mistaking you're in a neighborhood bar when you're here. But the food is cheap, and solidly tasty, like the $15 "Midnight Special" Cuban sandwich, and the $13 Chicago dog. Best bargain of all is the $10 Sloppy Jose sandwich of Cuban picadillo on a soft potato roll served with a side of chips—it's a savory stew of spices and sauce on a bun that calls for lots of napkins and maybe even a nap after. Need a late-night snack? This place serves 'til 3am, except on Sundays.

157 E. Flagler St. lostboydrygoods.com. **305/372-7303.** Main courses $10–$15. Mon–Sat noon–3am; Sun noon–1am.

Miami Slice ★★ PIZZA   Pizza places serving just a slice in Miami are as rare as a snowstorm, but this downtown spot near the performing arts center allows you to order just that. And this is a slice you will probably want more than one of: classic margherita or go a little fancier with garlic confit cream, leeks, bacon, and mozzarella. Slices are tasty and range from $5.75 to $10.75 for a mushroom truffle version. There's bar seating with views of the pizza-making action, or tables inside and out.

1335 NE Miami Court. miamislicepizza.com. ✆ **305/21-SLICE** [217-5423]. Slices $5.75–$11. Wed–Mon 5–11pm.

Midtown & Wynwood

Located north of downtown, the area roughly bound by North 20th Street to the south, I-195 to the north, I-95 to the west, and Biscayne Bay to the east, is a restaurant lover's mecca, with both white-tablecloth joints and some seriously excellent budget spots.

Tip: If you find yourself in Wynwood jonesing for java, head to **Panther Coffee** (2390 NW 2nd Ave.; PantherCoffee.com; ✆ **305/677-3952;** daily 'til 8pm), where the beans are roasted right on-site. There are several other locations throughout the city, and many Miami restaurants serve only Panther Coffee.

To locate the restaurants in this section, see the map "Downtown Miami, Midtown, Wynwood & Little Havana" (p. 73).

EXPENSIVE

Hiyakawa ★★★ JAPANESE/SUSHI   Straight out of a design magazine, the dining room here is framed by wood panels arranged in organically undulating concentric rings. It's a mesmerizing, minimalistic look and the minimalism is intentional, so that diners focus on their meals. Those consist of modern Japanese cuisine using traditional Japanese techniques not usually seen in these parts. From aged soy sauces to freshly grated wasabi, Hiyakawa is obsessively dedicated to its craft. Guests can order a la carte, or go for an omakase menu of 17 courses over approximately 2 hours ($250). For those not into raw food, there's tempura, steak, and more on the menu.

2700 N. Miami Ave. hiyakawamiami.com. ✆ **305/333-2417.** Main courses $14–$90. Wed–Sun 6–11pm.

> **Foodie Tours**
>
> Comprehensive tours of some of Miami's most delicious neighborhoods and districts, featuring local and global delicacies, are available from **Miami Culinary Tours** ★★★ (miamiculinarytours.com; ✆ **786/942-8856**). Sure, your souvenir may come in the form of a few extra pounds, but if you're interested in the interaction between food and culture, this is the tour for you.

MaryGold's Brasserie ★★★ AMERICAN   One of Miami's best chefs, Brad Kilgore, uses MaryGold's as his chef's lab. And foodies convene in Wynwood to see what's being plucked off his tweezer this week. What you'll be eating when you get here, and what the restaurant will look like, is up in the air, because Kilgore announced he'd be "transitioning to a new concept" just as we were going to press. Based on his track record, we trust that whatever goes into the space will be a winner.

2217 NW Miami Court in the Arlo hotel. marygoldsbrasserie.com. ✆ **786/522-6601.** Main courses $20–$195. Sun, Wed, Thurs 6–10pm; Fri–Sat 6–11pm. Closed Mon and Tues.

MODERATE

Morgans ★ AMERICAN   In 2024, Wynwood's breakfast and lunch go-to left the lavender house where it spent 14 years for a bigger location 6 blocks away. And though it's not nearly as homey as it was—the new location is much more chic and entirely indoors—Morgans is still where Miamians go for modern comfort food. "Voluptuous Grilled Cheese," sensational skinny fries, brioche French toast, meatloaf with "smokey mash"—well, you get the picture. Morgans serves three meals a day, but we prefer the daytime menu (breakfast, brunch, and lunch). However, a great 6–8pm special includes Morgans' Succulent Burger and a beer for $19—a bargain around here! The new location added more space for jazz nights, events, and bigger brunch crowds.

2800 NW 7th Ave. themorgansrestaurant.com. **305/573-9678.** Breakfast, lunch $14–$24; dinner main courses $16–$30. Daily 8am–9:30pm.

Pastis Miami ★★ FRENCH   A clone of the NYC Meatpacking District brasserie, Pastis brings a touch of Paris to Wynwood with its tobacco-stained sexiness, curved zinc bar, and signature banquettes. What's unique to this location is the gorgeous outdoor garden and courtyard under a black locust wrapped enclosed pergola from which to enjoy fab French onion soup, escargot, steak frites, croque madame and monsieur, and lots of raw bar bivalves. Oh, and don't forget the rose. This is a rose all day kind of place.

380 NW 26th St. pastismiami.com. **305/686-3050.** Main courses $18–$41 (more for steak). Mon–Wed 11:30am–11pm; Thurs–Fri 11:30am–midnight; Sat 10am–midnight; Sun 10am–11pm.

Sugarcane Raw Bar Grill ★★ SOUTH AMERICAN/ASIAN   Talented chef Timon Balloo presides over three kitchens—one for cooking meats, a raw bar, and one for everything else—seamlessly fusing South American, Asian, and global cuisine into tidy little (and not-so-little) plates of palate-pleasing foods. Loud and bustling, the 4,000-plus-square-foot hip, warehouse-style eatery packs in crowds with potent cocktails and signature dishes such as the duck and waffle—crispy leg confit, fried duck egg, and mustard maple syrup. Lots of emphasis on the raw bar here, too, with a sizeable sushi and sashimi menu. A huge cocktail crowd gathers at the indoor/outdoor bar and patio area after work and late on weekend nights. Sunday brunch is also extremely popular.

In the Shops at Midtown Miami, 3250 NE 1st Ave. sugarcanerawbargrill.com. **786/369-0353.** Sushi, main courses $11–$30. Mon–Fri 11:30am–midnight; Sat–Sun 10:30am–midnight.

Miami's Award-Winning Dining

The James Beard Awards are the Oscars of the culinary world. After a years-long drought of Miami having no winners, in the summer of 2024 young chef Valerie Chang brought home the badge of honor, and title of Best Chef: South when she scored a coveted James Beard Award for her Midtown Miami Peruvian restaurant **Maty's** ★★★, 3255 NE 1st Ave. (matysmiami.com; **786-338-3525**). Named for her late grandmother, and influenced by her Peruvian immigrant parents, the restaurant is known for creative spins on Peruvian classics including grilled grouper tail in beurre blanc, *lomo saltado* with oxtail, and tuna tiradito in lemon juice, orange juice, and aji Amarillo chiles. Maty's is also known for delicious brunch and cocktails. Book early, as the Beard Award just bumped it way up on Miami's hard-to-score reservations list.

Grab a seat outside at 1-800-Lucky . . . and you'll feel lucky, too.

INEXPENSIVE

1-800-LUCKY ★★ ASIAN A 10,000-square-foot Asian food hall, smack in the middle of pricey Wynwood, is the spot for fast, casual, and kitschy, with seven different Asian restaurants to choose from serving everything from bubble tea and chunky ube cream cheese chewies, to dim sum, sushi, Thai food, ramen, crispy Peking duck, and Gohan rice bowls. There's indoor and outdoor seating, booming soundtracks of everything from K-pop to hip-hop, two full bars, and a very fun—and loud—karaoke lounge.

143 NW 23rd St. 1800lucky.com. **305/768-9826**. Prices vary by restaurant. Mon–Wed noon–1am; Thurs–Sun noon–3am.

Enriquetta's Sandwich Shop ★★ CUBAN Before this area was filled with pricey condos, shops, restaurants, and hipsters, Enriquetta's was—and still is—a magnet for area workers looking for a fast and filling combo of Cafecito, Cuban sandwich, and croquettas—cheap (everything is under $10)! Even erstwhile resident David Beckham stopped in. This place is quintessential Miami: loud, fast, harried and a celebrity in its own right. Dine in or hop up to the window for takeout and a taste of old-school Miami.

186 NE 29th St. **305/333-6929**. Entrees all under $10. Mon–Fri 7am–2:45pm; Sat 7am–2pm.

Zak the Baker ★★★ BAKERY/CAFE An independent, artisan bakery from which many local restaurants source their breads, Zak the Baker is a kosher carb lovers' dream come true, with a full-service cafe and on-site bakery. Of the breads—oh, those breads!—the Jewish rye sourdough is a crunchy, crusty mashup of two two faves, and the pan au chocolat seems to have wandered in from the Left Bank. Those looking for meals have many classic choices, from fab Florida avocado toast to a sourdough grilled cheese with tomato bisque to bagels with salmon bacon (totally kosher!).

295 NW 26th St. zakthebaker.com. **786/294-0876**. $4-$15. Sun–Fri 7am–5pm. Closed Sat.

Design District, Little Haiti, Biscayne Corridor, Upper East Side

Little Haiti is the small, but culturally rich, heart of Miami's Haitian community west of Biscayne Boulevard between 54th and 52nd streets and minutes away from Wynwood and the Design District. Because of that, gentrification is in the works, much to the dismay of locals. South of Little Haiti and north of the Design District is Buena Vista, a mostly residential neighborhood with some hidden gems. Located along Biscayne Bay between downtown Miami and Little Haiti,

Miami's Upper East Side, also known as the MiMo district (Miami Modern) and the Biscayne Corridor (which is a fancy way of saying Biscayne Blvd. from 50th to 79th sts.), is full of funky shops, restaurants, and bars, and has been in a similar transition as Little Haiti for the last decade.

To locate the restaurants in this section, see the map "Miami Area Hotels & Restaurants" (p. 71).

MODERATE

Blue Collar ★★★ AMERICAN   Another winner from chef/owner Daniel Serfer (of Mignonette; see p. 91), this diner/bistro is about comfort food done so well it often ends up on "best of Miami" lists. In recent years, Blue Collar's burgers, french fries, brunch dishes, and Key lime pie have all been chosen as among the city's 10 best by local food writers. Daily specials are noteworthy, too: every day, the restaurant serves up different takes on ribs, parm, and braised meats (could be brisket, could be pork shoulder, you never know). And vegetarians are well taken care of here, with veggie plates crafted from 19 possible options (the diner chooses). Best of all: Only one menu item hits $35, with the rest under $30.

6789 Biscayne Blvd. bluecollarmiami.com. **305/766-0366.** Entrees $21–$25. Daily 11:30am–3:30pm and 5:30–10pm ('til 10:15 on Fri and Sat).

Boia de ★★★ ITALIAN   If you drive too fast out of the Design District and through residential Buena Vista, you'll miss this strip mall with laundromat and supermarket in it, and you'd think, so? Well, behind that pink neon exclamation point is this marvel, a tiny, dimly lit, cute 30-seat space where chefs Alex Meyer and Luciana Giangrandi turn out the tantalizing pastas that make this the hardest reservation score in the city. We're talking pappardelle with Florida rabbit; tortellini with foie gras, duck prosciutto, and duck consommé; and the big splurge, white truffle tagliatelle with truffle butter and parmesan. It's a fun place, not stuffy, with loud music. For those who don't score rezzies, walk-ins are welcome at the wine bar and Giangrandi offers this secret: Get there at 5:30pm on the dot and you'll get in.

Or, head to the team's second eatery, **Walrus Rodeo** ★★, a wood-fired restaurant serving an exquisite muffaletta panzanella, halibut puttanesca, and "proper Italian za" a few doors down at 5143 NE 2nd Ave. in the same strip. It's open 5:30 to 10:30pm Sunday through Thursday and 5:30 to 11pm Fridays and Saturdays, and is not as hard to get into as its sibling.

5205 NE 2nd Ave. in the Bravo Supermarket Plaza. BoiaDerestaurant.com. No phone. Main courses $26–$30 mostly. Daily 5:30–10:30pm.

Mandolin Aegean Bistro ★★ GREEK/MEDITERRANEAN   This bistro is like a set straight out of the film "Mamma Mia!" minus the painful wailing of Pierce Brosnan. Housed in a restored 1940s house in between the Design District and Buena Vista, the whitewashed building has a bougainvillea-studded back garden with taverna tables shaded by a lantern-lit tree. Cuisine pays homage to the simple, rustic fare found in villages of Greece and Turkey, with an emphasis on seasonal ingredients, local purveyors, and freshly caught fish. That means it serves typical Greek staples—Horiatiki salad, fried calamari, saganaki, and a gyro sandwich with tzatziki and moussaka—but it also throws in specialties such as olive oil–poached leeks with carrots and dill; Turkish spoon salad with pomegranate molasses; and homemade *pide,* or rustic village flatbread, made fresh daily.

4312 NE 2nd Ave. mandolinrestaurant.com. **786/749-9140.** Most entrees $20–$40. Daily noon–11pm.

Michael's Genuine Food & Drink ★★ NEW AMERICAN Since it opened in 2007, local foodies (and a few savvy visitors) have embraced this little Design District bistro wedged into a breezeway amid chichi showrooms and art galleries, because of its unassuming owner-chef Michael Schwartz and its mission to be Miami's locavore ground zero (though given the vagaries of Florida agriculture, Swartz sometimes has to go farther afield, but always keeping it organic). One thing I especially like is the variety of plate sizes for every budget and appetite. In the past, my faves on the constantly changing menu have included chargrilled octopus with gigante bean salad; wood oven–roasted yellowjack with kalamata olive tapenade, and creative wood-oven pizzas like the one with Fontina, slow-roasted pork, shaved onions, and—wait for it—peaches. The wine list is modest but well curated.

130 NE 40th St. michaelsgenuine.com. 📞 **305/676-0894.** Main courses $17–$42 (more for steak). Mon–Thurs 11:30am–10pm; Fri–Sat 11:30am–11pm; Sun 11am–10pm.

Tablé by Bachour ★★★ FRENCH/LEBANESE This Design District darling is owned by master baker Antonio Bachour, a man known for pastries worthy of a place in an art gallery. So it goes without saying that the breads and desserts are superb (camembert cheesecake: OMG!). But what's a surprise at this sherbet-colored, bustling bistro, is the way he mixes it up on the savory side of the menu, from delicious lamb meatballs and petite falafel to an oozy gruyere omelet and a Caesar salad with the best croutons on the planet. After you've tried the cauliflower escalope—with kibbeh, noisette herb salad and capers—you'll never underestimate that veggie again.

180 NE 40th St. tablebachour.com. 📞 **786/842-0551.** Most entrees $18–$38. Mon–Thurs 8am–9pm; Fri–Sat 8am–10pm; Sun 8am–5pm.

INEXPENSIVE

Andiamo! Brick Oven Pizza ★★ PIZZA This stretch of Biscayne Boulevard is known for its MiMo (Miami Modern, from the 1950s and early '60s) architecture, so it made sense to transform this retro-style 1960s tire shop into an indoor/outdoor pizza pit stop. It has a range of offerings from the simple Andiamo pie (tomato sauce, mozzarella, and basil) to designer combos of pancetta and caramelized onions. Very casual and family-friendly, there are picnic tables and TVs to keep everyone entertained, though watching the cars speed by on Biscayne is also fun.

5600 Biscayne Blvd. andiamopizzamiami.com. 📞 **305/762-5751.** Pizzas $12.50–$24.50. Mon–Thurs 11am–10pm; Fri 11am–11pm; Sat 11:30am–11pm; Sun 11:30am–10pm.

Dogma Grill ★ HOT DOGS A little bit of L.A. comes to a gritty stretch of Biscayne Boulevard in the form of this very tongue-in-cheeky hot dog stand. The brainchild of a former MTV executive, Dogma is a great option when you want something grilled fast, but not yellow arches fast, offering a plethora of choices, from your typical chili dog to Chicago-style, with celery salt, hot peppers, onions, and relish. The tropical version with pineapple is a bit funky but fitting for this stand, which attracts a very colorful, arty crowd from the nearby Design District. They also serve Philly cheesesteaks, hamburgers, sandwiches, and even a very good veggie burger.

7030 Biscayne Blvd. dogmagrill.com. 📞 **305/759-3433.** Hot dogs, hamburgers, sandwiches $5.25–$12.50. Mon–Sat 11am–10pm; Sun noon–9pm

Jimmy's Eastside Diner ★★ DINER   The only thing wrong with this quintessential greasy-spoon diner is that it's not open 24 hours. But it serves the cheapest breakfasts in town, not to mention lunches, so who is complaining? Try the banana pancakes, corned-beef hash, roasted chicken, or Philly cheesesteak. Located on the newly hip Upper East Side of Biscayne Boulevard, Jimmy's is a very neighborhoody place, where the late Bee Gee Maurice Gibb used to dine every Sunday and where the 2016 Oscar-winning Best Picture *Moonlight* was filmed.

7201 Biscayne Blvd. © **305/759-3433.** Main courses $10–$20. Daily 7am–3:30pm.

Little Havana

The main artery of Little Havana is a busy commercial strip called SW 8th Street, or Calle Ocho. Auto-body shops, cigar factories, and furniture stores line this street, and on every corner, there seems to be a pass-through window serving superstrong Cuban coffee and snacks. In addition, many of the Cuban, Dominican, Nicaraguan, Peruvian, and other Latin American immigrants have opened full-scale restaurants ranging from intimate candlelit establishments to bustling stand-up lunch counters. And then came the hipsters, an inevitable migration that has made Little Havana a nightlife and culinary hot spot for young scene chasers.

To locate the restaurants in this section, see the map "Downtown Miami, Midtown, Wynwood & Little Havana" (p. 73).

EXPENSIVE

Café La Trova ★★★ CUBAN   What started out as an homage to the fabulous supper clubs, music, and cocktail culture of pre-Castro Cuba by master mixologist Julio Cabrera, became an even more fabulous spot when Cabrera's bestie, James Beard Award–winning Miami chef Michelle Bernstein, brought her modern Cuban kitchen skills to the party. Trova, btw, is a style of music born in the eastern provinces of Cuba by traveling musicians well versed in guitar, vocal harmonies, and poetic lyrics. That's important, because nightly live music is a big part of the appeal here. As are such classic Cuban cocktails as the Hotel Nacional, a fruity fiesta of pineapple rum, apricot liqueur, pineapple juice, and lime juice. Creative tipples range from the Maduro Old Fashioned (plantain-infused whiskey, Demerara syrup, and chocolate bitters) to the award-winning Buenavista, a fusion of gin, cucumber, mint, elderflower liqueur, lime juice, and sugar. For food, start with the sweet corn and chicken empanadas with fermented garlic and charred scallions, some Cuban sandwich empanadas, or spinach and feta croquetas before moving on to the mains. We're partial to the oxtail stew, a savory symphony of its own juices, mascarpone, and pecorino over short, thin and twisted trofie pasta, and the arroz con pollo. For vegans, there's plant-based beef—it tastes like chicken! Kidding, it tastes beef-ish: picadillo with spices, tomatoes, peppers, onions, with *tostones* and white rice. There's a daily happy hour at the bar from 4 to 7pm.

971 SW 8th St. cafelatrova.com. © **786/615-4379.** Tapas, main courses $14–$87. Sun–Wed 4pm–midnight; Thurs 4pm–1am; Fri–Sat 4pm–2am.

MODERATE

Lung Yai Thai Tapas ★★★ THAI   However this Thai spot ended up in Little Havana doesn't matter. What matters is that you find it, you wait (no reservations accepted), and you enjoy every bit of Bangkok-born chef/owner Veenuthri

AREPA TO YUCA: MIAMI latin cuisine AT A GLANCE

Miami dining serves up a tasty culinary tour of Latin America—especially countries such as Cuba, Argentina, Peru, Colombia, Nicaragua, and Brazil. Although many restaurants have menus in English for the benefit of *norteamericano* diners, here are translations and suggestions for filling and delicious meals in case they don't:

Arepa: A corn flatbread common in Venezuela and Colombia, eaten with cheese and other accompaniments.

Arroz con pollo: Roast chicken served with saffron-seasoned yellow rice and diced vegetables.

Camarones enchilados: Shrimp in a slightly tangy-sweet, tomato-based sauce.

Ceviche: Raw seafood seasoned with spice and vegetables and marinated in vinegar and citrus to "cook" it; originally Peruvian but present in various Latin cuisines.

Chimichurri: A savory Argentine dressing based on parsley, garlic, and olive oil, paired with steak and sometimes chicken.

Croquetas: Golden-fried croquettes of ham, chicken, or codfish.

Empanada: A pastry with various fillings such as beef, chicken, tuna, or spinach, particularly a specialty of Argentina.

Feijoada: Brazil's national dish, a black-bean stew with beef, pork, and other items.

Flan: Bequeathed to all Latin countries by Spain, it's egg custard in liquid caramel, and is also made in variations including cheese and coconut.

Frijoles negros: Black beans, served in soup or over white rice.

Frita: A Cuban-style hamburger with beef, pork, chorizo sausage, garlic, and spices, served with potato sticks.

Mofongo: Popular especially in Puerto Rico and the Dominican Republic, a dish of mashed fried green plantains served in a broth with beef, shrimp, or chicken.

Palomilla: Thinly sliced beef, similar to American minute steak, usually served with onions, parsley, and a mountain of french fries.

Pan Cubano: Long, white, crusty Cuban bread. Ask for it *tostado*—toasted and flattened on a grill with lots of butter.

Papa a la huancaína: Peruvian sliced potatoes with very slightly spicy cheese sauce.

Picadillo: From the Caribbean, a ground-beef hash mixed with (depending on the island) peppers, onions, pimientos, raisins, and olives.

Plátanos (or maduros): Soft, mildly sweet bananas, fried and caramelized.

Pollo asado: Roasted chicken with onions and a crispy skin.

Pupusa: Originating in El Salvador and now part of other Central American cuisines, it's a thick, soft corn tortilla stuffed with cheese and served with various fillings.

Ropa vieja: A tomatoey shredded beef stew whose name literally means "old clothes."

Tostones: Green, unsweet plantains, flattened and fried.

Trisransri's Thai street food, served tapas-style and served Thai spicy, which is no joke. (They also do mild on request.) A massive menu has all the classics and some specialties, including perfect pad Thai and tom yum soup, curries in all colors, and crazy good and often sold-out *khao mam kai*—chicken poached with salt, sugar, garlic, and ginger, served over rice cooked in ginger and chicken broth and topped with a soybean garlic sauce that they should definitely bottle. It's a tiny spot and there are rules. Among them: You must order everything at once, but you can "always ask for more water and beers," and when you're done pay your check so others can take your seat. They even tell you the best times to be seated: between noon and 3pm and 5 to 7pm. Easy enough to follow for some of the best Thai in town.

1731 SW 8th St. lungyai.com. **786/334-6262.** Main courses $15–$24. Tues–Sat noon–3pm and 5–10pm; Sun 5–10pm. Closed Mon.

INEXPENSIVE

El Rey de Las Fritas ★★ CUBAN

Accurately billing itself as the home of the original Frita Cubana, El Rey schools other places on the art of the Cuban burger: a ground-beef patty with chorizo sausage mixed in, spices such as paprika, a secret-ingredient dressing, and sauteed onions, topped with crispy shoestring fries between a pillowy Cuban roll. The Frita Suprema adds fried cheese and sweet plantains to the party but stick to the original for the full—emphasis on full—experience. There are all sorts of other delicious Cuban dishes here, like the tamale with fried pork chunks, the $10 steak special with salad and fries, *croquetas* and so much more, but go for the original *frita*. There are three other locations throughout the city, but this is the best and the original.

1821 SW 8th St. elreydelasfritas.com. **305/644-6054.** $5–$15. Daily 8am–10pm.

Lung Yai Thai Tapas.

El Rey de Las Fritas.

La Camaronera Seafood Joint ★★ SEAFOOD   A casual spot with an open kitchen and constant crowds, this is the place to go for fried seafood in various incarnations—sandwiches, platters, and even burritos. The most famous dish here is the *pan con minuta,* a whole, lightly fried snapper filet (tail included) on a Cuban bun with diced white onions, ketchup, and tartar sauce. It's a sensory overload of crunch, crisp, sweet, tart, and briny. For those in your group not into fried, the shrimp or fish of your choice in the tacos are served blackened and are delicious. For a splurge, the whole spiny lobster is seasoned and fried and out of this world. A Monday through Friday happy hour from 4 to 7pm features oysters and beer specials.

1952 W. Flagler St. lacamaronera.com. ✆ **305/642-3322.** Main courses $12–$22. Sun–Thurs 11:30am–8pm; Fri–Sat 11:30am–9pm.

Sanguich ★★ CUBAN   After wowing crowds with its Cuban sandwiches crafted inside a shipping container, Sanguich transformed into a walk-up window and tiny (and cute) Little Havana luncheonette. It has counter seating and a few tables, and turns out some of the best sandwiches you will ever eat. The big draw here: the Cuban sandwich (Cubano) featuring ham, Swiss cheese, pickles, mustard, and pork butt marinated for a week in garlic and spices, then pressed between grilled slices of house-made bread. The *pan con lechón* runs a close second, with shredded pork, pickled mojo onions, and garlic cilantro aioli. A second location is in Little Haiti at 6500 NE 2nd Ave., a third in Coral Gables at 111 Palermo Ave., and another expected downtown at Bayside Marketplace.

2057 SW 8th St. sanguich.com. ✆ **305/539-0969.** $12–$15. Daily 10am–6pm.

Sanpocho ★★ COLOMBIAN   For Colombian food, this strip-mall sensation is it, with only 14 tables and takeout, with long lines especially at lunch. Come with an empty stomach because they don't skimp here: The national dish, *bandeja paisa,* is a massive plate of beans, rice, arepa, chorizo, plantain, chicharrón, fried egg, corn cake, avocado, and either ground or grilled beef. It can feed an entire football team. For lighter appetites, just order a few of the crispy Colombian empanadas with a squirt of lime and spicy *aji.* There's also delicious daily breakfast until 11:45am—the refried rice with beans and scrambled eggs, onions, and tomatoes is a wakeup call to your tastebuds and a bargain at only $6. Servers are super friendly. Check out the tchotchkes on the walls around the place—some are even for sale.

901 SW 8th St. sanpocho.com. ✆ **305/854-5954.** Main courses $9–$20. Mon–Thurs 7am–8pm; Fri–Sun 7am–9pm.

Terras Rooftop ★★ LATIN AMERICAN   Little Havana's only rooftop bar and restaurant, Terras, is located on the fourth floor of the Life House Hotel, which also features gardens from which the fruits, vegetables, and herbs in many of the cocktails and dishes are sourced. It has a small menu of South American, Caribbean, and Latin American–inspired, street-food shareables including sweet corn "cachapa" cheese pancakes, which are basically arepas with quesillo, avocado, salsa verde, and radish (add on *ropa vieja* or red mole chicken for a heartier share); *ropa vieja* birria tacos with consommé dip and Oaxaca cheese; and the favorite here, the *frita* burger with caramelized onions, guava marmalade, shoestring potatoes, and spicy ketchup. Spectacular views!

528 SW 9th St. in the Life House Hotel. lifehousehotels.com. ✆ **305/642-3322.** $6–$17. Tues 4–10pm; Wed–Sat 4pm–midnight; Sun 4–9pm.

Versailles ★ CUBAN   Calle Ocho's most famous mainstay, as well as Miami's best known Cuban icon, Versailles (pronounced "ver-SIGH-yes") is something of a marvel not just for longevity (est. 1971) but also its prices and look. We don't know if its kitschy mirrors and chandeliers were meant to evoke the Sun King's palace for real or with tongue in cheek, but they sure make an unforgettable backdrop to a parade of local characters, from blue-haired *abuelitas* to late-night club kids. Versailles still delivers the goods menu-wise, with fare that's tasty, authentic, and still quite affordable. Plantain soup, Cuban sandwiches, roast pork with onions, *vaca frita* (shredded grilled beef), guava pastries, Cuban-style coffee that's as sweet as it is strong—all the classics are here, and then some.

3555 SW 8th St. VersaillesRestaurant.com. **305/444-0240.** Main courses $10–$25. Mon–Thurs 8am–midnight; Fri–Sat 8am–1am; Sun 9am–midnight.

Key Biscayne

Key Biscayne is home to some of the world's nicest beaches, but it is not known for great food. Locals, or "Key rats," as they're known, tend to go off-island for meals, but here is the best on-the-island choice.

To locate the restaurants in this section, see the map "Miami Area Hotels & Restaurants" (p. 71).

Rusty Pelican ★ SEAFOOD   A landmark Key Biscayne waterfront restaurant since 1972, Rusty Pelican has gone through many incarnations. While some consider it a, well, rusty tourist trap, its location on the water on the Rickenbacker Marina makes it worth a go, even if it's just for appetizers and drinks. In fact, it's an excellent happy-hour spot where, from 4 to 6:30pm Monday through Thursday,

The spectacular view from the Rusty Pelican . . . plus some shrimp.

the lounge offers deeply discounted drinks and half-priced dishes. ***Bottom line:*** The food here is pricey and not the best, but if you go around sunset, the beauty of your surroundings—the million-dollar view over Biscayne Bay with birds (pelicans included) swooping by, and in the distance downtown Miami's high-rise skyline—make up for what they lack culinarily speaking.

3201 Rickenbacker Causeway. therustypelican.com. © **305/361-3818.** Main courses $30–$160. Mon–Fri noon–4pm; Sun–Thurs 4–10pm; Fri–Sat 4–11pm; Sat 11am–4pm; Sun 10am–4pm.

Coconut Grove

Coconut Grove was long known as the artists' haven of Miami, but the rush of developers turned parts of it into an overgrown mall. But today, the Grove has taken back its reputation as a hip spot, and there are several great dining spots both inside and outside the confines of Mayfair and CocoWalk.

To locate the restaurants in this section, see the map "Coral Gables & Coconut Grove" (p. 77).

EXPENSIVE

Ariete ★★★ NEW AMERICAN   Chef Michael Beltran grew up in Little Havana on his Cuban exile family's cuisine—his grandparents worked at a bakery called Ariete—and honed his skills in the kitchens of the Floribbean pioneers who put the Miami food scene on the map: namely chefs Norman van Aken and Michael Schwartz. The result is this Michelin-starred mecca with a rustic-chic indoor dining room (white subway tiles, low ceilings with exposed ducts, open kitchen, dim lighting, and loud music), and a resplendent, lush outdoor patio. On the meat-heavy menu: venison, not something you see much in these warm climes, with truffle twice-baked potatoes, and foie gras sauce Diane; pastrami-style short rib with an oyster and short rib croquette; and a divine duck for two—a 14-day-dry-aged breast with roasted *calabaza* (pumpkin) tamal, wild mushroom foie gravy, and duck fricassee *pastelitos*. If this one is outside your budget, know that Beltran owns a slew of area restaurants including affordable **Chug's Diner** (see below), and his newest, **Eva**, in neighboring CocoWalk, a dinner-only, oyster- and seafood-focused restaurant.

3540 Main Hwy. arietecoconutgrove.com. © **786/615-3747.** Main courses $42–$160. Sun–Thurs 5:30–10pm; Fri–Sat 5:30–11pm.

MODERATE

Chug's Diner ★★ CUBAN AMERICAN   Michael Beltran of Ariete fame decided to experiment with the greasy spoon concept, but when a chef as talented as Beltran goes budget, the result is never greasy. This riff on a retro Cuban American diner has booths, counter seating, and a lovely outdoor patio. It serves all-day breakfast—the breakfast sandwich of sunny side up egg, Taylor ham, American cheese, mayo, *papitas* (potatoes), on Cuban bread is something you will want to eat at any meal—lunch and dinner. Other menu champs include malanga latkes with guava apple sauce and sour cream, and the *frita* patty melt with Swiss, caramelized onions, and 1000 Island dressing. For huge eaters: the Abuelas Plate, inspired by Beltran's grandparents, features suckling pig, crispy pork and chicken with white rice, black beans and banana. There are also delicious cocktails, milkshakes, and a magnificent mac and cheese skillet. Happy hours from Thursday to Sunday offer discounted booze and eats.

3444 Main Hwy. chugsdiner.com. © **786/353-2940.** Main courses $10–$28. Mon–Wed 7:30am–3pm; Thurs–Sat 7:30am–10pm; Sun 7:30am–7pm.

CARIBBEAN CAFFEINE: cuban coffee

Café cubano is a longstanding tradition in Miami, and despite the more than a dozen Starbucks that dot the Miami landscape, many locals still rely on the Cuban joints for their daily caffeine fix. You'll find it served from the takeout windows of hundreds of *cafeterías* or *loncherías* around town, especially in Little Havana, downtown, Hialeah, and the beaches. Depending on where you are and what you want, you'll drop between 40¢ and $1.50 per cup.

The best *café cubano* has a thin but rich layer of foam on top formed when the hot espresso shoots from the machine into the sugar below. The result is the caramely, sweet, potent concoction that's a favorite of locals of all nationalities. And try asking for it *en español: "Un cafecito, por favor!"*

Glass & Vine ★★ INTERNATIONAL Housed in the former Coconut Grove Library, this massive, mostly outdoor, 200-seat restaurant spreads out in a sprawling garden beneath the twinkly-lit trees dotting Peacock Park. As gorgeous as it is at night, daytime doesn't disappoint, with excellent breakfasts and a bustling brunch. This is a family-friendly spot, where parents chug cocktails as kids run around in the park. The comprehensive menus cover everything from skirt steak and gnocchi to burgers, chicken, and salads. Happy hour from 3 to 7pm Monday through Friday is always packed, as is "Throw It Back Thursdays" from 5pm until closing, featuring $9 stone crab claws in season and snacks and bar bites for $4 and $7. You can even order your pooch a plate of grilled salmon and pasta for $12. Live music makes the place especially magical.

2820 McFarlane Rd. glassandvine.com. **305/200-5268.** Main courses $12–$44. Mon–Fri 11:30am–4pm; Mon–Thurs 4–10pm; Fri–Sat 4–11pm; Sun 4–10pm; Brunch 10am Sat and Sun.

Le Bouchon du Grove ★★ FRENCH This very authentic bistro is French right down to the waitstaff. The food, prepared by an animated French (what else?) chef, is good, sometimes very good, sometimes great. A delicious starter that's always reliable is the *gratinée Lyonnaise* (traditional French onion soup). Fish is also a smart pick, brought in fresh daily; try the pan-seared sea bass with sweet pea puree and truffle butter. If dinner's not in the cards, we highly recommend breakfast and lunch—a traditional French breakfast of café au lait, bread, butter, and jam hits the spot, and the croque monsieur is, well, *magnifique.*

3430 Main Hwy. lebouchondugrove.net. **305/448-6060.** Main courses $28.50–$50. Tues–Sat 11:30am–9:30pm; Sun 8:30am–3pm. Closed Mon.

OMAKAI ★★ SUSHI Stellar sushi is what's on the menu at this fast-paced Japanese restaurant, where for $50 (the Oma Deluxe), you'll get an appetizer, 10 pieces of nigiri and two handrolls, which is an excellent deal for excellent quality fish. The sleek, 65-seat space considers itself "fine casual," as opposed to fast-casual, even though it can get harried in here. There are four other locations around Miami.

3304 Mary St. omakai.com. **786/644-6494.** Sushi $5–$95. Sun–Thurs noon–10:30pm; Fri–Sat noon–11:30pm.

INEXPENSIVE

Regatta Grove ★★ INTERNATIONAL   An outdoor version of a food hall, Regatta Grove has what the aforementioned doesn't: waterfront views. It also has four restaurants by Michelin-starred and James Beard Award–nominated chefs. *Top Chef* season 13 winner Jeremy Ford's JJ's (Guilty Pleasures) slings fancy burgers and tacos; chef Jose Mendin of Pubbelly Sushi fame takes on pizza at "The Piefather"; a rare offering of Australian cuisine comes to Miami via "Sunny Side Aussie Bites + Ice" by chef Janine Booth, also a *Top Chef* alum, whose partner and fellow contestant, chef Jeff McInnis serves seafood at the "Tackle Box." Lastly, yet another *Top Chef* alum, this time season 7, Kenny Gilbert, serves excellent fried chicken at "House of Birds." There are also three huge bars and live entertainment, making for a one-stop night out, but only from Thursday to Sunday.

3415 Pan American Dr. regattagrove.com. **305/707-4667.** Main courses $7–$25. Thurs 4pm–1am; Fri 4pm–3am; Sat noon–3am; Sun noon–midnight.

Coral Gables & Environs

What Starbucks is to most major cities, excellent gourmet and ethnic restaurants are to Coral Gables, where there's a restaurant on every corner and everywhere in between.

Note that we sang the praises of pastry chef Antonio Bachour earlier in the chapter (p. 97). He has a killer sit-down restaurant cum bakery in Coral Gables, as well, called **Bachour** ★★★ (2020 Salzedo St.; antoniobachour.com; **305/203-0552;** Mon–Sat 7am–9pm, Sun 7am-5pm). It serves elevated sandwiches, salads, arroz con pollo, and other savory treats, along with some of the most exquisite desserts you've ever tasted. Also, if you're in the mood for Cuban, but don't want to trek to Little Havana, **Havana Harrys** ★★ (4612 S. Le Jeune Rd.; havanaharrys.com; daily 8am–10pm) will scratch that itch.

To locate the restaurants in this section, see the map "Coral Gables & Coconut Grove" (p. 77).

EXPENSIVE

Bouchon ★★★ FRENCH   The grand poobah of California cuisine, Thomas Keller, has his place in the Four Seasons Surfside (p. 84) and also this branch of his West Coast bistro. Housed in a historic 1924 building, Bouchon brings Keller's seasonally changing French fare to the Gables in all its glory, including roast chicken, steak frites, croque madame, and the signature raw bar with a selection of fruits de mer, all complemented by an extensive French and domestic wine list. Classy Coral Gables is the perfect location for this piece of culinary excellence.

2101 Galliano St. thomaskeller.com. **305/990-1360.** Main courses $28–$55. Mon–Wed 5–9pm; Thurs 5–10pm; Fri noon–10:30pm; Sat 11am–10:30pm; Sun 11am–9pm.

Caffe Abbracci ★★ ITALIAN   As newcomers to the Coral Gables culinary scene come and go, this venerable Italian classic stays put, and for good reason. Though its affable owner passed away in 2022, his legacy lives on through his two daughters, who would make their dad proud with their polished and warm hospitality. Abbracci serves classic Italian fare in a comfortably elegant dining room. You won't find foams or tweezers in this kitchen, but that doesn't stop it from putting out Italian delights. A classic.

318 Aragon Ave. caffeabbracci.com. **305-441-0700.** Main courses $24–$60. Mon–Thurs 11:30am–3:30pm and 6–10:30pm; Fri 11:30am–3:30pm and 6–11pm; Sat 6–11pm; Sun 6–10:30pm.

Christy's ★★★ STEAKHOUSE
Old-school Coral Gables is alive and well at this steakhouse in all its red-hued and woodsy glory, in biz since 1978. The scene of many power lunches, Cristy's is an upper crusty classic that exudes old Coral Gables. Always known for its stellar Caesar salad and prime rib, Cristy's has come into the 21st century with some updated sides including fried Brussels sprouts with jalapeno aioli and a now-requisite truffle mac and cheese. Service is as professional as it gets, and cocktails are stiff—the ideal ingredients for a mainstay meatery such as this one.

3101 Ponce de Leon Blvd. christysrestaurant.com. © **305-446-1400.** Main courses $28–$125. Tues–Thurs 5:30–9:30pm; Fri–Sat 5:30-10pm. Closed Sun and Mon.

Eating House ★★★ MODERN AMERICAN
When then-rising chef Giorgio Rapicavoli won Food Network's *Chopped,* he parlayed his win into a pop-up restaurant that was so widely acclaimed it became one of Miami's most in demand reservations for an impressive 10-year run. It has now reopened bigger and better, in a huge, 3,300-square-foot space with L-shaped bar, white walls, high ceilings, and sleek black furniture. The menu reflects the chef's playfulness, like an American caviar starter that's served with tater tots and "everything" seasoned crème fraiche. Other menu musts: buttermilk fried chicken thighs with a fiery carrot hot sauce; and a bucatini carbonara soaked in heritage bacon and black truffle. Brunch is the most fun menu of all, with Cap'n Crunch pancakes slathered in vanilla butter, condensed milk syrup, and candied cereal. *Tip:* Happy hour Tuesday through Saturday from 3 to 7pm at the bar features $9 cocktails—try the Ya Filthy Animal if you like dirty martinis—and bar snacks from $6 to $22. Rapicavoli also opened an Italian restaurant, **Luca Osteria,** a few doors down at 1156 Giralda (lucamiami.com; © **305/381-5097**), whose menu features Italian classics.

A bartender crafts a cocktail at Eating House.

128 Giralda Ave. eatinghousemiami.com. © **786/580-3745.** Main courses $29–$64. Tues–Fri 11:30am–3pm; Tues–Thurs 6–10pm; Fri–Sat 6–11pm. Brunch Sat–Sun 11am–3pm.

Zitz Sum ★★★ ASIAN FUSION
Chef Pablo Zitzmann beat Bobby Flay in his own kitchen, and you'll see why at this sexy, dark and windowless spot. Zitzmann, who grew up in a German/Mexican immigrant household in Bogota, Colombia, says that Asian flavors were "The Ramones" of food for him, and you'll taste that punk influence in his daily changing menus, on which you'll find things like a Kinoko Hot Pot with spicy Hong Kong XO Sauce, Koshihikari rice,

soft egg, oyster mushrooms and herbs, or a blue crab and Thai basil cavatelli pasta with sake beurre monte and *ikura* (salmon caviar). Dumplings, in whatever incarnation of the day, are always outstanding. The HK Style French Toast is an example of dessert served here, with milk iced tea gelato, peanut crumble, and condensed milk.

396 Alhambra Circle. zitzsum.com. *786/409-6920.* Main courses $18–$64. Tues–Thurs 6–9:30pm; Fri–Sat 6–10pm. Closed Mon and Tues.

MODERATE

Bulla Gastrobar ★★ SPANISH   The kind of place where you can speak with a Catalonian lisp and fit right in, Bulla is the quintessential Spanish tapas bar, with small plates of chorizo, olives, Manchego cheese, shrimp in garlic and brandy, croquetas, gazpacho, *patatas bravas,* and so much more. Large plates of paella for those who are hungry and patient—it takes at least 30 minutes to prepare—and sangria, lots of sangria. It's moderately priced compared to other area eateries, lively—especially during happy hours and weekend brunch—and informal, and because of that we're bully for Bulla.

2500 Ponce de Leon Blvd. bullagastrobar.com. *786/810-6215.* Tapas $9–$15, main courses $17–$40. Mon–Tues 11:30am–10pm; Wed–Thurs 11:30am–11pm; Fri 11:30am–midnight; Sat 11am–midnight; Sun 11am–10pm.

INEXPENSIVE

The Café at Books & Books ★★ CAFE   There's nothing like the smell of a just-cracked new book along with your grilled cheese or tuna melt, which is why this indie bookstore cafe is one of our favorites. Grab a book, a magazine (they still have those!), and a seat in the alfresco courtyard and sit as long as you want over a glass of wine, a cup of coffee, or one of their many salads, sandwiches, wraps, and sweets. Plus, you never know who you'll see here, as this remains a literati's living room, a real, well-read, well-fed spot, indeed.

265 Aragon Ave. booksandbooks.com. *305/448-9599.* Main courses $13–$19. Mon–Sat 10am–11pm; Sun 10am–8pm.

West Miami, Kendall & Homestead

Though mostly residential, these areas nonetheless have one eating establishment apiece worth the drive.

To locate the restaurants in this section, see the map "Miami Area Hotels & Restaurants" (p. 71).

EXPENSIVE

Fiola ★★★ ITALIAN   This Michelin-starred Washington, D.C.. import is as fancy as it gets, featuring Fabio Trabocchi's feastworthy cuisine, perfect for special occasions. Dinner is an experience here, with tasting menus and all kinds of rare and pricey caviars, plus a bison steak tartare as rare in these parts as a Kardashian without fillers. The pastas will have you singing an Italian aria. Sunday brunch is also quite the scene, with Delmonico steak and eggs and Panettone Toast with Vermont maple syrup and all sorts of boozy, bottomless offerings. *Tip:* Happy hour (Mon 5–7pm, Tues–Fri 4–7pm) is the best way to do this place if you're on a budget; you can indulge in tuna tartare or a *radiatore cacio e pepe* for $12 or indulgent foie gras *budino* for $10. Get here a half-hour before it starts to score a highly coveted bar stool.

But wait, there's more. Located a few steps away is **La Terrazza,** Fiola's rooftop bar and grill on the penthouse level of the 1515 Sunset Building, featuring a retractable roof, bar, and a so-called "bespoke" menu by Fiola's executive chef Danny Ganem that's similar to Fiola's happy-hour menu. It's a much more casual way to enjoy the finery, plus there's often live entertainment.

1500 San Ignacio Ave. fiolamiami.com. **305/912-2639.** Main courses $28–$55. Mon 5:30–9pm; Tues–Thurs noon–3pm and 5:30–9pm; Fri noon–3pm and 5:30–10pm; Sat 5:30–10pm; Sun 11:30am–3:30pm and 5–8:30pm.

Ghee Indian Kitchen ★★★ INDIAN   Oh. Em. Ghee. This Indian spot put sleepy South Miami suburb Kendall (or as it's now known as, "Downtown Dadeland") on the map for culinary excellence. Here, chef Nivel Patel, former chef de cuisine at the Design District's Michael's Genuine Food & Drink, has drawn Michelin and Miami's persnickety food crowd all the way to Kendall to try some of the best, most refined Indian cuisine in town. Patel makes guests feel like they're in his home kitchen, with a cozy ambiance and walls of shelves packed with spices. Standout snacks off the dinner menu include the spicy, smoky, tandoori peri peri wings which will have you viewing your corner bar's buffalo wings with scorn, and a short rib dosa, which is a fermented rice crepe filled with melt-in-your-mouth short rib with sambar dal and chutney dipping sauces. Main courses include the best chicken tikka masala I've had—and I've had some spectacular ones in London—and the vegetarian Saag Paneer, a flavor bomb of epic proportion, featuring cubes of spice-marinated paneer cheese, grilled and served over a curry sauce. Best of all? The ingredients—bronze fennel, sunchokes, purple sugar apple, lychee, everglade tomatoes, and 10 varieties of mango—come from Rancho Patel, the chef's 2-acre farm in Homestead. A second location opened in Wynwood at 70 NW 25th St. as we went to press.

8965 SW 72nd Pl., Kendall. gheemiami.com. **305/968-1850.** Main courses $18–$38. Tues–Sun noon–2:30pm and 5–9pm.

MODERATE

Tropical Chinese ★★ CHINESE   Over the years, this attractively decorated space, tucked into the unprepossessing Tropical Park Plaza strip mall, has become a beloved institution for residents of a region with a dearth of decent Chinese restaurants. In addition to a tasty regular menu, Tropical serves some of the most delicious dim sum this side of Hong Kong, 7 days a week—*siu mai,* steamed pork buns, leek and scallion dumplings, stuffed bean curd skin, and of course those queasily photogenic chicken feet. Favorites on the menu include the roast duck, sizzling black pepper beef, pepper-salt tofu squares, and Singapore rice noodles. The crowd and vibe are usually lively without ever getting overwhelming. I'd say this one's worth the drive even all the way from Miami Beach—and being right off one of the expressways, not even much of a schlep.

7991 Bird Rd., West Miami. tropicalchinesemiami.com. **305/262-7576.** Main courses $10–$35, dim sum items $6.75–$11. Mon–Sat 11am–9:30pm; Sun 11am–9pm. Take U.S. 1 to Bird Rd. and go west on Bird, all the way down to 78th Ave. The restaurant is btw. 78th and 79th on the north side of Bird Rd.

INEXPENSIVE

El Palacio de los Jugos ★★ CUBAN   Although the original is on West Flagler Street, this outpost of the Cuban culinary landmark is just as good, if not better, serving fresh squeezed juices (guava, papaya, sugar cane, mango), tropical shakes, and some of the most authentic Cuban fare this side of Havana at prices that go back to the old days. Here, you'll find everything from oxtail to roasted chicken, pork ribs, and roast pork, and pretty much anything comes dished from a steam table with a heaping helping of either arroz con pollo or red beans and rice. You also get a generous hunk of boiled yucca with its traditional accompaniment of garlic and citrus mojo sauce. They also serve a fantastically cheap breakfast. It's loud, it's frenzied, it's almost 100% in Spanish, and it's one of the most delicious Miami experiences you will have for under $20.

1545 SW 27th Ave. *305/635-0166.* Juices and main courses $5–$20. Daily 7am–8:45pm.

White Lion Cafe ★★ SOUTHERN   The White Lion Cafe is a hidden gem serving Southern-style blue-plate specials, including delicious meatloaf and fried chicken. Or, for the high rollers with a sense of humor, order the P.J. and Dom—a gigantic PB&J sandwich with a "complimentary" bottle of Dom Perignon for $200. There's also an extensive entertainment calendar here, with everything from live jazz to karaoke. If you're in the Homestead area en route to the Keys, it's definitely worth a stop here, where time seems to stand still, at least until the band starts playing.

146 NW 7th St., Homestead. whitelioncafe.com. *305/248-1076.* Main courses $10–$30. Tues–Fri 11am–3pm and 5pm until "the fat lady sings"; Sat noon–5pm. Closed Sun and Mon. Take the 836 E. to the 826 S., at exit 6 make a left and head west on 8th St. (Campbell Dr.), after crossing Krome Ave. take a left at 1st Ave. (the very next light), and turn right on 7th St. The cafe is on the left.

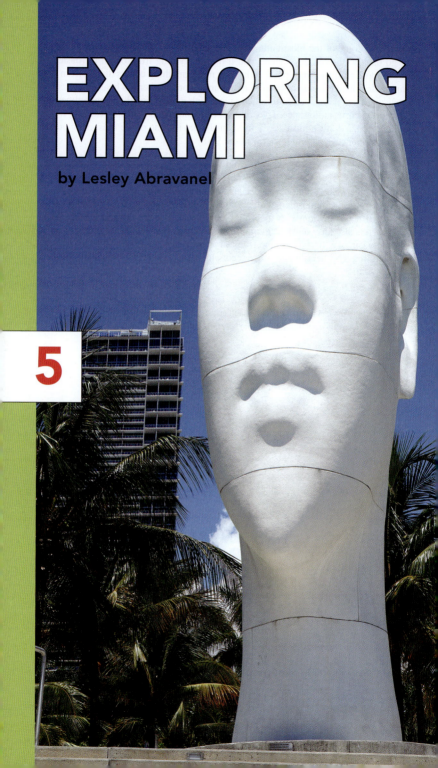

EXPLORING MIAMI

by Lesley Abravanel

5

f there's one thing Miami doesn't have, it's an identity crisis—multiple personalities, maybe, but hardly a crisis. In fact, it's the city's vibrant, multifaceted personality that attracts millions each year from all over the world. South Beach may be on the top of many Miami to-do lists, but the rest of the city—a fascinating assemblage of multicultural neighborhoods—should not be overlooked. Once considered "God's Waiting Room," the Magic City now attracts a mix of old and young, celebs and plebes, American and international, and geek and chic with an equally varied roster of activities.

For starters, Miami boasts some of the world's most natural, albeit fragile, beauty, with dazzling blue waters, fine sandy beaches, and lush tropical parks. The city's man-made brilliance, in the form of crayon-colored architecture, never seems to fade in Miami's unique Art Deco district. For cultural variation, you can experience the tastes, sounds, and rhythms of Cuba in Little Havana (as well as the rest of Latin America, there and elsewhere in the city).

As in any metropolis, though, some areas aren't as great as others. Downtown Miami, for instance, is still in the throes of a major, albeit slow, renaissance, in which the warehouse sections of the city are being transformed into hubs of all things hip. But there are the still poverty-stricken areas of downtown such as Overtown, Liberty City, and Little Haiti (though Overtown is striving to transform itself into the Overtown Historic Village, showcasing its landmarks such as the famous Lyric Theater and the home of D. A. Dorsey, Miami's first African-American millionaire). While we advise you to exercise caution when exploring the less-traveled parts of the city, we would also be remiss if we were to tell you to bypass them completely.

Lose yourself in the city's nature and its neighborhoods and, best of all, its people—a sassy collection of artists and intellectuals, beach bums and international transplants, dolled-up drag queens and bodies beautiful.

MIAMI'S BEACHES

Perhaps Miami's most popular attraction is its incredible 35-mile stretch of beachfront, which runs from the tip of South Beach north to Sunny Isles, then circles Key Biscayne and numerous other pristine islands dotting the Atlantic. The characteristics of Miami's many beaches are as varied as the city's population: There are beaches for swimming, socializing, or serenity; for family, seniors, or gay singles; some to make you forget you're in the city, others darkened by huge condominiums. Whatever type of beach vacation you're looking for, you'll find it in one of Miami's two distinct beach areas: Miami Beach and Key Biscayne. And in keeping up with technology, Miami Beach is now officially a hot spot—as in a

FACING PAGE: Jaume Plensa's 40-foot-tall statue *Looking into My Dreams, Awilda* stands outside the Pérez Art Museum.

wireless hotspot, offering 95% coverage outdoors (70% indoors) of free Wi-Fi throughout the entire city and, yes, even on the sand.

MIAMI BEACH'S BEACHES Collins Avenue fronts more than a dozen miles of white-sand beach and blue-green waters from 1st to 192nd streets. Although most of this stretch is lined with a solid wall of hotels and condos, beach access is plentiful. There are lots of public beaches here, wide and well maintained, complete with lifeguards, restroom facilities, concession stands, and metered parking (see p. 60 for info). Except for a thin strip close to the water, most of the sand is hard packed—the result of a $10-million Army Corps of Engineers Beach Rebuilding Project meant to protect buildings from the effects of eroding sand.

> **Impressions**
>
> *Is Miami America? Is it a state? Is it the South? . . . I love Miami for the same reason I love the places I love most around the world . . . it's the mix here, this big, messy, dysfunctional hell broth of people from all over the world that make it so awesome and make it a place I want to keep coming back to. Also, the food's good.*
>
> —Anthony Bourdain

In general, the beaches on this barrier island (all on the eastern, ocean side of the island) become less crowded the farther north you go. A wooden boardwalk runs along the hotel side of the beach from 21st to 46th streets—about

It's always a lively scene on Miami Beach's beaches.

1½ miles—offering a terrific sun-and-surf experience without getting sand in your shoes. Miami's lifeguard-protected public beaches include 21st Street, at the beginning of the boardwalk; 35th Street, popular with an older crowd; 46th Street, next to the Fontainebleau; 53rd Street, a narrower, more sedate beach; 64th Street, one of the quietest strips around; and 72nd Street, a local old-timers' spot.

KEY BISCAYNE'S BEACHES If Miami Beach doesn't provide the privacy you're looking for, try Virginia Key and Key Biscayne. Crossing the Rickenbacker Causeway ($1.50 toll), however, can be a lengthy process, especially on weekends, when beach bums and tan-o-rexics flock to the Key. The 5 miles of public beach there, however, are blessed with softer sand and are less developed and more laid-back than the hotel-laden strips to the north. Key Biscayne's historic **Virginia Key Beach Park,** 4020 Virginia Beach Dr. (virginiakeybeachpark.net; ⓒ **305/960-4600**) was a former "colored only" beach that opened in 1945. The 83-acre historic park features picnic tables and grills, a playground for children with special needs, and a miniature railroad. There are free eco-tours Friday through Sunday at 10am and 2pm. The beach eventually plans to open a civil rights museum as well. Open from 7am to sunset daily, with free admission Monday through Thursday and $8 on Friday through Sunday.

SOUTH BEACH: ART DECO DISTRICT

The Art Deco District within South Beach has the largest concentration of Deco architecture in the world (in 1979, much of South Beach was listed in the National Register of Historic Places). The district is roughly bounded by the Atlantic Ocean on the east, Alton Road on the west, 6th Street to the south, and Dade Boulevard (along the Collins Canal) to the north. Most of the finest examples of the whimsical Art Deco style are concentrated along three parallel streets—Ocean Drive, Collins Avenue, and Washington Avenue—from about 6th to 23rd streets.

Art Deco got its name in 1925 at an exposition in Paris at which it set a stylistic tone, with buildings based on early neoclassical styles but with exotic motifs taken from ancient Greece, Rome, and Egypt, often in the form of geometric patterns, and stylized floral patterns. Very vertical windows are also a hallmark of the style. In Miami, Art Deco is marked by the pastel-hued buildings that line South Beach and Miami Beach. But it's a lot more than just color. If you look carefully, you will see the intricacies and impressive craftsmanship that went into each building in Miami back in the 1920s, '30s, '40s, and today, thanks to intensive restoration.

Classic Art Deco architecture is on display at the Carlyle on Collins Avenue.

art deco **WALKING TOURS**

The **Miami Design Preservation League** offers several tours of Miami Beach's historic architecture, all of which leave from the Art Deco Welcome Center at 1001 Ocean Dr., in Miami Beach. These include guided tours conducted by local historians and architects, which offer an in-depth look at the structures and their history. The 90-minute Official Art Deco walking tour (offered daily at 10:30am) takes you through the district, pointing out the differences between Mediterranean Revival and Art Deco for $35 for adults, $30 for seniors 65 and over, veterans, and students. As well, the League has created a **self-guided audio tour** (available in the Apple app store and Google Play store) which turns the streets into a virtual outdoor museum, taking you through Miami Beach's Art Deco district at your own leisure, with tours in several languages for just $25 for adults, $15 for seniors 65 and over, veterans, and students. For more information on tours or reservations, call ✆ **305/672-2014** or log on to mdpl.org.

After years of neglect and calls for the wholesale demolition of its buildings, South Beach got a new lease on life in 1979. Under the leadership of Barbara Baer Capitman, a dedicated crusader for the Art Deco zone, and the Miami Design Preservation League, founded by Baer Capitman and five friends, an area made up of an estimated 800 buildings was granted a listing on the National Register of Historic Places. Designers then began highlighting long-lost architectural details with soft sherbet shades of peach, periwinkle, turquoise, and purple. Developers soon moved in, and the full-scale refurbishment of the area's hotels was underway.

Not everyone was pleased, though. Former Miami Beach commissioner Abe Resnick said, "I love old buildings. But these Art Deco buildings are 40, 50 years old. They aren't historic. They aren't special. We shouldn't be forced to keep them." But Miami Beach kept those buildings, and Resnick lost his seat on the commission.

Today hundreds of establishments—hotels, restaurants, and nightclubs—have renovated these older, historic buildings, bringing them new life.

If you're touring this unique neighborhood on your own, start at the **Art Deco Welcome Center,** 1001 Ocean Dr. (mdpl.org; ✆ **305/531-3484;** daily 9am–5pm), which is run by the Miami Design Preservation League. The only beachside building across from the Clevelander Hotel and bar, the center gives away lots of informational material, including maps and pamphlets, and runs guided tours around the neighborhood (see above). Art Deco books (like *The Art Deco Guide,* an informative compendium of all the buildings here), T-shirts, postcards, and other paraphernalia are for sale.

Take a stroll along **Ocean Drive** for the best view of sidewalk cafes, bars, colorful hotels, gigantic cocktails in fishbowls, and even more colorful people. Another great place for a walk is **Lincoln Road,** which is lined with boutiques, large chain stores, cafes, and stores. The **Community Church,** at the corner of Lincoln Road and Drexel Avenue, was the neighborhood's first church and is one of its oldest surviving buildings, dating from 1921. Do not miss **Espanola Way,** a pedestrian-only block between 14th and 15th streets built in the 1920s as an artists' colony modeled after those in France and Spain, and featuring more character than Lincoln Road, with an assortment of unique shops, restaurants, bars, and culturally colorful events (yoga in the morning, salsa dancing at night).

Miami didn't used to be known as a cultural mecca, but that has changed, thanks largely to the international attention brought to the scene by such esteemed fairs as Switzerland's Art Basel, which comes to Miami for a few days every December. The focal point of Art Basel is **Collins Park Cultural Center,** which comprises a trio of arts buildings on Collins Park and Park Avenue (off Collins Ave.), bounded by 21st to 23rd streets: the expanded art museum **The Bass** (see below), the Arquitectonica-designed home of the Miami City Ballet, and the **Miami Beach Regional Library,** an ultramodern building designed by architect Robert A. M. Stern. Collins Park is also now the site of large sculpture installations and cultural activities planned jointly by the organizations that share the space.

Near to the Collins Park neighborhood is the **Miami Beach Botanical Garden,** 2000 Convention Center Dr. (mbgarden.org); ⓒ **305/673-7256**). Because so many people are focused on the beach itself, it remains a secret garden. The lush, tropical 4½-acre garden is a fabulous natural retreat from the hustle and bustle of the silicone-enhanced city. Open Tuesday through Sunday from 9am to 5pm; admission is free.

South Pointe Park, 1 Washington Ave. (ⓒ **305/673-7730**), is another strollable area, featuring 18 waterfront acres of green space, walkways, a playground, and an observation deck. From the **Smith and Wollensky** steakhouse's outdoor patio, you can watch cruise ships depart.

The Bass Museum of Art ★★★

The Bass is Miami Beach's contemporary art crown jewel. World-renowned Japanese architect Arata Isozaki teamed with designers Jonathan Caplan and Mani Colaku to zhuzh up the place in 2017 and what resulted is a magnificent Art Deco–inspired facility, surrounded by a lush public park and outdoor sculptures, with a sun-drenched indoor courtyard, a museum cafe, unique gift shop, and a center for education. The constantly rotating exhibitions feature contemporary works by the likes of Hernan Bas, Tracey Moffatt, Carola Bravo, and Nam June Paik, as well as works from the museum's contemporary art permanent collection which includes other major names. *Tip:* On the third Thursday of every month from 6 to 9pm and on the last Sunday of every month, admission is free and special events take place.

2121 Park Ave. (1 block west of the beach in the heart of Collins Park). thebass.org. ⓒ **305/673-7530.** Admission $15 adults, $8 students and seniors, free for children 6 and under. Wed–Sun noon–6pm. Third Thurs of every month noon–9pm. Closed Mon–Tues.

Holocaust Memorial ★★★

This heart-wrenching memorial is hard to miss and would be a shame to

Holocaust Memorial.

Part of the displays at the Jewish Museum of Florida: *Tefillin* (also called phylacteries), small black leather boxes containing scrolls of parchment.

overlook. The powerful centerpiece, Kenneth Treister's *A Sculpture of Love and Anguish,* depicts victims of the concentration camps crawling up a giant yearning hand stretching up to the sky, marked with an Auschwitz number tattoo. Along the reflecting pool is the story of the Holocaust, told in cut marble slabs. Inside the center of the memorial is a tableau that is one of the most solemn and moving tributes I've seen to the millions of Jews who lost their lives to the Nazis. You can walk through an open hallway lined with photographs and the names of camps and their victims. From the street, you'll see the outstretched arm, but do stop and tour the sculpture at ground level.

1933 Meridien Ave. (at Dade Blvd.). holocaustmemorialmiamibeach.org. **305/538-1663.** Free admission. Daily 10am–10pm.

Jewish Museum of Florida ★★★
Why is this one of South Beach's most relevant museums? Many people don't realize that the world-celebrated Deco District was built back in the 1920s and '30s essentially as a Jewish ghetto. Developers in what were then more desirable Miami neighborhoods refused to sell to the sons and daughters of Abraham (illustrated here by a sign quoting a charming local hospitality industry boasting, "Always a View, Never a Jew"). However, this pair of buildings, including a 1929 former synagogue, doesn't dwell on the negative but focuses more on the myriad, sometimes surprising, ways Jews have made their mark not just in Miami but throughout Florida all the way back to the

conversos (Jews masquerading as Christians) thought to have arrived with Ponce de León. Groundbreakers also include mobster Meyer Lansky, whose name is on a stained-glass window on the right-hand side of the main exhibition hall, and the first Jewish Miss America, Bess Myerson, who donated photos and memorabilia. This exhibit of 250 years of Jewish history in Florida, supported by video, artifacts and more, is likely to be an eye-opener. The museum also delves into the Jewish roots of Latin America.

301 Washington Ave., South Beach. jmof.fiu.edu. © **305/672-5044.** Admission $12 adults, $10 seniors and students. Wed–Sun 10am–4pm. Closed Mon, Tues, and Jewish holidays.

Jungle Island ★★   Not exactly an island and not quite a jungle, Jungle Island is an excellent diversion for the kids and for animal lovers. The 19-acre park doubles as a protected bird sanctuary, and features an Everglades exhibit, trails, a playground, shows, a two-toed sloth, and aviaries. Watch your head because flying above are hundreds of parrots, macaws, peacocks, cockatoos, and flamingos. The most popular attractions here are the animal encounters, which cost extra but allow you to get up close and personal with lemurs, sloths, bunnies, wallabies, and giant tortoises. Another extra on top of regular admission is **Treetop Trekking,** an aerial adventure park for those who like to zip, climb, and swing above and through the trees. *Note:* The former South Miami site of (Parrot) Jungle Island is now known as **Pinecrest Gardens,** 11000 Red Rd. (© **305/669-6942**), which features a petting zoo, a mini water park, lake, natural hammocks, and banyan caves.

A flock of flamingos at Jungle Island.

Open daily from 9am to 5pm; admission is $5, $3 for seniors 65 and up, and free for children under age 2.

1111 Parrot Jungle Trail, Watson Island (on the north side of MacArthur Causeway/I-395). jungleisland.com. ✆ **305/400-7000.** Admission $19.95 adults, $16.95 children 3–10. Parking $15/vehicle. Daily 9:30am–5pm. From I-95, take I-395 E. (MacArthur Causeway); turn right on Parrot Jungle Trail, which is the first exit after the bridge. Follow the road around and under the causeway to the parking garage on the left side.

Miami Children's Museum ★★

Kids really take to practically every corner of this multimedia, fairly high-tech, 56,500-square-foot facility, starting with the pretend professions areas where they can try out jobs in a construction zone or learn about what it's like to be a veterinarian. There's also a re-creation of a Carnival cruise ship and a multi-sensory room for children with autism and other disabilities. Perhaps the coolest thing of all is the Music Makers Studio, in which aspiring rock stars can lay down a few tracks and play instruments. The Children's Museum is located on the MacArthur Causeway, across from Jungle Island (see above). Along with 17 galleries, it has an educational gift shop, a 200-seat auditorium, a Subway restaurant, and an outdoor, interactive play area.

980 MacArthur Causeway, Miami. miamichildrensmuseum.org. ✆ **305/373-5437.** Admission $24 adults and children 13 months and over, $16 Florida residents. Daily 10am–6pm.

Wilzig Erotic Art Museum ★★

Opened in 2005 by then-70-year-old grandmother, the late Naomi Wilzig, this wacky, 12,000-square-foot, X-rated museum features Wilzig's collection of more than 4,000 pieces of erotic art, including Kama Sutra temple carvings from India, peekaboo Victorian figurines that flash their booties, the notorious white phallus sculpture from the film *A Clockwork Orange,* and occasional comic relief (Mickey Mouse, is that you?). You'll spot names such as Picasso, Gauguin, Dali, and Miro, along with special exhibitions. This is a great place to spend an hour on a rainy day, but more than anything, the stuff is more amusing than racy.

1205 Washington Ave., South Beach. weammuseum.com. ✆ **305/532-9336.** Admission $25 adults. Children 17 and under not admitted. Mon–Thurs 11am–6pm; Fri–Sun 11am–11pm.

The Wolfsonian ★★★

Mitchell Wolfson, Jr., heir to a family fortune built on movie theaters, was known as an eccentric, but we'd call him a pack rat. A premier collector of propaganda and advertising art, Wolfson was spending so much money storing his booty that he decided to buy the warehouse that was housing it. It ultimately held more than 70,000 of his items, from controversial Nazi propaganda to King Farouk of Egypt's match collection. Thrown into the eclectic mix are also zany works from great modernists such as Charles Eames and Marcel Duchamp. It all adds up to a thought-provoking reflection of history, society, politics, and socio-economic issues. So yes, those 1926 stained-glass panels, for example, are luminous and lovely, but they also reflect themes and allegories relating to Ireland's independence. Wolfson then gave this incredibly diverse collection to Florida International University. The former 1927 storage facility has been transformed into a museum that is the envy of curators around the world, featuring over 200,000 objects today. The museum is unquestionably fascinating and hosts lectures and rather swinging events surrounding exhibits. The museum's design store and coffee shop is a funky spot serving drinks and nibbles, whose focal point is a large library shelving system from 1915. The design represents the first modular book-stacking system ever created. Leave it to the Wolfsonian to make the store a piece of art!

1001 Washington Ave. wolfsonian.org. © **305/531-1001.** Admission $12 adults; $8 seniors, students with ID, and children 6–12; free Fri 6–9pm. Wed–Sun 10am–6pm; Fri 10am–9pm.

NORTH MIAMI

The **Oleta River State Park,** 3400 NE 163rd St., North Miami (floridastateparks.org/oletariver; © **800/326-3521;** open 9am to 1 hr. before sunset Mon–Fri, 8am to 1 hr. before sunset Sat–Sun), consists of 993 acres—the largest urban park in the state—on Biscayne Bay. The beauty of the Oleta River, combined with the fact that you're essentially in the middle of a city, makes this park especially worth visiting. With miles of bicycle and canoe trails; a sandy swimming beach; a kayak, canoe, paddleboard, and mountain bike rental shop; an eatery and shaded picnic pavilions; and a fishing pier, Oleta River State Recreation Area allows for an outstanding outdoor recreational experience. Admission for pedestrians and cyclists is $2 per person. By car: Driver plus car costs $4; driver plus one to seven passengers and car costs $6. *Lodging tip:* There are 14 rustic cabins on the premises that sleep four people. The cost is $55 per night, and guests are required to bring their own linens. Bathrooms and showers are outside, as is a fire circle with a grill for cooking.

To get here, take I-95 to exit 17 (S.R. 826 E.) and go all the way east until just before the causeway. The park entrance is on your right. Driving time from downtown Miami is about a half-hour.

Ancient Spanish Monastery.

Ancient Spanish Monastery ★★

Most of the "historic" buildings throughout Greater Miami are "neo" this and ersatz that, but this gorgeous cloister is the real deal: a Cistercian monastery built in Segovia, Spain, in the 12th century, then dismantled and brought to the United States in 1925 by none other than Citizen Kane newspaper tycoon William Randolph Hearst. It's a beautiful place to wander. *Warning:* This isn't merely a tourist attraction, but also home to an Episcopal church, St. Bernard de Clairvaux. It's super-popular for weddings, photo shoots, and other special occasions, and thus is closed to the public as often as it is open, so check the website before heading over. Tours are often offered from 10am to 4:30pm.

16711 W. Dixie Hwy. (btw. NW 167th and NW 170th sts.). SpanishMonastery.com. Admission $10. Wed–Thurs 10:00am–4:00pm; Fri–Sat 10am–2:00pm; Sun 2:00–5:00pm.

Museum of Contemporary Art (MOCA) ★★ Founded in 1996, MOCA is quite small for a major museum—some 12,000 square feet—but it does boast a well-curated collection of today's art scene, even if you'd need to be a real maven to recognize most of the names, besides maybe Keith Haring, Purvis Young, George Segal, and Edward Ruscha. It's one of the few U.S. contemporary art museums that collects, as opposed to mostly hosting rotating shows, and it also is home to the Jazz at MOCA series of evening performances by leading musicians.

770 NE 125th St. (btw. NE 7th and 8th aves.). mocanomi.org. ✆ **305/893-6211.** Admission $10 adults, $5 seniors and students with ID, free for children 12 and under. Wed noon–7pm; Thurs–Sun 10am–5pm. Closed Tues.

KEY BISCAYNE

Named after the late champion of the Everglades, the **Marjory Stoneman Douglas Biscayne Nature Center,** 6767 Crandon Blvd. (biscaynenaturecenter.org; ✆ **305/361-6767;** daily 9am–4pm), offers hands-on marine exploration through its excellent **Seagrass Adventure** program (see below). Those on their own find this a top area for hikes through maritime forests, bike trips, and beach walks. Admission is free. To get there, take I-95 to the Rickenbacker Causeway exit (no. 1) and take the causeway all the way until it becomes Crandon Boulevard. The center is on the Atlantic Ocean side of the street about 25 minutes from downtown Miami.

At **Bill Baggs Cape Florida State Park** ★, 1200 Crandon Blvd. (floridastateparks.org; ✆ **786/582-2673;** daily 8am–sunset), at the southern tip of Key Biscayne about 20 minutes from downtown Miami, you can explore some of the most secluded beaches in Miami. In fact, Bill Baggs has been consistently rated as one of the top 10 beaches in the U.S. for its 1¼ miles of wide, sandy beaches and

A wraparound balcony at the top of Cape Florida Lighthouse gives visitors awe-inspiring 360-degree views.

its serene atmosphere. Admission is $8 per car with up to eight people (or $4 for a car with only one person; $2 to enter by foot or bicycle). The oldest lighthouse in South Florida (1825) is also here. It was damaged during the Second Seminole War (1836) and again in 1861 during the Civil War, but restored to working lighthouse condition in 1978 by the U.S. Coast Guard. As we went to press the lighthouse was closed for renovations (check online before going over to see if tours have resumed). A rental shack here leases bikes, and it's a great place to picnic, or eat at one of the two on-site restaurants. Just be careful that the raccoons don't get your lunch—the furry black-eyed beasts are everywhere. Take I-95 to the Rickenbacker Causeway and take that all the way to the end.

Seagrass Adventure ★★   Naturalists from the Marjory Stoneman Douglas Biscayne Nature Center (see above) introduce kids and adults to an amazing variety of creatures during these tours. Most live in the sea grass beds of the Bear Cut Nature Preserve near Crandon Beach on Key Biscayne. To see them, visitors wade in the water and catch an assortment of sea life in nets provided by the guides. At the end of the program, participants gather on the beach while the guide explains what everyone has just caught, passing the creatures around in miniature viewing tanks. *Important:* They don't take reservations on the web, so you'll need to call to reserve a tour.

Marjory Stoneman Douglas Biscayne Nature Center, 6767 Crandon Blvd., Key Biscayne. biscaynenaturecenter.org. © **305/361-6767.** Free admission to the center, $15/person tours. Daily 9am–4pm.

DOWNTOWN

Frost Science Museum ★★★   Part of the massive complex at Museum Park, this tri-level natural light and solar-powered homage to science and tech is a place to marvel at many things, including the human body and mind, flight, and the frontiers of innovation and technology. Its cone-shaped, three-level **aquarium** takes you through South Florida's various, vibrant ecosystems, featuring a colorful collection of coral reefs, fish, devil rays, and hammerhead sharks. The best views of all come from a 31-foot oculus lens that forms the bottom of the aquarium from which you can view the same sharks you saw at eye level swimming overhead. A cutting-edge, 250-seat **planetarium** offers other-worldly views of space, a coral reef, or a DNA strand. The **Power of Science** exhibit takes you on a trippy journey through the leading frontiers of scientific exploration, where bacteria transform Martian rock into 3D-printed homes and innovative marine infrastructure encourages coral regeneration. The **Feathers to the Stars** exhibit covers the story of flight, from dinosaurs to spacecraft, and the **meLab** features all sorts of fun, interactive games and hands-on exhibits, and even an AI mirror to help understand the marvels of being human. The **Food@Science** cafe has outdoor seating and a variety of snacks. *Warning:* Because this is an uber-popular attraction, pricing here is much like, well, Uber, and there are surges based on dates, times, and season.

1101 Biscayne Blvd. frostscience.org. © **305/434-9600.** Base admission $29.95 adults; $24.95 children 4–11; free for children 3 and under. Peak pricing $37.95 adults; $26.95 children 4–11.

The meLab at the Frost Science Center takes an interactive look at how the human brain and body interact.

HistoryMiami Museum ★★ This small Smithsonian-affiliate gives the lowdown on the Magic City, with an impressive collection of over 30,000 artifacts covering everything from Miami's prehistoric history to 20th-century Afro-Cuban art. The permanent exhibition, *Tropical Dreams: A People's History of South Florida*, presents 10,000 years of South Florida history. The museum is also known for its events and tours conducted by local historians like Miami's lauded Dr. Paul George. Try to take one of his free walking tours of Miami—his knowledge is encyclopedia-caliber.

101 W. Flagler St., downtown Miami. historymiami.org. ✆ **305/375-1625.** Admission $15 adults, $10 seniors, $8 children 6–12. Wed–Sat 10am–5pm; Sun noon–5pm. Closed Mon–Tues.

Museum of Sex Miami ★★ Miami's newest homage to the three-letter-word that gets everyone's attention, this 32,000-square-foot museum opened near the Rubell Museum in January 2024 with the first U.S. solo museum exhibition by pioneering Japanese artist, Hajime Sorayama, and a retrospective look at the design and marketing of sexual health products from the 1920s to today. As this is the city's second museum with a sexy theme, the difference between this and the World Erotic Art Museum is shock value—this one is a more erudite take on sex as opposed to the latter's homage to sex toys and tchotchkes. Visitors will also experience an enhanced edition of the museum's blockbuster installation: Super Funland: Journey into the Erotic Carnival. There are three exhibition galleries, a retail shop, and cocktail bar.

2200 NW 24th St., Miami. museumofsex.com. ✆ **786/206-9210.** Admission $25 adults. Children 17 and under not admitted. Mon–Thurs 11am–6pm; Fri–Sun 11am–11pm.

Pérez Art Museum Miami ★★★   Located in downtown Miami's sprawling Museum Park, a $200-plus-million project on an underused 29-acre property on the bay in downtown Miami, this extraordinary museum was designed by Pritzker Prize–winning architects Herzog & de Meuron. It features a heady collection of artists such as Louise Nevelson, Wifredo Lam, Marcel Duchamp, and Roy Lichtenstein, as well as exhibitions like that of Chinese dissident artist Ai Weiwei, Canadian installation artist Geoffrey Farmer, and more. Also very cool is their collection of self-taught artists including Leroy Almon, known for wood carvings and paintings depicting the African diaspora. This being Miami, there's a particular emphasis on Latin America and the Caribbean. There's also a nice restaurant called **Verde**, and a browse-able shop. On the second Saturday of every month, admission is free and there are art classes, live music, and more.

1103 Biscayne Blvd. (at NW 11th St.). PAMM.org. **305/375-3000.** Admission $18 adults; $14 seniors 62 and over, youth 7–18, and students with ID; free for children 6 and under. Mon 11am–6pm; Thurs 11am–9pm; Fri–Sun 11am–6pm. Closed Tues–Wed.

MIDTOWN MIAMI

Bay of Pigs Brigade 2506 Museum ★   Although it's in a temporary location in a strip mall, this tiny Little Havana museum packs a historical wallop, thanks to its knowledgeable staff, many of whom are veterans of the historic 1961 event. The museum displays a cool collection of artifacts related to the invasion, including the Brigade 2506 flag held up by President John F. Kennedy during a 1962 speech at the since-destroyed Orange Bowl. A 30-minute tour of the space includes videos, lectures, and interesting conversations with the staff. A permanent location is underway at the site of the actual Brigade 2506 HQ at 1821 SW 9th St. Check the website before heading over, in case they've moved there.

1338 SW 8th St. bayofpigsbrigade2506.com. **305/649-4719.** Free admission. Mon–Thurs 10am–4pm; Fri–Sat 10am–2pm.

Rubell Museum ★★★   This exciting collection, owned by one of the modern art world's biggest collector families (that happens to include the late Steve

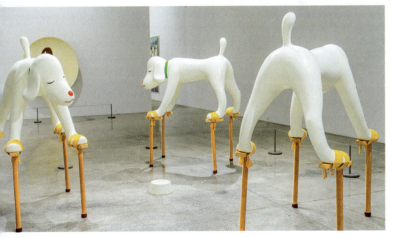

An installation by Japanese artist Akashi Murakami at the Rubell Museum.

Rubell of Studio 54 fame), is housed in a former industrial complex of six interconnected buildings in a sketchy area northwest of downtown Miami. It's a priceless assemblage of more than 1,000 works of contemporary art by the likes of Keith Haring, Damien Hirst, Richard Prince, Julian Schnabel, Jean-Michel Basquiat, Paul McCarthy, Charles Ray, and Cindy Sherman. But *be forewarned:* Some of the art is extremely graphic and may be off-putting. An artist-in-residence program features a diverse mix of emerging contemporary artists. The museum features 36 galleries, a flexible performance space, an extensive research library, a bookstore, and an indoor-outdoor restaurant that opens onto a courtyard garden filled with plants native to South Florida.

1100 NW 23rd St., Miami. https://rubellmusem.org/miami. ✆ **305/573-6090.** Admission $15 adults, $12 seniors, $10 students with ID and kids 7–18. Sun, Wed, Thurs 11:30am–5:30pm; Fri–Sat 11:30am–7:30pm.

CORAL GABLES

South Beach's Art Deco District is but one of many colorful neighborhoods that can boast dazzling architecture. The rediscovery of the entire Biscayne Corridor (from downtown to about 80th St. and Biscayne Blvd.) has given light to a host of ancillary neighborhoods on either side, which are filled with Mediterranean-style homes and Frank Lloyd Wright gems. Coral Gables is home to many large and beautiful homes, mansions, and churches that reflect architecture from the 1920s, 1930s, and 1940s. Some of the homes, or portions of their structures, have been created from coral rock and shells. The Biltmore Hotel is also filled with history; see p. 76.

Coral Gables Museum ★ Since its founding in the 1920s by developer George Merrick, Coral Gables has become one of Florida's most beautiful, historic, cultural, and well-heeled cities—yet it wasn't until a bit over a decade ago that local leaders finally created a city museum. The result occupies 24,000 square feet in downtown's original fire and police HQ, a creamy coral-stone Mediterranean-Revival affair adorned with carved heads of long-ago firemen. At the core of the nine light, airy galleries lies the story of how the Gables was carved out of orange groves and wilderness, including plenty of period documents, artifacts, and fascinating photos and artwork. Beyond that, rotating exhibitions cover architecture, Latin American art, and sustainable development.

285 Aragon Ave. coralgablesmuseum.org. ✆ **305/603-8067.** Admission $12 adults, $8 students and seniors, $5 children 7–12. Tues–Fri 11am–5pm; Sat 10am–6pm; Sun 11am–5pm. Closed Mon.

Fairchild Tropical Garden ★★★ A veritable rainforest of both rare and exotic plants, this is the largest tropical garden in the continental United States. It spreads around an 83-acre property with 2.1 miles of walking pavement, 11 lakes, 7 pools, and countless meadows. Palmettos, vine pergola, palm glades, and other unique species create a scenic, lush environment. The 2-acre **Richard H. Simons Rainforest** will save you a trip to the Amazon. More than 100 species of birds have been spotted at the garden (ask for a list at the front gate), and it is home to a variety of animals. For fans of butterflies, the **Wings of the Tropics** exhibit features hundreds of them of over 40 different species. The best way to get an overview is the 30-minute narrated tram tour (tours leave on the hour 10am–3pm Mon–Fri, 10am–4pm Sat–Sun). There is also a museum, a cafe, a picnic area, and

The serene Fairchild Tropical Garden feels worlds away from the hustle and bustle of Miami.

a gift shop. Fairchild often hosts major art exhibits by the likes of Dale Chihuly and Roy Lichtenstein. Expect to spend a minimum of 2 hours.

10901 Old Cutler Rd. fairchildgarden.org. ✆ **305/667-1651.** Admission $24.95 adults, $17.95 seniors, $11.95 kids 6–17, free for those 5 and under. Daily 10am–5pm. Take I-95 south to U.S. 1, turn left onto Le Jeune Rd., and follow it straight to the traffic circle; from there, take Old Cutler Rd. 2 miles to the park.

Lowe Art Museum ★★ Located on the University of Miami campus, Miami's oldest art museum has a dazzling collection of 19,500 works representing five millennia of human creativity on every inhabited continent. That includes the art of ancient Americas, the Mediterranean, Africa, and Asia, American paintings, Latin American art, Navajo and Pueblo Indian textiles, and Renaissance and baroque art. In the permanent collection are a who's who of art history, both classic and recent: El Greco, Monet, Gainsborough, Goya, Liechtenstein, and Stella. Traveling exhibits, such as the pop art of John Miller, Southern Photography from the Do Good Fund, and Susan Grant Lewin and the Art Jewelry World, also stop here.

University of Miami, 1301 Stanford Dr. (at Ponce de León Blvd.), Coral Gables. lowe.miami.edu. ✆ **305/284-3603.** Free Admission, but reserve tickets online well in advance. Wed–Sat 10am–4pm.

Venetian Pool ★★★ Miami's most beautiful and unusual swimming pool, dating from 1924, is hidden behind pastel stucco walls and is honored with a listing in the National Register of Historic Places. Underground artesian wells feed the free-form lagoon, which is shaded by three-story Spanish porticos and has both fountains and waterfalls. During summer, the pool's 820,000 gallons of water are drained and refilled nightly, thanks to an underground aquifer, ensuring a cool, *clean* swim. Visitors are free to swim and sunbathe here, just as Esther Williams and Johnny Weissmuller did decades ago. The pool is closed during fall and winter, reopening in the spring.

2701 DeSoto Blvd. (at Toledo St.). coralgables.com/attractions/venetian-pool. **305/460-5356.** Admission $21 for those 13 and older, $16 for children 3–12. Children must be at least 3 (parents must provide proof of child's age with birth certificate) or 38 in. tall to enter. Tues–Sat 11am–5:30pm; Sat–Sun 10am–4:30pm. Closed Mon.

COCONUT GROVE

Barnacle State Historic Site ★★
The former home of naval architect and early settler Ralph Middleton Munroe is now a museum in the heart of Coconut Grove. It's the oldest house in Miami and it rests on its original foundation, which sits on 5 acres of natural hardwood forest and landscaped lawns. The house's quiet surroundings, wide porches, and period furnishings illustrate how Miami's first snowbird lived in the days before condo-mania. Enthusiastic and knowledgeable state park employees provide a wealth of historical information to those interested in quiet, low-tech attractions such as this one. On Mondays and Wednesdays from 6:30 to 7:45pm, they have sunset yoga by the sea.

3485 Main Hwy. (1 block south of Commodore Plaza). FloridaStateParks.org. **305/442-6866.** Admission $2. Tours $3 adults, $1 children 6–12. Fri–Wed 9am–5pm. Tours Sat–Wed at 10 and 11:30am, and 1 and 2:30pm. From downtown Miami, take U.S. 1 south to 27th Ave., turn left, and continue to S. Bayshore Dr.; then turn right, follow to the intersection of Main Hwy., and turn left.

Vizcaya Museum and Gardens ★★★
Sometimes referred to as the "Hearst Castle of the East," this magnificent villa is more Gatsby-esque than anything else you'll find in Miami. It was built in 1916 as a winter retreat for James Deering, cofounder and former vice president of International Harvester. The industrialist was fascinated by 16th-century art and architecture, and his ornate mansion, which took 1,000 artisans 5 years to build, became a celebration of that period. If you love antiques, this place is a dream come true, packed with European relics and works of art from the 16th to the 19th

One of the many fine artworks at Vizcaya Museum and Gardens.

centuries. Most of the original furnishings, including dishes and paintings, are still intact. You will see very early versions of a telephone switchboard, central vacuum-cleaning system, elevators, and fire sprinklers. A free guided tour of the 34 furnished rooms on the first floor takes about 45 minutes. The second floor, which consists mostly of bedrooms, is open to tour on your own. The spectacularly opulent villa wraps itself around a central courtyard. Outside, lush formal gardens, accented with statuary, balustrades, and decorative urns, front an enormous swath of Biscayne Bay. Definitely take the tour of the rooms, but immediately thereafter, you will want to wander and get lost in the resplendent gardens.

3251 S. Miami Ave. (just south of Rickenbacker Causeway), north Coconut Grove. vizcaya.org. ⓒ **305/250-9133.** Admission $25 adults, $10 children 6–12, free for children 5 and under. Holiday prices are higher. Wed–Mon 9:30am–4:30pm. Gardens daily 9:30am–5:30pm.

WYNWOOD

Superblue Miami ★★ A worthy nearby add-on to the Wynwood Walls experience, Superblue was described by the *New York Times* as a "blue-chip contestant in the rapidly growing field of immersive art." If you've experienced the mirrored infinity rooms of Yayoi Kusama, or the wrapped structures and islands of Christo, you know the drill: art that you enter into, that you can (often) touch, and that uses high technology to create dazzling new ecosystems. Though the exhibits

The curators at Wynwood Walls transformed a former warehouse district into a street art mecca.

are supposed to change regularly at Superblue, some have proved so popular they've hung around since the 2021 opening, and hopefully will still be there when you visit. These include the "Massless Clouds Between Sculpture and Light" room in which visitors interact with mystical, high-tech soap bubbles; and a dazzling light installation from James Turrell.

1101 NW 23rd St. superblue.com/miami. *786/697-3405*. Admission $39 adults, $14 children. Mon–Thurs 11am–7pm; Fri–Sat 10am–8pm; Sun 10am–7pm.

Wynwood Walls ★★★ Wynwood Walls, Miami's world-renowned street art museum, showcases cutting-edge works from leading fine artists, graffiti writers, and muralists from 21 countries. Wandering around this technicolor maze of masterpieces by the likes of Kenny Scharf, Krink, Kobra, Mantra, Mojo, and Momo, is like being Alice in a graffiti wonderland. The Walls encompass 35 murals, two street-art galleries, and lots of cool retail shops and a restaurant. Plan on spending at least an hour here, more if you plan to take a lot of selfies as this is one of Miami's most in-demand spots for pix. For those who want to know more about what you're looking at, they offer excellent, in-depth tours.

266 NW 26th St. thewynwoodwalls.com. No phone. Admission $12 adults, $10 seniors 65 and up, $5 students with ID, free for children 12 and under. Sun–Thurs 11am–7pm; Fri–Sat 11am–8pm.

SOUTH MIAMI-DADE COUNTY

Monkey Jungle ★ Not everyone's a fan of this place. It's smelly, the monkeys are often sleeping or in heat, and it's really far from the city, even farther than the zoo. But if primates are your thing and you'd rather pass on the zoo, it could well be a good option. You'll see rare Brazilian golden lion tamarins and Asian macaques. There are no cages to restrain the antics of the monkeys as they swing, chatter, and play. Screened-in trails wind through acres of "jungle," and daily shows feature the talents of the park's most progressive pupils. People who come here aren't monkeying around—many of the park's frequent visitors are scientists and anthropologists. In fact, an interesting archaeological exhibition excavated from a Monkey Jungle sinkhole displays 10,000-year-old artifacts, including human teeth and animal bones. If you can stand the humidity, the smell, and the bugs (flies, mosquitoes, and so on), expect to spend about 2 hours here. For those REALLY into the primates, there's an interactive guided tour that brings you into Jane Goodall–caliber contact with monkeys. Your $150 ticket gets you a show, an after-show, and the photo ops: You get to feed monkeys, feed rhino iguana and tortoise, and then go exploring in the Amazon rain forest where the squirrel and capuchin monkeys live. Best of all, when feeding the monkeys, they jump on your head, sit on your shoulders, and do whatever it takes to get that food from you. If that's too much moneying (not a spelling error) around, the regular ticket should do.

14805 SW 216th St., South Miami. monkeyjungle.com. *305/235-1611*. Admission $20 adults, $10 children 3–9. Daily 9:30am–5pm (tickets sold until 3pm). Take U.S. 1 south to SW 216th St., or from Florida Tpk., take exit 11 and follow the signs.

Patricia and Phillip Frost Art Museum ★★ This is the only art museum in Florida to attempt to exhibit paintings in natural light. Housed in a $16-million building designed by architect Yann Weymouth, the museum's permanent collection includes a strong representation of American printmaking from the 1960s and '70s, notable photography, pre-Columbian objects dating from A.D. 200 to 500, and a growing number of works by contemporary Caribbean and Latin American artists. (The museum has recently begun presenting exhibitions in Latin America and is working on future collaborations with leading art institutions in that region.)

Florida International University, 10975 SW 17th St. thefrost.fiu.edu. © **305/348-2890.** Free admission. Tues–Sat 10am–5pm; Sun noon–5pm.

Zoo Miami ★★ This 750-acre complex is quite a distance from Miami proper and the beaches—about 45 minutes—but worth the trip. Isolated and never really crowded, it's also completely cageless: The over 2,500 animals are kept at bay by cleverly designed moats. This is a fantastic spot to take younger kids; there are wonderful play areas, and safari cycles for rent, and the zoo offers several daily programs designed to educate and entertain. Mufasa and Simba of Disney fame were modeled on a couple of Zoo Miami's lions. Other residents include blue poison dart frogs, a bald eagle, a sloth bear, an Orinoco crocodile, chimpanzees, Komodo dragons, koalas, kangaroos, and meerkats. **Amazon & Beyond** features jaguars, anacondas, giant river otters, harpy eagles, a stingray touch tank, an interactive water-play area, the Flooded Forest building with a unique display of a forest before and during flood times, and an indoor Cloud Forest that houses reptiles. At 27 acres and a cost of $50 million, this exhibit is massive and made Zoo Miami the third zoo in the country to have giant river otters when it opened.

Cool activities include the **Samburu Giraffe Feeding Station,** where, for $5, you get to feed the giraffes veggies; the **Rhino Encounter,** where you can touch, brush, and feed a rhino for $35; and a **black bear encounter** for $25 per person. *Note:* The distance between animal habitats can be great, so you'll do *a lot* of walking here. A $99.95 per person VIP tour includes a 2-hour golf cart tour of the zoo, which is actually worth the splurge because you get a private guide and food voucher. Also, because the zoo can be miserably hot during summer months, plan your visit in the early morning or late afternoon. Expect to spend all day here if you want to see it all.

A lemur at Zoo Miami.

12400 SW 152nd St., Miami. zoomiami.org. © **305/251-0400.** Admission $22.95 adults, $18.95 children 3–12. Daily 9:30am–5:30pm (ticket booth closes at 4pm). Free parking. From U.S. 1 south, turn right on SW 152nd St., and follow signs about 3 miles to the entrance. From FL Tpk. S., take exit 16 west to the entrance.

HOMESTEAD

A testament to Miami's unusual climate, the **Preston B. Bird and Mary Heinlein Fruit and Spice Park,** 24801 SW 187th Ave., Homestead (www.fruitandspicepark.org; © **305/247-5727;** $10 adults, $3 ages 6–11; daily 10am–5pm), harbors over 500 varieties of fruits, vegetables, nuts, spices, and herbs as well as rare fruit trees that cannot survive elsewhere in the country. If a volunteer is available, you'll learn some fascinating things about this 30-acre living plant museum, where the most exotic varieties of fruits and spices—ackee, mango, ugli fruit, carambola, and breadfruit—grow on strange-looking trees with unpronounceable names. There are also original coral rock buildings dating back to 1912. The Strawberry Folk Festival in February and an art festival here in January are among the park's most popular—and populated—events. The best part? You're free to take anything that has *naturally* fallen to the ground (no picking here). If the ground is bare, don't worry: You'll find samples of interesting fruits and jellies made from the park's bounty, as well as exotic ingredients and cookbooks, in the gift store.

Take U.S. 1 south, turn right on SW 248th Street, and go straight for 5 miles to SW 187th Avenue. The drive from Miami should take 45 minutes to an hour.

Coral Castle ★

There's plenty of competition, but Coral Castle is probably the strangest attraction in Florida. In 1923, the story goes, a 26-year-old crazed Latvian, suffering from the unrequited love of a 16-year-old who left him at the altar, immigrated to South Miami and spent the next 25 years of his life carving huge boulders into a prehistoric-looking roofless "castle." It seems impossible that one rather short man could have done all this, but there are scores of affidavits on display from neighbors who swear it happened. Apparently, experts have studied this phenomenon to help figure out how the great pyramids and Stonehenge were built. Rocker Billy Idol was said to have been inspired by this place to write his song "Sweet 16." An interesting 25-minute audio tour guides you through the spot, now on the National Register of Historic Places. Although Coral Castle is overpriced for its small size, it's wacky enough for a visit when you're in the area, which is about 37 miles from Miami.

28655 S. Dixie Hwy., Homestead. coralcastle.com. © **305/248-6345.** Admission $18 adults, $8 children 3–12. Sun–Mon and Thurs 9am–6pm; Fri–Sat 9am–7pm. Take 836 W (Dolphin Expwy.) toward Miami International Airport. Merge onto 826 S. (Palmetto Expwy.) and take it to the Florida Tpk. toward Homestead. Take the 288th St. exit (no. 5) and then take a right on S. Dixie Hwy., a left on SW 157th Ave., and then a sharp left back onto S. Dixie Hwy. Coral Castle is on the left side of the street.

Flamingo Time

Historic **Hialeah Park Casino,** 100 E. 32nd St. (hialeahparkcasino.com; © **305/885-8000**), and its lush 200 acres, was once known for horse racing, its 16th-century, French-Mediterranean landscaping, and its legendary flock of neon-pink flamingos, which still roam the property. After decades of decay, the park was spruced up for the most part, although experts say the restoration of the National Historic Landmark to its former glory will take years and hundreds of millions of dollars to complete. In the meantime, the historic structure has been turned into a casino. For now, go just for the flamingos—it *is* an Audubon Bird Sanctuary despite the slot machines.

"You Will Be Seeing An Unusual Accomplishment" a sign at Coral Castle reads. Yes, you will.

ORGANIZED TOURS
Specialized Tours

In addition to the tours listed below, **Miami Culinary Tours** is an excellent outfit. See our review on p. 93.

As well, **Dr. Paul George,** a historian and former Miami Dade College history professor, conducts a variety of tours throughout the city, all fascinating for history buffs. Tour focus is either on such neighborhoods as Little Havana, Brickell Avenue, or Key Biscayne, or on themes such as Miami cemeteries, the Miami River, and Stiltsville, the "neighborhood" of houses on stilts in the middle of Biscayne Bay. Most tours are through **HistoryMiami Museum** (historymiami.org/city-tours) for which Dr. George is resident historian.

Design District ★★   The **Design District** (miamidesigndistrict.com) conducts free walking tours exploring the art and architecture that characterize this neighborhood. Tours typically visit outdoor installations and murals including Buckminster Fuller Fly's Eye Dome, Criola's Interdimensional Portal, Virgil Abloh's Dollar a Gallon, Amani Lewis's Baltimore's Finest, and more.

Duck Tours South Beach ★   Hands down the corniest way to see Miami, these 90-minute tours take place on a "vesicle," and no, that's not a body part, but a hybrid name that means part vessel, part vehicle (technical name: Hydra Terra

Amphibious Vehicle). Each vesicle seats 49 guests, plus a captain and tour guide, and leaves from the corner of Lincoln Road and James Avenue on South Beach. After driving the streets in "The Duck," the vesicle transforms into a boat so that you can cruise Biscayne Bay. Embarrassing or downright hilarious, Duck Tours are definitely unique and if you want to take the cringe factor a step further, you can buy an actual duck whistle at the tour office for a buck.

1661 James Ave., South Beach. ducktours southbeach.com. ✆ **305/673-2217.** Tickets $45 adults, $39 seniors and military, $28 children 12 and under, $10 infants 3 and under.

Eco-Adventure Tours ★★★
The Miami-Dade Parks and Recreation Department offers guided nature, adventure, and historic tours involving biking, canoeing, snorkeling, hiking, and bird-watching all over the city.

miamiecoadventures.com. ✆ **305/365-3018.**

Little Havana Cultural Walking Tour ★★★

If it quacks like a Duck, you're probably on a tour!

A historian will guide you on this 2-hour tour of Little Havana, starting with a Cuban coffee, and even stopping to play dominoes with the locals. Tours include a visit to the Bay of Pigs Museum (p. 125), area social clubs, and a *botanica,* a shop that caters to followers of the Santeria or Voudon religions. *Tip:* While this walking tour is great and available daily, if you happen to be in town the third Friday of the month, you can take a *free* walking tour with HistoryMiami maven Dr. Paul George (see above). The free tour is part of the monthly **Viernes Culturales** arts and culture festival that starts at noon on Calle Ocho and continues into the night. The tour

---

Vintage Miami

Although it's hardly Napa Valley, Miami does have an actual winery: **Schnebly Redland's Winery,** 30205 SW 217th Ave., Homestead (schneblywinery.com; ✆ **305/242-1224**). Oenophiles can sample a number of vintages in its $1.5-million tasting room. We've tried some, and while they're too fruity for our taste, many will enjoy watching the press deck where fruit becomes juice and eventually wine. There are 30- to 45-minute tours for $16 per person and daily tastings for $25 per person. There are also Friday date nights with tastings and dinners under the stars. Open noon to 5pm Monday to Thursday, 11am to "close" Friday and Saturday, and 11am to 8pm Sunday.

leaves at 7pm from the historic **Tower Theater,** 1508 SW 8th St. Sign up at viernesculturales.org.

littlehavanawalkingtour.com. Tour $35.

Redland Tropical Trail Tours ★★★
Dade County agriculture is the focus here. A circuit of stops, tastings, and sightseeing will take you from gardens and jungles to an orchid farm, an actual working winery (see below), a fruit stand, and more, in the farming area called the Redlands (it's near Homestead). There's no cost to follow the trail with a map (available on the website) on a self-guided tour, but we think the guided tours are more enjoyable (and you don't run the risk of going to closed attractions).

redlandtrail.com. ℂ **305/245-9180.**

WATERSPORTS

BOATING Private rental outfits include **Boat Rental Miami,** 401 Biscayne Blvd., downtown Miami (boatrentalmiami.net; ℂ **786/295-2628**), where powerboats rent for some of the best prices in the city. Here, you can rent a 20-footer for 2 hours starting at $199. A captained boat starts at $299. They offer 2- and 4-hour rentals. Cruising is permitted only in and around Biscayne Bay (ocean access is prohibited), and renters must be 21 or older to rent a boat. The rental office is on Pier 5 right next to the arena. For longer, fancier, or specific rentals anywhere in Miami, **Boatsetter.com** and **GetMyBoat.com** are your best bets, virtual Vrbos of boat rentals, with ratings, instant bookings, and special deals.

Note: Visitors who do not already possess a valid boating education certificate must take an online test. See more on p. 29.

JET SKIS/WAVERUNNERS Bravery is a prerequisite for renting one of these bad boys, as Miami's waterways are full of speeding jet-skiers and boaters who think they're in the Indy 500. Many beachfront concessionaires rent a variety of these popular (and loud) water scooters. **MDQ Watersports,** at 5225 Collins Ave. (mdqwatersports.com; ℂ **305/301-8607**), is the area's most popular spot for jet-ski rental. Rates begin at $80/half-hour and $120/hour and include life jacket, gas, and instructor. Must be 14 to ride.

KAYAKING For kayaking and paddleboarding, **i paddle Miami,** 1275 NE 79th St. (ipaddlemiami.com; ℂ **305/472-3353**), offers rentals in Pelican Harbor on Biscayne Bay in North Bay Village (near Bal Harbour), and Chapman Bay Park in Coral Gables, as well as guided, 2½-hour tours. Rates start at $65 for 2 hours, $85 for 4 hours, and $70 for tours. The night tours are especially cool but start at a steep $185 per person.

SCUBA DIVING & SNORKELING In 1981, the U.S. government began a wide-scale project designed to increase the number of habitats available to marine organisms. One of the program's major accomplishments has been the creation of nearby artificial reefs, which have attracted all kinds of tropical plants, fish, and animals. In addition, Biscayne National Park (see the park's section in chapter 7, beginning on p. 230) offers a protected marine environment just south of downtown. Several dive shops around the city offer organized outings, either to the reefs or to one of more than a dozen old shipwrecks around Miami's shores.

Windsurfers carve the waves in front of downtown Miami.

Diver's Paradise, of Key Biscayne, 4000 Crandon Blvd. (www.keydivers.com; © **305/361-3483;** daily 9am–5pm), offers one dive expedition per day during the week and two per day on the weekends to the more than 30 wrecks and artificial reefs off the coast of Miami Beach and Key Biscayne. You can take a 3-day certification course for $699, which includes all the dives and gear. If you already have your C-card, a dive trip costs about $95 per person plus gear. For snorkeling, they will set you up with equipment and maps to the best underwater sights. Rental for mask, fins, and snorkel is $20.

Tarpoon Lagoon Diving Center, 300 Alton Rd., Miami Beach (tarpoonlagoon.com; © **305/532-1445**), is a full-service dive shop on South Beach. In addition to daily dive and snorkel charters, they offer dive certification courses at their on-site pool. Two-day courses start at $645, and dive trips start at $115. For those who have no interest in getting wet, for $100, you can spend the day on the boat while the others sink to new depths.

The most amusing and apropos South Beach diving spot has to be the **Jose Cuervo Underwater Bar,** located 150 yards southeast of the Second Street lifeguard station—a 22-ton concrete margarita bar that was sunk on May 5, 2000. Nicknamed "Sinko De Mayo," the site is designed with a dive flag roof, six bar stools, and a protective wall of tetrahedrons.

WINDSURFING Many hotels rent windsurfers to their guests, but if yours doesn't have a watersports concession stand, head for Key Biscayne. **Miami Watersports,** Dinner Key Marina, Key Biscayne (miamiwatersports.com; © **786/713-8006**), offers rentals and, as importantly, beginner lessons, from one of the hottest windsurfing spots in the city, where there's an average of 12–15 knots of wind year-round. Lessons range from $130 for group lessons to $250 for one-on-one private lessons. Rentals start at $75 per hour for beginner gear, or $95 per hour for advanced gear.

MORE WAYS TO PLAY, INDOORS & OUT

BIKING Bikers can also enjoy more than 130 miles of paved paths throughout Miami. The cement promenade on the southern tip of **South Beach** is a swell place to ride. The beautiful and quiet streets of **Coral Gables** and **Coconut Grove** (several bike trails are spread throughout these neighborhoods) are particularly bike friendly. Old trees form canopies over wide, flat roads lined with grand homes and quaint street markers. The terrain in **Key Biscayne** is also perfect for biking, especially along the park and beach roads. If you don't mind the sound of cars whooshing by your bike lane, **Rickenbacker Causeway** is also primo, as it is one of the only bikeable inclines in Miami from which you get elevated views of the city and waterways. However, be warned that this is a grueling ride, especially going up the causeway.

Most of the big beach hotels rent bicycles, as does the **Miami Beach Bicycle Center,** 746 5th St., South Beach (bikemiamibeach.com; © **305/674-0150;** Mon–Sat 10am–7pm, Sun 10am–5pm), which rents e-bikes, beach cruisers, road bikes, sand bikes, and kids bikes starting at $30/day. **Key Cycling,** 61 Harbor Dr., Key Biscayne (keycyclingkb.com; © **305/361-0061;** Mon–Fri 10am–7pm, Sat 9am–5pm), rents hybrid and mountain bikes for $20 for 2 hours, $25 a day, or $100 a week.

Biking note: Children 15 and under are required by Florida law to wear a helmet, which can be purchased at any bike store or retail outlet selling biking supplies.

FISHING Fishing licenses are required in Florida. If you go out with one of the fishing charter boats listed below, you are automatically accredited because the companies are. If you go out on your own, however, you must have a Florida fishing license, which costs $17 for 3 days and $30 for a week. Visit myfwc.com/license/recreational/saltwater-fishing/ for more info.

Some of the best surfcasting in the city can be had at **Haulover Beach Park** (Collins Ave. and 105th St.), and there's a bait-and-tackle shop right on the pier. **South Pointe Park,** at the southern tip of Miami Beach, is another popular fishing spot and features a long pier, comfortable benches, and a view of ships passing through Government Cut, the deep channel made when the Port of Miami was dug.

You can also do deep-sea fishing in the Miami area. One bargain outfitter, the **Kelley Fishing Fleet,** at the Haulover Marina, 10800 Collins Ave. (at 108th St.), Miami Beach (miamibeachfishing.com; © **305/945-3801**), has half-day, full-day, and night fishing aboard diesel-powered "party boats." The fleet's emphasis on drifting is geared toward trolling and bottom-fishing for snapper, sailfish, and mackerel. Half-day and night-fishing trips are $69 for adults and $59 for children up to 10 years old, and full-day, 8-hour trips are $99 for adults and $89 for children. Daily departures are scheduled at 9am and 1:45 and 8pm; reservations are recommended.

Outfitters on Key Biscayne offer deep-sea fishing to those willing to get their hands dirty and pay a bundle. The competition among the boats is fierce, but the prices are basically the same, no matter which you choose. The going rate is about $1,200 for a half-day and $1,800 for a full day of fishing. These rates are usually for a party of up to six, and the boats supply you with rods and bait as well as instruction for first-timers. Some will also take you out to the Upper Keys if the fish aren't biting in Miami. **Cutting Edge** is a reliable outfitter on the Key, 4000 Crandon Blvd. (miamicharterfishing.com; © **305/360-9740**), as is Captain Jimmy, who sails a tournament fishing charter boat out of the Key Biscayne marina: *L & H* (landhsportfishing.com; © **305/361-9318**).

Bridge fishing in Biscayne Bay is also popular in Miami; you'll see people with poles over almost every waterway. But look carefully for signs telling you whether it's legal to do so wherever you are: Some bridges forbid fishing.

GAMBLING Thanks to plenty of loopholes and laws that allow wagering, gambling in Miami has come a long way, though it's still no Vegas. Gamblers can try their luck at offshore casinos or on shore at bingo, jai alai, card rooms, horse tracks, dog races, and Native American reservations. **Hialeah Park Racing** (hialeahparkracing.com) has thoroughbred and quarter horse racing and, sometime in the near future, because no racetrack in Florida is complete without it, poker and slot machines. For slots and poker, you can check out the **Magic City Casino,** 5 minutes from the airport and downtown Miami at 450 NW 37th Ave. (magiccitycasino.com; © **888/56-MAGIC** [566-2442]), or **Calder Casino,** located by Hard Rock Stadium at 21001 NW 27th Ave. in Miami Gardens (caldercasino.com; © **305/625-1311**), featuring 1,100 slot machines, poker, and an outdoor, "backyard" smoking casino. You can also drive up to Broward County, where the **Seminole Hard Rock Hotel and Casino** (seminolehardrockhollywood. com), **Seminole Casino Coconut Creek** (seminolecoconutcreekcasino.com), **The Big Easy Casino** (playmardigras.com), **Harrah's Pompano Beach** (caesars. com/harrahs-pompano-beach), and **Gulfstream Park Casino and Racing** (gulfstreampark.com) in Hallandale offer slots, poker, and horse racing. The Hard Rock and Seminole Coconut Creek offer blackjack, craps, roulette, and all sorts of Vegas-style gambling.

Despite the Hard Rock in Hollywood's behemoth presence on the gambling circuit (and its many imitators), some people prefer the **Miccosukee Casino & Resort,** 500 SW 177th Ave. (off S.R. 41, in West Miami, on the outskirts of the Everglades; miccosukee.com; © **800/741-4600** or 305/222-4600). This tacky casino ain't Caesars Palace, but you can play tab slots, high-speed bingo (watch out for the serious blue-haired players who will scoff if you make too much noise), and even poker. With more than 85,000 square feet of playing space, the complex even provides overnight accommodations for those who don't want to make the approximately 1-hour trip back to downtown Miami. Take the Florida Turnpike south toward Florida City/Key West. Take the SW 8th Street exit (no. 25) and turn left onto SW 8th Street. Drive for about 3½ miles and then turn left onto Krome Avenue, and left again at 177th Street; you can't miss it.

GOLF There are nearly 50 private and public golf courses in the Miami area. The **Greater Miami Convention and Visitor's Bureau** (miamiandbeaches.com) has a list of all the courses and costs.

The best hotel courses in Miami are found at **JW Marriott Miami Turnberry Isle Resort & Spa** (19999 West Country Club Drive, Aventura; marriott. com), with two Robert Trent Jones, Sr.–designed courses for guests and members, and the **Biltmore ★★★** (p. 76), which is our pick for best public golf course because of its modest greens fees (starting at $57), and an 18-hole, par-71 Donald Ross course located on the hotel's spectacular grounds.

Crandon Golf at Key Biscayne ★★, formerly known as the Links, 6700 Crandon Blvd., Key Biscayne (golfcrandon.com; ⓒ **305/361-9129**), was the site of the Senior PGA Tour for 18 years, attracting golf's greats. The course is considered one of the most beautiful and difficult par-72 courses in the state of Florida. The park is situated on 200 bayfront acres and offers a pro shop, rentals, lessons, carts, and a lighted driving range. It is open daily from dawn to dusk; greens fees (including cart) range from $89 to $199, depending on the season, for nonresidents and include a cart. Special twilight rates are also available.

The **Miami Beach Golf Club** ★, 2301 Alton Rd., South Beach (miamibeachgolfclub.com; ⓒ **305/532-3350**), is a gorgeous, 79-year-old 18-hole, par-72 course that, par for the, er, course in Miami Beach, received a fabulous face-lift. Miami Heat players and Matt Damon have been known to tee off here. There's also a Jim McClean golf school on the premises and a restaurant. Greens fees range from $149 to $250, depending on the season.

For those who like golf on a smaller scale, champ Rory McIlroy is a backer of **Puttery,** 239 NW 28th St., Wynwood (puttery.com; ⓒ **786/733-0770**), a 21-and-over indoor minigolf bar and restaurant featuring three fun, themed 9-hole courses for $27 unlimited play.

PICKLEBALL/TENNIS Hundreds of tennis courts in South Florida are open to the public for a minimal fee, with pickleball courts opening on what seems like a daily basis. Most courts operate on a first-come, first-served basis and are open from sunrise to sunset. For info and directions, look at the website of the **City of Miami Parks and Recreation Department** (miamibeachfl.gov).

Of the 590 public tennis courts throughout Miami, the 27 courts, including 13 that are lighted, at the **Crandon Park Tennis Center**, 6702 Crandon Blvd. (miamidade.gov/parks/crandon-tennis.asp; ⓒ **305/361-5263**), are the best, most beautiful and the venue for one of the world's biggest annual tennis events, the Sony Ericsson Open. Lendl, Graf, Evert, McEnroe, Federer, the Williams sisters, and other greats have all competed here. Because of this, they often get crowded on weekends. If you reserve at least 24 to 48 hours in advance, you can usually take your pick of courts. Hard courts cost $5 per person per hour during the day, $9 per person per hour at night. Clay courts cost $7 per person per hour during the day. You can also channel your best Williams sister or Federer on

Crandon Park Tennis Center.

the stadium courts, which cost $18 per person per hour. The courts are open daily from 8am to 7pm.

We also highly recommend the first-come, first-served **Flamingo Tennis Center,** 1001 12th St., in South Beach (© **305/673-7761;** Mon–Thurs 7:30am–9pm, Fri–Sun 7:30am–8pm). It has 17 Har-Tru clay courts which are $5 per person per hour for Miami Beach residents, $17 for nonresidents. Playing at night adds an extra $6 "light fee."

Miami's pickleball scene is a hot one, with several courts, including one at the aforementioned **Miami Beach Golf Club,** where there are six outdoor hard courts. They're free, but it's first come, first served. There are also free courts at **Haulover Park,** 10800 Collins Ave., in the north part of Parking Lot 2, and at **Douglas Park,** 2755 SW 37th Ave. near Coral Gables.

Hotels with the best tennis facilities are the Ritz-Carlton Key Biscayne and the Biltmore (p. 76).

SPECTATOR SPORTS

For last-minute tickets, contact the venue directly, as many season-ticket holders sell singles and return unused tickets. Expensive tickets are available from brokers, Ticketmaster, or StubHub.

BASEBALL In 2020 the **Miami Marlins** became the first team in any American major league sports league to hire a woman, Kim Ng, as GM. In 2023, Ng became the first woman GM in MLB history to take her team to the playoffs. Pretty cool! If you're interested in catching a game, ***be warned:*** The summer heat in Miami can be unbearable, even in the evenings. The stadium, 501 Marlins Way (mlb.com/marlins/ballpark; © **305/480-1300**), has a retractable roof to make things a bit more pleasant. Tickets cost from $26 to $165. The team currently holds spring training at Roger Dean Chevrolet Stadium, 4751 Main St. (rogerdeanchevroletstadium.com) in Jupiter, Florida.

BASKETBALL The **Miami Heat** (nba.com/heat; © **786/777-1000**) is still one of Miami's hottest tickets, even if their star lineups have aged out. Courtside seats are often full of visiting celebrities. The season lasts from October to April, with most games beginning at 7:30pm. The team plays in the waterfront **Kaseya Center,** downtown on Biscayne Boulevard. Tickets are $30 to $650 or much more.

CAR RACING **Homestead-Miami Speedway,** One Speedway Blvd., Homestead (homesteadmiamispeedway.com; © **866/409-7223** or 866/409-RACE [7223]) is a place where you can channel your inner speed demon via open-to-the-public events that allow regular folk to put the pedal to the metal, including **Hooked on Driving** (hookedondriving.com) and **Florida Track Days** (floridatrackdays.com). Ticket prices vary by event.

FOOTBALL Miami's golden boys are the **Miami Dolphins** (miamidolphins.com), the city's most recognizable team, followed by legions of devoted "dolfans." The team plays at least eight home games during the season, between September and December, at **Hard Rock Stadium,** 347 Don Shula Dr., Miami Gardens (hardrockstadium.com; © **305/943-8000**). Tickets start around $60 and go up much, much more, especially when they're playing well.

HORSE RACING Located on the Dade–Broward County border in Hallandale (just north of North Miami Beach/Aventura), **Gulfstream Park Racing,** at U.S. 1 and Hallandale Beach Boulevard (gulfstreampark.com; © **305/454-7000**), is South Florida's version of Churchill Downs, but without the hats. This horse track is a haven for serious gamblers and voyeurs alike. Large purses and important races are commonplace at this sprawling suburban course, and the track is typically crowded. Admission and parking are free. January 3 through April 23, post times are 1:15pm Wednesday through Sunday. The track is closed Mondays and Tuesdays, though the on-site casino remains open. And while not exactly racing, a newish event on the sands of South Beach is the **Beach Polo World Cup** (miamipolocup.com), featuring hard-core sand-kicking matches, a parade of the ponies down the beach, and chic parties. General admission is free to the public.

SOCCER So yes, David Beckham bent all the rules and brought Major League Soccer to South Florida in the form of **Inter Miami,** featuring none other than star player Lionel Messi. But here's the kicker—until the stadium is finished in Miami, the team plays in Fort Lauderdale at the **DRV Pink Stadium,** 1350 NW 55th St., Fort Lauderdale (intermiamicf.com; ✆ **305/428-0611**), and tickets are impossible to come by ever since Messi took to the field If you *can* snag one, they'll likely set you back from $135 to $1,000.

SHOPPING

Miami has many, many malls. In addition to the strip malls, Miami offers a choice of megamalls, from the upscale **Village of Merrick Park** and mammoth **Aventura Mall** to the ritzy **Design District** and **Bal Harbour Shops** and touristy yet scenic **Bayside Marketplace** (just to name a few). The city also offers more unique shopping spots, such as the edgy Biscayne Corridor and Wynwood, where funky boutiques thrive, and Little Havana, where you can buy hand-rolled cigars and *guayaberas*.

> **Impressions**
>
> We're the only city that has big-butt mannequins.
> —Anna Maria Diaz-Balart, Miami-based fashion designer

Shopping Hours & Taxes

As a general rule, shop hours are Monday through Saturday from 10am to 6pm, and Sunday from noon to 5pm. Many stores stay open late (until 9pm or so) at least one night of the week, usually Thursday, but oftentimes Fridays and Saturdays. Shops in Coconut Grove, South Beach, Aventura Mall, and Wynwood are often open later. With all these variations, you may want to call specific stores to find out their hours.

A 7% state and local sales tax is added to the price of all nonfood purchases.

Shopping Areas

Most of Miami's shopping happens at the many megamalls scattered from one end of the county to the other. However, excellent boutique shopping and browsing can be found in the following areas (see "The Neighborhoods in Brief," on p. 54, for more information):

AVENTURA On Biscayne Boulevard between Miami Gardens Drive and the county line at Hallandale Beach Boulevard is a 2-mile stretch of the usual big-box retail stores. Also here is the mammoth **Aventura Mall,** a shopping destination housing a constantly growing, fabulous collection of shops and restaurants.

Books and Books isn't just one of the best independent bookstores in Miami; its expert staff and curation make it one of the finest of its kind in the U.S.A.

BISCAYNE CORRIDOR Amid the ramshackle old motels of yesteryear exist several funky, kitschy, and arty boutiques along the stretch of Biscayne Boulevard from 50th Street to about 79th Street known as the Biscayne Corridor. Everything from hand-painted tank tops to expensive Juicy Couture sweat suits can be found here, but it's not just about fashion: Several furniture stores sell modern pieces and antiques, so look carefully, as you may find something here that would cause the appraisers on *Antiques Road Show* to lose their wigs. More mainstream stores are at the **Shops at Midtown Miami** on the gritty yet developing edge of Wynwood at North Miami Avenue and NE 36th Street.

CALLE OCHO In Little Havana, take a walk down 8th Street between SW 27th Avenue and SW 12th Avenue, where you'll find lively street life and many shops selling cigars, baked goods, shoes, furniture, and record stores specializing in Latin music. Have a translation app handy.

COCONUT GROVE Downtown Coconut Grove, centered on Main Highway and Grand Avenue, and branching onto the adjoining streets, is one of Miami's most pedestrian-friendly zones. The Grove's wide sidewalks, lined with cafes and boutiques, can provide hours of browsing. The area has few funky holdovers from the days when the Grove was a bit more bohemian, plus some good sidewalk cafes and lively bars.

CORAL GABLES **Miracle Mile** is the heart of the shopping district here. Actually only a half-mile long, this stretch of Coral Way (btw. LeJeune Rd. and Douglas Rd.) was an integral part of George Merrick's original city plan. Today the strip is known for its bridal stores, ladies' shops, haberdashers, and gift shops. The hyper-upscale **Village of Merrick Park,** a mammoth, 850,000-square-foot outdoor shopping complex between Ponce de León Boulevard and Le Jeune Road, just off the Mile, houses Nordstrom, Neiman Marcus, Armani, and Yves St. Laurent, to name a few. Also in Coral Gables is the flagship store of **Books and Books ★★★** (265 Aragon Ave; booksandbooks.com; ✆ **305/442-4408;** Mon–Sat 10am–11pm, Sun 10am–8pm), Miami's world-class bookstore chain, with six stores around the city. The staff are reading savants: Tell them what you like, and they'll find the right book for you. It has a nice cafe, too (p. 107).

DESIGN DISTRICT An interior design, art, and furniture hub, including uber-high-end shops like Gucci, Alexander McQueen, Chanel, and Dior.

DOWNTOWN MIAMI If you're looking for discounts on all types of goods—especially watches, fabric, shoes, luggage, and leather—Flagler Street, just west of Biscayne Boulevard, is the best place to start. We wouldn't necessarily recommend buying expensive items here, as many stores seem to be on the shady side and do not understand the word *warranty*. However, you can still have fun here as long as you are a savvy shopper and don't mind haggling. Most signs are printed in English, Spanish, and Portuguese; however, many shopkeepers are not entirely fluent in English. The area is also known for jewelry: The **Seybold Building** and the **International Jewelry Center** have bigtime bling. Nearby, the **Mary Brickell Village,** a 192,000-square-foot urban entertainment center west of Brickell Avenue and straddling South Miami Avenue between 9th and 10th streets downtown, offers a few independently owned boutiques, but it's the **Brickell City Centre** that has forever changed the area's retail landscape, spreading across four floors and three city blocks, anchored by Saks Fifth Avenue and featuring over 120 shops and restaurants. And because traffic isn't bad enough now, coming eventually to the area: **Miami Worldcenter,** a 750,000-square-foot retail center next to where the Heat play.

> **Impressions**
>
> I love coming to Miami because it's a real melting pot. And it's hot, so people can wear little bits of clothing.
> —Shakira, international pop star

SOUTH BEACH South Beach has ebbed, flowed, and ebbed again as far as trendy shopping is concerned. While **Ocean Drive** is only tourist schlock today, the southern blocks of **Collins Avenue** have better options including Armani Exchange, Free People, and The Webster. Alas, South Beach's legendary **Lincoln Road,** once known for art galleries and indie boutiques, is now just an outdated, outdoor shopping mall with chains instead of funky boutiques. For the vibe Lincoln used to have, head to **Espanola Way** instead, a pedestrian-only, Mediterranean shopping destination.

WYNWOOD Wynwood is now a haven for those who cringe at the conspicuous consumption of the Design District, and instead like to wear things as groovy as the art on the area's walls. It has one-of-a-kind shops for clothing, shoes, records (yup, vinyl), home goods, and more. By the time the stuff you see here arrives in the Design District shops, it will be rendered passe in Wynwood.

MIAMI AFTER DARK

Miami's nightlife is hotter than ever before—and getting cooler with the opening of each funky, fabulous watering hole, lounge, and club. Not always cool, however, is the presence of ubiquitous, closely guarded velvet ropes used to create an air of exclusivity. Don't be fooled or intimidated by them: *Anyone* can party like a rockstar in the Magic City, and throughout this section, we've provided tips to ensure that you gain entry to your desired venue.

South Beach was once Miami's nocturnal nucleus, but more and more diverse areas, such as the Design District, Midtown/Wynwood, Brickell, South Miami, and even Little Havana, are increasingly providing fun alternatives without the ludicrous cover charges, "fashionably late" hours of operation (things don't typically get started on South Beach until after 11pm), lack of sufficient self-parking, and outrageous drink prices that are standard in South Beach. Parts of downtown, such as Brickell, the Biscayne Corridor, the Miami River, Midtown, Wynwood, and the Design District, have become nightlife destinations in their own rights, as well.

While South Beach dances to a more electronic beat, other parts of Miami dance to a Latin beat, from salsa and merengue to tango and cha-cha. If you're looking for a less frenetic good time, Miami's bar scene has something for everyone, from sleek, loungey watering holes to friendly dives.

Miami also provides a variety of first-rate diversions in theater, music, and dance, including a world-class ballet, a recognized symphony, and a talented opera company. The circa-2006 Cesar Pelli–designed, $446-million Adrienne Arsht Center for the Performing Arts is the focal point for the arts, created to prove to the world that Miami isn't as shallow and devoid of culture as people once thought.

The Performing Arts

In recent years, Miami's performing arts scene has improved greatly, though in the summer of 2024, culture warrior Governor DeSantis vetoed a massive chunk of the entire state's arts budget because of, inexplicably, "sexual festivals," which do not even exist. As we go to press, it's unclear whether that action will lead to the closing of any of the city's arts organizations, as government funding was a large part of many of their budgets. The city's **Broadway Series** ★★ (arshtcenter.org) features Tony Award–winning shows (the touring versions, of course), which are not nearly as pricey as they are in New York City. Local arts groups, such as the **Miami Light Project** ★★★ (miamilightproject.com), a not-for-profit cultural organization that presents performances by innovative dance, music, and theater artists, have had huge success in attracting big-name artists to the city. Also, a burgeoning bohemian movement in Little Havana has given way to performance spaces that are nightclubs in their own right.

THEATER

The **Actors' Playhouse at the Miracle Theatre** ★★, 280 Miracle Mile, Coral Gables (actorsplayhouse.org; © **305/444-9293**), is the largest self-producing professional theater in South Florida. Its shows, musicals, and children's theater are performed in a grand 1948 Art Deco movie palace with a 600-seat main theater and a smaller theater/rehearsal hall.

The **GableStage** ★★, at the Biltmore Hotel (p. 76), 1200 Anastasia Ave., Coral Gables (gablestage.org; © **305/445-1119**), stages at least one Shakespearean play, one classic, and one contemporary piece a year. This well-regarded professional theater usually tries to secure the rights to a national or local premiere, as

The Adrienne Arsht Center lights up Miami's performing arts scene.

well. Tickets cost $35 to $65. GableStage was expected to take over the abandoned landmark Coconut Grove Playhouse using $20 million in designated county improvement funds to create a larger, 600-seat theater, but politics, permitting, and preservation issues have held that up.

CLASSICAL MUSIC

In addition to a number of local orchestras and operas (see below), which regularly offer quality music and world-renowned guest artists, each year brings a slew of classical-music special events and touring artists to Miami.

New World Symphony ★★★ Founded by Artistic Director Laureate Michael Tilson Thomas, and currently led by Stéphane Denève, New World Symphony is a steppingstone for gifted young musicians seeking professional careers. The orchestra specializes in innovative, energetic performances, and often features renowned guest soloists and conductors. The season lasts from October to May, and the NWS plays in a spectacular, $200-million-plus Frank Gehry–designed campus featuring a grand performance space. Even if you're not into the music, it's something to see. *Tip:* It's possible to see concerts for free, throughout the season, at **SoundScape Park,** where they are projected on a soaring, 7,000-square-foot wall. It's a high-tech endeavor, meaning both the audio and visuals of WALLCAST are crystal clear. These free concerts are so popular NWS added a mobile 23×13-foot projection wall to extend viewing areas and allow more people to attend. 500 17th St., South Beach. nws.edu. © **305/673-3330.** Tickets free to $200 and up.

OPERA

Florida Grand Opera ★★ Around since 1941, this company regularly features singers from top houses in both America and Europe. All productions are sung in their original language and staged with projected English supertitles. The season runs roughly from November to April, with five performances each week. Performances take place both at the **Arsht Center for the Performing Arts** and at the **Broward Center for the Performing Arts** in Fort Lauderdale. Box office: 1300 Biscayne Blvd., Miami. fgo.org. © **800/741-1010.** Tickets $25–$230.

DANCE

Ballet Flamenco La Rosa ★★ For a taste of local Latin flavor, see this lively troupe perform impressive flamenco and other styles of Latin dance on Miami stages. 74 NE 150th St. balletflamencolarosa.com. ✆ **305/899-7729.**

Miami City Ballet ★★★ This acclaimed and innovative company, founded by Edward Villella, and led today by Jerome Robbins and George Balanchine–mentored dancer Lourdes Lopez, features a repertoire of more than 60 ballets, many by Balanchine, and has had more than 20 world premieres. The City Ballet season runs from September to April and shows are at the Arsht Center. Ophelia and Juan Jr. Roca Center, 2200 Liberty Ave., at Collins Ave. and 22nd St., South Beach. miamicityballet.org. ✆ **929-7010** for box office. Tickets $40–$235.

Major Venues

The **Colony Theatre** ★★, 1040 Lincoln Rd., South Beach (miaminewdrama.org; ✆ 305/674-1040), an architectural showpiece of the Art Deco District, currently houses the non-profit **Miami New Drama** company. The latter is the largest professional bilingual theater company in the United States. It often uses major talent (like Tony-winning director Gregory Mosher) in its productions.

At the 1,700-seat **Olympia Theater** ★★★, 174 E. Flagler St., downtown Miami (olympiaarts.miami/olympia-theater.html; ✆ **305/209-1233**), seating is tight, and so is funding (in 2020 the City of Miami took over management), but the sound is superb. The auditorium was built as the Olympia Theater in 1926, and its ornate palace interior is typical of that era, complete with fancy columns, a huge pipe organ, and twinkling "stars" on the ceiling. In addition to hosting the Miami Film Festival, the elegant theater features concerts, plays, and more.

Last, but definitely not least, the **Adrienne Arsht Center for the Performing Arts of Miami-Dade County** ★★★, 1300 Biscayne Blvd. (arshtcenter.org; ✆ 305/949-6722), is the performing space of choice for the **Florida Grand Opera, Miami City Ballet,** and **New World Symphony,** as well as the premier venue for a wide array of local, national, and international performances, ranging from Broadway musicals and visiting classical artists to world and urban music, Latin concerts, and popular entertainment from many cultures. It's often the setting for the city's most intriguing performances.

Designed by world-renowned architect Cesar Pelli, the **Carnival Center,** also part of the sprawling Arsht Center, is the focal point of a planned Arts, Media, and Entertainment District in mid-Miami. The complex is wrapped in limestone, slate, decorative stone, stainless steel, glass curtain walls, and tropical landscaping.

The biggest joke in town, however, is that after spending millions to create these state-of-the-art performance venues, the planners forgot to include parking facilities. As a result, valet parking is available for $35 or you can park in nearby lots for $10 to $28, but it's truly a pain; so to make things easy, just take an Uber. It'll cost you the same and you won't have to deal with traipsing across Biscayne Boulevard in your fine theater threads. For more information, check out the website at arshtcenter.org.

Bars & Lounges

There are countless bars and lounges in and around Miami, with the highest concentration on South Beach. The selection here is a sample of the ones we find most intriguing. Oh, yes, and when going out in South Beach, make sure to take a so-called disco nap, as things don't get going until at least 11pm. If you go earlier, be prepared to face an empty bar. Off of South Beach and in hotel bars in general, the hours are earlier, with the action starting as early as, say, 7pm.

In addition to the bars listed below, several full-service restaurants have noteworthy bar and nightlife scenes including **Café La Trova** (see p. 98 for a full review) and **Sweet Liberty Drinks & Supply Company** (p. 81).

The Abbey Brewing Co. ★★   Dark, dank, and hard to find, this local microbrewery is a favorite for locals looking to escape the $20 candy-flavored martini scene. Best of all, there's never a cover and it's open 'til 5am. 1115 16th St., South Beach. ⓒ **305/538-8110.** Mon–Fri 3pm–5am; Sat 1pm–5am; Sun noon–5am.

Bar Nancy ★★   This Little Havana liquor lounge is a nautical- and Colonial American–themed bar, with a crowd who come here for—wait for it, it gets even weirder—Canadian-style poutine. Drinks include the "Smile You Son of a Bitch" (a Don Julio Casa Noble cocktail of blue nectar, tequila blend, mango, blackberry shrub, and lime), and the "I Don't Know What I Want," about which they say, "Arrrgh, no worries, matey, it has Tito's." Live music here ranges from Bowie and Pink Floyd tribute bands to post-punk, industrial, and synth wave. 2007 SW 8th St., Little Havana. nancy305.com. No phone. Mon–Tues 6pm–2am; Sun, Wed–Thurs 4pm–2am; Fri–Sat 4pm–3am.

Broken Shaker ★★★   A visionary in all things boozy, Broken Shaker is a place where mustachioed bartenders make like mad scientists with tinctures, potions, and garnishes not seen at your typical corner bar. It's lauded for its cocktail programs, and gets creative with its ingredients, like bourbon infused with Reese's Puffs candy, mango-kiwi-habanero syrups, and an array of rare spirits. There's also a small menu of snacks, including a hipster's version of a Happy Meal which comes sided by Miller High Life or soda. At the Freehand Hotel, 2727 Indian Creek Dr., Miami Beach. BrokenShaker.com. ⓒ **786/476-7011.** Sun–Thurs 5pm–1am; Fri–Sat 5pm–2am.

The Corner ★★★   Located west of Museum Park in downtown Miami, this neighborhood bar built out of 150-year-old repurposed wood, is as close to *Cheers* as it gets, where everybody knows your name and your preferred poison. Open until 5am Sunday through Thursday and 8am (!) Friday and Saturday, The Corner is where people typically end up after a night of supping or clubbing around town. On Tuesday nights, there's live jazz. There's also a highly regarded craft beer selection, excellent cocktails (try the Sazerac or the Hot and Smokey), and decent bar food including grilled cheese and hot dogs. 1035 N. Miami Ave., downtown Miami. thecornermiami.com. ⓒ **305/961-7887.** Sun–Thurs 4pm–5am; Fri–Sat 4pm–8am.

A bartender creates a cocktail at Broken Shaker.

147

Fox's Lounge ★★★ This circa 1946 lounge and package store was originally a place where people went when they didn't want to be found. It's now a hot spot of sorts, a dark, windowless cavern of cocktailing, with wood paneling and red vinyl booths. The jukebox that used to play Sinatra tunes has now been modified to play some, but not much, more modern music, but the old-school pay phone is still hanging on the wall to the delight of younger generations who pose for Instagram pix with it. A food menu features old faves including the original Fox's thumb bits of beef with au jus, as well as frog legs in garlic butter. A daily happy hour features $7 cocktails from 4 to 7pm, which is as throwback as things get here. 6030 S. Dixie Hwy., South Miami. foxslounge.com. ⓒ **305/703-6553.** Daily 4pm–2am.

Gramp's ★★★ This delightful dive bar is a little bit tiki and a lot of local color. Live music, fantastic local DJs spinning everything from '70s disco to Taylor Swift, bingo nights, and decent pizza make Gramp's a go-to for fun, come-as-you-are cocktailing, or chugging PBR out of the can—anything goes. Gramp's also has a location on Key Biscayne called, appropriately, **Gramp's Getaway,** 3301 Rickenbacker Causeway, with a focus on frozen drinks and fresh Florida seafood. 176 NW 24th St., Wynwood. gramps.com. ⓒ **305/699-2669.** Sun–Thurs noon–1am; Fri–Sat noon–3am.

> **Impressions**
>
> There are two shifts in South Beach. There's 9 to 5. And then there's 9 to 5.
> —South Beach artist Stewart Stewart

Mac's Club Deuce ★★★ Set in a sea of trendiness, Mac's Club Deuce is the quintessential dive bar, with cheap drinks and a cast of characters ranging from your typical barfly to your atypical drag queen. The late Anthony Bourdain ranked it as one of his top five best dive bars in the world. It's got a well-stocked jukebox, friendly bartenders, and a pool table. Best of all, it's an insomniac's dream, open daily from 8am to 5am. 222 14th St., South Beach. macsclubdeuce.com. ⓒ **305/673-9537.** Daily 8am–5am.

Mode Downtown ★★ One of the hottest trends in Japanese nightlife is listening lounges, places where the music (spun by a DJ) is as important as the tipples. Mode is an American version of that, set in downtown Miami's burgeoning Flagler District, with multiple rooms on two floors, all of which boast superb acoustics and state-of-the-art sound systems. Dimly lit and inviting, one room is a vinyl bar for old-school music lovers, another plays electronic music. Mode also regularly plays host to a pop-up called **Jezebel,** a cutting-edge dance club known for attracting top DJs. For more information on what night Jezebel makes her appearance at Mode, go to linktr.ee/jezebelsound. 2 S. Miami Ave., downtown Miami. mode.miami. ⓒ **305/942-7240.** Tues–Thurs 7pm–2am; Fri–Sat 7pm–5am. Closed Sun–Mon.

Segafredo l'Originale ★★ Although Segafredo is technically a cafe, it has become an integral part of Miami's nightlife as command central for expats who miss that very special brand of European cafe society. It's a place to hear groovy lounge music, sip a few cocktails, snack on delicious sandwiches and pizza, and sit outside on a prime corner of Lincoln Road and people-watch. 1040 Lincoln Rd., South Beach. sze-originale.com. ⓒ **305/673-0047.** Sun–Thurs 11am–midnight; Fri–Sat 11am–1am.

BOWLING & booze (GOLF, TOO)

Bowling in Miami gives new meaning to partying in the gutter. Think of it as the Big Lebowski meets Studio 54. Not into bowling? Try some indoor golf. Thumping music, cocktails, and food turn a hole-in-one into a much more challenging endeavor. Here's where to go:

- **Bowlero:** One of Miami's biggest bowling alleys, with glow-in-the-dark bowling. In the Dolphin Mall, 11401 NW 12 St. bowlero.com. © **305/594-0200.** $30–$40/hour depending on day and time, including shoe rental.

- **Pinstripes:** The newest and fanciest bowling alley has an Italian restaurant, wine cellar, and bocce courts. Esplanade at Aventura, 19505 Biscayne Blvd. pinstripes.com. © **786/998-2180.** $17–$25 per person, per hour for bowling depending on day and time, including shoe rental.

- **Puttery:** This Rory McIlroy–backed indoor minigolf restaurant and bar is the place to be in Wynwood, especially on a rainy day. Unlimited play is a downright bargain at $27. 239 NW 28th St., Wynwood. puttery.com. © **786/733-0770.**

- **Topgolf:** Climate-controlled hitting bays, loud music, food, and cocktails. 17321 NW 7th Ave., Miami Gardens. topgolf.com. © **305/357-6151.** $16–$62 per hour, per bay plus a $5 membership fee for new players. Sun–Thurs 10am–11pm; Fri–Sat 10am–1am.

Wet Bar at the W South Beach ★★   As wholly unoriginal as the name is, the poolside Wet Bar & Grille, along with lush (heh) outdoor Irma's and lobby-level Living Room at the W South Beach are among the city's most buzz-worthy nightspots thanks to master mixologists who shake and stir up some of the most creative cocktails you'll ever drink. The decor at all three is also an eye-popping delight. 2201 Collins Ave., South Beach. marriott.com. © **305/938-3000.** Daily 3pm–midnight.

Wet Willie's ★   A well-liked pre- and post-beach hangout, Wet Willie's inspires serious drinking. Popular with the Harley-Davidson set, tourists, and beachcombers (the bar is right off the sands), this bar is best known for its rooftop patio (get there early if you plan to get a seat) and its half-nude bikini beauty patrons. 760 Ocean Dr., South Beach. wetwillies.com/south-beach. © **305/532-5650.** Sun–Thurs 11am–1am; Fri–Sat 11am–2am.

Dance Clubs

Clubs were once as much a cottage industry in Miami as is, say, cheese in Wisconsin. That is, until the smartphone became a third appendage and people began to zone out on their phones instead of on the dance floor. That being said, there are still dance clubs in the city, they're just rare these days, and yep, go to one and you will see people on their phones on the dance floor—or at the very least, on their phones sitting on the sidelines. It's sad, really, but there are some clubs where phones are actually put away as dance moves are put on.

SAVING MONEY, TIME & SANITY AT MIAMI CLUBS   As we said before, Miami is a very late town, with nightlife rarely starting before 11pm. The

WINTER music CONFERENCE

During the second or third week of March Miami is flooded by the most unconventional conventioneers the city sees, here for the **Miami Music Week** (MMW) and the **Winter Music Conference** (WMC). These are the world's biggest and most important gatherings of DJs, remixers, agents, artists, and pretty much anyone who makes a dime off of the booming electronic music industry. They hail from more than 60 countries.

But unlike most conventions, this one, described as "a masterclass in dance music," is completely interactive and open to the paying public as South Beach and Miami's hottest clubs transform into showcases. For 5 consecutive days and nights, DJs, artists, and software producers play for audiences composed of industry bigwigs and locals just along for the ride. Parties take place everywhere, from hotel pools to street corners. There's always something going on every hour on the hour, and most people who really get into the throes of MMW get little or no sleep.

The week(s) culminate in the Woodstock for EDM fans known as **Ultra Music Festival** (ultramusicfestival.com), a 3-day outdoor electronic music festival featuring the who's who in that world spinning beats.

At any rate, MMW is worth checking out if you enjoy such artists as Diplo, Carl Cox, Marshmello, Martin Garrix, David Guetta Purple Disco Machine, among many, many others. For more information on MMW/WMC events, go to **miamimusicweek.com** or **wintermusicconference.com**.

Catch-22 is that if you don't arrive, say, on South Beach early enough, you may find yourself driving around aimlessly for parking, as it is very limited outside of absurd $50-plus valet lots. So your best bet is to arrive on South Beach somewhat early and kill time by strolling around, having something to eat, or sipping a cocktail in a hotel bar or lounge. Another advantage of arriving a bit earlier than the crowds is that some clubs don't charge a cover before 11pm or midnight, which could save you a wad of cash over time.

Club hours are unreliable, and that includes the info on club websites. Call ahead to get the most up-to-date information possible: Things change very quickly around here, and a call in advance can help you make sure that the dance club you're planning to go to hasn't become a Lululemon.

Cover charges are haphazard, too. If you're not on the ubiquitous guest list (ask your concierge to put you on the list—he or she usually has the ability to do so, which won't help you with the wait to get in, but will eliminate the cover charge), you may have to fork over a ridiculous $20 or more to walk past the ropes. Don't fret, though. There are many clubs and bars that have no cover charge—they just make up for it by charging $30 for a martini!

Club Space ★ This now landmark, cavernous (30,000 square feet) downtown warehouse of a club is a mecca of EDM (electronic dance music). On Saturday and Sunday nights, the party usually extends to the next morning, sometimes as late as 11am. Known as the venue of choice for world-renowned DJs, Club Space sometimes charges ludicrous admission fees. *Note:* Club Space doesn't really get going until around 3am. 34 NE 11th St., Miami. clubspace.com. **786/357-6456.** Cover up to $50. Fri–Sat 11pm–11am; Sun 10pm–11am.

LIV ★★★   LIV at the Fontainebleau remains Miami Beach's A-list and still-hard-to-get-into dance club, where Kardashians hole up in one VIP area and the latest, hottest rapper and his or her squad are in another. Believe it or not, people do dance here, but with their phones in the air, hoping to catch a viral moment to share with the world. Go early for a better chance at entry before the throngs arrive. 4441 Collins Ave., South Beach. livnightclub.com. ✆ **305/538-2000.** Cover $60–$80. Thurs–Sun 11pm–5am.

Nikki Beach ★★   A little bit of St. Barth reaches South Beach in the form of this circa 1998 beach club that has since expanded to the actual St. Barth as well as 11 other locations worldwide. If you want a locals' scene, you won't find it here. The allure is mostly for day drinking, and dartying (day partying). The daybeds and sexy Tiki hut/Polynesian theme, makes for great Insta posts, as do the huge bottles of rosé for the rosé-all-day set. There's a dress code, unbelievably, since less is more here, that forbids hoodies, athletic wear, and whatever else they deem as unsightly. 101 Ocean Dr., South Beach. miami-beach.nikkibeach.com. ✆ **305/538-1111.** Mon–Thurs noon–6pm; Fri–Sat noon–8pm; Sun 11am–8pm.

The LGBTQIA+ Scene

Miami Beach used to be a capital of the gay circuit party scene, rivaling San Francisco, Palm Springs, and Sydney, Australia. Today, not so much. In fact, in 2023, gay-rights organization Equality Florida issued a travel advisory warning of the risks posed to the health, safety, and freedom of those considering short- or long-term travel, or relocation, to Florida. Though Miami-Dade has a gay-rights ordinance, controversial, oppressive laws like the "Don't Say Gay" laws of Governor Ron DeSantis are hurting the cause of equal protection under the law across Florida. The LGBTQIA+ community hangs on, though many have moved out of state or to northern parts like Fort Lauderdale and Orlando.

Still the LGBTQIA+ community finds ways to thrive, albeit, sadly, less loudly than they used to.

Palace ★★★   Just steps away from the men preening on the 12th Street Beach is this gay bar and drag show venue, which loudly and proudly plants its rainbow flag on the Ocean Drive sidewalk. Snag a table before a show (nightly 7–11:30pm, Tues–Thurs noon–3pm, Fri–Sun 11am and 2pm) if you want Tiffany Fantasia to get all up in your Cobb salad. Drag shows are 18 and over. 1200 Ocean Dr. palacesouthbeach.com. ✆ **305/531-7234.** Mon–Thurs 11am–1am; Fri–Sun 11am–2am.

A daytime drag show at the Palace.

R House Wynwood ★★★ So that whole drag dustup by Governor DeSantis started when someone said they saw children at the very popular drag brunch at this Wynwood hot spot. The drag brunch is for the 18 and over crowd only, as are the "drag extravaganzas" on Friday, Saturday, and Sunday nights, and they're mad fun. (So, somebody was lying.) Beyond politics, the queens who perform here are some of the city's sparkliest, sassiest, and savviest stars. The Saturday night shows have a Latin twist, with salsa music and dancing. Wednesday through Friday happy hours are also festive, with beat-the-clock specials from 4 to 7pm. As to be expected, they are VERY strict on ID because of their issues with the drag-obsessed Florida governor, who unintentionally, like the books he banned, made this place ESPECIALLY in demand and popular, so reserve your spot early. 2727 NW 2nd Ave., Wynwood. rhousewynwood.com. ✆ **305/576-0201.** Wed–Thurs 4–10pm; Fri 4pm–midnight; Sat 11:30am–midnight; Sun 11:30am–6pm.

Twist ★ One of the most popular (and only remaining) gay bars (and hideaways) on South Beach, Twist is an LGBTQIA+ landmark that has a casual, yet lively atmosphere. Founded in 1993, the place has seen it all, and despite its continued popularity, never charges a cover and welcomes all. 1057 Washington Ave., South Beach. twistsobe.com. ✆ **305/538-9478.** Daily 3pm–5am.

Live Music & Latin Clubs

Unfortunately, Miami's live music scene is not thriving. Local DJs are more admired than FL-based bands, thanks to the city's lauded dance-club scene. However, there are still several places to go, like the aforementioned **Bar Nancy** (p. 147), **Café La Trova** (p. 98), and **Gramp's** (p. 148). **The Corner** (p. 147) often features live music.

The **Fillmore Miami Beach at Jackie Gleason Theater,** located in South Beach at Washington Avenue and 17th Street (livenation.com; ✆ **305/673-7300**), may be a mouthful, but when it comes to live music, it truly rocks. In addition to its Hard Rock–meets–Miami Beach decor, complete with chandeliers, and an homage to the original legendary Fillmore in San Francisco, the classic 1950 theater, which was taken over by Live Nation, brings major talent to the beach, from Madonna and Elvis Costello to Busta Rhymes.

Considering that Hispanics make up a large part of Miami's population and that there's a huge influx of Spanish-speaking visitors, it's no surprise that there are some great Latin nightclubs in the city. Plus, with the meteoric rise of the international music scene based in Miami, many international stars come through the offices of MTV Latino, Univision, and a multitude of Latin TV studios based in Miami—and they're all looking for a good club scene on weekends. *Tip:* If you're feeling shy about hitting a Latin club because you have two left feet, take a lesson or two from **Luz Pinto** (latin-heat.com; $10/class). She teaches 7 days a week and you can take just one class and see improvement.

Ball and Chain ★★★ A historic Little Havana hot spot with a colorful past involving Jewish mafia, bootlegging, and gambling, it looks quite like Ricky Ricardo's Tropicana supper club, and is the best place in Little Havana for salsa dancing and live Cuban music. There's also decent food and very potent mojitos. No cover charge. 1513 SW 8th St. ballandchainmiami.com. ✆ **305/643-7829.** Mon 11am–midnight; Tues–Thurs, Sun 11am–1am; Fri–Sat 11am–3am.

The front of Mango's Tropical Café.

Mango's Tropical Café ★★   Claustrophobic types do not want to go near Mango's—ever. One of the most popular spots on Ocean Drive, this outdoor enclave shakes with the intensity of a Richter-busting earthquake. Mango's is *Cabaret,* Latin-style. Nightly live Brazilian and other Latin music, not to mention scantily clad male and female dancers, draws huge crowds in from the sidewalk. But pay attention to the music, if you can: Incognito international musicians often lose their anonymity and jam with the house band on stage. Salsa classes are given nightly at 7:30pm and include food and drink for $89 per person. Dinner shows are nightly at 8pm and cost $98 to $117 per person including $60 food and beverage credit. General reservations are accepted at no charge but have no views of the show. 900 Ocean Dr., South Beach. mangos.com. **305/673-4422.** Mon–Fri noon–5am; Sat–Sun 11am–5am.

6

THE KEYS & THE DRY TORTUGAS

by Lesley Abravanel

The drive from Miami to the Keys is a slow descent into an unusual but breathtaking American ecosystem: On either side, for miles ahead, are nothing but emerald waters. (On weekends, however, you will also see plenty of traffic in front of and in back of you.) Strung out across the Atlantic Ocean like loose strands of cultured pearls, more than 400 islands make up this 150-mile-long necklace.

Despite the usually calm landscape, these rocky islands can be treacherous, as tropical storms, hurricanes, and tornadoes are always possibilities. The exposed coast poses dangers to those on land as well as at sea.

When Spanish explorers Juan Ponce de León and Antonio de Herrera sailed amid these craggy, dangerous rocks in 1513, they and their men dubbed the string of islands "Los Martires" (The Martyrs) because they thought the rocks looked like men suffering in the surf. It wasn't until the early 1800s that rugged, ambitious pioneers, who amassed great wealth by salvaging cargo from ships sunk nearby, settled the larger islands (legend has it that these shipwrecks were sometimes caused by "wreckers," who removed navigational markers from the shallows to lure unwitting captains aground). At the height of the salvaging mania (in the 1830s), Key West had the highest per-capita income in the country.

However, wars, fires, hurricanes, mosquitoes, and the Depression took their toll on these resilient islands in the early part of the 20th century, causing wild swings between fortune and poverty. In 1938, the spectacular **Overseas Highway** (U.S. 1) was finally completed atop the ruins of Henry Flagler's railroad (which was destroyed by a hurricane in 1935, leaving only bits and pieces still found today), opening the region to tourists, who had never before been able to drive to this sea-bound destination. These days, the highway connects more than 30 of the populated islands in the Keys. The hundreds of small, undeveloped islands that surround these "mainline" Keys are known locally as the "backcountry" and are home to dozens of exotic animals and plants. Therein lie some of the most renowned outdoor sporting opportunities, from bonefishing to spearfishing and—at appropriate times of the year—diving for lobsters and stone crabs. To get to the backcountry, you must take to the water—a vital part of any trip to the Keys. Whether you fish, snorkel, dive, or cruise, include some time on a boat in your itinerary; otherwise, you haven't truly seen the Keys.

Of course, people go to the Keys for the peaceful waters and year-round warmth, but the sea and the teeming life beneath and around it are the main attractions here: Countless species of brilliantly colored fish can be found swimming above the ocean's floor, and you'll discover a stunning abundance of tropical and exotic plants, birds, and reptiles.

The warm, shallow waters (deeper and rougher on the eastern/Atlantic side of the Keys) nurture living coral that supports a complex, delicate ecosystem of plants and animals—sponges, anemones, jellyfish, crabs, rays, sharks, turtles, snails, lobsters, and thousands of types of fish. This vibrant underwater habitat

FACING PAGE: **A snorkeler swims past the Christ of the Abyss statue in John Pennekamp Coral Reef State Park.**

Anne's Beach **9**
Crane Point Hammock **5**
Dolphin Research Center **7**
Florida Keys Aquarium Encounters **6**
Florida Keys Wild Bird Center **15**
History of Diving Museum **13**
Indian Key Historic Park **12**
John Pennekamp Coral Reef State Park **16**

Lignumvitae Key State Park **11**
Long Key State Recreation Area **8**
Pigeon Key **2**
Robbie's Pier **10**
Seven-Mile Bridge **1**
Sombrero Beach **4**
Theater of the Sea **14**
Turtle Hospital **3**

The Florida Keys

thrives on one of the few living tropical reefs on the entire North American continent. As a result, anglers, divers, snorkelers, and watersports enthusiasts of all kinds come to explore.

Heavy traffic has taken its toll on this fragile eco-scape, but conservation efforts are underway (traffic laws are strictly enforced on Deer Key, for example, due to deer crossings that have been contained, thanks to newly installed fences). In fact, environmental efforts in the Keys exceed those in many other high-traffic visitor destinations.

Although the atmosphere throughout the Keys is that of a laid-back beach town, don't expect many impressive beaches. Nice beaches are mostly found in a few private resorts, though there are some small, sandy strips in John Pennekamp Coral Reef State Park, Bahia Honda State Park, and Key West. One great exception is **Sombrero Beach,** in Marathon (p. 160), which is well maintained by Monroe County and is larger and considerably nicer than other beaches in the Keys.

The Keys are divided into three sections, both geographically and in this chapter. The Upper and Middle Keys are closest to the Florida mainland, so they are popular with weekend warriors who come by boat or car to fish or relax in such towns as Key Largo, Islamorada, and Marathon. Farther on, just beyond the impressive Seven Mile Bridge (which actually measures 6½ miles), are the Lower Keys, a small, unspoiled swath of islands teeming with wildlife. Here, in the protected regions of the Lower Keys, is where you're most likely to catch sight of the area's many endangered animals—with patience, you may spot the rare eagle, egret, or Key deer. You should also keep an eye out for alligators, turtles, rabbits, and a huge variety of birds.

Key West, the most renowned—and last—island in the Lower Keys, is the southernmost point in the continental United States (made famous by Ernest

Hemingway). This tiny island is the most popular destination in the Florida Keys, overrun with cruise ship passengers and day-trippers, as well as franchises and tacky T-shirt shops. More than five million visitors pass through it each year. Still, this "Conch Republic" (pronounced "Conk") has a tight-knit community of permanent residents who cling fiercely to their live-and-let-live attitude—an atmosphere that has made Key West famously popular with painters, writers, and free spirits, despite the recent influx of money-hungry developers.

The last section in this chapter is devoted to the Dry Tortugas, a national park located 68 nautical miles from Key West.

Exploring the Keys by Car

After you've left the Florida Turnpike and landed on U.S. 1, which is also known as the Overseas Highway (see "Getting There" under "Essentials," below), you'll have no trouble negotiating these narrow islands, as only one main road connects the Keys. The scenic, lazy drive from Miami can be very enjoyable if you have the patience to linger and explore the diverse towns and islands along the way. We recommend allowing at least 2 days to work your way down to Key West, and 3 or more days once there.

Encouraging you to slow down is the 90-mile **Florida Keys Overseas Heritage Trail,** a scenic, multiuse paved trail for bikers, hikers, runners, fishermen, and sightseers running parallel to the Overseas Highway and extending from Key Largo all the way down to Key West.

Most of U.S. 1 is a narrow two-lane highway, with some wider passing zones along the way. The speed limit is usually 55 mph (35–45 mph on Big Pine Key and in some commercial areas). There has been talk of expanding the highway, but

> ### Alabama Jack's: Card Sound's Favorite Dive
>
> On its own, there's not much to the waterfront shack that is **Alabama Jack's**, 58000 Card Sound Rd., Key Largo (no phone or website). The bar is a big beer spot for bikers, and the restaurant specializes in inconsistent bar fare and good conch fritters. But this quintessential Old Floridian dive, in a historic fishing village called Card Sound between Homestead and Key Largo, is a colorful "must" on the drive south, especially on Sunday, when bikers mix with barflies, anglers, line dancers, and Southern belles in all their fabulous frills. There's live country music, so pull up a bar stool, order a cold one, and take in the sights—in the bay and at the bar. The views of the mangroves are spectacular. To get here, pick up Card Sound Road (the old Rte. 1) a few miles after you pass Homestead, heading toward Key Largo. Alabama Jack's is on the right side and can't be missed. Open daily from 11am to 5pm.

plans have not been finalized. Even on the narrow road, you can usually get from downtown Miami to Key Largo in just over an hour. If you're determined to drive straight through to Key West, allow at least 3½ hours. Weekend travel is another matter entirely: When the roads are jammed with travelers from the mainland, the trip can take upwards of 5 to 6 hours (when there's an accident, traffic is at an absolute standstill). We *strongly* urge you to avoid driving anywhere in the Keys on Friday afternoon or Sunday evening.

Most addresses in the Keys (except in Key West and parts of Marathon) are delineated by **mile markers** (MM), small green signs on the roadside that announce the distance from Key West. The markers start at no. 127, just south of the Florida mainland. The zero marker is in Key West, at the corner of Whitehead and Fleming streets. Addresses in this chapter are accompanied by a mile marker (MM) designation when appropriate.

THE UPPER & MIDDLE KEYS

58 miles SW of Miami

The Upper Keys are a popular year-round refuge for South Floridians, who take advantage of the islands' proximity to the mainland. This is the fishing and diving capital of America, and the swarms of outfitters and billboards never let you forget it.

Key Largo, once called Rock Harbor but renamed to capitalize on the success of the 1948 Humphrey Bogart film (which wasn't filmed here), is the largest Key and is more developed than its neighbors to the south. Dozens of chain hotels, restaurants, and tourist information centers service the water enthusiasts who come to explore the nation's first underwater state park, **John Pennekamp Coral Reef State Park,** and its adjacent marine sanctuary. **Islamorada,** the unofficial capital of the Upper Keys, has the area's best atmosphere, food, fishing, entertainment, and lodging. It's an unofficial "party capital" for mainlanders seeking a quick tropical excursion. Here (Islamorada is actually composed of four islands), nature lovers can enjoy walking trails, historic exploration, and big-purse fishing tournaments. For a more tranquil, less party-hearty experience, other Keys besides Key West and Islamorada are better choices. **Marathon,** smack in the middle, is known as the heart of the Keys and is one of the most populated. But don't judge it by its main drag. To appreciate Marathon, you need to go beyond U.S. 1. It is part fishing village, part tourist center, part nature preserve. This area's highly developed infrastructure includes resort hotels, a commercial airport, and a highway that expands to four lanes.

Essentials

GETTING THERE From Miami International Airport (there is also an airport in Marathon), take Le Jeune Road (NW 42nd Ave.) to Route 836 West. Follow signs to the Florida Turnpike South, about 7 miles. The turnpike extension connects with U.S. 1 in Florida City. Continue south on U.S. 1. For a scenic option, take Card Sound Road, south of Florida City, a backcountry drive that reconnects with U.S. 1 in upper Key Largo. The view from Card Sound Bridge is spectacular and well worth the $1 toll.

If you're coming from Florida's west coast, take Alligator Alley to the Miami exit and then turn south onto the turnpike extension. The turnpike ends in Florida City, at which time you will be dumped directly onto the two-lane U.S. 1, which leads to the Keys. Have around $25 for the tolls, which are either in cash or toll by plate. If you take U.S. 1 straight down and bypass the turnpike, it's free, but a lot longer.

Greyhound (greyhound.com; © **800/231-2222**) has two buses leaving Miami for Key West every day, with stops in Key Largo, Tavernier, Islamorada, Marathon, Big Pine Key, Cudjoe Key, Sugarloaf, and Big Coppit on the way south. Prices range from $26 to $30 one-way and $52 to $60 round-trip; the trip takes from 1 hour and 40 minutes to 4 hours and 40 minutes, depending on how far south you're going. Seats fill quickly in season, so come early. It's first-come, first-served.

VISITOR INFORMATION Make sure you get your information from an official not-for-profit center. The **Key Largo Chamber of Commerce,** U.S. 1 at MM 106, Key Largo (keylargochamber.org; © **800/822-1088** or 305/451-1414; daily 9am–6pm), gives good advice and is headquartered in a handsome clapboard house. It operates as an information clearinghouse for all of the Keys.

The **Islamorada Chamber of Commerce,** housed in a little red caboose, U.S. 1 at MM 82.5 (islamoradachamber.com; © **800/322-5397** or 305/664-4503), offers maps and literature on the Upper Keys.

You can't miss the big, blue visitor center at MM 53.5, **Greater Marathon Chamber of Commerce,** 12222 Overseas Hwy., Marathon, (floridakeysmarathon.com; © **305/743-5417**). Here you can receive free info on local events, festivals, attractions, dining, and lodging.

On your smartphone, check out the **Florida Keys & Key West Travel App,** available for all mobile devices. With it, users can access information on weather, events, venues, and maps, as well as GPS and audio driving tours. Best of all, the app is free.

Outdoor Sights & Activities

Anne's Beach (MM 73.5, on Lower Matecumbe Key, at the southwest end of Islamorada) is more picnic spot than full-fledged beach, but die-hard tanners congregate on this lovely, tiny strip of coarse sand that was damaged beyond recognition by storms in 1998 and then again in 2019 by Hurricane Irma. The place has

Sombrero Beach is one of the best stretches of sand in the Keys.

since been spruced up a bit and features a 1,300-foot boardwalk that winds through mangroves, six pavilions with picnic tables, and clean(ish) restrooms. Windsurfers like this spot, as do people with dogs, who sometimes don't like to clean up after them. The beach was named for local environmentalist Anne Eaton upon her death in 1992.

A better choice for real beaching is **Sombrero Beach** ★★, in Marathon, at the end of Sombrero Beach Road (near MM 50). This wide swath of uncluttered beachfront boasts more than 90 feet of sand and is dotted with palms, Australian pines, and royal poincianas, as well as with grills, picnic tables, volleyball courts, clean restrooms, and tiki huts for relaxing in the shade. It's also a popular nesting spot for turtles that lay their eggs at night. The beach was redeveloped in recent years to make it fully accessible.

If you're interested in seeing the Keys in their natural, pre–modern development state, you must venture off the highway and take to the water. Two backcountry islands that offer a glimpse of the "real" Keys are **Indian Key** and **Lignumvitae Key Botanical State Park** ★★★. Visitors come here to relax and enjoy the islands' colorful birds and lush hammocks (elevated pieces of land above a marsh).

Named for the lignum vitae ("wood of life") trees found there, Lignumvitae Key supports a virgin tropical forest, the kind that once thrived on most of the Upper Keys. Human settlers imported "exotic" plants and animals, irrevocably changing the botanical makeup of many backcountry islands and threatening much of the indigenous wildlife. Over the past 25 years, however, the Florida

Department of Natural Resources has successfully removed most of the exotic vegetation from this key, leaving the 280-acre site much as it existed in the 18th century. The island also holds the **Matheson House,** a historic structure built in 1919 that has survived numerous hurricanes. You can go inside, but it's interesting only if you appreciate the coral rock of which the house is made. It's a museum dedicated to the history, nature, and topography of the area. More appealing are the **Botanical Gardens,** which surround the house and are a state preserve. Lignumvitae Key has a visitor center at MM 88.5 (floridastateparks.org/LignumvitaeKey; ⓒ **305/664-2540;** $2.50 entry, plus $2 for tours; Thurs–Mon 8am–4pm).

Indian Key Historic State Park, a much smaller island on the Atlantic side of Islamorada, was occupied by Native Americans for thousands of years before European settlers arrived. The 10-acre historic site was also the original seat of Dade County before the Civil War. You can see the ruins of the previous settlement and tour the lush grounds on well-marked trails (off Indian Key Fill, Overseas Hwy., MM 79). As of 2021, the park was only accessible by kayak launch, as the boat ramp was closed due to storm damage. For more info on Indian Key, check out floridastateparks.org/IndianKey.

If you want to see both islands, plan to spend at least half a day. You can rent your own skiff, powerboat, paddleboard, or kayak from **Robbie's of Islamorada ★★**, U.S. 1 at MM 77.5 (on the bay side; robbies.com; ⓒ **305/664-9814**), on Islamorada. Robbie's also does fishing trips and jet-ski and eco-tours through passages among the seagrass beds that rim the many protected shallow bays. You'll get to cruise among the hundreds of small, uninhabited mangrove and hardwood hammock islands, which host an amazing variety of wildlife and create the island network of the Florida Bay. *Note:* See p. 29 for info on the necessary educational courses required by the state of Florida for boat rentals.

Crane Point Hammock Museum & Nature Trails ★★

Crane Point Hammock is a little-known but worthwhile stop, especially for those interested in the rich botanical and archaeological history of the Keys. This privately owned, 64-acre nature area is considered one of the most important historic sites in the Keys. It contains what is probably the last virgin thatch-palm hammock (forests on higher ground in wetlands) in North America, as well as a rainforest exhibit and an archaeological site with prehistoric Indian and Bahamian artifacts. It's home to Bahamian-style Adderly House, the oldest house in the Keys outside of Key West.

The hammock's impressive nature museum has simple, informative displays of the Keys' wildlife, including a walk-through replica of a coral-reef cave and life-size dioramas with tropical birds and Key deer. There's also a 600-year-old dugout canoe and remnants of pirate ships. Kids can make art projects, see 6-foot-long iguanas, go birding, climb through a scaled-down pirate ship, and touch a variety of indigenous aquatic and landlubber creatures. Also included in your admission fee? A fish pedicure. Yup. You dip your feet into a tidal pool and let the Gambusia fish nibble on your barking dogs.

5550 Overseas Hwy. (MM 50), Marathon. cranepoint.net. ⓒ **305/743-9100.** Admission $14.95 adults, $12.95 seniors, $9.95 children 5–13; free for kids 4 and under. Mon–Sat 9am–5pm; Sun noon–5pm.

History of Diving Museum ★★

For over 4,000 years, human beings have been trying to explore the undersea world. This passion project, created by Drs. Joe and Sally Bauer, unpacks that history, with interactive exhibits, and artifacts from the Bauer's vast collection of hand-operated air pumps, armored suits, helmets, submarines, and more. One especially compelling exhibit looks at the development of underwater photography from 1856 through today. Another shows the wacky homemade diving helmets that were inspired by a 1932 issue of the magazine *Popular Mechanics* which featured an article on the how-to's of creating this underwater headgear (one was crafted from a chamber pot!). It will take about an hour to see all the exhibits here.

82990 Overseas Hwy., Islamorada. divingmuseum.org. **305/664-7537.** Admission $15 adults, $13 seniors, $7 children. Daily 10am–5pm.

Pigeon Key ★★ At the curve of the old bridge on Pigeon Key is an intriguing historic site that has been under renovation for the last 30 years (no joke). This 5-acre island once served as the camp for the crew that built the old railway in the early 20th century, and later served as housing for the bridge builders. From here, the vista includes the vestiges of Henry Flagler's old Seven Mile Bridge and the one on which traffic presently soars, as well as many old wooden cottages and a tranquil stretch of lush foliage and sea. If you miss the shuttle tour from the Pigeon Key visitor center or would rather walk or bike to the site, it's about 2½ miles. Either way, you may want to bring a picnic to enjoy after a brief self-guided walking tour and a museum visit to what has become an homage to Flagler's railroad, featuring artifacts and photographs of the old bridge. An informative 28-minute video of the island's history is shown every hour starting at 10am, and there are daily tours at 10and 11:30am, and 1 and 2:30pm. The train departs from the Pigeon Key gift shop. When the 1pm tour ends, you can help feed the sharks in the saltwater pool. Parking is available at the Knight's Key end of the bridge, at MM 48, or at the visitor center at MM 47, on the ocean side.

East end of the Seven Mile Bridge near MM 47, 1090 Overseas Hwy., Marathon. pigeonkey.net. **305/743-5999.** Admission $25 adults, $23 veterans with ID, $20 children 12 and under. Prices include shuttle transportation from the visitor center. Daily 9am–4pm.

Seven Mile Bridge ★★★ A stop at the Seven Mile Bridge is a rewarding and relaxing break on the drive south. Built alongside the ruins of oil magnate Henry Flagler's incredible Overseas Railroad, the "new" bridge (btw. MMs 40 and 47) is considered an architectural feat. The apex of the wide-arched span, completed in 1985 at a cost of more than $45 million, is the highest point in the Keys. The new bridge and its now-defunct neighbor provide excellent vantage points from which to view the stunning waters of the Keys. In the daytime, you may want to walk, jog, or bike along the 4-mile stretch of old bridge. The Old Seven Mile Bridge (the original Knights Key Bridge) to Pigeon Key is listed on the National Register of Historic Places. Local anglers love it here, catching barracuda, yellowtail, and dolphin (the fish, not the mammal) on what is known as "the longest fishing pier in the world." Parking is available on both sides of the bridge.

Btw. MMs 40 and 47 on U.S. 1. **305/289-0025.**

Visiting with Animals

Dolphin Research Center ★★★ Of the several such centers in the continental United States (all located in the Keys), the Dolphin Research Center is a nonprofit facility and one of the most organized and informative. Although some people argue that training dolphins is cruel and selfish, this is one of the most respected of the institutions that study and protect the mammals, which have

The new Seven Mile Bridge consists of 440 precast, prestressed concrete spans. At its side, the old bridge is used by cyclists, pedestrians, and fishermen.

arrived here from other facilities, or were rescued, rehabbed, and deemed unreleasable back into the wild by the government. Trainers at the center will also tell you that the dolphins need stimulation and enjoy human contact. They certainly seem to. They nuzzle and seem to smile and kiss the people who get to interact with them in daily interactive programs. The "family" of 27 dolphins swims in a 90,000-square-foot natural saltwater pool carved out of the shoreline. If you can't get into an interactive program, you can watch the sessions that cover a variety of topics from fun facts about dolphins, to therapeutic qualities of dolphins, to research projects in progress. There are also sea lions (which swim with the dolphins), exotic birds, iguanas, and tortoises here. Because the Dolphin Encounter swimming program is the most popular, advance reservations are required and can be made up to 6 months in advance. The cost is $199 to $225 per person, including entrance fees. If you're not brave enough to swim with the dolphins or if you have a child under age 5 (not permitted to swim with dolphins), try the Meet a Dolphin program, in which participants stand on a submerged platform from which they can "meet and greet" the critters. A participating adult must hold children younger than 5. Cost for this program is $70 per person (free for children 4 and under).

Readers of a certain age will remember that this was the place where the movie *Flipper* was filmed. The dolphin who played the lead in that film was named Mitzi. She's buried here.

Note: Swimming with dolphins has both its critics and its supporters. You may want to visit the Whale and Dolphin Conservation Society's website at **www.wdcs.org**.

U.S. 1 at MM 59 (on the bay side), Marathon. dolphins.org. © **305/289-1121**. Admission $35 adults, $20 military and veterans with ID, $25 children 4–12. Prices are cheaper online. Daily 9am–4:30pm. Narrated behavior sessions with bottlenose dolphins and sea lions and educational presentations approximately every half-hour.

Florida Keys Aquarium Encounters ★★
An immersive aquarium, this attraction is entirely outdoors (there are tiki huts for shade where needed) and

includes 20-minute-long biologist-led educational tours of the facility at 10 minutes before each hour. In addition, the staff's biologists conduct 15-minute-long introductions to different animals around the compound throughout the day (snapping turtles, sharks, and more), and oversee touch tanks with all manner of critters in them. Those who want to (sorry) dive deeper can sign up for a feeding encounter with nurse sharks, a guided snorkeling or scuba diving trip to their coral reef or lagoon, and more. There's lots to see and do here, so allot a full 2 hours for a visit (more if you do an encounter).

11710 Overseas Hwy., Marathon. floridakeysaquariumencounters.com. 305/407-3262. Base ticket $30 ages 13 and up, $20 ages 4–12. Daily 9am–5pm.

Florida Keys Wild Bird Center ★★
Wander through lush canopies of mangroves on wooden walkways to see some of the Keys' most famous residents—native birds, including broad-winged hawks, great blue and white herons, roseate spoonbills, cattle egrets, and pelicans at the Lara Quinn Wild Bird Sanctuary. This not-for-profit center also operates as a bird hospital for those that have been injured by accident or disease. In 2002, the World Parrot Mission was established here, focusing on caring for parrots and educating the public about the birds. Visit at feeding time, usually about 3:30pm, when you can watch the staff feed the hundreds of hungry birds.

U.S. 1 at MM 93.6 (bay side), Tavernier. keepthemflying.org. 305/852-4486. Donations suggested. Daily 7am–sunset.

Robbie's Pier ★★★
One of the best and definitely one of the cheapest attractions in the Upper Keys at famed Robbie's Pier are fierce steely tarpons, a

Here you go, little fishy! Feeding the tarpon at Robbie's Pier.

prized catch for the backcountry anglers who have been gathering for the past 20 years. You may recognize these prehistoric-looking giants that grow up to 200 pounds; many are displayed as trophies and mounted on local restaurant walls. To see them live, head to Robbie's Pier, where tens and sometimes hundreds of these behemoths circle the shallow waters waiting for you to feed them. You can also hop on a fishing charter, rent a jet ski or kayak, or take a guided tour on a variety of watercraft. Robbie's also has an open-air shopping village and restaurant.

U.S. 1 at MM 77.5, Islamorada. robbies.com. ✆ **305/664-9814.** Admission to see the tarpon $2.50. Bucket of fish to feed them $5. Daily 8am–5pm. Make a hard-right U-turn off the highway, then it's a short drive before you'll see a HUNGRY TARPON restaurant sign. Robbie's driveway is just before that.

Theater of the Sea ★ Established in 1946, the Theater of the Sea is one of the world's oldest marine zoos. But while the Dolphin Research Center is a legitimate, scientific establishment, Theater of the Sea is more like a theme-park attraction. Still, the park's dolphin and sea lion shows are entertaining, especially for children. Theater of the Sea also permits visitors to swim with sea lions, dolphins, and sting rays; get up close to alligators and parrots; and to paint with sea lions and dolphins. (Children 4 and under cannot participate.) The animals seem well taken care of and the place is well maintained, but there are serious ethical issues involved with keeping dolphins in captivity (see p. 162).

U.S. 1 at MM 84.5, Islamorada. theaterofthesea.com. ✆ **305/664-2431.** Admission $47.95 adults, $29.95 children 3–10. Dolphin swim $155–$1,995; sea lion swim from $165. Reservations are a must. Daily 9:30am–5pm (ticket office closes at 4pm).

Turtle Hospital ★★★ At this crucial rehab center, visitors learn about turtles' life cycles and the challenges that confront them. They also see these shelled critters being treated for various issues. What makes the visitor experience so involving are the passionate, knowledgeable guides who lead these experiences, and make it clear that the entry fee will do a lot of good.

2396 Overseas Hwy., Marathon. TurtleHospital.org. No phone. Admission $35 adults, $17.50 children 3-12. Daily 9am–6pm by 90-min. guided tour (every half-hour from 9am–4pm).

Two Exceptional State Parks

One of the best places to discover the diverse ecosystem of the Upper Keys is its most famous park, **John Pennekamp Coral Reef State Park ★★★**, located on U.S. 1 at MM 102.5, in Key Largo (pennekamppark.com; ✆ **305/451-6300**). Named for a former *Miami Herald* editor and conservationist, the 188-square-mile park, which will celebrate its 65th anniversary in 2025, is the nation's first undersea preserve: It's a sanctuary for part of the only living coral reef in the continental United States.

The park extends 3 miles into the Atlantic Ocean and is approximately 25 miles in length. Because the water is extremely shallow, the 40 species of coral and more than 650 species of fish here are accessible to divers, snorkelers, and glass-bottom-boat passengers. To experience this park, visitors must get in the water—you can't see the reef from the shore. Your first stop should be the visitor center, which has a mammoth 30,000-gallon saltwater aquarium that re-creates a reef ecosystem. At the adjacent dive shop, you can rent snorkeling and diving equipment and join one of the boat trips that depart for the reef throughout the day. Visitors can also rent motorboats, sailboats, sailboards, and canoes. The 2½-hour glass-bottom-boat tour is the best way to see the coral reefs if you don't want to get wet. Watch for the lobsters and other sea life residing in the fairly shallow ridge walls beneath the coastal waters. ***Remember:*** These are protected waters, so you can't remove anything from them.

Canoeing around the park's narrow mangrove channels and tidal creeks is also popular. You can go on your own in a rented canoe or, in winter, sign up for a tour led by a local naturalist. Hikers have two short trails from which to choose: a boardwalk through the mangroves, and a dirt trail through a tropical hardwood hammock. Ranger-led walks are possible for groups if booked in advance.

Park admission is $8 per vehicle of two to eight passengers plus a 50¢ Monroe County surcharge per person. If you have more than eight in the car, it's $2.50 per person over the eight, $4.50 for a single driver, $2.50 for pedestrians and bicyclists. On busy weekends, there's often a line of cars waiting to get into the park. On your way in, ask the ranger for a map. Glass-bottom-boat tours cost $50 for adults and $26 for children ages 4 to 11. Tours depart three times daily, at 9:15am, 12:15pm, and 3:15pm. Snorkeling tours depart four times daily and last approximately 2½ hours with an hour and a half underwater and are $49.95 for adults and $45.95 for children 17 and under; masks, fins, and snorkels cost $25 and the snorkel is yours to keep. Two-tank scuba tours are offered twice daily at 9am and 1:30pm and cost $105 per person including tanks and weights.

Canoes rent for $35 per hour; kayaks are $30 per hour for a single, $35 per hour for a double; and paddleboards $35 per hour. For experienced boaters only, four different sizes of reef boats (powerboats) rent for $400 for four hours to $500 for a full day. Reservations are recommended and you need proof of proficiency to

A surgeon fish forages for food in John Pennekamp Coral Reef State Park. See the park's famous statue on p. 154.

rent a boat (see p. 29). Also see below for more options on diving, fishing, and snorkeling off these reefs.

Long Key State Recreation Area ★★★, U.S. 1 at MM 68, Long Key (floridastateparks.org; © **305/664-4815**), is one of the best places in the Middle Keys for hiking, camping, snorkeling, and canoeing. This 965-acre site is situated atop the remains of an ancient coral reef. At the entrance gate, ask for a free flyer describing the local trails and wildlife.

Three nature trails can be explored via foot or canoe. The **Golden Orb Trail** is a 40-minute walk through mostly plants; the **Layton Trail** is a 15-minute walk along the bay; and the **Long Key Canoe Trail** glides along a shallow-water lagoon. The excellent 1.5-mile canoe trail is short and sweet, allowing visitors to loop around the mangroves in about an hour. Long Key is also a top spot to stop for a picnic. Long Key sustained significant damage from Hurricane Irma in 2017, and efforts are continuing to restore the full-facility, oceanfront campsites. Although construction to rebuild these sites is in progress, the park currently offers hike-in, tent-only campsites.

The swimming and saltwater fishing (license required) are top-notch here, as is the snorkeling, which is shallow and on the shoreline of the Atlantic. For novices, educational programs on the aforementioned are available, too.

Railroad builder Henry Flagler created the Long Key Fishing Club here in 1906, popular among the Gilded Age's rich and famous including U.S. presidents and author Zane Grey, and the waters surrounding the park are still popular with game fishers. The fishing club was destroyed by a hurricane in 1935 and never rebuilt. In summer, sea turtles lumber onto the protected coast to lay their eggs. Educational programs are available to view this phenomenon.

Admission is $5 per car of two to eight people plus 50¢ per person, $4.50 for a single-occupant vehicle, $2.50 per pedestrian or bicyclist, The recreation area is open daily from 8am to sunset. At the time of this writing, kayak rentals were temporarily suspended.

Watersports from A to Z

There are hundreds of outfitters in the Keys who will arrange all kinds of water activities, from cave dives to parasailing.

BOATING In addition to the rental shops in the state parks, and such peer-to-peer online resources as **GetMyBoat.com** and **BoatSetter.com,** you'll find dozens of outfitters along U.S. 1 offering a range of runabouts and skiffs for boaters of any experience level. **Captain Pip's,** U.S. 1 at MM 47.5, Marathon (captainpips.com; © **800/707-1692** or 305/743-4403), is a top operator. They charge $269 to $429 per day. Overnight accommodations ($129–$269) are available at their marina and include a 10% discount on boat rentals. Rooms are Key West comfortable and recently revamped with new linens, hardwood floors, pine paneling, and in some, full kitchens.

Robbie's Rent-a-Boat, U.S. 1 at MM 77.5, Islamorada (robbies.com; © **305/664-9814**), is another reliable source. It rents 16- to 24-foot boats for $195 to $325 for a half-day and $275 to $385 for a full day.

If you want to see the Keys by water without captaining your own rig, consider **Dolphin Bay Watersports,** 13201 Overseas Hwy (behind the Holiday Inn Express), Marathon (dolphinbaywatersports.com; © **305/902-8655**), whose 1-hour jet-ski tours will take you on a guided tour of the area and its marine life. Tours are $109 per jet ski and carry up to three to four passengers, including children.

CANOEING, KAYAKING & PADDLEBOARDING We can think of no better way to explore the uninhabited backcountry on the Gulf side of the Keys than by kayak, paddleboard, or canoe, as you can reach places that big boats just can't get to. Manatees will sometimes cuddle up to kayaks, thinking them to be another friendly species.

Many area hotels rent kayaks and canoes to guests, as does **Florida Bay Outfitters,** U.S. 1 at MM 104, Key Largo (FloridaBayOutfitters.com; © **305/451-3018**), which rents its vessels for use in and around John Pennekamp Coral Reef State Park for $40 to $55 for a half-day, $55 to $70 for a full day. **Florida Keys Kayak and Sail,** U.S. 1 at MM 75.5, Islamorada (KayakTheFloridaKeys.com; © **305/664-4878**), the Kayak Shack at Robbie's Pier, offers kayak, paddleboard, and jet-ski backcountry tours, botanical-preserve tours of Lignumvitae Key, historic-site tours of Indian Key, and sunset tours through the mangrove tunnels and saltwater flats. Tour prices and times vary, so consult their website.

Big Pine Kayak Adventures, operating out of the Old Wooden Bridge Fishing Camp, 1791 Bogie Dr., MM 30, Big Pine Key (keyskayaktours.com; © **305/872-2241**), rents kayaks for self-guided tours, and will even ferry you and your kayak on a shallow-water powerboat into the backcountry. Or, take a guided tour for $150 per person for 4 hours.

Nature lovers can slip through the silent backcountry waters off Key West and the Lower Keys in a kayak, discovering the flora and fauna that make up the unique Keys ecosystem, on **Blue Planet Kayak Tours'** (blue-planet-kayak.com; © **305/809-8110**) 2½- to 3-hour, $60 starlight tour. All excursions are led by an environmental scientist. No previous kayaking experience necessary.

FISHING **Robbie's Partyboats & Charters,** U.S. 1 at MM 77.5, Islamorada (robbies.com; © **305/664-8070** or 664-8498), located at Robbie's Marina on Lower Matecumbe Key, offers day and night deep-sea and reef fishing trips aboard a 65-foot party boat. Big-game fishing charters are also available, and "splits" are

Paddleboarding is growing in popularity in the Keys.

A couple snorkels in the waters off Islamorada.

arranged for solo fishers. Party-boat fishing costs about $100 for a half-day morning tour or 5-hour night trip. A 4-hour afternoon trip is $75 per person. Charters run about $365 for three-quarters of a day, $450 for a full day.

Bud n' Mary's Fishing Marina, U.S. 1 at MM 79.8, Islamorada (budmarys.com; *©* **800/742-7945** or 305/664-2461), one of the largest marinas between Miami and Key West, is packed with sailors offering backcountry fishing charters. This is the place to go if you want to stalk tarpon, bonefish, and snapper. If the seas are not too rough, deep-sea and coral fishing trips can also be arranged. Sportfishing charters range from $1,000 to $1,200 for a half-day, to $1,600 to $2,500 for a full day; backcountry fishing trips are much cheaper, starting at $600 for a half-day to $950 for a full day based on two people, though some can take more.

SCUBA DIVING & SNORKELING Just 6 miles off Key Largo is a U.S. Navy Landing Ship Dock, the latest artificial wreck site to hit the Keys—or, rather, to be submerged 130 feet *below* the Keys.

The **Florida Keys Dive Center,** 840001 Overseas Hwy., Islamorada (floridakeysdivecenter.com; *©* **305/852-4599**), takes snorkelers and divers to the reefs of John Pennekamp Coral Reef State Park and environs every day. PADI (Professional Association of Diving Instructors) training courses are available for the uninitiated. Cost is $60 per person to snorkel including gear, and $105 per person to dive (plus an extra $25 if you need to rent all the gear).

Key Largo Scuba Diving, 102900 Overseas Hwy., Key Largo (keylargoscubadiving.com; *©* **305/391-4040**), offers over 100 reef and wreck dives and snorkeling excursions to places such as the famous Christ of the Abyss statue, the USS *Spiegel Grove,* and more. Snorkeling trips start at $70, and dive trips start at $100.

Where to Stay

Because the real beauty of the Keys lies mostly beyond the highways, there is no better way to see this area than by boat. So why not stay in a floating hotel? If

> **Price Categories**
>
> We're listing double room rates only. Please assume that suites will be pricier. Also note that some hotels fall into one price range in high season and a different one in low, hence the hybrid categories below.
> **Inexpensive:** $199 and under
> **Moderate:** $200–$325
> **Expensive:** $326 and up

you're traveling with a group, houseboats are not only fun, they can be super economical. You'll find plenty to rent on both Vrbo or Airbnb, but if you go with a full-service rental you'll have someone to turn to if there are problems. We recommend **KeySea Houseboats**, in Key Largo (KeyseaHouseboats.com; *C* **305/394-3096**), which has slightly higher rates than you might find online ($970 for 2 nights to $2,485 for 7 nights), but that's for personalized service and a boat that can sleep up to six people and includes kayak rental, snorkel equipment, fishing equipment, and your first fill-up of ice. All KeySea boats have flat-screen TVs, linens, bath amenities, touchscreen GPS, and propane barbecue grill.

Or you could stay *below* the waves at **Jules Undersea Lodge ★★★** (51 Shoreland Dr., Key Largo; jul.com; *C* **305/451-2353**). Generally booked by honeymooners, and other celebrating events that make the high rates here palatable (they're $1,350–$1,575 per person), this two-guest-room hotel was once an underwater research station. It rests on pillars on the ocean floor, and now operates as a two-room hotel. To get inside, guests scuba dive 21 feet under the structure and pop up into the unit through a 4×6-foot "moon pool" that gurgles soothingly all night long. Food, drink, and unlimited diving is part of the nightly rate here.

For our more traditional recommendations, see below.

EXPENSIVE

Baker's Cay Resort Key Largo, Curio Collection by Hilton ★★★

A short drive from Miami, this property is very peaceful, and actually quite beautiful, which you'd never guess from its motel-esque facade. Almost all rooms face the ocean, and the decor pulls from beachy places around the globe, with *ikat* (Indonesian) and Mediterranean-style patterned pillows, dark wood floors, conch-shaped lamps, and Turkish tiling in the bathrooms. The resort has two pools (one adults only), but most guests head instead to the hotel's private, white-sand beach for watersports, nature trails, and a tiki bar. The dining and drinking options are so good you won't really need to leave. **Calusa** features a contemporary American menu with Creole-Caribbean accents, and **DryRocks** is the hopping bar with live music, fire pits, and an impressive selection of tequila. Resort fee gets you use of bikes, paddleboards, fishing rods with bait, and assorted fun events, such as the one we ran into during our stay—a huge foam party for kids and the young at heart.

97000 S. Overseas Hwy., Key Largo. hilton.com. *C* **305/852-5553.** 200 units. $340–$683 double, plus $49 resort fee. Pet fee $75. **Amenities:** 2 restaurants; 3 bars; children's activities; fitness center; 2 outdoor pools; watersports equipment/rentals; free Wi-Fi.

The Moorings Village ★★★

You can stay on this 18-acre resort, a former coconut plantation with only eight guesthouses, without ever running into another soul. There isn't even maid service unless you request it—that's the level of serenity here. The units, from cozy cottages to three-bedroom houses, are spacious, painted in soft pastels, with billowy white curtains, pillowtop mattresses, and fully equipped kitchens. Most have washers and dryers, and all have TVs with

Amazon Fire Sticks. Key perk: a 1,000-plus-foot beach (one of the only real beaches around). Guests use loaner bikes, kayaks, and paddleboards on and around the property, but there are no motorized water vehicles in the waters surrounding the hotel. There are plenty of hammocks, though. There's no room service or restaurant, but Morada Bay and Pierres across the street are excellent. This is a place for people who like each other a lot. Leave the kids at home unless they're extremely well behaved and not easily bored.

123 Beach Rd., near MM 81.5, on the ocean side, Islamorada. mooringsvillage.com. ✆ **305/664-4708.** 8 units. One-bedroom cottages start at $950. **Amenities:** Outdoor heated pool; spa; watersports equipment; excursions on the resort's boat; free Wi-Fi.

EXPENSIVE/MODERATE

Casa Morada ★★ The closest thing to a boutique hotel in the Florida Keys is the brainchild of a trio of New York women who used to work for hip hotelier Ian Schrager. The 16-suite Casa Morada is tucked off a sleepy lane, radiating serenity and style in an area where serenity abounds, but style not so much (decor is decidedly island, but think Cabo cool rather than Gilligan's). Sitting on 1¾ acres of prime bayfront, it has a limestone grotto, freshwater pool, and poolside drinks service. Each of the rooms has either a private garden or a terrace; request the one with the open-air Jacuzzi facing the bay. There's no restaurant, but breakfast is included daily. Bird-watchers alert: Casa Morada partners with the renowned Cornell Lab of Ornithology to educate guests about native species and sustainability issues. Enjoy free use of bikes, paddleboards, snorkel equipment, bocce pitch, and morning yoga. Despite the games, this place is not for kids (only those 16 and older can stay).

136 Madeira Rd., Islamorada. casamorada.com. ✆ **888/881-3030** or 305/664-0044. 16 units. $294–$386 double. Pet fee $70. Rates include continental breakfast. From U.S. 1 S., at MM 82.2, turn right onto Madeira Rd. and continue to the end of the street. The hotel is on the right. **Amenities:** Bikes; kayaks; paddleboards; freshwater pool; free Wi-Fi.

Isla Bella Beach Resort ★★★ Located right before you head onto the Seven Mile Bridge, Isla Bella Beach Resort is truly an oasis away from the grit of Overseas Highway and smack on the water, with sandy beach, a mile of waterfront, and five oceanfront pools. Best of all, every room and suite features oceanfront views. And unlike some of the newer, Floribbean-decored hotels in the Keys, this one has a much-welcome Greek-inspired vibe, with whitewashed buildings and bold blue and white room decor. As elegant and upscale as it is, it's also very family friendly and laid back (this is the Keys after all, where pretentiousness also goes fishin'). Daily activities, from diving for treasures and popsicles to nature scavenger hunts, will keep the kids busy. There's also bocce ball, minigolf, giant chess, and even an 8am Seven Mile Bridge guided run for those who feel the need to do that sort of thing. For food, there's a Polynesian-inspired oceanfront restaurant, and a brand-new sushi restaurant. There's also our fave, the beach bar, where more casual fare is served until 6pm, with drinks served until 11pm. A spa stands by to spruce up hair, nails, skin, and sore muscles. From the on-site marina, explore the nearby mangroves by paddleboard, or take a guided kayak expedition. Or do like we do, and do nothing by the pool.

1 Knights Key Blvd. at MM 47, Marathon. islabellabeachresort.com. ✆ **800/405-1948.** 199 units. $247–$629 double. Self-parking $25; valet $50. **Amenities:** 2 restaurants; bar; marketplace; 24-hr. fitness center; 5 pools; bikes; kayaks; minigolf; paddleboards; watersports rentals; free Wi-Fi.

Lime Tree Bay Resort ★★ The only place to stay in the tiny town of Layton (pop. 183), Lime Tree is midway between Islamorada and Marathon and is on a pretty piece of waterfront graced by hundreds of mature palm trees and tropical foliage. There are two pools, a nice white-sand beach, fishing pier, and free use of kayaks, paddleboards, and tennis court. Staff are super friendly. Rooms have been upgraded with shiplap and requisite Caribbean-esque decor; some have kitchenettes or full kitchens. Avoid rooms that are "off property." There are also efficiencies and town houses for those looking for more room and comforts of home. Next door, the Florida Boy Bar and Grill is a popular local hangout thanks to its Florida version of the New Orleans po'boy with grouper, and the 'gator bites, which do taste like chicken. Rates include a good continental breakfast that goes beyond the typical and features hot dishes and eggs.

U.S. 1 at MM 68.5, Layton, Long Key. limetreebayresort.com. ✆ **800/723-4519** or 305/664-4740. 47 units. $278–$426 double. **Amenities:** Jacuzzi; 2 outdoor pools; tennis court; free Wi-Fi

MODERATE

Kona Kai Resort, Gallery & Botanic Garden ★★★ This little haven is an exquisite, adults-only property right on Florida Bay, offering sunset views overlooking Everglades National Park. Guest rooms and suites are very comfortable, painted in cheerful sherbet colors, with quirky details (like a headboard made of oars, or a seashell-adorned dresser). They're all nestled in a lush 2-acre botanic garden brimming with tropical vegetation and fruit trees, from which guests are free to sample. A beachfront pool (heated in winter, cooled in summer), complimentary bottled water and fresh fruit poolside, a Jacuzzi, and one of the largest private beaches on the island, make Kona Kai the perfect place for escape and relaxation. The concierge organizes tours, fishing trips, snorkeling/diving excursions, and parasail, kayak, paddleboard, bicycle, and kiteboard outings. Kayaks, paddleboats, pingpong, cornhole, Wi-Fi, and parking are all included at no extra charge.

97802 Overseas Hwy. (U.S. 1 at MM 97.8), Key Largo. konakairesort.com. ✆ **305/852-7200.** 14 units. $269–$388 double. Children 15 and under not permitted. **Amenities:** Concierge; Jacuzzi; heated/cooled pool; in-room and on-beach spa treatments; watersports equipment/rentals; free Wi-Fi.

Ragged Edge Oceanfront Resort & Marina ★★★ Honestly, I'm not sure where the "ragged" thing comes in, because this oceanfront property's neat units are spread along more than a half-dozen gorgeous, grassy waterfront acres. All are immaculately clean and comfy, and most are outfitted with full kitchens and pleasant if not fancy furnishings. There's no bar, or restaurant, but the retreat's affable owner is happy to lend bicycles and give advice on area offerings. A large dock attracts boaters and a variety of local and migratory birds. An outdoor heated freshwater pool is a bonus for those months when temperatures get a bit cooler. They also rent out camping spots to RVs. A throwback to simpler times.

243 Treasure Harbor Rd. (near MM 86.5), Islamorada. ragged-edge.com. ✆ **305/852-5389.** 11 units. $212–$240 motel room, more for efficiencies, less for camping. **Amenities:** Free use of bikes; outdoor pool; free Wi-Fi.

INEXPENSIVE

Fairfield Inn and Suites Marathon Florida Keys ★★ Sometimes a caring staff can elevate a motel. That's certainly the case here, thanks to the folks who keep this pleasant if boring-looking property spotless, and make sure every guest feels taken care of. The motel also has some surprising extras, like two spiffy pools; an on-site marina that rents jet skis, paddleboards, and kayaks; and a fab tiki bar overlooking the water.

13201 Overseas Hwy. (MM 54), Marathon. marriott.com; © **305/289-0222.** $143–$226 double. **Amenities:** Restaurant/bar; marina; free breakfast; free Wi-Fi.

CAMPING

John Pennekamp Coral Reef State Park ★★   One of Florida's best parks (p. 165), Pennekamp has 42 well-separated campsites, each with 30-amp, 50-amp, and 110 electrical outlets. Each site also has water and sewer hookup, a picnic table, and a grill. Most sites can fit an RV of 40 feet max; a few sites can fit larger. Located at the end of the campground drive is a primitive group camp with a large grill, campfire circle, picnic table, and water faucet. Electricity is not available at the site, but a restroom is right next to it. *Note:* The local environment provides fertile breeding grounds for insects, particularly in late summer, so bring repellent. Two man-made beaches and a small lagoon attract many large wading birds. Reservations are held until 5pm; the park must be notified of late arrival by phone on the check-in date. Pennekamp opens at 8am and closes around sundown.

U.S. 1 at MM 102.5, Key Largo. pennekamppark.com. © **305/451-1202.** Reservations: Reserve America (© **800/326-3521**). 42 campsites. $36 (with electricity) per site, 8 people maximum. Park entry $8/vehicle with driver (plus 50¢/person up to 8 people).

Where to Dine

Not known as a culinary hot spot (though it's improving), the Upper and Middle Keys do have some fresh seafood specialists. Often, visitors (especially those who fish) take advantage of accommodations that have kitchen facilities and cook their own meals. Some restaurants will even clean and cook your catch, for a fee.

> **Price Categories**
>
> Meal per person, not including drinks or tip:
> **Inexpensive:** $20 and under
> **Moderate:** $21–$40
> **Expensive:** $40 and above

If you're in the market for breakfast in Marathon, the classic pit stop is **Seven Mile Grill** ★★ (1240 Overseas Hwy.; sevenmilegrill.com; © **305/743-4481**), which has a famous Greek omelet with lots of feta, friendly service, and reasonable prices.

And in Islamorada **Florida Keys Food Tours** (flkeysfoodtour.com; © **305/394-1028;** $109/person) leads a walking tour downtown, which includes tastings at family-owned eateries and places featured on Food Network, a visit to a brewery, the chance to learn to blow a conch horn, and photo ops at spots filmed in the popular Netflix series *Bloodline*. The tour is 4 hours long.

EXPENSIVE

Atlantic's Edge ★★ SEAFOOD   Atlantic's Edge is a Caribbean-American seafood specialist. Menu highlights include steamed mussels in a creole curry sauce; poached mahimahi with coconut, ginger, and a jalapeno broth; yellowtail snapper with zippy Haitian pikliz and pineapple chutney; and roast half chicken with Caribbean spice rub and fried plantains. If you were lucky on the water earlier, they'll cook your catch however you want, and give you two side dishes for

$30. The restaurant has panoramic views of, yes, the Atlantic, and a glassed-in wine cellar featuring more than 150 wines. Breakfast and lunch here are very good, but it's better for dinner.

Cheeca Lodge, U.S. 1 at MM 82, Islamorada. cheeca.com/dine-drink/atlantics-edge. **305/664-4651.** Main courses $30–$60. Daily 7am–5pm and 6–10pm.

Butterfly Café ★★ SEAFOOD

With water views and a menu of fresh local seafood, this is an excellent special occasion place. Among the dishes not to miss: mahimahi grilled or blackened with Key lime butter; the yellowtail snapper with tropical coulis, and roasted red pepper brandy cream sauce; and a fab nutty-crust Key lime pie with white chocolate mousse.

2600 Overseas Hwy., in the Tranquility Bay Resort, Marathon. tranquilitybay.com. **305/289-7177.** Main courses $34–$65. Daily 6–9pm.

Chef Michael's ★★★ SEAFOOD

A fine-dining, white-tablecloth experience with a small indoor dining room, and a charming outdoor patio, here the food, not the views, is paramount. Though the fresh seafood selection changes daily, signature dishes typically star hogfish or lionfish, prepared in a multitude of ways, including the New Orleans–style Pontchartrain (blackened and topped with crawfish in a Creole cream), or Adriatic ("grilled and napped with our olive oil and herb concoction.") Dishes are a production—in a good way. Other than seafood there is a daily vegetarian dish and a delicious roasted duck with mandarin oranges, cashews, coconut rice, and vegetables. Save room for the Key lime pie.

81671 Overseas Hwy., Islamorada. foodtotalkabout.com. **305/664-0640.** Main courses $40–$70. Mon–Sat 5am–10pm.

Green Turtle Inn ★★ SEAFOOD

The iconic Keys restaurant got its name when it started serving green turtle steaks along with gas back in 1947. While the name has stuck, owners have changed, the original building was demolished and revamped for the 21st century (much to the dismay of locals), but the place is still a landmark. Sadly, it's no longer a throwback to the old Florida Keys visually, but some original menu items remain, including the famous turtle chowder with pepper sherry, and luscious conch chowder. The new menu items are nothing to sneer at either. Skillet corn bread is a signature starter, and the fish dip with creole mustard and capers is also a top way to begin. Main courses peak with Chef Big Jean's Famous Shrimp Scampi and the mutton snapper with andouille Cajun cream sauce. For dessert: macadamia nut Rice Crispy crust Key lime pie or bread pudding. Or both. After dinner, check out the art gallery and gourmet shop. Green Turtle also serves excellent breakfast and lunch. Primo Bloody Marys, too.

81219 Overseas Hwy., at MM 81.2, Islamorada. greenturtleinn.com. **305/664-2006.** Main courses $24–$55. Daily 7–10am and 11:30am–10pm.

Marker 88 ★★ SEAFOOD

Upper Keys institution Marker 88 has been *the* spot for sunset dinners since the 1970s. That's still the case, but today new chefs and owners are aiming to make the food equal to the views. They're doing that by serving fish caught in the Keys' waters, perhaps in a homemade curry sauce, or blackened, or expertly grilled with a Key lime Tabasco butter. For those not into seafood, there's fajitas, steaks, and crisp and complex salads. No matter what you choose for entrees, ask for the banana fried roti with caramel and vanilla ice cream—it's the bomb.

U.S. 1 at MM 88 (bay side), Islamorada. marker88.info. **305/852-9315.** Main courses $16–$48. Sun–Thurs 11am–9pm; Fri–Sat 11am–10pm.

Pierre's ★★★ FRENCH FUSION   Set in a two-story British West Indies–style plantation home, candlelit inside with tiki torches outside, and bursting with Moroccan, Indian, and African artifacts, Pierre's may well be one of the most romantic restaurants in Florida. Especially on the second-floor veranda overlooking the water. The food matches the setting: gorgeously plated, and toothsome, whether you go for the yellowfin tuna tartare with lychee, jalapeno, and shrimp chips, or brioche with truffled goat cheese, two top appetizers. After dinner, the Green Flash Lounge downstairs is a sexy setting for a nightcap.

U.S. 1 at MM 81.6 (bay side), Islamorada. moradabaykeys.com/dining/pierres-restaurant. **305/664-3225.** Main courses $34–$68. Upstairs dining room daily 6–10pm. Lounge open at 5pm daily.

Ziggie and Mad Dog's ★★★ STEAKHOUSE   When former Miami Dolphins player Jim Mandich, aka Mad Dog, bought Ziggie's Crab Shack from Sigmund "Ziggie" Stockie, he decided to keep the ex-owner's name up there with his own. Mandich passed away in 2011, but his carnivorous (and football) legacy lives on at this Keys landmark. In fact, many famous athletes make a pilgrimage here when passing through. Dishes are pricey, but many, like the cowboy cut bone-in, and the truffle mac and cheese, are massive, so don't be shy about sharing. The old-school beef stroganoff is a bargain and a welcome throwback. Service is friendly and the vibe is fun.

83000 Overseas Hwy., Islamorada. ziggieandmaddogs.com. **305/664-3391.** Main courses $18–$58. Daily 5:30–10pm.

MODERATE

Barracuda Grill ★★ SEAFOOD   This small, casual lunch and dinner spot has outlasted many of its neighbors thanks to friendly service and appealing fare: fish tacos, local yellowtail snapper with nut butter, crispy Brussels sprouts in curry sauce. For fans of spicy food, the red-hot calamari and shrimp is accurately described as "vicious, but delicious." And even if it's 200 degrees out, Julia's Cream of Tomato Soup, their signature soup, sooths the soul. Decorated with barracuda-themed art, the restaurant has a well-priced wine list with lots of California vintages.

U.S. 1 at MM 49.5 (bay side), Marathon. **305/743-3314.** Main courses $20–$46. Daily 11am–2:30pm and 6–9pm.

Key Largo Conch House Restaurant & Coffee Bar ★★★ AMERICAN   A funky, pet-friendly spot for breakfast, lunch, and dinner, Key Largo Conch House is exactly that: a gingerbread Victorian set amid lush foliage, complete with resident dog and parrot, wraparound veranda for outdoor dining, and a grandma-core indoor dining room. Food is fresh and kindly priced, from the heaping plate of spicy shrimp and grits, to twists on the usual eggs Benedict, including our favorite, the crab cakes Benedict. The Key Lime Macadamia pancakes are winners here, too. They also have a great vegan menu, and it's beer and wine only, but the craft beer selection is stellar. Featured on the Food Network, Conch House should be a stop on everyone's trip down to the Keys.

U.S. 1 at MM 100, Key Largo. keylargoconchhouse.com. **305/453-4844.** Main courses $8–$39. Daily 8am–10pm.

Keys Fisheries ★★★ SEAFOOD   For many visitors, it's not a trip to the Keys until you grab a plate of coconut shrimp (or a lobster Reuben) at the counter of this beloved seafood market, plop down at a picnic table overlooking the water, and open up a cold one. Food here is among the freshest in the region, the stone crab claws, especially (when they're in season Nov–May). Conch, be it frittered, fried, or in ceviche form, is another a classic order. Come see what the fuss is about.

3502 Gulfview Ave., Marathon. keysfisheries.com. *866/743-4353*. Main courses $24–$30. Daily 11am–9pm.

Lazy Days ★★ SEAFOOD/BAR FARE

True to its name, this laid-back oceanfront eatery is the quintessence of Keys lifestyle. The chefs here, however, are far from lazy, preparing savory seafood pastas, vegetarian pastas, fish filets, sandwiches, steaks, and chicken. They'll also cook your catch. Choose from toes-in-the-sand beach dining, upstairs patio seating, indoor dining, or a table on the porch. Both upstairs and downstairs bars are always packed, especially during daily happy hours from 4 to 6pm featuring two-for-a-buck peel-and-eat shrimp and dollar wings, conch fritters, and jalapeno poppers, along with half-priced drinks. The original owners of Lazy Days opened Lazy Days South, at the Marathon Marina (lazydayssouth.com; *305/289-0839*), and while the two are unrelated now, it has a similar menu and oceanfront dining.

79867 Overseas Hwy., Islamorada. lazydaysislamorada.com. **305/664-5256**. Main courses $18–$29. Daily 11am–10pm.

INEXPENSIVE

Truly accomplished craft beers are on tap at the tasting room/beer garden of the **Florida Keys Brewing Company** ★★★ (81611 Old Hwy., Islamorada; floridakeysbrewingco.com; *305/664-9722*; daily 11am–8:30pm). There's often live music too, and food trucks provide grub to accompany the suds. It's a really good time, and quite family friendly (cornhole and other games for the kids).

Islamorada Fish Company ★ SEAFOOD

Pick up a cooler of stone crab claws in season (mid-Oct to Apr), or try the fried-fish sandwiches. It's a bit of a tourist trap, but it's a very Keys-y place to stop even if it's just for a drink. Lunch is served until 4pm and dinner until 9pm. Keep your eyes open while dining outside—the last time we were here, baby manatees were floating around, waiting for their close-ups.

81532 Overseas Hwy., Islamorada. islamoradafishco.com. **305/664-9271**. Main courses $17–$35. Mon–Thurs 11am–8pm; Fri–Sun 11am–9pm.

Island Grill ★★ SEAFOOD

If you drive too fast over Snake Creek Bridge, you may miss one of the best Keys dining experiences. Just under the bridge and on the bay, Island Grill is a locals' favorite, with an expansive, breezy deck and bar, and cozy waterfront dining room. Like many spots, they try to do it all here, but their "famous" ahi tuna nachos really do deserve their local acclaim. Also tops: the whole yellowtail snapper with Thai sweet chili sauce. On Fridays, they serve prime rib from noon to 9pm for $26 for 12 ounces. Live entertainment near nightly brings in a colorful Keys crowd. Although they serve breakfast too, we say skip the food and just stick to the Bloody Marys. Speaking of, on "Thirsty Thursdays," happy hour is from 11am to 9pm (not a typo) at the bar only.

MM 88.5 (ocean side at Snake Creek Bridge), Islamorada. keysislandgrill.com. **305/664-8400**. Main courses $14–$34. Daily 9am–9pm.

Porky's Bayside Restaurant & Marina ★★★ BBQ/SEAFOOD

Porky's is a waterfront tiki hut serving down home barbecue (smoked daily on-site); fried, raw, and taco-ed seafood dishes; and Bloody Marys. Food is served speedily and is reasonably priced, and the vibe is laid back, making you almost not want to hop back in the car and hit the road, but alas . . . have one slice of deep-fried Key lime pie and then go. There's live music from 6 to 9pm nightly. Porky's is pet friendly.

1410 Overseas Hwy., at MM 47.5, Key Largo. porkysbaysidebbq.com. ✆ **305/289-2065.** Main courses $9–$28. Daily 8am–10pm.

Sal's Ballyhoo's ★★★ SEAFOOD/SOUTHERN   If you're driving a bit too fast down south, you may miss this unassuming gem of a restaurant that has been serving fresh seafood for over 3 decades. A casual space with indoor and outdoor seating, Ballyhoo's serves fish with a southern twist. The whole fried snapper, for instance, is dusted with fried chicken flour, fried, and drizzled with garlic butter, and the shrimp and oyster po'boy comes on a Cuban roll with Tabasco mayo, a kicky take on the Nola staple. On weekend nights, chef/owner Sal serves up slow-cooked oxtail. It's. So. Good. Sandwiches, salads, sliders, snacks, a fantastic vegan/vegetarian menu (try the fried pink tomatoes) make this one of the Keys' most popular eateries. Good wine list and sangria, too.

97860 Overseas Hwy., at MM 97.8, Key Largo. ballyhoosrestaurant.com. ✆ **305/664-5256.** Main courses $12–$25. Daily 11am–10pm.

Snapper's ★★ SEAFOOD   Another waterfront hang, Snapper's serves fresh seafood caught by local fishermen—or by you (they'll cook it for you at $16 for 8 ounces a person)! The blackened mahimahi is exceptional and a bargain, complete with salad, vegetable, and choice of starch. There are also three bars, live music nightly and a lively, colorful crowd. A popular Sunday brunch features live jazz from the barge out back and a make-your-own-Bloody-Mary bar. Kids love feeding the tarpon off the docks. Also here: **Turtle Club,** an entirely outdoor, waterfront bar and grill located out back and featuring live music and a more casual menu of sandwiches, snacks, and pub grub.

139 Seaside Ave., at MM 94.5, Key Largo. snapperskeylargo.com. ✆ **305/852-5956.** Main courses $8–$33. Mon–Fri 11:30am–10pm; Sat–Sun 11am–10pm.

The Upper & Middle Keys After Dark

Nightlife in the Upper Keys tends to start before the sun goes down, often at noon, as most people—visitors and locals alike—are on vacation. Also, many anglers and sports-minded folk go to bed early.

Locals and tourists in Islamorada mingle at the outdoor cabana bar at **Lorelei** ★★, U.S. 1 at MM 82, Islamorada (loreleicabanabar.com). Most evenings after 5pm, you'll find local bands playing on a thatched-roof stage, mainly rock or reggae, and sometimes blues. **Hog Heaven** ★★★, MM 85.3, just off the main road on the ocean side, Islamorada (hogheavenbarandgrill.com; ✆ **305/664-9669;** Fri–Sat 11am–4am, Sun–Thurs 11am–2am), opened in the early 1990s, the joint venture of young locals tired of tourist traps. This whitewashed biker bar is a welcome respite from the neon-colored cocktail circuit. It has a waterside view and diversions such as big-screen TVs and video games. The food isn't bad, either. The atmosphere is cliquish because most patrons are regulars, so start up a game of pool to break the ice.

In Key Largo, **The Caribbean Club** ★★, 10480 Overseas Hwy. (caribbeanclubkl.com; ✆ **305/451-4466**), is a divey waterfront spot for karaoke Wednesdays and nightly live music. Plus, it's the place where many movies, including Bogie and Bacall classic *Key Largo,* were filmed, so the locals and staff have good, salty

> ### Key Largo Vikings?
>
> Thirsty Vikings back in the day drank mead, a fermented alcoholic beverage made from honey, believed to be one of civilization's first boozy bevs. So how did it make its way into Key Largo? Not via Thor, but via **Keys' Meads**, 99411 Overseas Hwy. (keysmeads.com; © **305/204-4596**), which offers tours, a tasting room, and retail space if you love the stuff enough to take some home. Traditional mead from the family-operated Keys' Meads is made from honey, water, and yeast. The meads are dry, semi-dry, or sweet, with "characteristics of whatever honey it was made from, along with any added ingredient," said Jeff Kesling, Keys' Meads owner. A far cry from the Keys' usual beer and frozen concoctions, but worthy of a stop if you are in the area. Skal!

stories. It's open from 7am(!) until 1am-ish daily and it's cash only, but there's an ATM inside. For a higher end nightlife, **Pierre's** ★★★, 81600 Overseas Hwy., (moradabaykeys.com; © 305/664-3225) is *the* place, or, cross the sand to neighboring **Morada Bay** for a toes-in-the-sand scene.

Located on the bay side in Key Largo, **Jimmy Johnson's Big Chill** ★★, 10400 Overseas Hwy. (jjsbigchill.com; ©305/453-9066), is a massive entertainment and boozing complex owned by the legendary football coach featuring several bars, restaurants, a pool, and nightly entertainment. It's more for early birds as it closes at 9pm. Nearby is another popular day and night drinking spot, **Skippers Dockside** ★★★, 528 Caribbean Dr., MM 100, Key Largo (skippersdockside.com; © 305/453-9794), featuring an outdoor tiki bar, live entertainment, and a Monday through Friday happy hour from 3 to 6pm that often keeps people happy until the place closes around 10pm on weeknights and 11pm on weekends. **Snook's Bayside Restaurant & Grand Tiki Bar** ★★★, 99470 Overseas Hwy., Key Largo (snooks.com; © 305/453-5004), is a guaranteed good time, featuring three bars, fab views, live music every night from 5:30 to 9:30pm, daily happy hours from 4 to 6pm, and good food.

Sundowners Key Largo ★★, 103900 Overseas Hwy., (sundownerskeylargo.com; © 305/451-4502), has fabulous views from its bustling bar, as well as live music nightly until at least 10 or 11pm, but get this, leaving from Sundowners is **Cruisin' Tikis** ★★★ (cruisintikiskeylargo.com; © 800/941-7080), a floating tiki bar offering BYOB day and night trips starting at $60 per person.

In Marathon, **Sunset Grille** ★★★, 7 Knights Key Blvd. (sunsetgrille7milebridge.com; © 305/396-7235), has spectacular sunset sips overlooking the Seven Mile Bridge and a daily 3 to 5pm happy hour, as well as a very popular, splashy Sunday pool party with DJs, cornhole tournaments, food and drink specials, and a beach barbecue. And, although it closes somewhat early, around 8:30pm, **Burdine's Waterfront** ★★★ is a Marathon hideaway, 1200 Oceanview Ave. (burdineswaterfront.com; © 305/743-9204), featuring a wide variety of drinks and views of the water.

THE LOWER KEYS

128 miles SW of Miami

Unlike their neighbors to the north and south, the Lower Keys (including **Big Pine, Sugarloaf,** and **Summerland**) are devoid of rowdy spring break crowds, boast few T-shirt and trinket shops, and have almost no late-night bars. What they do offer are the best opportunities to enjoy the vast natural resources on land and water that make the area so rich. Stay overnight in the Lower Keys, rent a boat, and explore the reefs—it might be the most memorable part of your trip.

Essentials

GETTING THERE See "Essentials" for the Upper and Middle Keys (p. 159) and continue south on U.S. 1. The Lower Keys start at the end of the Seven Mile Bridge. There are also airports in Marathon and Key West.

VISITOR INFORMATION Big Pine and Lower Keys Chamber of Commerce, 31020 Overseas Hwy., Big Pine Key (lowerkeyschamber.com; © **305/872-2411**), is open daily from 10am to 5pm. The pleasant staff will help with anything a traveler may need.

What to See & Do

Once the centerpiece (these days, it's Big Pine Key) of the Lower Keys and still a great asset, **Bahia Honda State Park** ★, U.S. 1 at MM 37.5, Big Pine Key (bahiahondapark.com; © **305/872-2353**), has one of the most beautiful coastlines in South Florida. Bahia (pronounced *Bah-ya*) Honda is a great place for hiking, bird-watching, swimming, snorkeling, and fishing. The 524-acre park encompasses a wide variety of ecosystems, including coastal mangroves, beach dunes, and tropical hammocks. There are miles of trails packed with unusual plants and animals, plus a small white-sand beach. Shaded seaside picnic areas are fitted with tables and grills. Although the beach is never wider than 5 feet, even at low tide, this is the Lower Keys' best beach area.

True to its name (Spanish for "deep bay"), the park has relatively deep waters close to shore—perfect for snorkeling and diving. Easy offshore snorkeling here gives even novices a chance to lie suspended in warm water and simply observe diverse marine life passing by. Or else head to the stunning reefs at Looe Key, where the coral and fish are more vibrant than anywhere else in the United States. Snorkeling trips go from the Bahia Honda concessions to Looe Key National Marine Sanctuary (4 miles offshore). They depart twice daily (9:30am and 1:30pm) March through September and cost $30 for adults, $25 for children 6 to 17, and $12.95 for mask, fin, and snorkel rental.

Bahia Honda State Park with a view of the highway.

Entry to the park is $8 per vehicle of two to eight passengers, $4 for a solo passenger, $2 per pedestrian or bicyclist, free for children 5 and under, with a 50¢-per-person Monroe County surcharge. Open daily from 8am to sunset.

The most famous residents of the Lower Keys are the tiny Key deer. Of the estimated 300 existing in the world, two-thirds live on Big Pine Key's **National Key Deer Refuge/Floria Keys National Wildlife Refuge ★**, 30587 Overseas Hwy. (fws.gov/refuge/national-key-deer; ⓒ **305/872-0774**). The refuge is also home to over 20 endangered and threatened plant and animal species. The helpful people at the nature center will give you an informative brochure and map of the area. Some of the refuge is paved, some is more rustic, so wear sturdy shoes. Also keep an eye out for snakes, crocodiles, and alligators—sightings of which are very rare, but they are in there. The refuge is open daily at a half-hour prior to sunrise and closes a half-hour after sunset.

If the nature center is closed, head out to the **Blue Hole,** a former quarry now filled with the fresh water that's vital to the deer's survival. To get there, turn right at Big Pine Key's only traffic light at Key Deer Boulevard (take the left fork immediately after the turn) and continue 1½ miles to the observation-site parking lot, on your left. The .5-mile **Watson Hammock Trail,** about ⅓ mile past the Blue Hole, is the refuge's only marked footpath. The deer are more active in cool hours, so try coming out to the path in the early morning or late evening to catch a glimpse of these gentle dog-size creatures. There is an obser-

A tiny Key deer.

vation deck from which you can watch and photograph the protected species. Don't be surprised to see a lazy alligator warming itself in the sun, particularly in outlying areas around the Blue Hole. If you do see a gator, do not go near it, do not touch it, and do not provoke it. If you must get a photo, use a zoom lens. Also, whatever you do, do not feed the deer—it will threaten their survival. Contact the **park office** (see above) to find out about the infrequent free tours of the refuge, scheduled throughout the year.

Outdoor Activities

BIKING Get off busy U.S. 1 to explore the beautiful, and reasonably safe, back roads of the Lower Keys. On Big Pine Key, cruise along Key Deer Boulevard (at MM 30). Those with fat tires can ride into the National Key Deer Refuge. Many lodgings offer bike rentals.

BIRD-WATCHING A stopping point for migratory birds on the Eastern Flyway, the Lower Keys are populated with many West Indian bird species, especially in spring and fall. The small, vegetated islands of the Keys are the only nesting sites in the U.S. for the white-crowned pigeon. They're also some of the few breeding places for the reddish egret, roseate spoonbill, mangrove cuckoo, and black-whiskered vireo. Look for them on Bahia Honda Key and the many uninhabited islands nearby.

BOATING Dozens of shops rent powerboats for fishing and reef exploring. Most also rent tackle, sell bait, and have charter captains available. **Aqua Boat Rental** (aquaboatrentals.com) in Summerland Key offers an impressive selection of boats from $350 to $500 per day, less for multi-day rentals. They can also find captains. *Note:* Visitors need a valid boating education certificate; see p. 29 for more information.

CANOEING & KAYAKING The Overseas Highway (U.S. 1) touches on only a few dozen of the many hundreds of islands that make up the Keys. To really see the Lower Keys, rent a kayak or canoe—perfect for these shallow waters. **Big Pine Kayak Adventures,** 1791 Bogie Dr., MM 30, Big Pine Key (keyskayaktours.com; © **305/872-2241**), which has been operating out of the Old Wooden Bridge Fishing Camp for more than 30 years, offers kayak and charter boat ecotours of the lower Keys' wildest, most remote National Wildlife Refuge backcountry on your own or with an expert. The expert, U.S.C.G.-licensed Captain Bill Keogh, wrote the book on the subject. *The Florida Keys Paddling Guide* (Countryman Press) covers all the unique ecosystems and inhabitants, as well as launches and favorite routes from Key Biscayne to the Dry Tortugas National Park. Self-guided, single kayak and paddleboard rentals start at $40 for the half-day and tandems are $50. An expertly guided mangrove creek kayak adventure is offered daily at $75 per person. There are also custom, private charters, with mothership motor vessel and paddlecraft aboard to reach the remote wilderness, run by Cap'n Bill himself a few times a week.

FISHING A day spent fishing, either in the shallow backcountry or in the deep sea, is a great way to ensure a fresh-fish dinner, or you can release your catch and just appreciate the challenge. Whichever you choose, **Captain Hook's Looe Key Reef Adventures,** 29675 Overseas Hwy., Big Pine Key (captainhooks.com; © **305/872-9863**), is the charter service to call. Prices for fishing boats start at $650 for a half-day and $1,000 for a full day. If you have enough anglers to share a boat (they take up to six people), you can amortize the cost. The outfitter may also be able to match you with other interested visitors. There are also daily snorkeling trips to Looe Key National Marine Sanctuary ($49/ person), and sightseeing only at $39 per person, or diving from $99 per person.

HIKING You can hike throughout the flat, marshy Keys on both marked trails and meandering coastlines. The best places to trek through nature are **Bahia Honda State Park,** at MM 29.5, and **National Key Deer Refuge,** at MM 30 (for more information on both, see "What to See & Do," above). Bahia Honda Park has a free brochure describing an excellent self-guided tour along the Silver Palm Nature Trail. You'll traverse hammocks, mangroves, and sand dunes, and cross a lagoon. The walk (less than a mile) explores a great cross section of the natural habitat in the Lower Keys and can be done in less than half an hour.

SNORKELING & SCUBA DIVING Snorkelers and divers should not miss the Keys' most dramatic reefs at the **Looe Key National Marine Sanctuary.** Here you'll see more than 150 varieties of hard and soft coral—some centuries old—as well as every type of tropical fish, including gold and blue parrotfish, moray eels, barracudas, French angels, and tarpon. **Looe Key Dive Center,** 27340 Overseas Hwy., Ramrod Key (diveflakeys.com; © **305/872-2215**), offers a 4-hour tour aboard a 45-foot catamaran with two shallow 1-hour dives for snorkelers and scuba divers. Snorkelers pay $49.99; divers pay $94.99, and those who just want to come along for the ride pay $34.99. Friday night trips start at $59.99 and give you an hour and a half under water in the dark. You can do a fascinating dive to the *Adolphus Busch, Sr.,* a shipwreck off Looe Key in 100 feet of water, for $109.99 per person.

Where to Stay

There are still a few bare-bones fish shacks along the highway for those who want cheap accommodations. Your best bet for bargains here are Vrbo and Airbnb. So far, there are no national hotel chains in the Lower Keys.

EXPENSIVE

Little Palm Island Resort & Spa ★★★ Built on a private 5½-acre island, this exclusive escape—host to presidents, royalty, and, recently, Howard Stern—is accessible only by boat or seaplane. Guests stay in thatched-roof duplexes amid flowering tropical plants and Key deer, which are to this island what cats are to Key West. Many bungalows have ocean views and private decks with hammocks. Inside, the suites have all the comforts of a swank beach cottage, but without phones, TVs, or alarm clocks (there's Wi-Fi for those who must be connected). The pool is small, but tranquil—a favorite gathering spot for the Key deer. A tiny, yet pristine, white-sand beach has lounge chairs and umbrellas. Mosquitoes can be a problem here, even in winter. (Bring spray and lightweight, long-sleeved clothing.) Known for a stellar spa and innovative and pricey food, Little Palm also hosts visitors just for meals. Speaking of pricey, the nightly rate is subject to a steep 12.5% resort fee, but that does cover welcome cocktail, valet parking at the launch office, non-alcoholic minibar beverages, Wi-Fi, paddleboards, kayaks, Hobie Cat, and Boston Whaler.

Launch is on the ocean side of U.S. 1 at MM 28.5, Little Torch Key. littlepalmisland.com. **888/413-0560** or 305/684-8341. 30 units. $2,290–$3,290 double plus resort fee. No children 17 and under. **Amenities:** Restaurant; bar; concierge; fitness center; pool; room service; spa; watersports equipment/rentals; free Wi-Fi.

MODERATE

Parmer's Resort ★★ As mom and pop as the Keys gets these days, Parmer's, a fixture since the '70s, is known for its warm hospitality and helpful staff. This downscale resort is spread out over 5 acres of waterfront with an impressive 90 feet of beach and offers modest, no frills, but comfortable cottages. Some are waterfront, many have kitchenettes, and others are just a bedroom. The Wahoo room (no. 26), a one-bedroom efficiency, is especially nice, with a small sitting area that faces the water. All units are very clean, though housekeeping is only by request at least 24 hours in advance. The well-maintained property also has bocce ball, a 4-hole putting green, and a heated pool. Loaner kayaks and paddleboards, and breakfast, are covered by the resort fee (2-hr. time limit). Parmer's is within walking distance of **Kiki's Sandbar Bar & Grille,** which is a fun spot for live music, views, drinks, and food. The hotel's waterfront location, not to mention the fact that it's only a half-hour from Key West, are huge bonuses.

565 Barry Ave., MM 28.5, Little Torch Key. parmersresort.com. **305/872-2157.** 45 units. $185–$320 double. Pet fee $50/day. From U.S. 1, turn right onto Barry Ave. Resort is ½ mile down on the right. **Amenities:** Concierge; heated pool; putting green; watersports equipment; free Wi-Fi.

CAMPING

Bahia Honda State Park ★★★ This state park offers some of the best camping in the Keys. It is as loaded with facilities and activities as it is with campers. But don't be discouraged by its popularity—this park encompasses more than 500 acres of land, 80 campsites spread throughout three areas, and three spacious, comfortable duplex cabins. Cabins hold up to eight guests each and come complete with linens, kitchenettes, wraparound terraces, barbecue pits, and rocking chairs.

36850 Overseas Hwy., at MM 37, Big Pine Key. www.floridastateparks.org/BahiaHonda. © **305/872-2353.** Campsites $36 (for up to 4 people), cabins $120–$160.

Sugarloaf Key/Key West KOA Resort ★★
Another excellent value, this newly spruced up oceanside facility has the largest tent camping area in the Keys, with rustic sites including shade structure, 25×32-ft. cement pad power and water, picnic table, and your very own fire pit. Private tent sites have water and electric hookup for those who need a little more modernity with their camping. There are also a ton of pull-through and back-up RV hookups with ocean views, patios, and even private mangroves with rates around $265 a night. And then there's the on-site **Sugarloaf Key Hotel** (sugarloafkeyhotel.com), for those of us, ahem, who prefer to sleep in A/C and on actual, comfortable full-size beds off the ground and a window's view away from nature. There are suites that hold up to six people, with bunk beds and even washers and dryers. Now that's what we call glamping! Rates range from $225 to $450. The best part of it all is the pool and poolside pub open to campers and hotel guests. This place is especially nice because of its private beaches and access to diving, fishing, snorkeling, and boating; its grounds are also well maintained. There's also a ton of amenities, from bike and boat rental to trivia nights, live music, and an interactive dog park.

Near MM 20 at 251 SR 939 in Sugarloaf Key. koa.com/campgrounds/sugarloaf-key. © **786/876-7724** or 305/745-3549. Campsites $80–$170 depending on season, type of vehicle, and more.

Sun Outdoors Sugarloaf Key ★★
Near Sugarloaf Key, this facility has 17 premium, back-in full hookup 20-, 30-, and 50-amp RV sites, offering a patio, Wi-Fi, and a picnic table. There are also lakefront sites, a variety of waterfront hookups, retro-fab fully outfitted Airstream trailers with full bathroom, coffeemaker, mini-fridge, and air-conditioning, and pet-friendly, air-conditioned bungalows, some with water views. Amenities are nice and include heated pool; kayak, paddleboard, and golf cart rentals; tiki bar with fire pit; dog park; lawn games; weekly live music parties; and Aquabana rentals—floating cabanas with table—these are cool and definitely a little luxe.

311 Johnson Rd., Summerland Key. sunoutdoors.com. © **305/745-1079.** $99–$199 per night.

Where to Dine

There aren't many fine-dining options in the Lower Keys, with the exception of the **Dining Room at Little Palm Island,** MM 28.5, Little Torch Key (© **305/422-4236**), where you'll be wowed with French and Pan Latin fare (see p. 182 for the hotel listing). You need to take a ferry to this private island to dine there.

MODERATE

Mangrove Mama's Restaurant ★★ AMERICAN As the locals who come daily for happy hour will tell you, this is a dive in the best sense of the word. The restaurant is a shack that used to have a gas pump as well as a grill. Diners share the property with stray cats and some miniature horses out back. It's run-down, but in a charming Keys sort of way. A handful of tables, inside and out, are shaded by banana trees and palm fronds. New owners have retooled the menu to include standard comfort food (meatloaf, country fried pork chops, sandwiches), and less standard options like braised duck tacos with spicy mandarin orange drizzle (a deelish special when I was last there). But it's the newly converted outdoor tiki bar and pontoon boat stage that are the real draws.

U.S. 1 at MM 20, Sugarloaf Key. mangrovemamas20.com. ⓒ **305/745-3030.** Main courses $16–$32. Mon–Fri 11am–9pm; Sat–Sun 11am–10pm.

INEXPENSIVE

Coco's Kitchen ★★ CUBAN/AMERICAN This storefront has been dishing out black beans, rice, and shredded beef since 1969. When Coco retired, locals took over and continue to cook not only superior Cuban food, but also local specialties, Mexican and Caribbean choices. Top dishes include fried shrimp, whole fried yellowtail, *carne con papas* (beef chunks with potatoes in spicy red salsa served with tortillas), and Cuban-style roast pork. The best bet is the daily special, which may be roasted pork or fresh grouper, served with rice and beans or salad and crispy fries. Breakfast burritos, biscuits and gravy, and delicious Cuban coffee make it a breakfast hot spot. Top off the huge meal with a rich caramel-soaked flan.

283 Key Deer Blvd. (in the Winn-Dixie shopping center), Big Pine Key. cocoskitchen.com. ⓒ **305/872-4495.** Main courses $8.50–$17; breakfast $2.75–$8; lunch $3.75–$6. Tues–Sun 7am–3pm. Turn right at the traffic light near MM 30.5; stay in the left lane.

No Name Pub ★★ PUB FARE/PIZZA Founded as a general store and bait-and-tackle shop in 1931, this hard-to-find honky-tonk out in the boondocks (tagline: "You Found It") is an affable hangout. Pizzas are tasty—try one topped with local shrimp—or consider a bowl of chili with all the fixings. Everything is served on paper plates. One of the Keys' oldest bars, blanketed with thousands of signed dollar bills, this rustic is all about drinking beer and listening to a jukebox heavy with 1980s tunes.

¼ mile south of No Name Bridge on N. Watson Blvd., Big Pine Key. nonamepub.com. ⓒ **305/872-9115.** Entrees $5–$20. Daily 11am–10pm. Turn right at Big Pine's only traffic light (near MM 30.5) onto Key Deer Blvd. Turn right on Watson Blvd. At the stop sign, turn left. Look for a small wooden sign on the left marking the spot.

The Lower Keys After Dark

Although the mellow islands of the Lower Keys aren't exactly known for wild nightlife, there are some friendly bars and restaurants where locals and tourists gather. **No Name Pub** (see above) is a legendary dive bar. One of the most scenic nightspots is **Kiki's Sandbar & Grille** ★★, Barry Avenue near MM 28.5 (kikis sandbar.com; ⓒ **305/872-9989**), in Little Torch Key, the only waterfront restaurant between Key West and Marathon. The upstairs, air-conditioned dining room is enclosed with windows looking out onto the water, and there's a beachside tiki bar, games beach, and raw bar. The huge menu has seafood, burgers, sandwiches, and tacos, and they'll cook your catch—grilled, blackened, or fried, for $18 per person, including fries and coleslaw. Kiki's attracts an odd mix of bikers and bluehairs daily, and is a great place to overhear local gossip. There's also live music every night. Open 11am to 11pm.

Square Grouper Bar & Grill ★★, oceanside at 22658 Overseas Hwy., in Cudjoe Key (squaregrouperbarandgrill.com; ✆ **305/745-8880**), offers fresh local seafood, innovative small plates, changing specials, homemade desserts, and a boutique wine list and microbrews at its upstairs bar, **My New Joint ★★**, whose website is cheekily, mynewjoint420lounge.com. Nearby is **The Bent Prop Bar & Grill ★★★**, 457 Drost Dr., Cudjoe Key (bentpropkeys.com; ✆ **305/741-7017**), with daily happy hour from 3 to 5pm to go with the fabulous waterfront views.

KEY WEST ★★★

159 miles SW of Miami

If you're looking for a party, you'll find it in Key West. More than any other place in the U.S., this is the land of the eternal vacation, where no one wears a watch or tie and the phrase "hasta mañana" could have been invented. It seems the sun is always shining in this part of Florida, making the island a perfect destination for sunbathers, deep-sea fishermen, divers, and motorcyclists. Munch on fresh seafood, watch the jugglers in Mallory Square, and have another margarita. You can think about work tomorrow.

Things to Do The preferred leisure activity in Key West is relaxing. Visitors inclined toward more active pursuits head to the docks, where divers explore submarine reefs, and anglers head off from **Garrison Bight Marina** in hopes of landing sailfish and tarpon in the azure waters of the Gulf of Mexico. There are also some surprisingly compelling museums and historic homes in town.

Shopping You'll soon become convinced the predominant island souvenir is a tacky T-shirt. But if you can make it past the crude shirts, art fans will find some colorful and nautical themed pieces for their collections in local shops and galleries.

Nightlife & Entertainment When the sun begins to drop, Sunset Celebration goes into full swing in **Mallory Square ★★★**. Magicians, jugglers, and one-man bands entertain the crowds each evening as the sun tints the sky and waves with orange and purple. After dark, do the **Duval Street** crawl. Favorite bars include Sloppy Joe's (p. 210), reputed to be an old Hemingway haunt, and Hog's Breath Saloon.

Restaurants & Dining So many good choices! For a dinner of "conch fusion cuisine," stop in at Hot Tin Roof (p. 205), in the Ocean Key Resort. Or head off the beaten track to enjoy a fish dinner at Hogfish Bar and Grill (p. 209), where tattooed bikers and yacht owners alike gather to eat freshly caught fish at picnic tables.

Essentials

GETTING THERE For directions by car, see "Essentials" (p. 159) for the Upper and Middle Keys and continue south on U.S. 1. When entering Key West, stay in the far-right lane onto North Roosevelt Boulevard, which becomes Truman Avenue in Old Town. Continue for a few blocks and you'll find yourself on **Duval Street ★**, in the heart of the city. If you stay to the left, you'll also reach the city center after passing the airport and the remnants of historic houseboat row, where a motley collection of boats once made up one of Key West's most interesting neighborhoods.

Crowds gather at Mallory Square, which means buskers are there too, filling the air with music.

Several regional airlines fly nonstop (about 55 min.) from Miami to Key West. **American, Delta, United, Silver Airways, Jet Blue,** and **Allegiant** land at the recently expanded **Key West International Airport,** South Roosevelt Boulevard (eyw.com; © 305/296-5439), on the southeastern corner of the island.

Greyhound (greyhound.com; © **800/231-2222**) has five buses heading to Key West every day starting as low as $9.99. Seats fill up in season, so come early. The ride takes about 4½ hours.

You can also get to Key West from Ft. Myers or Marco Island via the **Key West Express** (keywestexpress.net; ©**866/KW-FERRY** [593-3779]), a 155-foot-long catamaran that travels to Key West at 40 mph. *The Big Cat* features two enclosed cabins, sun seated deck, observation deck, satellite TV, and full galley and bar. Prices range from $130 one-way and $155 to $185 round-trip per person.

GETTING AROUND Old Town Key West has limited parking, narrow streets, and congested traffic, so driving is more of a pain than a convenience. Unless you're staying in one of the more remote accommodations, consider trading in your car for a bicycle. The island is small and flat as a board, which makes it easy to negotiate, especially away from the crowded downtown area. Many tourists choose to cruise by moped, an option that can make navigating the streets risky, especially because there are no helmet laws in Key West (only children 16 and under must wear them). Hundreds of visitors are seriously injured each year, so spend the extra few bucks to rent a helmet.

Rates for simple one-speed cruisers start at about $10 per day. Mopeds start at about $20 for 2 hours, $35 per day for a one-seater, and $100 per week. The best shops include the **A&M Scooter and Bicycle Center,** 523 Truman Ave. (amscooters keywest.com; ⓒ **305/294-4556**); and **Pirate Scooter Rentals,** across from the Green Parrot bar at 401 Southard St. (piratescooterrentals.com; ⓒ **305/928-2138**).

PARKING Parking in Key West's Old Town is limited, but there is a well-placed **municipal parking lot** at Simonton and Angela streets, just behind the firehouse and police station. If you've brought a car, you may want to stash it here while you enjoy the very walkable downtown.

VISITOR INFORMATION The **Key West Visitors Center** (keywest123.com; ⓒ **305/296-8881**), 31281 Overseas Hwy. on Big Pine Key, is the area's best for information on goings-on, and restaurants; it's open every day except Tuesday from 10am to 5pm. Queer travelers may want to surf to the **Key West Business Guild** (gaykeywestfl.com), which promotes LGBTQIA+ travel to Key West and has an online directory of gay-friendly hotels, restaurants, bars, and businesses in the area.

ORIENTATION A mere 2×4-mile island, Key West is simple to navigate, even though there's no real order to the arrangement of streets and avenues. As you enter town on U.S. 1 (Roosevelt Blvd.), you will see most of the moderate chain hotels and fast-food restaurants. The higher end restaurants, shops, and outfitters are crammed onto Duval Street, the main thoroughfare of Key West's Old Town. On surrounding streets, many inns and lodges are set in picturesque Victorian/Bahamian homes. On the southern side of the island are the coral-beach area and some of the larger resort hotels.

The area called Bahama Village has trendy restaurants and guesthouses, but this hippie-ish neighborhood, complete with street-roaming chickens and cats, is the roughest and most urban you'll find in the Keys.

A look-alike participates in the annual Hemingway Days fest.

Seeing the Sights

The **Florida Keys Eco-Discovery Center** ★★, overlooking the waterfront at the Truman Annex (35 E. Quay Rd.; floridakeys.noaa.gov/eco_discovery.html; ⓒ **305/ 809-4750**), is an informative, entertaining, and free (!) attraction featuring 6,000 square feet of interactive exhibits depicting Florida Keys underwater and upland habitats, with emphasis on the ecosystem of North America's only living contiguous barrier coral reef, which parallels the Keys. Kids dig the interactive yellow submarine while adults enjoy the cinematic depiction of an underwater abyss. Open 9am to 4pm Friday and Saturday only.

Before shelling out for any of the dozens of worthwhile attractions in Key West, we recommend getting an overview on either of the two comprehensive island tours, the **Conch Tour Train** or the **Old Town Trolley** (p. 194).

Audubon House & Tropical Gardens ★★

This well-preserved 19th-century home stands as a prime example of early Key West architecture. Built by one of the many rich shipwreck salvagers on the island, and named for the painter and bird expert John James Audubon, who is said to have visited the house in 1832, the graceful two-story structure is a retreat from the bustle of Old Town. Included in the price of admission is a self-guided, half-hour audio tour that spotlights rare Audubon prints, antiques, historical photos, and tropical gardens. With voices of several characters from the house's past, the tour never gets boring—though it is a bit hokey at times. Even if you don't want to explore the grounds and home, check out the gift shop, which sells a variety of fine mementos at reasonable prices. Expect to spend 30 minutes to an hour.

205 Whitehead St. (btw. Greene and Caroline sts.). audubonhouse.com. **305/294-2116.** Admission $15 adults, $5 children 6–12, $10 students of any age. Daily 9:30am–4:15pm.

Ernest Hemingway Home and Museum ★★★

Papa may have been a rolling stone, but this genteel, two-story limestone manse and grounds built in 1851 was as close as it got to home. He spent most of the 1930s here, the decade in which most of his best-known works were written (including *For Whom the Bell Tolls, A Farewell to Arms,* and *The Snows of Kilimanjaro*). He also stayed here in the '50s during stopovers in Key West between his newer home bases in Cuba and Idaho. A museum since 1964, it remains the centerpiece of the Hemingway legend and lore that's so much a part of this island's history. You can hop on a half-hour guided tour or just show yourself around the eight rooms—which, by the way, reflect the taste of wife number two, Pauline, as much or more than the writer himself (I find more of Papa's own personality in his spread outside Havana). It makes for a fascinating visit, both inside and on the rest of the grounds (get a load of that impressive pool out back, built in the late '30s on the spot where Hemingway used to have a boxing ring). You'll likely spot some of the dozens of famous six-toed cats, descendants of the 50 felines Hemingway kept on property —and see if you can spot the fountain adapted from a pissoir taken from Sloppy Joe's saloon. If you're feline phobic (or allergic), beware:

Descendants of Hemingway's cats still roam freely through the author's home, just as they did when he was alive.

There are cats everywhere. Guided tours are given every 15 minutes; expect to spend an hour on the property.

907 Whitehead St. (btw. Truman Ave. and Olivia St.). hemingwayhome.com. ✆ **305/294-1136.** Admission $18 adults, $6 children 6-12. Daily 9am–5pm.

Fort East Martello Museum ★★ Key West was controlled by the Union during the Civil War, which built this small brick fortress on the Atlantic coast, but it never saw action—or indeed, was even finished. In 1950 the island historical society restored the circa 1862 structure and opened it as a museum curating an overview of local history, including cigar-making, wreck-salvaging, sponge-diving, and Cuban heritage. This being Key West, the weird and wacky are well-represented, including the story of a doctor who spent years sleeping with the corpse of his wife and a creepy larger-than-life doll named Robert, who even today some believe to be possessed (it's on display right across from an antique horse-drawn hearse, to play up the spookiness). Other galleries display island folk artists such as Stanley "Barefoot" Papio and Mario Sanchez, the much-ballyhooed local counterpart to Grandma Moses. Before leaving, head up to the roof for the sweeping view out over the ocean. Expect to spend 1 hour.

3501 S. Roosevelt Blvd. kwahs.org. ✆ **305/296-3913.** Admission $17 adults, $13 seniors, $9 children 7–18. Daily 10am–5pm (last entry at 4:30pm). Rates are cheaper online.

Harry S. Truman Little White House ★★ It may not jump to mind as readily as other Key West associations, but the U.S. Navy has been a big presence here for nearly 2 centuries. The naval station, now known as the Truman Annex, was thrust into the public eye when U.S. President Truman made the former commandant's quarters his winter White House from 1946 to 1952. It was later used for both business and pleasure by Eisenhower, JFK (including during the Cuban Missile Crisis), and other presidents and government officials to this day—symposia, receptions, and negotiations occasionally close the house to visitors, but at other times you never know when you might bump into a U.S. senator or Cabinet member in town on a fishing trip. Historic decisions were made here (including dropping the atom bomb on Japan), and the docents do a nice job of bringing it all alive as they walk visitors through the '40s vintage interior (which is the only way you can see the place). Tours run every 15 minutes and last between 45 and 50 minutes, so plan to spend more than an hour here. For fans of all things Oval Office–related, there's a presidential gift shop on the premises.

111 Front St. trumanlittlewhitehouse.com. ✆ **305/294-9911.** Admission $22.95 adults, $10 children 4–10. Daily 9am–4:30pm.

Key West Aquarium ★★ There's something I find endearing about this very old-fashioned little aquarium at water's edge, founded in 1934. Although it's not big, high-tech, or flashy, it just may end up charming you with its well-designed, informative exhibits showcasing Florida and Caribbean marine and shore environments and their denizens, with highlights including alligators, huge marine turtles, plenty of sharks, and a stingray touch tank. Speaking of sharks, it's very much worth timing your visit to take one of the free guided tours. Not only do the guides put things into context, but you can witness the dramatic feeding frenzy of the sharks, tarpon, barracudas, stingrays, and turtles. Expect to spend 1 hour here.

1 Whitehead St. (at Mallory Sq.). keywestaquarium.com. ✆ **305/910-2791.** Admission $20.99 adults, $11.99 children 4–12. Daily 10am–6pm; tours at 11am and 1, 3, and 4pm.

Key West Butterfly & Nature Conservatory ★★
In a 13,000-square-foot pavilion, this attraction has nature lovers flitting with excitement, thanks to the 5,000-square-foot, glass-enclosed butterfly aviary as well as a gallery, learning center, and gift shop exploring all aspects of the butterfly world. Inside, more than 1,500 butterflies and 3,500 plants, including rare orchids, and even fish and turtles coexist in a controlled climate. You'll walk freely among the butterflies. Expect to spend 1 hour.

1316 Duval St. keywestbutterfly.com. ✆ **305/296-2988.** Admission $17.50 adults, $14.50 seniors, $12.50 children 4–12. Rates cheaper online. Daily 9am–5pm; last ticket sold at 4:30pm.

> **A Smokin' Park**
>
> **Gato Village Pocket Park,** 616 Louisa St., pays homage to the island's once-flourishing cigar-making industry. Located on the site of a former cigar maker's cottage in what was once called Gatoville—a housing community built by cigar baron Eduardo Gato for his factory workers—the park features a re-creation of the cottage's front porch and facade, a 13-foot-tall metal cigar and signage telling the community's ashy history.

Key West Cemetery ★★★
This cemetery is the epitome of quirky Key West: irreverent and humorous. Many tombs are stacked several high, condominium-style, because the rocky soil made digging 6 feet under nearly impossible for early settlers. Epitaphs reflect residents' lighthearted attitudes toward life and death. I TOLD YOU I WAS SICK is one of the more famous, as is the tongue-in-cheek widow's inscription AT LEAST I KNOW WHERE HE'S SLEEPING TONIGHT. Plan to spend 30 minutes to an hour or more, depending on how morbid your curiosity is.

Entrance at the corner of Margaret and Angela sts. Free admission. Daily dawn–dusk.

Key West Lighthouse & Keeper's Quarters Museum ★★
When the Key West Lighthouse opened in 1848, it signaled the end of a profitable era for the pirate salvagers who looted reef-stricken ships. The story of this and other area lighthouses is illustrated in a small museum that was formerly the keeper's quarters. It's worth mustering the energy to climb the 88 claustrophobic steps to the top, where you'll be rewarded with magnificent panoramic views of Key West and the ocean. Expect to spend 30 minutes.

938 Whitehead St. kwahs.org. ✆ **305/294-0012.** Admission $17 adults, $13 seniors and locals, $9 children 7–18. Rates cheaper online. Daily 10am–5pm (last admission 4:30pm).

Key West Museum of Art and History at the Custom House ★★
Built in 1891 to house both the government's customs office and postal service and courts, this imposing four-story red-brick landmark alongside Mallory Square made an early mark as the site of inquiry into the sinking of the USS *Maine* in Havana harbor, which led the United States into the Spanish-American War. Since 1999 it's been home to a bright, appealing museum showcasing local artists—especially Mario Sanchez, Key West's answer to Grandma Moses—and exhibitions focusing on historical periods and events that defined and changed the island, including the arrival of the railroad, the hurricane of 1935, cigar making, the impact of Ernest Hemingway, and more.

281 Front St. (at Greene St.). kwahs.org. ✆ **305/295-6616.** Admission $17 adults, $13 seniors 62 and over, $9 youth 7–18, free kids 6 and under. Daily 10am–5pm.

Key West Shipwreck Treasure Museum ★
Shipwreck salvaging was the source of Key West's first great boom in the early to mid-19th century, so

although this slick multimedia bit of business has a certain theme-park feel to it, if you're curious about the phenomenon, and that era in general, this is probably the single most comprehensive collection there is. The two-story re-creation of an 1850s warehouse mixes film, actors playing period roles, and artifacts from salvaged cargo items. These include artifacts from the *The Isaac Allerton,* a merchant ship carrying cargo throughout the Caribbean, Gulf of Mexico, and the North Atlantic Ocean until August 28, 1856, when it was caught in a hurricane off Saddlebunch Keys, 15 miles off of Key West, and sank. Over 130 years later, it was rediscovered. As a bonus, you can climb the 65-foot lookout tower atop the museum for a great view over this corner of the island and out to sea.

1 Whitehead St. (at Mallory Sq.). keywestshipwreck.com. **305/292-8990.** Admission $17.99 adults, $8.99 children 4–12. Rates are cheaper online. Daily 9am–5pm.

Mel Fisher Maritime Museum ★★★   The name Mel Fisher ring any bells? In 1985, after 16 years of trying, a team led by this chicken-farmer-turned-dive-operator-turned-treasure-hunter bagged one of the biggest prizes in treasure-hunting history: the wreck of the Spanish galleon *Our Lady of Atocha,* which sank off the Keys in a 1622 hurricane. Fisher's crew brought up a batch of the boodle that went down with the ship—nearly half a billion dollars' worth of silver and gold bars, coins, jewels, and artifacts. Though he died in 1998, the for-profit salvage operation continues. An interesting part of this museum, established in 1992 in a historic firehouse, is a shop; here you'll find replicas, but can also drop anywhere from a few hundred bucks to six figures on various items of treasure from the *Atocha.* Displays do a nice job of telling the story of both ship and salvage operation, including a good representative cross section of the loot and historic artifacts. On its second floor, the museum—the only fully accredited museum in the Florida Keys—covers a more sober story: that of a 1700 English merchant slave ship, the only tangible evidence of the transatlantic slave trade. A gripping exhibition tells the story of more than 1,400 African slaves captured in Cuban waters and brought to Key West for sanctuary. The museum is also a nationally recognized research and archaeology institution, so if you geek out for those things, you can do a lab tour ($30).

200 Greene St. melfisher.org. **305/294-2633.** Admission $17.50 adults, $8.50 children 6–12. Daily 10am–5pm (last ticket sold at 4pm). Take U.S. 1 to Whitehead St. and turn left on Greene.

Oldest House Museum & Garden ★   Dating from 1829, this old New England Bahama House has survived pirates, hurricanes, fires, warfare, and economic ups and downs. The one-and-a-half-story home was designed by a ship's carpenter and incorporates many features from maritime architecture, including portholes and a ship's hatch designed for ventilation before the advent of air-conditioning. Especially interesting is the detached kitchen building outfitted with a brick "beehive" oven and vintage cooking utensils. Though not a must-see on the Key West tour, history and architecture buffs will appreciate the finely preserved details and the glimpse of a slower, easier time in the island's life. They also have an excellent speaker series. Plan to spend 30 minutes to an hour.

322 Duval St. oirf.org. **305/294-9501.** Free admission. Daily 10am–4pm.

San Carlos Institute ★   As the closest bit of the United States to Cuba, 90 miles south, this island has had a history intertwined with that of the Latin island since at least the 1870s, when Cubans arrived after fleeing fallout from uprisings against colonial ruler Spain. Founded in 1871 as a center of Cuban culture and education, the San Carlos is today a museum, library, gallery, theater, and school.

Over the decades it moved once, burned down once, and was destroyed by a hurricane once, so the gracious building with columns, arches, and stained glass we see now actually dates from 1924. Have a peek inside at the lovely tile work and decor (entry is free). There are also exhibitions on Cuban aviation, Cuban postage stamps, and a photo exhibit on Cuban patriot and poet José Martí, but they're relatively modest.

516 Duval St. institutosancarlos.org. 786/251-3399. Free admission. Thurs–Sun noon–6pm.

Tennessee Williams Museum ★★★ Some say Williams finished the final draft of *A Streetcar Named Desire* in 1947 while staying at the La Concha Hotel. Whatever the truth is, this giant of 20th-century theater visited and lived in Key West from 1941 until his death in 1983. In 1950, he bought a house at 1431 Duncan St., where he lived for years. While that house is no longer here, a scale model of that home is at the museum which highlights Williams' literary accomplishments and life in Key West through an extensive collection of photographs, first edition plays and books, rare newspaper and magazine articles, videos, and even the typewriter he ticked on while writing in Key West. Members of the local literati, including resident and author Judy Blume, love this place.

513 Truman Ave. kwahs.org. 305/204-4527. Admission $9 adults, $6 seniors, free for children 18 and under. Daily 10am–5pm (last admission 4:30pm).

Organized Tours

BY TRAM & TROLLEY BUS The city's entire story is packed into a neat, sometime raunchy 90-minute package on the **Conch Tour Train** ★★ (conch tourtrain.com; 305/77-5775; $42–$54 adults, $20 children 12 and under). In operation since 1958, the engine of the "train" is a propane-powered jeep disguised as a locomotive, so yes, it does feel hokey to ride the thing. Tours depart from both Mallory Square and the Welcome Center, near where U.S. 1 becomes North Roosevelt Boulevard, on the less-developed side of the island. Daily departures are every half-hour from 9am to 4:30pm.

The **Old Town Trolley Tours** ★★ (keylimebiketours.com; 855/623-8289; $52–$70 adults, $20 children 4–12) is the choice in bad weather (the Conch Train is open to the elements) or if you're staying at one of the hotels on its route. Humorous drivers maintain a running commentary as the enclosed trolley loops around the island's streets past all the major sights. Trolley buses depart from Mallory Square and other points around the island, including many area hotels. Departures are daily every half-hour (though not always on the half-hour) from 9am to 4:30pm.

Visitors debarking the Conch Train.

Also from Old Town Trolley: **Ghosts & Gravestones Frightseeing Tour ★★★**, an hour of horrors passing through the shadowy streets and lanes of Old Town, stopping at allegedly haunted Victorian mansions, and covering island lore, superstitions and rituals, a scorned wife who haunted her ex, a cursed silver bar at the Key West Shipwreck Treasure Museum, and other bizarre yet true aspects of this eerie place. Tours depart from 501 Front St. at 7, 8, 8:30, 9:30, and 10pm. Tickets are $37 per person. Children 12 and under will find the tour too scary. Call © 305/294-4678 (it spells out GHOST) for more info.

Whichever you choose, all of these historic, trivia-packed tours are well worth the price of tickets, and you'll get discounts on all if you pre-book online.

BY AIR **Florida Keys Flight Academy,** at Key West Airport, 3469 S. Roosevelt Blvd. (floridakeysflightacademy.com; © 844/KEYS-AIR [539-7247]), offers scenic airplane tours including one in a WWII trainer, a Vultee BT-13 Warbird. Tours range from 20 minutes to an hour, and all include the Seven Mile Bridge and assorted Key West landmarks. Prices range from $199 to $399, and most are for up to three passengers. They also do custom air tours.

BY BIKE Besides walking, one of the best ways to explore Key West is by bike. With **Key Lime Bike Tours ★★**, 122 Ann St. (keylimebiketours.com; © 305/340-7834), you can pedal around the Old Town district on a 2-hour bicycle tour led by a knowledgeable guide who will offer insight into everything from Key West's seafaring history to architecture, foliage, and even local gossip. Included in the $45-per-person tour are a 25-ounce bottle of water, a slice of Key lime pie (work it off!), sunscreen, and ponchos. Tours are daily at 10am and 2pm. Bike rentals are $20 per day to $110 for the week.

BY BOAT The catamarans and the glass-bottom boat of **Fury Water Adventures ★**, 237 Front St. (furycat.com; © 305/296-6293), depart on daytime coral-reef tours and evening sunset cruises. It also offers jet-ski tours, eco-tours, and parasailing. Prices are cheaper on the website, and range from $40 to $120 for adults and $20 to $100 for children ages 4 to 10.

The schooner *Appledore Star* **★★★** (keywestschooners.com; © 305/563-8157) is the last known Chesapeake Bugeye ever built. Its unique shallow draft design allows it to navigate Key West's backcountry with ease on daily eco-tours exploring mangrove islands. In addition to the eco-tours, there's a gorgeous champagne sunset sail, a Windjammer Day Sail, and, our personal fave, the Key West Bloody Mary Sail. Sails are 2 hours and range from $50 per adult and $25 for kids 4 to 11 and include alcoholic beverages, water, and soft drinks. It's a deal.

For shark sightings with a Key West flair, contact **Capt. Ken Harris ★★★** (kwextremeadventures.com; © **305/508-1951;** 2-hr. tours $89 adults, $49 children 6–16, $29 children 5 and under), one of the area's more famous captains known, along with relatives and fellow captains Dave and Clay Harris, as the Key West Shark Whisperers, working these docks for more than 30 years. He operates the 34-foot *Tiger Cat*, a custom-built eco-adventure catamaran.

OTHER TOURS **Sharon Wells ★★★** (sharonwellskeywestart.com; © **305/923-5133**), historian and artist, leads a number of tours throughout the island, focusing on such diverse topics as literature, architecture, and places connected with the island's LGBTQIA+ culture. Her Key West House tours are especially fascinating.

For a spirited take on Key West, try the **Key West Pub Crawl** (keywestwalkingtours.com; © 305/998-8599), a tour of the island's most famous bars. It's given on Tuesday through Sunday nights at 8pm, lasts 2½ hours, costs $34.95, and includes five (!) drinks.

Two other fun options are, first, the 90-minute **Bone Island Ghost Tour** ★★ (boneislandghosttours.com; $25), leaving nightly at 8:30pm. This spooky tour gives participants insight into many old island legends. The other is **Ghosts & Gravestones** (above).

Since the early 1940s, Key West has been a haven for LGBTQIA+ luminaries such as Tennessee Williams and Broadway legend Jerry Herman. The **Gay and Lesbian Historic Trolley Tour** ★★★ (gaykeywestfl.com; $20–$25) showcases the history, contributions, and landmarks associated with the island's flourishing LGBTQIA+ culture. Highlights include Williams's house, the art gallery owned by Key West's first gay mayor, and a variety of guesthouses whose gay owners fueled the island's architectural-restoration movement. The 70-minute tour takes place Saturday at 10:50am, starting and ending at City of Key West parking lot, corner of Simonton and Angela streets. Look for the trolley with the rainbow flags.

Outdoor Activities

BEACHES Key West actually has a few small beaches, although they don't compare with the state's wide natural wonders up the coast; the Keys' beaches are typically narrow and rocky. Here are the top ones:

A magnet for partying teenagers, **Smathers Beach** is Key West's largest and most overpopulated. Despite the number of rowdy teens, the beach is actually quite clean. If you go early enough in the morning, you may notice people sleeping on the beach from the night before. It's off South Roosevelt Boulevard, west of the airport.

Higgs Beach, along Atlantic Boulevard, between White Street and Reynolds Road, is a favorite among Key West's gay crowds. But what many people don't know is that beneath the sand is an unmarked cemetery of African slaves who died while waiting for freedom. Higgs has a playground and tennis courts, and is near the minute Rest Beach, which is actually hidden by the White Street pier. The sand here is coarse and rocky and the water tends to be a bit mucky, but if you can bear it, Higgs is known as a great snorkeling beach. If it's sunbathing you want, skip Higgs and go to Smathers.

Although there is an entrance fee ($6/car of two to eight plus 50¢/person for Monroe County surcharge, $4.50 single-occupant vehicle, $2.50 pedestrians and bicyclists), we most recommend the beach at **Fort Zachary Taylor Historic State Park** ★★★, 601 Howard

Fort Zachary Taylor.

England Way (floridastateparks.org/parks-and-trails/fort-zachary-taylor-historic-state-park; © **305/292-6713**), located off the western end of Southard Boulevard. Beyond the sands it has a historic fort; a museum with the largest collection of Civil War armaments on the planet; and a large picnic area with tables, barbecue grills, restrooms, and showers. Large trees scattered across 87 acres provide shade for those who are reluctant to bake in the sun. *Tip:* We highly recommend the 11am daily tour of the fort, as the guides are talented at bringing its history to life.

BIKING & MOPEDING A popular mode of transportation for locals and visitors, bikes and mopeds are available at many rental outlets in the city. Escape the hectic downtown scene and explore the island's scenic side streets by heading away from Duval Street toward South Roosevelt Boulevard and the beachside enclaves along the way. See p. 189.

FISHING As any angler will tell you, there's no fishing like Keys fishing. Key West has it all: bonefish, tarpon, dolphin, tuna, grouper, cobia, and more—sharks, too.

Step aboard a small, exposed skiff for an incredibly diverse day of fishing. In the morning, you can head offshore for sailfish or dolphin (the fish, not the mammal), and then by afternoon get closer to land for a shot at tarpon, permit, grouper, or snapper. Here in Key West, you can probably pick up more cobia—one of the best fighting and eating fish around—than anywhere else in the world. For a real fight, ask your skipper to go for the tarpon, the greatest fighting fish there is, famous for its dramatic "tail walk" on the water after it's hooked. Shark fishing is also popular.

> **Reel Deals on Fishing**
>
> When looking for the best deals on fishing excursions, know that the bookers from the kiosks in town generally take a large chunk of a captain's fee in addition to an extra monthly fee. You can usually save yourself money by booking directly with a captain in advance (just Google "fishing charters Key West") or by going straight to one of the docks. For reviews on charters, we recommend checking captainexperiences.com/locations/florida/key-west.

The advantage of the smaller, more expensive charter boats is that you can call the shots. They'll take you where you want to go, to fish for what you want to catch. These "light tackles" are also easier to maneuver, which means you can go to backcountry spots for tarpon and bonefish, as well as out to the open ocean for tuna and dolphin fish. You'll really be able to feel the fish, and you'll get some good fights, too. Larger boats, for up to six or seven people, are cheaper and are best for kingfish, billfish, and sailfish. If you're not comfortable wading through web reviews, the experts at **Southbound Sportfishing** (southboundsportfishing.com; © **305/780-6281**) can book for you, and will take responsibility for finding the right boat, though you will pay more going through them than you would simply booking direct.

The huge commercial party boats are more for sightseeing than serious angling, though you can be lucky enough to get a few bites at one of the fishing holes. One especially good deal is the ***Gulfstream IV*** ★★ (gulfstreamkeywest.com; © **305/296-8494**), an all-day charter that goes out daily from 10am to 4pm. You'll pay $67.95 for adults, $42.95 for kids 11 and under, and $45.95 for riders not fishing. Price includes parking, bait, tackle, and license. Rod rentals are $5. This 58-foot party boat usually is licensed for 67 passengers, but they keep it at 45 anglers max. There's a full-service galley on board.

Serious anglers should consider the light-tackle boats that leave from Stock Island 1½ miles off U.S. 1 (stockislandfishing.com; ✆ **305/509-2201**). It's a 20-minute drive from Old Town on the Atlantic side. There are more than 30 light-tackle guides, which range from flatbed, backcountry skiffs to 28-foot open boats. There are also a few larger charters and a party boat that goes to the Dry Tortugas.

GOLF The area's only public golf club is **Key West Golf Club** ★★ (keywestgolf.com; ✆ **305/294-5232**), an 18-hole course at the entrance to the island of Key West at MM 4.5 (turn onto College Rd. to the course entrance). Designed by Rees Jones, the 200-acre course has plenty of mangroves and water hazards on its 6,526 yards. It's open to the public and has a pro shop. Call ahead for tee-time reservations. Rates range from $75 to $140 for adults and $49 to $64 for those 18 and under. Rates include cart. Club rental is $55.

KAYAKING **Lazy Dog Adventure** ★★★, 5114 Overseas Hwy. (lazydog.com; ✆ **305/295-9898**), operates first-rate, 2-hour daily kayaking tours through the backcountry of Key West ($35). For the really adventurous, they also offer a 4-hour kayak and snorkel tour combo through the mangroves ($60/person ages 12 and over).

SCUBA DIVING One of the area's largest scuba schools, **Captain Hook's Dive Key West,** 3128 N. Roosevelt Blvd. (divekeywest.com; ✆ **800/426-0707** or 305/296-3823), offers instruction at all levels; its dive boats take participants to scuba and snorkel sites on nearby reefs.

Key West Marine Park and Snorkel Trail ★★★ (reefrelief.org/key-west-marine-park; ✆ **305/294-3100**), a 40-acre dive park along the island's Atlantic shore, incorporates no-motor "swim-only" lanes marked by buoys, providing swimmers and snorkelers with a safe way to explore the waters. The park's boundaries stretch from the foot of Duval Street to Higgs Beach.

Wreck dives and night dives are two of the special offerings of **Lost Reef Adventures,** 261 Margaret St. (lostreefadventures.com; ✆ **305/296-9737**). Regularly scheduled runs and private charters can be arranged. Phone for departure information.

For a map of the **Florida Keys Shipwreck Heritage Trail** ★★★, an entire network of nine wrecks from Key Largo to Key West, go to floridakeys.noaa.gov/shipwrecktrail. It should include the *General Hoyt S. Vandenberg,* a 524-foot former U.S. Air Force missile-tracking ship, that was sunk 6 miles south of Key West in 2009 to create an artificial reef. For location and more info, go to keywest.com/vandenberg/about.

For hard-core and high-tech wreck divers, check out the **Wreck Trek Passport Program** (www.fla-keys.com/diving/wrecktrek), spotlighting the Florida Keys Shipwreck Trail from Key Largo to Key West and allowing certified divers to explore the trail and be rewarded with bragging rights for logging back-to-back wreck dives. Dive passport highlights nine shipwrecks. Even if you don't compete, it's worth a look just for the trail information alone.

Shopping

You'll find both unique gifts and schlocky souvenirs in Key West, from coconut postcards and Key lime pies to lewd clothing and tchotchkes. On Duval Street, T-shirt shops outnumber almost any other business. *Be careful:* Unscrupulous salespeople have been known to rip off unwitting shoppers on custom tees. You are entitled to a written estimate of any T-shirt work before you pay for it.

At Mallory Square, you'll find the **Clinton Square Market,** an overly air-conditioned mall of kiosks and stalls housed in an old U.S. Navy customs building and designed for the many cruise ship passengers who never venture beyond this supercommercial zone. Beyond the high-priced hat and shoe shops, the real reason to head here is for its free and clean restroom.

Once the main industry of Key West, cigar making is enjoying renewed success at the handful of factories that survived the slow years. Though you will no longer find *viejitos* (little old men) rolling fat stogies in the streets just as they used to do in their homeland across the Florida Straits, the **Original Key West Cigar Factory** ★★, 1075 Duval St. (kwcigarfactory.com; ✆ **305/998-9141**), has an excellent selection of imported and locally rolled smokes. Also consider booking the 10:30am or 1:30pm tour at **Rodriguez Cigar Factory** ★★★, 113 Fitzpatrick St. (rodriguezcigarskeywest.com; ✆ **305/296-0167**), where you'll learn about the family's history in Key West as cigar makers dating back to 1831, and watch them prepare, wrap, construct, and roll. Cost is $35 for the 90-minute tour which includes a cigar and Cuban espresso. Remember, buying or selling Cuban-made cigars is illegal. Shops advertising "Cuban cigars" are usually referring to domestic cigars made from tobacco grown from seeds that were brought from Cuba decades ago. To be fair, though, many premium cigars today are grown from Cuban seed tobacco but in Latin America and other areas of the Caribbean.

If you're looking for local or Caribbean art, you'll find nearly a dozen galleries and shops on Duval Street between Catherine and Fleming streets. There are also some excellent shops on the side streets, including the **Key West Collective** ★★★, 720 Caroline St. (keywestcollective.com; ✆ **305/396-1328**), a very cool, curated collection of locally crafted artwork.

Literature and music buffs will appreciate the many bookshops and record stores on the island. **Key West Island Bookstore** ★★, 513 Fleming St. (✆ **305/294-2904;** Mon–Sat 10am–8pm, Sun noon–6pm), carries new, used, and rare books, and specializes in fiction by residents of the Keys, including Ernest Hemingway, Tennessee Williams, Shel Silverstein, Ann Beattie, Richard Wilbur, and John Hersey. For a glimpse of a literary legend or two, check out the small, but cozy and comprehensive **Books & Books @ The Studios** ★★★, 533 Eaton St. (booksandbookskw.com; ✆ **305/320-0208**), a branch of Miami's lauded, beloved indie bookstore that was co-founded by a local whose name you may recognize: Judy Blume. She's often working behind the counter here.

Where to Stay

From resorts with all the amenities to seaside motels, quaint bed-and-breakfasts, and clothing-optional guesthouses, there's a wide variety of lodgings in Key West. You can almost always find a place to stay at the last minute, unless you're in town during the most popular holidays: **Fantasy Fest** (around Halloween), when Mardi Gras meets South Florida and most hotels have outrageous rates and 5-night minimums; **Hemingway Days** (in July), when Papa is seemingly and eerily alive and well; and **Christmas, New Year's,** and big fishing tournaments (many are held Oct–Dec) and boat-racing tourneys. As well, in winter prime properties fill up and many require 2- or 3-night minimum stays. Prices at these times are extremely high. Finding a decent room for less than $300 a night is a real trick.

There are many rentals available through Airbnb and Vrbo. As always with these sites you can avoid extra fees by figuring out the name of the property manager and booking with them directly (easier on Vrbo than Airbnb). LGBTQIA+ travelers should check out the website of the **Key West Business Guild** (gaykeywestfl.com), which represents and recommends gay-friendly and gay-owned businesses. Be advised that many gay guesthouses have a clothing-optional policy.

EXPENSIVE

The Capitana ★★★ B&B meets boutique hotel at this chic, 75-room waterfront spot, well away from the Duval Street madness. It offers suites, cottages, and guest rooms decorated in, yep, coastal decor, but here it actually works because the water views complement, not contradict, the shiplap. Family rooms have bunk beds, and cottages have furnished decks and two king bedrooms. A handsome pool, and actual private beach area (a rarity in these parts except for Casa Marina), are big pluses as are the restaurant, tiki bar, on-site paddleboard, kayak, and bike rentals, and waterfront fitness center. The staff here, too, are unusually gracious and helpful. The $35 per day resort fee covers breakfast and self-parking.

2401 N. Roosevelt Blvd. thecapitanakeywest.com. **305/296-6925.** 75 units. $309–$631 double. Pet fee $100. **Amenities:** Restaurant; bar; outdoor pool; bike rental; concierge; fitness center; watersports gear rental; free Wi-Fi.

The Gardens Hotel ★★★ Believe it or not, the true Garden of Eden has been located . . . and it's on Angela Street. Once Key West's largest private estate–cum–botanical garden, created in the 1930s from an 1880s manse, this has been an inn since the 1990s. A clutch of Bahamian-style buildings house elegant rooms, suites, and cottages (with hardwood floors and plantation beds with Tempur-Pedic mattresses, Apple+ streaming on TVs, and marble bathrooms), and surround two pools and poolside bar. The gardens here are lush and mazelike with bubbling fountains, funky sculptures, a gazebo, a big fancy birdcage; and several huge, antique clay jars from Cuba called *tinajones*. On Sunday afternoons the hotel features live jazz in the gardens. **d'Vine Wine Gallery,** an on-site, self-serve wine bar offers 36 different vintages for hotel and non–hotel guests from 5 to 10pm daily. *Note:* If you plan to party, do *not* stay here. Guests at this adults-only property tend to be on the quieter side.

526 Angela St. gardenshotel.com. **800/526-2664** or 305/294-2661. 21 units. $367–$1,039 double. Rates include continental breakfast. Parking $30. Pet fee $100. **Amenities:** 2 bars; bike rental; concierge; 2 outdoor heated pools; spa services; laundry service; free Wi-Fi.

Marquesa Key West ★★★ Back in 1986, a forward-thinking local transformed a pair of 1880s clapboards into a complex that today houses one of Key West's most fetching small hotels and a beloved restaurant (p. 205). Rooms are good-size, with slanted ceilings and cherrywood floors, appointed with a tasteful mix of the antique and the contemporary, and more often than not have porches for enjoying room-service breakfast, a glass of wine, or just some veg-out time. They're arranged around three pools (one heated) with comely landscaping (love the hanging orchids). But apart from the elegance and blessed tranquility, what takes the experience to the next level is the low-key but attentive service from staff. *Tip:* Famous authors tend to stay here during the annual Key West Literary Seminar. *One caveat:* Those with mobility issues should mention that when booking, because there are no elevators. *Note:* Its sister property, **Marquesa 414,** has more modern rooms in a newer building with its own pool.

600 Fleming St. (at Simonton St.). marquesa.com. **800/869-4631** or 305/292-1919. 44 units. $399–$821. Self-parking $25/day. No children 13 and under. **Amenities:** Restaurant; bike rental; concierge; access to nearby health club; 3 outdoor pools (1 heated); limited room service; free Wi-Fi.

Ocean Key Resort & Spa ★★

You can't beat the location of this 100-room resort, at the foot of Mallory Square, the epicenter of the sunset ritual. Ocean Key also features a Gulf-side heated pool and the lively Sunset Pier, where guests can wind down with cocktails and live music. Guest rooms start at a generous 300 square feet, and go up from there, and have views of the Gulf, the harbor, or Mallory Square and Duval Street. The property is adorned in classic Key West decor (tile floors and lots of aqua), with deep soaking tubs and high-quality mattresses. The Indonesian-inspired **SpaTerre** is perhaps the best in town. The resort's restaurant, **Hot Tin Roof** (p. 205), is also one of Key West's finest. **The Liquid Lounge** is a VIP pool lounge with nightclub-style bottle service and music. Downside to staying here? The ridic $56 resort fee, which, shockingly, does not cover parking, though it does get you a welcome cocktail.

Zero Duval St. (near Mallory Square). oceankey.com. ⓒ **844/330-3852** or 305/809-8072. 100 units. From $546–$1,439 double. Valet $45. **Amenities:** 2 restaurants; 3 bars; bike rental; concierge; fitness center; heated pool; room service; watersports equipment/rentals; free Wi-Fi.

Simonton Court Historic Inn & Cottages ★★★

Behind the unassuming, palm-hidden facade of a onetime cigar factory is a lushly landscaped little world unto itself: converted Bahamian-style houses and cottages dating from the 1880s. Though all have the usual modern amenities, units vary quite a bit, from the rustic-feeling cigar-factory rooms, paneled in Dade County pine, to suites with a more contemporary, Asian-inflected flavor. Some even have their own pools, and all are adorned with for-sale paintings by local artists. The two corners of the main pool are fragments of the brick walls of the water cistern that once stood on this very spot. Atmosphere like this, plus the friendly, helpful staff, keep regulars coming back, and also means it can be tough to score a reservation, especially in season. People love the place so much, they book years in advance.

320 Simonton St. simontoncourt.com. ⓒ **305/294-6386.** 30 units. $337–$447 Queen room, more for bigger units. Rates include continental breakfast. **Amenities:** Concierge; 4 outdoor pools; free Wi-Fi.

Southernmost Beach Resort ★★★

Why at the lower end of Duval Street is there a cluster of hostelries labeled "Southernmost"? Well, right down the block on South Street is that famous, garish, buoy-looking thingy marking the southernmost point in the continental U.S. (though actually, this is still true only if you're counting natural landmass—the manmade Truman Annex reaches farther south). The recipient of a recent facelift, this beachfront hotel—one of the few in Key West on an actually sandy beach—is a collection of different buildings: the beachfront resort, with 127 rooms, all with views of the Atlantic, and several historic guesthouses. At the resort, rooms are done up in soothing neutrals, with aqua throw pillows and fine wood and wicker furnishings. The newly restored guesthouses are called **Le Mer & Dewey,** the **Avalon,** and **Duval Gardens.** All are located off the big resort's premises on the quieter end of Duval Street and feature a bit more personality (lots of coral pink accents, tray ceilings, and colorful, artistically mismatched furniture and wallpaper). Some have French doors that open to a heated pool. Our fave is the adults-only, Victorian-style Le Mer & Dewey House, which is quaint and cottagey with its own innkeeper. Guesthouse guests are welcome to use the amenities at the more bustling resort just a few steps away. These include the open-air **Southernmost Beach Café,** and two poolside bars. Because of its impressive beach, Southernmost is the site of many weddings.

1319 Duval St. southernmostbeachresort.com. ⓒ **800/354-4455.** 261 units. $389–$641 double. Parking $42/night. **Amenities:** Restaurant; 3 bars; bike rental; concierge; fitness center; 3 pools; spa; watersports equipment rental; free Wi-Fi.

EXPENSIVE/MODERATE

Ambrosia Key West ★★★
Ambrosia is a private compound set on 2 lush acres, hidden just a block from Duval Street. Three lagoon-style pools, suites, town houses, and a cottage are spread around the grounds. Town houses have living rooms, kitchens, and spiral staircases leading to master suites with vaulted ceilings and private decks. The cottage, overlooking a dip pool, is a perfect family retreat, with two bedrooms, two bathrooms, a living room, and a kitchen. All rooms have private entrances, most with French doors opening onto a variety of intimate outdoor spaces, including private verandas, patios, and gardens with sculptures, fountains, and pools. The Alligator room is large and spacious, with an enormous, covered porch, just steps from the pool, and with plenty of amenities: microwave, Keurig machine, fridge. Topnotch service explains why Ambrosia has a 90% year-round occupancy, a record in seasonal Key West.

622 Fleming St. ambrosiakeywest.com. **800/535-9838** or 305/296-9838. 20 units. $303–$444 double. Rates include breakfast buffet. Pet fee $25/night. **Amenities:** Concierge; 3 outdoor heated pools; free Wi-Fi.

The Grand Guesthouse ★★
Built in the 1880s as a boardinghouse for workers at a nearby cigar factory, this guesthouse is tucked away on a quiet residential street a half-dozen blocks away from Duval. It's also an easy several-block stroll from Higgs Beach—especially helpful because there's no pool. Apart from some nice landscaping and a hammock out back, on-premises bells and whistles are at a minimum, but the 10 rooms are clean, comfy, and tasteful and come with all the expected mod-cons and private entrances. The hosts here are friendly and accommodating. No children under age 12 allowed.

1116 Grinnell St. (btw. Virginia and Catherine sts.). thegrandguesthouse.com. **888/947-2630** or 305/294-0590. 10 units. $304–$780 double. Rates include expanded continental breakfast, evening happy hour, and parking. **Amenities:** Bike rental; concierge; free Wi-Fi.

Island City House Hotel ★★
Another charmer of a variation on the Key West theme of historic architecture with a heated pool set amid palmy gardens. Behind a striking, balustraded, triple-decker facade, Island City House also brings a particular distinction to the table: It's the island's oldest still-operating guesthouse, established in 1912 from a merchant's home built in 1880 (if you're looking for period decor, the original building is the place, with hardwood floors, lace curtains, wainscoting, four-posters, and antiques). Two adjacent, also historic buildings house half of the units, which lean

Island City House Hotel.

toward a more contemporary flavor; some, for example, with white pickled-wood paneling, others with a more Tommy Bahama/rattan vibe. It's also great for folks who want to do a little cooking, as all have full kitchens. *Warning/perk:* Kitties are part of the scene here, so this is not a place for those allergic to cats.

411 William St. islandcityhouse.com. **305/294-5702.** 22 units. $273–$531 double. **Amenities:** Bike rental; concierge; access to nearby health club; outdoor heated pool; free Wi-Fi.

Seascape Inn Bed & Breakfast ★★

For a low-key, intimate, and adults-only stay just a half-block from Duval Street, the Seascape makes for a sweet little oasis. It was built from native pine in the Bahamas in the 1840s and transported by ship to Key West, where it was rebuilt in 1889. Fast forward to 2025 and you have a smartly renovated, tropical-style inn with turn-of-the-19th-century charm. Rooms are decorated in colorful, tropical decor with wicker furnishings and local art. Most have French doors that open out to a heated pool and Jacuzzi, upstairs sun deck, or gardens and courtyard where guests get a champagne continental breakfast. The two-story Havana Suite has a private entrance as well as a kitchenette. In the lobby is an honor bar with beer, wine, and sodas.

420 Olivia St. seascapetropicalinn.com. **888/765-6438** or 305/296-7776. 7 units. $272–$702. Rates include breakfast and parking. **Amenities:** Concierge; bike rental; Jacuzzi; outdoor heated pool; free Wi-Fi.

Silver Palms Inn ★★

Emerging from the wreckage of the mom-and-pop El Rancho Motel is this family-friendly 50-room hotel on the edge of Duval Street featuring modern, immaculately clean rooms and suites surrounding a courtyard, deck, and saltwater pool. Free parking and free breakfast are two favorite perks here, but eco-conscious travelers will also appreciate Silver Palm's green initiatives, including water and energy conservation and use of eco-friendly insulation and products. Guests can use the pool at the inn's sister property, La Pensione, whose own guests come here for the big breakfast.

830 Truman Ave. silverpalmsinn.com. **305/294-8700.** 50 units. $247–$639 double. Rates include free breakfast and parking. **Amenities:** Concierge; bike rental; fitness room; pool; free Wi-Fi.

Southernmost Point Guest House By the Beach ★★

One of the few inns here that welcomes children and pets, this romantic, Victorian-era Queen Anne–style guesthouse is a real find. White-glove clean, modern coastal-style rooms are located either in the main guesthouse or in one of the adjoining buildings. The Pointe View Suite is one of the best, with a private, wraparound porch, and full kitchen. For those on a budget, the Petite Sugar Apple Queen Room is tiny, but adorable, with all the amenities of a more expensive room. Every unit comes with a complimentary drink ticket for one tipple per guest, per day. There's also a daily happy hour with free wine and live music. The inn also supplies chairs and towels for the beach, just a block away. Breakfast is served in the garden from 8 to 10am, and you actually can order prepared food from a menu. Kids will enjoy the grounds where they can chase the lizards, the roosters, and the pet rabbits.

1327 Duval St. southernmostpoint.com. **305/294-0715.** 13 units. $232–$527 double. Rates include breakfast, happy hour, and parking. **Amenities:** Bar; bike rental; pool; Wi-Fi.

Weatherstation Inn ★

Weather can be a big deal in the Gulf of Mexico, which is why the U.S. Navy built this two-story, neoclassical-style storm-tracking station in 1912. Presidents Truman, Eisenhower, and JFK all visited the station. By the 1990s, it had been transformed into a bed-and-breakfast of just eight

> ### Taking Stock (Island)
>
> Ten minutes east of Key West is Stock Island, a salty, rusty, fishy spot that some love for its rustic, uh, charm, while others find it depressing. Its working boatyards and fishing docks can be fascinating, but the rest of this impoverished area is all trailers, empty dirt lots, and run-down homes. That hasn't stopped developers from staking claim here, bizarrely enough, planting two upscale hotels on the island: **Perry Hotel & Marina,** 7001 Shrimp Rd. (perrykeywest.com; ⓒ **877/496-8712**), and **Ocean's Edge Resort & Marina,** 5950 Peninsular Ave. (oceansedgekeywest.com; ⓒ **877/935-0862**). Neither, however, uses "Stock Island" in their names for a reason. Yes, these hotels are nice once you are inside, and less expensive than those in Key West proper, but they're a stark contrast to their surroundings. After my last stay on Stock Island (I did a night in each hotel), I didn't feel the need to return, and this is coming from someone who loves dive bars and met her spouse of nearly 2 decades at a dirt floor watering hole, **Schooner Wharf** in Key West. I *would* return for the **Hogfish Bar & Grill** (p. 209), or if I had kids in tow for the **Sheriff's Animal Farm,** 5501 College Rd. (www.facebook.com/KeysAnimalFarm; ⓒ **305/293-7300**), the country's only jailhouse animal farm and petting zoo, run by the Monroe County Sheriff's office to rehab rescued animals, including a one-eyed ostrich, a three-legged kinkajou, and more. It's free of charge and open from 1 to 3pm twice monthly on the second and fourth Saturdays.

genteel rooms (though weather balloons are occasionally still launched from the roof). I'd have to say that because of its unusual history and small size, as well as unique location—on a very peaceful residential block of the former Navy base, yet a short, no-sweat stroll to Mallory Square and Duval Street—this is one inn that's definitely for a very particular type of vacationer. There are no gregarious cocktail hours by the pool or extensive gardens; here the allure is tranquility. Spacious and uncluttered, each guest room is uniquely furnished to complement the interior architecture: hardwood floors, tall sash windows, and high ceilings. The large, modern bathrooms are especially appealing. The staff are professional and warm. The only downside to staying here: a musty odor in some of the rooms (ask to move if you're bothered).

57 Front St. weatherstationinn.com. ⓒ **305/294-7277.** 8 units. Winter $224–$528 double. Rates include continental breakfast. **Amenities:** Concierge; outdoor pool; free Wi-Fi.

INEXPENSIVE

Seashell Motel & Key West Hostel This well-run hostel is a 3-minute walk to the beach and Old Town. Very popular with European backpackers, it's a great place to meet people. The newly renovated dorm rooms are sparse, but livable if you want a cheap stay. There are all-male, all-female, and co-ed dorm rooms for couples. The higher-priced, also recently renovated, private motel rooms are a good deal, especially those equipped with kitchens. Amenities include a courtyard with gas grill which many guests use to cook up what they caught that day.

718 South St. keywesthostel.com. ⓒ **305/296-5719.** 92 dorm beds, 10 motel rooms. Shared dorm bed $49–$199; private rooms $224–$329. Free parking. **Amenities:** Bike rental; free Wi-Fi.

Where to Dine

With its share of fast-food franchises—mostly on Duval Street and Roosevelt Boulevard—you might be surprised to learn that Key West now also has a damn high quality dining scene. We have a number of exciting recommendations below.

Tip: If you're staying in a condo or an efficiency, you may want to stock your fridge with goods from the area's oldest grocer, **Fausto's Food Palace** (faustos.com). Open since 1926, Fausto's has two locations: 1105 White St. and 522 Fleming St. The latter will deliver with a $25-minimum order.

EXPENSIVE

Antonia's ★★ ITALIAN From the perfectly seasoned homemade focaccia to an exemplary amaretto coconut cream pie, this elegant little standout is amazingly consistent. The menu includes a small selection of classics (linguine with shrimp, pillowy gnocchi, and *zuppa di pesce*), but it also does well with more inventive dishes like the warm goat-cheese soufflé appetizer. And you can't go wrong with any of the handmade pastas. Bottom line: The food is great, but the atmosphere is a bit fussy for Key West. And if you don't have a reservation in season, don't even bother to stop by. This place books up months in advance.

615 Duval St. antoniaskeywest.com. © **305/294-6565.** Reservations suggested. Main courses $23–$74. Daily 5–10pm.

Café Marquesa ★★★ CONTEMPORARY AMERICAN One of Key West's best boutique hotels (p. 200) also houses one of its finest restaurants, a single-room, yellow-sponge-painted 50-seater with large mahogany mirrors on one side, and on the other, large windows out onto the tranquil surrounding streets. Chef Laurence brightens his menu with plenty of international influences and ingredients, and as you might expect, he's also big on both local sourcing and seasonality. A recent menu included grilled tenderloin of beef "Oscar" with bearnaise sauce and lump crabcake, and a miso glazed grouper with wasabi mashed potatoes, bok choy, and dashi mushrooms. The she-crab soup is always a big hit, and don't overlook the delish breakfasts here.

In the Marquesa Hotel, 600 Fleming St. marquesa.com. © **305/292-1919.** Main courses $52–$88. Daily 8–11am and 5:30–9:30pm.

Hot Tin Roof ★★★ FUSION SEAFOOD Ever hear of conch fusion cuisine? Neither had we, until we experienced it firsthand at Hot Tin Roof, Ocean Key Resort's (p. 201) elegant, harborfront restaurant which melds South American, Asian, French, and Keys cuisine together into flavor profiles you won't find anywhere else. We're talking plantain-crusted swordfish with roasted corn salsa and tequila poblano sauce, or a whole, crispy yellowtail snapper with maduros and cilantro dipping sauce. Cuban bread pudding is a stunner, and breakfast is top-notch here, too. Last time we ate here, Meryl Streep was sitting next to us, looking as impressed as she was impressive.

In the Ocean Key Resort, Zero Duval St. oceankey.com. © **305/296-7701.** Main courses $39–$79. Daily 8–11:30am and 5–9:15pm. Sunday brunch 11:45am–12:45pm.

Latitudes ★ SEAFOOD All the superlatives in the world can't describe the beauty of this place, located on the pristine, private island that houses the swanky Sunset Key cottages. As for the food . . . it's good, but the views are better. When the tiki torches are lit at night it's especially magical. Plus, you get a "free" boat ride here, the only way to get here if you aren't a guest of Sunset Key resort. On the dinner menu, expect items like Key West pink shrimp carbonara with smoked bacon or braised beef short rib. Dinners are pricey, so consider going for the simpler (and less expensive) breakfasts and lunches—you'll still get those views!

By boat only at 245 Front St. 305/292-5394. opalcollection.com. Main dinner courses $44–$72. Daily 7am–2:15pm; Sun–Thurs 5–10pm; Fri–Sat 5–11pm.

La Trattoria ★★ ITALIAN   It's near impossible to choose between here, and Antonia's (see above). Both serve high-quality Italian, and Italian-American, fare, with genuine smiles. From the simple dishes, like breadcrumb-stuffed mushroom caps, to a Venetian pasta of sun-dried tomatoes, crabmeat and mushrooms, it's hard to go wrong dining here. Many end the evening at **Virgilio's,** the restaurant's indoor/outdoor cocktail lounge with live jazz until 2am.

524 Duval St. latrattoria.us. 305/296-1075. Main courses $17–$50. Sun–Thurs 5–10:30pm; Fri–Sat 5–11pm.

Louie's Backyard ★★★ CARIBBEAN   Still going strong after more than 50 years, both the setting and the creative island menu help make Louie's one of Key West's most cherished and romantic—not to mention pricey—upper-end restaurants. Set in a big ol' 19th-century clapboard house right on the Atlantic, the restaurant's interior is elegant, but ambience-wise, it's all about the great outdoors, with three levels and a beachside bar. For the full-blown fine-dining experience, longtime chef Doug Shook's creative menu (Florida meets the Caribbean, then they tour the world together) includes highlights such as silky splendid Bahamian conch chowder with Bird Pepper hot sauce, and grilled, root beer–glazed Berkshire pork chop with bourbon sweet potato mash and caramelized cipollini onions. To keep your tab down, come for lunch, weekend brunch, or world-cuisine tapas on the "Upper Deck," with the likes of flaming ouzo shrimp, Moroccan-spiced grilled quail, and duck confit pizza. *Tip:* Reservations are only taken by phone, and they are *very* hard to get. Either call way in advance, hope that your hotel concierge has some pull, or find a seat at the casual oceanfront bar or upstairs cafe.

700 Waddell Ave. www.louiesbackyard.com. 305/294-1061. Main courses $39–$48. Daily 11:30am–3pm and 6–10:30pm.

Seven Fish ★★★ SEAFOOD   Seven Fish serves some of the best fish on the island. Consensus faves here include the yellowtail snapper curry, sea scallops with split pea puree and sauteed spinach, and the simple sauteed fish. For the people in your party who won't do fish (there's always one of them, right?), there is a fab banana chicken, as well as burgers, pesto pasta, and meatloaf. For dessert, bananas win again in the form of banana flambe.

921 Truman Ave. 7fish.com. 305/296-2777. Main courses $25–$57. Wed–Mon 6–10pm.

MODERATE

Banana Café ★★ FRENCH   Banana Café benefits from a French-country-cafe look and feel. It's set on the less-congested end of Duval Street and has retained its loyal clientele with affordable prices and delightfully light preparations. This is especially true of their exceptional crepes, filled with everything from ham and eggs at breakfast, to chicken cordon bleu or blackened mahimahi for lunch or dinner. Speaking of dinner, they do Gallic classics here quite well (duck l'orange, steak frites) as well as a number of locally sourced fish dishes. There's beer and wine only, but at brunch that translates to bellinis and mimosas (this is a top brunch spot).

1211 Duval St. bananacafekw.com. 305/294-7227. Main courses $10–$34. Daily 7:30am–9:30pm.

Blue Heaven ★★★ SEAFOOD/AMERICAN/NATURAL   A one-of-a-kind local institution, founded by artist-and-writer couple Richard and Suanne in 1992, this, more than any other eatery I can think of, captures the barefoot quirkiness of Key West (see p. 12). Interior dining rooms are cute, but what defines the place is the rustic courtyard with its hippie-commune vibe and roaming cats and chickens (ambulatory poultry aren't an uncommon sight anywhere here in the Bahama Village section). Back in the day, this space hosted gambling, whoring, cockfighting, even boxing (some matches refereed by Ernest Hemingway himself). These days the menu is more sophisticated than the surroundings, in fact we'd say the food is some of the best in town, especially at breakfast, which features homemade granola, tropical-fruit pancakes (owner Richard often makes his pancakes with beer), and seafood Benedict. Dinners run the gamut from fresh-caught fish and Jamaican jerk chicken to curried soups and vegetarian stews. This is as authentic as Key West gets.

729 Thomas St. (at the corner of Petronia and Thomas). blueheavenkw.com. **305/296-8666.** Main courses $12–$45. Daily 8am–2:30pm and 5–10pm.

Nine One Five ★★★ ECLECTIC FUSION   Housed in a restored and romantic Victorian mansion, Nine One Five has such good food that it was selected to host a six-course dinner at the James Beard House in NYC. Twice. The menu opens with sharing-size appetizers, like the aptly named "absurdly addictive asparagus" (with pancetta, pinenuts, garlic, and lemon zest) and the grilled octopus over chickpea ragu. Always fresh raw bar options include daily changing ceviche. There are also toothsome homemade pastas and a slew of seafood-forward entrees like the whole yellowtail snapper flash fried in Thai fish sauce or the Soul Mama Seafood Soup (with mild Thai green curry in it). Service is attentive, although if you sit up on the quaint second-floor porch, you may be there for a while. But this is the kind of place where you want to linger.

915 Duval St. 915duval.com. **305/296-0669.** Reservations recommended. Main courses $23–$38. Daily 5–11pm. Upstairs lounge daily until 2am.

Pepe's ★★ AMERICAN   The island's oldest still-operating eatery was founded by Pepe Peláez back in 1909, and it's definitely got that old-timey look and feel, with rustic wooden booths, tables, and all manner of Key Westiana crowding the walls and hanging from the ceiling. Another good option is the brick patio alongside, which besides its big ol' spreading mahogany in the middle is also cooled by canvas shades overhead and an enormous fan at back. Whether it's French toast or a hearty omelet for breakfast/brunch (which some consider Pepe's best meals), a fresh fish sandwich at lunchtime, or a nice juicy dinner steak, both quality and portions are satisfying. Apalachicola oysters from Florida's Panhandle are a house specialty. Expect a wait for a table, especially on weekends.

806 Caroline St. (btw. Margaret and Williams sts.). pepeskeywest.com. **305/294-7192.** Main courses $12.50–$64. Daily 7:30am–9:30pm.

INEXPENSIVE

BO's Fish Wagon ★★★ SEAFOOD   If you happen to pass by this ramshackle joint without knowing what it is, you might be afraid to go in. It looks like someone upended a junk shop in the corner of a parking lot. But go in. I urge you. In his younger years, Buddy Owen (nicknamed B.O.) ran a little fried-fish shack in a lot on Duval Street. It was the ideal life: He'd cook the perfect grouper for folks at mealtimes, but when he wasn't working, he'd be out fishing all day and carousing all night. Life changes, though, and Buddy got married, had a kid, and

BO's Fish Wagon's junkyard elan put it on the map, but it's the excellent sandwiches that draw large crowds daily.

when his Duval Street lot was developed, he set up shop on this corner, cobbling together a shelter out of old lobster pots, mannequin legs, concrete, license plates, and an entire vintage pickup truck. He's been here for over 2 decades now, raising a family through sales of the perfect fish sandwich, greasy burger, endless refills of Key limeade, fried grouper and cracked conch, non-seafood "Landwiches," hand-cut fries, and Friday music nights that have attracted locals for years. The free-spirited kitchen staff may sit on the serving counter while they casually take your order, the food may take its sweet time, and if you're very lucky indeed, Buddy himself, now a pillar of the Conch community, may make an appearance. You'll know him because he looks like Hemingway himself. Usually, though, he lets the party he started rock on without him. Oh, and dress code? "No shirt, no shoes, no problem!"

801 Caroline St. bosfishwagon.com. **305/294-9272.** Sandwiches and platters $15–$20. Wed–Mon 11am–9:30pm; Tues 9am–9:30pm.

Boat House Bar & Grill at Turtle Kraals ★ BARBECUE/SEAFOOD

You'll join lots of locals at this out-of-the-way converted warehouse at the historic Key West seaport, with indoor and dockside seating, which serves everything from coconut shrimp and lobster tempura to skirt steak, prime rib, lamb chops, and barbecue ribs. But it's the daily happy hour from 4:30 to 6pm that packs the place (food and drink specials aplenty). Blues bands play most nights, and for drinks the restaurant's roof deck, **The Tower Bar,** has fabulous views of the marina.

220 Margaret St. (at Caroline St.). facebook.com/boathousekeywest.com. **305/294-2640.** Main courses $10–$25. Daily 11am–10pm.

Hogfish Bar & Grill ★ SEAFOOD A ramshackle seafood bar and grill on Safe Harbor in "downtown" Stock Island (there's no town, just fisheries, boats, and shacks), Hogfish is the place to try its namesake sandwich. Similar to grouper, hogfish is a delicious, rare fish with a scalloplike flavor. The sandwich they make out of it, served on Cuban bread, is so popular it's often sold out by noon. Live music and a salty (or rude and crude, depending on your POV) bar scene make Hogfish a quintessential Keys experience. Kids like feeding the fish in the harbor.

6810 Front St., Stock Island. hogfishbar.com. ✆ **305/293-4041.** Main courses $14–$38. Daily 11am–10pm. Take U.S. 1 N. out of Key West and across the Cow Key Channel Bridge. At the 3rd stoplight, bear to the right and onto MacDonald Ave. Follow this for approx. 1 mile and turn right on 4th Ave. (across from Boyd's Campground). Take your next left on Front St. and drive almost to the end—you'll see the Hogfish Bar and Grill on the right.

Island Dogs Bar ★ AMERICAN This islandy bar is a cool spot to throw back a few while catching a game or a live band. The upscale pub fare includes everything from wings and sliders to pizzas and even a very tasty bacon-wrapped hot dog with mango, pineapple, and banana peppers. Sit at the bar or at one of the few outdoor tables ideally placed for watching the crowds stumble—literally—off Duval Street.

505 Front St. islanddogsbar.com. ✆ **305/509-7136.** Main courses $10–$20. Daily 9am–"close."

Key West After Dark

Duval Street is the Bourbon Street of Florida. Amid the tacky T-shirt shops, you'll find bar after bar serving neon-colored frozen drinks to revelers who bounce from one saloon to the next from noon 'til dawn. If you want to join the throngs, start at Truman Avenue and head up Duval. Cover charges are rare, except in LGBTQIA+ clubs (see below), so stop into a dozen and see which you like. Key West is a late-night town, and most bars and clubs don't close until around 3 or 4am.

Alonzo's Oyster Bar ★ SEAFOOD At Alonzo's it's all about the location, on the ground floor of the A&B Lobster House, at the end of Front Street in the marina. There's excellent people-watching, and the staff are cheerful and quick. Because of that, it's a fun place to go for a glass of wine, beer, or a cocktail and some oysters. But don't bother with food beyond that. 700 Front St. ✆ **305/294-5880.** Daily 11am–10pm.

Captain Tony's Saloon ★★ Just around the corner from Duval's beaten path, this smoky old bar is about as authentic as it gets. It comes complete with old-time regulars who remember the island before cruise ships

A bride and groom commemorate their love . . . for Captain Tony's Saloon.

You can't say you've "done" Key West until you've bellied up to the bar at Sloppy Joe's.

docked here; they say Hemingway drank, caroused, and even wrote here. The late owner, Capt. Tony Tarracino, was a former controversial Key West mayor, immortalized in Jimmy Buffett's "Last Mango in Paris." 428 Greene St. capttonyssaloon.com. 📞 **305/294-1838.**

The Green Parrot Bar ★★★ A Key West landmark since 1890, the Green Parrot is a locals' favorite featuring stiff drinks, salty drinkers, and excellent live music from bluegrass and country to Afro-punk. 601 Whitehead St. greenparrot.com. 📞 **305/294-6133.**

Sloppy Joe's ★★ You'll have to stop in here just to say you did. Scholars and drunks debate whether this is the same Sloppy Joe's that Hemingway wrote about, but there's no argument that this classic bar's early-20th-century wooden ceiling and cracked-tile floors are Key West originals. There's live music nightly. Also check out **Joe's Tap Room,** a separate bar within the complex that serves an excellent selection of craft beers. 201 Duval St. sloppyjoes.com. 📞 **305/294-5717.**

The LGBTQIA+ Scene

Key West's live-and-let-live atmosphere extends to its thriving and quirky LGBTQIA+ community. Before and after Tennessee Williams, Key West has provided the perfect backdrop to a gay scene unlike that of many large urban areas.

Seamlessly blended with the prevailing culture, there is no "gay ghetto" in Key West, where the whole place is fabulous.

In Key West, the best music and dancing can be found at the predominantly LGBTQIA+ clubs. While many of the area's other hot spots are geared toward tourists who like to imbibe, these clubs are for those who want to rave, queer or not. Covers vary, but are rarely more than $20.

Two popular adjacent late-night spots are the **801 Bourbon Bar/One Saloon** ★★ (801 Duval St. and 504 Petronia St.; 801Bar.com; ✆ **305/294-4737** or 305/294-4727), featuring great drag and lots more disco. While a mixed crowd comes for the drag shows, a mostly male clientele frequents the bar from noon to 4am. Another Duval Street favorite is **Aqua** ★★, 711 Duval St. (aquakeywest.com; ✆ **305/294-0555**), where you might catch drag queens belting out torch songs or judges voting on the best package in the wet-jockey-shorts contest.

Sunday nights are fun at La-Te-Da, proper name: **La Terraza de Martí** ★★★, 1125 Duval St. (lateda.com; ✆ **305/296-6706**), the former Key West home of Cuban exile José Martí. This is a great spot to gather poolside for the best martini in town—don't bother with the food. Upstairs is the **Crystal Room** ★★★ (✆ **305/296-6706**), with a high-caliber cabaret performance featuring the popular Randy Roberts, who does a fabulous Cher, Bette Midler, and more.

The dress code at 801 Bourbon Bar on Duval Street is "anything goes."

THE DRY TORTUGAS ★★

70 miles W of Key West

Few people realize that the Florida Keys don't end at Key West; about 70 miles west is a chain of seven small islands known as the Dry Tortugas. Because you've come this far, you might wish to visit them, especially if you're into bird-watching, their primary draw.

Ponce de León, who discovered this far-flung cluster of coral keys in 1513, named them Las Tortugas because of the many sea turtles, which still flock to the area during nesting season in the warm summer months. Oceanic charts later carried the preface "dry" to warn mariners that fresh water was unavailable here. Modern intervention has made drinking water available, but little else.

These undeveloped islands make a lovely day trip for travelers interested in seeing the natural anomalies of the Florida Keys—especially the birds. The Dry Tortugas are nesting grounds and roosting sites for thousands of tropical and subtropical oceanic birds. Visitors will also find a historic fort, good fishing, and terrific snorkeling around shallow reefs.

Getting There

There are only two ways to get here—by boat or seaplane. If you rented your own boat, you will have to pay entrance fees in cash: $15 per person, ages 16 and older. That fee is good for 7 days from the time of purchase at Garden Key's main dock, or you can purchase a digital pass online at recreation.gov.

BY BOAT *Yankee Freedom II* (yankeefreedom.com; © **800/634-0939**), a high-speed boat complete with A/C, cushioned seats, three restrooms, freshwater rinse shower, and full galley selling snacks, soft drinks, beer, wine, mixed drinks (on return trip only), film, and souvenirs, zips you to and from the Dry Tortugas in 2 hours and 15 minutes. The round-trip fare ($220 adults, $210 seniors, $165 children 4–16) includes continental breakfast, water, lunch, and a 40-minute guided tour of the fort led by an expert naturalist. The boat leaves Key West for Fort Jefferson at 8am and returns by 5:30pm.

BY PLANE Key West Seaplane Adventures at the Key West International Airport (keywestseaplanecharters.com; © **305/293-9300**) offers morning, afternoon, and full-day trips to the Dry Tortugas National Park via 10 passenger DHC-3T Turbine Otter seaplanes. Prices are steep: $451 and $792 for adults, $360.80 and $633.60 for children 12 and under, not including the $15-per-person park entry fee—cash only for that fee. Flights include free soft drinks and snorkeling equipment.

Exploring the Dry Tortugas

Of the seven islands that make up the Dry Tortugas, Garden Key is the most visited because it is where Fort Jefferson and the visitor center are located. Loggerhead Key, Middle Key, and East Key are open only during the day and are for hiking. Bush Key is for the birds—literally! It's a nesting area for birds only, though it is open from October to January for special excursions. Hospital and Long keys are closed to the public.

Fort Jefferson, a six-sided, 19th-century fortress, is set almost at the water's edge of Garden Key, so it appears to float in the middle of the sea. The

An aerial shot of Fort Jefferson in the Dry Tortugas.

monumental structure is surrounded by 8-foot-thick walls that rise from the sand to a height of nearly 50 feet. Impressive archways, stonework, and parapets make this 150-year-old monument a grand sight. With the invention of the rifled cannon, the fort's masonry construction became obsolete and the building was never completed. For 10 years, however, from 1863 to 1873, Fort Jefferson served as a prison, a kind of "Alcatraz East." Among its prisoners were four of the "Lincoln Conspirators," including Samuel A. Mudd, the doctor who set the broken leg of fugitive assassin John Wilkes Booth. In 1935, Fort Jefferson became a national monument administered by the National Park Service. Today, Fort Jefferson is struggling to resist erosion from the salt and sea, as iron used in the gun openings and the shutters in the fort's walls has accelerated the deterioration, and the structure's openings needed to be rebricked. The National Park Service designated the fort as the recipient of a $15-million facelift, a project that took nearly a decade to complete. In 2020, Fort Jeff received another $4.5-million facelift and its lighthouse was restored and preserved.

For more information on Fort Jefferson and the Dry Tortugas, call the **Everglades National Park Service** (nps.gov/drto/index.htm; *℡* **305/242-7700**). Fort Jefferson is open during daylight hours. A self-guided tour describes the history of the human presence in the Dry Tortugas while leading visitors through the fort. Because of various storms and weather incidents, parts of the park are often closed, so definitely check ahead to see what's what there.

Outdoor Activities

BIRD-WATCHING Bring your binoculars and your bird books: Bird-watching is *the* reason to visit this cluster of tropical islands. The Dry Tortugas, in the middle of the migration flyway between North and South America, serve as an important rest stop for the more than 200 winged varieties that pass through annually. The season peaks from mid-March to mid-May, when thousands of birds show up, but many species from the West Indies can be found here year-round.

> ### Camping on Garden Key
>
> The rustic beauty of the 14-acre **Garden Key** (the only island of the Dry Tortugas where you can pitch tents) is a camper's dream. There are no RVs or motor homes: They can't get here. The abundance of birds doesn't make it quiet, but the camping—a stone's throw from the water—is as beautiful as it gets. Picnic tables, cooking grills, and toilets are provided, but there are no showers. All supplies must be packed in and out.
>
> Sites are $15 and $30 per night and available on a first-come, first-served basis. The 10 sites book up fast. In 2022, Hurricane Ian damaged much of Garden Key, so check in advance for updates on conditions. As we went to press there was still some damage to the pier. For more information, call the **National Park Service** (nps.gov/drto/planyourvisit/camping.htm; ✆ **305/242-7700**).

FISHING A federal law prohibits fishing in a 90-square-mile tract of ocean called the Tortugas North and a 61-square-mile tract of ocean called the Tortugas South. However, some sport fishing is now allowed in Dry Tortugas. We recommend a charter such as **Two Fish Charters** (tortugasfishing.com; ✆ **305/797-6396**), which will take you on a 50-foot sport-fishing catamaran into deep water where you'll catch dolphin (fish, not mammals), tuna, wahoo, king mackerel, sailfish, and an occasional marlin. Trips are overnight and rates are steep: from $5,400 to $5,600, and $2,000 per extra day. If you don't have the money or the time, **Captain Eddie Griffiths** (fishcapteddie.com; ✆ **305/587-3747**) will take you on 4-hour custom fishing trips to the Tortugas at $600 for six people.

SCUBA DIVING & SNORKELING The warm, clear, shallow waters of the Dry Tortugas produce optimum conditions for snorkeling and scuba diving. Four endangered species of sea turtles—green, leatherback, Atlantic Ridley, and hawksbill—can be found here, along with myriad marine species. The region just outside the seawall of Fort Jefferson is excellent for underwater touring; an abundant variety of fish and coral live in 3 to 4 feet of water.

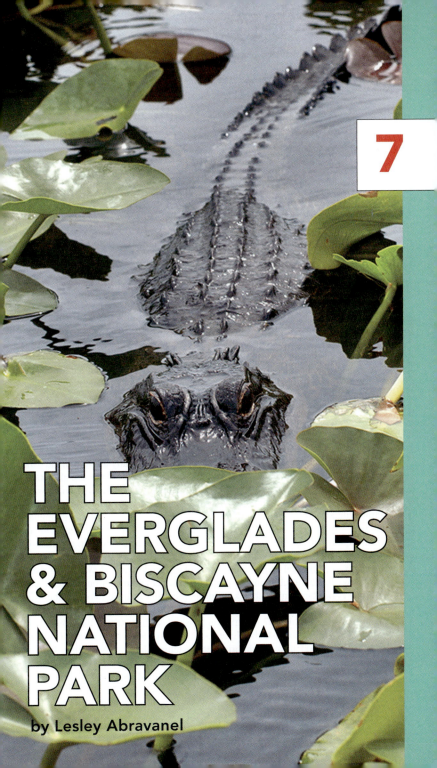

THE EVERGLADES & BISCAYNE NATIONAL PARK

by Lesley Abravanel

7

The vast ecosystem of Everglades National Park—and most of South Florida, really—is a shallow, 50-mile-wide, slow-moving river. Its current 1.5 million acres is less than 20% of its mass when preserved in 1947, but the park has since been designated as an International Biosphere Reserve, a Wetland of International Importance, and a World Heritage Site. It remains one of few places to see endangered American crocodiles, leatherback turtles, and West Indian manatees. Take your time: The rustling of a bush might be a tiny, red-throated anole lizard; that splash of purple might be a mule-ear orchid.

EVERGLADES NATIONAL PARK ★★

On December 6, 1947, when President Harry S. Truman was dedicating Everglades National Park, he called it "an irreplaceable primitive area." While those words don't exactly do justice to the Everglades and the surrounding Biscayne National Park, he clarified what he said: "Here are no lofty peaks seeking the sky, no mighty glaciers or rushing streams wearing away the uplifted land. Here is land, tranquil in its quiet beauty, serving not as the source of water, but as the last receiver of it. To its natural abundance, we owe the spectacular plant and animal life that distinguishes this place from all others in our country."

It's a smart way to describe this majestic area, which inevitably surprises visitors with its variety of sights and experiences.

The absolute best way to see the 'Glades is via canoe, which allows sightseers to get very close to nature. For those with mobility impairments, or dubious athletic skills, another option is airboats, which aren't actually allowed in the park proper, but cut through the saw grass on the park's outskirts. There are also some powerboats allowed in the park (see p. 223), a quieter but pricier option. A walk on one of the park's many trails provides a different vantage point: up-close interaction with an assortment of wildlife. Whichever method you choose, I guarantee that you will marvel at the sheer beauty of the Everglades. And that's even with all the mosquito bites you'll likely get (the bugs seem to be immune to repellent—wear long pants and cover your arms).

This vast, unusual ecosystem is actually a 50-mile-wide, slow-moving river. How slow? It takes a full month for 1 gallon of water to move through Everglades National Park. Rarely more than knee-deep, the water is the lifeblood of this wilderness, and the subtle shifts in water level dictate the life cycles of the native plants and animals. In 1947, 1.5 million acres—less than 20% of the Everglades' wilderness—were established as Everglades National Park. At that time, few lawmakers understood how neighboring ecosystems relate to each other. Consequently, the park is heavily affected by surrounding territories and is at the butt end of every environmental insult that occurs upstream in Miami.

PREVIOUS PAGE: **An alligator slithers through lily pads in Everglades National Park.**

While there has been a marked decrease in indigenous wildlife, Everglades National Park remains one of the few places where you can see dozens of endangered species in their natural habitat, including the American alligator, American crocodile, West Indian manatee, wood stork, snail kite, and Florida panther.

Take your time on the trails. Follow the rustling of a bush, and you might see a small green tree frog or tiny brown anole lizard, with its bright-red spotted throat. Crane your neck to see around a bend, and discover a delicate, brightly painted mule-ear orchid. The slow and subtle splendor of this exotic land may not be immediately appealing to kids raised on smartphones, but they'll certainly remember the experience and thank you later. There's enough dramatic fun around the park, such as airboat rides, hiking, and biking, to keep them satisfied for at least a day.

Essentials

GETTING THERE & ACCESS POINTS

Although the Everglades may seem overwhelmingly large, it's easy to drive to the park's two main areas: the northern section, accessible via Shark Valley and Everglades City, and the southern section, accessible through the Ernest F. Coe Visitor Center, near Homestead and Florida City.

NORTHERN ENTRANCES A popular day trip for Miamians, **Shark Valley,** a 15-mile paved loop road (with an observation tower in the middle of the loop) overlooking the pulsating heart of the Everglades, is the easiest and most scenic way to explore the park. Just 25 miles west of the Florida Turnpike, Shark Valley is best reached via the Tamiami Trail, South Florida's pre-Turnpike, two-lane road, which cuts across the southern part of the state along the park's northern border. Road-

A great egret in Everglades National Park.

side attractions (boat rides and alligator farms, for example) along the Tamiami Trail are operated by the Miccosukee Indian Village and are worth a quick, fun stop. An excellent tram tour (leaving from the Shark Valley Visitor Center) goes deep into the park along a trail that's also terrific for biking. Shark Valley is about an hour's drive from Miami.

A little less than 10 miles west along the Tamiami Trail from Shark Valley, you'll discover **Big Cypress National Preserve,** in which stretches of vibrant green cypress and pine trees make for a fabulous photo op. If you pick up S.R. 29 and head south from the Tamiami Trail, you'll hit a modified version of civilization in the form of Everglades City (where the Everglades meet the Gulf of Mexico), where there's another entrance to the park and the brand-new (2024) **Marjory Stoneman Douglas (MSD) Visitor Center.** From Miami to Shark Valley: Go west on I-395 to S.R. 821 South (Florida Tpk.). Take the U.S. 41/Southwest 8th Street (Tamiami Trail) exit. The Shark Valley entrance is just 25 miles west. To get to Everglades City, continue west on the Tamiami Trail and head south on S.R. 29. Everglades City is an approximately 2½-hour drive from Miami, but because it is scenic, it may take longer if you stop or slow down to view your surroundings.

SOUTHERN ENTRANCE (VIA HOMESTEAD & FLORIDA CITY) If you're in a rush to hit the 'Glades and don't care about the scenic route, this is your best bet. Just southeast of Homestead and Florida City, off S.R. 9336, the southern access to the park will bring you to the Ernest F. Coe Visitor Center. Inside the park, 4 miles beyond the Ernest F. Coe Visitor Center, is the **Royal Palm Visitor**

Center, the starting point for the two most popular walking trails, Gumbo Limbo and Anhinga, where you'll witness a plethora of birds and wildlife. Thirteen miles west of the Ernest F. Coe Visitor Center, you'll hit **Pahayokee Overlook Trail,** which treks across the boardwalk to reach the observation tower, over which vultures and hawks hover protectively. It offers a resplendent, bird's-eye view of the Everglades. From Miami to the southern entrance: Go west on I-395 to S.R. 821 South (Florida Tpk.), which will end in Florida City. Take the first right through the center of town (you can't miss it) and follow signs to the park entrance on S.R. 9336. The Ernest F. Coe Visitor Center is about 1½ hours from Miami.

VISITOR CENTERS & INFORMATION Along with the **Marjory Stoneman Douglas (MSD) Visitor Center** (see above), the following are the best places to stop before exploring the park. The **Ernest F. Coe Visitor Center** (© 305/242/7700; Apr to mid-Dec 9am–5pm, mid-Dec to Mar 8am–5pm), at the park headquarters entrance, west of Homestead and Florida City, can give details on tours and boat rentals, plus free brochures outlining trails and activities. It also has state-of-the-art educational displays, films, and interactive exhibits. A bookstore sells an impressive selection of books about the Everglades, unusual gift items, and your most important gear: insect repellent.

The **Royal Palm Visitor Center** (© 305/242-7237; daily 10am–4pm), a small nature museum located 3 miles past the park's main entrance, is no great shakes, but the center, which includes a small bookstore, bathrooms, and vending machines, is the departure point for the popular Anhinga and Gumbo Limbo trails.

Knowledgeable rangers provide brochures and personal insights into the park's activities at both the **Guy Bradley Flamingo Visitor Center** (© 305/242-7700; daily 8am–5pm), 38 miles from the main entrance, at the park's southern access, and the **Shark Valley Visitor Center** (daily 9am–5pm), at the park's northern entrance.

Everglade wonders great and small: a Cuban treefrog on the bark of a pine tree.

ENTRANCE FEES, PERMITS & REGULATIONS Permits and passes can be purchased at the MSD and Guy Bradley Flamingo Visitor Centers, the Shark Valley and Homestead pay stations, and online at recreation.gov. Even if you are just visiting for an afternoon, you'll need to buy a 7-day permit, which costs $35 per vehicle. Pedestrians and cyclists are charged $20 each. An **Everglades Park Pass,** valid for a year's worth of unlimited admissions, is available for $70. You may also purchase a 12-month America the Beautiful National Parks and Federal Recreation

Lands Pass–Annual Pass for $80, which is valid for entrance into any U.S. national park. U.S. citizens ages 62 and older pay only $20 for the America the Beautiful National Parks and Federal Recreation Lands Pass–Senior Pass that's valid for life. An America the Beautiful National Parks and Federal Recreation Lands Pass–Access Pass is available free to U.S. citizens with disabilities.

Permits are required for campers to stay overnight either in the backcountry or at the primitive campsites. See p. 227.

Those who want to fish without a charter captain must obtain a State of Florida saltwater fishing license. These are available in the park, at any tackle shop or sporting-goods store nearby. Nonresidents pay $30 for a 7-day license or $17 for a 3-day license. Florida residents pay $17 for an annual fishing license. A snook license must be purchased separately at a cost of $10; a lobster permit is $5. For more information on fishing licenses, go to **myfwc.com/license/recreational/saltwater-fishing**.

Most of the area's freshwater fishing is limited to murky canals and artificial lakes near housing developments, so it's hardly worth the trouble with so much good saltwater fishing here. That being said, freshwater fishing licenses are available at bait-and-tackle stores outside the park at the same rates as those offered inside the park. A good one nearby is **Don's Bait & Tackle,** 90 N. Homestead Blvd., right on U.S. 1 in Homestead (donsbait.com; *✆* **305/247-6616**).

SEASONS There are two distinct seasons in the Everglades: high season and mosquito season. High season is also dry season and lasts from late November to May, a time that's generally warm, sunny, and breezy—a good combination for keeping the bugs away. And trust us, you will want to keep away from those bugs. They are brutal and relentless, even with repellent and proper clothing. Winter, though not completely bug free—ever—is also the best time to visit because low water levels attract the largest variety of wading birds and their predators. As the dry season wanes, wildlife follows the receding water; by the end of May, the only living things you are sure to spot will make you itch. The worst, called no-see-ums, are not even swattable. If you choose to visit during the buggy season, be vigilant in applying bug spray. Also, realize that many establishments and operators either close or curtail offerings in summer.

RANGER PROGRAMS Ranger-led walks and talks are offered year-round from Royal Palm Visitor Center, and at the Flamingo and MSD visitor centers, as well as Shark Valley Visitor Center during winter months. Park rangers tend to be helpful, well informed, and good humored. Some programs occur regularly, such as the informative Royal Palm Visitor Center's Glade Glimpses (daily 10:30am and 1:30pm), a walking tour on which rangers point out flora and fauna, and discuss issues affecting the Everglades' survival. The Anhinga Amble, a similar program that takes place on the Anhinga Trail, starts at 10:30am daily and lasts about 50 minutes. Because other programs vary from month to month, check the schedule, available at any of the visitor centers and online.

SAFETY There are many dangers inherent in this vast wilderness area. *Always* let someone know your itinerary before you set out on an extended hike. It's mandatory that you file an itinerary when camping overnight in the backcountry (which you can do when you apply for your overnight permit at either the Flamingo Visitor Center or the MSD Visitor Center). When you're on the water, watch for weather changes; thunderstorms and high winds often develop rapidly. Swimming is not recommended because of the presence of alligators, sharks, and barracudas. Watch out for the region's four indigenous poisonous snakes: diamondback and pygmy rattlesnakes, coral snakes (identifiable by their colorful rings), and water moccasins (which swim on the surface of the water). Bring insect repellent to ward off mosquitoes and biting flies. First aid is available from park rangers. The nearest hospital is in Homestead, 10 miles from the park's main entrance.

Seeing the Highlights

Shark Valley, a 15-mile paved road (ideal for biking) through the Everglades, provides a fine introduction to the wonders of the park. For those not into cycling, a guided tram tour (p. 227) is a smart way to cover the highlights. With either method of getting around, you'll want to devote at least a day to exploring the park.

The Anhinga and Gumbo Limbo trails provide a thorough introduction to the Everglades' flora and fauna and are highly recommended to first-time visitors. Each is a half-mile round-trip, and they start right next to each other, 3 miles from the park's main entrance. **Gumbo Limbo Trail** (my pick for best walking trail in the Everglades) meanders through a gorgeous, shaded, junglelike hammock of gumbo-limbo trees, royal palms, ferns, orchids, air plants, and a general blanket of vegetation, though it doesn't put you in close contact with much wildlife. **Anhinga Trail** is one of the most popular trails in the park because of its abundance of wildlife: There's more water and wildlife in this area than in most parts of the Everglades, especially during dry season. Alligators, lizards, turtles, river otters, herons, egrets, and other animals abound. Arrive early to spot the widest selection of exotic birds, such as the anhinga bird, the trail's namesake, a large black fishing bird so accustomed to humans that many of them build their nests in plain view. Take your time: At least an hour is recommended for each trail. If you treat the trails and modern boardwalk as pathways to get through quickly, rather than destinations to savor, you'll miss out. Both are wheelchair accessible.

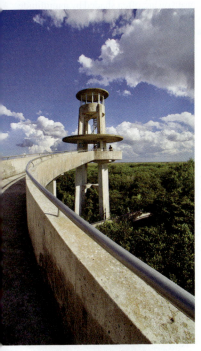

A viewing tower in Shark Valley.

To get closer to nature, a few hours in a canoe along any of the aforementioned trails allows paddlers the chance to sense the park's fluid motion and to become a part of the ecosphere. Visitors who choose this option end up feeling more like explorers than observers. (See "Sports & Outdoor Activities," below.)

No matter which option you choose, I strongly recommend staying for the 45-minute 7pm program, held Mondays, Wednesdays, and Fridays January through March 31 at the Long Pine Key Amphitheater. This ranger-led talk and slide show will give you a detailed and fascinating look at the park's history, natural resources, wildlife, and threats to its survival.

A non-nature-oriented highlight of the park is the **Nike Hercules Missile Base HM-69** ★, completed in 1965, not long after the Cuban Missile Crisis. The base was decommissioned in 1979, and looks almost exactly like it did then (it wasn't open to the public until 2009). From December to March 31, free ranger-led tours take visitors on a 90-minute driving and walking tour of the missile assembly building, three barns where 12 missiles were stored, the guardhouse and guard dog kennel, and the underground control room. Tours depart from the **Daniel Beard Center,** 40001 S. R. 9336 in Homestead. The tour is free, but the park admission still applies. The site is open most days between early December and late March, but program schedules fluctuate due to staffing capability. View the online park calendar for info on programming at **www.nps.gov/ever/planyourvisit/calendar.htm**.

Sports & Outdoor Activities

BIKING The relatively flat, 38-mile paved **Main Park Road** is great for biking, not just because there are no hills, but because you are often shaded by a multitude of hardwood hammocks (treelike islands or dense stands of hardwood trees that grow only a few inches above land) and a dwarf cypress forest (stunted and thinly distributed cypress trees, which grow in poor soil on drier land).

Shark Valley, however, is the best biking trail by far. If the park isn't flooded from excess rain (which it often is, especially in spring), this is South Florida's most scenic bicycle trail. You'll share the flat, paved road only with other bikers, trams, and a menagerie of wildlife. (Don't be surprised to see a gator lounging in the sun or a deer munching on some grass. Otters, turtles, alligators, and snakes are common companions in the area.) There are no shortcuts, so if you become tired or are unable to complete the 15-mile trip, turn around and return on the same road. Allow 2 to 3 hours to bike the entire loop.

Those who love to mountain bike and who prefer solitude might check out the **Southern Glades Trail,** a 14-mile unpaved trail lined with native trees and teeming with wildlife, such as deer, alligators, and the occasional snake. The trail runs along the C-111 canal, off S.R. 9336 and Southwest 217th Street.

A couple biking in Shark Valley.

Bike rentals are available from **Shark Valley Tram Tours,** at the park's Shark Valley entrance (sharkvalleytramtours.com; ⓒ **305/221-8455;** $25/day). Rentals can be picked up anytime between 8:30am and 3pm but must be returned by 4pm.

BIRD-WATCHING More than 400 species of birds make their home in the Everglades. Tropical birds from the Caribbean and temperate species from North America can be found, along with exotics that have flown in from more distant regions. The park is a critical stopover habitat for birds migrating along the Atlantic Flyway, such as the yellow-throated warbler. It's also ground zero for the impacts of rising seas. Accelerating the pace of Everglades restoration is key to giving managers flexibility to cope with extreme weather patterns and climate change, as healthier ecosystems are more resilient.

Eco and **Mrazek ponds,** located near Flamingo, are two of the best places for birding, especially in early morning or late afternoon in the dry winter months. Pick up a free birding checklist from one of the visitor centers (p. 219) and inquire about what's been spotted in recent days. For a guided birding tour, contact **Everglades Area Tours** (evergladesareatours.com; ⓒ **239/695-3633**), which does an excellent birding/photography tour, or **Everglades Boat Tours** (everglades-boat-tours.com; ⓒ **239/695-3633**), which offers a **National Park and Grand Heritage Birding Tour,** a comprehensive, 7-hour naturalist-led tour with multiple forms of transportation—powerboats, kayaks, and even a beach walk, so you don't miss any of the spectacular feathered (among others) species who call the park home. The tour is a steep $299.95 per adult and $159.95 per child 11 and under and limited to six per tour. The powerboats are a good option for noise sensitive folks (who should avoid airboats, as they're quite loud).

CANOEING Canoers in the Everglades coexist with the gators and birds in an almost mystical way: The creatures behave as if you're part of the ecosystem, something that won't happen on an airboat. Everglades National Park's longest "trails" are designed for boat and canoe travel, and many are marked as clearly as walking trails. The **Noble Hammock Canoe Trail,** a 2-mile loop, takes 1 to 2 hours and is recommended for beginners. The **Hell's Bay Canoe Trail,** a 3- to 6-mile course for hardier paddlers, takes 2 to 6 hours, depending on how far you choose to go. Fans of this trail like to say, "It's hell to get in and hell to get out." Park rangers can recommend other trails that suit your abilities, time limitations, and interests.

A ranger-guided boat tour is your best bet if you're not a seasoned paddler, and oftentimes they are either free or very inexpensive. As always, a ranger will help you understand your surroundings and what you're seeing. They don't take reservations, but for more information on the various boat tours, go to **www.nps.gov/ever/planyourvisit/rangerprogram.htm** or call ⓒ **239/695-3311.** An outfit that *does* take reservations, and has very good guides, is **Everglades Adventures Kayak & Eco Tours** (evergladesadventures.com; ⓒ **239/977-8904**). Try them if you can't get a ranger tour. They are also a good source for canoe rentals ($49–$85 daily, based on boat size with free delivery to the Everglades National Park). Kayaks and tandem kayaks are also available. Rental facilities are open daily from November to mid-April from 8am to 9pm. You can also take a canoe tour from the Parks Docks on Chokoloskee Causeway on S.R. 29, ½ mile south of the traffic circle at the MSD ranger station in Everglades City. More info at **NPS** address above.

Kayakers navigate the reeds of Nine-Mile Pond.

During ideal weather conditions (stay away during bug season!), you can paddle right out to the Gulf and camp on the beach. However, Gulf waters at beach sites can be extremely rough, and people in small watercraft such as a canoe should exercise caution.

FISHING About a third of Everglades National Park is open water. Freshwater fishing is popular in brackish **Nine-Mile Pond** (25 miles from the main entrance) and other spots along the Main Park Road, but because of the high mercury levels found in the Everglades, freshwater fishers are warned not to eat their catch. Here, you'll see alligators, birds, crocs, and even the endangered snail kite. Before casting, check in at a visitor center, as many of the park's lakes are preserved for observation only. Fishing licenses are required (p. 220).

Saltwater anglers will find snapper and sea trout plentiful. Capt. George LeClair leads expertly guided, affordable fishing trips through the backcountry with **Adventures in Backwater Fishing** (fishing-florida.com/adventures; © **239/ 774-6765**). Fly-fishing and spin casting, among other things, are part of the trip. Six-hour trips will set you back around $385. A full list of charters and guides can be found at nps.gov/ever/planyourvisit/permittedtours.htm.

MOTORBOATING In recent years, environmentalists have been taking stock of the damage inflicted by motorboats (especially airboats) on this delicate ecosystem. If you choose to motor, remember that most of the areas near land are "no wake" zones and that, for the protection of nesting birds, landing is prohibited on most of the little mangrove islands. Motorboating is allowed in certain areas, such as Florida Bay, the backcountry toward Everglades City, and the Ten Thousand Islands area. In all the freshwater lakes, however, motorboats are prohibited if they're above 5 horsepower. There's a long list of restrictions and restricted areas, so get a copy of the park's boating rules from park headquarters before setting out. You don't want to get a ticket, or more importantly, inflict damage unwittingly.

The Everglades' only marina—accommodating about 50 boats with electric and water hookups—is **Flamingo Marina,** 1 Flamingo Lodge Hwy., Everglades City (flamingoeverglades.com/flamingo-marina; © **239/695-1095**). The well-marked channel to the Flamingo is accessible to boats with a maximum 4-foot draft and is open from 7am to 7pm November 1 to April 30 and 8am to 6pm from May 1 to October 31. An activities booth is open daily from 8am to 4pm. Reservations can be made through the marina store (flamingoeverglades.com; © **239/695-1095**). Skiffs with 40-horsepower motors are available for rent for $60 to $195 for a half-day or $260 to $295 for a full day. *Note:* Visitors require a valid boating education certificate. See p. 29.

If you don't plan on renting a boat, know that both Florida Bay and backcountry motorboating tours are offered Thursday to Monday at the **Flamingo Marina** (see above). Florida Bay tours cruise nearby estuaries and sandbars, while six-passenger backcountry boats visit smaller sloughs. Passengers can expect to see birds and a variety of other animals (I once saw a raccoon and some wild pigs). Both cost $48 for adults, $24 for children 5 to 12. Tours depart throughout the day; reservations are recommended. The Florida Bay tour is given November through April only, and can be booked on their website at flamingoeverglades.com/boat-tours. If you're on the Gulf Coast side of things, the naturalist-guided Gulf Coast 2-hour boat tour of the Ten Thousand Islands departs from 929 Dupont St. in Everglades City (evergladesnationalparkadventures.com; © **239/330-1902**). Tour prices are the same as the tours at the Flamingo Marina.

Tours

AIRBOAT TOURS Shallow-draft, fan-powered airboats were invented in the Everglades by frog hunters who were tired of poling through the brushes. Airboats cut through the saw grass and are sort of like hydraulic boats; at high enough speeds, a boat actually rises above the saw grass and into the air. Even though airboats are the most efficient (not to mention fast and fun!) way to get around, they are not permitted in the park—these shallow-bottom runabouts tend to inflict severe damage on animals and plants. Just outside the boundaries of the Everglades, however, you'll find a number of outfitters offering rides. *Tip:* Consider bringing earplugs, as these high-speed boats are *loud.*

The most informative and entertaining airboat tour operators around is **Gator Park,** 12 miles west of the Florida Turnpike at 24050 SW Eighth St. (gatorpark.com; © **800/559-2255;** daily 9am–5pm). They're also the only one to give out free earplugs. After the boat ride, there's a free interactive wildlife show that features alligator wrestling and several other frightening acts involving scorpions. Take note of the peacocks that live in the trees here. Admission for the boat ride and show is $29.99 for adults, $19.99 for children 6 to 11.

Another outfitter we recommend is **Coopertown Airboat Tours** (coopertownairboats.com; © **305/226-6048;** daily 9am–5pm), about 11 miles west of the Florida Turnpike on the Tamiami Trail (U.S. 41), in a town that boasts a total

Airboat tours are an adrenaline-pumping way to see this ecosystem, but they are loud, and can damage the areas they're in.

population of eight humans! The superfriendly staff have helped the company garner the title of "Florida's Best" by the *Miami Herald* for 75 years in a row. You never know what you're going to see, but with these guides, you're sure to see *something* of interest on the 40-minute, 8-mile round-trip tours, including, perhaps, the purple gallinule, which has been described as the most colorful bird in Florida. There's also a restaurant and a small gator farm on the premises. Airboat rides cost $29.95 for adults, $18.95 for children 6 to 11. Tours leave frequently and the last airboat ride leaves at 4:30pm.

The **Miccosukee Indian Village,** just west of the Shark Valley entrance on U.S. 41/Tamiami Trail and MM 70 (miccosukeeairboats.com; © **786/385-3502**), offers 40-minute airboat tours for $40 for adults and $30 for kids 7 to 12. For those not into boating, there's a casino at which you can kill some time or your budget.

The **Everglades Alligator Farm,** 4 miles south of Palm Drive on Southwest 192nd Avenue (everglades.com; © **305/247-2628**), offers half-hour guided airboat tours daily from 9am to 6pm. The price, which includes admission to the park, is $37 for adults and $29 for children 4 to 11. There are also alligator encounters (starting at $67) where anyone brave enough and 6 years or older can hold a three-foot alligator and feed over 250 larger ones in a breeding pond.

Another reputable company is **Captain Doug's,** 35 miles south of Naples and 1 mile past the bridge in Everglades City (captaindougs.com; © **800/282-9194**).

ECO-TOURS Everglades Area Tours (evergladesareatours.com; © **239/695-9107**) offers not only guided kayak fishing, but also guided half-day kayak ecotours, customized bird-watching expeditions, and full-moon paddling, as well as bicycle and aerial tours of the Everglades. A motorboat-assisted eco-tour takes six kayaks and six passengers on a trip out to the Wilderness Waterway, deep within Everglades National Park's Ten Thousand Islands, where you will paddle in the wilderness, spotting birds, dolphins, manatees, sea turtles, and perhaps even the elusive American crocodile. The shuttle then brings you back to Everglades City. Rates start at $199.95 per adult and $129.99 per child and includes transportation, guides, outfitted kayaks, and safety equipment.

TRAM TOURS At the park's Shark Valley entrance, open-air tram buses take visitors on 2-hour naturalist-led tours that delve 7½ miles into the wilderness and are the best quick introduction you can get to the Everglades. At the trail's midsection, passengers can disembark and climb a 65-foot observation tower with good views of the 'Glades (though the tower on the Pahayokee Trail is better). Visitors will see plenty of wildlife and endless acres of saw grass. Tours run December through April, daily on the hour between 9am and 4pm, and May through December at 9:30 and 11am, and 2 and 4pm. The tours are sometimes stalled by flooding or particularly heavy mosquito infestation. Reservations are recommended from December to March. The cost is $31 for adults, $24 for seniors 62 and older, $16 for children 12 and under. For further information, contact **Shark Valley Tram Tours** (sharkvalleytramtours.com; ✆ **305/221-8455**).

Where to Stay

In 2023 the National Park Service and its concessionaire finally addressed a long-standing problem in the park: the lack of non-camping lodgings. It opened the 24-unit **Flamingo Lodge and Restaurant** ★★, 1 Flamingo Lodge Hwy. (flamingoeverglades.com/flamingo-lodge; ✆ **855/708-2207**), and while its claim that the rooms are "Miami Modern" seems like a stretch, the studios and one- and two-bedroom suites—all crafted from former shipping containers— have been given a nice dash of color, have quality beds, plus kitchenettes and balconies overlooking Florida Bay. There are also some nice glamping units and campsites. Rates range from $188 to $399 per night for the lodge rooms (less for glamping and camping). Their stand-alone 75-seat restaurant serves casual fare from 7 to 10am, with lunch and dinner from 11am to 9pm.

Just outside the park, the **Miccosukee Casino & Resort,** 500 SW 177th Ave. (miccosukee.com; ✆ **877/242-6464**), is located along the southeastern edge of the Everglades and is another decent option.

CAMPING IN THE EVERGLADES

Although bugs can be a major nuisance, especially in the warm months, camping is the best way to fully experience South Florida's wilderness. Campgrounds are open year-round in Flamingo and Long Pine Key. Flamingo has several hiking and canoe trails, plentiful opportunities for saltwater fishing, solar-heated showers, two dump stations, picnic tables, grills, and an amphitheater for seasonal ranger programs. Fees are $50 to $60 for RV hookup with electricity, $33 to $38.50 for tent and non-electric RV camping. Long Pine Key campground has more trees than Flamingo and feels more rustic, but is only open seasonally (Nov–May). Reservations are available for RVs and tents along with first-come, first-served sites. If sites are booked, more camping may be available further down the Main Park Road in Flamingo. Fees are $33 to $38.50. Long Pine Key and Flamingo are popular and require reservations in advance, which can be made through the National Park Reservations Service (recreation.gov; ✆ **800/365-CAMP** [2267]).

Camping is also available year-round in the **backcountry** (those remote areas accessible only by boat, foot, or canoe—basically, most of the park), on a first-come, first-served basis. The sites are either on ground, beach, or elevated "chickee" platforms. Campers must register with park rangers and get a permit in person or by phone no less than 24 hours before the start of their trip. The permit costs $21 plus $2 per camper per night. For more info, check nps.gov/ever/plan yourvisit/wilderness-trip-planner.htm or call ✆ **305/242-7700**.

Many backcountry sites are **chickee huts**—covered wooden platforms (with toilets) on stilts. They're accessible only by canoe and can accommodate freestanding tents (without stakes). Ground sites are located along interior bays and rivers, and beach camping is also popular.

LODGING IN EVERGLADES CITY

Everglades City is 35 miles southeast of Naples and 83 miles west of Miami. Many visitors use it as a hub for exploring the western entrance to Everglades National Park, located off the Tamiami Trail, on S.R. 29. An annual seafood festival held the first weekend in February is a major event here. Everglades City (gateway to the Ten Thousand Islands), where the 'Glades meet the Gulf of Mexico, is the closest thing you'll get to civilization in this swampy frontier, with a few tourist traps—er, shops—a restaurant, and a few motels.

Four of those motels are sister properties, with small differences from one to the next. **Captain's Table Hotel,** 202 Broadway Ave. E., Everglades City (captainstableeverglades.com; ✆ **239/360-3937**), is the oldest of the group, and feels like it because of the small windows in guest rooms, its (sometimes) hard beds, and the grungy carpeting. It has some bigger efficiencies, and a lakeside pool, and is the least expensive at $79 to $109 a night. **Everglades Adventures Hotel Suites,** 107 Camelia St. E. (evergladeshotelsuites.com; ✆ **239/695-7105**), is the newest, and newest looking, of the properties (lots of blond woods, colorful art), built in 2020, with rooms and suites for $119 to $179. And in between those two, in terms of looks and amenities, are **Ivey House Everglades Adventure Hotel,** at 605 Buckner Ave. N. (iveyhouse.com; ✆ **239/323-9826**; $119–$179 per night), and **Everglades City Motel,** 309 Collier Ave. (evergladescitymotel.com; ✆ **239/695-4224**; $99–$149 per night). The last is a fave for anglers because it has boat parking. Ivey House is also a tour operator, offering fishing trips, walks, bike rides, and tours.

Rod & Gun Lodge ★★

Set on the banks of the sleepy Baron River, this old white-clapboard house has plenty of history: President Herbert Hoover vacationed here after his 1928 election victory, and President Truman flew in to sign Everglades National Park into existence in 1947 and stayed over as well. Other guests have included Richard Nixon, Burt Reynolds, and Mick Jagger. The public rooms are beautifully paneled and hung with tarpon, wild boar, deer antlers, and other trophies. Guest rooms in this single-story building have been revamped with "Florida Everglades casual style" (read: Rooms to Go, or some other big-box furniture store, but with shiplap) and all have porches looking out on the river. Out by the pool, a screened veranda with ceiling fans is a pleasant place for a cocktail. The seafood restaurant serves breakfast, lunch, and dinner, and the bar is straight out of a Teddy Roosevelt cosplay with all sorts of taxidermy and wood paneling. There's also a full-service marina, and, for those looking to make a grand entrance, a pad for helicopter landings. But wait—it's so historic, it's cash only.

200 W. Broadway, Everglades City. rodandguneverglades.com. ✆ **239/695-2101.** 17 units. $140–$218 double. CASH ONLY! **Amenities:** Restaurant; 2 bars; bike rental; pool.

LODGING IN HOMESTEAD & FLORIDA CITY

Homestead and Florida City, two adjacent towns, are located 10 miles from the park's main entrance, along U.S. 1, 35 miles south of Miami. These somewhat rural towns offer several budget options, including chain hotels. The spiffiest of these are in Florida City: **The Best Western Gateway to the Keys,** 411 Krome Ave. (U.S. 1; bestwestern.com; ⓒ **800/528-1234** or 305/246-5100), and the **Hoosville Hostel,** 20 SW 2nd Ave. (hoosvillehostel.com; ⓒ **305/363-4644**).

Where to Eat in & Around the Park

You won't find fancy nouvelle cuisine in this suburbanized farm country, but there are plenty of fast-food chains along U.S. 1 and a few old favorites worth a taste. Housed in a one-story, windowless building that looks something like a medieval fort, the **Capri Restaurant** ★★, 935 N. Krome Ave., Florida City (dinecapri.com; ⓒ **305/247-1542;** Mon–Fri noon–9:30pm, Sat until 10:30pm), has been serving hearty Italian-American fare—and fried alligator—since 1958. Tasty pastas and salads complement a menu of meat and fish dishes; portions are big. The **White Lion Cafe** ★★★, 146 NW 7th St., Homestead (whitelioncafe.com; ⓒ **305/248-1076;** Tues–Fri 11am–3pm, Fri 5pm "till the fat lady sings," Sat noon–5pm), is a quaint house-and-gardens with a menu with Blue Plate specials and cheekily named appetizers and entrees such as Dirty Shrimp and the $200 P.J. & Dom, which they claim to be the "World's largest PB&J sandwich for two with a bottle of Dom Perignon." Fancy! Try the Romanian steak, skirt steak sliced thin and served with fresh mushrooms, spinach, and garlic over real mashed potatoes and gravy. On Friday evenings, the only day they're open late, there's often live music.

Craving gator ribs? Near the Miccosukee reservation is the **Pit Bar-B-Q** ★★★, 16400 SW 8th St. (facebook.com/thepitbbqmiami; ⓒ **305/226-2272;** daily 11am–8pm), a total pit of a place (sorry!) known for some of the best smoked ribs, barbecued chicken, and corn bread this side of the Deep South. For even more gator, head to Homestead's **Everglades Gator Grill** ★★, 36650 SW 192nd Ave. (facebook.com/evergladesgatorgrill; ⓒ **786/243-0620;** daily 11am–6pm), where gator tacos have a distinct bite.

The first Cuban restaurant in the Everglades, **Captain Morgan's Seafood Grill** ★★★, 102 S. Copland Ave., Everglades City (captainmorganssea foodgrill.com; ⓒ **239/232-0041;** Wed–Sun 11am–8pm), serves excellent ceviches and tostones, delicious ice cream, and an eye-opening cafe con leche.

A happy customer at Captain Morgan's Seafood Grill.

Finally, **Camellia Street Grill** ★★, 208 Camellia St. (camelliastreetgrill. net; ✆ **239/695-2003;** daily 11am–9pm), a rusty waterfront fish joint fuses Southern hospitality with outstanding seafood. An on-site herb and veggie garden provides the freshest ingredients for sides and stellar salads. Everything is homemade, including the Key lime pie, and there's live music weekends.

7 BISCAYNE NATIONAL PARK ★★

With only about 700,000 visitors each year (mostly boaters and divers), Biscayne National Park is one of the least-crowded parks in the country. Perhaps that's because the park is a little more difficult than most to access—more than 95% of its 172,971 acres is underwater.

The park's significance was first formally acknowledged in 1968 when, in an unprecedented move (and despite intense pressure from developers), President Lyndon B. Johnson signed a bill to conserve the barrier islands off South Florida's east coast as a national monument—a protected status just a rung below national park. After being twice enlarged, once in 1974 and again in 1980, the waters and land surrounding the northernmost coral reef in North America became a full-fledged national park, the largest of its kind in the country.

To be fully appreciated, Biscayne National Park should be thought of as more preserve than destination. Use your time here to explore underwater life, but also to relax. The park's small mainland mangrove shoreline and keys are best explored by boat. Its extensive reef system is beloved by divers and snorkelers.

The park consists of 42 islands, but only a few are open to visitors. The most popular is **Elliott Key,** a former community of pioneers, pineapple farmers, sponge farmers and wreckers, which has campsites and a visitor center, plus freshwater showers (cold water only), restrooms, trails, and a buoyed swim area. It's about 9 miles from the **Dante Fascell Visitor Center,** the park's official headquarters on land. During Columbus Day weekend, there is a very popular regatta for which a lively crowd of partiers gathers—sometimes in the nude—to celebrate the long weekend. The 29-acre island known as **Boca Chita Key,** once an exclusive haven for yachters, has become a popular spot for all manner of boaters. Visitors can camp and tour the island's restored historic buildings, including the county's second-largest lighthouse and a tiny chapel.

Essentials

GETTING THERE & ACCESS POINTS   The **Dante Fascell Visitor Center,** 9700 SW 328th St., Homestead (nps.gov/bisc/planyourvisit/hours.html; ✆ **305/230-1144**), the park's mainland entrance, is 9 miles east of Homestead. To reach the park from Miami, take the Florida Turnpike to the Tallahassee Road (SW 137th Ave.) exit. Turn left, then left again at North Canal Drive (SW 328th St.), and follow signs to the park. Another option is to rent a speedboat in Miami and cruise south for about 1½ hours. From U.S. 1, whether you're heading north or south, turn east at North Canal Drive (SW 328th St.). The entrance is approximately 9 miles away. The rest of the park is accessible only by boat.

Because most of Biscayne National Park is accessible only to boaters, mooring buoys abound, as it is illegal to anchor on coral. When no buoys are available, boaters must anchor on sand or on the docks surrounding the small harbor off Boca Chita. Boats can also dock here overnight for $25. Even the most experienced boaters should carry updated nautical charts of the area, which are available

Visit the old lighthouse at the tip of Boca Chita Key.

at the Dante Fascell Visitor Center. The waters are often murky, making the abundant reefs and sandbars difficult to detect—and there are more interesting ways to spend a day than waiting for the tide to rise. There's a boat launch at adjacent Homestead Bayfront Park and 36 slips on Elliott Key, available for a $25 docking fee. Docking fees must be paid in advance at recreation.gov.

Three-and-a-half-hour boat trips to Boca Chita and Elliott Key are available at biscaynenationalparkinstitute.org/boat-cruise and cost $83 for adults and $49 for kids 5 to 12.

VISITOR CENTERS & INFORMATION Open daily from 9am to 5pm, the **Dante Fascell Visitor Center** (often referred to by its older name, Convoy Point Visitor Center), at the park's main entrance, is the natural starting point for any venture into the park without a boat. It provides comprehensive info about the park.

For info on transportation, glass-bottom boat tours, and snorkeling and scuba-diving expeditions, contact the park concessionaire, **Biscayne National Park Institute,** located at the Dante Fascell Visitor Center (biscaynenational parkinstitute.org; ⓒ **786/465-4058**).

ENTRANCE FEES & PERMITS Park entrance is free, but there is a $25 overnight docking fee at both Boca Chita Key Harbor and Elliott Key Harbor, which includes a campsite. Campsites are $35 for those staying without a boat. You can book your sites at recreation.gov. See p. 220 for info on fishing permits.

Backcountry camping permits are free and can be picked up from the Dante Fascell Visitor Center.

Seeing the Highlights

Because the park is primarily underwater, the only way to truly experience it is with snorkel or scuba gear. Beneath the surface of Biscayne National Park, the aquatic universe pulses with multicolored life: bright parrotfish and angelfish, gently rocking sea fans, and coral labyrinths. After your dive, take a picnic out to Elliott Key and taste the crisp salt air blowing off the Atlantic. Or head to Boca Chita, an intriguing island that was once the private playground of wealthy yachters.

Sports & Outdoor Activities

CANOEING, KAYAKING & PADDLEBOARDING Biscayne National Park has excellent paddling, both along the coast and across the open water to nearby mangroves and artificial islands dotting the longest uninterrupted shoreline in the state. Because tides can be strong, only experienced paddlers should attempt to travel far from shore. **The Biscayne National Park Institute** concession at the Dante Fascell Visitor Center (biscaynenationalparkinstitute.org) offers first-rate guided kayaks and paddleboard tours ($39–$109). Unfortunately canoe, kayak, and paddleboard rentals are not available at the park.

FISHING & LOBSTERING Ocean fishing is excellent year-round at Biscayne National Park; many people cast their lines from the breakwater jetty at Convoy Point near the Dante Fascell Visitor Center. A fishing license is required. (See p. 220 for more info.) Stone crabs and Florida lobsters can be found here, but you're allowed to catch these only on the ocean side when they're in season. For more info on lobstering, go to nps.gov/bisc/planyourvisit/lobstering.htm. There are strict limits on size, season, number, and method of take (including spearfishing) for both freshwater and saltwater fishing. The latest regulations are available at most marinas, bait-and-tackle shops, and the park's visitor center.

HIKING & EXPLORING As the majority of this park is underwater, hiking is not the main attraction here, but there are some interesting sights and trails nonetheless. At Convoy Point, you can walk along the 370-foot boardwalk and along the half-mile jetty trail that serves as a breakwater for the park's harbor. From here, you can usually see brown pelicans, little blue herons, snowy egrets, and a few exotic fish. Check out the map and guide to the jetty trail at nps.gov/bisc.

Elliott Key is accessible only by boat, but once you're there, you have two good trail options. True to its name, the Loop Trail makes a 1.5-mile circle from the bayside visitor center, through a hardwood hammock and mangroves, to an elevated oceanside boardwalk. You'll likely see land crabs scurrying around the mangrove roots.

Boca Chita Key was once a playground for wealthy tycoons, and it still has the peaceful beauty that attracted elite anglers from cold climates. Many of the historic buildings are still intact, including an ornamental lighthouse that was never put to use. Take advantage of the **Biscayne National Park Institute's** 3-hour tours, including a Boca Chita heritage boat trip, available twice daily from the Dinner Key Marina in Coconut Grove. Tickets are $83 for adults and $49 for children 5 to 12. Go to biscaynenationalparkinstitute.org to book.

SNORKELING & SCUBA DIVING The clear, warm waters of Biscayne National Park are packed with colorful tropical fish that swim in the offshore reefs. If you didn't bring your own gear, you can rent snorkeling and scuba gear at the Biscayne National Park Institute at the Dante Fascell Visitor Center. A snorkeling bundle of all the essentials costs $16 per person, or you can rent masks and snorkels for $5 and fins for $6. A short wetsuit is $10.

The best way to see the park from underwater is to take a snorkeling or diving tour operated by **Biscayne National Park Institute** at the Dante Fascell Visitor Center (biscaynenationalparkinstitute.org). A 6-hour, sail, snorkel, and paddle trip offers the greatest hits of the park for $209 per passenger ages 8 and up.

Before entering the water, be sure to apply waterproof sunblock—once you begin to explore, it's easy to lose track of time, and the Florida sun is brutal, even during winter.

SWIMMING You can swim off the protected beaches of Elliott Key, Boca Chita Key, and adjacent Homestead Bayfront Park, but none of these matches the width or softness of other South Florida beaches. Check the water conditions before heading into the sea: The strong currents that make this a popular destination for windsurfers and sailors can be dangerous, even for strong swimmers. Homestead Bayfront Park is really just a marina next to Biscayne National Park, but it does have a beach and picnic facilities, as well as fishing areas and a playground. It's located at Convoy Point, 9698 SW 328th St., Homestead (miamidade.gov/parks/homestead-bayfront.asp; ⓒ **305/230-3033**).

Where to Stay

Besides campsites, there are no facilities available for overnight guests in this watery park. Most noncamping visitors come for an afternoon, on their way to the Keys, and stay overnight in nearby Homestead. The good news is that Biscayne National Park boasts some of the state's most pristine campsites. Because they are inaccessible by car, you'll be sure to avoid the mass of RVs so prevalent in many of the state's other campgrounds. Boca Chita has only saltwater toilets (no showers, sinks, or drinking water); Elliott Key has freshwater, cold-water showers and toilets, but is otherwise no less primitive. If you didn't pay for the overnight docking fee, campsites are $35. Ask for a map and be sure to bring plenty of bug spray. It is approximately 9 miles from the Dante Fascell Visitor Center and offers hiking trails, fresh water, boat slips, showers, and restrooms. While there, hike the Old Road, a 7-mile tropical hammock trail that runs the length of Elliott Key. This trail is one of the few places left in the world to see the critically endangered Schaus swallowtail butterfly, recognizable by its black wings with diagonal yellow bands. These butterflies are usually out from late April to July. Oh, and cell phone connectivity on both sites is abysmal, so you really are going off the grid here.

THE GOLD COAST:

HALLANDALE TO THE PALM BEACHES

by Lesley Abravanel

amed not for the sun-kissed skin of the area's residents, but for the gold salvaged from shipwrecks off its coastline, the Gold Coast embraces more than 60 miles of beautiful Atlantic shoreline—from the pristine sands of Palm Beach to the legendary strip of beaches in Fort Lauderdale.

If you haven't visited the cities along Florida's southeastern coast in the past few decades, you'll be amazed at how much has changed. Miles of grassland and empty lots have been replaced with luxurious resorts and high-rise condominiums. The glut of condos has also led to a hybrid of lodging type: former condos-turned-hotel. Taking advantage of their proximity to Miami, the cities that make up the Gold Coast have attracted millions looking to escape the everyday routines of life.

Fortunately, amid all the building, much of the natural appeal of the Gold Coast remains. There are still 300 miles of Intracoastal Waterway, Fort Lauderdale's Venetian-inspired canals, and the swampy splendor of the Everglades just a few miles inland.

The most popular areas in the Gold Coast are Fort Lauderdale and Palm Beach. There has also been a great revitalization of these area's urban downtowns, especially Hollywood, Fort Lauderdale, and West Palm Beach. These once-desolate city centers have been spruced up and now attract a younger crowd.

Farther north is Jupiter, best known for spring training at the Roger Dean Stadium. In between these more-visited destinations are a number of attractions worth stopping for. Driving north along the coastline is one of the best ways to fully appreciate what the Gold Coast is all about.

Unfortunately, like its neighbors to the south, the Gold Coast can be prohibitively hot and buggy in summer. The good news is that bargains are often plentiful May through October, when many locals take advantage of package deals and uncrowded resorts.

For the purposes of this chapter, the Gold Coast consists of the towns of Hallandale, Hallandale Beach, Hollywood, Pompano Beach, Fort Lauderdale, Dania Beach, Deerfield, Boca Raton, Delray Beach, West Palm Beach, Palm Beach, and Jupiter.

Exploring the Gold Coast by Car

Like most of South Florida, the Gold Coast consists of a mainland and adjacent barrier islands. Interstate 95, which runs north-south, is the area's main highway. Farther west is the Florida Turnpike, a toll road that can be worth the expense, as the speed limit is higher and it's often less congested than I-95. Also on the mainland is U.S. 1, which generally runs parallel to I-95 (to the east) and is a narrower thoroughfare that is mostly crowded with strip malls and seedy hotels.

We recommend taking Fla. A1A, a slow oceanside road that connects the long, thin islands of Florida's east coast. Although the road is narrow, it is the most scenic and ushers you properly into the relaxed atmosphere of these resort towns.

FACING PAGE: Players compete for the gold cup at the U.S. Polo Association championship in Palm Beach.

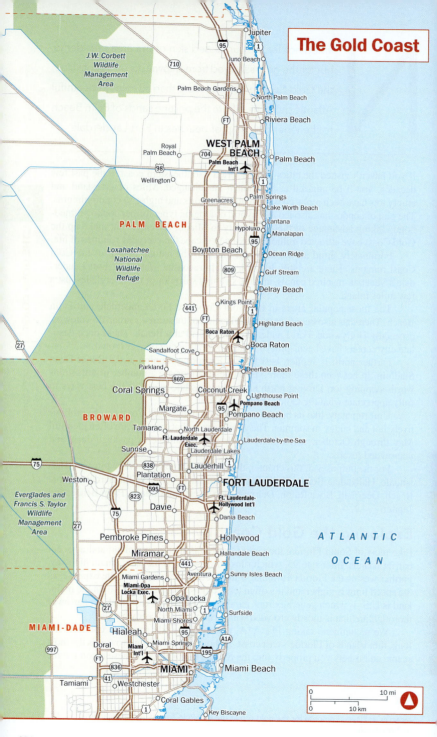

FORT LAUDERDALE

23 miles N of Miami

Once famous (or infamous) for the annual mayhem it hosted during spring break, **Fort Lauderdale** now attracts a more affluent, better-behaved crowd. Known as the "Venice of America," its 300 miles of navigable inland waterways and innumerable canals—in addition to the Atlantic Ocean—permit thousands of residents to anchor boats in their backyards. On land, institutions like the Museum of Art Fort Lauderdale and Museum of Discovery & Science give the city cultural resonance.

Things to Do Spend at least an afternoon or evening cruising Fort Lauderdale's waterways by water taxi. Stroll the Hollywood Beach Broadwalk for a people-watching extravaganza. Head to Fort Lauderdale Beach to sun and swim or hike the nature trails at Dr. Von D. Mizell-Eula Johnson State Park. Get in 18 holes at Emerald Hills or take a dive off Pompano Beach.

Shopping Bargain hunters bring suitcases to **Sawgrass Mills,** an outlet mecca west of Fort Lauderdale in Sunrise featuring over 350 stores. For upscale boutiques, **Las Olas Boulevard,** a tree-lined thoroughfare located between Fort Lauderdale Beach and downtown, has a mix of chain and boutique stores as well as art galleries.

Restaurants & Dining Fort Lauderdale can finally boast the presence of a number of fine restaurants and authentic ethnic eateries. They now join the legions of surf-and-turf joints in **Pompano Beach** and **downtown. Las Olas Boulevard,** especially, is packed with good eateries.

Nightlife & Entertainment Over the years, Fort Lauderdale has vastly improved the quality of its nightlife by welcoming earthy and sophisticated bars

A boat glides through one of Fort Lauderdale's many canals.

and clubs, especially downtown and on **Las Olas Boulevard.** Then there's the **Seminole Hard Rock Hotel & Casino,** as well as some less flashy, but still lively casinos. For a quieter night out, consider **Hollywood.**

Visiting Broward County

Even with the shine of Fort Lauderdale, the city's home county of Broward is still less well known and a lot calmer than hyped Miami-Dade County. According to some, it's much friendlier, too. In fact, a bit of a rivalry exists between residents of both counties. Miamians consider themselves more cosmopolitan than their northern neighbors, who, in turn, dismiss the alleged sophistication as snobbery and prefer their own county's gentler pace.

With more than 23 miles of beachfront and 300 miles of navigable waterways, Broward County is also a top outdoor destination. Scattered amid the shopping malls, condominiums, and tourist traps is a landscape lined with hundreds of parks, golf courses, tennis courts, and, of course, beaches.

The City of **Hallandale Beach** is a small, peaceful oceanfront town just north of Miami-Dade County's Aventura. Condos are the predominant landmarks in Hallandale, which is still pretty much a retirement community.

Just north of Hallandale is the more energetic city of **Hollywood.** A bustling community with a noted arts and culture scene and a walkable downtown, it has a much younger, more bohemian vibe than you'll find on Fort Lauderdale's Las Olas Boulevard. A spate of redevelopment has made the pedestrian-friendly center along Hollywood Boulevard and Harrison Street, east of Dixie Highway, a popular destination for travelers and locals alike. Prices are a fraction of those at other tourist areas, but a gritty undercurrent prevents it from becoming *too* trendy. The behemoth **Seminole Hard Rock Hotel & Casino** (p. 252), shaped like a giant guitar, looms over the city. It opened in 2019, and is illuminated with an LED light show most nights.

Huge cruise ships also take advantage of Florida's deepest harbor, Port Everglades. The seaport is on the southeastern coast of the Florida peninsula, near the Fort Lauderdale–Hollywood International Airport on the outskirts of Hollywood and Dania Beach.

Essentials

GETTING THERE If you're driving from Miami, it's a straight shot north to Hollywood or Fort Lauderdale. Visitors on their way to or from Orlando should take the Florida Turnpike to exit 53, 54, 58, or 62, depending on the location of your accommodations. The **Fort Lauderdale–Hollywood International Airport (FLL)** is usually easy to negotiate, and just 15 minutes from both of the downtown areas it services. However, the airport is undergoing an expansion not slated for completion until the end of 2026 and that often renders it just as maddening to navigate as any other major metropolitan airport. Some two dozen plus airlines, large and small, serve the airport, with plenty of connections to and from the U.S., Canada, and the Caribbean.

The airport has a car-rental center where at least a dozen rental companies are under one roof—very convenient.

Amtrak (amtrak.com; © **800/USA-RAIL** [872-7245]) stations are at the **Tri Rail Station,** 200 SW 21st Terrace (Broward Blvd. and I-95), Fort Lauderdale

ATTRACTIONS
Bonnet House Museum & Gardens **9**
Butterfly World **1**
Hillsboro Inlet Lighthouse **3**
International Swimming Hall of Fame **18**
Jungle Queen Riverboat **19**
Museum of Discovery & Science **25**
NSU Art Museum Fort Lauderdale **26**
Stranahan House **27**

HOTELS
The Atlantic Hotel & Spa **10**
Conrad Fort Lauderdale **12**
Four Seasons Hotel & Residences Fort Lauderdale **13**
High Noon Beach Resort **6**
Lago Mar Resort and Club **20**
Margaritaville Beach Resort Hollywood Beach **37**
Napoli Belmar **11**
Pelican Grand Beach Resort **8**
The Pillars Hotel & Club **15**
Riverside Hotel **28**
Sea Downs (and the Bougainvillea) **36**
Seminole Hard Rock Hotel & Casino Hollywood **35**
snooze **16**

RESTAURANTS
Anthony's Runway 84 **31**
Café Martorano **7**
Cafe Maxx **4**
Cap's Place Island Restaurant **2**
Casa D'Angelo **21**
Coconut's **17**
Foxy Brown **22**
Gilbert's 17th St. Grill **29**
Jaxon's Ice Cream Parlor & Restaurant **32**
The Katherine **23**
La Spada's Original Hoagies **5**
Le Tub **38**
Lester's Diner **30**
Rustic Inn Crabhouse **33**
Sistrunk Marketplace **24**
Steak 954 **14**
Tropical Acres Steakhouse **34**

Fort Lauderdale, Hollywood & Pompano Beach

239

ONE IF BY LAND, taxi IF BY SEA

The **Water Taxi** (watertaxi.com; © **954/467-6677**) is one of the greatest innovations for water lovers since waterproof smartphones. Especially in a city like Fort Lauderdale's which has 300 miles of scenic waterways. A trusty fleet of older port boats serves the dual purpose of transporting and entertaining visitors as they cruise through the "Venice of America." Because of its popularity, the water taxi fleet has welcomed several sleek, 70-passenger "water buses" (featuring indoor and outdoor seating with an atrium-like roof).

Taxis operate on demand and also along a fairly regular route, carrying from 19 to 200 passengers, depending on the size of the vessel, to 20 stops. If you're staying at a hotel on the route, you can be picked up there, usually within 15 minutes of calling, and then be shuttled to any of the dozens of restaurants, bars, and attractions on or near the waterfront. If you aren't sure where you want to go, ask one of the personable captains, who can point out historic and fun spots along the way.

Boats operate daily from 10am to 10pm, depending on the weather. The cost is $40 for an all-day pass with unlimited stops on and off, $35 for seniors, $20 for children 5 to 11, and $25 for adults and seniors and $20 for children 5 to 11 if you board after 5pm.

(© **954/587-6692**); and 3001 Hollywood Blvd. (northwest corner of Hollywood Blvd. and I-95), Hollywood.

The high speed **Brightline,** which runs as far south as Miami and north as Orlando has a station in downtown Fort Lauderdale at 101 NW 2nd Ave. (gobrightline.com; © **831/539-2901**), with airport connector locations at FLL at terminals 1, 2, 3, and 4.

GETTING AROUND The coolest—literally—way to get around Fort Lauderdale is by **Water Taxi** (see box, above), which may not necessarily be the cheapest, but when in Fort Laudy, it's the most fun. **The Fort Lauderdale Sun Trolley** (luxurylivingfortlauderdale.com/fort-lauderdale-sun-trolley; $1/ride, $3/day pass), is a hop-on bus with seven routes covering the beaches, downtown, and more, with a free airport connection, and only two routes, the Las Olas and beach route, that charge. For those looking to put the pedal to the asphalt, the **Broward B-Cycle** (fortlauderdale.gov) bike-share service has 16 stations throughout town. Rentals are $5 per half-hour or $25 for a 7-day pass.

VISITOR INFORMATION Visit **Lauderdale,** 101 NE 3rd Ave. (visitlauderdale.com; © **954/765-4466**), is an excellent resource for area information.

The **Greater Hollywood Chamber of Commerce,** 330 N. Federal Hwy. (at U.S. 1 and Taylor St.), Hollywood (hollywoodchamber.org; © **954/923-4000**), has the lowdown on all of Hollywood's events, attractions, restaurants, hotels, and tours. Another good website is VisitHollywoodFL.com.

Hitting the Beach

The southern part of the Gold Coast, Broward County, has the region's most amenity-laden beaches, which stretch for more than 23 miles. Most do not charge for access, and all are well maintained. Here's a selection of some of the county's best, from south to north:

Hollywood Beach, stretching from Sheridan Street to Georgia Street, is a major attraction in the city of Hollywood, a veritable carnival of young hipsters, big families, and sunburned French Canadians who dodge bicyclers and skaters along the rows of tacky souvenir shops, T-shirt shops, game rooms, snack bars, beer stands, hotels, and miniature-golf courses. **Hollywood Beach Broadwalk,** modeled after Atlantic City's legendary boardwalk, is a cement promenade that's 30 feet wide and stretches along the shoreline for 3 miles. On it, you'll also find a concrete bike path, a crushed-shell jogging path, and beach showers at each street end (all of them are accessible for people with disabilities). Popular with runners, skaters, and cruisers, the Broadwalk is renowned as a hangout for thousands of retirement-age snowbirds who get together for frequent dances and shows at a faded outdoor amphitheater. Despite efforts to clear out a seedy element, the area remains a haven for scammers, so keep alert.

Beyond Hollywood's Broadwalk there's the natural beauty of the beach itself, which is wide and clean. There are lifeguards, showers, restroom facilities, and public areas for picnics and parties.

The **Fort Lauderdale Beach Promenade** along the beach is especially peaceful in the mornings, when there's just a smattering of joggers and walkers; but even at its most crowded on weekends, the expansive promenade provides room for everyone. Note, however, that the beach, while clean and lovely, isn't exactly zen; it is across the street from an uninterrupted stretch of hotels, bars, and retail outlets. On the sand just across the road, most days you'll find hard-core volleyball players who always welcome anyone with a good spike, and you'll find an inviting ocean for swimmers of any level. The waters are under the careful watch of at least 20 lifeguards in stands up and down the beach. Clean showers and restrooms are conveniently located along the strip. Pets have been banned from most of the beach in order to maintain the impressive cleanliness; a designated area for pets exists away from the main sunbathing areas.

Hollywood is home to 7 miles of pristine beaches.

> ### Turtle Trail
>
> In June and July, the beach at **Dr. Von D. Mizell-Eula Johnson State Park** is home to the spectacular **Sea Turtle Awareness Program** (www.floridastateparks.org/mizell). Park rangers begin the evening with a lecture and slide show, while scouts search the beach for nesting loggerhead sea turtles. If a turtle is located—plenty of them usually are—a beach walk allows participants to see the turtles nest and, sometimes, their eggs hatch. The program begins at 9pm on Wednesdays and Fridays in June and July. Walks last between 1 and 3 hours. Comfortable walking shoes and insect repellent are necessary, as are reservations. The park entrance fee of $4 to $6 per carload applies.

Especially on weekends, parking at the oceanside meters is nearly impossible. Try biking, skating, Ubering, or hitching a ride on the water taxi instead. The strip is located on Fla. A1A, between SE 17th Street and Sunrise Boulevard.

Dania Beach's **Dr. Von D. Mizell-Eula Johnson State Park,** 6503 N. Ocean Dr., Dania Beach (floridastateparks.org/mizell; © **954/923-2833**), consists of 251 acres of barrier island, situated between the Atlantic Ocean and the Intracoastal Waterway, from Port Everglades on the north to Dania on the south. Its natural setting contrasts sharply with the urban development of Fort Lauderdale, making it the last example of an undeveloped coastal ecosystem in Broward County. The park's beach, one of Broward County's most important nesting beaches for sea turtles, produces some 10,000 hatchlings a year. The park's broad, flat beach is popular for both swimming and sunning. It's named for Civil Rights Movement leaders who led "wade-in" protests to desegregate South Florida beaches in the 1950s and 1960s (this was once the county's designated "colored beach" and bore the name of the Broward County attorney who was instrumental in transferring ownership of the land to the state, in lieu of being developed for residential highrises). Over 3 miles of self-guided nature trails are great for those too restless to sunbathe. There's also a full-service restaurant, **Whiskey Creek Hideout,** overlooking a scenic creek, which also happens to rent umbrellas, kayaks, and paddleboards in addition to serving a very good burger. Admission to the park is $6 per vehicle with two to eight people, $4 for a single occupant, and $2 for pedestrians and bicyclists. The park is open daily from 8am until sunset.

A block in from the beach, the **Hugh Taylor Birch State Park,** 3109 E. Sunrise Blvd., Fort Lauderdale (floridastateparks.org/HughTaylorBirch; ©**954/564-4521;** daily 8am–sunset), is a rare and worthy spot of greenery set amid the waterways, the sands, and the sprawl. It preserves a peaceful patch of hammock (subtropical hardwood forest) in which you're welcome to hike, bike, skate, kayak, fish, or canoe in the park's coastal dune lakes. Known as Fort Lauderdale's "Central Park," it has 1.9 miles of shaded bike paths, and a 20-minute Coastal Hammock Trail for hiking. There's even a happening bar and restaurant, **The Grove.** A free ranger-guided tour of the entire park is offered from 10:30 to 11:30am every Friday and Saturday where you will learn about the flora and fauna of the park's five different natural communities. The park is also listed on Florida's Great Birding Trail, with over 250 species of birds, as well as gopher tortoise, diamondback terrapin turtles, and terrifying snakes. Fees are $6 per car with up to eight people, $4 for single occupant car, scooter, or motorcycle, and $2 for pedestrians and bicyclists.

Outdoor Activities & Spectator Sports

BOATING Often called the "yachting capital of the world," Fort Lauderdale provides ample opportunity for visitors to get out on the water, either along the Intracoastal Waterway or on the open ocean. If your hotel doesn't rent boats, try **Aloha Watersports,** across from Casablanca Café, 3008 Alhambra St., Fort Lauderdale (alohawatersports.com; © **954/462-7245**). It can outfit you with a variety of craft, including jet skis, WaveRunners, and catamarans. Rates start at $100 per half-hour for WaveRunners ($15 each additional rider; doubles and triples available), $80 to $125 for catamarans, $30 an hour for paddleboards or $100 for a 1-hour lesson, and $105 to $125 per person for a 15-minute parasailing ride. Aloha also offers a thrilling speedboat ride for $50 for a half-hour or $100 for a 90-minute excursion, a surfing school ($100—though the waves are hardly rippin' here!), and a water playground with trampoline and waterslide for $25 for a half-hour or $40 for an hour. Treasure hunters can rent a metal detector here for $25 for an hour or $30 for a longer hunt. For larger bareboats, often the most effective way to book, cost-wise, is via marketplace sites **Boatsetter.com** or **GetMyBoat.com.**

Note: Visitors who wish to rent a boat to operate in Florida waters are required to take an online course; see p. 29.

FISHING The newly revamped **Fisher Family Pier,** 222 N. Pompano Beach Blvd. (parks.pompanobeachfl.gov/facilities/fisher-family-pier; © **954/532-9724;** daily 7am–10pm), in Pompano Beach is a fun place to drop a line. Look closely and you'll notice the end of the pier is shaped like a—wait for it—pompano fish! Snapper, mackerel, snook, and cobia are the popular catches here. Daily fishing rate is $6, and you can rent rods for $27 which includes bait, bucket, towel, and knife.

A Fort Lauderdale drawbridge opens to let a boat in.

Over at the 976-foot **Deerfield Beach International Fishing Pier,** 200 NE 21st Ave. (deerfield-beach.com/1420/International-Fishing-Pier; © **954/480-4407**), you can rent rods, bait, and other fishing accessories. Check for conditions at this pier's three live cameras with views of the pier, the beach, and even underwater. And in laidback Dania Beach, the fishing pier (daily 6am–11pm) is a relaxing spot to cast your line or look at what the locals are catching. Fishing is $4, rod rental is cash only from $18 to $25.

GOLF More than 35 golf courses in all price ranges compete for players in this area. Among the best is **Eagle Trace Golf Club** ★★, 1111 Eagle Trace Blvd. West, Coral Springs (eagletrace.clublink.com; © **954/753-7222**), located east of the Sawgrass Expressway in west Broward County, and featuring six sets of tees. The course also has an island green, three greens surrounded by wooden bulkheads, and not a single palm tree on the property— a rarity in these parts. Greens fees start at $65 per person and include cart.

Designed by famed golf course architect Donald Ross in 1924, the **Hollywood Beach Golf Club** ★★★, 1600 Johnson St., Hollywood (hollywoodbeachgolf.com; © 954/927-1751), is situated on a 110-acre property far from commercial and residential areas, and features a tree-lined, 18-hole par-70 layout, including five par-3s. Greens fees are a bargain, from $20 to $65, including cart.

The **Pompano Beach Municipal Golf Course** ★★★, 1801 NE 6th St. (parks.pompanobeachfl.gov/golf; © 954/786-4111), has two 18-hole courses, including the recently redesigned Greg Norman Signature Pines Course that has already gained a reputation as a golfer's paradise. Greens fees start at $50 with cart, $44 without.

SCUBA DIVING In Broward County, the best dive wreck is the *Mercedes I*, a 197-foot freighter that washed up in the backyard of a Palm Beach socialite in 1984 and was sunk for divers the following year off Pompano Beach. The artificial reef, filled with colorful sponges, spiny lobsters, and barracudas, is 97 feet below the surface, a mile offshore between Oakland Park and Sunrise boulevards. Dozens of reputable dive shops line the beach. Ask at your hotel for a nearby recommendation, or contact **American Dream Dive Charters,** at the Hilton Fort Lauderdale Marina (scubafortlauderdale.com; © 954/577-0338).

SPECTATOR SPORTS During the season, the Miami Dolphins and University of Miami Hurricanes football teams play just south of Hallandale at **Hard Rock Stadium,** near the Dade–Broward County line, 347 Don Shula Dr., Miami Gardens (hardrockstadium.com; © 305/943-8000).

Gulfstream Park Racing and Casino, at U.S. 1 and Hallandale Beach Boulevard, Hallandale (gulfstreampark.com; © 954/454-7000), is known for large purses and important horse races (like the Florida Derby), so the track is often crowded at this recently refurbished suburban course. There's also a casino with slots and electronic table games.

South Florida's only remaining fronton, **Dania Jai Alai,** at the **Casino Dania Beach,** 301 E. Dania Beach Blvd., at Fla. A1A and U.S. 1 (casinodaniabeach.com/jai-alai; © 954/920-1511), is a great place to catch what has become a dying sport, at least in South Florida.

Lionel Messi playing for Inter Miami CF.

The National Hockey League's **Florida Panthers** (panthers.nhl.com; © 954/835-7000) play in Sunrise at the **Amerant Bank Arena,** 2555 NW 137th Way. Tickets are exceptionally inexpensive, starting as low as $11.

Last, but not the least bit least, David Beckham has bent the rules and brought Major League Soccer to South Florida in the form of **Inter Miami CF,** featuring the one, the only, legendary soccer star Lionel Messi. So why are we including this in the Fort Lauderdale chapter? Because Inter Miami plays in the DRV Pink Stadium, 1350 NW 55th St., Fort Lauderdale (intermiamicf.com; © **954/428-0611**). Tickets, ever since Messi signed on (through 2025), are either impossible to get or upwards of tens of thousands of dollars!

TENNIS/PICKLEBALL There are hundreds of courts in Broward County, and plenty are accessible to the public. Many are at resorts and hotels. If yours has none, try the **Jimmy Evert Tennis Center,** in **Holiday Park,** 701 NE 12th Ave. (off Sunrise Blvd.), Fort Lauderdale (parks.fortlauderdale.gov; © **954/828-5378;** daily 6am–9:30pm), famous as the spot where Chris Evert trained with her dad. There are 18 lighted clay courts and 3 hard courts here. Nonresidents of Fort Lauderdale pay $9 per hour before 5pm and $10.50 after. There are also six pickleball courts here; cost is $4.50 per person before 5pm, and $6 after 5pm.

In early 2024, the city announced it was breaking ground near the Fort Lauderdale International Airport within **Snyder Park** (parks.fortlauderdale.gov), to open **The Fort** (playthefort.com), a pickleball stadium featuring 43 professional courts—14 of them weatherproof—as well as lakefront beach area, bocce, shuffleboard, and more. It should be completed by the time we go to press. For info on pickleball courts throughout the Fort Lauderdale area, go to **FTL Pickleball Club** (ftlpb.org), which has a comprehensive list of courts.

Seeing the Sights

Bonnet House Museum & Gardens ★★★
Little do most beachgoers suspect what lies behind the fence and wall of greenery a few yards away. This

View the fascinating grounds and furnishings of Bonnet House.

35-acre spread named after the Bonnet lily is a trip back in time to 1921, when artist and collector Frederic Clay Bartlett built a gracious two-story manse in a kind of Caribbean plantation style, filled with art and surrounded by lush tropical gardens, where he wintered with a first, then a second wife (the latter of whom, Evelyn, some of the friendly and talkative volunteer guides even met). The 1¼-hour self-guided tour introduces visitors to quirky Floridians, whimsical artwork, lush grounds, and intriguing design. For history buffs, the $30 docent-led tour gives a more in-depth look at the stories of those who lived here. There's also a $40 VIP tour, with access to normally closed areas, but that's more than most visitors need, or enjoy, quite frankly.

900 N. Birch Rd. (1 block west of the ocean, south of Sunrise Blvd.), Fort Lauderdale. bonnethouse.org. **954/563-5393.** Admission to house and grounds $25 adults, $8 kids 6–17. Grounds only admission $10. Tues–Fri 11am–3pm; Sat–Sun 11am–4pm.

Butterfly World ★★ After moving to Florida from Illinois in 1968, electrical engineer Ronald Boender decided to actively pursue his passion, raising local butterflies at his home and recording data on each. After realizing there was a need for farmed butterflies, Boender set up a company in 1984 and went one step further, building this butterfly house along with the founder of the world-renowned London Butterfly House across the pond. Enter Butterfly World, renowned globally for its butterfly farm and research facility as well as its 10 acres of aviaries and botanical gardens, home to over 20,000 exotic butterflies and birds. Butterfly World has been instrumental in saving the endangered Schaus Swallowtail, a species of butterfly that is becoming reestablished in South Florida (Biscayne National Park), and may, one day soon, be taken off the endangered species list. Kids especially love the "bug zoo," which features some of the insect world's biggest celebrities—all of which kids are able to touch, if they dare, with the help of an expert. There's lots to see here so set aside at least 2 hours to, uh, flit around yourself.

Tradewinds Park, 3600 W. Sample Rd., Coconut Creek. butterflyworld.com. **954/977-4400.** Admission $32.50 adults and seniors, $22.50 children 3–11. Mon–Sat 9am–5pm; Sun 11am–5pm.

Hillsboro Inlet Lighthouse ★★ Completed in 1907, the Hillsboro Inlet Lighthouse, which rises 136 feet above water and marks the northern end of the Florida Reef, isn't just any lighthouse. It contains a 5,500,000-candlepower light and is the most powerful light on the East Coast of the United States. And there's more history. This lighthouse was also made famous thanks to one of the "barefoot mailmen," carriers of the first U.S. mail route between Palm Beach and Miami. Because there was no paved road on that route, the mailmen had to get through by boat and by walking the sand along the beach. James Hamilton was the most famous of these after disappearing delivering mail on the route just after October 10, 1887, presumably the victim of drowning or an encounter with a hungry alligator while trying to swim across the Hillsboro inlet to retrieve his boat from the far side. His body was never recovered, and his death still remains a mystery today. An original stone statue called *The Barefoot Mailman* by Frank Varga is displayed on the shores of the Hillsboro inlet next to the Hillsboro lighthouse with an inscription dedicated to Hamilton. A fascinating story, it can be told in much more detail with a tour by the Hillsboro Lighthouse Preservation Society, which is given once every other month, usually on Saturdays. Boats typically depart on the hour from the departing docks and depart from the lighthouse (USCG) docks on the half-hour. If the tour isn't available, check out the museum.

Hillsboro Inlet, off A1A, Pompano Beach. hillsborolighthouse.org. © **954/942-2102.** Tours $35/person or $75 for a family of 4. Museum open daily 11am–3pm. Take I-95 to Atlantic Blvd. Go east across the Intracoastal and left at A1A for 2 miles to Pompano Beach City Park. Stop at the SE corner of the Hillsboro Inlet bridge where there's an excellent view of the Hillsboro Lighthouse. Tours meet on the dock across from Riverside Dr. To get there, go east, cross the Intracoastal and make an immediate left on North Riverside Dr. Go 1 block to the parking lot. Park and head west to the dock across Riverside Dr.

International Swimming Hall of Fame (ISHOF) ★★★

Any aspiring Michael Phelps (who was inducted in 2023), or those who appreciate the sport, will love this splashy homage to the best backstrokers, front crawlers, and divers in the world. The museum houses the world's largest collection of aquatic memorabilia and is the single largest source of aquatic books, manuscripts, and literature. Among the highlights are Johnny Weissmuller's Olympic medals, Mark Spitz's starting block used to win six of his seven 1972 Olympic gold medals, and more than 60 Olympic, national, and club uniforms, warm-ups, and swimsuits. For those who don't mind getting their feet wet, the ISHOF Florida Aquatic Center is the only one of its kind in the world with two 50m pools, a diving well, a swimming flume, and one of the world's highest diving platforms at 27 meters. As of this writing, only the east side of the museum was open, as the ISHOF was undergoing a $190-million makeover to add new buildings, an aquarium, and rooftop restaurant. Completion is expected in late 2025.

1 Hall of Fame Dr., Fort Lauderdale. ishof.org. © **954/462-6536.** Admission by donation. Check website for current hours.

Hillsboro Inlet Lighthouse.

Jungle Queen Riverboat ★★

A staple of family vacations since its debut in 1935, this old-timey-looking riverboat glides along the New River past mansions and through downtown, stopping at a pavilion for a variety of entertainments and a barbecue dinner before making a return trip after dark. If your kids are between 3 and 12 years of age, they'll love this dinner cruise.

junglequeen.com. © **954-462-5596.** Tues–Sun 6pm departures from 801 Seabreeze Blvd. (be there 30 min. before). 4-hr. experience. $75 adults, $50 ages 3-12.

Museum of Discovery & Science ★★★
A science museum that successfully leverages high tech and interactivity to make science fun for kids—and just as engaging for grownups—starting with a funky, 52-foot "kinetic-energy" sculpture out front called the "Great Gravity Clock." Another highlight here is the Florida Ecoscapes exhibit which delves into the science behind living coral reefs, bees, bats, frogs, turtles, and alligators. Especially popular is the To Fly exhibit, where visitors can find out what it feels like to soar the open skies in the cockpits of history-making aircraft, and explore the red landscapes of Mars. When my daughter was around 4, she "landed a plane" here magnificently and still talks about it.

401 SW 2nd St., Fort Lauderdale. mods.org. 📞 **954/467-6637.** Admission (includes 1 documentary IMAX film) $27 adults, $25 seniors 65 and over, $22 children 2–12. Mon–Sat 10am–5pm; Sun noon–5pm. Movie theater closes later. From I-95, exit on Broward Blvd. E. Continue to SW 5th Ave., turn right; garage is on the right.

NSU Art Museum Fort Lauderdale ★★
It's a surprise to some to find the largest collection of works by William Glackens here, the seminal American Realist painter who was one of the founding members of the Ashcan School of Art, but there you have it. This regional powerhouse owns some 7,500 important works, including the largest American collection of CoBrA Movement pieces (acronym for Copenhagen, Brussels, and Amsterdam, the avant-garde artists who resisted the Nazis during World War II and gained prominence soon thereafter); stunning Picasso ceramics; Latin American modern and contemporary art by Frida Kahlo, Diego Rivera, and Wilfredo Lam; and contemporary works from more than 90 Cuban artists in exile around the world. A recent acquisition, centered on multicultural and women artists, includes works from Nan Golden, Cindy Sherman, and Cara Walker. *Tip:* On the first Thursday of the month, admission is waived and the cafe and wine bar have a two-for-one happy hour (11am–7pm).

1 E. Las Olas Blvd., Fort Lauderdale. nsuartmuseum.org. 📞 **954/525-5500.** Admission $16 adults, $10 seniors, free for children 5 and under. Tues–Sat 11am–5pm; Sun noon–5pm.

Stranahan House ★★
Granted, Fort Lauderdale doesn't exactly ooze history, but it's here if you look for it. A case in point is the city's oldest remaining edifice, tucked away alongside downtown's New River. It dates back to 1901, when the eponymous Frank Stranahan built it as a trading post when this was still a frontier settlement and Seminole Indians would pull up in dugout canoes. It's been a post office, town hall, and general store, and now serves as a worthwhile little museum of South Florida pioneer life, containing turn-of-the-20th-century furnishings and historical photos of the area. *Note:* Self-guided tours are not allowed, and the house usually offers one tour a day. Tours last about an hour.

335 SE 6th Ave. (Las Olas Blvd. at the New River Tunnel), Fort Lauderdale. 📞 **954/524-4736.** stranahanhouse.org. Admission $13 adults, $11 seniors, $8 students and children. One tour daily. Check online for times.

Shopping

It's all about malls in Broward County with a few exceptions. **Dania** is known as a place for antiques because within 1 square mile of Federal Highway, the city has more than two dozen dealers selling everything from small collectibles to historic furnishings. Alas, the number of shops has dwindled in recent years, but there's still enough here to appeal to antique hunters. The website **Antiques.com** has a good listing of stores, including addresses and websites, so you can get an idea of what they carry before heading over.

If you're looking for unusual boutiques, especially art galleries, head to quaint **Las Olas Boulevard,** located west of A1A and a block east of Federal Highway/U.S. 1, off SE Eighth Street, where there are hundreds of shops with alluring window decorations and intriguing merchandise such as mural-size oil paintings.

Malls in Broward County include the **Galleria,** at Sunrise Boulevard near the Fort Lauderdale Beach, and **Broward Mall,** west of I-95 on Broward Boulevard, in Plantation. Both are, well, like most malls these days, meh. Right near the Fort Lauderdale International Airport is a brand-new outdoor shopping, dining, and entertainment complex, **Dania Pointe,** 139 S. Compass Way (daniapointe.com; ⓒ **833/800-4343**), featuring stores like H&M and a Nike Outlet.

For bargains, there's no better place than **Sawgrass Mills,** 12801 W. Sunrise Blvd. (simon.com; ⓒ **954/846-0179**), which has more than 350 name-brand outlets from Gucci, Boss, Louboutin, and Prada to the more accessible shops (Ann Taylor, Adidas, etc.). There's a hotel right on-site (**AC Hotel For Lauderdale Sawgrass Mills/Sunrise**) for those who literally want to shop and drop.

Where to Stay

For rentals for a few weeks or months, check the annual list of small lodgings compiled by **Visit Lauderdale** (visitlauderdale.com; ⓒ **954/765-4466**); they're especially helpful if you're looking for privately owned, charming, affordable lodgings. You'll also, of course, find a slew of listings on **Airbnb** and **Vrbo.**

EXPENSIVE

Conrad Fort Lauderdale ★★★ This 24-story resort is one of the many once-empty condo buildings on the beach that were taken over by hotels. This building, however, isn't just any building. It was designed by the late postmodern icon Michael Graves, and inspired by the area's yachting culture. A blue-and-taupe-hued lobby carries that theme out, with white Italian marble, wood, and textured walls. Rooms have a seafaring look as well, with walnut wood floors and Spanish leather furniture. All are quite large (they once were full apartments), with Italian marble bathrooms, rainfall showers, and soaking tubs. The *piece de resistance* here is the 20,000-square-foot oceanfront sixth floor Sky Deck, with heated pool, cabanas, Jacuzzi, restaurant, and fire pit for those chilly nights at—er, across from the—sea. There's also a nice spa, two restaurants (Italian and Japanese), and an

> **Price Categories**
>
> We're listing double room rates only. Please assume that suites will be pricier. Also note that some hotels fall into one price range in high season and a different one in low, hence the hybrid categories below.
> **Inexpensive:** $199 and under
> **Moderate:** $200–$325
> **Expensive:** $326 and up

excellent program for families traveling with infants and young children. Resort fee includes 2 hours of bike rental a day.

551 N. Fort Lauderdale Beach Blvd., Fort Lauderdale. conradfortlauderdale.com. ✆ **954/414-5100.** 290 units. $333–$788 double. Valet parking $55. **Amenities:** 5 restaurants; bar; concierge; spa; kids camp; bike rentals; 2 pools; fitness center; free Wi-Fi.

Four Seasons Hotel & Residences Fort Lauderdale ★★★

Yet another yacht-themed hotel, right down to the travertine-floored lobby cafe named after President JFK's yacht, the Honey Fitz. Rooms are boaty too, adorned in lots of white and navy blue, curvaceous walnut furnishings, and beds that have rattan and wood headboards. But it's the third floor that really makes you feel like you're the king (or queen) of the world: a sundeck reminiscent of an exclusive beach club, with both adult and kid pools, unobstructed ocean views, and a Mediterranean restaurant that has a "rosé all day" ambiance. Also on-site: the excellent **Maass by Chef Ryan Ratino ★★★**, an elegant dining experience, with food (mostly) cooked in a wood-fired stove. The hotel's spa is notable for its salt-wall saunas and aromatherapy steam rooms. A kids club, beach concierge to set you up across the street, and free use of bikes to explore the area, are also nice perks.

525 N. Fort Lauderdale Beach Blvd., Fort Lauderdale. fourseasons.com. ✆ **754/336-3100.** 189 units. $566–$954 double. Valet parking $50. Pet fee $100. **Amenities:** 3 restaurants; bar; babysitting; bike rentals; concierge; 2 pools; fitness center; free Wi-Fi.

Margaritaville Beach Resort Hollywood Beach ★★

If you feel like wasting away on Hollywood Beach, this would be the best place to do it, a family-friendly, fun resort that exudes the late Jimmy Buffett's barefoot and fancy-free vibes. The 17-story property is huge, with spacious rooms that are very cute (blond wood furnishings, lots of aqua, balconies). On the roof is an adults-only pool that's less harried than the two beachfront pools. Yes, one of those below has a Flow Rider surf simulator that kids LOVE, but it is open to the public and tends to get overcrowded. The bars and restaurants here are also always packed and often have live entertainment. For those looking for loud, lively, and boozy, this is the place to be on Hollywood Beach.

1111 N Ocean Dr., Hollywood. margaritavillehollywoodbeachresort.com. ✆ **954/923-4968.** 369 units. $423–$463 double. Valet parking $48, self-parking $43. Pet fee $250. **Amenities:** 4 restaurants; 3 bars; 3 outdoor pools; Flow Rider surf machine; spa; kids club; watersports rentals; room service; free Wi-Fi.

EXPENSIVE/MODERATE

The Atlantic Hotel & Spa ★★

Overlooking 23 miles of white sand, the Atlantic is a 16-story study in minimal modernity with soothing colors and comfortable, stylish decor. Rooms were spruced up in the summer of 2023 and all have kitchenettes and exceptionally comfortable beds. For those looking for more room, there are two- and three-bedroom suites, ranging from 3,500 to 4,000-plus square feet, some with private elevators. Most notable may be the Atlantic's state-of-the-art 10,000-square-foot spa. On the hotel's fifth-floor ocean terrace you'll find a heated pool, casual bar, and restaurant. It's a nice spot for a frozen drink and a sensational view.

601 N. Fort Lauderdale Beach Blvd., Fort Lauderdale. atlantichotelfl.com. ✆ **954/567-8020.** 100 units. $270–$633 double. Valet parking $45. Pet fee $150. **Amenities:** 2 restaurants; bar; bike rentals; concierge; outdoor heated pool; room service; spa; watersports equipment/rentals; free Wi-Fi.

Lago Mar Beach Resort and Club ★★ A charming lobby with a rock fireplace and saltwater aquarium sets the tone of this old-school, off-the-beachy-path resort, a piece of Old Florida that occupies its own 10-acre, lush little island between Lake Mayan and the Atlantic. Guests have access to the broadest and best 500-foot strip of private beach in the entire city, not to mention three pools: one an adults-only oceanfront pool, another large enough for lap swimming, and the third a 9,000-square-foot swimming lagoon edged with tropical plants. Lago Mar is very family oriented, with many facilities and supervised activities for children. It's more like a country club than your typical chain beach resort. There's tennis, pickleball, putting course, beach volleyball, and a playground, too. Service is warm and gracious. The rooms and suites have Mediterranean or Key West influences and remind me of a guest room in your grandparents' Florida home. A full-service spa offers a wide array of treatments.

1700 S. Ocean Lane, Fort Lauderdale. lagomar.com. **954/523-6511.** 204 units. $311–$481 double. Free valet and self-parking (one car per room). From Federal Hwy. (U.S. 1), turn east onto SE 17th St. Causeway; turn right onto Mayan Dr.; turn right again onto S. Ocean Dr.; turn left onto Grace Dr.; then turn left again onto S. Ocean Lane to the hotel. **Amenities:** 4 restaurants; bar; wine room; room service; children's programs during holiday periods; concierge; minigolf course; 3 pools; tennis/pickleball courts; watersports equipment/rentals; free Wi-Fi.

Pelican Grand Beach Resort ★★ There's quite a bit to like about this family-friendly but luxe hotel. Elegant public spaces, 159 bright, cheery, oversized rooms; ocean-facing suites with balconies; a huge veranda out back where you can sit in rocking chairs and gaze out to sea; a zero-entry pool and "lazy river" right alongside it. But if you're coming to Fort Lauderdale for the beach (and really, who on vacation isn't?), one key difference about the Pelican Grand is that it's astride its own 500-foot stretch of sand instead of across the street, as is the case with most every other property hereabouts. Sweet. That, plus a laid-back atmosphere, and other amenities like an old-fashioned ice-cream parlor and location near, yet an arm's length away from "the scene," make it especially suited for families. *Tip:* Some rooms are showing their age, so ask to move if you're not satisfied.

2000 N. Ocean Blvd., Fort Lauderdale. pelicanbeach.com. **954/568-9431.** 159 units. $242–$665 double, plus $50 resort fee. Parking $48. **Amenities:** Restaurant; ice-cream parlor; bar; fitness center; pool; free Wi-Fi.

The Pillars Hotel & Club ★★★ Hidden away several blocks off the beach, the Pillars is a more intimate luxury option, the prime pick of the enclave known as North Beach Village, between Atlantic Boulevard and the Intracoastal Waterway. A genteel, island-plantation-style vision in yellow and white, it's got just two floors and 18 luxurious rooms with eclectic decor (a touch of midcentury modern here, some rattan there) and of course the up-to-date amenities you'd expect at a Small Luxury Hotels of the World member. Out back is a modest-size kidney-shape pool, along with a dock where you can dine with sweet views of yachts gliding by. There's also an annex with 6 more rooms of the same level of luxury. The service is discreet, friendly, and attentive. A library area (with more than 500 books) is at guests' disposal . . . as is pretty much anything else you request here.

111 N. Birch Rd., Fort Lauderdale. pillarshotel.com. **954/467-9639.** 24 units. $211–$610. Free off-street parking. **Amenities:** Restaurant; concierge; pool; room service; free Wi-Fi.

Seminole Hard Rock Hotel & Casino Hollywood ★★ The Seminole Tribe of Florida has created a miniature Vegas in Florida, and it's doing a booming business, especially at the massive, 130,000-square-foot casino. One caveat though: Unlike in Vegas, there are no free cocktails while you gamble. The humongous **Guitar Hotel** debuted on the property in 2019 in all its rock-star, lit-up glory—allegedly even seen by NASA up in space. In addition to the 638 rooms in the Guitar Hotel, there are 168 rooms in the seven-story **Oasis Tower,** complete with swim-up suites overlooking the lagoon pool, and 465 rooms in the original building, the **Hard Rock Hotel.** All rooms have high-tech amenities and mood lighting, plus Egyptian cotton sheets, and comfortable beds, though we have heard some complaints about maintenance standards. Each hotel complex has its own lagoon-style pools, with cabanas, DJ music, and splashy scenes. The entire complex has six fine dining restaurants, seven more casual eateries, and bars. So many bars. Ten of them, last we counted. There's also a

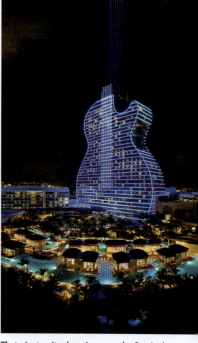

That giant guitar looming over the Seminole Hard Rock—and all of Broward County—cost $1.5 billion to construct.

food court, shops, two nightclubs—one open during the day, so it's called **Daer,** much to our chagrin, and the signature **Hard Rock Live,** where all the A-listers perform. If all this action has you feeling wiped out, there's always the **Rock Spa,** which, in Seminole Hard Rock fashion, is also pretty sizable. Although they're welcome, we don't recommend this place for kids.

1 Seminole Way, Hollywood. seminolehardrockhollywood.com. © **866/502-7529.** 1,271 units. $268–$745. Valet parking $35, free self-parking. Pet fee $100. **Amenities:** 13 restaurants; 2 nightclubs; 10 bars; Jacuzzi; 3 pools; room service; fitness center; spa; free Wi-Fi.

MODERATE

High Noon Beach Resort ★★★ The only complaint we have ever heard about this place is that reservations are tough to score here. So, as one regular guest told us, "Don't wait 'til high noon to book your stay here." This spick-and-span, family-owned property has been in biz for 60 years, and they know what they're doing. They even specifically state on their website: If you are looking for a big party crowd, with packed pool, loud music, smoking, etc., this isn't your place. Located directly on the ocean in fun beach town Lauderdale-By-The-Sea, the resort's four buildings have many rooms overlooking the two freshwater heated pools, which are in turn surrounded by the ocean and lush landscaping. All of these cheerful rooms (done up in striking ocean blues and white) have a fridge, microwave, and toaster, and apartments have full kitchens. Staff couldn't be better: friendly, responsive, and smart. The use of bikes is complimentary, as is parking.

4424 El Mar Dr., Lauderdale-By-The-Sea. highnoonresort.com. © **954/776-1121.** 40 units. $245–$296 double. **Amenities:** Free use of bikes; 2 outdoor heated pools; free Wi-Fi.

Riverside Hotel ★★ There's no beach here, but this 1936-built hotel is set on the sleepy and scenic New River, capturing the essence of that ever-elusive Old Florida. Guest rooms, outfitted in Mexican tile and wicker furnishings, are spacious and well maintained. Such details as intricately tiled bathrooms and old-style furniture enhance the charm of the otherwise stark building. The best units face the river, but it's hard to see the water past the parking lot and trees.

620 E. Las Olas Blvd., Fort Lauderdale. riversidehotel.com. © **954/467-0671.** 231 units. $124–$314 double. Valet parking $36, self-parking $26. From I-95, exit onto Broward Blvd.; turn right onto Federal Hwy. (U.S. 1); turn left onto Las Olas Blvd. **Amenities:** 4 restaurants; concierge; outdoor pool; fitness room; limited room service; free Wi-Fi.

INEXPENSIVE/MODERATE

snooze ★★★ Here, you snooze you win. That's because this adorbs little motel is directly across the street from the beach and has staff that care and so keep the place sparklingly clean. Rooms are cute and comfy, with vintage Fort Lauderdale photos on the walls, white-slatted headboards on the good quality beds, and pops of aqua to remind you that the sea is right outside. Staff loan out chairs, towels, and umbrellas for the beach for free, there's a shared barbecue grill for guests, and self-parking is a reasonable $10 a day. They get a lot of cruise passengers here because the motel is quite near to the main cruise port; and some students and backpackers, too, because one room has a bunk bed in it (the rest are regular hotel rooms).

205 N. Fort Lauderdale Beach Blvd., Fort Lauderdale. takeasnooze.com. © **954/761-9933.** $101–$322 double rooms. 18 units. **Amenities:** Rooftop lounge; loaner beach gear; barbecue grill; free Wi-Fi.

INEXPENSIVE

Napoli Belmar ★★ This North Beach Village mom-and-pop complex (actually three double-decker properties, including the Birch Patio Motel and Summerland Suites) is a good-value holdout—not fancy, but clean, friendly, and well managed. Mom and pop are Angela and Tony de Santo, who treat guests like family, while their 74 rooms, efficiencies, and suites are on the basic side but cheerful, well priced, and reasonably well equipped. The only tricky part about staying here is getting a reservation: Many folks take a room or efficiency for 4 to 6 weeks in high season, so call early (bookings are by phone only, surprisingly enough).

617 N. Birch Rd. (btw. Auramar and Belmar sts.), Fort Lauderdale. $90–$130 standard room. napolibelmar.com. © **954/564-3205.** 74 units. **Amenities:** 4 pools; barbecue area; picnic tables; bocce court; shuffleboard; washer/dryer; efficiencies/suites include full kitchens; free Wi-Fi

Sea Downs (and the Bougainvillea) ★★ This bargain lodging on the quiet end of the bustling Hollywood Broadwalk is often booked months in advance by return guests (mostly Europeans) who want to be directly on the beach without paying a fortune. The hosts of this superclean 1950s motel, Claudia and Karl

Herzog, live on the premises and keep things running smoothly. All rooms have fully equipped kitchens with fridges, stoves, utensils, and glassware and have been redecorated here and at the Herzogs' other, even less expensive property next door, the 11-unit Bougainvillea. Guests at both hotels share the Sea Downs' pool.

2900 N. Surf Rd., Hollywood. seadowns.com or bougainvilleahollywood.com. **954/923-4968.** 12 units. $135–$195 efficiency double. From I-95, exit Sheridan St. E. to A1A and go south; drive ½ mile to Coolidge St.; turn left. **Amenities:** Concierge; freshwater outdoor pool; free Wi-Fi.

Where to Eat

For years, Fort Lauderdale's food scene has been the Jan Brady of South Florida, with Michelin-saturated Miami being Marcia, Marcia, Marcia, and Palm Beach being not necessarily the youngest, but the most precocious sibling in highly curated curls. But as all siblings do, each has grown into their own distinct personalities, and to some seasoned foodies' surprise, the 954 has become one to watch when it comes to cuisine appealing to almost every tastebud and every budget. Take that, Marcia!

> **Price Categories**
>
> Meal per person, not including drinks or tip:
> **Inexpensive:** $20 and under
> **Moderate:** $21–$40
> **Expensive:** $40 and above

Beyond the restaurants below, don't sleep on **Maass by Chef Ryan Ratino** ★★★ (p. 250), which is serving some of the most exciting meals in town. As well, local institution **Lester's Diner** has four spots around the area (see LestersDiner.com for locations) and comes to the rescue when you need breakfast—at any time of day. You may also hear tell of **Le Tub** at 1100 N. Ocean Dr., Hollywood (Le-tub.com). It started life in 1959 as a Sunoco gas station, then was transformed in 1974 into a waterfront restaurant by a man who saw beauty in the flotsam, jetsam, and ocean-borne treasures he gathered over 4 years of jogging on Hollywood Beach. Today Le Tub is a wackily decorated dive bar with food, but it's fun to see the hand-painted bathtubs and toilet bowls used as planters lining the walkway.

EXPENSIVE

Anthony's Runway 84 ★★★ ITALIAN Red velvet chairs, monogrammed plates, chandeliers, and a Frank Sinatra sing-alike crooning on a small stage: Yes, it does feel like you're dining on an updated set of *Goodfellas* here (or *The Godfather*. Or *The Sopranos*). And that's a big part of the fun of this contemporary supper club, which just underwent an impressive reno that upped the glam factor. But the real stars are the huge portions of old-school Italian fare, like Caesar salad tossed table side, baked clams oreganata, or a big slab of veal scallopini. Bring your appetites, your checkbooks, and your breath mints, and don't forget the cannoli. For Anthony's take on pizza, try nearby **Anthony's Coal Fired Pizza,** 2203 S. Federal Hwy. (anthonyscoalfiredpizza.com; **954/462-5555**), which is quickly on its way to becoming a bona fide chain with locations all over South Florida and more up north (New York, New Jersey, Pennsylvania). This one is the original though.

330 S.R. 84, Fort Lauderdale. runway84.com. **954/467-8484.** Main courses $28–$85. Tues–Thurs and Sun noon–10pm; Fri–Sat 5–11pm.

Café Martorano ★★ ITALIAN Yo, cuz! Steve Martorano is quite the character—a big, tattooed lug of a South Philly DJ-turned-restaurant-guy who set up shop in a strip mall on a busy thoroughfare in 1993, and went on to become a Lauderdale icon. His cafe is loud, it's festive, it's got classic, Italian, and mafia-themed movies showing on the walls, and the menu is tasty Italian-American soul food all the way (the humongous, delicious meatballs especially have a deserved rep). Honestly, it's turned into a bit of a mozzarella-cheesy shtick by now, and it's not everyone's cup of chianti—did we mention it's LOUD?—but the place remains a crowd pleaser and even something of a celebrity magnet.

3343 E. Oakland Park Blvd., Fort Lauderdale. cafemartorano.com. **954/561-2554.** Main courses $31–$50. Tues–Thurs 6–11pm; Fri–Sat 6pm–1:30am.

Cafe Maxx ★★★ FLORIBBEAN Despite its bleak location, Darrel & Oliver's Cafe Maxx is still one of the best restaurants in Broward County. When it opened in 1984, it was the first restaurant to have an open kitchen, and what a stir that caused! Now, the marvel is what comes out of that kitchen, like Southern BBQ glazed pork chop risotto; or the green peppercorn-seared Faroe salmon with garlic broccolini. There's so much to choose from. But save room for dessert: the deep-dish bourbon and chocolate pecan pie, or the cookies and crème bread pudding are just two of many diet- and mind-blowing options. Sunday brunch goes beyond the usual with caviar pie, a luxe, luscious slice of caviar-slathered whole wheat toast, with two hard boiled eggs, sour cream, and onions.

2601 E. Atlantic Blvd., Pompano Beach. cafemaxx.com. **954/782-0606.** Main courses $34–$95. Tues–Sat 5–10pm; Sun–Mon 5–9pm; Sun 10:30am–2:30pm. From I-95, exit at Atlantic Blvd. E. The restaurant is 3 lights east of Federal Hwy.

Casa D'Angelo ★★★ ITALIAN Although Fort Lauderdale may be transforming into a thoroughly modern 21st-century beach city, Casa D'Angelo remains steeped in old-school, old-world style and service with an impeccable reputation for some of the best Tuscan-style Italian food in South Florida. Don't be intimidated by the 40-plus-page wine list of regional Italian varietals. The waiters here are friendly and knowledgeable and will help guide you through it. As for chef/owner Angelo Elio's cuisine, insert superlatives here, but you won't truly understand until you taste some of the handmade pastas (bucatini cacio and pepe with Maine lobster medallions is beyond). There are also expertly grilled chops and fresh and simply prepared seafood and superb crispy calamari. A Boca Raton sibling at 171 E. Palmetto Park Rd. (**561/996-1234**) is quieter than the original, but the food is just as exceptional, and the newest location in Aventura, 2906 NE 207th St. (**305/699-5500**), is good, but still, none are as good as the Fort Lauderdale original.

1201 N. Federal Hwy., Fort Lauderdale. casa-d-angelo.com. **954/564-1234.** Reservations recommended. Main courses $28–$66. Sun–Thurs 5:30–10pm; Fri–Sat 5:30–11pm.

Rustic Inn Crabhouse ★★ SEAFOOD The word "rustic" in the name isn't just a marketing ploy. This seafood joint just west of the airport has been kicking around since the year Disneyland opened (1955), and the fact that it has practically zero ambience doesn't bother anybody a whit. Sitting in a noisy, woody dining room with fluorescent interrogation-style lighting and hanging lobster traps (or outside on the covered deck next to a canal), all they care about is whacking away at crustaceans with wooden mallets. The house specialty is garlic crabs, but there's plenty else on the menu (the fried clams are especially good). A word of

BEACHY dining scenes

Fort Lauderdale's A1A is an expansive strand, packed with eateries and bars. But there are two other beach blocks nearby also worthy of a visit. **Lauderdale-By-The-Sea** (lauderdalebythesea-fl.gov) first, where there's a bustling block of restaurants, bars, and shops at the eastern end of Commercial Boulevard. Among the hot spots there, **Even Keel Fish Shack,** 112 Commercial Blvd. (evenkeelfish.com; *©* **954-530-6276**), has excellent seafood and outdoor seating; and **The Village Grille & Pump,** 4400 El Mar Dr. (villagegrille.com; *©* **954/776-5092**), serves up live music, stiff drinks, and salty scenery since 1949.

There is also a public plaza right at the ocean's edge, with Adirondack chairs, which are ideal from which to people-watch, especially on packed weekend nights. Don't drive here, take public transportation or ride-sharing service.

Ten miles north is the sandy street of North Ocean Drive in Deerfield Beach, where barefoot surfers, families, and couples pack into tropically themed restaurants like **The Whale's Rib** 2031 NE 2nd St. (whalesrib.com; *©* **954/421-8880**), a seaside dive known for "Whale fries," excellent Bloody Marys, and a starring role on an episode of Guy Fieri's *Diners, Drive-ins, and Dives;* and, for front row views of the ocean with your mahi sandwich, **Oceans 234,** 234 N. Ocean Dr. (oceans234.com; *©* **954/428-2539**), and **JB's on the Beach,** 300 NE 21st Ave. (jbsonthebeach.com; *©* **954/571-5220**).

Oceans 234.

advice: If you do go for the crabs, do Dungeness, and don't wear anything you wouldn't want to see ruined.

4331 Ravenswood Rd., Fort Lauderdale. rusticinn.com. *©* **954/584-1637.** Reservations not accepted. Main courses $20–$70. Mon–Sat 11:30am–10pm; Sun noon–9pm.

Steak 954 ★★ STEAKHOUSE   Housed in the W Fort Lauderdale, this playful creation of restaurant mogul Stephen Starr (of Morimoto fame) is tops for ambience: dark woods and bold floral silk wall panels, with the restaurant's centerpiece being a 15-foot-long reef aquarium, home to hypnotic jellyfish. It is definitely an "it" girl, a place where locals come to see and be seen, which makes it, well, a scene. But the heart of the experience is, ultimately, the dry-aged, expertly cooked meats. They do also have some well-executed seafood dishes and a popular brunch.

W Fort Lauderdale, 401 N. Fort Lauderdale Beach Blvd., Fort Lauderdale. steak954.com. *©* **954/414-8333.** Main courses $38–$225. Daily 5–10pm; Sat–Sun 11am–3pm and 3–5pm.

MODERATE

Cap's Place Island Restaurant ★ SEAFOOD Opened in 1928 by a bootlegger who ran in the same circles as gangster Meyer Lansky, this barge-turned-restaurant is the oldest eatery in Broward County. Although it's no longer a rum-running operation, its illustrious past (FDR and Winston Churchill dined here together) landed it a spot on the National Register of Historic Places. To get here, you hop on a ferryboat, provided by the restaurant. Although you can drive to the restaurant, the short ride across the Intracoastal definitely adds to the Cap's Place experience. The separate bar area has more ambiance than the dining room and is worth a drink or two. The food is good, not great, consisting of traditional seafood dishes such as Florida or Maine lobster, clams casino, and oysters Rockefeller.

2765 NE 28th Court, Lighthouse Point. capsplace.com. **954/941-0418.** Main courses $20–$40. Daily 5:30pm–midnight. Motor-launch from I-95, exit at Copan's Rd., and go east to U.S. 1 (Federal Hwy.). At NE 24th St., turn right and follow the double lines and signs to the Lighthouse Point Yacht Basin and Marina (8 miles north of Fort Lauderdale). From here, follow the CAP'S PLACE sign pointing you to the shuttle.

Coconut's ★★ SEAFOOD If you drive too quickly north off A1A you will miss this, the most Fort Lauderdale of restaurants, a hidden waterfront gem serving oysters, smoked fish dip, lobster rolls, coconut shrimp, and more. There is always a long wait here, so if you can snag a seat at the adjacent **G&B Oyster Bar,** do it asap! There is also a dockside bar where you can have a drink while watching boats and waiting for a table. Sunday brunch is particularly mobbed here, so go early and prepare to wait. The scenery—and the food—when you eventually get some—makes it all worth it.

429 Seabreeze Blvd., Fort Lauderdale. coconutsfortlauderdale.com. **954/525-2421.** Main courses $14–$28. Mon–Sat 11:30am–10pm; Sun 10am–10pm.

A feast from Coconut's restaurant.

Foxy Brown ★★ AMERICAN "Comfort food with a twist" is served at this neighborhood favorite. Its outdoor patio is breezy, the inside bar area is buzzy, and both are good places to tuck into grilled artichoke with garlic butter or Philly pretzel bread with bacon onion jam or the green fries (fried green beans battered and served golden brown). There are also big salads, sandwiches (like their gooey short rib grilled cheese), fish and chips, veggie plates, and, for brunch, s'mores waffles, and sometimes, a Barbie waffle in all its pink, glittery glory. It's a fun place with friendly service.

476 N. Federal Hwy., Fort Lauderdale. foxybrownftl.com. **754/200-4236.** Main courses $15–$30. Mon–Fri 11:30am–10pm; Sat 9:30am–10pm; Sun 9:30am–9pm.

The Katherine ★★★ MODERN AMERICAN   Once upon a time, no Miamian of a certain level of epicurean snobbery would ever cross into Fort Lauderdale to eat. But that was then. Today, they're hopping in their cars to come to this joint, created by former Magic City wunderkind, Timon Balloo. You'll understand why after trying the accomplished, very particular culinary combinations that made him so beloved in Miami (he's of Chinese descent, and his wife Columbian, and he brings both traditions, and others, to the table). We're talking addictive fish sauce caramel wings with radish pickles, and the slapping squid ink carbonara with bacon gremolata and lemon zest, to name just two. Miami's calling, but the Katherine says, "New area code, who 'dis?"

723 E. Broward Blvd., Fort Lauderdale. katherinerestaurant.com. ✆ **754/216-0690.** Main courses $18–$38. Wed–Sun 5–9pm; Fri–Sat 5–10pm.

Tropical Acres Steakhouse ★★★ STEAKHOUSE   A SoFlo dining landmark, this time, an old-school steakhouse dating back to 1949, when New York restaurateur Gene Harvey decided to turn an old frame house into a carnivorous club of sorts. Fast forward to the 2020s and people are still packing it for prime rib, and lobster specials at old-school, reasonable prices. Also charmingly old fashioned: the '80s decor, and the fact that a piano player softly pounds out standards as you dine. Food is delicious though, and service is exceptional. In keeping with the old-school vibe, reservations are only taken on the phone and are highly recommended, though there is a bar area up front in which you can also dine in case you can't score a table—which is likely if not booked ahead of time.

2500 Griffin Rd., Dania Beach. tropicalacres.com. ✆ **954/923-4445.** Main courses $24–$57, but many options under $40. Mon–Sat 4:30–10pm.

INEXPENSIVE

Gilbert's 17th St. Grill ★★ AMERICAN   While some places brag about having the best burgers in town, family-owned, unpretentious Gilbert's actually *has* the best and doesn't need to brag because legions of regulars keep this place packed. Tucked away off the bustling 17th Street Causeway en route to the Fort Lauderdale strip, Gilbert's has angus beef burgers of all styles, from the Louisiana Cajun and Havarti bacon on a toasted garlic-buttered English muffin to the Dominican burger with grilled salami, fried queso blanco, egg, and pickled onions with chipotle cilantro mayo. Read that without having your mouth water. Better yet, go there instead.

1821 Cordova St., Fort Lauderdale. gilberts17thstgrill.com. ✆ **954/768-8990.** Burgers $14–$18, other dishes in that range, except for the ribs. Mon–Sat 11am–9pm.

Jaxon's Ice Cream Parlor & Restaurant ★ ICE CREAM   Yes, it's a bit of a tourist trap. But this is also South Florida's best and only authentic old-fashioned ice-cream parlor/country store, so it attracts sweet tooths from all over. Kids love the candy store in the front, and all enjoy hand-churned flavors. Jaxon's most famous everything-but-the-kitchen-sink sundae has countless scoops and endless toppings. Sugar-free offerings, too.

128 S. Federal Hwy., Dania Beach. jaxonsicecream.com. ✆ **954/923-4445.** Ice cream $11–$23. Sun–Thurs 11:30am–11pm; Fri–Sat 11:30am–midnight.

La Spada's Original Hoagies ★★ SANDWICHES   An institution since 1973, La Spada's is a hero to every sandwich fan (sorry!) whether you call it a sub, grinder, or a hoagie. The artful arranging of layers of fresh meats piled into a chewy roll with lettuce, tomato, onion, pickles, and their own blend of marinated sweet peppers is unmatched. Try some.

233 Commercial Blvd., Lauderdale-By-The-Sea. laspadashoagies.com. © **954/776-7893.** Sandwiches $8–$15. Daily 10am–8pm.

Sistrunk Marketplace ★★★ FOOD HALL   This hip food hall located in Fort Lauderdale's art district, offers 40,000 square feet of foodstuffs, craft beer, artisan coffee, local art, and live music. Highlights include **Crunly Churros & Ice Cream,** from the West Palm Beach food truck of the same name, Wynwood pizza palace **Made in Italy, Henry's Sandwich Station,** and Bahamian cuisine fave, **Island Made,** which won the space in the food hall's inaugural Fired Up Food

FLL'S MOST FABULOUS "gayborhood"

With politics turning Florida's LBGTQIA+ community into a persecuted one, forcing Equality Florida to issue a travel warning to the community, the Fort Lauderdale hamlet of **Wilton Manors** (wiltonmanors.gov) has remained a safe haven for the community. It refers to itself as the area's most fabulous "gayborhood"—and rightly so. The heart of the 'hood is on Wilton Drive, described as the "epicenter of the gay community in south Florida," where bars, clubs, restaurants, and shops wave their pride flags and welcome everyone into their businesses with open arms and maybe even a cocktail. It's home to restaurants with serious bar scenes like **Georgie's Alibi,** 2266 Wilton Dr. (alibiwiltonmanors.com; © **954/565-2526**), **Pub on the Drive,** 2283 Wilton Dr. (thepubwm.com; © **754/200-5244**), **Rosie's Bar & Grill,** 2449 Wilton Dr. (rosiesbarandgrill.com; © **954/563-0123**), **Voo La Voo Café,** 2430 NE 13th Ave. (voolavoocafe.com; © **754/200-5285**), **La Mexicana Taco Bar,** 2430 NE 12th Ave. (lamexicana.online; © **754/701-5977**), and **Thai Me Up,** 2389 Wilton Dr. (thaimeupfl.com; © **954/202-0000**). Wilton Manors is home to the annual Stonewall Pride Festival and Parade, which attracts some 30,000 people yearly, and the expanded **Stonewall National Museum,** 1300 E. Sunrise Blvd. (stonewall-museum.org; © 954/763-8565), featuring an impressive collection of items documenting LGBTQIA+ political, cultural, and social history. It contains more than six million pages of materials and archives of the plight and the fight of the community, which has never been more important—especially in Florida—than it is today.

Fort Lauderdale's annual Pride Parade.

Concept Competition. **Shady Distillery** has a tasting room here, serving their seven-times distilled Shady Vodka, along with their own rum (made with Florida molasses). They also have cooking classes, champagne brunches, distillery dinners, and even a Vegas-style "girls' night out" with male dancers.

116 NW 6th St., Fort Lauderdale. sistrunkmarketplace.com. 954/357-2616. Tues–Thurs 11am–10:30pm; Fri 11am–11:45pm; Sat 10am–11:45pm; Sun 11am–9pm. Closed Mon.

Fort Lauderdale Nightlife

While Fort Lauderdale is no Miami, it has vastly improved the quality of its nightlife by welcoming places that wouldn't dare host wet T-shirt or beer-chugging contests. It also lacks that city's attitude, which is part of the attraction.

In recent years, a crop of posh places to go for a spritzer or an espresso martini has emerged. The best is **No Man's Land** ★★★, 666 N. Federal Hwy. (nomanslandftl.com; 954/280-6291), a strip-mall speakeasy (not an oxymoron) that has some of the some of the tastiest tipples in town. Check out the various tinctures on the bar and ask the bartender to craft you a customized spirit that matches your mood. Oyster shooters with Bloody Mary hot sauce, and Los Magos Sotol (mezcal's grassy cousin) are the bar nosh of choice, sided by a plate of deviled eggs with caviar.

Another speakeasy-esque spot is **The Wilder** ★★★, 701 E. Broward Blvd. (intothewilder.com; 954/918-7212), which, despite its name, is more sultry than wild and serves "elevated bites" and handcrafted cocktails in a very cool, dimly lit three-room lounge and leafy terrace.

And for most legit speakeasy, check out **Rm. 901** ★★★, a swank cocktail lounge in an actual guest room at the Hyatt Centric, 100 E. Las Olas Blvd. (roomnine01.com). It's open 5:30 to 11:30pm Wednesday through Sunday and serves serious cocktails with a small menu of fancy fare (think: caviar and wagyu beef katsu on Japanese milk bread) for a very well-heeled crowd. It's tough to get into, so book in advance; there are rules and time limits since it's so small.

If those scenes are too posh, consider **Yot Bar & Kitchen** ★★★, 2015 SW 20th St. (yotmlc.com; 954/953-9000), tucked away in an actual boatyard and featuring live music, good food, and great cocktails. You may see some familiar faces from Bravo's *Below Deck* here. We're also big fans of the **Elbo Room** ★★ (241 S. Fort Lauderdale Beach Blvd.; elbowroom.com), which has been an unabashed dive since its founding in 1939. Take a seat at the deeply grooved bar and make some new friends.

For beer lovers, the **Funky Buddha Brewery** ★★, 1201 NE 38th St. (funkybuddha.com; 954/440-0046), has locally brewed suds, a taproom, games, and entertainment. If you prefer wine, **Vino's** ★★★, 901 E. Las Olas Blvd. (vinoswinebars.com; 954/765-6730), is a dimly lit oenophile's den, hidden off the main drag and featuring cozy seating and excellent wines by the glass.

BOCA RATON & DELRAY BEACH

26 miles S of Palm Beach; 40 miles N of Miami; 21 miles N of Fort Lauderdale

Boca Raton is a well-manicured, but mostly soulless suburban city, home to ladies who lunch, country clubbers, and retirees. The city's name is often mistranslated as "rat's mouth," but the phrase is actually a nautical term meaning rocky or jagged inlet. The original settlers were the people of the Glades Culture,

Boca Raton & Delray Beach

ATTRACTIONS
Boca Raton Museum of Art **19**
Daggerwing Nature Center **1**
Gumbo Limbo Nature Center **18**
Morikami Museum and
 Japanese Gardens **2**

HOTELS
The Boca Raton **25**
Colony Hotel & Cabana Club **12**
Crane's Beach House Boutique
 Hotel & Luxury Villas **15**
Opal Grand Resort **14**
The Ray **5**

RESTAURANTS
Brule Bistro **4**
City Oyster **10**
Cut 432 **11**
Dada **7**
Elisabetta's **8**
Farmer's Table **17**
The Grove **6**
J&J's Seafood Bar & Grill **13**
La Nouvelle Maison **20**
Luff's Fish House **23**
New York Prime **16**
Old Key Lime House **3**
The Tin Muffin Café **22**
Tramonti **9**
Trattoria Romana **21**
Twenty Twenty Grille **24**

who lived here for a thousand years before being driven out in the 1800s by pineapple farmers and land speculators, the latter drawn there by the development of the Intracoastal Waterway and the railroad. Today the greater Boca Raton area is home to some 250,000 people.

If you're looking for funky, wacky, and eclectic, look elsewhere. Boca is a resort community that, though it has come a long way from Seinfeld's Del Boca Vista visions of old people and HOAs, is still pretty boring. With minimal nightlife, entertainment in Boca is restricted to leisure sports, good dining, and upscale shopping. Its 2-mile stretch of beach is well maintained and crowded, though never mobbed.

Delray Beach ★★, named after a suburb of Detroit, is a sleepy-yet-starting-to-awaken beachfront community. Its bustling, buzzy downtown area includes Atlantic Avenue, which is known for restaurants, quaint shops, and art galleries. Delray's bars and restaurants make for a lively scene after nightfall especially, and lodging costs are lower here than in Boca Raton. Because of their proximity, Boca and Delray can easily be explored together. Still, compared to Boca, Delray is much more laid-back; it's trendy, but hardly as chichi, and definitely a cuter little beach town than sprawling, suburban Boca.

Essentials

GETTING THERE   Like the rest of the cities on the Gold Coast, Boca Raton and Delray are easily reached from I-95 or the Florida Turnpike. Both the Fort Lauderdale–Hollywood International Airport and the Palm Beach International Airport are about 20 minutes away. **Amtrak** (amtrak.com; ✆ **800/USA-RAIL** [872-7245]) trains make stops in Delray Beach at an unattended station at 345 S. Congress Ave. High speed rail **Brightline** (gobrightline.com) has a station at 101 NW 4th St. in downtown Boca Raton, taking you as far north as Orlando and south to downtown Miami, and there's also a **TriRail** (tri-rail.com) station at 680 Yamato Rd., which goes as far north as West Palm Beach and south to the Miami International Airport.

GETTING AROUND   A car in these parts is ideal, but new in 2024 is the **BocaConnect** (ridecircuit.com), an on-demand shuttle seating six people and offering free rides in the city's downtown area, and some rides within a mile radius outside for $2 per rider, capped at $5 for groups per one-way trip. Delray Beach offers a similar service called **Freebee** (delraybeachfl.gov; ✆ **855/918-5733**), which is exactly as its name implies: a free, downtown electric shuttle service between A1A and close to 1-95 that you can either flag down or download an app on your phone to order.

VISITOR INFORMATION   The **Greater Boca Raton Chamber of Commerce,** 1800 N. Dixie Hwy., 4 blocks north of Glades Road, Boca Raton (bocaratonchamber.com; ✆ **561/395-4433**), has information on attractions, accommodations, and events in the area. You can also try the **Greater Delray Beach Chamber of Commerce,** 140 NE 1st St., Delray Beach (delraybeach.com; ✆ **561/278-0424**), for information on Delray-specific events and festivals—there are many of those.

Beaches & Outdoor Activities

BEACHES   Thankfully, Florida had the foresight to set aside some of its most beautiful coastal areas for the public's enjoyment. Among those are Delray

Beach's **Atlantic Dunes Beach** ★★★, 1600 S. Ocean Blvd., which charges no admission to access a 7-acre developed beach with lifeguards, restrooms, changing rooms, and a family park area; and Boca Raton's **South Beach Park** ★★, 400 N. Ocean Blvd., with 1,670 feet of beach, 25 acres, lifeguards, picnic areas, restrooms, showers, and 850 feet of renourished beach south of the Boca Inlet, accessible for an admission charge per vehicle (up to 11 passengers) of $35 Monday through Friday, and $50 Saturday and Sunday.

Delray Beach ★★★, on Ocean Boulevard at the east end of Atlantic Avenue, is one of the area's most popular hangouts. Weekends especially attract a young and lively crowd. Refreshments, snack shops, bars, and restaurants are just across the street. Families enjoy the protection of lifeguards on the clean, wide strip. Gentle waters make it a good swimming beach, too. Restrooms and showers are available, and there's limited parking at meters along Ocean Boulevard.

Spanish River Park Beach ★★, on North Ocean Boulevard (3001 N. A1A), 2 miles north of Palmetto Park Road in Boca Raton, is a huge 95-acre oceanfront park with a half-mile-long beach with lifeguards as well as a large grassy area, making it one of the best choices for picnicking. Facilities include picnic tables, grills, restrooms, showers, and a 40-foot observation tower. You can walk through tunnels under the highway to access nature trails that wind through fertile grasslands. Volleyball nets always have at least one game going on. The park is open from 8am to 8pm. Admission is $35 for vehicles Monday through Friday; $50 on Saturday, Sunday, and major holidays.

Also see the description of **Red Reef Park** under "Scuba Diving & Snorkeling," below. Please note that many of the area's best beaches are located in state parks and are free to pedestrians and bikers, though most do charge for parking.

GOLF This area has plenty of top courses. The **Red Reef Family Golf Course** ★★ in Boca, 1221 N. Ocean Blvd. (myboca.us/538/Alan-C-Alford-Red-Reef-Family-Golf-Cours; ⓒ **561/391-5014**), is a 9-hole course with magnificent views of the Intracoastal and Atlantic, designed by Charles Ankrum, and open daily from 7am to sunset. Greens fees range from $29 and up.

A young child joyfully runs onto Delray Beach.

Also loved by golfers is the **Southwinds Golf Course** ★★★, 19557 Lyons Rd., Boca Raton (pbcsouthwindsgolf.com; © **561/483-1305**), an 18-hole course with water on every hole, plus cameos by wildlife including Canada geese, otters, foxes, and more. It's actually a certified Audubon International Cooperative Sanctuary. But keep your eye on the ball! Greens fees range from $16 to $36.

In 2022, the gated community, **Boca Raton Golf and Racquet Club,** 17751 Boca Club Blvd. (myboca.us/2043/Boca-Raton-Golf-Racquet-Club; © **561/367-7000**), became an official open-to-the-public premiere course, plus pickleball, tennis, and more. It's known for its driving range, and reasonable greens fees ($40–$75). We also recommend **The Boca Raton** (p. 267).

Tiger Woods got playful by backing **Popstroke** (popstroke.com), a minigolf course with two 18-hole putting courses and restaurant with several locations in Palm Beach County, including Delray Beach at 1314 N. Federal Hwy. (© **561/800-4520**), West Palm Beach, and the equestrian suburb of Wellington. There's also a Treasure Coast location in Port St. Lucie, Sarasota, Tampa, and Orlando.

SCUBA DIVING & SNORKELING **Moray Bend** ★★★, a 58-foot dive spot about ¾ mile off Boca Inlet, is the area's most popular. It's home to three moray eels that are used to being fed by scuba divers. There are several others within 30 minutes of the Boca Inlet. For a good list of those, go to thediversity.com/reefs. Moray Bend and others are accessible by boat from **Force E Dive Center,** 2621 N. Federal Hwy., Boca Raton (force-e.com/dive-shops/boca-raton; © **561/368-0555**). Phone for dive times. Dives cost $55 to $70 per person.

Red Reef Park ★★★, 1400 N. Ocean Blvd. (© **561/393-7974**), a 67-acre oceanfront park in Boca Raton, has good swimming and year-round lifeguard protection. There's snorkeling around the shallow rocks and reefs that lie just off the beach. The park has restrooms and a picnic area with grills. Located a half-mile north of Palmetto Park Road, it's open daily from 8am to 10pm. The cost is $35 per car Monday through Friday, $50 on Saturday and Sunday; walkers and bikers get in free.

TENNIS/PICKLEBALL The snazzy **Delray Beach Tennis Center,** 201 W. Atlantic Ave. (delraytennis.com; © **561/243-7360**), the place where champ Coco Gauff honed her skills, has 14 lighted clay courts and 14 hard courts, and pickleball courts available by the hour. Rates range from $10.75 to $15.

The 13 public lighted hard courts and 12 lighted pickleball courts at **Patch Reef Park,** 2000 NW 51st St. (patchreefpark.org; © **561/367-7090**), are available by reservation. The fee for nonresidents per 90 minutes is $12 for adults, $8 for juniors. To reach the park from I-95, exit at Yamato Road West and continue past Military Trail to the park.

Seeing the Sights

Boca Raton Museum of Art ★★

Much like Florida, the collection here ranges from very old to very young: statuettes from 800 B.C. to 21st-century paintings by the likes of Kehinde Wiley (who did the famous portrait of President Obama surrounded by greenery). It's a relatively small, but well-chosen permanent collection, with photographs, contemporary sculptures and paintings, studio glass and ceramics, and African Art and the Art of the Ancient Americas. The museum also stages a wide variety of excellent temporary exhibitions by local and international artists. Lectures and films are offered on a regular basis.

Mizner Park, 501 Plaza Real, Boca Raton. bocamuseum.org. © **561/392-2500.** Admission $16 adults, $12 seniors 65 and over, free for children 17 and under. Wed and Fri–Sun 11am–6pm; Thurs 11am–8pm.

Daggerwing Nature Center ★   Seen enough snowbirds? Head over to this 39-acre swampy splendor way out in suburban West Boca, where birds of another feather reside, including herons, egrets, woodpeckers, and warblers. The trails come complete with a soundtrack provided by songbirds hovering above (watch your head). The park's night hikes will take you on a search for owls at 6pm. Bring a flashlight. There's also a 3,000-square-foot exhibit hall, a laboratory classroom, butterfly garden, and interesting wet forest and conservation exhibits. An elevated boardwalk over a swamp features two trails and an observation tower from which a keen eye can view the abundant plant and animal life, including osprey, woodpeckers, butterflies (including the park's namesake S. Ruddy Daggerwing), endangered wood storks, alligators, and a wide variety of bromeliads.

South County Regional Park, 11200 Park Access Rd., Boca Raton. discover.pbcgov.org. © **561/629-8760.** Free admission. Wed–Fri 1–4pm; Sat 10am–4pm. Boardwalk open sunrise–sunset.

Gumbo Limbo Nature Center ★★★   Named for an indigenous tree, the 20-acre complex protects one of the few surviving coastal hammocks (subtropical hardwood forests) in South Florida. Nature trails feature lush canopies and a butterfly garden. Walk through the hammock on a half-mile-long boardwalk that ends at a 40-foot observation tower, from which you can see the Atlantic Ocean, the Intracoastal Waterway, and much of Boca Raton. From mid-April to September, sea turtles come ashore here to lay eggs. In fact, Florida Atlantic University's Department of Biological Sciences keeps an active research lab here that's open to the public, where you can gawk at the adorable sea turtle hatchlings in the summer and fall months. Another big attraction here is the aquariums, featuring native fish and organisms, and naturalistic habitats representing the coastal mangrove community, a nearshore reef, tropical coral reef, and artificial reef/shipwreck, whose resident rescued sea turtle, Morgan, seems to love hamming it up for visitors. The small indoor nature center has all sorts of slithery creatures as well as a sea turtle garden and educational tidbits.

1801 N. Ocean Blvd. (on A1A btw. Spanish River Blvd. and Palmetto Park Rd.), Boca Raton. myboca.us/2096/Gumbo-Limbo-Nature-Center. © **561/544-8605.** Free admission ($5 donation suggested). Tues–Sun 9am–4pm; Mon noon–4pm. Nature trails daily 7am–sunset.

Buddha statue, Morikami Museum and Japanese Gardens.

Morikami Museum and Japanese Gardens ★★★   This serene Japanese garden dates from 1905, when an entrepreneurial farmer, Jo Sakai, came to Boca Raton to build a tropical agricultural community. The Yamato Colony, as it was known, was short-lived; by the 1920s, only one tenacious colonist remained: George Sukeji Morikami. But Morikami was quite successful, eventually running one of the largest pineapple plantations in the area. The 200-acre Morikami Museum and Japanese Gardens, which opened to the public in 1977, was Morikami's gift to Palm Beach County and the state of Florida. The museum is devoted specifically to the acquisition, research, preservation, and exhibition of the story of George Sukeji Morikami and the Yamato Colony as well as the visual culture created by Japanese and Japanese Americans. The result of this effort over more than 40 years is not just a catalog of objects, but rather a collection of diverse ideas and unique stories illuminated by the objects. Fans of Japanese anime love it here, and you will likely see a lot of anime cosplay around the museum and gardens. A stroll through the garden is almost a mile long. An artificial waterfall that cascades into a koi- and carp-filled moat; a small rock garden for meditation; and a large bonsai collection with miniature maple, buttonwood, juniper, and Australian pine trees are all worth contemplation. There's also a cafe and fun events here, including films, lectures, walks, tea ceremonies, flower-arranging classes, fabric wrapping, and Zen garden raking.

4000 Morikami Park Rd., Delray Beach. morikami.org. **561/495-0233.** Museum $18 adults, $16 seniors, $10 children 6–17. Museum and gardens Tues–Sun 10am–5pm.

Shopping

Once a high-end shopping mecca, Boca Raton's **Mizner Park** (on Federal Hwy., between Palmetto Park and Glades rds.; miznerpark.com; **561/362-0606**) has sadly become a retail desert, but still remains a place for freshly coiffed women to lunch at outdoor cafes. It has a bowling alley, small indoor theater, outdoor amphitheater, and movie theater.

Outdoor cafes for the ladies-who-lunch crowd in Boca.

Boca's **Town Center Mall,** on the south side of Glades Road, just west of I-95, has a few remaining department stores, including Nordstrom, Bloomingdale's, Neiman Marcus, and Saks Fifth Avenue. Add hundreds of specialty shops, an extensive food court, and a range of other restaurants, and you have the area's most comprehensive shopping center.

On Delray Beach's **Atlantic Avenue,** especially east of Swinton Avenue and in the Pineapple Grove area, you'll find a few shops, clothing stores, and galleries shaded by palm trees and colorful awnings.

Where to Stay

Although you won't find rows of cheap hotels as in Fort Lauderdale and Hollywood, a handful of mom-and-pop motels have survived along A1A between the towering condominiums of Delray Beach. Look along the beach just south of Atlantic Boulevard. Vrbo and Airbnb have plenty of rentals in these condos, and elsewhere in the area.

Even more economical options can be found in Deerfield Beach, Boca's neighbor, south of the county line. A number of beachfront efficiencies offer great deals, even in the winter months. Again, you'll find a lot of options on the major online lodgings marketplaces.

EXPENSIVE

The Boca Raton ★★ This landmark resort was built in 1926, the brainchild of architect Addison Mizner, who based its first building on the cloister of an 11th-century Spanish convent. Today, it's a sprawling 350-acre collection of oddly matched buildings: the original, and still spectacular, **Cloister** building; and the drab pink 27-story **Tower** with **Tower Suite Collection** guest rooms as well as a brand-new, family-friendly **Harborside Pool Club** with a 450-foot lazy river, waterslides, games, and kids club. Accessible by water shuttle or bus is the **Beach Club** and its three pools, two restaurants, oceanfront bar, beach access, Vilbrequin-designed cabanas, and 207 modern rooms all revamped in late 2024, many with "outdoor living spaces." The **Bungalows** is another group-friendly option, with apartment-style suites for longer stays. Those are all for families. For those who don't want kids around, there's the adults-only **Yacht Club,** a Venetian-style wing of 112 luxury rooms and suites. Whew! All rooms, suites, and efficiencies throughout are looking suavely contemporary, thanks to a recent $200-million renovation.

The resort straddles the Intracoastal, and is so massive it provides transportation to guests via a shuttle every 10 minutes. Amenities include a state-of-the-art spa, a championship golf course, 16 tennis Hydro Grid courts and 6 Hydro Grid pickleball courts, beachside fitness club, a 30-slip marina, and a small private beach with watersports equipment. The resort's also foodie haven, with a choice of 16 places to dine and drink, including an outpost of NYC's beloved brunch spot **Sadelle's.** The fabulously redesigned and transformed **Palm Court** within the Cloister (think: White Lotus) has live jazz nightly at its cocktail bar.

Service, alas, is spotty, ranging from exceptional to downright nonexistent. The resort is exclusive to guests and members only, so you can't pop by for a meal, drink, or swim unless you're a guest.

501 E. Camino Real, Boca Raton. thebocaraton.com. ✆ **855/774-8530.** 1,041 units. $407–$850 double. Valet parking $55. Pet fee $195. From I-95 N., exit onto Palmetto Park Rd. E. Turn right onto Federal Hwy. (U.S. 1), then left onto Camino Real. **Amenities:** 16+ restaurants and bars; children's programs; concierge; fitness centers; golf course; 8 pools; room service; spa; tennis/pickleball courts; watersports equipment/rentals; free Wi-Fi.

Crane's Beach House Boutique Hotel & Luxury Villas ★★
Crane's Beach House, meticulously run and maintained by husband-and-wife Michael and Cheryl Crane, is located just 1 block from the beach and right in the middle of Delray Beach. Reminiscent of a cute apartment complex, Crane's is family friendly, but gives off a more couples and singles vibe. Studios and one-bedrooms have kitchenettes, while suites have full kitchens. Guest rooms are comfy and clean if a bit spare, with plantation shutters and very good pillowtop mattresses. Villas are more high style and luxe with private balconies or patios, upscale bathroom amenities, and spa bathrooms with river rock showers. Lush gardens, hammocks, a tiki hut, and two saline pools leave you with little reason to flee the premises, but when you do—and you will need to for food, which is just steps away in "downtown" Delray—you'll want to return as quickly as possible.

82 Gleason St., Delray Beach. cranesbeachhouse.com. **866/372-7263.** 28 units. $355–$627 double. Pet fee $50. Free parking. **Amenities:** Concierge; 2 small outdoor pools; free Wi-Fi.

Opal Grand Resort ★★★
A former Marriott, with a priceless location across from the beach and at the end of bustling Atlantic Avenue, the Opal Grand has been zhuzhed up with "coastal chic" decor (light woods, whites, blues), and a new rooftop lounge. Guests' favorite space is likely the handsome pool, which is surrounded by cabanas, day beds, and has a charming staff. But it's in competition with the hotel's very Zen spa. Opal is also a very family-friendly place with a kids club and activities. If you feel like going to the beach, you can order a picnic basket in advance. The resort fee of $35 is low for the area, especially because it includes self-parking.

10 N. Ocean Blvd., Delray Beach. opalcollection.com. **866/240-6316.** 276 units. Winter $333–$627 double. Pet fee $100. **Amenities:** 4 restaurants; 3 bars; pool; room service; fitness center; spa; kids club; watersports; free Wi-Fi.

MODERATE/EXPENSIVE

The Ray ★★★
Located close enough to the beach (1 block) but in the heart of Delray's arty Pineapple Grove, this Hilton property is more reminiscent of a Miami boutique hotel than a chain. Its public areas are awash in sculptures and contemporary paintings, with living walls and other immersive installations, plus a chic, 22,000-square-foot roof deck with bar, pool, three restaurants, and views for miles. Room decor is kicky, with "Barbie at the Beach" photos on the walls (no joke), quality shiplap and wainscotting, crisp Eucalyptus linens on the beds, and Frette bath towels and robes. Hilton, who are you? The hotel offers free transportation to the beach via the golf cart's hipper cousin, the Moke, and rents surfboards.

233 NE 2nd Ave., Delray Beach. hilton.com. **561/739-1700.** 141 units. $184–$563 double. Valet parking $42. **Amenities:** 3 restaurants; 3 bars; outdoor heated pool; concierge; fitness center; watersports rental; free Wi-Fi.

INEXPENSIVE/MODERATE

Colony Hotel & Cabana Club ★★★
Built in 1935, and family-owned since then, this Art Deco hotel is on the National Historic Register. You'll see photos of the property's early days all around the rattan-clad lobby. Rooms are painted in bold sunset colors (deep oranges, reds, or golds—it works), many of the furnishings look antique, but beds are modern and quite sleepable. Two miles away, the Colony has its own private beach club, included in the nightly rate for hotel guests. Along with 250 feet of sand, the Cabana Club has a friendly pool area and

bar (service is tops throughout the property). Guests can drive their own cars to the club or take the hotel's free shuttle there. By the way, parking is included in the reasonable nightly rates. Overall: a well-located find, right on the best stretch of Atlantic Avenue, and a wonderfully evocative trip back in time.

525 E. Atlantic Ave., Delray Beach. thecolonyflorida.com. © **561/276-4123.** 66 units. $149–$289 double, including parking and breakfast. **Amenities:** Restaurant; bar; saltwater pool; beach club; guest laundry; fitness room; free Wi-Fi.

Where to Eat

Boca Raton and its surrounding area is the kind of place where you discuss dinner plans at the breakfast table. Nightlife in Boca means going out to a restaurant. But who cares? This is some of the best dining in South Florida. Delray Beach, on the other hand, has both excellent cuisine *and* nightlife.

Newest in Boca's dining scene is an area right near—where else?—the mall, laughingly called **Restaurant Row,** 5377 Town Center Rd., which has a popular Mexican restaurant **El Camino** (elcaminobocaraton.com), an Italian joint, a sushi place, and several other options. **Boca Center** mall at 5150 Town Center Circle (bocacenter.com) is another dining hub, as is **Mizner Park** mall (p. 266) and **Royal Palm Place.**

Delray Beach's Atlantic Avenue is known familiarly as "The Ave" and has a ton of very popular restaurants like **City Oyster,** 213 E. Atlantic Ave. (cityoysterdelray.com; © **561/272-0220**), beloved for its happy hour; **Cut 432,** a sceney steakhouse at 432 E. Atlantic Ave. (cut432.com; © **561/272-9898**); and **Tramonti,** high-end Italian, at 119 E. Atlantic Ave. (tramontidelray.com; © **561/272-1944**). A new place seems to open daily. Be sure to check out the side streets, where sometimes the best places are hiding.

EXPENSIVE

The Grove ★★★ GLOBAL   While there are no Michelin-starred restaurants in Delray Beach, this is as close to one as it gets, a dimly lit, indoor/outdoor modern spot in Pineapple Grove featuring an always-changing menu created by chef Michael Haycook. On recent visits, we've enjoyed such creative treats as a brioche-crusted chicken with chorizo-braised collard greens, and roasted sea scallops with braised leeks and vermouth butter. Reservations here are tricky to snag. They open 30 days in advance on the Tock website, accessible via the restaurant's website, so set a reminder. If you can't get one of those, try your luck at the handsome bar behind the garage doors.

187 NE 2nd Ave., Delray Beach. © **561/266-3750.** Main courses $32–$65. Tues–Sat 6–11pm. Closed Sun–Mon.

J&J's Seafood Bar & Grill ★★★ SEAFOOD   Before Atlantic Avenue became *the* place for dining, J&J's was doling out fresh seafood to a satisfied clientele. Changing not a thing since 1999, this tiny seafoodery is still the place to go in Delray for fresh fish, fairly priced. Among the standouts on the menu are the fish tacos, the grilled scallops over risotto with orange habanero, the coconut curry shrimp, and a grilled grouper with shrimp in a pink guava hollandaise. The restaurant gets a very local, somewhat mature crowd, many of whom congregate at the bar for oysters and rosé. It's an affable scene.

634 E. Atlantic Ave., Delray Beach. jjseafooddelray.com. © **561/272-3390.** Main courses $28–$49. Tues–Thurs 11am–3pm and 4:30–9pm; Fri 11am–3pm and 4:30–10pm; Sat 11:30am–3pm and 4:30–10pm. Closed Sun–Mon.

La Nouvelle Maison ★★★ FRENCH It's fancy, it's a bit stuffy, but Nouvelle Maison is also quite special, and the food is *parfait*. They deliver expert renditions of such Gallic treats as duck liver pate (from the Hudson Valley), *escargots bourguignonne,* a cash-heavy cornucopia of caviars, Holland Dover sole, and a twice-cooked duck a l'orange that will make you rethink that dish. As for the ambiance: It gets almost laughably froufrou, especially around the bar, where multiple generations, dressed in the very latest fashion trends, gather. But who can blame them? The complimentary homemade potato chips are divine, and pair perfectly with a good cocktail, which is what you'll get here.

455 E. Palmetto Park Rd., Boca Raton. inmbocaraton.com. **561/338-3003.** Main courses $25–$60. Sun–Thurs 5:30–10pm; Fri–Sat 5:30–11pm.

New York Prime ★★★ STEAKHOUSE So what's the difference between New York Prime, and the other ninety-or-so steakhouses in Boca? Vibe. New York Prime is your great-granddaddy's steakhouse, old-school, even kitschy, down to the keyboardist belting out the best in '70s, '80s, and '90s music like a Catskills opening act. And if you are craving huge hunks of steak, simply prepared, with old-school sides like sauteed spinach, hash browns, and a classic Caesar salad, this is the place. Tuxedoed servers are skilled in slicing, serving, and shmoozing. A who's who of Boca's monied set love this place in all its paddled fan glory, they know the maître d' by his first name, and they know the birthdates of the bartenders. There is even a Boca Raton police officer stationed up front, and when we asked him why he was there, he gave us a shady, inscrutable answer. But we know why he's there. It's smells good, the singer can belt out Sinatra and Hall and Oates like nobody's business, and it's a lot more amusing than a night patrolling the sleepy streets.

2350 NW Executive Center Dr., Boca Raton. newyorkprime.com. **561/998-3881.** Main courses $32–$130. Mon–Sat 5–10pm; Sun 4–9pm.

Trattoria Romana ★★★ ITALIAN Trattoria Romana is a bustling trattoria that looks like it's been airlifted from Roma (read: purposefully mottled walls, leather chairs, white tablecloths, and waiters who take their jobs very seriously). When you enter, you'll be greeted by the aroma of garlic, and the sight of people jostling to try and get a seat at the popular bar. If you can snag one, take it and don't leave (bar seats are a hot commodity here). You can eat at the bar, too, if you don't mind being jabbed in the back by all the hoverers. Better (probably) to head into the dining room, where you'll be gifted with pre-dinner amuse-bouches, like bruschetta and chunks of freshly cut Parmesan cheese, before you tuck into one of their marvelous pastas. We like the pitch perfect *penne arabiata,* but the short rib pappardelle is also primo. Other recommended dishes: the veal and chicken parm, and the branzino with white wine, mushrooms, and Kalamata olives.

499 E. Palmetto Park Rd., Boca Raton. trattoriaromanabocaraton.com. **561/393-6715.** Main courses $28–$60. Daily noon–3pm and 5–10pm.

Twenty Twenty Grille ★★★ AMERICAN Chef Ron Weisheit's 40-seat modern American restaurant (20 inside, 20 outside) combines artful cooking from the chef, with the genuinely warm hospitality of his wife, Rhonda. Menus change, but if it's being offered, the "Duck Duck Taco," with margarita gastrique and oven-dried tomato pico de gallo, is revelatory. We're also huge fans of the Puerto Rican clam chowder with coconut milk, plantain, and banana pepper; and horchata-brined wild boar with Peruvian refried beans, in a dulce de leche chile sauce. Insane. And insanely creative. Dessert is no less inventive, from the chocolate peppermint patty flourless cake with "minty mallow filling," to the guava sticky toffee pudding cake.

141 Via Naranjas in Royal Palm Place, Boca Raton. twentytwentygrille.com. 561/990-7969. Main courses $32–$52. Wed–Thurs, Sun 5–9:30pm; Fri–Sat 5–10pm.

MODERATE

Brulé Bistro ★★ AMERICAN   One of Pineapple Grove's most appealing spots, Brulé is a small bistro serving big flavors: pork belly banh mi sliders, an exceptionally juicy burger, tempura squash blossoms, crispy octopus with serrano Kabayaki, and more. There's much to choose from here and at surprisingly decent prices considering its surroundings in downtown Delray. The bar scene is big here (especially at happy hour Mon–Fri 3–6pm), as is weekend brunch.

200 NE 2nd Ave., Delray Beach. brulebistro.com. 561/274-2046. Main courses $12–$40 (more for steak). Wed–Sun 11:30am–3pm; Wed–Thurs 4–10pm; Fri–Sat 4–11pm.

Dada ★★ AMERICAN   Located in the historic 1924 Tarrimore House and surrounded by lush landscaping and banyan trees, Dada may have been named for a surrealist movement, but the food is real—and really good. With twinkly lights and a garden setting, outdoor seating is most popular, but we also like the cozier, moodier vibe inside. As for the food, it consists of deeply satisfying regional

Outdoor seating at Dada restaurant.

American fare, like pork belly burnt ends with honey BBQ; meatloaf with horseradish mashed potatoes and wild mushroom gravy; and a perfect burger with American cheese on a challah bun. On a budget? No worries: The "Starving Artist Grilled Cheese Sandwich" is now and forever only $10, and that's with a side of cream of tomato soup. We think the Dadaists would approve.

52 N. Swinton Ave., Delray Beach. sub-culture.org. 561/330-3232. Entrees $18–$37. Daily 5pm–midnight. Sunday brunch 11am–2:30pm.

Elisabetta's ★★ ITALIAN

An always hoppin' Italian joint smack on the Ave, Elisabetta's has delicious pastas, pizzas, and cocktails, served either at a few outdoor tables or inside—which we prefer—in the two-story dining room. The ground floor has a busy bar scene and comfy booths, while upstairs is a more intimate dining room with speakeasy-esque bar and terrace seating. We love both. The food here is quality: All pastas, breads, pastries, and gelati are made in-house, and specials are always just that, truly special. Martini Mondays features the shaken or stirred cocktail at half off along with $3.95 meatball sliders all day. Or, hit their Aperitivo Hour, daily at the bar from 4pm featuring $10 pizzas and $2 off all drinks. Weekend late night menu served 11am to midnight. There's another location at 185 Banyan Blvd. in downtown West Palm Beach (561/342-6699).

32 E. Atlantic Ave., Delray Beach. elisabettas.com. 561/560-6699. Main courses $18–$45. Mon–Thurs 11:30am–10pm; Fri 11:30am–11pm; Sat 11am–4pm and 4–11pm; Sun 11am–4pm and 4–10pm.

Farmer's Table ★★ HEALTHY

At Farmer's Table none of the proteins served have been exposed to outside chemicals, hormones, pesticides, or antibiotics. And while some of those proteins are meats, they also have many vegan and/or vegetarian options, like their excellent sweet potato noodles with veggies and tofu. Gluten-free folks are taken care of here, too (love their spaghetti squash with either chicken or vegan meatballs). Sometimes the food needs extra salt, but overall it's tasty. Best seating is outdoors around the courtyard pool. On weekends and evenings, they have live music. Tables book fast here, so do make a reservation. There's another location in North Palm Beach at 951 U.S. Hwy. 1 (561/691-3430).

1901 N. Military Trail, Boca Raton. dinefarmerstable.com. 561/417-5836. Entrees $17–$36. Mon–Fri 7:30–11am and 11am–5pm; Sat–Sun 7:30–10am and 10am–5pm; Sun–Thurs 5–9pm; Fri–Sat 5–10pm.

Luff's Fish House ★★★ SEAFOOD

This Key West–style, historic 1920s bungalow has been transformed into a topnotch boat-to-plate restaurant. It's not on the beach, but close enough to it that you can smell the salty air, especially if you choose the outdoor seating (which you should). Start your meal with some fresh oysters and the signature honey jalapeno cornbread. If you have a large appetite, or a large group, the Spanish-style garlic shrimp is another fab appetizer. As for mains: The whole Key West snapper in a shrimp creole sauce, or the seared diver scallops with crab fried rice, are two of the best. For those who don't dig seafood, the country-fried pork chop or the grilled steak sandwich with truffle gouda are the way to go. And wouldn't you know it? The place that looks most like the Keys has the best Key lime pie in town.

390 E. Palmetto Park Rd., Boca Raton. luffsfishhouse.com. 561/609-2660. No reservations accepted. Main courses $17–$42 (steak pricier). Sun–Thurs 11am–9pm; Fri–Sat 11am–10pm.

INEXPENSIVE

Old Key Lime House ★ SEAFOOD   This family-owned, waterfront spot is a welcome respite from the bougie eateries that are popping up all over the Palm Beaches. Old Key Lime House brags that it has the largest tiki bar in South Florida—and we have no reason to doubt them. They also claim that it's the oldest waterfront restaurant in the state. While that's doubtful, what's not is the place's popularity, always packed, no matter what time it is. The food is okay, it's your typical waterfront bar and seafood fare, but you really come here for the views and live music.

300 E. Ocean Ave., Lantana. oldkeylimehouse.com. © **561/582-1889.** Main courses $10–$40. Mon–Thurs 11am–10pm; Fri–Sat 11am–11pm.

The Tin Muffin Cafe ★★ BAKERY/SANDWICH SHOP   Popular with the downtown lunch crowd, this excellent storefront bakery serves big sandwiches on fresh bread, plus muffins, quiches, and good homemade soups such as split pea or lentil. The curried-chicken sandwich is stuffed with chunks of white meat doused in a creamy curry dressing and fruit. Homemade desserts such as the dreamy banana cake are worth every calorie. There are a few cafe tables inside the cozy, quaint cafe that's country bumpkin authentic in a way Cracker Barrel wishes it was, and even one outside on a tiny patio. Be warned, however, that service is (forgivably) slow and parking is a nightmare. Try looking for a spot a few blocks away at a meter.

364 E. Palmetto Park Rd. (btw. Federal Hwy. and the Intracoastal Bridge), Boca Raton. © **561/392-9446.** Sandwiches and salads $11–$14. No credit cards. Mon–Thurs, Sat 11am–4pm; Fri 11am–5pm. Closed Sun.

Boca Raton & Delray Beach After Dark

THE BAR, CLUB & MUSIC SCENE

Atlantic Avenue ★★★ in Delray Beach has finally gotten quite hip to nightlife and is now lined with sleek and chic lounges, and bars that attract a young crowd. Although it's hardly South Beach or Fort Lauderdale's Las Olas and Riverfront, Atlantic Avenue can definitely be fun after dark. In Boca Raton, **Mizner Park** ★★ and nearby "downtown" Boca is the nucleus of nightlife, with restaurants masking themselves as nightclubs or, at the very least, sceney bars.

Boston's on the Beach ★★   Chill nightlife, for post-sunbathing, is the draw here, with happy hours Monday through Friday from 4 to 7pm, and live music nightly. Boston's two decks overlook the ocean, making it an ideal place to mellow out and take in the scenery. Directly next door is Boston's all outdoor **Sandbar,** an oceanfront tiki bar where bottle service, DJs, and bathing suits are de rigueur. While Boston's is open daily from 11am to 9pm, Sandbar stays open later. 40 S. Ocean Blvd., Delray Beach. bostonsonthebeach.com. © **561/278-3364.**

Cosmo's ★★   The cheesiest—and only—dance club in the entire area, Cosmo's is a disco lover's dream come true, an old-school, dark, somewhat dingy, neon-lit discotheque where people, gasp, actually dance. That's because the median age here is about 60, but still, it is the most fun you will have since your cousin's bar mitzvah. No need to dress up, though tank tops and shorts are not allowed. So, get ready to do the Hustle, the Macarena, the Electric Slide, and the Moon Walk until the wee hours. Cover charge ranges from $10 to $20. 99 SE 1st Ave., Boca Raton. cosmosnightclublounge.com. © **561/617-1873.**

Crazy Uncle Mike's ★★   A sprawling brewery, restaurant, and live music venue, Crazy Uncle Mike's is a magnet for some of the best traveling bands in the country. There's a daily happy hour from 3 to 7pm that attracts a huge crowd of locals waiting to hear who's up next onstage. There's also Taco, Tango and Salsa Tuesdays for those looking for a more Latin beat, and Boot Scootin' Boogie: free country line-dancing lessons every Monday at 8pm. 6450 N. Federal Hwy., Boca Raton. CrazyUncleMikes.com. **561/931-2889.**

Dada ★★★   This is where the area's neo-bohemian types (think: beards and tattoos) linger on cozy couches, listening to music, poetry, or dissertations on life. Live music, great food, a tiny bar, an outdoor patio area, and a very eclectic crowd make Dada the coolest hangout in Delray. Open daily from 5pm to midnight. 52 N. Swinton Ave., Delray Beach. sub-culture.org. **561/330-3232.**

The Funky Biscuit ★★   Live music is alive and well in this Boca Raton club dedicated to just that. A favorite for Deadheads, Funky Biscuit is home to some local jam bands, but they also host blues, funk, jazz, and rock bands. Oftentimes you may get a show by a musician who is passing through with a major A-lister. Keep your ears open for the next big thing. There's food here, but we'd just stick with the bar. 303 SE Mizner Blvd., in Royal Palm Plaza, Boca Raton. funkybiscuit.com. **561/395-2929.**

Johnnie Brown's ★★   This open-air Delray Beach institution is right on the train tracks, but you'll probably never hear the train' a comin' unless it's from a band singing "Long Train Coming" or "Folsom Prison Blues." For rockin', honky-tonkin' live music, this is the place to go. It gets mobbed, so crowds spill out onto the streets. It's also open late every night and drinks are relatively cheap here. 301 E. Atlantic Ave., Delray Beach. johnniebrowns.com. **561/243-9911.**

Boynton & Lake Worth Beach

North of Delray Beach and just before Palm Beach are two communities, both worthy of a quick visit.

Scuba divers dig **Boynton Beach** for "Lofthus," an underwater shipwreck preserve. Daily dive charters depart from the **Boynton Harbor Marina,** 735 Casa Loma Blvd. (boyntonbeachcra.com; **561/735-7955**). Anglers love fishing for snook, pompano, mackerel, bluefish, and redfish at **Boynton Beach Inlet,** 646 Ocean Inlet Dr. For kids, the **Schoolhouse Children's Museum,** 129 E. Ocean Ave. (schoolhousemuseum.org; **561/742-2680;** Tues–Sat 9am–4:30pm; $6.50), provides an interactive look at the ways Florida pioneers lived.

Just 8 miles north of Boynton is **Lake Worth Beach,** which has a stylish, revitalized downtown area concentrated around Lucerne and Lake avenues. It seems to host more than the usual number of street fairs, and is known for its bar and restaurant scene. Just over the bridge and on the beach is the **Lake Worth Beach and Casino Complex,** 10 S. Ocean Blvd., where there's no casino, but there are restaurants. Bonfires are a weekly treat there, Fridays and Saturdays 6 to 10pm from November through February. For golfers, the **Lake Worth Beach Golf Club,** 17th Ave. N. (lakeworthbeachgolfclub.com; **561/582-5713**), has vintage charm, magnificent views, 18 challenging holes, and waterfront restaurant. Greens fees range from $23 to $70.

Vino Wine Bar & Kitchen ★★   This tiny, candle-lit five-table restaurant and bar serves solid Italian fare, but we tend to come here for a glass of late-night, expertly chosen red—especially on nights they have live music (usually a singer/songwriter). 114 NE 2nd St., Boca Raton. © **561/869-0030.**

THE PERFORMING ARTS

For live concerts, featuring one-hit wonders, cover bands, and, once in a blue moon someone you actually would pay to hear live, the **Count de Hoernle Amphitheater** aka the **Mizner Park Amphitheater Centre for the Arts** in Mizner Park (myboca.us/2021/Mizner-Park-Amphitheater; © **561/393-7890**) is the place to see them in an open-air format, under the stars and, at times, in the rain. *Tip:* If you don't want to splurge for an admission ticket, you can still hear (but not see) the concerts from Mizner Park. Also within Mizner is **The Studio at Mizner Park ★** (thestudioatmiznerpark.com; © **561/203-3742**), a 300-seat black-box theater for nationally recognized comedians, musicians, and shows.

The **Wick Theatre & Costume Museum ★★★**, 7901 N. Federal Hwy. (thewick.org), features dramas, comedies, classics, off-Broadway hits, and new works throughout the year, plus, a fabulous costume museum housing original wardrobes from over 35 Broadway productions and revivals, including the Julie Andrews production of "My Fair Lady" and the Sarah Jessica Parker production of "Once Upon A Mattress."

PALM BEACH & WEST PALM BEACH

65 miles N of Miami; 193 miles E of Tampa; 45 miles N of Fort Lauderdale

For generations, Palm Beach has been the traditional winter home of American aristocracy: the Kennedys, Rockefellers and others, have all fled northern climes for this slice of paradise. Beyond the upscale resorts that cater to such a crowd, Palm Beach holds some surprises, including the renowned Norton Museum of Art, some stellar restaurants, top-notch birding, and the sparkling Intracoastal Waterway.

Beaches   Public beaches are a rare commodity in Palm Beach. **Midtown Beach** is a notable exception, a golden island of undeveloped strand in a sea of glitz and glamour. Groomed beach sand, picnic facilities, and outdoor recreation dominate at **Phipps Ocean Park,** another public beach especially popular with families.

Things to Do   Wherever there is an abundance of sun, sand, and sightseers, there is **golf,** and Palm Beach is no exception. Downtown, the **Norton Museum of Art** displays works by the world's most recognizable names: O'Keeffe, Pollock, Monet, Renoir, and Picasso.

Eating & Drinking   Leave the Bermuda shorts behind in favor of crisply ironed linen and Lily Pulitzer prints for swanky, oceanfront dining in Palm Beach. Overlook the surf dining on platters of freshly caught **seafood,** from Florida lobster to snapper, at beachside dining rooms. **Southern barbecue** reminds visitors that Florida *is* part of the South.

Nightlife & Entertainment Artists' lofts, sidewalk cafes, bars, restaurants, and galleries dot **Clematis Street,** the pumping heart of Palm Beach nightlife, which is technically in West Palm, which has its own burgeoning downtown nightlife scene on assorted side streets and in nicknamed neighborhoods (SoDo, SoSo—no joke). On weekends, Boomers, Gen Z, and everyone in between mingle at sidewalk tables or **dance** to EDM at youthful bars. The moneyed set in Palm Beach is most likely found sipping high-end ports, rosés, and brandies at **oceanfront hotel bars.**

Essentials

GETTING THERE If you're driving up or down the Florida coast, you'll probably reach the Palm Beach area by way of I-95. Exit at Belvedere Road or Okeechobee Boulevard, and head east to reach the most central part of Palm Beach.

Visitors on their way to or from Orlando or Miami should take the Florida Turnpike, a toll road with a speed limit of 65 mph. Tolls are pricey, though; the entire length from Miami to Orlando will set you back about $23. If you're coming from Florida's west coast, you can take either S.R. 70, which runs north of Lake Okeechobee to Fort Pierce, or S.R. 80, which runs south of the lake to Palm Beach.

Drop by the historic Breakers hotel (p. 285) to see Palm Beach–style luxury.

All major airlines fly to the **Palm Beach International Airport,** at Congress Avenue and Belvedere Road (pbia.org; ✆ **561/471-7400**). **Amtrak** (amtrak.com; ✆ **800/USA-RAIL** [872-7245]) has a terminal in West Palm Beach, at 201 S. Tamarind Ave., as does the **Brightline** train at 260 Quadrille Plaza Dr. (gobrightline.com; ✆ **831/539-2901**), and **Tri-Rail,** 203 S. Tamarind Ave. (tri-rail.com; ✆ **561/260-1838**).

The **Brightline** costs about $15 from Miami to West Palm and from $79 for adults, $39 for kids from West Palm to Orlando.

GETTING AROUND Although a car is pretty much a necessity in this area, the public transportation system will get you to some attractions in both West Palm and Palm Beach. **Palm Tran** (palmtran.org) covers 31 routes with more than 192 buses. The fare is $2; children 8 and under are free.

In downtown West Palm, free electric shuttles zip passengers to CityPlace, Brightline station, downtown, Worth Avenue, Ocean Boulevard, and more daily from 7am to 9pm. Go to ridewpb.com.

VISITOR INFORMATION The **Palm Beaches Florida** (thepalmbeaches.com) has info on events, activities, and more.

Beaches & Outdoor Activities

BEACHES Public beaches are a rare commodity here in Palm Beach. Most of the island's best beaches are fronted by private estates and inaccessible to the general public. However, there are a few notable exceptions, including **Midtown Beach,** east of Worth Avenue, on Ocean Boulevard between Royal Palm Way and Gulfstream Road, which boasts more than 100 feet of undeveloped sand. This newly widened coast is a centerpiece and a natural oasis in a town dominated by commercial glitz. There are no restrooms or concessions here, though a lifeguard is on duty until sundown. A popular hangout for locals lies about 1½ miles north of here, near Dunbar Street; they prefer it to Midtown Beach because of the relaxed atmosphere. Parking is available at meters along A1A. At the south end of Palm Beach, there's a less-popular but better-equipped beach called **Phipps Ocean Park.** On Ocean Boulevard, between the Southern Boulevard and Lake Avenue causeways, there's a lively public beach encompassing more than 1,200 feet of groomed oceanfront. With picnic and recreation areas and plenty of parking, the area is especially good for families.

BIKING **Palm Beach Bicycle Trail Shop,** 50 Cocoanut Row in Royal Poinciana Plaza (palmbeachbicycle.com; © **561/659-4583**), rents a wide range of bikes, everything from an English single-speed to a full-tilt mountain bike. Rates are $25 per hour, $35 for 90 minutes, and $49 for 24 hours, and include a basket and lock (not that a lock is necessary in this fortress of a town). The most scenic route is called the Lake Trail, running the length of the island along the Intracoastal

---

THE sport OF KINGS

The **Palm Beach Polo and Country Club** (11809 Polo Club Rd.; © **561/793-1440**) and the **International Polo Club** (3667 120th Ave.; © **561/204-5687**) are two of the world's premier polo grounds and host some of the sport's top-rated players. These fields are on the mainland in a rural area called Wellington, the "Equestrian Winter Capital of the World," they say. Most of the spectators, and many of the players, are pure Palm Beach. But you need not be a Vanderbilt or a Kennedy to attend—matches are open to the public and are surprisingly affordable.

Even if you haven't a clue how the game is played, you can spend your time people-watching. In recent years, stargazers have spotted King Charles, Prince Harry, Sylvester Stallone, Tommy Lee Jones, Bruce Springsteen, Bill Gates, and Michael Bloomberg, among others.

Dress is casual; a navy or tweed blazer over jeans or khakis is the standard for men, while neat-looking jeans or a pantsuit is the norm for women. On warmer days, shorts and, of course, polo shirts are fine, too.

General admission is $10 to $45; box seats cost $150 and up but are usually for members only. Special polo brunches are often available, too, at $85 per person. Matches are held throughout the week. Schedules vary, but the big names usually compete on Sunday at 3:30pm from January to April.

The fields are located at 11809 Polo Club Rd. and 3667 120th Ave., South Wellington, 10 miles west of the Forest Hill Boulevard exit off I-95. Visit internationalpoloclub.com for tickets and a detailed schedule of events.

Waterway. On it, you'll see wildlife, magnificent mansions, and downtown West Palm Beach in the distance.

GOLF There's good golfing in the Palm Beaches, but many private-club courses are maintained exclusively for members' use. In the offseason, some private courses open to visitors at Palm Beach County hotels.

The best hotel for golf in the area is the **PGA National Resort** ★★★ in Palm Beach Gardens (p. 288; pgaresort.com; ✆ **800/863-2819**), which features a whopping 99 holes of golf.

The Park West Palm ★★, 7301 Georgia Ave. (theparkwestpalm.com; ✆ **561/530-3810**), is a fab, family-friendly golf park that offers caddie services, putting course, night putting, lessons, two restaurants and a bar, and a course designed by Gil Hanse, Jim Wagner, and Dirk Ziff. The Lit 9 is a challenging, par-3 course that has extended hours under lights. Cost for the Lit 9 is $30, and greens fees for the golf course range from $60 to $250.

The **Palm Beach Public Golf Course** ★, 2345 S. Ocean Blvd. (golfontheocean.com; ✆ **561/547-0598**), a popular public 18-hole course, is a par-3 that was redesigned in 2009 by Raymond Floyd and includes a new layout, more holes by the ocean, and, down the road, a state-of-the-art clubhouse. The course opens at 8am on a first-come, first-served basis. Club rentals are available. Greens fees are $35 to $86 per person depending on the time, season, and number of holes played. Cart fees are an extra $14 to $19.

SCUBA DIVING Year-round warm waters, barrier reefs, and plenty of wrecks make South Florida one of the world's most popular places for diving. One of the best-known artificial reefs in this area is a vintage Rolls-Royce Silver Shadow, which was sunk offshore in 1985. Nature has taken its toll, however, and divers can no longer sit in the car, which has been ravaged by time and saltwater. For gear and excursions contact **The Kyalami Scuba Club,** 200 E. 13th St., Riviera Beach (thescubaclub.com; ✆ **561/844-2466**).

SPECTATOR SPORTS The **Washington Nationals** (mlb.com/nationals/spring-training) and **Houston Astros** (mlb.com/astros/spring-training) do their spring training at **CACTI Park of the Palm Beaches,** 5444 N. Haverhill Rd. (cactipark.com; ✆ **561/500-4487**). Tickets range from $20 to $65.

TENNIS There are hundreds of tennis courts in Palm Beach County. Wherever you are staying, you're bound to be within walking distance of one. In addition to the many hotel tennis courts, you can play at **Okeeheelee Park,** 7715 Forrest Hill Blvd., West Palm Beach (okeeheeleepark.com; ✆ **561/966-6600**), featuring six lighted tennis courts and no fees. First-come, first-served, of course. **The Palm Beach Gardens Tennis & Pickleball Center,** 5110 117th Court N., Palm Beach Gardens (pbgfl.com/356/Tennis-Pickleball-Center; ✆ **561/630-1180**), has 20 Har-Tru courts, and 10 permanent and 6 temporary pickleball courts. Fees range from $12 to $15.

WATERSPORTS Contact the **Blue Water Boat Rental,** 200 E. 13th St., Riviera Beach (www.bluewaterboatrental.com; ✆ **561/840-7470**), to arrange sailboat, jet-ski, bicycle, kayak, water-ski, and parasail rentals. At the aforementioned **Okeeheelee Park** is **Shark Wake Park** ★, 1440 Eshelman Trail, West Palm Beach (sharkwakepark.com/561; ✆ **561/323-3937**), a water park on the lake featuring obstacle courses, ziplining, wakeboarding, kneeboarding, and more. We asked if there were any alligators around since it is a brackish lake, and they told us, "Not today there aren't." Oof. Prices range from $28 for one attraction to $70 for all-day access. There's a concession stand and restrooms.

Note: Visitors who do not already possess a valid boating education certificate must take a course. See p. 29 for more information.

Seeing the Sights

Ann Norton Sculpture Gardens ★★★
Designed by world-renowned botanist Sir Peter Smithers, these gardens, established in 1977 by sculptor Ann Norton, boast over 250 rare palm and cycads surrounded by over 100 of Norton's creations, including nine sculptures, eight in brick, one in granite—they make for excellent social media posts. Also here is the home, listed on the National Register of Historic Places, where Norton and her husband Ralph resided during their lifetime. In 2019, Ann, who died in 1982, was inducted into the Florida Artists Hall of Fame.

253 Barcelona Rd., West Palm Beach. ansg.org. ✆ **561/832-5328.** Admission $15 adults, $10 seniors, $7 children/students. Wed–Sun 10am–4pm.

Cox Science Center & Aquarium ★★★
How does the human brain grow and develop over the course of a lifetime? That's the topic for the Cox's fascinating "Journey Through the Human Brain" exhibit. It's a 2,500-square-foot wonder with 30 integrated displays, created in tandem with a major, Palm Beach–based neurological research institute at a cost of $2.5 million. It's the centerpiece for this enlightening museum, which ranges across a number of scientific disciplines thanks to its state-of-the-art planetarium, a soon-to-be-massive aquarium (opening sometime in 2026), interactive galleries, and traveling exhibitions. There's also an early childhood exhibit, a science lab, and a science-themed 18-hole miniature golf course designed by local legends Gary Nicklaus and Jim Fazio. Outside, the quarter-mile-long Fisher Family Science Trail connects 15 exhibits, including a Physics Forest, FPL SolarScape, interactive splash pad, gem panning station and dinosaur walk. An open-air amphitheater features daily live science shows and trivia sessions.

4801 Dreher Trail N., West Palm Beach (at the north end of Dreher Park). coxsciencecenter.org. ✆ **561/832-1988.** Admission $24 adults, $22 seniors, $20 children. Planetarium shows $5 addition to museum admission. Mon–Fri 9am–5pm; Sat–Sun 10am–6pm.

---

unreal ESTATE

No trip to Palm Beach is complete without at least a glimpse of **Mar-a-Lago,** the residence of Donald Trump. In 1985, Trump purchased the estate of cereal heiress Marjorie Merriweather Post for a meager $8 million (for a fully furnished beachfront property of this stature, it was a relative bargain), to the great consternation of locals, who feared that he would turn the place into a casino. Instead, Trump, who resides in a portion of the palace, opened the house to the public—for a price, of course—as a tony, albeit musty and allegedly bedbug-riddled country club (membership fee: $200,000). Trump continues to make his presence loudly known in Palm Beach, as do fans who, despite Secret Service presence, often stand outside with flags.

While there are currently no tours open to the public, you can glimpse the manse as you cross the bridge from West Palm Beach into Palm Beach. You can't miss the massive American flag and the Secret Service vehicles. It's located at 1100 S. Ocean Blvd., Palm Beach.

Ostriches gawk at visitors to Lion Country Safari.

Flagler Museum ★★★ The Gilded Age is preserved in this luxurious mansion commissioned by Standard Oil tycoon Henry Flagler as a wedding present to his third wife. Whitehall, also known as the Taj Mahal of North America, is a classic Edwardian-style mansion containing 55 rooms, including a Louis XIV music room and art gallery, a Louis XV ballroom, and 14 guest suites outfitted with original antique European furnishings. Out back, you can climb aboard the *Rambler,* Mr. Flagler's private restored railroad car. Allow at least 1½ hours to tour the stunning grounds and interior. Group tours are available, but for the most part, this is a self-guided museum.

1 Whitehall Way (at Cocoanut Row and Whitehall Way), Palm Beach. flaglermuseum.us. **561/655-2833.** Admission $26 adults, $13 children 6–12. Tues–Sat 10am–5pm; Sun noon–5pm.

Lion Country Safari ★★ More than 1,000 animals roam this 4-mile, 500-acre preserve (the nation's first cageless drive-through safari). They're divided into their indigenous regions, from the East African preserve of the Serengeti to the American West. Elephants, lions, wildebeest, ostriches, American bison, buffalo, Watusi, pink flamingos, and many other unusual species live on the preserve. When we last visited, most of the lions were asleep; when awake, they travel freely throughout the cageless grassy landscape. In fact, you're the one who's confined in your own car without an escort (no convertibles allowed). You're given a detailed pamphlet with photos and descriptions, and are instructed to obey the 15 mph speed limit—unless you see the rhinos charge (a rare occasion), in which case you're encouraged to floor it. Driving the loop takes slightly more than an hour, though you could make a day of just watching the chimpanzees play on their secluded islands. Though some consider this a tourist trap, I've very much enjoyed my visits here.

The best time to go is late afternoon, right before the park closes; it's much cooler then, so the lions are more active. For those without cars, limited vans are available for rent for $35 for 90 minutes.

Beyond the safari experience there are also few rides here (a train, carousel, and flying elephant ride), but it's no Disney—Animal Kingdom maybe, but not Disney. Also on-site: **Safari Splash,** a water park with 23 interactive water features and a 10,000-square-foot play area and wading pool.

There are also cabins, tent sites, and RV sites for those who feel like spending the night (away from the animals, of course). Rates range from $140 for cabins (four people), $65 for tent sites, and $125 for RV sites.

2003 Lion Country Safari Rd. (Southern Blvd. W. at S.R. 80), Loxahatchee. lioncountrysafari.com. **561/793-1084** or 561/793-9797 for camping reservations. Admission $49 ages 10 and up, $37 children 3–9. Daily 9:30am–5:30pm (last vehicle admitted at 4:30pm). From I-95, exit on Southern Blvd. Go west for about 18 miles.

Norton Museum of Art ★★★

The Norton is world famous for its prestigious permanent collection and top temporary exhibitions. The museum's major collections are divided geographically. The American galleries contain major works by Hopper, O'Keeffe, and Pollock. The French collection contains Impressionist and post-Impressionist paintings by Cézanne, Degas, Gauguin, Matisse, Monet, Picasso, Pissarro, and Renoir. The contemporary collection has works by Jenny Saville, Nick Cave, Sylvie Fleury, John McCracken, and Dahn Vo. The Chinese collection contains more than 200 bronzes, jades, and ceramics, as well as monumental Buddhist sculptures. Allow about 2 hours to see this museum. Every Friday night after 4pm is Art After Dark, featuring music, film, special tours with curators and docents, hands-on art activities, a cash bar, and menu options from **The Restaurant,** a gorgeous midcentury modern space with floor-to-ceiling windows overlooking the garden, which features works by the likes of Fernand Léger.

1451 S. Olive Ave., West Palm Beach. norton.org. **561/832-5196.** Admission $18 adults, $5 ages 13–21; $10 adults and seniors every Fri after 4pm. Mon–Thurs, Sat 10am–5pm; Fri 10am–10pm; Sun 11am–5pm. Closed Tues during the summer. Take I-95 to exit 52 (Okeechobee Blvd. E.). Travel east on Okeechobee to Dixie Hwy., then south ½ mile to the Norton. Access parking through entrances on Dixie Hwy. and S. Olive Ave.

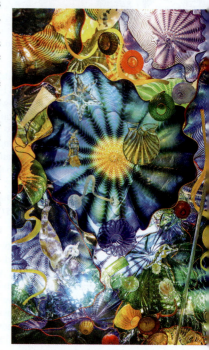

Part of a Dale Chihuly ceiling sculpture at Norton Museum of Art.

Palm Beach Zoo & Conservation Society ★

Miami's Zoo is spread across 800 acres. This intimate venue has just 23, so it's not an all-day excursion (budget 2 hr. tops). That said, for animal fans (and small children) it'll do the trick as it houses more than 500 animals representing 100+ different species. The Tropics of the Americas exhibit showcases jaguars, bush dogs, Baird's tapirs, and giant anteaters on a 3-acre re-creation of a Central and South American rain forest. An Everglades Center features the endangered Florida panther, among other animals. Other animal highlights include Malayan tiger, Queensland koala, Komodo dragon, black bear, river otter, and the Florida Reptile House. And if the tots get antsy, there's a colorful wildlife carousel, an interactive water-play fountain, a full-service restaurant, and daily performances of the "Wings Over Water" bird show and the "Wild Things" stage show. The zoo also offers zookeeper talks and animal training sessions.

1301 Summit Blvd. (east of I-95 btw. Southern and Forest Hill blvds.). palmbeachzoo.org. ℂ **561/547-WILD** [9453]. Admission $29 adults, $26.95 seniors, $23 children 3–12. Tickets cheaper online. Daily 9am–5pm.

Rapids Water Park ★

It may not be on the same grand scale as the theme parks in Orlando, but the seasonal Rapids is a great way to cool off on a hot day. There are 12 acres of water rides, including an aquatic obstacle course, a children's area, a miniature-golf course, the Superbowl (a tubeless water ride that spins and swirls before dumping riders into the pool below), and the Big Thunder, a giant funnel that plunges riders down 50 feet in a four-person tube (claustrophobia, anyone?). New in 2024: Mega Mayhem, Florida's only dueling water coaster.

6566 N. Military Trail, Riviera Beach (1 mile west of I-95 on Military, btw. 45th St./exit 54 and Blue Heron Blvd./exit 55 in West Palm Beach). rapidswaterpark.com. ℂ **561/842-8756.** Admission $59.99 (down $5 Mon–Fri with advance online purchase); free for children 2 and under. Parking $15. Mid-Mar to Sept Mon–Fri 10am–5pm; Sat–Sun 10am–6pm. Open until 7pm in summer months.

Richard and Pat Johnson Palm Beach County History Museum ★

There's more to Palm Beach history than Donald Trump and well-preserved octogenarians. Located within the historic 1916 Courthouse in downtown West Palm Beach, the museum has two permanent exhibits: the **People Gallery,** a tribute to approximately 100 individuals and families who have contributed to the growth of Palm Beach County; and the **Place Gallery,** featuring models and photographs of Palm Beach County's natural environment and the animals and ecology that make it unique.

300 N. Dixie Hwy., West Palm Beach. Entrance is on 2nd floor of courthouse. pbchistory.org. ℂ **561/832-4164.** Free admission. Mon–Sat 10am–4pm.

Shopping

Worth Avenue (worth-avenue.com) is known as the "Rodeo Drive of the South," and it is a window-shopper's mecca. Between South Ocean Boulevard and Cocoanut Row, there are more than 200 boutiques, shops, art galleries, and restaurants, including the **Lily Pulitzer** flagship, **Gucci, Chanel, Ferragamo,** and more. Besides the boldface collection of couturiers, there are also a good number of unique, independent boutiques. For privileged feet, **Stubbs & Wooton ★★**, 340 Worth Ave. (stubbsandwooton.com; ℂ **561/655-6857**), sells velvet slippers that are a favorite of the loofahed locals. For rare and estate jewelry, **Richter's of Palm Beach ★★**, 224 Worth Ave. (ℂ **561/655-0774**), has been specializing in priceless

> ## quintessential PALM BEACH WALK
>
> Along the west side of the fashionable barrier island **Town of Palm Beach,** hugging the **Intracoastal Waterway** (here known as Lake Worth) is the recently renovated and very high-tech **superyacht marina** (the only one of its kind in the town itself, it welcomes boats that measure 60 to 294 feet in length), and the adjacent and picturesque **Lake Park,** where you can go to watch the docked boats—er, superyachts, sorry—bobbing in the background. (Alas, only those who own these megaliths can go onto the docks at the marina, but you'll get a good view from the park.) Then walk all, or part of, the 5.5-mile palm tree–lined **Lake Trail** that starts there and take in Palm Beach's historical sights (like the **Flagler Museum**) and some of the town's grandest homes.

gems since 1893. Just off Worth Avenue is **Church Mouse** ★★★, 378 S. County Rd. (bbts.org/church-mouse; ✆ **561/659-2154**), a consignment/thrift shop with antique furnishings and tableware, as well as lots of good castoff clothing and shoes from socialites who've moved on to the next designers or, worse than that, to the big gala in the sky. This shop usually closes for 2 months during the summer.

CityPlace ★★, 700 S. Rosemary Ave., West Palm Beach (cityplace.com; ✆ **561/366-1000**), is a Mediterranean-style shopping, dining, and entertainment complex slash condo that's responsible for revitalizing what was once a lifeless downtown West Palm Beach. Across the street in the magnificent **Restoration Hardware** furniture gallery—and it is a work of art—**RH Rooftop Restaurant** is a wine bar and restaurant with a small menu and lots of photo ops.

Nearby on South Dixie Highway between Belvedere Road and Southern Boulevard in downtown West Palm is **Antique Row Art & Design District** (westpalmbeachantiques.com), with over 40 antique shops offering a wide selection of 17th- to 20th-century relics, decorative arts, furniture, and more, all within walking distance. Because of its proximity to filthy-rich Palm Beach, there are some fabulous finds here from various estate sales and, sadly, bankruptcies from people living above their means.

Where to Stay

The island of Palm Beach is the epitome of *Lifestyles of the Rich and Famous* or, for our younger readers: [insert Instagram influencer account here]. Royalty and celebrities come to winter here, and there are plenty of lavishly priced options to accommodate them. Most of the more modest places surround the island, including a number of decently priced chain motels near the airport. In West Palm Beach, chain hotels are mostly on the main arteries close to the highways and a short drive from downtown.

Doing a rental through Airbnb or Vrbo can be a smart move here, as there are a number of nice options at half the price of most hotels in this area.

EXPENSIVE

The Brazilian Court Palm Beach ★★★ This elegant, old-world, Mediterranean-style hotel dates to the 1920s, but like many Palm Beach residents it has a youthful glow, thanks to a recent facelift. The 80 custom-designed,

Spanish colonial–style rooms and suites all feature mahogany case goods and crown molding, handsome wood shutters, and king-size beds topped with imported linens. A large hotel by Palm Beach standards (the Breakers notwithstanding), Brazilian Court sprawls over half a block and features fountains and private courtyards. It is 2 blocks from the beach and if you're lazy, the hotel provides complimentary rides to and from the sand. A fleet of old-school and electric bikes are also available to explore (the first 2 hr. are included in your room rate). The only downside here, perhaps? A tiny, yet intimate, pool where you feel you have to whisper. A small Jacuzzi hidden from the pool is where shy types and celebs like to hide. Especially swanky is the hotel's 44-foot Italian **Solaris Power Yacht** on which guests get free 2-hour tours around the island, thrice daily from Sunday through Wednesday. An on-site salon will leave you well-coiffed thanks to expert stylists. With the addition of renowned chef Daniel Boulud's **Café Boulud,** which has a fun bar scene with live music, Brazilian Court is one of Palm Beach's places to see and be seen.

301 Australian Ave., Palm Beach. thebraziliancourt.com. **800/552-0335** or 561/655-7740. 80 units. $499–$1,490 double. Valet parking $29. Pet fee $100. **Amenities:** Restaurant; bar; concierge; exercise room; heated outdoor pool; game room; room service; fitness center; spa treatments; free Wi-Fi.

The Breakers Palm Beach ★★★ This 140-acre beachfront hotel is quintessential Palm Beach. Founded by tycoon Henry Flagler in 1896 to house well-heeled passengers at the last stop of his railway, it was rebuilt twice after devastating fires (in 1903 and 1926). The current Neo-Renaissance main building cost $7 million to construct (the equivalent of $142 million today), and employed

This magnificent fountain greets guests to the Breakers.

1,200 workers, including 72 artisans who did the splendid frescoes in the lobby. Since people were smaller in the 1920s, rooms tend to be, er, cozier than what you'll find at neighboring resorts, but they're plenty plush, featuring marble bathrooms, fine wood furnishings, and views of the ocean or the magnificently manicured grounds. For those seeking next-level luxe, **The Flagler Club** is a 21-room hotel within the hotel, featuring private lounge, terrace, staff, and a Mercedes Maybach car at your disposal.

After a $15-million beachfront redevelopment project, the **Beach Club** now features five pools; four whirlpool spas; 20 private, luxury beach bungalows, and 10 pool cabanas for daytime rental, with a dedicated staff of concierges; a beach gazebo; and two casual oceanside restaurants. The hotel's available spa treatments can be performed indoors or out. Florida's oldest existing golf course is here, but millions have been lavished on it, and its sister course, to transform them into championship-level par-70 places to play. Kids aren't neglected either at the impressive **Family Entertainment Center,** a 6,160-square-foot space that includes an arcade, a toddler's playroom, an arts-and-crafts area, a children's movie theater, and a video-game room. The hotel is also home to a coterie of notable bars and restaurants.

1 S. County Rd., Palm Beach. thebreakers.com. **833/777-8363.** 534 units. $951–$1,837 double. From I-95, exit Okeechobee Blvd. E., head east to S. County Rd., and turn left. **Amenities:** 9 restaurants; 5 bars; babysitting; bike rentals; children's programs; concierge; 2 championship golf courses; 2 fitness centers; 5 outdoor pools; room service; indoor/outdoor spa; 10 Har-Tru tennis courts; watersports equipment/rentals; free Wi-Fi.

Eau Palm Beach Resort and Spa ★★

If the Breakers is too mammoth for your taste, consider this former Ritz Carlton. A lot warmer than the Four Seasons, Eau (pronounced "oh?" and French for water), located on a beautiful beach in a tiny town about 8 miles from Worth Avenue, lacks pretension and feels more like a boutique hotel. Rooms all have balconies with hanging chairs from which to view ocean, pool, and gardens. They're decorated in the bright blues and yellows of whimsical interior designer Jonathan Adler. The 42,000-square-foot Eau Spa—one of only 48 in the world with Forbes' five-star rating—has 19 treatment rooms, scrub and polish rooms, steam room, saunas, and a garden featuring swings, dipping pools, and water-massage benches. Four restaurants, an ice-cream parlor, and a spa cafe keep guests well fed. Kids ages 3 to 12 are welcome at **Loggers,** an immersive kids' club, while teens have their own space, the **Hide Away,** featuring gaming, movies, and sports. Kids 4 and under eat free throughout the resort except at Angle. There are also three Har-Tru tennis courts.

100 S. Ocean Blvd., Manalapan. eaupalmbeach.com. **561/533-6000.** 309 units. $572–$1,091 double. Valet parking $40. Pet fee $250. From I-95, take exit for Lantana Rd., heading east. After 1 mile, turn right onto Federal Hwy. (U.S. 1/Dixie). Continue south to the next light and turn left onto Ocean Ave. Cross the Intracoastal Waterway and turn right onto A1A. **Amenities:** 4 restaurants; 3 bars; ice-cream parlor; coffee bar; bike rental; children's programs; concierge; fitness center; Jacuzzi; 2 pools; room service; spa; 3 Har-Tru tennis courts; watersports equipment/rentals; free Wi-Fi.

Four Seasons Resort Palm Beach ★★★

Situated on a lovely and private swatch of beach, Four Seasons is a quiet retreat from Worth Avenue—just a quick Uber ride from the hotel or a longer, scenic bike ride (bikes and helmets are included in your room rate). Guest rooms have a chic beach-house vibe (as opposed to a stuffy, swanky hotel vibe) and are quite spacious, with private balconies and lavish bathrooms. The full-service spa is top notch, featuring 11 treatment rooms including a "Man Room," wet room, and full-service salon. Of the on-site eateries, **Moody Tongue Omakase** is best, a 15-course Japanese tasting menu by sushi chef Hiromi Iwakiri paired with specialty beers from the only Michelin-starred brewery in the world. Fancy! The resort offers a complimentary kids' program (ages 4–12) and a teen game room. Kids 4 and under eat free at some restaurants. Two outdoor pools—one for families and the other adults-only—have fabulous ocean views.

2800 S. Ocean Blvd., Palm Beach. fourseasons.com/palmbeach. **800/432-2335** or 561/582-2800. 207 units. $1,164–$1,915 double. Valet parking $45. Pet fee $100. From I-95, take the 6th Ave. exit east and turn left onto Dixie Hwy. Turn east onto Lake Ave. and north onto A1A (S. Ocean Blvd.); the resort is just ahead on your right. **Amenities:** 3 restaurants; bar; babysitting; children's programs; concierge; fitness center; outdoor heated pool; spa; 2 tennis courts; watersports equipment/rentals; free Wi-Fi.

MODERATE/EXPENSIVE

The Colony ★★★   Opened in 1947, the Colony was a storied hangout—hideout, perhaps—for socialites and celebrities for years. Presidents Bush, Clinton, Carter, and Ford, plus Judy Garland, Frank Sinatra, Sofia Loren, and Lena Horne all stayed here on the DL. The Duke and Duchess of Windsor spent part of their time in exile here. And the very old-school Polo Lounge was command central for an eclectic mix of local lounge and A-list cabaret singers and entertainers. Somewhere in the mid-1990s the hotel fell out of fashion, until 2014, when the

Lovely hand-painted wall murals at the historic Colony Hotel.

owners recruited interior designer Carleton Varney, of the storied Dorothy Draper and Company, to revamp the place, and that he did, painting the facade Palm Beach pink and creating what is now known as the "Brazilliance" pattern in the hallways. In 2016, when the place was sold again, interior designers Celerie Kemble, Mark D. Sikes, and Aerin Lauder (yep, Estee's granddaughter) were hired for the refresh, and brought a delightfully retro sensibility to the task, hand-painting all of the guest rooms in one of four "Palm Beach" colors, adding whimsical floral motifs to the headboards, and piling on luxe amenities in each room (like Dyson hair dryers). The Colony is once again a jet set fave, with the villas and bungalows going to the real high rollers. But regular rooms can, surprisingly, be quite affordable, especially in the offseason. Each section has its own pools, and the one next to bar/restaurant **Swifty's** is shaped like the state of Florida! The beach is located a few steps away, and a beach butler will escort you and set you up on the sand like regular Palm Beach royalty. Various complimentary modes of island transport include beach cruiser bikes and a vintage pink Land Rover Defender with roll-down sides. Seasonal exercise classes are taught by wintering fitness gurus.

155 Hammon Ave., Palm Beach. thecolonypalmbeach.com. **800/521-5525** or 561/655-5430. 93 units. $320–$517 double. Valet parking $35. Pet fee $150. From I-95, exit onto Okeechobee Blvd. E. and cross the Intracoastal Waterway. Turn right on S. County Rd. and then left onto Hammon Ave. **Amenities:** 2 restaurants; 2 bars; concierge; 3 heated pools; room service; spa services; free Wi-Fi.

Hilton West Palm Beach ★★

Ideally located adjacent to the shops, restaurants, and bars of CityPlace, and across from the Kravis Center for the Performing Arts, this Hilton is for those wanting to explore the area without trashing their 401K. An oasis from the area's bustle, it has a nice resort-style pool with a bar and live music and outdoor fire pits. Rooms are cookie-cutter Hilton rooms, but well maintained. Staff are caring. The resort fee gives you a $15 food and beverage credit at any of the restaurants or bars as well as a 1-hour bike rental daily, beach chairs, towels, and complimentary transportation around town via electric shuttle.

600 Okeechobee Blvd., West Palm Beach. hiltonwestpalmbeach.com. **561/231-6000.** 400 units. $183–$528 double. Valet parking $40. **Amenities:** 3 restaurants; bar; concierge; heated pool; room service; free Wi-Fi.

Palm Beach Historic Inn ★★

Built in 1923, the Palm Beach Historic Inn is an area landmark within a block's walking distance of Worth Avenue, several good restaurants, and the beach (chairs and towels are provided for guests of the hotel). All bedrooms are uniquely and elegantly decorated and have hardwood floors, goose down comforters, Egyptian-cotton linens, fluffy bathrobes, and plenty of good-smelling toiletries. There's no restaurant on-site, but snacks and drinks are available around the clock in the lobby. They provide guests with Palm Beach Town parking placards. *Note:* All rooms are on the second floor and there is no elevator.

365 S. County Rd., Palm Beach. palmbeachhistoricinn.com. **561/832-4009.** 13 units. $210–$763 double. **Amenities:** Concierge; in-room spa treatments; bike rental; access to nearby fitness center; free Wi-Fi.

PGA National Resort ★★★

The name gives away the focus here. With five 18-hole championship courses and one 9-hole course on more than 2,300 acres, plus Leadbetter and Pelz golf schools, and tour-level club fitting, golfers and other sports-minded travelers will find plenty to keep them occupied. The

Champion Course opened in 1981 and was originally designed by George and Tom Fazio. It was the site of the Ryder Cup in 1983, the PGA Championship in 1987, and the Senior PGA Championship for 19 years from 1982 to 2000. The course has undergone several renovations by Jack Nicklaus over the years, with the latest completed in 2018. In addition to golf, there's tennis, pickleball, a complete health and fitness center, six pools (but no beach), and a top-rated 40,000-square-foot European spa (which could be a destination in itself). Posh, tropical-themed guest rooms are comfortable, and bordering on residential in size, with immense bathrooms, and private terrace or patio. On-site is the retro-fab 1950s-style steakhouse by *Top Chef* season 13 winner Jeremy Ford, **The Butcher's Club** and modern American spot **Honeybelle** by *Top Chef*'s Lindsay Autry. An interactive kids' club has a slew of activities for the young 'uns.

400 Ave. of the Champions, Palm Beach Gardens. pgaresort.com. © **800/863-2819.** 339 units, 21 cottages. $265–$497 double. Valet parking $35. Pet fee $150. From I-95, take exit 57B (PGA Blvd.) going west and continue for approx. 2 miles to the resort entrance on the left. **Amenities:** 9 restaurants and lounges; concierge; 5 18-hole tournament-ready golf courses; 9-hole course; kids' club; 7 pools; room service; European spa; 16 Har-Tru clay tennis courts; 12 pickleball courts; free Wi-Fi.

INEXPENSIVE

Pioneer Inn ★★ This is, unapologetically, a motel. When you look back at your time in this area 5 years from now, you'll likely have no memory of what your room looked like, because it will have looked like the rooms in dozens of other motels around the U.S. But you probably *will* remember the affable owner, who never seems to leave the front desk, and runs a tight ship. You may also remember all of the fun things you got to do because you paid a reasonable rate for your room, a big deal in an area where the cost of sleeping has gotten astronomical. Might I add that you also won't have any flashbacks to unpleasant memories here? The hotel is eat-off-the-floor clean, with strong showers, and quality beds. Many concertgoers stay at the Pioneer as it's walking distance to the amphitheater.

9121 Southern Blvd., West Palm Beach. pioneerinn.us. © **561/855-6055.** $109–$158 double. 32 units. **Amenities:** Free Wi-Fi.

Where to Eat

Palm Beach has some of the area's swankiest restaurants. Thanks to the development of downtown West Palm Beach, however, there is also a selection of less expensive, but still mighty tasty spots. Dress here is slightly more formal than in most other areas of Florida: Men wear blazers, and women generally put on modest dresses or chic suits when they dine out, even on the oppressively hot days of summer. Beyond the listings below, we are also fans of hotel-based eateries like **The Butcher's Club** (see above), **Swifty's** (p. 288), and **Flories.**

EXPENSIVE

Buccan ★★★ MODERN AMERICAN Buccan is Palm Beach, 21st-century style, a hopping, contemporary American eatery, with excellent lighting, a current soundtrack, and Clay Conley, a rock-star chef with multiple James Beard awards. On the plates here: crudo including a fantastic Hamachi tiradito with Peruvian chiles and yuzu; plant-based beauties in the form of crispy squash blossom Rangoon with lion's mane mushrooms, cream cheese, and a sweet and sour sauce; an elevated hot dog panini with sauerkraut, gruyere, mustard, and chili; homemade pastas (such as the sweet corn agnolotti with ricotta and bacon); and a fabulous

Florida grouper Scaloppine. Service is fast and friendly, but those who want a quiet dinner should go elsewhere. The bar is small, but always busy, and worthy of an after-dinner drink if you can squeeze in.

Located directly next door is 40-seat sibling sushi spot whose name literally means "Little Sister" in Japanese, **Imoto at Buccan** (imotopalmbeach.com; 𝒞 **561/833-5522**). Also adjacent to the restaurant is **Buccan Sandwich Shop** (buccansandwichshop.com; 𝒞 **561/833-6295**), serving fab made-to-order hot and cold sandwiches. Another location is at 1901 S. Dixie Hwy. in West Palm (𝒞 **561/469-1917**), which also houses **Grato** (gratowpb.com; 𝒞 **561/404-1334**), Conley's swell Italian joint. Conley has plans to bring his greatest hits to Coral Gables in Miami in 2025, taking Buccan, Imoto, and Buccan Sandwich Shop into a collective 9,600-square-foot space at 100 Miracle Mile.

350 S. County Rd., Palm Beach. buccanpalmbeach.com. 𝒞 **561/833-3450.** Main courses $17–$60. Sun–Thurs 5–9:30pm; Fri–Sat 5–10pm.

Cafe l'Europe ★★★ CONTINENTAL

Is it the ginormous displays of fresh flowers around the blue velvet–clad dining room, or the fact that a pianist softly tinkles the ivories nightly, that makes this Palm Beach's most romantic restaurant? Superlative service certainly puts patrons in the mood, as does the sexy, surprising menu, which includes starters like crispy veal sweetbreads with wild mushroom and asparagus, and entrees of yellowtail snapper in a caper beurre blanc (two favorites, but there are no losing dishes here). And those celebrating really special occasions can order from the cafe's famed champagne and caviar bar (a definite splurge). Whatever the secret, it's worked to make Café l'Europe one of the most coveted reservations in town for some 30-odd years now. A classic.

331 S. County Rd. (at Brazilian Ave.), Palm Beach. cafeleurope.com. 𝒞 **561/655-4020.** Main courses $49–$87. Tues–Sun "from 5pm."

Okeechobee Steakhouse ★★ STEAKHOUSE

Founded by the Lewis family and staking claim to the title of the oldest steakhouse in Florida, this old-school meatery on a gritty block west of West Palm is known for its prime dry-aged steaks, hand-cut meats, 800-bottle wine collection, and even a free steak on your birthday! It's dark, clubby, and always packed. Reservations are booked well in advance. Last time we were there, we saw Maury Povich at the bar. TBH we prefer Tropical Acres down in Dania and Bern's in Tampa, but when you're up this way and have a hankering for a hunk of meat with a side of old-school Florida scene, this is where to go.

2854 Okeechobee Rd., West Palm Beach. okeesteakhouse.com. 𝒞 **561/683-5151.** Main courses $28–$150. Mon–Fri 11:30am–10pm; Sat 4–10pm; Sun 4–9pm.

MODERATE

City Cellar Wine Bar & Grill ★★ AMERICAN

If the Palm Beach proper dining scene is too stuffy, head over to CityPlace to find this fun, casual, brick-and-pressed-tin-ceiling enclave. City Cellar offers a varied menu, from pizzas and pastas to steak and blue crab–crusted sea bass. Of note: the onion-and-mushroom soup with pinot grigio, and chicken schnitzel with house-made roasted onion and bacon spaetzle. This place gets mobbed on weekends, especially for brunch, so plan for a long wait that's best spent at the action-packed bar.

700 S. Rosemary Ave., West Palm Beach. citycellarwpb.com. 𝒞 **561/659-1853.** Main courses $17–$42 (more for steak). Mon–Thurs 11:30am–10pm; Fri–Sat 11:30am–10:30pm; Sun 11am–10pm. Bar daily until midnight.

Coolinary and the Parched Pig ★★ AMERICAN
As groovy as its name, you won't get the same old, same old FL meal here. Instead, chef Tim Lipman crafts palate-pleasing dishes by combining a number of ingredients and cuisine types. Comfort food staple mac and cheese, for example, gets a welcome kick from the addition of hot sauce, jalapeno, and fine smoked gouda (bonus: it's half off during happy hour). Duck rillettes become even richer with the addition of cognac, mustard, pickled kohlrabi, and sourdough. And they serve some of the best chicken and cheddar jalapeno waffles you'll ever try. The creamsicle creme brulee is the way to end a meal. Cocktails are expertly crafted, and the ambiance is chill.

4580 Donald Ross Rd., Palm Beach Gardens. thecoolpig.com. ✆ **561/249-6760.** Main courses $23–$49. Mon–Thurs 4–10pm; Fri–Sat 4–11pm.

Fern Street Wine Bar & Kitchen ★★★ AMERICAN
On a quiet side street near the much louder, bustling scene at CityPlace is this very special wine bar and restaurant. It has a small, dimly lit dining room and humming bar, and a sprawling outdoor patio. The food theme here is ranch-to-kitchen, with said kitchen smack in the middle of the bar and featuring a Palvesi wood fire oven, straight from Modena, Italy. On it, they're grilling bison, vegetables, Spanish octopus, Berkshire pork, you name it. Pair your dish with whatever wine the knowledgeable server tells you will go with it. Staff are very welcoming and real experts. Happy hour is daily from 4 to 7pm and 9 to 11pm, featuring all sorts of well-priced food and drink specials.

501 Fern St., West Palm Beach. fernstreetwpb.com. ✆ **561/328-9745.** Main courses $27–$42 (more for steaks). Mon–Sat 4–11pm. Closed Sun.

The Honor Bar ★★ AMERICAN
What Houston's and Hillstone is to your average American suburb, the Honor Bar is to Palm Beach. By which we mean a dark, cozy eatery that's way less froufrou than many others in these parts. The menu here is small and simple: a bargain $22 burger or delicious prime rib sandwich, Carolina-style beef ribs or a classic omelet with goat and Reggiano cheese (served all day). The bar is always a party, they don't take reservations, but they do have a strict dress code: no tank tops, hats, or athletic attire. Directly next door is swanky sister restaurant, **Palm Beach Grill** (palmbeachgrill.com), with a more upscale menu and higher prices.

340 Royal Poinciana Way, Palm Beach. honorbar.com. ✆ **561/209-2799.** Main courses $18–$35. Sun–Thurs 11:30am–9pm; Fri–Sat 11:30am–9:30pm.

PB Catch ★★ SEAFOOD
A nice, upscale neighborhood raw bar and seafood spot, PB Catch is an advocate for sustainable fishing and harvesting practices. Small plates or "seacuterie" include a delicious smoked mussel piperade, salmon pastrami, and a sensational cured white tuna with crispy shitake and sake aioli. A pan-seared tuna with fried potatoes deserves many chefs' kisses, and even the beer-battered fish and chips are excellent, though it hurt to spend $43 on that one. Oyster selection here is stellar, and the bar has a good selection of cocktails, bubbles, and wines.

251 Sunrise Ave., Palm Beach. PBCatch.com. ✆ **561/659-1853.** Main courses $19–$46. Mon–Thurs 11:30am–10pm; Fri–Sat 11:30am–10:30pm; Sun 11am–10pm. Bar open daily until midnight.

Rhythm Café ★★★ ECLECTIC AMERICAN
This funky hole-in-the-wall, set in a 1950s drugstore complete with lunch counter and stools, is where

WEST PALM'S warehouse district

Once a desolate collection of run-down 1920s industrial buildings, West Palm's burgeoning **Warehouse District** (thedistrictwpb.com) is an 85,000-square-foot, 3-block bastion of all things hip, arty, and whatever word the kids are using these days to describe what's cool, including **Grandview Public Market** food hall, 1401 Clare Ave. (grandviewpublic.com; © 561/206-2148), an industrial-chic space featuring several excellent eateries like **Ramen Lab Eatery, Pizza Paradise,** and the Caribbean **Fire Side Bistro.** Also in Grandview is local brewery, **Steam Horse Brewing Co.,** 1500 Elizabeth Ave. (steamhorsebrewing.com; © 561/623-0091), and rum and vodka distillery, **Steel Tie Spirits Co.,** 1615 Clare Ave. (steeltiespirits.com; © 561/623-9061), but if coffee is more your poison, the 8,000-square-foot cafe and roastery, **Pumphouse Pouratorium,** 1016 Clare Ave. (pumphousecoffee.com; © 561/557-3118), is the wakeup call java junkies need.

---

those in the know come to eat some of West Palm Beach's most satisfying food. On the handwritten, photocopied menu (which changes daily), you'll always find a fish specialty, cooked four possible ways, accompanied by a hefty dose of greens and garnishes. The tenderloin tips, inspired, as they say, by Julia Child's legendary beef bourguignon, are reliably delish. Specials may include blackened scallops with Cajun seasoning on a refreshing mango slaw, or veal sweetbreads. The kitschy decor is a hoot: vinyl tablecloths and a changing display of paintings by local amateurs.

3800 S. Dixie Hwy., West Palm Beach. rhythmcafe.com. © **561/833-3406.** Main courses $20–$55. Wed–Sun 5:30–10pm. From I-95, exit east on Southern Blvd. Go 1 block north of Southern Blvd.; restaurant is on the right.

Stage ★★★ MODERN INDIAN In 2024, Stage was named one of the 47 best restaurants in the United States by *USA Today,* and chef Pushkar Marathe was a finalist for the James Beard Award for Best Southern Chef. The accolades are well deserved for a restaurant that's upending expectations for what an Indian meal is like. Here the cocktails are accomplished, the indoor and outdoor dining rooms are breezy and sophisticated, and the menu is a wickedly smart mashup of Indian fare with specialties of other world cuisines. So that might mean Spanish octopus with Vietnamese green apple *nuoc cham,* or a bruleed pate of chicken liver, or truffled naan bread. Dishes are mostly small plates, so diners get a number of flavors in the course of a meal. And the menu for vegans and vegetarians is substantial. Daily happy hour (2–6pm) means drink and food specials. Sunday brunch in two words: breakfast naan. Chef Marathe also has a nearby restaurant, **Ela Curry & Cocktails** (4650 Donald Ross Rd; elacurryandcocktails.com), that serves more traditional Indian fare. Both eateries are in suburban Palm Beach Gardens, but we think they're worth the drive.

2000 PGA Blvd., Palm Beach Gardens. stagepga.com. © **561/408-3685.** Main courses $13–$45. Sun–Thurs 11:30am–11pm; Fri–Sat 11:30am–midnight.

INEXPENSIVE

Green's Pharmacy ★★ AMERICAN This neighborhood pharmacy and luncheonette dates back to 1939 and offers one of the best meal deals in Palm Beach. Both breakfast and lunch are served coffee-shop-style, either at a Formica bar or at tables on a black-and-white checkerboard floor. Breakfast specials include eggs and omelets served with home fries and bacon, sausage, or corned-beef hash. The grill serves burgers and sandwiches, as well as ice-cream sodas and milkshakes, to a loyal crowd of pastel-clad Palm Beachers.

151 N. County Rd., Palm Beach. *561/832-0304.* Main courses $5–$20. Mon–Sat 7am–3pm; Sun 7am–1pm.

Howley's ★★ AMERICAN   A diner with full bar, jukebox, tin ceilings, and retro '50s-meets-21st-century decor, Howley's is where the cool kids eat all five meals a day (we're counting brunch and late-night snacks). Fun, friendly servers slinging comfort food (including "snackaroos" like fried green tomatoes, buffalo wings, or artichoke dip) are thoroughly modern throwbacks, with multiple piercings, fluorescent hair, and masterpiece tattoos—much like the crowd. The menu is all over the place as a diner's should be, from Coney Island hot dogs and cheeseburgers to pastas, meatloaf, and all-day breakfast dishes. Best of all, Howley's is open late.

4700 S. Dixie Hwy., West Palm Beach. sub-culture.org. *561/832-0304.* Main courses $5–$20. Sun–Thurs 7am–midnight; Fri–Sat 7am–2am.

Pig Beach BBQ ★★ BARBECUE   A smoked-meat sanctuary from Kentucky, you'll smell this place well before you get there (a good thing). Chef Jeff's salt-and-pepper-crusted brisket with pickles, crispy onions, and his award-winning barbecue sauce is what keeps the crowds packing in as early as 9:30 on Sunday mornings. For sides, the purple coleslaw with smoked jalapeno and pineapple is outstanding. The mac and cheese and collards are also mainstays. For dessert—it is called PIG Beach, you know—there's soft serve ice cream and a fantastic Key lime pie. Oink.

2400 S. Dixie Hwy., West Palm Beach. pigbeachnyc.com. *561/803-0333.* Main courses $12–$23. Mon 4–9pm; Tues–Fri 11:30am–9pm; Sat 11:30am–10pm; Sun 9:30am–6pm.

Tropical Smokehouse ★★★ BARBECUE   This James Beard-nominated spot features chef Rick Mace's magnificently smoked meats, seafood, and SoFlo-inspired sides and starters including smoky black beans, plantains, crispy yuca, chorizo queso, brisket empanada, and more. It's an order-at-the-counter spot with long waits in season, but it's worth it. There's a full bar with a fabulous daily happy hour from 4:30 to 5:30pm featuring $5 burgers, and for those who don't want to wait, a downtown **Tropical BBQ Market,** 206 S. Olive Ave., where you can take out items.

3815 S. Dixie Hwy., West Palm Beach. eattropical.com. *561/323-2573.* $10–$20 main dishes (more for full racks of ribs). Tues–Sun 11:30am–9pm.

Chef Rick Mace of Tropical Smokehouse.

Palm Beach After Dark

Clematis Street, West Palm Beach's hub of nightlife, and its surroundings, also known as the Clematis District, has experienced an immense resurgence, with a slew of new dining destinations, retailers, and nightspots. Among them are luxe lounges like the modern **123 Datura,** 125 Datura St. (123datura.com; ✆ **561/619-8902**), and **Camelot,** 114 S. Narcissus Ave. (sub-culture.org; ✆ **561/408-1001**), a nautical spot that pays homage to the halcyon days of the Kennedy family on Palm Beach. Then there's **E.R. Bradley's Saloon,** 104 S. Clematis St. (erbradleys.com; ✆ **561/833-3520**), a former Palm Beach landmark that crossed over the bridge and is now a West Palm watering hole and landmark for locals. Back on "the island," in addition to the stalwarts like **Swifty's** (in the Colony, p. 287), **Lola 41** at the White Elephant, and **HMF** at the Breakers, there's a big late-night (meaning it goes at least until past 11pm) scene at Italian restaurant **Cucina Dell'Arte,** 257 Royal Poinciana Way (cucinapalmbeach; ✆ **561/655-0770**), catering to a motley mixture of young and old locals who moved here from the now defunct Worth Avenue mainstay Ta'boo. Then there's **Le Bar a Vin,** 380 S. County Rd. (lebarpalmbeach.com; ✆ **561/490-1456**), which prides itself on being the island's only wine bar, where locals come and sip vintages almost as, um, aged as them, with over 45 wines and champagnes by the glass, as well as charcuterie, cigars, and a white piano as shiny as the shoes on some of the dapper dapplers.

THE PERFORMING ARTS

With a number of dedicated patrons and enthusiastic supporters of the arts, this area happily boasts many good venues for those craving culture. Check the *Palm Beach Post* (palmbeachpost.com) or the *Palm Beach Daily News* (palmbeachdailynews.com) for up-to-date listings and reviews.

The **Raymond F. Kravis Center for the Performing Arts,** 701 Okeechobee Blvd., West Palm Beach (kravis.org; ✆ **561/832-7469**), is the area's largest and most active performance space. With a huge curved-glass facade and more than 2,500 seats in two lushly decorated indoor spaces, plus a new outdoor amphitheater, the Kravis stages more than 300 performances each year. Phone or check the website for a current schedule of Palm Beach's best music, dance, and theater.

THE TAMPA BAY AREA

by Lesley Abravanel and Beth Luberecki

9

When some people hear the word *Tampa*, they think of Busch Gardens and never even mention Tampa's bay area. They're missing out: Tampa is a stunning city, one that has morphed into a bustling urban metropolis that rivals Miami. The two are totally different, of course, but Tampa has definitely come into its own. If you haven't had a chance to explore Florida's bay area, here's your chance. There's so much more to the area than beer and amusement parks.

As Florida's own city by the bay, Tampa has a vibrant culture, with roots planted in Cuban and American history.

The city of Tampa is the commercial center of Florida's west coast—a growing seaport and center of banking and high-tech manufacturing. You can come downtown during the day to observe the sea life at the Florida Aquarium and stroll through the Henry B. Plant Museum, housed in an ornate, Moorish-style hotel built more than a century ago to lure tourists to the city. A short trolley ride will take you from downtown Tampa to Ybor City, the historic Cuban enclave, now a bustling, often rowdy, nightlife and dining hot spot.

Two bridges and a causeway will whisk you west across Old Tampa Bay to St. Petersburg, Pinellas Park, Clearwater, Dunedin, Tarpon Springs, and other cities on the Pinellas Peninsula, one of Florida's most densely packed urban areas. Over here on the bay, photo-ready downtown St. Petersburg is famous for wintering seniors, a shopping and dining complex built on a pier, and, surprisingly, the world's largest Salvador Dalí collection.

Keep driving west and you'll come to a line of barrier islands, where St. Pete Beach, Clearwater Beach, and other Gulf-side communities boast 28 miles of sunshine, surf, and white sand.

Heading south, I-275 will take you across the mouth of Tampa Bay to Sarasota and another chain of barrier islands that stretches 42 miles along the coast. One of Florida's cultural centers, affluent Sarasota is the gateway to St. Armands and Longboat keys, two playgrounds of the rich and famous, and to Lido and Siesta keys, both attractive to families of more modest means.

TAMPA

200 miles SW of Jacksonville; 85 miles SW of Orlando; 254 miles NW of Miami

Even if you stay on the beaches 20 miles to the west, you should consider driving into Tampa for a taste of metropolis. If you have children, they may *demand* that you go there so they can enjoy the rides and see the animals at Busch Gardens Tampa Bay. Once there, you can also educate them (and yourself) at the Florida Aquarium and the city's other museums. And historic Ybor City has some of the bay area's liveliest nightlife.

PREVIOUS PAGE: **Stargazing on the beach in Sarasota.**

Tampa was a sleepy little port when Cuban immigrants founded Ybor City's cigar industry in the 1880s. A few years later, Henry B. Plant put Tampa on the tourist map by building a railroad that ran into town and by constructing bulbous minarets atop his garish Tampa Bay Hotel, now a museum. During the Spanish-American War, Teddy Roosevelt trained his Rough Riders here and walked the Ybor City streets with Cuban revolutionary José Martí. A land boom in the 1920s gave the city its charming, Victorian-style Hyde Park suburb just across the Hillsborough River from downtown.

Today's downtown skyline is the product of booms across the last 40 years. Banks built skyscrapers and the city put up an expansive convention center, a performing arts center, and Amalie Arena (formerly the St. Pete Times Forum), a 20,000-seat bayfront arena that is home to professional hockey's Tampa Bay Lightning. In recent years, the seaport area east of downtown has been redeveloped. That's the area of the Florida Aquarium and the Garrison Seaport Center (a major home port for cruise ships bound for Mexico and the Caribbean) plus a big shopping-and-dining center known as Sparkman Wharf.

You won't necessarily want to spend your *entire* vacation in Tampa, but it offers a lot as a modern city on the go.

Essentials

GETTING THERE **Tampa International Airport** (tampaairport.com; © **813/870-8770**), 5 miles northwest of downtown Tampa, is the major air gateway to this area. **St. Petersburg–Clearwater International Airport** has limited service; see "St. Petersburg," later in this chapter. Most major and many no-frills airlines serve Tampa International. All of the major car rental companies have offices here, too.

The **SuperShuttle Express** (supershuttle.com; © **800/258-3826**) operates van services between the airport and hotels throughout the Tampa Bay area. **Yellow Cab** (yctampa.com; © **813/253-0121**) and **United Taxi** (© **727/777-7777**) serve the airport. Minimum fare from the airport is $15, and the average fare to downtown Tampa is $25.

Amtrak trains arrive downtown at the **Union Station,** 601 Nebraska Ave. N. (amtrak.com; © **800/872-7245**).

GETTING AROUND The public transportation situation has improved dramatically with its nostalgic and free **TECO Line Street Car System** (tecolinestreetcar.org; © **813/254-4278**), a new but old-fashioned 2⅓-mile streetcar system, complete with overhead power lines, that hauls passengers between downtown and Ybor City via Centennial Park, with 11 stops. The cars run every 15 minutes (every 12 min. during peak hours Fri–Sun 1–9pm). It's a fun way to explore the city, but most visitors will find they still need a car to see everything they wish to see.

VISITOR INFORMATION **Visit Tampa Bay,** 201 N. Franklin St. (visittampabay.com; © **813/223-2752**) has advice, maps, and brochures. The **Ybor City Visitor Information Center,** 1600 E. 8th Ave. (in the Centro Ybor Complex; centroybor.com; © **813/241-8838;** Mon–Sat 10am–4pm, Sun noon–4pm), also distributes info and has good exhibits on the area's history.

Animal & Theme Parks

Adventure Island ★ If the summer heat gets to you before one of Tampa's famous thunderstorms brings late afternoon relief, you can take a break at this

30-acre outdoor water theme park near Busch Gardens Tampa Bay (see below). You can also frolic here during the cooler days of spring and fall, when the water is heated. The Aruba Tuba, Rapids Racer, Solar Vortex, the Water Moccasin, and the super-scary Vanish Point will drench the teens, while other, calmer rides are geared toward younger kids. New in 2024 is Castaway Falls, a kid-friendly interactive splash and play area. There are places to picnic and sunbathe, restaurants, and stores.

10001 Malcolm McKinley Dr. (btw. Busch Blvd. and Bougainvillea Ave.). adventureisland.com. **813/987-5600.** Admission at least $47.99 ages 3 and up. Parking $30. Hours change seasonally; check website. Take exit 50 off I-275 and go east on Busch Blvd. for 2 miles. Turn left onto McKinley Dr. (N. 40th St.); entry is on the right.

Busch Gardens Tampa Bay ★★★

Although its heart-pounding thrill rides get most of the ink, this venerable theme park (it predates Disney World) ranks among the largest zoos in the country. It's a don't-miss attraction with wild animals from across the globe—and you'll get better views of them here than at Disney's Animal Kingdom in Orlando (p. 382). Busch Gardens Tampa Bay has more than 2,000 exotic animals living in natural-style environments. Most authentic is the 65-acre plain, reminiscent of the real Serengeti of Tanzania and Kenya, upon which zebras, rhinos, giraffes, and other animals graze. Unlike the animals on the real Serengeti, however, these grazing creatures have nothing to fear from lions, hyenas, crocodiles, and other predators, which are confined to enclosures—as are the hippos and elephants. Located in the area that formerly housed the Budweiser Clydesdales, a cheetah habitat gives visitors the opportunity to get closer to them than ever with elevated, glass-paneled viewing areas.

Thrills galore at Busch Gardens.

But back to those thrill rides. The park's seventh roller coaster—there are 10 in total—**SheiKra,** was the nation's first dive coaster, carrying riders up 200 feet at 45 degrees and then hurtling them 70 mph back at a 90-degree angle. **Cheetah Run,** a Linear Synchronous Motor (LSM) Launch Coaster, uses the force of repelling magnets to launch riders from 0 to 60 in a matter of seconds. For the real thrill seekers, the wood-and-steel hybrid coaster **Iron Gwazi** plunges brave riders from a 206-foot-tall peak into a 91-degree drop at 76 miles an hour. Experts voted it best new coaster in 2022 and best hybrid coaster in the world in 2023. A more family-friendly coaster, **Phoenix Rising,** opened in 2024.

The park has 11 areas, each with its own theme, animals, live entertainment, thrill rides, kiddie attractions, dining, and shopping. A Skyride cable car soars over the park, offering a bird's-eye view of it all. The first "world" many visitors hit is **Morocco,** which is just beyond the entry gate to the right. A walled city with North African architecture, it features crafts demonstrations, and an exhibit of alligators and turtles. Over in **Egypt,** a replica of King Tut's tomb is the big lure; youngsters can dig for their own ancient treasures in a sand area. Adults and kids 54 inches or taller can ride **Montu,** once the tallest and longest inverted roller coaster in the world until its Williamsburg, Virginia, sibling opened.

From Egypt it's a short stroll to **Edge of Africa,** home to most of the large animals. Go to the Adventure Tours tent and see if you can get on a **Serengeti Safari,** one of the park's best zoologist-led wildlife tours. Added up-close experiences are also available, including a 6-hour zookeeper-for-a-day program and a nighttime safari by lantern light.

Next stop is **Nairobi,** with gorillas and chimpanzees in a lush rainforest habitat (the Myombe Reserve) as well as a 270-gallon aquarium that focuses on fish breeding methods (outside of collecting them from the wild). In the middle of all the excitement, you will find **Pantopia,** where Scorpion, one of the smaller roller coasters, is located along with the horrifying freefall ride, **Falcon's Fury.**

The **Congo** is next geographically, where the highlights are the rare white Bengal tigers that live in **Jungala,** the park's 4-acre attraction within the Congo featuring up-close animal interactions, multistory family play areas, rides, and live entertainment. The Congo is also home to **Kumba,** which plunges riders from 110 feet into a diving loop, where you get a full 3 seconds of feeling weightless while spiraling 360 degrees, before tearing through one of the world's largest vertical loops (54-in. minimum height for riders). The **Congo River Rapids** is here: round boats that float down a swiftly flowing "river" (42-in. height minimum). Most riders get drenched on this one.

From the Congo, **Stanleyville,** a prototype African village, is next, with a shopping bazaar, and the Stanleyville Theater, featuring shows for all ages. Three rides are here: **Tigris,** the park's ninth coaster, **Stanley Falls Flume** (an aquatic version of a roller coaster), and the floorless **SheiKra,** which goes 200 feet up and 90 degrees straight down. It has a water-feature finale. *Tip:* Zambia Smokehouse here serves some of the best grub in the park (chicken and ribs).

Up next is **Sesame Street Safari of Fun** for the young ones and those, ahem, too frightened to partake in some of the other rides. It has tiny tot-friendly attractions like the Air Grover junior coaster, Elmo's Tree House (a jungle gym on steroids), and Bert and Ernie's water play area. The Sesame Street characters take part in shows, and you can have a meal with them.

Final stop, if you're doing this geographically, is **Bird Gardens,** the park's original core, offering lagoons and Florida flamingos. In 2024 **Walkabout Way,** an immersive Australian animal attraction, opened here. Visitors can hand-feed kangaroos and wallabies in Kangaloom during scheduled feedings throughout the day. Kookaburra's Nest is a free flight aviary. **Springs Taproom,** a casual restaurant and bar, also opened here in 2024.

3000 E. Busch Blvd. (at McKinley Dr./N. 40th St.). buschgardens.com. **888/800-5447.** Single-day tickets start at $99.99 ages 3 and up. Parking $30. Normal park hours 10am–6pm; hours extended during select weekends, summer, and holidays. Take I-275 north of downtown to Busch Blvd. (exit 50) and go east 2 miles. From I-75, take Fowler Ave. (exit 54) and follow the signs west.

The Florida Aquarium ★★★ Both *USA Today* and the Travel Channel ranked this aquarium as one of the 10 best in the United States and for good reason: Not only does it shine a spotlight on more than 20,000 aquatic animals and plants, it does so in innovative ways. In 2023 it debuted the exhibit **MORPH'D,** part of an ongoing $40-million expansion to the facility, which concentrates on the weirdos of the ocean, those creatures that are able to camouflage themselves, or have adapted to their environments in odd ways, like walking sharks, four-eyed fish, and electric eels. Not only do visitors get to view these critters, interactive displays allow them to quickly learn where they come from, what they eat, and how they adapt, the last via well-executed videos. On the touch tank front, it not only has the usual one for stingrays (yawn), but the only one in the Northeast that allows visitors to pet those otherworldly invertebrates known as moon jellies (head to **Moon Bay**). It also jumps briefly from land to sea with **Journey to Madagascar** displaying lemurs, tomato frogs, and, gag, hissing cockroaches. The **Coral Reef** is the aquarium's largest habitat with over 500,000 gallons of water in which tiger sharks, sea turtles, and giant stingrays swim.

The Florida Aquarium.

The aquarium also hosts a number of extra-charge, but pretty remarkable experiences, like an underwater walking tour—no swimming necessary—at the bottom of the 15-foot Heart of the Sea habitat ($95/person) during which visitors come face-to-face with all sorts of friendly sea creatures. A 45-minute interactive penguin encounter allows guests to get up close and personal with the cute creatures ($75). Most affordable is the 90-minute Eco Tour cruises on the *Bay Spirit II,* a 72-foot catamaran ($17 adults, $16 seniors, $15 kids 3–11) where zoologists help guests spot birds and fish. Expect to spend 3 to 4 hours here.

701 Channelside Dr. flaquarium.org. ✆ **813/273-4000.** Admission from $30.95 adults, $27.95 seniors, $26.45 children 3–11. Valet parking $40 for 3 hr. or more, $20 for up to 3 hr. Daily 9:30am–5pm.

ZooTampa at Lowry Park ★★ While it's not as extensive as Busch Gardens, Tampa's beloved zoo features over 1,000 animals from Africa, Asia, Australia, South America, and Florida, on nearly 60 acres of natural outdoor habitats year-round. Guests will find many interactive exhibits and opportunities to get closer to wildlife: feed a giraffe, ride a dromedary camel, hold a lorikeet, and more. The zoo's **David A. Straz, Jr., Manatee Critical Care Center** expands the traditional boundaries of a zoo, focusing efforts on critical care for injured, sick,

TWO safari SIDE TRIPS

Just 43 miles east of Tampa is Lakeland, home to the corporate offices of ubiquitous Florida supermarket chain Publix and the **Safari Wilderness Ranch ★★**, 10850 Moore Rd., Lakeland (✆ **813/382-2120**), a 260-acre piece of Old Florida smack in the middle of the Green Swamp, the second largest wilderness area in the state after the Everglades, as well as the heart of the Florida Aquifer. You can explore the wilderness in many ways—on ATVs, kayaks, open-air safari truck, your own car, or on a camel! The ranch specializes in wetland exotic species like African Watusi and Irish Dexter cattle, though it also has zebras, ostriches, ring-tailed lemurs, cheetahs, and other creatures. Tours range from $89 to $239 with optional add-ons, including encounters with cheetahs and lemurs.

Dade City is equidistant from Tampa as Lakeland, but north rather than east, and has a similar attraction: the 50-acre **Giraffe Ranch ★★**, 38650 Mickler Rd. (girafferanch.com). It's a bit pricier, starting at $150 per car per tour, but has some intriguing activities, including the ability to hand feed cabbage leaves to the giraffes, see lots of animals from Africa, and do the safari in their goofy Tesla cybertruck.

---

and orphaned wild manatees. The zoo also offers splash ground/water play areas, wild rides, educational shows, animal encounters, and a cafe.

1101 W. Sligh Ave. zootampa.org. ✆ **813/935-8552**. Admission $47.95 ages 12 and up, $37.95 children 3–11. Daily 9:30am–5pm. Take I-275 to Sligh Ave. (exit 48) and follow the signs.

Visiting the Museums

Glazer Children's Museum ★ Most notable for exhibiting the largest triceratops fossil in the world, this museum is a toddler paradise (but a bit dull for older kids). A good rainy-day option.

110 W. Gasparilla Plaza. glazermuseum.org. ✆ **813/443-3861**. Admission $24.95. Tues–Sun 9:30am–5pm.

Henry B. Plant Museum ★★ Built in 1891 by railroad tycoon Henry B. Plant as the 511-room Tampa Bay Hotel, this ornate building is worth a trip across the river from downtown to the University of Tampa campus. Its 13 silver minarets and Moorish architecture, modeled after the Alhambra in Spain, make this National Historic Landmark a focal point of the Tampa skyline. Although the building is the highlight of a visit, don't skip its contents: art and furnishings from Europe and Asia, plus exhibits that explain the history of the railroad resort, Florida's early tourist industry, and the hotel's role as a staging point for Theodore Roosevelt's Rough Riders during the Spanish-American War. If you're here in December, lucky you: The museum becomes the site of a Victorian Christmas Stroll, with each room dolled up in 19th-century Yuletide garb and carolers crooning.

401 W. Kennedy Blvd. (btw. Hyde Park and Magnolia aves.). plantmuseum.com. ✆ **813/254-1891**. Admission Jan–Nov $12 adults, $10 seniors and students, $9 children 4–18 (add $6 to all rates in Dec). Jan–Nov daily 10am–5pm. Take Kennedy Blvd. (Fla. 60) across the Hillsborough River.

MOSI (Museum of Science and Industry) ★
Like the Glaser, MOSI is a decent rainy-day option for families, but don't go out of your way to visit it. MOSI features 40,000 square feet of interactive activities and experiences, including a 36-foot-high ropes course, and virtual-reality explorations (under the sea, into space, back to the days of dinosaurs) that vary in effectiveness. A minigolf course explains the principles of physics. Outside, trails wind through a nature preserve with a butterfly garden.

4801 E. Fowler Ave. (at N. 50th St.). mosi.org. **813/987-6100.** Admission $14 adults, $10 children 3–17. Daily 9am–5pm or later. From downtown, take I-275 N. to Fowler Ave. E., exit 51. Take this 2 miles east to museum on right.

Tampa Bay History Center ★★
No dusty artifacts behind glass here! This engaging, and highly interactive, 60,000-square-foot museum brings to life some 500 years of recorded history, and 12,000 years of human habitation in the region. That includes the sports legends who called Florida home, the tycoons who reshaped the state, the Tocobaga people who lived here for centuries, the cigar makers who rolled in a new industry to Ybor City, and more. The museum's videos, especially, are quite well done. On the top floor is the favorite of adults and kids alike: a replica pirate ship, with actual artifacts from shipwrecks, that's a heckuva lot of fun to explore (it has a lot of bells and whistles I won't give away). Most visitors dedicate 2 to 3 hours to seeing it all, and include a meal at the museum's eatery, an offshoot of Columbia Café, the classic Ybor City Cuban restaurant.

The museum also offers 90-minute, 1-mile **walking tours** through some of Tampa's most historic areas. These take place every Saturday at 10am ($20/adult, $10/child 7–17). The tours depart from the Cuban Club, 2010 N. Avenida Republica de Cuba (aka N. 14th St.).

801 Old Water St. tampabayhistorycenter.org. **813/228-0097.** Admission $17 adults, $15 seniors, $13 children 7–17, free for ages 6 and under. Free parking. Mon–Fri 9am–5pm.

Tampa Museum of Art ★★★
In 2023, the Tampa Museum of Art added seven new gallery spaces, and an education center, to its already comely $43.6 million waterfront building. A near-future expansion will double the gallery space again, adding a dramatic, mostly glass, rectangular building to the current one. All of this will house what has long been one of the region's most impressive collections of classical antiquities, bronze sculptures, modern decorative arts, and sculpture by neoclassicist Hiram Powers and cubist Jacques Lipchitz. The museum's other treasures include prints by James Rosenquist, Robert Rauschenberg, and Vik Muniz, and photographs by Cindy Sherman, Henri Cartier-Bresson, Garry Winogrand, and Andy Warhol. Temporary exhibits are sometimes blockbusters, featuring big names in contemporary art. ***Tip:*** A 14,000-square-foot site LED installation on the building's facade is an iconic fixture on the city's skyline. It's best viewed from Curtis Hixon Park.

120 W. Gasparilla Plaza, downtown. tampamuseum.org. **813/274-8130.** Admission $25 adults, $15 seniors, $5 children grades K-12. Mon–Sun 10am–5pm; Thurs 10am–8pm. Take I-275 to exit 44 (Ashley Dr.).

Ybor City

Northeast of downtown, the city's historic Latin district takes its name from Don Vicente Martinez Ybor (*Eeee*-bore), a Spanish cigar maker who arrived here in

1886 via Cuba and Key West. Soon, his factory and others in Tampa were producing more than 300,000 hand-rolled stogies a day.

It may not be the cigar capital of the world anymore, but Ybor is still a smokin' part of Tampa, and it's one of the best places in Florida to buy hand-rolled cigars. It's not on par with New Orleans's Bourbon Street, Key West's Duval Street, or Miami's South Beach, but good food and great music dominate the scene, especially on weekends when the streets bustle until 4am. Live-music offerings run the gamut from jazz and blues to rock.

At the heart of it all is **Centro Ybor,** a brick-paved, wrought-iron-balconied dining-shopping-entertainment complex between 7th and 8th avenues and 16th and 17th streets (centroybor.com; ✆ **813/242-4660**). Here you'll find a comedy club, an arcade, several restaurants and bars.

Tampa Bay Tours (tampabay-tours.com; ✆ **813/406-2180**) offers four fascinating tours of the area, including the **Ybor City Ghost Tour,** taking you to the sites of the strange and creepy happenings of Tampa's historic Latin district. Cost is $30 for adults, $10 for kids 6 to 12. For a different kind of sinister, the **Tampa Mafia** (tampamafia.com; ✆ **813/358-3455**) has a 90-minute tour usually led by Scott M. Deitche, author of *Cigar City Mafia: A Complete History of the Tampa Underworld* and *The Silent Don: The Criminal Underworld of Santo Trafficante Jr.* (Tampa historian Manny Leto sometimes also leads this tour.) It goes through some of Tampa's shadier alleys, street corners, and spots where alleged wise guys conducted business. You'll learn about the rumored tunnels of Ybor and the area's so-called Era of Blood. They also do happy hour tours with booze. Cost is $30 per person.

Even if you're not a cigar smoker, you'll enjoy a stroll through the **Ybor City Museum State Park,** 1818 9th Ave., between 18th and 19th streets (ybormuseum.org; ✆ **813/247-1434;** daily 9am–5pm,), covering about half of a city block and consisting of the **Ybor City Museum,** an ornamental garden, and several restored worker's "casitas." The museum is housed in the former Ferlita Bakery (1896–1973). You can take a self-guided tour to see the collection of cigar labels, cigar memorabilia, and works by local artisans. Admission is $4, free for children 6 and under. Admission includes a 15-minute guided tour of **La Casita,** a renovated cigar worker's cottage adjacent to the museum; it's furnished as it was at the turn of the 20th century. You have the best chance for the guided tour if you visit between 11am and 3pm. Better yet, plan to catch a cigar-rolling demonstration, held Friday through Sunday from 10am to 3pm.

The Ybor City Museum Society also operates the **Tampa Baseball Museum** in the historic Al Lopez House, 2003 N. 19th St. (tampabaseballmuseum.org; ✆ **813/247-1434**), featuring over 125 years of ball history.

Outdoor Activities & Spectator Sports

BIKING, SKATING & JOGGING Bayshore Boulevard, a 7-mile-long promenade on the shores of Hillsborough Bay, is a favorite with runners, walkers, and in-line skaters. The route goes from the western edge of downtown in a southward direction, passing stately old homes in Hyde Park, high-rise condos, retirement communities, and houses of worship, ending at Ballast Point Park. The view from the promenade across the bay to the downtown skyline is matchless. (Bayshore Blvd. is also great for a drive.)

CANOEING & KAYAKING Rent your own canoe or kayak and take a self-guided tour through **Upper Tampa Bay Conservation Park,** 8001 Double

Branch Rd. (hcfl.gov; ✆ **813/855-1765**), a 596-acre peninsular park with mangrove forests, salt- and freshwater marshes, coastal hammocks, and flatwoods. There's also an abundance of wildlife including bottle-nosed dolphins and manatees. Rentals and paddling maps are available at the park's entry station. Rates are $25 for 4 hours and $10 for each additional hour. Entry fee to the park is $2 per vehicle. Park is open from 8am to 6pm.

FISHING For charters, try **Tampa Fishing Charters** (fishnfl.com; ✆ **813/945-7830**), which offers inshore, offshore, tarpon, and shark fishing charters. Rates are $800 to $1,200 for a half-day for up to four, $1,600 to $1,800 for a full day. Then there's **Tampa Fishing Charters, Inc.** (tampafishingcharters.com; ✆ **813/245-4738**), more for beginners and with affordable rates starting at $425 for four.

GOLF Tampa has three municipal golf courses where you can play for about $30 to $35, a relative pittance compared to fees at private courses. The **Babe Zaharias Golf Course** ★★, 11412 Forest Hills Dr., north of Lowry Park (babezahariasgolf.net; ✆ **813/631-4374**), is an 18-hole, par-70 course with a pro shop, putting greens, and a driving range. It is the shortest of the municipal courses, but its small greens and narrow fairways present ample challenges. Water provides obstacles on 12 of the 18 holes at **Rocky Point Golf Course** ★★, 4151 Dana Shores Dr. (rockypointgolf.net; ✆ **813/673-4316**), between the airport and the bay. It's a par-71 course with a pro shop, a practice range, and putting greens. On the Hillsborough River in north Tampa, the **Rogers Park Golf Course** ★★, 7910 N. 30th St. (rogersparkgolf.net; ✆ **813/673-4396**), is an 18-hole, par-72 championship course with a lighted driving and practice range. The courses are open daily from 7am to dusk. Club rentals are available.

You can book starting times and get info about area courses by contacting **Tee Times USA** (teetimesusa.com; ✆ **800/374-8633**).

If you want to do some serious work on your game, book a lesson at **Saddlebrook Golf Academy,** 5700 Saddlebrook Way, Wesley Chapel, 12 miles north of Tampa (saddlebrook.com; ✆ **800/729-8383** or 813/973-1111). Half-day and hourly instruction is available, as well as multi-day programs.

SPECTATOR SPORTS The **Tampa Bay Rays** are a hugely popular draw for sports fans. The Rays' home base, Tropicana Field, 1 Tropicana Dr., St. Petersburg (mlb.com/rays; ✆ **727/825-3137**), was significantly damaged during 2024's Hurricane Milton. The team is playing at **George M. Steinbrenner Field** (gmsfield.com; ✆ **813/875-7753**) for the 2025 season, and a repair plan for Tropicana Field was still being developed as we went to press. Steinbrenner Field is also the spring-training home of the **New York Yankees** from mid-February to the end of March. This scaled-down replica of Yankee Stadium is the largest spring-training facility in Florida, with a 10,000-seat capacity. Tickets for the Yankees are $45 to $120. Season tickets are expensive and hard to come by.

National Football League fans can catch the **Tampa Bay Buccaneers** at the modern, 66,000-seat Raymond James Stadium, 4201 N. Dale Mabry Hwy., at Dr. Martin Luther King, Jr., Boulevard (buccaneers.com; ✆ **813/879-2827**), August through December. Single-game tickets are very hard to come by, as they are usually sold out to season-ticket holders. This is a huge football city.

The National Hockey League's **Tampa Bay Lightning,** winners of the 2020 and 2021 Stanley Cup, play in the Amalie Arena starting in October (nhl.com/lightning; ✆ **813/301-6500**). You can usually get single-game tickets ($63–$271) on game day.

The only thoroughbred racetrack on Florida's west coast is **Tampa Bay Downs,** 11225 Racetrack Rd., Oldsmar (tampadowns.com; ✆ **813/855-4401**), home of the Tampa Bay Derby. Races are held Wednesday, Friday, Saturday, and Sunday from December to May (free on Wed, $3 Fri–Sun), and the track presents simulcasts year-round.

TENNIS/PICKLEBALL The **Sandra W. Freedman Tennis Complex,** 59 Columbia Dr. (tampa.gov; ✆ **813/259-1664**), is a staffed facility with eight clay courts and a practice wall open Monday through Friday from 8am to 9pm and Saturday and Sunday from 8am to 6pm. Rates are $6.45 per adult during prime hours (Mon–Fri 9am–noon and 4–9pm; Sat–Sun 8am–noon and 4–6pm) and $5.38 during non-prime hours. The **Tampa Pickleball Crew** (tampapickleball crew.com) opened an eight-court, open-air facility in Ybor at 1701 E. 2nd Ave. A day pass is just $14.

Shopping

Hyde Park Village, 1602 W. Snow Ave. (hydeparkvillage.com; ✆ **813/251-3500**), is a terrific alternative to cookie-cutter malls. This cluster of 50 upscale shops is set in a village layout in one of the city's most historic and picturesque neighborhoods. There's a free parking garage on South Oregon, Rome, and Swann avenues. Most shops are open Monday through Saturday from 10am to 8pm and Sunday from noon to 5pm. The village concerts, art festivals and other events.

The centerpiece of the downtown seaport renovation is **Sparkman Wharf,** 615 Channelside Drive (sparkman wharf.com; ✆ **813/618-5844**). It has stores, restaurants, bars, and a bowling alley. The Wharf is open Sunday through Thursday from 11am to 9pm, and 11am to 11pm on Fridays and Saturdays.

In Ybor City, **Centro Ybor,** on 7th Avenue East at 16th Street (centroybor.com; ✆ **813/242-4660**), is primarily a dining-and-entertainment complex, but you'll find a few retail shops. While Ybor City is no longer a major producer of hand-rolled cigars, you can still watch artisans making stogies at the **Columbia Restaurant Cigar Store** (columbiarestaurant.com). Rollers are on duty Monday through Friday from 11am to 3pm. You can stock up on domestic and imported cigars at **King Corona Cigars Bar and Cafe,** 1523 E. 7th Ave. (kingcoronacigars.com; ✆ **813/241-9109**); and **Tabanero Cigars,** 1601 E. 7th Ave. (tabanerocigars.com; ✆ **813/402-6316**).

A cigar roller plies his trade in Ybor City.

307

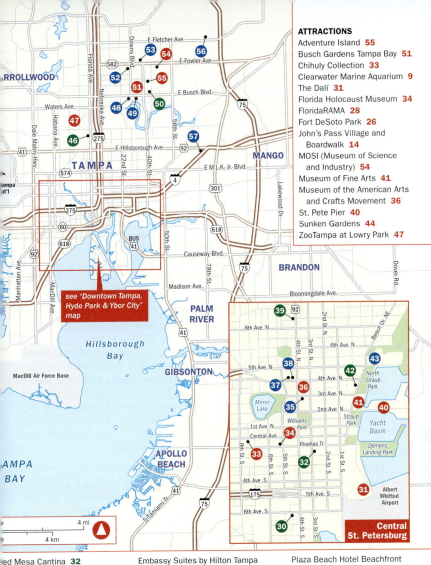

ATTRACTIONS

Adventure Island 55
Busch Gardens Tampa Bay 51
Chihuly Collection 33
Clearwater Marine Aquarium 9
The Dalí 31
Florida Holocaust Museum 34
FloridaRAMA 28
Fort DeSoto Park 26
John's Pass Village and Boardwalk 14
MOSI (Museum of Science and Industry) 54
Museum of Fine Arts 41
Museum of the American Arts and Crafts Movement 36
St. Pete Pier 40
Sunken Gardens 44
ZooTampa at Lowry Park 47

Red Mesa Cantina 32
Rooster & The Till 46
The Salt Rock Grill 13
The Studio Public House 27
Ted Peters' Famous Smoked Fish 15
Whiskey Joe's Bar & Grill 45

HOTELS
Avalon 37
Barefoot Bay Resort and Marina 6
Beach Haven 21
The Don CeSar 23

Embassy Suites by Hilton Tampa USF Near Busch Gardens 53
Hampton Inn & Suites 49, 56
Holiday Inn Express & Suites 48
The Hollander Hotel St. Petersburg Downtown 38
Hyatt Place Tampa/Busch Gardens 52
The Inn on Third 35
Innisbrook Golf Resort 1
Island's End Resort 25
JW Marriott Clearwater Beach Resort & Spa 8

Plaza Beach Hotel Beachfront Resort 22
The Saint Hotel 16
Sandpearl Resort 2
Seminole Hard Rock Hotel & Casino Tampa 57
Shephard's Beach Resort 7
Sheraton Sand Key Resort 11
Sirata Beach Resort 19
St. Pete Beach Suites 18
Vinoy Resort and Golf Club, Autograph Collection 43
Wyndham Grand Clearwater Beach 5

309

Where to Stay

The listings below are organized into two geographic areas: **near Busch Gardens Tampa Bay** and **downtown** (including **Ybor City** and **Hyde Park**). If you're going to Busch Gardens, Adventure Island, the zoo, or the Museum of Science and Industry (MOSI), the motels near Busch Gardens are much more convenient than those downtown, about 7 miles to the south. The downtown hotels are geared to business travelers, but staying there will put you near the city's museums, the Tampa Bay Performing Arts Center, scenic Bayshore Boulevard, and the dining and shopping opportunities in the Channelside and Hyde Park districts. Lodging in Ybor City is for those who want to be within walking distance of the city's liveliest nightspots.

The Westshore area, near the bay, west of downtown, and south of Tampa International Airport, is another commercial center, with a wide range of chain hotels catering to business travelers and conventioneers. It's not far from Raymond James Stadium and the New York Yankees' spring-training complex.

Room rates at most hotels in Tampa vary little from season to season. This is especially true downtown, where the hotels do a brisk convention business year-round. Hillsborough County adds 12% tax to your hotel bill.

NEAR BUSCH GARDENS TAMPA BAY

You won't find luxe near the park. But there are clean, comfortable motels like **Hampton Inn & Suites,** both the one at 3333 E. Busch Blvd. (hilton.com; © 813/605-5233) and the one at 8210 Hidden River Pkwy. (© **813/903-6000**). Also reliable is **Holiday Inn Express & Suites,** 2807 E. Busch Blvd. (ihg.com; © **813/936-8200**). The 500-room d Suites by Hilton Tampa USF Near Busch Gardens (yes, that's its entire name), 3705 Spectrum Blvd., facing Fowler Avenue (hilton.com; © **813/977-7066**), is a Busch Gardens "preferred partner hotel" that offers a free shuttle to the park, which is just 5 minutes away. Just south of Fowler Avenue **Hyatt Place Tampa/Busch Gardens,** 11408 N. 30th St. (hyatt.com; © **813/979-1922**) is another well-maintained, friendly option.

DOWNTOWN/YBOR CITY/HYDE PARK

Epicurean Hotel, Autograph Collection ★★ Located right across the street from famed Bern's Steak House (p. 313), this is, appropriately, a foodie-themed hotel. When guests check in, they're offered a complimentary glass of wine to sip in a lounge area decorated with boxes from famous wineries. Rooms pay homage to the culinary lifestyle with butcher block cabinetry, cutlery-patterned throw pillows, and pantries stocked with local craft beers, premium liquors, coffee, espresso, and half bottles of wine with snack pairings. A lobby restaurant, rooftop bar, and restaurant, **Élevage,** offer plenty of epicurean opportunities, including cooking and mixology classes. There's also a spa, a quiet pool, and for those looking to work off what they've eaten, a fitness center and an hour of free bike rental per stay. The hotel is partnered with Bern's so you get priority making reservations or can book a package that already includes one.

1207 S. Howard Ave., Tampa. epicureanhotel.com. © **813/999-8700**. 137 units. $238–$540 double. Valet parking $20. **Amenities:** Restaurant; 2 bars; concierge; fitness center; heated outdoor pool; room service; spa; bike rentals; free Wi-Fi.

Hotel Haya Ybor City ★★★ Named for Ybor City's first cigar roller, Ignacio Haya, this hotel's mission is to reflect and celebrate the character and culture of Ybor City, and it more than succeeds. Set in a historic brick building, many rooms have wood-tiled floors (like those on the streets of Havana), ovoid lamps reminiscent of the area's streetlamps, and abstract paintings by local artist Kristin Texeia. She's just one of the many local artisans represented in the hotel's decor, and much of the food and drink served here. Guest rooms have walkout balconies overlooking a bustling street, and the pool area is command central for DJs, pop-ups, and assorted "activations" which bring in the area's young and beautiful set. Dining options include the Latin-inspired **Flor Fina,** and contemporary Cuban coffee shop **Café Quiquiriquí.** The Haya is an evocative place to stay.

Downtown Tampa.

1412 E. 7th Ave., Tampa. hotelhaya.com. © **813/568-1200.** 178 units. $391–$553 double. Valet parking $28. Pet fee $75. **Amenities:** 2 restaurants; bar; concierge; fitness center; heated outdoor pool; room service; free Wi-Fi.

JW Marriott Tampa Water Street ★★   Many stay here specifically for the hotel's "Stay Well" guest rooms, designed to zap jet lag with circadian mood lighting, foil allergies with high-tech air purification systems and non-toxic cleaning products, and soften skin with shower infusers that reduce the amount of chlorine in the water. If only they could cure the boredom created by these luxurious but seriously cookie-cutter rooms. Ah well! Most won't mind, thanks to guest rooms' expansive views of the city and water. On the sixth floor are two pools, cabanas, a substantial spa and fitness area, and **SiX,** a bistro with magnificent views. The hotel also has a steakhouse, and rooftop bar/restaurant on the 27th floor (the city's highest). Connected to the JW via a third-floor glass skybridge is the Tampa Marriott Water Street (see below), an older property.

510 Water St., Tampa. marriott.com. © **813/221-4950.** 519 units. $369–$564 double. Valet parking $45. **Amenities:** 5 restaurants; 3 bars; 2 outdoor heated pools; gym; room service; spa; free Wi-Fi.

Seminole Hard Rock Hotel & Casino Tampa ★★   Tampa's Seminole Hard Rock Hotel & Casino is a place of nonstop action, which some travelers may enjoy. The casino has 178,000 square feet of Vegas-style slots, blackjack, baccarat, sports betting, and other games of chance. The hotel's 26,000-square-foot spa has a hammam plus a "Rhythm & Motion Room," in which music, vibration, bass, and treble are used to therapize. For meals, there's an even dozen restaurants on-site, of all types. Want to take a dip? There are three pools to choose from, each with its own set of cabanas. A newly constructed tower (East) rises 17 stories and has 550 rooms with modern amenities and large bathrooms (it's nicer than the older West building, so move if you get assigned there). The biggest mark against the place? Its location, in a somewhat run-down part of town.

5223 Orient Rd., Tampa. seminolehardrocktampa.com. © **866/388-4263.** 800 units. $342–$527 double. Pet fee $250. **Amenities:** 12 restaurants (including a food court); 8 bars; 3 pools; full-service spa; fitness center; free Wi-Fi.

The Tampa EDITION ★★★

The EDITION is a destination hotel, not a convention hub like the neighboring Marriotts. With a sleek, curvy exterior by celebrated architect Morris Adjmi, guest rooms are both Zen and sexy, with white oak floors, faux fur throws on the beds, and walls of windows. The lobby is a surreal take on a jungle, thanks to dozens of large potted plants bisected by a sculptural white spiral staircase. The five bars and restaurants on property are also high design scenes, from the **Arts Club** (a cocktail lounge swathed in red velvet, with a sea of disco balls on the ceiling) to the **Punch Room** (Caribbean cocktails, and again, lots of velvet). Most coveted reservation here is at **Lilac ★★**, a Mediterranean restaurant helmed by star chef John Fraser. A rooftop pool and bar underneath a canopy of bougainvillea and Japanese blueberry trees remind you that this isn't Busch Gardens' Tampa. The spa is also spectacular.

500 Channelside Dr., Tampa. marriott.com. © **813/221-4600.** 172 units. $385–$682 double. Valet parking $49. Pet fee $250. **Amenities:** 5 restaurants and bars; babysitting; concierge; fitness center; Jacuzzi; heated outdoor pool; room service; spa; free Wi-Fi.

Tampa Marriott Water Street ★★

Connected by a third-floor glass bridge to the swankier JW Marriott, the hotel was fully renovated in 2018. Rooms are Marriott-bland, but comfortable and most feature balconies. The hotel's "Stay Well" rooms, 35 of them, have the same types of wellness features that are available at the JW (see above) but at a lower price. There are also concierge-level rooms with free breakfast and honor bar. A large third-floor heated pool is surrounded by cabana pods, wicker couches, and requisite bar and grill. There's also a 32-slip marina, which is nice to walk through when the weather is nice.

505 Water St., Tampa. marriott.com. © **813/221-4900.** 727 units. $317–$476 double. Valet parking $45. Pet fee $150. **Amenities:** 4 restaurants; 3 bars; babysitting; concierge; concierge-level rooms; fitness center; Jacuzzi; heated outdoor pool; room service; spa; free Wi-Fi.

The Westin Tampa Waterside ★★

Close enough to downtown but still worlds away on its own 177-acre island, this newly renovated hotel is all about vacations (no conventions here). Rooms overlook the harbor and are hyper-comfortable, with pillow top mattresses and large bathrooms featuring dual shower heads. Stroll the boardwalk to fully appreciate your surroundings.

725 S. Harbour Island Blvd., Tampa. marriott.com. © **813/229-5000.** 309 units. $202–$357 double. Valet parking $45. Pet fee $50/night. **Amenities:** Restaurant; 3 bars; babysitting; concierge; fitness center; Jacuzzi; heated outdoor pool; room service; free Wi-Fi.

Where to Dine

The restaurants below are organized by geographic area: near Busch Gardens, downtown, in or near Hyde Park (across the Hillsborough River from downtown), and in Ybor City. Although Ybor City is better known, Tampa's trendiest dining scene is along South Howard Avenue—"SoHo" to the locals—between West

> **Price Categories**
>
> Meal per person, not including drinks or tip:
> **Inexpensive:** $20 and under
> **Moderate:** $21–$40
> **Expensive:** $40 and above

Kennedy Boulevard and the bay in Hyde Park, where there is a location of Palm Beach and Boca Raton's very sceney steakhouse, **Meat Market,** 1606 W. Snow Ave. (meatmarket.net; ✆ **813/280-1113**). We also highly recommend **Lilac** (see above) and **Olivia** (p. 319), which we feature in our nightlife section for their hopping bar, but the Italian food earlier in the evening is also highly recommendable.

NEAR BUSCH GARDENS

You'll find the national fast-food and family restaurants east of I-275 on Busch Boulevard and Fowler Avenue.

Inexpensive

Mel's Hot Dogs ★ AMERICAN   Former Chicagoland hippie Mel Lohn's red-and-white cottage offers everything from traditional Chicago-style to bacon/cheddar Reuben-style hot dogs. All choices are served on poppy seed buns and can be ordered with fries and a choice of coleslaw or baked beans. Even the decor is dedicated to wieners: The walls and windows are lined with hot dog memorabilia, and a wiener-mobile is usually parked out front. Mel's chili is outstanding, too. Other menu options: chicken sandwich, veggie burgers, Chicago beef, and terrific onion rings.

4136 E. Busch Blvd., at 42nd St. melshotdogs.com. ✆ **813/985-8000.** $3–$11. Daily 11am–8pm.

HYDE PARK

Expensive

Bern's Steak House ★★★ STEAKHOUSE   The unassuming exterior of this famous steakhouse, in business for over 70 years, is a stark contrast to its opulent interior, eight ornate dining rooms decorated with late 1950s elan and lots of mahogany paneling, marble busts, and chandeliers. The way plates are piled high also has its roots in the '50s: All entrees come with French onion soup, salad, baked potato, onion rings, and a selection of organic vegetables. Most diners go for Bern's strips, porterhouses, Delmonicos, and T-bones, all USDA Prime, and aged in-house for 5 to 8 weeks before being charbroiled over natural hardwood charcoal. Bern's also serves elk loin. The phonebook-size wine list—one of the restaurant's most famous attributes—has more than 6,800 labels, 150 by the glass. When you book your reservation, ask for a wine cellar tour. Upstairs, the restaurant's other most famous attribute—the **Harry Waugh Dessert Room**—has 48 romantic, semiprivate booths paneled in aged California redwood; each can privately seat from 2 to 12 guests. All of these little chambers are equipped with phones for placing your requests with the piano player. The dessert menu has 35 to 40 tough choices—and with ice-cream flavors, choices become 100 times harder—plus some 1,400 after-dinner drinks, wines, and spirits. You can go here just for desserts, but the dessert room is first-come, first-served unless you have dinner. For those who love cheese, Bern's has two indoor caves storing artisanal cheeses from around the world.

The big secret here is that steak sandwiches are available at the bar but are not mentioned on the menu. That bar was recently redesigned and is more modern than the rest of the spaces, but you can't just snag a barstool or table there: You must put your name on a wait list for either.

Haven, 2208 W. Morrison Ave., at South Howard Avenue (haventampa.com; ✆ 813/258-2233), is the restaurant's New American offshoot. It's also quite, quite good, but if you have only 1 night, choose the original.

1208 S. Howard Ave. (at Marjory Ave.). bernssteakhouse.com. ✆ 813/251-2421. Main courses $36–$158. Sun–Thurs 5–10pm; Fri–Sat 5–11pm. Haven: Tues–Thurs 5–9pm; Fri–Sat 5–10pm.

edison: food+drink lab ★★★

FUSION If you guessed from the name that this restaurant has molecular gastronomy ambitions you'd be somewhat right. Chef Jeannie Pierola isn't turning out foams or freeze-dried meats, but is, instead, experimenting with flavor profiles in a sophisticated, and quite appealing, way. Take the burrata appetizer. It's served with charred shishito peppers and pepita pesto, but also—here's the culinary alchemy—chipotle lime sorbet. The coffee-rubbed NY strip is elevated by potato mochi and a pumpkin seed gremolata. For dessert, a brown butter blondie is served with rose water, sumac caramel, nutmeg orange curd, and a saffron ice cream. It all works.

At Sparkman Wharf, Periola runs **edison's swigamajig** (swigamajig.com), a self-professed dive bar and seafood joint. She has another more upscale eatery called **Counter Culture** at 2909 W. Bay (cc-tampa.com).

912 W. Kennedy Blvd. edison-tampa.com. ✆ 813/254-7111. Main courses $26–$48. Mon–Thurs 4–9pm; Fri 4–10pm; Sat 5–10pm; Sun 5–9pm.

Chef/owner Jeannie Pierola of edison: food+drink lab.

Restaurant BT ★★★ VIETNAMESE

Chef/owner Trina Nguyen-Batley began her career in the fashion industry, so it's no surprise her dining room is the epitome of chic minimalism (love the Philip Starck ghost chairs). Her food—tweaked recipes from her childhood in Vietnam—offers maximal flavors and uses the bounty of Florida, as in her bouillabaisse of Key West pink prawns, king salmon, lobster claw, clams, saffron crustacean broth, and black garlic rouille. An appetizer of grass-fed beef tartare with passion fruit jus, and opal basil and cilantro grown in her own garden, is equally stunning. Vegans and vegetarians have a number of excellent options here, and the croissant bread pudding is a wonder.

2507 S. MacDill Ave. restaurantbt.com. ✆ 813/258-1916. Main courses $35–$65. Tues–Sat 5–9pm.

Moderate

Bella's Italian Cafe ★★ ITALIAN

Bella's has been open for more than 30 years and for good reason. The restaurant's authentic Italian fare is delicious, from the paper-thin carpaccio, to the old-fashioned spaghetti and meatballs. You can also create your own combination of pasta and sauce, choosing from a large list of options, or just order a pizza cooked in the oak-burning oven. Executive chef and co-owner Joanie Corneil studied cooking in Italy, and you can tell.

1413 S. Howard Ave. bellasitaliancafe.com. 813/254-3355. Main courses $13–$43 Mon–Thurs 11:30am–10:30pm; Fri 11:30am–1am; Sat 3pm–1am; Sun 3–10:30pm.

Mise en Place ★★ NEW AMERICAN Look around at all those happy people soaking up the trendy ambience, and you'll know why chef Marty Blitz and his wife, Maryann, have been among the culinary darlings of Tampa since 1986. They present the freshest of ingredients in a creative menu that changes weekly. Main courses often include venison loin cooked sous vide, with celery root chowchow and hot vinegar kale; or for vegetarians, a seared tofu with Aegean spices, mushroom and farro hash, and a carrot tahini sage vinaigrette. Ingredients may read like an unabridged culinary dictionary, but trust us, the mouthfuls are worth every word. Desserts are ridiculously good: The milk chocolate s'mores tart is beyond.

442 W. Kennedy Blvd. (at S. Magnolia Ave., opposite the University of Tampa). miseonline.com. 813/254-5373. Main courses $20–$43 except for steak and lamb. Tues–Thurs 5–9pm; Fri–Sat 5–10pm.

Oxford Exchange.

Oxford Exchange ★★★ AMERICAN We want to live in this place. A combo bookstore, retail store, candle store, champagne bar, coffee bar, and brunch hot spot, Oxford Exchange is an urban oasis of, well, everything good in life. It also has a look that's straight out of an interior design magazine: brick-walled, chandeliered, with art-filled dining rooms and a sunlit conservatory with rambling vines and retractable glass roof. Be sure to have a reservation, however, as this place is always PACKED—especially on weekends. All-day menus include breakfast favorites like avocado toast, apple crumble pancakes, omelets, and seriously good stone-ground yellow grits with aged white cheddar, crispy bacon, chives, and maple drizzle. There are also delicious salads, sandwiches, and, if you're feeling especially swanky—and you may, because it has that vibe here—caviar.

420 W. Kennedy Blvd., across from the University of Tampa. oxfordexchange.com. 813/253-0333. Main courses $12–$26. Daily 7:30am–5pm.

Inexpensive

Whiskey Joe's Bar & Grill ★ AMERICAN Gorgeous ocean views are why you're here, not the bar menu of beer-battered chicken, tacos, burgers, nachos, raw bar, and gator bites. The food is fine, but not memorable. Insist on sitting on the deck and time your meal around sundown; the vantage point for sunsets here makes developers drool. Live reggae on Sunday and happy hours Monday through Friday (3–6pm) make Whiskey Joe's a popular gathering spot for locals. *Note:* Whiskey Joe's is nearer to the airport and located on the causeway, so be sure to budget for the time it takes to get there. There are also locations in Port Richey, Pensacola Beach, Manatee River, and Port Charlotte.

7720 Courtney Campbell Causeway. whiskeyjoestampa.com. **813/281-0770.** Main courses $14–$25. Daily 11am–11pm.

YBOR CITY/CENTRAL TAMPA/DOWNTOWN TAMPA

Expensive

Ebbe–Chef's Counter ★★★ SCANDINAVIAN   Minimally processed foods that are locally sourced and sustainably produced: Those are the hallmarks of a meal at this tasting-menu-only restaurant from Michelin-starred Swedish chef Ebbe Vollmer. Eating here is an intimate experience, with diners tucking into either a five-course tasting menu, or an 11-course degustation, at a marble bar surrounding an open kitchen filled with hard-working chefs. Menus change seasonally but may include beet roulade with a brown butter and black cherry sauce; turbot and sturgeon caviar with fermented white asparagus beurre monté; or braised oxtail with seared foie gras and a brunoise of sunchoke. It's very fancy, but not intimidating (or murderous like Ralph Fiennes in *The Menu*).

1202 N. Franklin St. chefebbe.com. Tasting menu only $155–$295 per person. Tues–Sat 5–11pm.

Kōsen ★★★ JAPANESE   Chef Wei Chen, who spent 6 years at acclaimed NYC restaurant Masa, brings his stellar omakase to Tampa in the form of this minimalist, dark-wood restaurant that features a 10-person sushi counter and 25-seat dining room. Tasting menus run from a 15-course, $150 per person, to upwards of $250 for a 20+-course event. And event is exactly what this restaurant is. The 15-course Nigiri menu includes a slew of nigiri (raw fish) that you may need to Google, plus luxe extras like shaved black truffle. It's all spectacularly over the top and an experience, to say the least.

307 W. Palm Ave. kosentampa.com. **813/999-1720.** Tasting menu only $150–$250 per person. Mon–Sat 5–11pm. Closed Sun.

Moderate

Columbia Restaurant ★★★ SPANISH/CUBAN   Columbia celebrates 120 years as Florida's oldest restaurant in 2025 and is still owned and operated by the fourth and fifth generations of the Hernandez/Gonzmart families. Its palatial building occupies an entire city block in the heart of Ybor City. The hot, fresh Cuban bread is so delicious you'll want to fill up on it, but don't, because portions are giant from flavorful grilled steaks and chicken, to paella, mojitos and other cocktails, and sangria by the glass or pitcher. My favorite, the 1905 Salad, is mixed tableside with ham, cheese, lettuce, olives, greens, and a garlicky wine vinegar dressing that won't help you consummate any courtships, but is deservedly on sale by the bottle in the gift shop. And it's so much fun to clap along during the fire-belching Spanish flamenco floor shows Monday through Saturday evenings ($10/person additional charge). Dining rooms are graced throughout with hand-painted tiles, wrought-iron chandeliers, dark woods, rich red fabrics, and stained-glass windows. There are Columbia locations in various forms throughout the state, as well as in airports, but this is the original.

2117 E. 7th Ave. (btw. 21st and 22nd sts.). columbiarestaurant.com. © **813/248-4961.** Reservations recommended, especially for flamenco shows. Main courses $15–$46. Sun–Thurs 11am–9pm; Fri–Sat 11am–10pm.

The Pearl ★★★ SOUTHERN/SEAFOOD It may seem odd that a seafood import from Ohio, of all places, is one of Tampa's best, but The Pearl is a Midwestern jewel. Their massive menu includes a zippy jalapeno corn spoon bread, chicken wing confit, a phenomenal twist on the Cuban sandwich (pork confit, sweet garlic pickles, smoked gouda, mustard, and black bean stew); shrimp and grits with kielbasa and gouda cheese grits. The oyster menu is comprehensive and includes our fave, the N'awlins-style baked oysters. This restaurant, in fact, reminds us of some of our favorite New Orleans oyster houses. Ohio, we hardly knew ye. Now we love ye.

823 Water St. thepearlrestaurant.com. © **813/709-7776.** Main courses $14–$44, except for steak. Mon–Thurs 11:30am–10pm; Fri 11:30am–11pm; Sat 10am–11pm; Sun 10am–9pm.

Rooster & The Till ★★★ AMERICAN What started in 2013 as a 37-seat restaurant with a few induction burners is now a Michelin-recognized 72-seat hot spot a few miles north of downtown in historic Seminole Heights, featuring some of Tampa's most innovative, exciting food, by a trio of talented chefs: Ferrell Alvarez, Ty Rodriguez, and Chon Nguyen. The always-changing menus include things you will not see or eat elsewhere: braised pork cheeks with Anson Mills corn pudding, smoked tomato sugo, and pig ear chicharron; cobia collar with nuoc cham, Thai chilis, and cilantro; and Parisian-style gnocchi with short rib, ricotta, and pickled pepperoncini. Drinks are also fantastic—the shot and a snack gives you a choice of aquavit, vodka, or brut, with a "bump" of Royal Sturgeon caviar. Happy hour (Wed–Fri 5–6:30pm) means food and drink specials, but only at the bar.

6500 N. Florida Ave. roosterandthetill.com. © **813/374-8940.** Main courses $17–$75. Wed–Thurs 5–9pm; Fri–Sat 5–9:30pm.

7th & Grove ★★ SOUTHERN Set in Ybor's bustling 7th Ave. district, they have a menu of cheekily titled—and terrifically tasty—dishes. For example, the Get Your M'fn Roll On is an appetizer of braised collard greens, macaroni and cheese, and jerk chicken wrapped in an egg roll. Cry Me A River is catfish nuggets, fried cornbread muffins, and four crispy fried shrimp. The Rude Boi features bold braised oxtail and collards. So. Good. Cocktails aren't too shabby, either, and named after the likes of Beyoncé, Snoop Dogg, and Megan Thee Stallion.

2930 E. 7th Ave. 7thandgrove.com. © **813/649-8422.** Main courses $17–$39. Tues–Fri 4–10pm; Sat 5–10pm.

Inexpensive

Armature Works ★★★ FOOD HALL Housed in a historic, mixed-use building in the trendy Tampa Heights neighborhood, Armature Works has an unobstructed view of the Hillsborough River and over 15 food choices in the building's Heights Public Market section, from sushi and pizza to empanadas and cookies. It's also the location of one of the area's best bars, **M. Bird** (see below). There are also some very cool local shops here, as well as various events and performances.

1910 N. Ola Ave. armatureworks.com. © **813/250-3725.** Mon–Thurs 7:30am–10pm; Fri 7:30am–midnight; Sat 8am–midnight; Sun 9am–9pm.

Carmine's Seventh Avenue ★

CUBAN/ITALIAN/SPANISH Bright blue poles hold up an ancient pressed-tin ceiling above this noisy corner cafe. It's a scruffy joint, but loyal local patrons still regularly gather here for genuine Cuban sandwiches: smoked ham, roast pork, Genoa salami, Swiss cheese, pickles, salad dressing, mustard, lettuce, and tomato on crispy Cuban bread. Folks from Miami will fight you on who has the better Cuban (Miami's do not have salami). There's a vegetarian version, too. The combination of a half-sandwich and choice of black beans and rice or a bowl of Spanish soup made with sausages, potatoes, and garbanzo beans is a filling meal just by itself. Main courses are led by Cuban-style roast pork, thin-cut pork chops with mushroom sauce, spaghetti with a blue crab tomato sauce, and a few seafood and chicken platters.

1802 E. 7th Ave. (at 18th St.). carminesybor.com. © **813/248-3834.** Main courses $10–$20. Mon–Tues 9am–5pm; Wed–Thurs 9am–9pm; Fri–Sat 9am–11pm; Sun 9am–6pm.

One of the many eateries at Armature Works.

Tampa After Dark

Racks in many restaurants and bars have copies of *Creative Loafing Tampa* (cltampa.com), a free publication and excellent website detailing what's going on in the entire bay area. You can also check the Friday edition of the *Tampa Bay Times* (tampabay.com).

THE PERFORMING ARTS With a prime downtown location on 9 acres along the east bank of the Hillsborough River, the huge **Straz Center** ★★★ (aka The Straz; strazcenter.org; © **800/955-1045** or 813/229-7827), 1010 N. MacInnes Place, next to the Tampa Museum of Art, is one of the largest performing arts centers in the country. This five-theater complex is the focal point of Tampa's performing arts scene, presenting a wide range of theater, classical and pop concerts, operas, and special events.

The restored **Tampa Theatre** ★★, 711 N. Franklin St., between Zack and Polk streets (tampatheatre.org; © **813/274-8286**), dates from 1926 and is on the National Register of Historic Places. It presents a varied program of classic, foreign, and alternative films, as well as concerts and special events (and it's said to be haunted!).

The 66,321-seat **Raymond James Stadium,** 4201 N. Dale Mabry Hwy. (raymondjamesstadium.com; © **813/673-4300**), is often the site of headliner concerts, from Taylor Swift to Billy Joel. The **Yuengling Center,** 12499 USF Bull Run Dr. (yuenglingcenter.com; © **813/974-3111**), on the University of South Florida campus, hosts major concerts by pop stars, rock bands, jazz groups, and other artists.

One of the busiest spots in town for live music, rustic-style, is **Skipper's Smokehouse** ★★, 910 Skipper Rd. (skipperssmokehouse.com; ✆ 813/971-0666), a Key West–esque former smokehouse turned blues, jazz, zydeco, and reggae hot spot.

THE CLUB, BAR & MUSIC SCENE Ybor City is Tampa's favorite nighttime neighborhood. Stroll along 7th Avenue East between 15th and 20th streets, and you'll hear music blaring from the clubs. On Friday and Saturday, from 9pm to 3am, the avenue is packed with people, the majority early-20-somethings; but you'll also find something going on Tuesday through Thursday, and even on Sunday. The clubs change names frequently, so you don't need names, addresses, or phone numbers; your ears will guide you. With all of the sidewalk seating, it's easy to judge what the clientele is like and make your choice from there. **Centro Ybor,** on 7th Avenue East at 16th Street (centroybor.com; ✆ **813/242-4660**), the district's large dining-and-entertainment complex, also has nightlife, but it tends to be of a tamer, more family-oriented variety, at least on nonweekend nights.

Hyde Park and **SoHo** (South of Howard) are two other nighttime downtown playgrounds, where restaurant bars buzz with late-night activity. This is especially the case at **Hattrick's** ★★, 107 S. Franklin St. (hattrickstavern.com; ✆ 813/225-4283); **Cru Cellars Wine Bar** ★★, 2506 S. MacDill Ave. (crucellars.com; ✆ 813/831-1117); and **Edge Rooftop Cocktail Lounge** ★ at the Epicurean Hotel, 1207 S. Howard (epicureanhotel.com; ✆ **813/999-8731**).

Other Tampa hot spots at night include the **Arts Club** ★★★ at the Tampa EDITION hotel (p. 312); the bar at **Boulon Brasserie** ★, 1001 Water St. (boulontampa.com; ✆ 813/768-9988); downtown rooftop bar **M. Bird** ★★ on the roof of the very cool **Armature Works,** 1903 Market St. (mbirdtampa.com; ✆ 813/296-2702); **CW's Gin Joint** ★★★, 633 N. Franklin St. (cwginjoint.com; ✆ **813/816-1446**); and the bar at **Olivia** ★★, 3601 W. Swann Ave. (oliviatampa.com; ✆ **813/328-8866**).

ST. PETERSBURG

20 miles SW of Tampa; 289 miles NW of Miami; 84 miles SW of Orlando

On the western shore of the bay, St. Petersburg stands in contrast to Tampa, much as San Francisco compares to Oakland. Whereas Tampa is the area's business, industrial, and shipping center, St. Petersburg was conceived and built a century ago primarily for tourists and snowbirds. Here you'll find one of the most picturesque and pleasant downtowns of any city in Florida, with a waterfront promenade, quality museums, interesting shops, and a few good restaurants. Thanks to an ongoing urban redevelopment program, St. Pete has become far more pedestrian-friendly, with restored streetscapes full of clubs, bars, and a vibrancy that goes beyond the excitement surrounding bingo night at the "adult" communities.

Essentials

GETTING THERE **Tampa International Airport,** approximately 16 miles northeast of St. Petersburg, is the prime gateway to the area (see "Essentials," earlier in this chapter). The primary carrier at **St. Pete–Clearwater International Airport,** on Roosevelt Boulevard (Fla. 686), about 10 miles north of downtown St. Petersburg (fly2pie.com; ✆ **727/453-7800**), is Allegiant; **Sun Country** also flies through here. **Amtrak** (amtrak.com; ✆ **800/USA-RAIL** [872-7245]) has bus connections from its Tampa station to downtown St. Petersburg (see "Getting There," p. 503).

> **Pier Around by Trolley**
>
> You can spend a small fortune in a parking garage or by feeding the meters in St. Petersburg, or you can cut costs substantially by parking at the **Pier** ($15–18 for 6 hr.) and taking the **Looper** (loopertrolley.com), the city's trolley service, which operates between the Pier and all major downtown attractions.

GETTING AROUND The **Pinellas Suncoast Transit Authority/PSTA** (psta.net; © **727/530-9911**) operates regular bus service throughout St. Petersburg and the rest of the Pinellas Peninsula. Rides cost $2.25.

If you need a cab, contact **BATS Taxi** (batstaxi.com; © **727/367-3702**), which encourages you to book your cab online.

VISITOR INFORMATION For info on St. Petersburg and the beaches, see **Visit St. Pete/Clearwater** (visitstpeteclearwater.com).

Seeing the Top Attractions

Those interested in American design may want to make a trip to the tiny but well-curated **Museum of the American Arts and Crafts Movement** ★ (355 4th St. N.; museumaacm.org; © **727/440-4859;** Tues–Sat 10am–4pm, Sun noon–4pm; $25 adults, $23 seniors, $10 children). It's the world's only museum on this topic and has pieces by Tiffany, Stieglitz, and Stickley, among others.

As well, you can't say you've been to St. Petersburg until you've set foot on the **St. Pete Pier** ★★★ at 600 2nd Ave. NE (stpetepier.org). Opened in 2020,

St. Pete Pier.

after 7 years of construction and a price tag of $92 million, this showplace park is 26 acres of fun. We're talking handsome and (often) massive works of public art, an imaginative kids' water park, a beach, a marine discovery center, and lots of places to dine, drink, shop, and soak in the views.

Chihuly Collection ★★★ Glass artist David Chihuly was involved in the creation of this dazzling museum and it shows: He even picked the perfect shade of paint (light gray) to offset his swirling, brilliantly colorful, translucent works of art. Included in the admissions costs are docent-led tours, which really add to the experience, as they go into the technical aspects of how the sculptures were crafted. Check the schedule before heading over so you can join one.

And if you're a big glass arts fan, consider also visiting the **Imagine Museum** ★ (1901 Central Ave.; imaginemuseum.com; **727/300–1700;** Tues–Thurs 10am–8pm, Fri–Sun 10am–5pm; $15 admission, $5 after 5pm Tues and Thurs), which holds more than 500 contemporary pieces by big names in the field.

720 Central Ave. moreanartscenter.org **727/896-4527.** Admission $20 adults, $18 seniors, $14 ages 6–18. Mon–Sat 10am–5pm; Sun noon–5pm.

The Dalí ★★★ This, well, surreal museum houses the world's most comprehensive (and most valuable, at $125 million) collection of works by the renowned Spanish artist Salvador Dalí. That includes oil paintings, watercolors, drawings, and more than 2,400 graphics, plus posters, photos, sculptures, *objets d'art,* and a 5,000-volume library on Dalí and surrealism. Take one of the free docent-led tours to get the most out of the museum. The building is a work of art, too, nicknamed "The Glass Enigma" and featuring 900 triangular-shaped glass panels—a 21st-century expression of Buckminster Fuller's geodesic dome, as utilized in Dalí's Teatro Museo in Figueres, Spain. The museum's dazzling **Dalí Alive 360°** is an immersive experience enveloping visitors in 360 degrees of light and sound, within a monumental new museum space, The Dalí Dome.

The architecture of The Dalí is as surreal as the art it holds.

1 Dali Blvd. thedali.org. **727/823-3767.** Admission $29 adults 18–64, $27 seniors, $20 students, $12 children 6–12, free for children 5 and under; Thurs 5–8pm $14.50 adults, $10 kids 6–12. Dali Alive 360° $15. Daily 10am–6pm (Thurs until 8pm).

FloridaRAMA ★★ Think dioramas, and you've got the picture. Or many pictures, because this immersive art installation features the work of 65 artists (both local and global) and has events like scavenger hunts to appeal to the art-averse. The focal point of St. Pete's burgeoning **Warehouse District** (which is filled with artists' galleries, trendy bars, and eateries), its exhibits are usually whimsical and appealing, though they change, so it's hard to clue you in on exactly what you'll see here.

2606 Fairfield Ave. S. floridarama.art. Admission $27 adults, $25 seniors, $26 children 6–12. See website for hours as they change.

Florida Holocaust Museum ★★★

This moving, thought-provoking museum has exhibits about the Holocaust (Jewish life before the Holocaust, the rise of the Nazi party, and so on), including a boxcar used to transport human cargo to Auschwitz and a gallery of art relating to the Holocaust. Its main focus, however, is to promote tolerance and understanding in the present. It was founded by Walter P. Loebenberg, a local businessman who escaped Nazi Germany in 1939 and fought with the U.S. Army in World War II. The museum underwent a major renovation in 2024 to make room for the Elie Wiesel collection, featuring his Nobel Prize, the entire contents of his personal office and library, unfinished manuscripts, letters from world leaders, art, photos, and never-heard-before recordings. In addition, the museum will be exhibiting *Thor*, one of the boats used during World War II to transport the Jews of Denmark to rural Sweden. Some 7,000 lives were saved; the new exhibit tells the story of this successful exodus.

> **Open-Air Mail**
>
> St. Petersburg residents don't have to go inside to get mail out of their boxes at St. Petersburg's open-air **post office,** 400 1st Ave. N. at the corner of 1st Avenue North and 4th Street North. Built in 1917, this granite, arcaded Spanish Colonial structure is a local landmark and is often photographed by those enchanted by its charm.

55 5th St. S. (btw. Central Ave. and 1st Ave. S.). thefhm.org. **727/820-0100.** Admission $20 adults, $15 seniors, $10 students, free for children 6 and under. Tues–Sun 10am–5pm.

Museum of Fine Arts ★★

Resembling a Mediterranean villa, this museum's collection has over 5,000 years of European, American, pre-Columbian, and Far Eastern art, with works by such big names as Fragonard, Monet, Renoir, Cézanne, and Gauguin. Other highlights include period rooms with antique furnishings, plus a gallery of Steuben crystal, a decorative-arts gallery, and world-class rotating exhibits. The best way to see it all is on a guided tour, given Saturdays and Sundays at 2pm, which takes about 1 hour.

255 Beach Dr. NE (at 3rd Ave. N.). mfastpete.org. **727/896-2667.** Admission $22 adults, $17 seniors 65 and over, $17 students with ID, $12 youth 7–17. Admission includes guided tour. Tues–Sat 10am–5pm; Sun noon–5pm. Guided tours Sat–Sun 2pm.

Sunken Gardens ★★

Dating from 1935, and now operated as a 7-acre botanical garden by the city of St. Petersburg, the garden contains 5,000 plants, including some of the oldest in the region, trees and flowers. There's also a butterfly garden, cascading waterfalls, demo gardens, a flock of flamingos, and a colorful array of rehomed tropical birds including macaws and cockatoos. The place defines serene.

1825 4th St. N. (btw. 18th and 19th aves. NE). sunkengardens.org. **727/551-3102.** Admission $15 adults, $12 seniors, $6 children 2–12. Mon–Sat 10am–4:30pm; Sun noon–4:30pm. Last ticket sold at 4pm.

Outdoor Activities & Spectator Sports

BIKING, SKATING & HIKING With miles of flat terrain, the St. Petersburg area is ideal for bikers, in-line skaters, and hikers. The **Pinellas Trail** ★★ (pinellas.gov/pinellas-county-trail-guide; © 727/464-8201) is especially good, as it follows an abandoned railroad bed 47 miles from St. Petersburg north to Tarpon Springs. The **St. Pete trail head** is on 34th Street South (U.S. 19), between 8th and Fairfield avenues south. It's packed on weekends. The 2½-mile-long **Friendship TrailBridge,** linking Tampa and St. Petersburg, is another popular venue for hikers, bikers, bicyclists, anglers, and in-line skaters, but be careful going up and down the steep center span, especially if you're on skates.

GOLF Located on 180 well-maintained acres in northeast St. Pete, the **Mangrove Bay Golf Course** ★★, 875 62nd Ave. NE (golfstpete.com/mangrove-bay; © 727/893-7800), hugs Old Tampa Bay and offers 18-hole, par-72 play. Facilities include a driving range. Lessons and golf-club rental are also available. Fees are about $53 with cart, $41 without, slightly lower during offseason.

In Largo, the **Bardmoor Golf & Tennis Club** ★★, 8001 Cumberland Rd. (bardmoorgolf.com; © 727/392-1234), is often the venue for major tournaments. Lakes punctuate 17 of the 18 holes on this par-72 championship course. Lessons and rental clubs are available, as is an impressive practice range. Call for info on greens fees, which usually range from $39 to $109 depending on the season/time. The course is open daily from 7am to dusk.

Contact **Tee Times USA** (teetimesusa.com; © 800/374-8633) to reserve times at these and other area courses.

For more area course information, go to golfstpete.com.

SAILING Steve and Doris Colgate's **Offshore Sailing School** (offshoresailing.com; © 888/454-7015) at the Hampton Inn & Suites, 80 Beach Dr. NE, and the **St. Petersburg Sailing Center,** 250 2nd Ave. SE (sailstpete.org; © 727/822-3113), will hoist up your skills. Various courses, lasting from 2 days to a week, are offered.

SPECTATOR SPORTS St. Petersburg has always been a baseball town, but Tropicana Field, the home of the **Tampa Bay Rays** (mlb.com/rays; © 888/326-7297 or 727/825-3137), was significantly damaged during 2024's Hurricane

A Town Runs Through It

The scenic **Pinellas Trail** happens to run right through downtown **Dunedin** ★★, a charming Gulf Coast town known for fishing, beaching, and the Toronto Blue Jays' (see below) spring training. The 6-block downtown area is dotted with shops, restaurants, breweries, old-fashioned streetlamps, and brick sidewalks, and it's a world apart from neighboring big-city Tampa and St. Pete. **Strachan's Ice Cream & Desserts** ★★★, 310 Main St. (strachansdesserts.com; © 727/733-3603), has the best ice cream in the state, and **Dunedin Mix** ★★, 990 Broadway (dunedinmix.com), a brand-new-in-2024 food hall and retail space, is garnering buzz for its rotating, 360-degree circular bar, **Circle 1852.** Just off the coast are Honeymoon and Caladesi islands (see later in this chapter). For more info, contact **Visit Dunedin** (visitdunedinfl.com).

ST. PETERSBURG'S SIDE TRIPS into nature & kitch

Drive north of St. Petersburg for an hour on congested U.S. 19, and you'll come to one of Florida's original tourist traps, the famous, and famously schlocky, **Weeki Wachee Springs State Park** (weekiwachee.com; ✆ **352/597-8484**). "Mermaids" have been putting on acrobatic swimming shows here every day since 1947. Whether you hate this spectacle, or think it's the essence of a Floridian vacation, seeing them doing their dances in waters that come from one of America's most prolific freshwater springs (pouring some 170 million gallons of 72°F/22°C water each day into the river) is a definite experience.

And there's more than mermaids here: There's a "Wilderness River Cruise Ride" on the springs that runs between 9:30am and 4pm; and a flume ride at Buccaneer Bay, a rickety remnant of roadside America featuring a manmade beach and four waterslides, two that plunge you into the natural springs. You can also rent an inner tube and float on the actual lazy river, but be forewarned: There are alligators here, even though they seem to avoid the crowds. Admission to Weeki Wachee is $13 for adults, $8 for children 6 to 12. Weeki Wachee Springs is open daily from 9am to 5:30pm.

For more of a classic nature experience, you can rent kayaks and paddleboards on the Weeki Wachee River for $35 for a one-person kayak, $51 for a two-person kayak, and $35 for a standup paddleboard per day (weekiwachee.com/reserve-online; ✆ **352/597-8484**).

From Weeki Wachee, travel 21 miles north to the **Ellie Schiller Homosassa**

A manatee greets a photographer at Three Sisters Springs.

Springs Wildlife State Park, 4150 S. Suncoast Blvd. (U.S. 19), in Homosassa Springs (floridastateparks.org; ✆ **352/423-5600**). (As of press time the park was still undergoing hurricane cleanup; be sure to check the status of things before visiting.) The highlight here is a floating observatory where visitors can "walk" underwater and watch manatees in a rehabilitation facility, as well as see thousands of fresh- and saltwater fish. You'll also spot deer, bear, bobcats, otters, egrets, and flamingos along unspoiled nature trails. The park is open daily from 9am to 5:30pm (last tickets sold at 4pm). There are also very educational, entertaining wildlife programs, including the alligator and hippo program and the manatee program. There's also a boat tour along the park's Pepper Creek ($3 ages 13 and up, $2 ages 6-12). Admission to the park is $13 for adults and $5 for children 6 to 12.

About 7 miles north of Homosassa Springs, more than 300 manatees spend the winter in Crystal River. You can **swim or snorkel with the manatees** ★★ in the warm-water natural spring of Kings Bay. **American Pro Diving Center,** 821 SE Hwy. 19, Crystal River (americanprodiving.com; ✆ **800/291-3483** or 352/563-0041), offers daily swimming and snorkel tours. Early morning is the best time to see the manatees, so try to take the 6:30am departure. Trips are $48 to $68 per person.

For those *really* into manatees, **Three Sisters Springs** (threesistersspringsvisitor.org; ✆ **352/586-1170**) is the preferred winter retreat for them, and a boardwalk circling the 1-acre springs complex allows you to get up close and personal with the mammals. It's open from 8:30am to 4:30pm, with last entry at 3:30pm. To get there, head to the Three Sisters Springs Center, 917 Three Sisters Springs Trail, and hop on a trolley that departs every hour. Admission is $12.50 for adults in summer, $20 in winter, $12.50 for seniors in summer, $17.50 in winter, and $7.50 for children ages 6 to 15 year-round.

Also check out the **Weedon Island Preserve,** 1800 Weedon Dr. NE (weedonislandpreserve.org; ✆ **727/453-6500**), in the upper Tampa Bay waters of Pinellas County, on the western shore of the entrance to Old Tampa Bay directly west of Port Tampa. The island was named for Dr. Leslie Weedon, a renowned authority on yellow fever, who acquired the 1,250-acre island in 1898 in what is now north St. Petersburg. Weedon had a fascination with Native American culture and developed a weekend retreat on the island, from which he began excavations that first revealed the importance of the site as an Indian burial mound. A Smithsonian expedition to the island in 1923 and 1924 further documented the importance, which is now managed as a 3,190-acre county preserve. Today it's home to an assortment of fish, snakes, raccoons, and dolphins. Rent a canoe to explore.

For more information about the area, contact the **Citrus County Chamber of Commerce,** 915 N. Suncoast Blvd., Crystal River (citruscountychamber.com; ✆ **352/795-3149**).

Milton. The Rays are playing at Tampa-based Steinbrenner Field (the Tampa-based spring-training site for the New York Yankees) for the 2025 season. Baseball season runs from April to October. Rays spring training, from mid-February through March, takes place 82 miles south at the **Charlotte Sports Park,** 2300 El Jobean Rd., Port Charlotte (charlottecountyfl.gov; © **941/235-5010**).

The **Philadelphia Phillies** play their spring-training season in Clearwater at BayCare Ballpark, 601 Old Coachman Rd. (milb.com/clearwater; © **727/712-4300**). Their minor-league affiliate, the **Clearwater Threshers** (milb.com/clearwater; © **727/712-4300**; $9–$12), plays in the stadium April through August. The **Toronto Blue Jays** do their spring thing at **TD Ballpark,** 373 Douglas Ave., in Dunedin (mlb.com/bluejays/spring-training; © **813/733-0429**; $16–$70), which is also home to their minor-league affiliate, the **Dunedin Blue Jays** (milb.com/Dunedin; © **727/733-9302**), April through August.

TENNIS/PICKLEBALL You can learn to play or hone your game at the **St. Petersburg Tennis Center,** 650 18th Ave. (stpetetenniscenter.com; © **727/823-2225**), which has 20 clay courts, 14 with lights, and is open to the public Monday through Thursday 8am to 8:30pm, Friday 8am to 7:30pm, Saturday and Sunday 8am to 2pm for a fee of $13 per person. Check the website for information on lessons, clinics, and matches. For tennis and pickleball, **The Bardmoor Golf & Tennis Club,** 8001 Cumberland Rd. (bardmoorgolf.com; © **727/392-1234**), has an impressive new pickleball center with 12 dedicated lit courts, ball machine rental, and more. Drop-in fee is $10. There are also 14 Har-Tru clay and hard courts as well as instruction by experts such as Harry Hopman, who trained John McEnroe. Tennis fees range from $70 to $130.

Where to Stay

Because most people who visit this area stay on the beach you can often find less expensive lodgings in the heart of St. Petersburg. *Note:* Sales and hotel taxes will add 13% to your bill.

EXPENSIVE

Vinoy Resort and Golf Club, Autograph Collection ★★★

Built in 1925 and opened a year later, this elegant Spanish-style establishment has hosted everyone from Calvin Coolidge and Bill Clinton to Jimmy Stewart, Babe Ruth, and Marilyn Monroe. It's on the National Register of Historic Places. The resort's History and High Tea tour, Thursday through Sunday from 2 to 4pm, is a fun way to learn the hotel's storied past (including ghostly tales) while sipping tea and eating finger sandwiches. Dominating the northern part of downtown, the Vinoy overlooks Tampa Bay and is within walking distance of the Pier, Central Avenue, and other attractions, though it's a 15-minute hike to the beach. All guest rooms offer the utmost in comfort and have been recently renovated. Many have views of the bay, but if you want a terrace that's big enough for a chair, request the Tower Wing (balconies in the original wing only allow standing). Along with several eateries, the hotel has an Old Florida lobby bar, 12 tennis courts, an 18-hole golf course (designed by Ron Garl), spa, and a large private marina.

501 5th Ave. NE (at Beach Dr.), St. Petersburg. thevinoycom. © **727/894-1000.** 354 units. $429–$538 double. Valet parking $39. Pet fee $150. **Amenities:** 4 restaurants; 2 bars; concierge; golf course; fitness center; Jacuzzi; heated outdoor pool; room service; spa; 12 tennis courts; free Wi-Fi.

INEXPENSIVE/MODERATE
The Hollander Hotel St. Petersburg Downtown ★★
A cute, youth-centric boutique hotel housed in a historic brick building (circa 1933) within walking distance of some of the area's bustling bars and restaurants, The Hollander has boldly colorful guest rooms, with the same good quality beds as sister property Avalon (see below). A hopping pool area with bar and cabanas, the popular **Tap Room Restaurant + Bar** with over 20 craft beers on tap, a coffee shop, and a spa round out the amenities.

421 4th Ave. N., St. Petersburg. hollanderhotel.com. **727/873-7900.** 96 units. $124–$270 double. Pet fee: $30/night. **Amenities:** Restaurant; 3 bars; coffee shop; concierge; outdoor heated pool; room service; spa; free Wi-Fi.

INEXPENSIVE

Avalon ★★
An Art Deco charmer, this updated 1930s-era hotel looks like it was ripped straight off of Ocean Drive in Miami Beach. Rooms are small but stylish, with pops of color (royal blue or deep red), bureaus that look like old-fashioned steamer trunks, and an overhead fan lazily rotating (there's air-conditioning, so this is just for the look). Beds are comfy. Guests get cookies upon check-in, and wine in the airy lobby nightly. All can use the amenities, including the fabulous pool, at Avalon's sister hotel right next door, the Hollander (see above).

443 4th Ave. N., St. Petersburg. hollanderhotel.com. **727/317-5508.** 50 units. $127–$191 double. Free parking. Pet fee $30/night. **Amenities:** Concierge; wine social hour; free Wi-Fi.

The Inn on Third ★★
Built in the 1930s, and with decor that seems borrowed from that era, this adorable little inn is run by an energetic and welcoming young couple. Rooms are small, but so is the nightly rate, and it includes breakfast, a glass of wine or beer at the nightly social, and free parking. Location can't be improved upon: walking distance to a number of good restaurants.

342 3rd Ave. N., St. Petersburg. theinnonthird.com. **727/317-5508.** 50 units. $119–$154 double. Free parking. **Amenities:** Wine social hour; continental breakfast; free Wi-Fi.

Where to Dine

The coolest block downtown is **Central Avenue,** a funky shopping, drinking, and dining district. The 600 block of Central is our favorite, with an assortment of cafes, coffee shops, and breweries. There are also a number of view-rich places to dine at the St. Pete Pier.

MODERATE

Ceviche Tapas Bar & Restaurant ★★ SPANISH
Pitchers of the area's best sangria, six different types of ceviche, authentic paellas, and tapas crafted from both Floridian seafood and ingredients imported from Spain—these are the potent lures at this long-standing eatery. A special Tapas Tuesday menu is offered from 4pm until closing featuring discounts on sangria and all sorts of tasty treats, and a daily happy hour from 3 to 6pm offers $7 to $9 bar bites. No reservations, so just show up.

332 Beach Dr. NE. ceviche.com. **727/209-2299.** $9–$42. Mon–Thurs 11am–10pm; Fri–Sat 11am–11pm; Sun 11am–9pm.

The Library ★★★ AMERICAN   Located on the campus of the Johns Hopkins All Children's Hospital in the downtown area, this restaurant was inspired by the George Peabody Library in Baltimore (original home town of Johns Hopkins), so it has bookshelves groaning with tomes, wingback armchairs, and portraits of dignified folks from the late 19th century or so. The folks behind Tampa's fab Oxford Exchange (p. 315) are in charge of the kitchen, so meals are expertly prepared and nicely inventive, like the black garlic Caesar salad with cured egg yolk; or salmon with a charred scallion gnocchi chard and apricot *mostarda*.

600 5th St. S. at Johns Hopkins All Children's Hospital. thelibrarystpete.com. © **727/369-9969.** Main courses $25–$42. Mon–Fri 10am–3pm; Sat–Sun 9am–4pm; Mon–Thurs 5–9pm; Fri 5–10pm; Sat 5:30–10pm.

INEXPENSIVE

Bodega on Central ★★ LATIN AMERICAN   Bodega has the best fast-casual Cuban fare in town, from Cuban sandwiches and fabulous *fritas* (fries), to vegetarian dishes that could convince hardcore carnivores to make the switch. The café con leche is one of the finest in St. Pete. For those looking for a healthy choice there are fresh-squeezed juices and smoothies like the "Greengo," a green juice with kale, apple, cucumber, cilantro, and *guarapo*. Service here is via walk-up window. Bodega's Mediterranean sibling, **Baba** ★★, 2701 Central Ave. (eatatbaba.com; © **727/954-3406**), is, uh, a-meze-ing, too. Heh.

1180 Central Ave. eatatbodega.com. © **727/623-0942.** Main courses $10–$12. Mon–Wed 11am–9pm; Thurs–Sat 11am–11pm; Sun 11am–9pm.

Fourth Street Shrimp Store ★★ SEAFOOD   If you're anywhere in the area, drive by to see the colorful, cartoonlike mural on the outside of this

The bar scene at Baba, a sister restaurant of Bodega on Central.

establishment just north of downtown—a gigantic drawing of people eating. Inside it gets even better, with paraphernalia and murals on two walls that make the main dining room seem like a warehouse, with windows that look onto an early-19th-century seaport (one painted sailor permanently peers in to see what you're eating). You'll pass a seafood market counter when you enter, from which comes the fresh shrimp, the star here. You can also pick from grouper, clam strips, catfish, or oysters fried, broiled, or steamed, all served in heaping portions. This is the best and certainly the most interesting bargain in town.

1006 4th St. N. (at 10th Ave. N.). theshrimpstore.com. © **727/822-0325.** $12–$24. Mon–Sat 11am–9pm.

Red Mesa Cantina ★★ MEXICAN   Although the vibe at this hip, downtown Mexican restaurant is unpretentious, the food's good enough to have a bit of attitude. Salsa and guacamole are made fresh and are addictive, as is the stuffed shrimp with chipotle sauce. The Grouper Al Mojo De Ajo (sautéed with garlic, tomato, parsley, and chile arbol) is a refreshing, spicy twist on our favorite Florida grouper. In fact, a lot of the menu is more creative than the typical Mexican combo-plate fare; we doubt you'll see duck enchiladas and filet mignon chimichurri at your corner Mexican joint! They also have an excellent mofongo, which is actually a Puerto Rican specialty of pork and chimichurri. We threw in an extra star for the restaurant's brick-walled and fountained courtyard and friendly bar scene.

128 3rd St. S. redmesarestaurant.com. © **727/510-0034.** Main courses $12–$29. Mon–Thurs 11am–10pm; Fri–Sat 11am–11pm; Sun 11am–9pm.

The Studio Public House ★★ PUB   Bangers and mash, shepherd's pie, Premier League soccer, and specialty teas evoke merry ol' England, at this very British pub set in a former recording studio. Best thing on the menu? Chef and owner Mike Crippen's habanero-infused Dragon Vindaloo curry (it will clear your sinuses and give you an endorphin high). There's live jazz Sundays and $10.99 fish and chips on Thursdays. On Mondays, Wednesdays, and Thursdays from noon to 9pm, beer fans can chug select brews for $3.

2950 Central Ave. thestudiopublichouse.com. © **727/873-6992.** Main courses $11–$24. Mon, Wed, Thurs noon–9pm; Fri noon–9:30pm; Sat 11:30am–9:30pm; Sun 11:30am–6pm.

St. Petersburg After Dark

Good sources of nightlife information are the *Tampa Bay Times* (tampabay.com) and *Creative Loafing Tampa* (cltampa.com), a tabloid available at visitor centers and in many hotel and restaurant lobbies.

The bars on Central Avenue—particularly the 600 block—and 3rd and 4th streets are the heart of downtown's nightlife.

THE PERFORMING ARTS   The **Duke Energy Center for the Arts-The Mahaffey** ★★★, 400 1st St. S. (themahaffey.com; © 727/892-5721), is a 2,031-seat theater with European box seating showing a variety of concerts, Broadway shows, big bands, ice shows, and more.

THE BAR, CLUB & MUSIC SCENE   Among the coolest bars in town are **The Mandarin Hide** ★★, 231 Central Ave. (mandarinhide.com; © 727/440-9231), a chic cocktail den with dim lighting and a dizzying array of drinks; **Crafty Squirrel** ★★, 259 Central Ave. (craftysquirrel.com; © 727/898-4888), a laid-back lounge serving poutine fries with your PBR every night until 3am; the very popular LGBTQ+ spot **The Garage on Central** ★★, 2729 Central Ave. (© 727/258-4850); the speakeasy-style **Ruby's Elixir** ★★★, 15 3rd St. N. (rubyselixir.com; © 727/898-2442), open daily until 3am and featuring live music nightly; and **The Landing at Jannus Live** ★★★, 200 1st Ave. N. (jannuslive.com; © 727/565-0550), a fantastic outdoor concert venue and bar.

A historic attraction, the Moorish-style **Coliseum Ballroom** ★★, 535 4th Ave. N. (stpete.org/visitors/attractions/coliseum.php; © 727/892-5202), has been hosting dancing, big bands, boxing, and other events since 1924 (it even made an appearance in the 1985 movie *Cocoon*). Come out and watch the town's many seniors jitterbug as if it were 1945 again!

ST. PETE & CLEARWATER BEACHES

St. Pete Beach: 20 miles SW of Tampa; 289 miles NW of Miami; 84 miles SW of Orlando. Clearwater Beach: 90 miles W of Orlando; 20 miles W of Tampa; 20 miles N of St. Petersburg.

If you're looking for sun and sand, you'll find plenty on the 28 miles of slim barrier islands that skirt the Gulf shore of the Pinellas Peninsula. With some one million visitors every year, don't be surprised if you have lots of company. But you'll also discover quieter neighborhoods and some of the nation's finest beaches, including some protected from development by parks and nature preserves.

At the southern end of the strip, St. Pete Beach is the granddaddy of the area's resorts: Visitors started coming here a century ago, and they haven't quit. Today St. Pete Beach is heavily developed and often overcrowded during the winter season. If you like high-rises and mile-a-minute action (albeit before 9pm, when things start to slow down a bit), St. Pete Beach is for you. But even here, Pass-a-Grille, on the island's southern end, is a quiet residential enclave with eclectic shops and a fine, though crowded, public beach.

A gentler lifestyle begins to the north on the 3½-mile-long Treasure Island. From here, you cross John's Pass to Sand Key, a 12-mile-long island occupied primarily by residential Madeira Beach, Redington Shores, Indian Shores, Indian

The bright pink Don CeSar Resort commands attention on St. Pete Beach.

Rocks Beach, and Belleair Beach. The road crosses a soaring bridge to Clearwater Beach, whose sands attract active families and couples.

If you like your great outdoors unfettered by development, the jewels here are **Fort DeSoto Park** ★★★, south of St. Pete Beach at the mouth of Tampa Bay, and **Caladesi Island State Park** ★★★, north of Clearwater Beach. They are consistently rated among America's top beaches. **Sand Key Park** ★★★, on the southern shores of Little Pass (which separates Clearwater Beach from Belleair Beach), is one of Florida's finest local beach parks. (As of press time, these parks were still undergoing cleanup from Hurricanes Helene and Milton; be sure to check the status of things before visiting.)

Essentials

GETTING THERE See our info on getting to St. Petersburg (p. 319).

GETTING AROUND The **Pinellas Suncoast Transit Authority/PSTA** (psta.net; © **727/530-9911**) runs the **Suncoast Beach Trolley,** which stretches from Clearwater Beach south to Indian Rocks Beach, Indian Shores, Redington Shores, North Redington Beach, Redington Beach, Madeira Beach, John's Pass Village, St. Pete Beach, and Pass-a-Grille. Take a short ride to one particular beach, shopping area or restaurant, or travel the entire route to get a view of some scenic Gulf Coast communities (you can hop on and off along the way). Trolleys arrive at each stop every 20 to 30 minutes between 5:20am and midnight. Fares are $2.25. Children 5 and under ride free.

Along the beach, the major cab company is **BATS Taxi** (batstaxi.com; © **727/367-3702**). Fares start at $5. Lyft and Uber will cost roughly the same (though all bets are off when surge pricing is on).

VISITOR INFORMATION In addition to **VisitStPeteClearwater.com**, visit **StPeteBeach.org** for info on fishing piers, parks, beaches, tours, and more. The **Clearwater Visitor Information Center,** in Pier 60 Park, 399 Mandalay Ave. (amplifyclearwater.com; © **727/331-1890**), is open from 9am to 8pm Monday through Friday.

Hitting the Beach

This entire stretch of coast is one long beach. But because hotels, condos, and private homes occupy much of it, and those beaches are often roped off for guests and residents, you'll swim at either your hotel's swatch of sand, or at one of the public parks. The best are described below, but there's also the fine **Pass-a-Grille Public Beach** (visitpassagrille.com), on the southern end of St. Pete Beach, where you can watch the boats going in and out of Pass-a-Grille Channel and quench your thirst at the Hurricane restaurant (p. 339). All Pinellas County public beaches have metered parking lots, but most are electronic, and can be paid with mobile apps (pinellas.gov/mobile-parking-apps). Public restrooms are available along the beach.

The 95-acre **Sand Key Park** (pinellas.gov/parks/sand-key-park), on the northern tip of Sand Key facing Clearwater Beach, has a wide beach and gentle surf, and is relatively off the beaten path in this commercial area. It's a great place to go for a morning walk or jog. The park is open from 7am until sunset and has restrooms. Admission is free, but the parking lot has meters. (As of press time, the park was still undergoing hurricane cleanup; be sure to check the status of things before visiting.)

Clearwater Public Beach (also known as **Pier 60;** myclearwater.com) has a 1,080-foot fishing pier, bait house, beach volleyball, watersports rentals, lifeguards, restrooms, showers, and concessions. The swimming is excellent, and the children's playground is huge. The park also throws a legendary nightly sunset celebration that features local merchants, musicians, and artists starting 2 hours before sunset and continuing 2 hours after. There's a $1 walk-on admission fee to the pier. Daily fishing fees are $10 for adults, $8 for seniors, and $7 for children 15 and under. Rod rental is $10. There's metered parking in lots across the street from the Clearwater Beach Marina, a prime base for boating, cruises, and other water activities (see "Outdoor Activities," below). A less crowded spot in Clearwater Beach is at the Gulf end of Bay Esplanade.

CALADESI ISLAND STATE PARK ★★★

Occupying a 3½-mile-long island north of Clearwater Beach, **Caladesi Island State Park** boasts one of Florida's top beaches, a lovely, relatively secluded stretch with fine, soft sand edged in seagrass and palmettos. Dolphins often cavort in the waters offshore. In the park is a nature trail, where you might see rattlesnakes, raccoons, armadillos, or rabbits. A concession stand, a ranger station, and bathhouses (with restrooms and showers) are available. New in 2025: the Caladesi Discovery Center, a three-story, open-air observation tower. Caladesi Island is accessible only by ferry from **Honeymoon Island State Recreation Area** (floridastateparks.org/honeymoon-island), which is connected by Causeway Boulevard (Fla. 586) in Dunedin, north of Clearwater. As for the name, well, the pioneers called it Hog Island, but in 1939 when a New York developer built 50 palm-thatched bungalows for honeymooners, its name was forever changed for the better.

Kayakers at Honeymoon Island State Recreation Area.

You'll first have to pay the admission to Honeymoon Island: $8 per car for two to eight people, $4 for single-occupant vehicle, $2 pedestrians, bicyclists, and extra passengers. Beginning daily at 10am, the ferry (caladesiferry.org; © **727/734-5263**) departs Honeymoon Island every hour. Round-trip rides cost $18 for adults, $9 for kids ages 4 to 12.

Pets are permitted on the island and on South Beach (bring a leash and use it at all times). The two parks are open daily from 8am to sunset (floridastateparks.org; © **727/469-5918**). (At press time, the two parks were still undergoing hurricane cleanup; be sure to check their status before visiting.)

FORT DESOTO PARK ★★★

South of St. Pete Beach at the very mouth of Tampa Bay, **Fort DeSoto Park** consists of 1,136 acres of five interconnected islands including Mullet Key, set aside by Pinellas County as a 900-acre bird, animal, and plant sanctuary. The entire area is home to 328 species of birds, including bald eagles, with new species added every year. Besides the stunning white-sugar sand, which is home to loggerhead sea turtle nests from April to September, it is best known for a Spanish-American War-era fort, and a Quartermaster Museum and Battery Laidley, the fort's primary defense, that's open daily from 9am to 4pm. Admission is free. Other diversions include fishing from piers (7am–sunset), large playgrounds for kids, a dog park, and 4 miles of trails winding through the park for in-line skaters, bicyclists, and joggers. Park rangers conduct nature and history tours, and you can rent canoes and kayaks from **Topwater Kayak** (topwaterkayak.com), located within the park, to explore the winding mangrove channels along the island's bay side. The park has changing rooms and restrooms as well.

Sitting by itself on a heavily forested island, the park's **campground** (pinellas.gov/camping-information; ⓒ **727/582-2100**) is one of Florida's most picturesque (many sites are beside the bay). It's such ideal camping that the 236 tent and RV sites usually are sold out, especially on weekends, so it's best to reserve well in advance. Sites cost $40 to $48. All sites have water and electricity hookups, picnic table, and charcoal grill. There's Wi-Fi at the camp store and office. Pets are permitted in Area 2 only.

Entry to the park is free. It's open daily from 8am to dusk, although campers and persons fishing from the piers can stay later. To get here, take the Pinellas Bayway (81¢ toll) east from St. Pete Beach and follow Florida 679 (75¢ toll) and the signs south to the park. For more information, contact the park (pinellas.gov/parks/fort-de-soto-park; ⓒ 727/582-2267). (Like the others above, the park was still undergoing hurricane cleanup as we went to press. We are betting it will be visitable, but do check online before making plans.)

Outdoor Activities

BOATING, FISHING & OTHER WATERSPORTS You can indulge in parasailing, boating, deep-sea fishing, wave running, sightseeing, dolphin-watching, water-skiing, and just about any other waterborne diversion your heart could desire in the St. Pete and Clearwater beaches area. All you have to do is head to one of two beach locations: **Hubbard's Marina,** at John's Pass Village and Boardwalk (hubbardsmarina.com; ⓒ **727/393-1947**), in Madeira Beach on the southern tip of Sand Key; or **Clearwater Beach Marina,** at Coronado Drive and Causeway Boulevard (myclearwater.com; ⓒ **727/562-4955**), which is at the beach end of the causeway leading to downtown Clearwater. Agents in booths there will give you the schedules and prices (expect to pay $700 for 4 hr for up to six passengers to $1,000 for 6 hr. up to six passengers), answer any questions you have, and make reservations, if necessary. Also look at the options on marketplace sites like **GetMyBoat.com** and **Boatsetting.com**.

Note: Visitors must possess a Florida-issued boating education certificate (see p. 29).

SCUBA DIVING You can dive on reefs and wrecks with **2 Shea Charters ★★**, 198 Seminole St., Clearwater (2sheacharters.com; ⓒ **813/385-2169**), which also operates fishing charters, sunset tours, and more.

Attractions on Land

Clearwater Marine Aquarium ★★
This little jewel of an aquarium on Clearwater Harbor is dedicated to the rescue and rehabilitation of marine mammals and sea turtles. Exhibits include dolphins, pelicans, otters, sea turtles, sharks, stingrays, reptiles, mangroves, and seagrass. There's a slew of education programs too, from dolphin encounters to trainer-for-a-day programs. The **Sea Life Safari,** a 90-minute boat trip that scouts dolphins, sea birds, and other marine life en route to a shell island, is quite worthwhile and not too pricey at $26 for ages 3 and up.

249 Windward Passage, Clearwater Beach. cmaquarium.com. **727/441-1790.** Admission $35.95 adults, $33.95 seniors, $26.95 children 3–12, free for children 2 and under. Daily 10am–5pm. The aquarium is off the causeway btw. Clearwater and Clearwater Beach; follow the signs.

John's Pass Village and Boardwalk ★★
Charming but very touristy, this Old Florida, turn-of-the-20th-century fishing village on John's Pass consists of a string of wooden structures topped by tin roofs and connected by a 1,000-foot boardwalk. Most have been converted into shops, art galleries, restaurants, and saloons. The focal points are the boardwalk and marina, where many watersports are available for visitors (see "Outdoor Activities," above).

12902 Village Blvd., Madeira Beach. johnspassvillage.net. **800/944-1847** or 727/394-0756. Free admission. Sun–Thurs 10am–10pm; Fri–Sat 10am–midnight.

John's Pass Village and Boardwalk.

Where to Stay

At press time, many St. Pete Beach hotels and resorts were still recovering from damage caused by Hurricanes Helene and Milton. The hotels listed below are properties that were ready to welcome guests when we went to press. By the time you're reading this, many others will have hopefully reopened. As well, there are more short- and long-term rental condominiums than hotel rooms here. Many of them are in high-rise buildings right on the beach (find them at Vrbo or Airbnb, but try to book directly with the management companies to save on fees).

ST. PETE BEACH

Expensive

The Don CeSar ★★★ This Moorish-style "Pink Palace" on the National Register of Historic Places (see photo on p. 330) has a rich history dating back to the Gatsby era (author F. Scott Fitzgerald actually stayed here). That history now unfortunately includes damage from Hurricanes Helene and Milton, but it should be in the midst of a phased reopening by the time you read this. Sitting majestically on 7½ acres of beachfront, its lobby is a classic, with high windows and archways, crystal chandeliers, marble floors, and original artwork. The 277 rooms are also evocative, light and airy with good beds and fun, flamingo-themed wallpaper. Rooms under the minarets of the original building are a bit smaller, but they offer views of the Gulf or Boca Ciega Bay. Some have balconies. If you want more space but less charm, go for one of the resort's luxe condos in the **Beach House Suites by The Don CeSar,** a midrise building ¾ mile to the north that is open post-storms. (There is typically 24-hr. complimentary transportation between the two properties). Back at The Don, as it's known, the two beachfront pools and an 11,000-square-foot spa have been joined by the brand-new Beacon Pool Bar & Lookout (dazzling views). The once musty, stuffy lobby bar has been transformed into a swellegant, 1920s-looking bar with stiff drinks and live jazz. The award-winning **Maritana** restaurant serves very fresh seafood. There's also a beach bar with fire pits, an ice cream shop and market, and another restaurant. The beach is spectacular, as is the service there, whether it's kids' activities on the sands or outdoor yoga classes. The $40 plus tax resort fee covers bikes and non-motorized watersports rentals. The hotel is completely cashless and accepts only credit cards for payment.

3400 Gulf Blvd. (at 34th Ave./Pinellas Byway), St. Pete Beach. doncesar.com. ✆ **844/338-1501.** $372–$802 double. Valet parking $38 overnight, $28 day. Pet fee $75. **Amenities:** 2 restaurants; 3 bars; market; babysitting; children's programs; concierge; fitness center; Jacuzzi; 2 heated outdoor pools; room service; spa; watersports equipment/rentals; free Wi-Fi.

Moderate/Expensive

Sirata Beach Resort ★★ It's super easy to get out on the sand from this well-situated resort. The decor of the property's 382 rooms (which include 170 one-bedroom suites) reflects the beachfront location, with bright tropical colors and other coastal touches. There's an attendant down at the beach to get you all set up for fun in the sun, and two pools offer another option for cooling off. A daily schedule of activities includes everything from kid-friendly scavenger hunts to live music, and complimentary bicycles, boogie boards, and pool noodles are available for guest use.

5300 Gulf Blvd., St. Pete Beach. sirata.com. ✆ **855/344-5999.** 382 units. $152–$422 double. Pet fee $50 daily cleaning fee. **Amenities:** Beach access; 2 pools; restaurants; complimentary bicycles; daily activities and watersports; free Wi-Fi.

Moderate
St. Pete Beach Suites ★★★
This boutique hotel has been in operation since 1948, when it was called the Dolphin Hotel. A complete remodel in 2016–17 modernized the property while still respecting and protecting its vintage past, at least in the public areas. (The retro dolphin pool fountain is kitchy beaut.) The hotel's 27 one-bedroom and studio suites and separate three-bedroom beach house are spacious and bright, with unusually comfortable beds, super speedy Wi-Fi, smart TVs, and usable kitchenettes. The beach is a block away, and guests have access to complimentary beach chairs, umbrellas, and towels, as well as complimentary bicycles. All sit within walking distance of the beach as well as bars and restaurants, and most suites have kitchenettes with cookware and eating utensils. We're giving the place three stars though for its bend-over-backward service (the staff here are topnotch).

6801 Sunset Way, St. Pete Beach. stpetebeachsuites.com. **727/360-7233.** 27 units. $125–$250. Pet fee $30/night. **Amenities:** 2 pools; barbecue grills; complimentary beach gear and bicycles; free Wi-Fi.

Inexpensive
Beach Haven ★
Right on the beach between two high-rise condos, these low-slung, pink-with-white-trim structures look like the early-1950s motel they are. On offer are standard motel rooms and one-, two-, and three-bedroom combo units, all done up in old-school, Florida grandma decor. The one-bedroom suite with sliding-glass doors opening onto a tiled patio beside an outdoor heated pool is the best. There's also a sunning deck with lounge furniture by the beach.

4980 Gulf Blvd. (at 50th Ave.), St. Pete Beach. beachhavenvillas.com. **727/433-5817.** 11 units. $83–$286 studio. **Amenities:** Heated outdoor pool; free Wi-Fi.

Plaza Beach Hotel Beachfront Resort ★
A no-frills, family-friendly beach resort that's part of a collection of three resorts on St. Pete Beach, this one features 39 rooms that are nothing fancy, but appealingly beachy (lots of aqua, with vintage beach photos on the walls), very clean, and all with full kitchens. In addition to the beachfront pool, there's shuffleboard, minigolf, human-size chess board, barbecue area, beach cabanas, and hammocks. Some rooms have balconies overlooking the Gulf of Mexico. The down-to-earth staff contribute to its reputation as the coolest mom-and-pop hotel in the area. Sibling hotels, **Bayview Plaza,** 4321 Gulf Blvd. (**800/257-8998**), is a seven-suite stay on Boca Ciega Bay, home to manatees and dolphins, featuring an outdoor pool, fitness center, and excellent fishing; and **Bay Palms,** 4237 Gulf Blvd. (same telephone), is a 15-room stay on Boca Ciega, recently renovated and with its own marina.

4506 Gulf Blvd. (at 50th Ave.), St. Pete Beach. plazaresorts.com. **727/257-8998.** 39 units. $108–$250. **Amenities:** Heated outdoor pool; free Wi-Fi.

CLEARWATER BEACH
Expensive
JW Marriott Clearwater Beach Resort & Spa ★★★
This $200-million, 16-story beachfront resort debuted in 2023 and it still has that new hotel smell. Located on the quieter, south end of Clearwater Beach, the J dub eschews hustle and bustle, with a secluded beach well away from the beer bong set. There's also a rooftop pool with views for days, a spa, kids' club, and three very good

restaurants. Rooms here are JW Marriott swanky: 36 of them were designed as residences and you, too, can move in here for upwards of a mil or much more.

691 S. Gulfview Blvd., Clearwater Beach. marriott.com. ✆ **727/677-6000.** 198 units. $491–$706 double. Valet parking $45. **Amenities:** 3 restaurants; 3 bars; market; children's programs; concierge; fitness center; heated pool; room service; full-service spa; watersports equipment/rentals; free Wi-Fi.

Sandpearl Resort ★★   For nearly a century, the original Clearwater Beach Hotel—built as a summer bungalow by a Florida lumberman in 1917—reigned as the crown jewel of the area, eventually passing its rich legacy onto its newest incarnation as the Sandpearl. The resort sits on 700 feet of beachfront. Rooms are open and airy, with balconies and high ceilings. The swank spa has treatments focusing on ocean therapy, and there's a lovely lagoon-style beachfront pool. Each evening, the Sunset Celebration invites a chosen guest to ring the dinner bell salvaged from the old Clearwater Beach Resort. The area's only AAA four diamond, fancy **Caretta on the Gulf** features stellar service, sushi, ceviche, seafood, and chops. Activities for children include dive-in movies, campfire storytelling, sing-alongs, and more. A $35 resort fee includes use of bikes. Sandpearl has a similarly chichi sibling nearby, **The Opal Sands,** 430 S. Gulfview Blvd. (opalcollection.com/opal-sands; ✆ **727/485-9497**), a 230-room resort with Gulf views from floor-to-ceiling windows in every room, as well as a spa, and gorgeous Gulf-front pool. Rates there range from $485 to $722 double.

500 Mandalay Ave., Clearwater Beach. opalcollection.com/sandpearl. ✆ **727/441-2425.** 253 units. $448–$684 double. Valet parking $40. Pet fee $100. **Amenities:** 2 restaurants; 2 bars; coffee bar; children's programs; concierge; fitness center; heated pool; room service; full-service spa; watersports equipment/rentals; free Wi-Fi.

Moderate/Expensive
Wyndham Grand Clearwater Beach ★★★   With sweeping views of the Gulf, clean and modern rooms (some with bunk beds), a massive oceanfront pool and sundeck, and a very good Asian fusion restaurant, this contemporary Wyndham is grand indeed. Part of the resort is a private residence, so you're sharing the facilities with people who live here, which is a plus because these people take much better care of the surroundings than the people checking out tomorrow. Staff are responsive and friendly. The $35 resort fee includes welcome cocktails, an on-site dining discount passport, and allows kids 5 and under to eat free breakfast per paying adult in Ocean Hai.

100 Coronado Dr., Clearwater Beach. wyndhamgrandclearwater.com. ✆ **727/281-9500.** 343 units. $299–$564 double. Valet parking $35. **Amenities:** 3 restaurants; 3 bars; babysitting; children's programs; concierge; fitness center; Jacuzzi; heated outdoor pool; room service; spa; watersports equipment/rentals; free Wi-Fi.

Moderate
Sheraton Sand Key Resort ★★   Set on 13 acres of beach next to Sand Key Park, this nine-story Spanish-style hotel is proof that not all Sheratons are schlocky. Its location, only a 450-foot walk across the broad beach in front of the hotel to the water's edge, is ideal. It also happens to be the only resort in the area that doesn't charge the dreaded resort fee and offers free parking. The pool deck has a bar, restaurant, and fire pits for those rare chilly nights. Moderately spacious guest rooms are bright, clean, and well-maintained, with balconies or patios with views of the Gulf or the bay. The gym is on the top floor, affording great workout

views. For those who love a little scandal, room no. 538 was the one where infamous former Praise the Lord Ministry leader Jim Bakker was busted with his then-assistant Jessica Hahn. Google it if you're unfamiliar. It's titillating.

1160 Gulf Blvd., Clearwater Beach. marriott.com. ✆ **727/595-1611.** 390 units. $270–$316 double. **Amenities:** 3 restaurants; 3 bars; babysitting; children's programs; concierge; fitness center; Jacuzzi; heated outdoor pool; room service; sauna; 3 tennis courts; watersports equipment/rentals; free Wi-Fi.

Inexpensive/Moderate
Barefoot Bay Resort and Marina ★★★ A family-owned-and-operated Old Florida motel on the bay, Barefoot Bay offers clean, comfortable, apartment-like accommodations at reasonable prices. There are four types of rooms, including a two-bedroom apartment with full kitchen. But the best part about the place, besides its location, is its backyard pool deck, complete with tropical landscaping and heated pool. It's more like hanging out at a friend's house than a motel. Even better, the beach is across the street and Pier 60 is just 3 minutes away.

401 E. Shore Dr., Clearwater Beach. barefootbayresort.com. ✆ **727/447-3316.** 16 units. $176–$255 double. **Amenities:** Heated pool; marina with watersports rentals; free Wi-Fi.

Shephard's Beach Resort ★ If you're looking for quiet, go elsewhere. Shephard's proudly bills itself as Clearwater's number one beachside entertainment resort, with a daily and nightly roster of bands, DJs, and laser shows at its famous Tiki Beach Bar & Grill, Soak Pool, and two-level Gulf-front nightclub. This is an ideal place for a bachelor/ette party or girls' weekend, where it feels like spring break on the daily. Rooms are comfortable and clean, but the resort does not make it a secret that rooms may hear noise from the nightclubs. The terrace pool is a splashfest of epic proportions, always filled with rowdy crowds bobbing up and down with their cocktails in the air. The beach is a bit more peaceful, but again, you aren't coming here for peace. While some have brought kids here, we recommend to go sans tots.

619 S. Gulfview Blvd., Clearwater Beach. shephards.com. ✆ **727/442-5107.** 140 units. $188–$374. **Amenities:** 3 restaurants; 4 bars; nightclub; heated pool; fitness center; bike rental; marina with watersports rentals; free Wi-Fi.

A NEARBY GOLF RESORT
Innisbrook Golf Resort ★★ *Golf Digest, Golf,* and others pick this as one of the country's best places to play golf. Between Palm Harbor and Tarpon Springs, this 900-acre, all-condominium resort has 72 holes on championship courses more like the rolling links of the Carolinas than the usually flat courses found in Florida. Some pros think the **Copperhead Course** is number one in Florida. If you want to learn, Innisbrook has one of the largest resort-owned-and-operated golf schools in North America. In addition, it has a tennis center with instruction. A free shuttle runs around the property, and another goes to the beach three times a day. There's an excellent spa and five good restaurants here, too. Ranging in size from suites to two-bedroom models, condo-style rooms are very cushy. There are tons of kids' camps and programs, and live music every Saturday night at the **Market Salamander Grille.** A $35 resort fee includes self-parking, minigolf, on-property transportation, and more.

36750 U.S. 19 N., Palm Harbor. innisbrookgolfresort.com. ✆ **855/790-1905.** 485 units. $226–$439 double. Dog fee $150. **Amenities:** 5 restaurants; 4 bars; babysitting; children's programs; concierge; 4 golf courses; health club; Jacuzzis; 6 heated outdoor pools; limited room service; sauna; 15 tennis courts; free Wi-Fi.

Where to Dine

The restaurants here are grouped by geographic location: St. Pete Beach, including Pass-a-Grille; Indian Rocks Beach, including Madeira Beach, Redington Beach, North Redington Beach, Redington Shores, and Indian Shores; and Clearwater Beach.

ST. PETE BEACH

Crabby Bill's Seafood ★★ SEAFOOD   This member of a local chain sits right on the beach. It has an open-air rooftop bar, as well as a large dining room enclosed by big windows. There are fine water views from picnic tables, which are equipped with paper towels and buckets of saltine crackers, the better with which to eat the blue, Alaskan, snow, and stone crabs. The crustaceans fall into the moderate price category or higher, but most other main courses, such as fried fish or shrimp, are inexpensive—and they aren't overcooked or overbreaded. A good place to feed the family.

5300 Gulf Blvd. (at 53rd Ave.), St. Pete Beach. stpetecrabbybills.com. ⓒ **727/360-8858.** Main courses $17–$33. Daily 11am–10pm.

Hurricane Seafood Restaurant ★★ SEAFOOD   An institution for over 4 decades, across the street from Pass-a-Grille Public Beach, this three-level gray Victorian building with white gingerbread trim is a swell place to toast the sunset, especially from the rooftop bar. It's more beach pub than restaurant, but the grouper sandwiches are tasty, and there's always fresh fish. Downstairs, you can dine inside the knotty-pine-paneled dining room or on the sidewalk terrace, where bathers from across Gulf Way are welcome (there's a walk-up bar for beach libation). You must be at least 21 to go up to the Hurricane Watch rooftop bar, where views are paramount.

807 Gulf Way (at 9th Ave.), Pass-a-Grille. thehurricane.com. ⓒ **727/360-9558.** Main courses $12–$40. Sun–Thurs 11:30am–9:30pm; Fri–Sat 11:30am–10:30pm.

Paradise Grille ★★★ BREAKFAST   Only on St. Pete Beach would the breakfast menu start out with a comprehensive list of cocktails, beer, and wine, because, when it comes to the beach, it's five o'clock all day, every day. Besides the great Bloody Marys, this beachfront eatery—which serves lunch and early dinner, too—has fantastic pancakes, French toast, and breakfast sandwiches at deliciously cheap prices. There's also live music. You can kind of spend your entire day here—literally—it's open from sunrise to sunset. There's another location at Pass-a-Grille, 900 Gulf Way (ⓒ **727/954-8957**).

6850 Beach Plaza, St. Pete Beach. paradisegrille.com. ⓒ **727/560-5399.** Main courses $7–$12. Daily sunrise to sunset.

Ted Peters' Famous Smoked Fish ★ SEAFOOD   This open-air eatery is an institution in these parts: Ted's has been around since the '50s. It's known for mullet, mackerel, salmon, and other fish slowly cooked over red oak. Some folks bring their catches for the staff to smoke. Ted's smoked fish dinners come with German potato salad and coleslaw. Enjoy the aroma—we'd turn it into a candle if we could.

1530 Pasadena Ave. (just across St. Pete Beach Causeway). tedpetersfish.com. ⓒ **727/381-7931.** Main courses $7–$28. No credit cards. Wed–Sun 11:30am–7:30pm.

INDIAN ROCKS BEACH AREA

Guppy's on the Beach ★★ SEAFOOD Locals love this bar and grill across from Indian Rocks Public Beach because they know they'll always get terrific chow. That includes Gulf grouper piccata; and the chargrilled Greek-style mahi (feta cheese, olives, banana pepper tapenade with spinach stuffed tomatoes). All entrees come with Caesar salad or their house specialty, Indian Rocks fish chowder, baked bread, fresh steamed veggies, and a choice of side dish. The atmosphere is beach-friendly, with a fun bar. You can dine outside on a patio beside the main road. A daily early-bird menu from 4 to 6:15pm is a bargain at $19.75.

1701 Gulf Blvd. (at 17th Ave.), Indian Rocks Beach. guppys.com. **727/593-2032.** Main courses $15–$50. Sun–Thurs 11:30am–9:30pm; Fri–Sat 11:30am–10pm.

The Salt Rock Grill ★★★ SEAFOOD/STEAK A beach landmark overlooking the Intracoastal, Salt Rock Grill is a staple for steaks and dayboat-caught seafood. The big dining room is built on three levels, affording every table a view over the creeklike waterway out back. In fair weather, you can dine out by the dock or slake your thirst at the lively tiki bar (bands play Sat–Sun during the summer). Thick, aged USDA steaks are offered, but it's the seafood everyone comes for, like salmon cooked on a cedar board or South African fire-roasted lobster tails. A fresh market cioppino gives you an all-in-one seafood experience with day-boat fish, king crab, shrimp, lobster, clams, mussels, and sourdough toast. Avoid spending a fortune by showing up for the early-bird specials, aka The Supper Club Menu (Mon–Fri 4–5:30pm and noon–5:30pm Sat–Sun).

19325 Gulf Blvd. (north of 193rd Ave.), Indian Shores. saltrockgrill.com. **727/593-7625.** Reservations strongly advised. Main courses $15–$39, more for steak and lobster. Mon–Fri 4–10pm; Sat–Sun noon–10pm.

CLEARWATER BEACH

Bobby's Bistro ★★ AMERICAN Son of Bob Heilman's Beachcomber (see below), this bistro draws a more urbane crowd. A wine-cellar theme is justified by the real thing: a walk-in closet with several thousand bottles kept at a constant 55°F (13°C). Walk through and pick your vintage, then listen to jazz while you dine inside at tall, bar-height tables or outside on a covered patio. The menu features classics like Heilman's New England clam chowder, plus imaginative offerings like New York strip steak pizza. The seafood dishes tend to be less adventurous but no less delicious, including the fresh Florida black grouper bronzed and topped with mild garlic butter.

447 Mandalay Ave. (at Papaya St., behind Bob Heilman's Beachcomber). bobbysbistro.net. **727/446-9463.** Main courses $18–$67. Wed–Sat from 5pm.

Bob Heilman's Beachcomber ★★ AMERICAN In biz since 1948, each dining room here is unique. One has a nautical theme with large models of sailing crafts, another features a pianist, the third looks like an art gallery (thanks to all the works on the walls), and booths and a fireplace make for a cozy fourth. The menu presents a variety of well-prepared fresh seafood and beef, veal, and lamb selections. If you tire of fruits-of-the-sea, the "back to the farm" fried chicken—from an original 1910 Heilman family recipe—is stellar. The Beachcomber shares valet parking, a New England clam chowder recipe, and an extensive wine collection with Bobby's Bistro.

447 Mandalay Ave. (at Papaya St.). bobheilmansbeachcomber.com. **727/442-4144.** Main courses $22–$64. Mon–Sat 11:30am–11pm; Sun noon–10pm.

Frenchy's Original Café ★★ SEAFOOD   Popular with locals and visitors in the know since 1981, this casual pub makes the best grouper sandwiches in the area and has the awards to prove it. The sandwiches are fresh, thick, juicy, and delicious, especially the one served Buffalo-style. Garlic crab fries come with (yum!). The atmosphere is pure Florida casual. There can be a wait during winter and on weekends year-round. For a similarly relaxed setting, directly on the beach, **Frenchy's Rockaway Grill**, at 7 Rockaway St. (✆ **727/446-4844**), keeps a charcoal grill going to cook fresh fish. Same goes for several more Frenchy's-owned eateries: **Frenchy's Salt Water Café,** 419 Poinsettia Ave. (✆ **727/461-6295**); **Frenchy's South Beach Café,** 351 S. Gulfview Blvd. (✆ **727/441-9991**); and **Frenchy's Outpost Bar & Grill,** 466 Causeway Blvd., Dunedin (✆ **727/286-6139**).

41 Baymont St. frenchysonline.com. ✆ **727/446-3607.** Main courses $12–$20. Sun–Thurs 11am–9pm; Fri–Sat 11am–10pm.

going GREEK

Just 13 miles north of Clearwater Beach is the so-called "Sponge Capital of the World," **Tarpon Springs** ★★ (exploretarponsprings.com), a charming seaside community straight out of the Greek islands, with a rich heritage of Greek history and food so good, Greek *yiayias* (grandmas) have been known to take road trips here instead of doing the home cooking. While the sponge biz brought the Greeks to this Gulf area, their culture and food bring the tourists, seeking authentic cuisine originating from the Dodecanese Islands region known for *Mizithra* cheese and *paximadia*, a barley bread cut into small pieces and baked repeatedly to dehydrate.

For the best gyro in town (fries inside!), **The Limani** ★★★, 776 Dodecanese Blvd. (✆ **727/945-8100**), is it, a tiny cafe on the sponge docks, with outdoor seating. On the same street, **Mykonos** ★★★, 628 Dodecanese Blvd. (✆ **727/934-4306**), has better spanakopita than my grandma's. Yep, I said it. And marinated lima beans that would make even the most lima-resistant happy. Across from Mykonos and right on the Anclote River is its sibling, **Dimitri's on the Water** ★★★, 690 Dodecanese Blvd. (dimitrisonthewater.com; ✆ **727/224-2902**), with more exceptional Greek fare.

It's a big fat Greek food fest in this town, but eating isn't the only thing to do. Tarpon Springs also has charming shops like **Conworlds Emporium** ★★★, 9 S. Safford Ave. (conworldsemporium.com; ✆ **727/314-3102**), a pop culture junkie's paradise, or, as the owners put it, "a haven for fellow dreamers, gamers, and creatives alike, fostering a community where the boundaries between reality and fantasy blur." Take a self-guided walking tour through **the Greektown Historic District** (tarponarts.org/walktarpon), which features 10 stops starting at the **Sponge Docks** ★★, which is the site of many a mouth-watering festival. While Tarpon makes for an excellent day trip or pit stop, an overnight stay is encouraged at **The 1910 Inn** ★★★, 32 W. Tarpon Ave. (the1910inn.com; ✆ **727/424-4091**), an historic Queen Anne–style inn on the National Register of Historic Places known for its 700-thread-count bed linens and rates beginning at $175 a night.

Island Way Grill ★★ SEAFOOD/SUSHI The glass-encased, wood-enhanced Island Way prepares the daily catch Pan-Asian style in its open kitchen. Everything is delicious, from the (cooked) fish to the sushi. Even the meatloaf is gourmet, with wasabi mashed potatoes and tumbleweed onions (a bargain at $17). The wine list is also superb. Intriguing people—like members and owners of the Tampa Bay Buccaneers—tend to hang out, talk shop, and scope the scene at the outdoor bar here.

20 Island Way. islandwaygrill.com. **727/461-6617.** Main courses $19–$59. Mon–Thurs 4–9pm; Fri 4–10pm; Sat 11am–10pm; Sun 10am–1:30pm and 4–9pm.

The Beaches After Dark

The funky fishing community of **John's Pass Village & Boardwalk,** 12945 Village Blvd., on Gulf Boulevard at John's Pass in Madeira Beach, has plenty of restaurants, bars, and shops to keep you occupied after the sun sets. Elsewhere, the nightlife scene at the beach revolves around bars that pump out music until midnight or later. All of the places listed in this section are bars with live music.

Pass-a-Grille has the always-lively lounge at **Hurricane** ★★, on Gulf Way at Ninth Avenue, opposite the public beach (p. 339). Over on Sunset Beach in nearby Treasure Island, **Ka'Tiki** ★★, 8803 W. Gulf Blvd. (katikisunsetbeach.com; **727/360-2272**), has live music 7 days a week—rock, blues, reggae, R&B, you name it—and is open daily from 9am to 2am. It's also known for its $3 cheeseburger!

In Clearwater Beach, **Frenchy's Rockaway Grill** ★★, at 7 Rockaway St. (frenchysonline.com; **727/446-4844**), is a popular hangout. Always booming—literally if the DJs are spinning heavy bass—is **Shephard's Tiki Beach Bar & Grill** ★★ and its sister nightclub **WAVES** ★★, 619 S. Gulfview (shephards.com; **727/441-6875**), where the party-hearty set channels their best spring break from early morning until the wee hours.

For a more highbrow evening, go to the Clearwater mainland and the 2,200-seat **Ruth Eckerd Hall** ★, 1111 McMullen-Booth Rd. (rutheckerdhall.com; **727/791-7400**), which hosts a varied program of Broadway shows, ballet, drama, symphonic works, popular music, jazz, and country music.

Also on the mainland, the **Cleveland Street District** has landscaped sidewalks with boutiques, bars, and restaurants, and plenty of public art. Among the hot spots here: **Clear Sky on Cleveland** ★★, 418 Cleveland St. (clearskyoncleveland.com; **727/754-7244**), a global bistro with an excellent craft-cocktail-tinged bar scene; LGBTQ+ landmark **Pro Shop Pub** ★★, 840 Cleveland St. (proshoppub.us; **727/447-4259**); and the always fun and lively, if sometimes intentionally off key, dueling piano bar, **The Nash Keys** ★★★, 520 Cleveland St. (thenashkeys.com; **727/881-6274**). The district begins at Clearwater Bay where Drew Street turns back toward the city center, and runs east to west, all the way to North Blecher Road. The first half-mile is the most rewarding/popular.

SARASOTA

52 miles S of Tampa; 150 miles SW of Orlando; 225 miles NW of Miami

Far enough away from Tampa Bay to have an identity of its own, Sarasota is one of Florida's cultural centers. In fact, many retirees spend their winters here because there's so much to keep them entertained and stimulated, including the Van Wezel

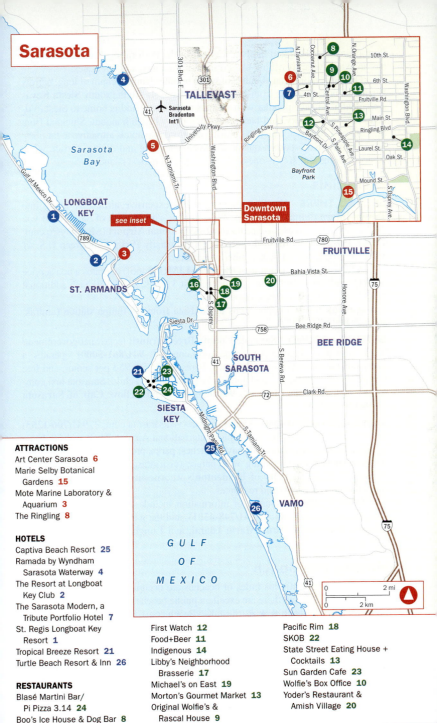

Sarasota

ATTRACTIONS
Art Center Sarasota 6
Marie Selby Botanical
  Gardens 15
Mote Marine Laboratory &
  Aquarium 3
The Ringling 8

HOTELS
Captiva Beach Resort 25
Ramada by Wyndham
  Sarasota Waterway 4
The Resort at Longboat
  Key Club 2
The Sarasota Modern, a
  Tribute Portfolio Hotel 7
St. Regis Longboat Key
  Resort 1
Tropical Breeze Resort 21
Turtle Beach Resort & Inn 26

RESTAURANTS
Blasé Martini Bar/
  Pi Pizza 3.14 24
Boo's Ice House & Dog Bar 8
First Watch 12
Food+Beer 11
Indigenous 14
Libby's Neighborhood
  Brasserie 17
Michael's on East 19
Morton's Gourmet Market 13
Original Wolfie's &
  Rascal House 9
Pacific Rim 18
SKOB 22
State Street Eating House +
  Cocktails 13
Sun Garden Cafe 23
Wolfie's Box Office 10
Yoder's Restaurant &
  Amish Village 20

343

Performing Arts Hall and the FSU Center for the Performing Arts. Sarasota also has an extensive array of first-class resorts, restaurants, and boutiques.

Offshore, more than 40 miles of white beaches fringe a chain of long, narrow barrier islands stretching from Tampa Bay to Sarasota. To the south, **Siesta Key** is a residential enclave popular with artisans and writers, and is home to Siesta Village, this area's funky, laid-back, and often noisy beach hangout. Shielded from the Gulf by **Lido Key,** which has a string of affordable hotels attractive to families, **St. Armands Key** sports a quaint and lively shopping and dining district, while adjacent **Longboat Key** is one of the country's swankiest islands.

Essentials

GETTING THERE You'll probably find less-expensive airfare by flying into **Tampa International Airport** (p. 297), an hour's drive north of Sarasota. If you fly directly here, **Sarasota-Bradenton International Airport (SRQ;** flysrq.com; © 941/359-2770), north of downtown, off University Parkway between U.S. 41 and U.S. 301, is served by a number of carriers.

ALD Limo (aldlimo.com; © 855/799-LIMO [5466]) operates a taxi service at SRQ, with rates starting at $25 for the first 3 miles, and $2.50 each additional mile. Lyft and Uber will be cheaper.

Amtrak has bus connections to Sarasota from its Tampa station (amtrak.com; © 800/872-7245).

GETTING AROUND **Sarasota County BreezeTransit** (scgov.net/government/breeze-transit or breezerider.tripsparkhost.com; © 941/861-5000) operates a fairly reliable bus service around town. Fares are $1.50, 75¢ per senior, and free for the first two children 5 and under, 75¢ per additional child. Sarasota taxi companies include **ALD Limo** (© **941/925-9535**) and **Yellow Cab of Sarasota** (© **941/955-3341**).

VISITOR INFORMATION **Visit Sarasota** (visitsarasota.com; © 941/706-1253) has a booth at the Sarasota–Bradenton International Airport. Their website has a useful section listing Sarasota's bays, beaches, parks, preserves, trails, rivers, and the best spots for communing with nature (visitsarasota.com/discover-natural-sarasota-county). The **City of Bradenton's** website (ityofbradenton.com/things todo) has info on events and resources.

Other excellent resources of information include the website of **Manatee County** (mymanatee.org; © 941/748-4501), and the website for **Florida's Gulf Islands, Bradenton, Anna Maria Island,** and **Longboat Key** (bradentongulf islands.com).

Hitting the Beach

Many of the area's 40-plus miles of beaches are occupied by hotels and condominium complexes, but there are excellent public beaches as well. The area's most popular is **Siesta Beach** ★★★ (SiestaKeyBeach.com), rated Florida's best beach in 2024 by *U.S. News & World Report,* with a picnic area, an 800-car parking lot, crowds of families, and quartz sand reminiscent of the white beaches in Northwest Florida. There's also beach access at **Siesta Village** ★★★, which has many casual restaurants and pubs with outdoor seating (see "Where to Dine," p. 356). The more secluded, quiet **Turtle Beach** ★★ is at Siesta Key's south end. It has shelters, boat ramps, picnic tables, and volleyball nets. Both beaches have restroom facilities. There's also **Passage Key** ★★, a nude beach off Anna Maria Island accessible only by boat, on a protected bird sanctuary in Tampa Bay.

Unless you're staying on Longboat Key, you won't be able to hit the beach there, as private houses and condos block access to the Gulf. However, do drive the length of Longboat Key and admire the luxury homes. Then take a right off St. Armands Circle onto Lido Key and **North Lido Beach.** The south end of the island is occupied by **South Lido Beach Park,** with plenty of shade—a good spot for picnics and walks.

Outdoor Activities & Spectator Sports

BIKING & SKATING The flat terrain in this area makes for good in-line skating and for fine, though not challenging, bike riding. You can bike and skate from downtown Sarasota to Lido and Longboat keys, because paved walkways/bike paths run alongside the John Ringling Causeway and then up Longboat Key. **Ride & Paddle by Siesta Sports Rentals** ★★, 6551 Midnight Pass Rd., in the Southbridge Mall, just south of Stickney Point Bridge on Siesta Key (rideandpaddle.com; ⓒ **941/346-1797;** daily 9am–5pm), rents bikes and electric bikes of various sizes (including trail attachments for kids), plus motor scooters, kayaks, paddleboards, and beach chairs and umbrellas. They offer kayak tours for $15. Bike rentals range from about $15 to $20 for 3 hours, to $25 to $60 per day; scooters go for $65 for 3 hours or $90 for a full day. They also rent three-wheeled scooter cars.

BOAT RENTALS **Siesta Key Water Sports** ★★, 1536 Stickney Point Rd. (siestakeywatersports.com; ⓒ **941/921-3030**), rents jet skis and kayaks and offers parasailing. At the island end of the bridge, **C. B.'s Saltwater Outfitters** ★★, 1249 Stickney Point Rd. (cbsoutfitters.com; ⓒ **941/349-4400**), and **Safe Harbor Siesta Key** ★★, 1265 Old Stickney Point Rd. (skmarina.com; ⓒ **941/349-1970**), rent runabouts, pontoon boats, and other craft. Bait and tackle are available at the marinas.

Note: Visitors who do not already possess a valid boating education certificate must get one (see p. 29).

Parasailers in Siesta Key.

CRUISES Sightseeing and nature cruises depart from several spots around Sarasota. **LeBarge Tropical Cruises** ★★ (lebargetropicalcruises.com; ⓒ **941/366-6116**) heads out for sunset cruises and dolphin-spotting trips from the Bayfront Park/Marina Jack area in downtown Sarasota. **Fun Boat Tours** ★★ (funboattours.com; ⓒ **941/400-2763**) does the same from Siesta Key Marina, but adds sandbar trips and private excursions to its offerings. And **Low Tide Tours** ★ (lowtidetours.com; ⓒ **941/405-0045**) offers its "floating tiki bar boat experiences" from several locations around the area.

ECO TOURS Make like *Little House on the Prairie* on a covered-wagon tour through the 20,000-acre **Duette Preserve** ★★, 2649 Rawls Rd. (mymanatee.org/departments/natural_resources/preserves/duette), the largest preserve in Manatee County, about 30 miles east of Bradenton, with the **Manatee Fish & Game Association**, 7611 9th Ave. NW (manateefishandgame.org; © **941/792-8314**), led by naturalists and park rangers who will point out the sights and wildlife as you travel through flatwoods, river floodplain, and scrub ecosystems. The tour is free and lasts around 3 hours.

FISHING Charter fishing boats dock at most marinas here; check out **4sarasota.com/Sarasota/Recreation/fish_charters.html** for a list. In downtown Sarasota, the **Flying Fish Fleet,** at Marina Jack's Marina, U.S. 41 at Island Park Circle (flyingfishfleet.com; © **941/366-3373**), offers party-boat charter-fishing excursions, with bait and tackle furnished. Prices for 4½-hour trips are $85 for adults, $75 for seniors and kids 4 to 12. All-day voyages cost $140 for all passengers.

GOLF The **Bobby Jones Golf Complex** ★★, 1000 Circus Blvd. (bobbyjonesgolfclub.com; © **941/365-4653**), is Sarasota's only municipal facility. It has two recently renovated (in 2023) 18-hole championship layouts—the American (par 71) and British (par 72) courses—and the 9-hole Gillespie executive course (par 30). Tee times are assigned 3 days in advance. Greens fees range from $74 to $114 including cart rental. **The Serenoa Golf Club** ★★★, 6773 Serenoa Dr. (serenoagc.com; © **941/925-2755**), has been rated one of the area's best thanks to existing wetlands, natural lay-of-the-land, and water on every hole. Greens fees range from $39 to $95. **Bent Tree Country Club** ★, 4700 Bent Tree Blvd. (benttreecc.net; © **941/371-8200**), boasts mature oaks, TifEagle Bermuda greens, newly excavated and filled bunkers as well as remodeled fairways and tee boxes. Greens fees range from $34 to $55.

The semi-private **University Park Country Club** ★★★, west of I-75 on University Parkway (universitypark-fl.com; © **941/359-9999**), is constantly ranked four stars by *Golf Digest*. Fees, including cart, are about $45 to $175.

Tiger Woods' minigolf complex **Popstroke,** 195 University Town Center Dr. (popstroke.com; © **941/500-9495**), in Sarasota, is a playful spot with two 18-hole putting courses and lively restaurant and bar.

HORSEBACK RIDING **Florida Beach Horses** ★★ (floridabeachhorses.com; © **941/527-9621**) offers horseback riding in the sand and the water at Bradenton's **Palma Sola Bay,** 8400 Manatee Ave. W. Rides are scheduled at low tide and take about an hour and a half. Tours start at $150 and include daytime and sunset options. Children as young as 3 are able to ride, and no experience is necessary.

KAYAKING/PADDLEBOARDING **Sea Life Kayak** ★★, 190 Taft Dr. (sealifekayak.com; © **941/400-2740**), launches very good 2-hour guided mangrove tunnel tours out of Ted Sperling Park on Lido Key daily at 9:30am and 1:30pm, with 4pm tours Wednesday through Saturday. Tours are $59 for adults and $49 kids 10 and under. They also rent kayaks for $45 to $67 for a half-day. **The Sarasota Paddleboard Company** has locations on Lido Key and Longboat Key (sarasotapaddleboardcompany.com; © **941/650-2241**), and offers tours, lessons, and rentals at both.

SAILING Take a sightseeing or sunset cruise on the waters of Sarasota Bay and the Gulf of Mexico with **Key Sailing** (siestakeysailing.com; © **941/346-7245**) on the *Key Breeze,* a 41-foot Morgan yacht that has competed in—and won—many regattas. Their most popular cruise is 3 hours long, but they also do 2-, 4-, and half-hour tours based on your budget.

You can also get to Egmont Key, 3 miles off the northern end of Anna Maria Island at the mouth of Tampa Bay, on a 30-foot Catalina yacht with **Spice Sailing Charters** (spicesailingcharters.com; © **941/778-3240**), based at the Galati Yacht Basin on Bay Boulevard on northern Anna Maria Island. Rates start at $50 per person for a 2½-hour sail to $75 per person for a 4-hour sail. The company has sunset cruises as well.

SPECTATOR SPORTS The **Baltimore Orioles** do spring training at **Ed Smith Stadium,** 2700 12th St. (mlb.com/orioles/spring-training; © **941/954-4101**). Tickets range from $18 to $48. The **Pittsburgh Pirates** (mlb.com/pirates/spring-training; © **941/748-4610**) do their February through March spring training at 5,170-seat **LECOM Park,** 9th Street West and 17th Avenue West, south of downtown Bradenton. Tickets are $21 to $36. After purchasing the Sarasota Reds when Cincinnati moved to Arizona for spring training, the Pirates got their own minor league team, the **Bradenton Marauders** (milb.com/bradenton), who also play at LECOM Park April through September. Tickets are $9 to $13.

The **Sarasota Polo Club,** 8201 Polo Club Lane (sarasotapolo.com; © **941/907-0000**), at Lakewood Ranch, a planned community midway between Sarasota and Bradenton, is the site of Sunday afternoon polo matches from mid-December to early April. Admission starts at $15.

TENNIS/PICKLEBALL The **IMG Academy** (formerly **Nick Bollettieri Tennis**) ★★★, 5650 Bollettieri Blvd., Bradenton (imgacademy.com; © **800/872-6425** or 941/755-1000), is one of the world's largest tennis training facilities, with over 55 grass, clay, and hard courts, and a pro shop. Serena Williams and Maria Sharapova are just two of the tennis titans who trained here. It's open year-round; reservations are required for all activities. The tennis legend for whom the street is named passed away at the age of 91 in 2022. For less intense tennis, the **Payne Park Tennis Center,** 2050 Adams Lane (letsplaysarasota.com; © **941/263-6641**), has 12 Har-Tru courts in downtown Sarasota, available for rent in 90-minute increments at $10 for adults, $5 for youth 17 and under. Public pickleball courts can be found at parks throughout Sarasota, including Longwood Park, 6050 Longwood Run Blvd., Sarasota (scgov.net; © **941/316-1383**), and Pompano Trailhead, 601 S. Pompano Ave., Sarasota (scgov.net; © **941/861-5000**).

WATERSPORTS You'll find watersports activities in front of the major hotels on the Keys (see "Where to Stay," p. 351). **Ride & Paddle by Siesta Sports Rentals,** 6551 Midnight Pass Rd., on Siesta Key (rideandpaddle.com; © **813/346-1797**), rents kayaks and paddleboards, plus beach chairs and umbrellas.

Exploring the Area

IN SARASOTA

Art Center Sarasota ★
In addition to the John and Mable Ringling Museum of Art (see below), Sarasota is home to more than 60 galleries and exhibition spaces, all open to the public. A convenient starting point for seeing a number of them is this downtown community art center. It contains four rotating galleries exhibiting local, regional, and international artists. It also has a small sculpture garden and hosts special events.

707 N. Tamiami Trail (at 6th St.). artsarasota.org. © **941/365-2032**. Free admission. Mon–Fri 10am–5pm; Sat noon–5pm. Closed Sun.

Marie Selby Botanical Gardens ★★★
A must-see for serious plant lovers and a should-see for those looking for good Instagram photo ops, this

A dazzling circus poster at The Ringling's Circus Museum.

peaceful retreat is set on 45 acres of bayfront sanctuaries on two campuses: 15 acres along Sarasota Bay in downtown, and 30 acres 10 miles south along Little Sarasota Bay at the Historic Spanish Point campus. It's said to be the only botanical garden in the world specializing in the preservation, study, and research of epiphytes—that is, "air plants" such as orchids. The downtown Sarasota campus (our favorite of the two) includes a tropical conservatory that showcases rotating displays of plants from the gardens' orchid and bromeliad collections and the Museum of Botany & the Arts in the site's historic Payne Mansion. A new welcome center, restaurant, gift shop, and parking garage topped by a 50,000-square-foot solar array recently opened as part of an ambitious master plan aimed at protecting the gardens' collections and increasing sustainability at the site. The Historic Spanish Point campus focuses on both local history and plant life. The site offers insight on the ancient and pioneer history of the area as well as native Florida plants. It's a peaceful place for a stroll and for gazing out over Little Sarasota Bay.

Downtown Campus, 1534 Mound St., Sarasota; Historic Spanish Point Campus, 401 N. Tamiami Trail, Osprey. selby.org. **941/366-5731**. Admission to each campus $26 adults, $11 children 5–17, free for children 5 and under with an adult. Daily 10am–5pm.

The Ringling ★★★

John Ringling's primary work was his traveling circus, which still entertains Americans to this day. But he also dabbled in oil, real estate, finance, and ranching, and the combination made him a very rich man. In 1926, he built a Venetian-style palazzo on the east edge of Sarasota Bay, filled it with European art and furniture he bought from other wealthy American collectors, and spent 2 or 3 months a year there, entertaining the cream of society. The dream didn't last long; his wife Mable died in 1929, aged 54, and he followed her to the grave in 1936. After that, his stunning estate, his mansion, and his stash of priceless art were bequeathed to the state. Today, the legacy of this circus magnate is the tent-pole (if that's the term) of Sarasota tourism, hosting a third of a million visitors a year.

Now under the aegis of Florida State University, the **John and Mable Ringling Museum of Art** is the state's official art museum. Over 500 years of the history of European and American art are represented in the collections of the Museum of Art, which also presents a vibrant schedule of special exhibitions. The collections of 17th-century baroque paintings are world-renowned, and include five vast, famous tapestry cartoons by Peter Paul Rubens.

At the western lip of Bayfront Gardens, 66 lovely acres of ponds, lawns, and gardens, stands Ringling's home **Ca' d'Zan** ("cah-duh-zan"; it takes its name from "House of John" in the Venetian dialect), a mishmash of furniture bought at auction and styles borrowed from the Continent. It was built between 1924 and October 1925 at a cost of $1.5 million and modeled after several Venetian palaces on the Grand Canal. This 56-room palatial mansion has been meticulously restored. A 13,000-square-foot marble terrace leads down to the lower dock where John and Mable Ringling moored several luxury yachts and a gondola.

But the attraction you will certainly be talking about is the **Circus Museum,** which is based here because Ringling once used Sarasota as a winter base for his crews. Here, the fascinating tale of the circus is retold intelligently and with some prime artifacts, including Buffalo Bill's spangled gloves and whip and Tom Thumb's miniature suit, boots, and umbrella. That's interesting enough, but the 3,800-square-foot illuminated diorama of an early 20th-century traveling circus in its unfurled glory (ostensibly on a Friday, October 23, in Knoxville) is truly astonishing and could suck you in for an hour: 1,300 workers, 152 wagons, dozens of tents, 55 train cars, and fine details down to the meals on the picnic tables of the catering tent. Artist Howard Tibbals began making it in 1956, the same year Ringling Bros. abandoned canvas tents for indoor arenas.

The grounds include a classical courtyard, a rose garden, a museum shop, and the historic **Asolo Theater,** an 18th-century Italian court theater, which the Ringling's first director, Chick Everett Austin, moved here in the 1950s.

The museum's on-site restaurant, **The Ringling Grillroom,** is an elegant spot serving modern American fare. A museum admission ticket isn't required to dine in the restaurant.

You'll need most of a day to see everything here. On Thursdays from 5 to 8pm admission is discounted to the art museum and the gardens, and the Museum of Art, Bayfront Gardens, and Glass Pavilion are free to the public on Mondays. Regular museum admission includes entry to the Museum of Art, Circus Museum, and the Bayfront Gardens, but not Ca' d'Zan.

5401 Bay Shore Rd., at N. Tamiami Trail (U.S. 41). ringling.org. **941/359-5700.** Regular admission $30 adults, $5 children 6–17, free for children 5 and under. Admission with access to Ca' d'Zan $40–$55 adults, $15–$30 children 6–17. Daily 10am–5pm. From downtown, take U.S. 41 N. to University Pkwy. and follow signs to the museum.

ON ST. ARMANDS KEY

Mote Marine Laboratory & Aquarium ★★ The main aquarium building here features a 135,000-gallon shark habitat plus exhibits highlighting the ecosystems studied by Mote scientists. They showcase everything from seahorses to mesmerizing jellyfish. Admission also includes access to the **Ann and Alfred E. Goldstein Marine Mammal Research and Rehabilitation Center** (just across the street), where you can see the Dolphin and Whale Hospital, resident manatee Buffet—as in Jimmy—along with resident sea turtles, and the cutest "Oh Baby!" gallery of ocean animal moms, dads, and babies. At press time, Mote was constructing a new site, **Mote Science Education Aquarium** (Mote SEA), at the University Town Center area off Interstate 75 in Sarasota. It should be open by the time you read this.

1600 Ken Thompson Pkwy. (on City Island). mote.org. **941/388-4441**. Admission $29 adults, $21 children 3–12, free for children 2 and under. Daily 9am–5pm. From St. Armands Circle, head north toward Longboat Key; turn right just before the Lido-Longboat bridge.

IN & NEAR BRADENTON

Bishop Museum of Science and Nature ★ Despite its name, the real highlight here is the Parker Manatee Rehabilitation Habitat, which nurses the ill and injured mammals back to health before releasing them into the wild. There's the rub, though. Sometimes they do such a good job, there are no manatees to see here, so check their website to see what's going on. When there are no manatees in residence, admission is reduced. The complex also features a museum with planetarium, and an outdoor area with scale models of the solar system, a freshwater pond filled with turtles, a science shed, and a 30-foot tree house. The museum itself is interesting, with fossil evidence of Florida's earliest animal inhabitants, the Montague Tallant collection of prehistoric and early post-contact archeological artifacts, and an exhibit hall focusing on Florida's ecology and biodiversity in the Pine Uplands and Riverine Galleries.

201 10th St. W. (on the riverfront, at Barcarrota Blvd.). bishopscience.org. **941/746-4131**. Admission $25 adults, $23 seniors, $16 children 5–17, free for children 4 and under. Jan–Apr and July Mon–Sat 10am–5pm, Sun noon–5pm; rest of year Tues–Sat 10am–5pm, Sun noon–5pm. Closed Mon. From U.S. 41, take Manatee Ave. west to 10th St. W. and turn right.

De Soto National Memorial ★ Right on the Manatee River, west of downtown, this 26-acre park recreates the look and atmosphere of the period when Spanish explorer Hernando de Soto landed in 1539. It includes a restoration of de Soto's campsite and a scenic .5-mile nature trail that circles a mangrove jungle and leads to the ruins of one of the first settlements in the area. The park was damaged by Hurricanes Helene and Milton and significant cleanup efforts were underway as we went to press. Make sure to check the website ahead of visiting to see what experiences will be available at the park when you get there.

8300 De Soto Memorial Hwy. (north end of 75th St. W.). nps.gov/deso/index.htm. **941/792-0458**. Free admission. Daily 9am–5pm. Take Manatee Ave. (Fla. 64) west to 75th St. W. and turn right; follow the road to its end and the entrance to the park.

Judah P. Benjamin Confederate Memorial at Gamble Plantation State Park ★ As states vote to remove confederate memorials and statues, leave it to Florida to change the name of a park to further highlight said memorial (it used to just be called the Gamble Plantation). In fact, the state was working on legislation that would punish people for removing such monuments. That being said, northeast of downtown Bradenton, this is the oldest structure on the southwestern coast of Florida, an antebellum plantation home—something that's rare in Florida. It was constructed during a 6-year period in the late 1840s by Maj. Robert Gamble, made primarily of "tabby mortar" (a mixture of oyster shells, sand, molasses, and water), with 10 rooms, verandas on three sides, 18 exterior columns, and eight fireplaces. Now maintained as a state historic site, it includes a fine collection of 19th-century furnishings. Entrance to the house is by tour only, although you can explore the grounds on your own.

3708 Patten Ave. (U.S. 301), Ellenton. floridastateparks.org/parks-and-trails/judah-p-benjamin-confederate-memorial-gamble-plantation-historic-state-park. © **941/723-4536.** Free admission. Tour $6 adults, $4 children 6–12, free for children 5 and under. Daily 8am–sunset; 30-min. guided house tour Thurs–Mon 9:30 and 10:30am and 1, 2, 3, and 4pm. Take U.S. 301 north of downtown to Ellenton; the site is on the left, just east of Ellenton-Gillette Rd. (Fla. 683).

Robinson Preserve ★★★
This 682-acre conservation land is an ecotourism haven featuring restored coastal habitat and 2.5 miles of kayaking and canoe trails. The Blueways Trails here connect to the Manatee River, Perico Bayou, and Palma Sola Bay, comprising over 3 miles of internal trails. A 5-mile round-trip adventure would start at the launch and meander through the preserve to Palma Sola Bay and back. In addition, there are 100 acres of open water tidal systems, 56 acres of marshland, and 30 acres of uplands. If you prefer to stay on land, there are two piers, a 500-foot boardwalk, six bridges, and 10 miles of coastal, shell, and paved trails, along with two 400-foot-long pathways through mangrove forests. A 40-foot-tall observation tower offers spectacular views of four counties and five bodies of water. The historic, 120-year-old Valentine House, moved to the preserve by boat, is Robinson's visitor center. Kayaks and paddleboards are available for rent though SurferBus.com for $23 to $26 for kayaks and $45 for paddleboards for a half-day.

1704 99th St. W., Bradenton. mymanatee.org/departments/natural_resources/preserves/robinson. © **941/748-4501.** Free admission. Daily 8am–sunset. From U.S. 41, head north toward 33rd Ave. W. Turn right and then left on 26th St. W. Turn left at Manatee Ave. W. and then right at 75th St. W. Turn left at 9th Ave. NW and then right at 99th St.

Solomon's Castle ★★
This attraction gets the award in the Weirdest and Wackiest (and, boy, are there many) of Florida category. In 1974, Howard Solomon began building what has become a 60-foot-tall, 12,000-square-foot castle in a Manatee County swamp. Solomon, a metal and wood sculptor by trade, built the huge structure (where he now lives) out of 22×34-inch offset aluminum printing plates discarded by a local newspaper. He and the other tour guides (try to get the tour led by Solomon, or at least talk with him about his work) lead guests on a pun-filled tour of the castle, which is decked out with some of his smaller artistic creations, mostly made of other people's "trash," including a chair made out of 86 beer cans, an elephant pieced together with seven oil drums, a unicorn fashioned out of coat hangers, and about 80 stained-glass windows. Howard is continually building new things—you never know what you'll find. If you're hungry, check out the **Boat in the Moat** restaurant, which is literally just that. You *have* to experience this to believe it.

4533 Solomon Rd., Ona. solomonscastle.com. © **863/494-6007.** Admission $35 adults, $32 seniors, $14 teens 13–17, $10 children 4–12. Less expensive tickets for shorter tours are available. Oct 2–Aug 1 Tues–Sun 10am–4pm. Closed Aug–Sept. Take Hwy. 64 east of I-75 29 miles to Hwy. 665, go south 9 miles, and turn left at the sign to the castle.

Where to Stay

The beaches here are lined with condominiums, many of which are actually all-condo projects operated as hotels. Yes, you can use Airbnb and Vrbo to book, but you may do better with **Florida Vacation Connection** (flvacationconnection.com; © **877/702-9981** or 941/387-9709). Its staff have a deep knowledge of the properties it reps, and it offers everything from studios and three-bedroom condos to five-bedroom homes. It's been in biz since 1994.

The hotels below are organized by geographic region: in downtown Sarasota, on Lido Key, on Longboat Key, and on Siesta Key. The high season is from January to April. The bed tax in Sarasota County of 6% plus 7% sales tax adds a 13% total tax to your bill.

DOWNTOWN SARASOTA

Most visitors stay out at the beaches, but cost-conscious travelers will find some decent deals on the mainland, such as the **Ramada by Wyndham Sarasota Waterfront,** 7150 N. Tamiami Trail (wyndhamhotels.com; ✆ **941/203-6439**). It's close to the beaches and overlooks the bay, with an on-site restaurant and bar, a swimming pool, a staff that care, and best of all, nightly rates that rarely pop above $200, even in high season (and usually cost far below that). We think it's head-and-tails better than the other area chain motels, though there are a number of those if you want to use loyalty points.

The Sarasota Modern, a Tribute Portfolio Hotel ★★

So, this is a Marriott, but if we didn't tell you, you'd never guess. Located in downtown's happening Rosemary Arts & Design District, the Sarasota Modern lives up to its name, as a fresh oasis of newness, with rooms that break the typical Marriott mold with updated midcentury modern furniture and genuinely handsome artwork. A pretty pool deck has the requisite bar and whirlpool, while two other pools include a hot tub pool with underwater speakers and a cold plunge pool with waterfall. The hotel's restaurant, **Wink Wink Food & Drink,** fuses old-school 1950s- and '60s-era Sarasota supper clubs with tiki culture of the same era.

1290 Boulevard of the Arts, Sarasota. marriott.com. ✆ **941/906-1290.** 89 units. $115–$395 double. Valet parking $35. Pet fee $150. **Amenities:** Restaurant, bar; concierge; fitness center; outdoor pool; Jacuzzi; room service; free Wi-Fi.

ON LONGBOAT KEY

After we went to press, the **St. Regis Longboat Key Resort** (marriott.com; ✆ **941/213-3300**) debuted on Longboat Key. It's the largest development on the island in over 50 years, located along an 18-acre stretch of beach and featuring a 4-acre saltwater lagoon with sea life, multiple pools, and a massive spat. We can't review it because of the timing, but if ultra-luxury is your jam, this will likely fit the (hefty) bill.

The Resort at Longboat Key Club ★★★

A 410-acre beachfront resort and private club on the southern end of Longboat Key, this award-winning, green-certified destination resort pampers the country club set with upscale restaurants and a variety of recreational facilities and social activities all in a lush, private tropical setting. The spacious, newly reimagined rooms and suites have shiplap walls, beachy beige furnishings, and private balconies. A tennis center has over 20 courts for both tennis and pickleball, and 45 holes of golf keep things active if you choose that route. A small spa has 10 treatment rooms and two for relaxation. The massive beachfront is a highlight, with excellent service, games, and even waterfront yoga and qigong.

220 Sands Point Rd., Longboat Key. opalcollection.com. ✆ **941/383-8821.** 225 units. $499–$1,299 double. From St. Armands Key, take Gulf of Mexico Dr. north; take 1st left after bridge. **Amenities:** 5 restaurants; 5 bars; complimentary bikes; concierge; 2 golf courses (45 holes); fitness center; Jacuzzi; heated outdoor pool; room service; sauna; spa; 25 Har-Tru tennis courts; pickleball; watersports equipment/rentals; free Wi-Fi.

ON SIESTA KEY

Many of the smaller, mom-and-pop-style hotels on Siesta Key suffered damage from Hurricanes Helene and Milton and had not reopened as of press time. Plenty of condo rentals, however, are available around the island, and companies like **Beachside Management** (beachsidemanagement.com; © **941/203-8058**) and **Tropical Sands Accommodations** (siestakey.com; © **941/312-6156**) can help travelers find rentals right on or close to Siesta Key's white-sand beaches, as can Airbnb and Vrbo.

The Residences on Siesta Key Beach ★★★

The most luxurious hotel option on the barrier island, these residential-style accommodations are massive, ranging from 1,800 to nearly 3,000 square feet for two- to four-bedroom options. (Perfect for families and groups.) Some of that space is devoted to state-of-the-art kitchens, with Viking stoves, Sub Zero fridges, and Nespresso coffee makers. The furnishings are as luxe, and all rooms have splendid views of the Gulf of Mexico. A pristine beach is right outside, with an attendant who will set you up with chairs, umbrellas, and even beach toys for the tots. More perks include a well-outfitted fitness center, a beachside firepit, and a cabana bar on the sands.

915 Seaside Dr., Siesta Key, Sarasota. hyatt.com/en-US/hotel/florida/the-residences-on-siesta-key-beach/fiesh. © **941/346-5900.** 44 units. $393–$589 double. **Amenities:** Pool; fitness center; beach service; grilling area; free Wi-Fi.

Siesta Key Beach Resort and Suites ★★

This 55-room hotel sits within Siesta Key Village, which means it's easy to walk to restaurants, bars, and

Siesta Key Beach is a lively stretch of sand.

shopping. Beach access is just across the street, and beach wagons, beach chairs, and coolers are available for use during a stay. Rooms are done up in bright and fresh beach-y style, and the property includes a zero-entry pool, hammocks, grilling stations, and beach cruisers that can be checked out at the front desk.

5311 Ocean Blvd., Siesta Key. siestakeybeachresortandsuites.com. © **941/349-3211.** 55 units. $151–$279 double. Pet fee $35/day. **Amenities:** Zero-entry pool and hot tub; grilling station; beach gear; free Wi-Fi.

Turtle Beach Resort ★★★   On Siesta Key's south end, this intimate bayside charmer is very family-friendly, but has some units that are honeymoon-worthy. The cottages are done in various styles, such as Caribbean and Southwestern, and have at least one bedroom each. Some units are close to a small, peaceful bayside swimming pool, but heavy tropical foliage provides a reasonable degree of privacy, and high wooden fences surround each unit's private outdoor hot tub. Sitting right on the bay, all units also have one-way privacy mirror windows. There's no restaurant on the grounds, but there are two waterfront restaurants and a pub right next door, and all units have kitchens. Guests can use bikes, fishing poles, kayaks, and canoes for free. Boaters especially love the property's 10-boat marina. Pets are welcome at the resort for $25 per pet, per night, or $75 weekly per pet.

9049 Midnight Pass Rd., Sarasota. turtlebeachresort.com. © **941/349-4554.** 10 units. $217–$435 double. **Amenities:** Free use of bikes; outdoor pool; free use of watersports equipment; free Wi-Fi.

Where to Dine

Whereas Sarasota has become a very buttoned up, wealthy enclave of conservative seniors, the **Rosemary Arts District** is the absolute antithesis. What was once Sarasota's first Black community has now become the city's hipster hub. It's still a bit gritty, but this entirely walkable area is now a shopping, eating, and drinking destination.

Among the most exciting drinking and dining outposts in the district: **Boo's Ice House & Dog Bar ★★**, 1314 10th St. (boosdogbar.com; © **941/960-2669**), features wood-fired pizza, a full bar, and an indoor/outdoor dog park; **Food+Beer ★★**, 1525 4th St. (eatfooddrinkbeer.com; © **941/444-1101**), serves the best hatch chili burger this side of New Mexico; **The Original Wolfie's & Rascal House ★★** and **Wolfie's Box Office,** 1420 and 1454 Boulevard of the Arts (originalwolfies.com; © **941/312-4072**), are Miami Beach–style, Jewish soul food throwbacks.

The Rosemary Arts District is bounded by Fruitville Road, Tamiami Trail (U.S. 41), 10th Street, and Orange Avenue.

ALSO IN DOWNTOWN SARASOTA

Downtown's best breakfast spot is the local branch of **First Watch,** 1395 Main St., at Central and Pineapple avenues (firstwatch.com; © **941/954-1395**). Like its siblings in Naples and elsewhere, First Watch offers a wide variety of breakfast and lunch fare. It's open daily from 7:30am to 2:30pm. If the wait's too long, just stroll along Main Street where you'll find several coffeehouses and cafes with sidewalk seating.

Indigenous ★★★ SEAFOOD   Chef/owner Steve Phelps is at the forefront of the sustainable seafood movement, acting as an advocate and educator, and getting most of his fish from the Gulf for this adorable restaurant, set in a former historic home. Veggies are just as fresh, most coming from the kitchen's garden. The menu changes every 2 weeks, and draws its inspiration from across the globe, so expect unusual spreads, Middle Eastern and Asian spices, crudo plates, and fish cooked every which way. It's all delish, and the service is kindly.

239 S. Links Ave. indigenoussarasota.com. © **941/706-4740.** Main courses $25–$39. Tues–Sat 5:30–8:30pm.

Michael's on East ★★★ NEW AMERICAN   The locals' favorite after-theater haunt, Michael's is set in the rear of the Midtown Plaza shopping center on U.S. 41 south of downtown. Though Michael Klauber's supper clubby bistro opened in 1987, it's still one of the top places for fine dining. Huge cut-glass walls create three intimate dining areas, one a piano bar for pre- or after-dinner drinks. Prepared with fresh ingredients and a creative flair, house specialties include Michael's "famous" angel hair onion rings (very addictive with house-made ketchup); Galician-style braised octopus with chorizo; and pan-roasted bluefin crabcakes with dill remoulade. There are also steaks, chops, and some seriously good sides including potato croquettes and truffled mac and cheese. ***Best bargain:*** the three-course $46.95 Epicurean Adventures menu. For just $20 more you can add wine pairings. There's live music nightly in the lounge starting at 7pm.

1212 East Ave. S. (btw. Bahia and Prospect sts.). michaelsoneast.com. © **941/366-0007.** Reservations recommended. Main courses $29–$70. Tues–Thurs 5–10pm; Fri–Sat 5–11pm.

State Street Eating House + Cocktails ★★ AMERICAN   While the building housing this restaurant was originally a bakery, its current iteration is a looker, with distressed brickwork in some areas, reclaimed lumber, iron, and concrete in others and fabulously chic wallpaper in still others. It all provides a cool backdrop for an even cooler crowd. On the menu, a magnificent mushroom toast (take that, avocado toast) with glazed hen of the woods, mushroom crème fraiche, chicken jus, herbs and charred ciabatta; red curry mussels with coconut, ginger, and lemongrass; an eye-opening Creole-style bouillabaisse; and a bangin' burger. For Sunday brunch, try the sweet potato pancakes. The bar here is booming and for those who stick around (many do), a late-night menu of snacks ($7–$14) is offered. The lounge is open Tuesday and Wednesday until 11pm, midnight on Thursdays, and 1am on weekends.

1533 State St. statestreetsrq.com. © **941/951-1533.** Main courses $11–$38. Tues–Sat 5–11pm; Sat–Sun brunch 10:30am–2:30pm.

Yoder's Restaurant & Amish Village ★ AMISH/AMERICAN   Sarasota and Bradenton have sizable Amish communities and several Amish restaurants. Just 3 miles east of downtown is the one we like best, an award-winning, good-value eatery that evokes Pennsylvania Dutch country, with the dining room displaying handicrafts, photos, and paintings celebrating the Amish way. The menu emphasizes straightforward, made-from-scratch cooking such as home-style meatloaf, Southern fried chicken, country-smoked ham, and fried filet of flounder. Mrs. Yoder's shoofly pie, and other homemade pies, are among the restaurant's biggest draws.

3434 Bahia Vista St. (west of Beneva Rd.). yodersrestaurant.com. © **941/955-7771.** Main courses $7–$20. Mon–Sat 7am–8pm.

IN SOUTHSIDE VILLAGE

Southside Village, centered on South Osprey Avenue between Hyde Park and Hillview streets, about 15 blocks south of downtown, has several fab restaurants, including Fred's and Pacific Rim (see below). The village landmark is **Morton's Gourmet Market,** 1924 S. Osprey Ave. (mortonsmarket.com; © **941/955-9856;** Mon–Sat 8am–8pm, Sun 10am–5pm), which offers a multitude of deli items, sandwiches, salads, fresh pastries, and desserts, and cooked meals dispensed from a cafeteria-style steam table. You can dine picnic-fashion at sidewalk tables. Most ready-to-go items cost less than $10.

Libby's Neighborhood Brasserie ★★★ AMERICAN

Libby's is a local favorite for sandwiches like the Krabby Patty (blue crab and local Gulf shrimp), its juicy brisket burger, garlicky shrimp scampi, and fall-off-the-bone Dr. Pepper ribs. A $29, 8-ounce sirloin with garlic herb butter, Yukon gold mashed potatoes, and veg of the day is a downright bargain. Homemade strawberry shortcake is a dessert specialty. Happy hour specials are daily, with all-day happy hour on Mondays and Tuesdays. A second location is at 8445 Lorraine Road (© **941/357-1570**).

1917 S. Osprey (at Hillview). libbysneighborhoodbrasserie.com. © **941/487-7300.** Main courses $15–$46. Sun–Thurs 11am–9pm; Fri–Sat 11am–10pm.

Pacific Rim ★★ JAPANESE/THAI

Pacific Rim looks nondescript from the outside, but it serves up the best Asian food in Sarasota: fresh fish, creative sushi rolls, and fiery Thai drunken noodles. For a sweet, saucy finish, try the coconut martini.

In Hillview Centre, 1859 Hillview St. (btw. Osprey Ave. and Laurent Place). pacrimsrq.com. © **941/330-8071.** Main courses $10–$25. Mon–Thurs 11:30am–2pm and 4:30–9pm; Fri 11:30am–2pm and 4:30–10pm; Sat 4:30–10pm; Sun 4:30–9pm.

ON SIESTA KEY

Ocean Boulevard, which runs through **Siesta Village,** the area's funky, laid-back beach hangout, is lined with restaurants and pubs. Most have bars and outdoor seating, which attracts the beach crowd during the day. At night, rock-'n'-roll bands draw students and young singles to this lively scene.

Blasé Martini Bar/Pi Pizza 3.14 ★★ PIZZA

Despite the double name, there's just one menu here—pizzas, wings, burgers, and sandwiches—though the place does have two very different vibes. For creative cocktails and live music, choose the indoor martini bar, where the owners have installed the original bar from Don CeSar Beach Resort & Spa in St. Pete Beach. For craft beers and a more relaxed, beachier vibe, choose the Pi Pizza 3.14's outdoor area on a wooden deck built around a palm tree in the center's asphalt parking lot.

In Village Corner, 5263 Ocean Blvd. (at Calle Miramar), Siesta Village. blasepisiesta.com. © **941/349-9822.** Reservations recommended. Main courses $12–$23. Martini Bar daily 5–11pm (bar until 2am); 3.14 Pi Mon–Wed 2pm–2am; Thurs–Sun noon–2am.

SKOB ★★ SEAFOOD

Siesta Key Oyster Bar, or SKOB, is the kind of beach bar where patrons tack dollar bills to the walls. It has live music, daily drink specials, and, of course, oysters of all varieties, raw on the half shell, fried, or steamed. That's in addition to sandwiches, salads, brunch, and a kids' menu, but what the place is known for is one of the best happy hours in town, daily from 3 to 6pm, when there are $12 dozen oysters, two-for-one appetizers, live bands, and drink specials.

5238 Ocean Blvd. skob.com. © **941/346-5443.** Main dishes $14–$32, except for crabs and the seafood boil, which are pricier. Mon–Thurs 11am–11pm; Fri–Sat 11am–midnight; Sun 9am–11pm.

Sun Garden Cafe ★★ BREAKFAST/LUNCH Hands down the best breakfast place on Siesta Key, this indoor-outdoor cafe features a breezy ambience and gracious service, along with a seasonal menu of freshly made egg dishes, breakfast sandwiches, waffles, pancakes (try the banana ones), French toast (cookie butter stuffed French toast is *the* one), omelets, and more. They also have something called Grateful Dead pudding with toffee sauce. Whatever you choose, you won't be disappointed, but if you do choose Elvis's fried chicken plate at lunch, you better come hungry.

210 Avenida Madera. sungardencafe.com. © **941/346-7170.** Main courses $12–$20. Daily 7:30am–1:30pm.

Sarasota After Dark

The cultural capital of Florida's west coast, Sarasota's performing arts scene is a vibrant one, especially during the winter season. Visit Sarasota has a comprehensive list of events, concerts, and performances at visitsarasota.com/node/23776. Also check alternative weekly *Creative Loafing Tampa Bay* (cltampa.com) and the "Ticket" section in Friday's *Herald-Tribune* (heraldtribune.com/entertainment/events), the local daily newspaper.

THE PERFORMING ARTS The historic **Asolo Repertory Theatre** ★★★ at 5555 N. Tamiami Trail in the Florida State Center for the Performing Arts (asolorep.org; © **800/361-8388** or 941/351-8000) is one of the finest regional theaters in the country, and hosts a conservatory for training professional actors. The 487-seat Harold E. and Ethel M. Mertz Theatre, originally constructed in Scotland in 1900

Downtown Sarasota at dawn.

and transferred piece by piece to Sarasota in 1987, serves as the main performing space for both the Asolo Repertory Theatre and the Sarasota Ballet. The 161-seat **Florida State Asolo Conservatory Theatre** is a venue for experimental and alternative offerings.

The city's other prime arts venue is the lavender, seashell-shaped **Van Wezel Performing Arts Hall** ★★, 777 N. Tamiami Trail (U.S. 41), at 9th Street (van wezel.org; ✆ **800/826-9303** or 941/953-3368). Restored after storm damage, it has excellent acoustics and sightlines, and offers a wide range of year-round programming, including touring Broadway shows and visiting orchestras and dance troupes. It and Holly Hall at the **Beatrice Friedman Symphony Center,** 709 N. Tamiami Trail, host performances by the **Sarasota Orchestra** (sarasotaorchestra.org; ✆ **941/953-4252**).

Built in 1926 as the Edwards Theater, **Sarasota Opera House** ★★★, 61 N. Pineapple Ave., between Main and 1st streets (sarasotaopera.org; ✆ **941/366-8450**), presents operas (in their original languages) as well as classical concerts. It's also a frequent venue for performances by the **Sarasota Ballet** (sarasotaballet.org; ✆ **800/361-8388** or 941/351-8000).

It's a good idea to check the schedules for the **Jazz Club of Sarasota** (jazzclubsarasota.org; ✆ **941/366-1552** or 941/316-9207) and the **Pops Orchestra of Bradenton and Sarasota** (thepopsorchestra.org; ✆ **941/926-7677**) to see if they're performing when you're in town. And you can't go wrong by taking in a show put on by **Westcoast Black Theatre Troupe** ★★, 1012 N. Orange Ave., Sarasota (westcoastblacktheatre.org; ✆ **941/366-1505**).

Downtown Sarasota's theater district is home to the **Florida Studio Theatre,** 1241 N. Palm Ave., at Cocoanut Avenue (floridastudiotheatre.org; ✆ **941/366-9000**), which produces contemporary plays and musicals from December to August. It also hosts a popular cabaret series in winter.

THE CLUB, MUSIC & BAR SCENE One of downtown's most popular places for a night out is **Mattison's City Grille** ★★★, 1 N. Lemon Ave. (mattisons.com; ✆ **941/330-0440**); it offers live jazz and local bands. Views, booze, and a piano bar are the draw at **Marina Jack,** also downtown at 2 Marina Plaza (marinajacks.com; ✆ **941/365-4232**).

In Siesta Key Village, the **Old Salty Dog** ★, 5023 Ocean Blvd. (theoldsaltydog.com; ✆ **941/349-0158**), has a big selection of British ales and an outdoor patio. The pubs and restaurants along Ocean Boulevard in Siesta Village have rock-'n'-roll bands entertaining a mostly young crowd—**SKOB** ★★, 5238 Ocean Blvd. (p. 356), is a major hot spot, featuring money-saving happy hours and live music nightly. Or you can retire to the pleasant confines of the martini bar at **Blasé** (p. 356) for live jazz.

On Longboat Key, the **Haye Loft** at **Euphemia Haye,** 540 Gulf of Mexico Dr. (euphemiahaye.com; ✆ **941/383-3633**), is command central for the cocktail set.

For a lofty view of the area, rooftop bars including the **Perspective Rooftop Pool Bar** at the **Art Ovation Hotel,** 1255 N. Palm Ave. (artovationhotel.com; ✆ **941/316-0808**); the one at **Sage SRQ,** 1216 1st St. (sagesrq.com; ✆ **941/445-5660**); and **The Roof Bar & Eats** at the Westin Sarasota, 100 Marina View Dr. (marriott.com; ✆ **941/217-4777**) are some of the city's best.

WALT DISNEY WORLD, UNIVERSAL & ORLANDO

by Jason Cochran

10

No matter who you are, no matter your politics or upbringing, when you were a kid growing up, you probably went at least once to Orlando. And if you didn't, you desperately wanted to. Which other aspect of culture can we all claim to share? Orlando is like a physical embodiment of America itself—how we dream, how we play, and how we spend. Orlando transformed the farmland and muggy swamps of Central Florida into "The Happiest Place on Earth." To experience the most popular tourist destination in the United States is to understand the values of the civilization that created it.

Walt Disney World (WDW), practically a city unto itself at 47 square miles, is home to four major theme parks; two water parks; an incredible shopping, dining, and entertainment complex; thousands of hotel rooms; scores of restaurants; and, an hour's drive to the coast, a cruise line.

That would be plenty, but add **Universal Orlando** (consisting of two major theme parks—and a third opening in 2025; a water park; an entertainment, dining, and shopping complex; and 11 fine hotels), **SeaWorld Orlando** (including Discovery Cove and Aquatica, a water park), and a handful of other smaller daylong attractions into Orlando's tourist mix. Considered together, it can get overwhelming.

We can help simplify things. To help you plan your Orlando stay, we've included the lowdown on the area's best hotels, restaurants, and attractions. You'll also find tips to help you plan and budget, making it not only easier to arrange, but, we hope, more affordable, too.

Note: For a deeper look at WDW as well as Orlando's many other experiences, hotels, and restaurants, check out the fuller coverage in our award-winning *Frommer's Disney World, Universal & Orlando,* available in paperback or as an e-book.

ESSENTIALS
Getting There

BY PLANE Orlando is served by some 40 airlines, and competition keeps airfares reasonable. More than 50 million trips begin or end at **Orlando International Airport** (www.orlandoairports.net) each year, making it the seventh busiest in the country. The airport, 25 miles east of Walt Disney World, was built during World War II as McCoy Air Force Base, which closed in the early 1970s but bequeathed the airport with its deceptive code, MCO. Midmornings and midafternoons can be crowded for outgoing passengers and weekends can be clogged with cruise passengers. Midafternoon summer thunderstorms frequently cause delays, so try to fly early in the morning then. Also, make sure you get on the correct tram

PREVIOUS PAGE: Mickey Mouse brings the sparkle to Disney's Hollywood Studios' Fantasmic! evening show.

Aquatica **9**
Charles Hosmer Morse
  Museum of American Art **2**
Discovery Cove **11**
Gatorland **12**
Islands of Adventure **7**
King's Landing **1**
Legoland Florida **17**
Orange County Regional
  History Center **4**
The Orlando Eye **8**
Scenic Boat Tour **3**
SeaWorld Orlando **10**
Universal Orlando **5**
Volcano Bay **6**
Walt Disney World:
  Disney's Animal Kingdom **16**
  Disney's Hollywood Studios **15**
  EPCOT **14**
  Magic Kingdom **13**

for your gate number, otherwise you'll have to go through security all over again. Most major rental car companies are in garages connected to the terminals—no shuttles required. The airport also puts out a free map app, **Orlando MCO.**

Comparatively few airlines use **Orlando Sanford International Airport** (orlandosanfordairport.com), or SFB, which despite the Orlando in its name is 42 miles northeast of Disney. SFB is connected to the Disney area by the Central Florida GreeneWay, or S.R. 417—the trip takes about 40 minutes and has tolls, so new arrivals should have U.S. money on them, preferably quarters. European visitors might fly into **Tampa International Airport** (tampaairport.com), or TPA, 90 minutes southwest.

BY CAR From Atlanta, take I-75 South to the Florida Turnpike to I-4 West. From the northeast, take I-95 South to I-4 West. From Chicago, take I-65 South to Nashville, then I-24 South to I-75, then south to the Florida Turnpike to I-4 West. From Dallas, take I-20 East to I-49 South, then head south to I-10, east to I-75, and south to the Florida Turnpike to I-4 West.

BY TRAIN The privately funded **Brightline** service (gobrightline.com; ✆ **831/539-2901**) connects a comfortable and well-provisioned station at Orlando International Airport with West Palm Beach (2 hr.), Fort Lauderdale (3 hr.), and Miami (3½ hr.). Trains hurtle at up to 110 mph in rural areas and have high on-board standards including charging ports and free Wi-Fi. Service begins daily at 5am and departures are scheduled roughly hourly until around 9pm.

Amtrak's (amtrak.com; ✆ **800/872-7245**) Silver Service/Palmetto route stops at Orlando and Kissimmee. Trains go direct between New York City, Washington, D.C., Charleston, and Savannah.

Package Tours

Vacation package companies that once competed with each other with lower prices on comprehensive air-and-hotel packages, like **Funjet Vacations** (funjet.com), **Southwest Vacations** (southwestvacations.com), and **United Vacations** (vacations.united.com), are now operated by one giant company, ALG Vacations. ALG still has buying power, so it's worth checking, but also broaden your search to include **JetBlue Getaways** (jetbluevacations.com; ✆ **844/528-2229**), **Delta Vacations** (deltavacations.com; ✆ **800/800-1504**), and **American Airlines Vacations** (aavacations.com; ✆ **800/321-2121**). Internationally, **Virgin Atlantic Holidays** (virginholidays.co.uk) is a player in the United Kingdom. These websites may sell hotel-only deals using their negotiated rates, and the best package deals won't be for Disney-run hotels.

Visitor Information

Orlando is lucky to have an excellent tax-supported visitors' bureau, **Visit Orlando** (visitorlando.com; ✆ **407/363-5872**), which provides basic but official planning resources online, hooks you up with discount codes, and answers questions by phone for free. Kissimmee, the town closest to Walt Disney World, maintains its own tourist bureau, the **Kissimmee CVB** (experiencekissimmee.com; ✆ **407/569-4800**). It works with the Orlando bureau, though, so you don't have to check in with both.

Walt Disney World (disneyworld.com; ✆ **407/939-5277**) provides lots of information, including menus and availability calendars, but information can be blindly positive, and not always forthright, and phone calls can result in long waits. **Universal Orlando**'s (universalorlando.com; ✆ **877/589-4783** or 407/363-8000) official information is just as suffused by marketing manipulation, but it can also answer many essential nuts-and-bolts questions. **SeaWorld Orlando** information is available at seaworldorlando.com or by calling ✆ **407/545-5500.**

Be wary of information gleaned from social media. Disney cultivates a large force of Disney-promoting influencers by granting them free access and gifts, but the company exiles accounts that it deems overly critical, which results in skewed coverage.

City Layout

Interstate 4 (I-4) sidewinds across Orlando diagonally from southwest to northeast and it will take you nearly everywhere you want to go. The tourist zones are generally segregated from residential ones: theme parks in the south, "real" Orlando in the north. Exits are numbered according to the mile marker at which they're found. Therefore, the Disney World exits (62, 64, 65, and 67) are roughly 10 miles from Universal Orlando's (74 and 75), which are about 9 miles from downtown (83). Like pretty much every urban American freeway, I-4 is often jammed, a situation made worse by the fact that lake-riddled Orlando offers few other direct routes. I-4 is least congested from late morning to midafternoon.

A few tolled or partially tolled roads are available. **Florida Turnpike** crosses I-4 and links with I-75 to the north. The **Beachline Expressway** runs east from I-4 past Orlando International Airport to Cape Canaveral and Cocoa Beach. Most of Central Florida's toll roads use transponders for payment and are not staffed, so if you're not from Florida, it's best to obtain a **Visitor Toll Pass** (highly recommended; visitortollpass.com), reserved ahead via a free app of the same name and picked up at vending machines located on Level 1 at Terminal A of the MCO airport. Instead of ripping you off like rental car transponder does, it charges your credit card with fair toll rates, and there's no surcharge to use it.

The Neighborhoods in Brief

WALT DISNEY WORLD First-time visitors aren't usually prepared for how large the area is: 47 square miles. Only a third of that land is truly developed, and

The iconic Cinderella Castle with the princess herself at Magic Kingdom.

another third has been set aside as a permanent reserve. Major elements are easily a 10-minute highway-style drive away from each other. Magic Kingdom is buried deep in the back of the resort campus—which is to say, the north of it, requiring the most driving time from I-4 to reach. EPCOT and Disney's Hollywood Studios are in the center, while Disney's Animal Kingdom is at the southwest of the property.

LAKE BUENA VISTA   Lake Buena Vista is a hotel enclave on the eastern fringe of Walt Disney World. It's mostly hotels and mid-priced chain restaurants with some schlocky souvenir stores thrown in, but it's convenient to Disney's side door and **Disney Springs,** WDW's pedestrianized shopping-and-entertainment district, where upscale restaurants and specialty shops attract locals and tourists alike.

KISSIMMEE   Kissimmee (Kiss-*imm*-ee) was the heart of Orlando tourism in the 1970s, but the center of tourist gravity shifted, and it now lags further behind every year. The tatty drag of U.S. 192, known also as the Irlo Bronson Memorial Highway (after a state senator who sold Walt a bunch of land), is its congested spine. U.S. 192 is mostly about ultra-cheap chains and buffets, but on weekend nights, it becomes a low-rent Rialto of cruising muscle cars.

INTERNATIONAL DRIVE AREA (HWY. 536)   The area from SeaWorld north to Universal Orlando, east of I-4 between exits 71 and 75, is probably the only district where you might comfortably stay without a car and still be able to see the non-Disney attractions, because I-Drive, as it's called, is chockablock with affordable hotels and plenty of crowd-pleasing things to do, such as arcades, wild minigolf courses, family restaurants, and the Orlando Eye (p. 398).

DOWNTOWN ORLANDO   Beneath the city's collection of modest skyscrapers (mostly banking offices), you'll find municipal buildings (the main library, historic museums) and some attractive lakes, but little shopping. Orange Avenue, once a street of proud stone buildings and department stores, now comes alive mostly at night, and mostly for the young. You'll be unlikely to stay this far north if your object is theme parks. Just north of downtown, **Winter Park** is one of the city's most interesting areas, and one of the few that hasn't taken pains to erase its history. Winter Park was where, more than 100 years ago, upstart industrialists built winter homes. Its most charming streets are still paved with brick.

GETTING AROUND

Probably 90% of what a tourist wants to do lies within a 10-minute drive of Interstate 4, or I-4, which is free. If you're traveling by highway, it's best to avoid the 7-day-a-week rush hour (7–9am and 4–6pm) whenever possible. Alternate routes can remain congested later into the evening.

The terrain of Orlando is pocked with lakes formed from sinkholes, and many minor roads have a way of dead-ending into them instead of taking you to your destination. Using a navigator app like **Waze** or **Apple Maps** can help. Roads can also go by both a number and a name. Also, don't rely on free maps that you find at tourist joints around town; laughably, some of the ones provided by Universal don't acknowledge that Disney exists at all.

Generally speaking, unless you will be confining your stay solely to Disney World or Universal Orlando (and staying exclusively at those parks' hotels), you're better off renting a car to get around Orlando. None of the theme parks (except SeaWorld and Epic Universe) can be easily accessed from town on foot. A large inventory means car rentals are cheaper here than in other American cities: $30 to $50 a day is common for a compact vehicle.

INTERNATIONAL DRIVE Traffic on I-Drive can be infuriating, compounded exponentially if you are visiting when conventions are in town. Two of the best ways to conquer the traffic are to travel by foot (points of interest can be reasonably close together, but heavy traffic can be hazardous to pedestrians) or by the **I-Ride Trolley** (iridetrolley.com; ✆ **407/354-5656;** adults $2 per ride, seniors 65 and over 25¢, kids ages 3–9 $1; day pass $6, 3-day pass $8, 5-day pass $10, 7-day pass $16; free transfers; passes not sold on board; daily 8am–10:30pm), an excellent shuttle bus with plenty of clearly marked and well-maintained stops, benches to wait on, and genuinely useful routes—except waits can be long and it doesn't go to Disney.

BY THE DISNEY TRANSPORTATION SYSTEM It's impossible to hoof it around Disney, but the company offers unlimited free transportation via bus, monorail, ferry, gondola, and water taxi to all WDW properties. Buses travel between the theme parks and Disney hotels, or between the hotels and Disney Springs, but no bus links Disney Springs directly to the parks. Bus service between Disney resort hotels and Disney theme parks begins 45 minutes prior to opening and ends 1 hour after closing. Buses tend to depart every 10 to 20 minutes.

The free system saves you money, but it can often be slow, crowded, and sometimes *very* indirect (especially from Disney's cheaper resorts). Check Disney's website (**disneyworld.com**), or ask your concierge to determine the best route.

BY SHUTTLE Mears Transportation (mearstransportation.com; ✆ **407/423-5566**) is the 800-pound gorilla of shuttles and taxis. It operates a coach service, **Mears Connect** (mearsconnect.com); fares vary slightly per hotel but a standard one-way rate to Disney would be $21 adult, $15 child. Mears Connect drops off and picks up at most major hotels, but it will stop a lot for other passengers and could take up to 90 minutes. If you just want to go straight there, no stopping, with your group, the rate for a private sedan or van will be around $110 to $130. Try **Mears** (✆ **407/422-2222**), **Tiffany Towncar** (tiffanytowncar.com; ✆ **888/838-2161** or 407/370-2196), or **Quicksilver Tours** (quicksilver-tours.com; ✆ **800/711-0080**).

Monorail Coral glides through EPCOT.

BY RIDE-SHARING SERVICE Taxis exist (**Diamond Cab Company;** diamondcabco.com; bookable by app; ℓ **407/523-3333** and **Yellow;** mearstransportation.com; ℓ **407/422-2222**), but they have been eclipsed by ride-share. Because huge theme park crowds compete for rides, it's not always easy to use Uber or Lyft for every journey you will make on vacation. Ride-shares between the rival resorts will cost you about $25 per ride. Uber trips within Disney World are about $10 to $14 (much cheaper than Disney's in-house, polka-dotted **Minnie Vans,** hailed via Lyft's app even though they cost triple what a standard Lyft ride does: $30–$70).

[FastFACTS] WALT DISNEY WORLD & ORLANDO

Babysitters
Few Orlando hotels, including Disney's resorts, still offer babysitting services. If you're staying in a luxury resort hotel, the management may offer some kind of paid babysitting or supervised kids' club service. **Kid's Nite Out** (kidsniteout.com; ℓ **800/696-8105;** reservations required) has been in business since 1998. Sitters will look after kids from 6 weeks to 12 years old, charging $30 per hour for the first child, $3 for each additional child, for a minimum of 4 hours. You also pay a $15 transportation fee, and there's a $5-per-hour surcharge for reservations that begin before 8am or after 8:59pm. The service is insured, bonded, and licensed, and it would appreciate advance warning of between 2 weeks and a month for reservations for in-room sitting. The **Four Seasons** resort (p. 403) includes a free daytime kids' club as part of its normal rates.

Doctors & Dentists
All the theme parks have first-aid centers. There's also a 24-hour number for the **Poison Control Center** (ℓ **800/222-1222**). To find a dentist, contact **Dental Referral** (dentalreferral.com; ℓ **855/289-6320**). If you don't have a car, **East-Coast Medical Network** (themedicalconcierge.com; ℓ **407/648-5252**) makes "hotel room calls" to area resorts or rental homes from 8am to 11pm daily for $150 to $275 for most ailments. It's available at all hours, accepts most insurance, and brings a portable pharmacy, although prescriptions cost more.

Emergencies
Dial ℓ **911** for the police, the fire department, or an ambulance.

Hospitals
Orlando Health Dr. P. Phillips Hospital, 9400 Turkey Lake Rd., Orlando (ℓ **407/351-8500**), is a short drive north up Palm Parkway from Lake Buena Vista. The 24-hour, full-service **AdventHealth ER at Flamingo Crossings Town Center,** 13323 Hartzog Rd., Winter Garden (ℓ **407/550-0700**), is on the western edge of Disney property, past Disney's Coronado Springs, and the 24-hour **AdventHealth Celebration,** 400 Celebration Place, Celebration (ℓ **407/303-4000**), is just east: from I-4, take the U.S. 192 exit, then at the first traffic light, turn right onto Celebration Avenue, and at the first stop sign, make another right. Clinics for simpler care: **Central Florida AdventHealth Centra Care Lake Buena Vista,** 12500 Apopka-Vineland Rd. (centracare.adventhealth.com; ℓ **407/934-2273;** daily 7am–midnight); and **AdventHealth Centra Care Dr. Phillips,** northwest of Universal at 8014 Conroy-Windermere Rd., Suite 104 (ℓ **407/291-8975;** Mon–Fri 8am–8pm, Sat–Sun 8am–5pm).

Kennels
None of the Disney resorts allow animals (except service dogs) to

stay (the only exception being Disney's Fort Wilderness Campground, where you can have your pet at the full-hook-up campsites). Disney offers **animal boarding**, usually for about $40 to $50 per day. Disney uses **Best Friends Pet Care,** at 2510 Bonnet Creek Pkwy. (bestfriendspetcare.com; ✆ 407/209-3126). For daycare, it opens 1 hour before the parks and closes 1 hour after the last closing. Overnight prices start at $60 to $65. Cheaper, and not much farther away, **Pet Paradise,** 7107 Palm Pkwy. (petparadise.com; ✆ 407/710-1966), also handles daycare and overnight boarding. **Universal** no longer boards pets. Off-property, there's **V.I.Pet Resort** (vipetresort.com; ✆ 407/355-3594; $75–$85 dogs, $45 cats overnight, $50 daytime with a 6:30pm pickup deadline), near where Sand Lake Road meets Florida's Turnpike. For all these services, you must have written proof of current vaccinations.

Pharmacies   The tourist area hosts national chains. **Walgreens,** 7650 W. Sand Lake Rd. at Dr. Phillips Blvd., Orlando (✆ 407/370-6742), has a pharmacy open until 9pm. **Turner Drugs,** 1530 Celebration Blvd., Suite 105-A, Celebration (turnerdrug.com; ✆ 407/828-8125), is not a 24-hour pharmacy, but during the day it delivers prescriptions to most Disney-area accommodations.

Post Office   The post office most convenient to Disney and Universal is at 10450 Turkey Lake Rd. (✆ 407/351-2492; Mon–Fri 8am–7pm, Sat 9am–5pm).

Taxes   A 6.5% to 7% sales tax is charged on all goods except for most edible grocery items and medicines. Hotels add another 2% to 5% in a resort tax, so the total tax on accommodations can run up to 12%. The United States has no VAT, but the custom is to not list prices with tax, so the final amount that you pay will be higher than the posted price.

Tipping   In the United States, the standard is to add at least 15%, but more often 20%, in gratuity to your pre-tax bill at a table-service restaurant. In the U.S., servers are paid a low hourly wage with the assumption that they will make the bulk of their income from gratuities. Because Orlando receives so many international visitors who don't expect this situation, you'll find reminders to tip posted everywhere. Other people to tip: Taxi or ride-share drivers (10%–15%), porters and valets ($2–$3 per bag or vehicle). Tips are optional at counter-service restaurants, but they're socially expected when tables are served by wait staff.

Weather   June to September is the heaviest season for excruciating sun (never go outside without sunscreen on), suffocating humidity, brief torrential rain, and flight delays. Winter can be chilly but never freezing.

EXPLORING WALT DISNEY WORLD

Walt Disney World is home to four major parks: Magic Kingdom (the world's most popular theme park, attracting about 17 million visits a year), EPCOT, Disney's Hollywood Studios, and Disney's Animal Kingdom.

PARKING   Each park has its own sunbaked lot ($30/day; free for Disney hotel guests and annual passholders; $45–$55 for "Preferred" to be extra close). The few **charging stations** for electric vehicles cost $0.35 per kilowatt with a minimum charge of $1.50, but there aren't nearly enough and they're first-come, first-charging, so if you drive an electric car, arrive early. Charging stations require both a credit card and a pre-ordered ChargePoint card (chargepoint.com); ask the toll attendant where they are.

SECURITY Everyone passes through scanners and bags may be searched. Eyeglass cases and big batteries seem to trigger closer inspection, so keep those visibly open as you pass through. Drawstring bags are quicker to search than zipper-laden ones, but you'll save the most time if you don't have a bag at all, because you'll use a faster screening line. ***Banned:*** Booze, glass containers, selfie sticks, wheelie sneakers, costumes on anyone age 14 and over.

BEST TIMES TO VISIT There isn't really an offseason in Orlando anymore, but crowds are usually thinner from early January to mid-March and from mid-September until the week before Thanksgiving. The busiest days are generally Saturday and Sunday, when more locals visit. Major holidays attract scores of visitors: Christmas to New Year's is by far the busiest time; with the week preceding and following Easter a close second. Summer (June–Sept) can be tough. The crowds are heavy, and the heat and humidity are decidedly uncomfortable.

> **Typical Adult Ticket Price Ranges at Disney**
>
> Magic Kingdom: $124–$189
> EPCOT: $114–$179
> Disney's Hollywood Studios: $124–$179
> Disney's Animal Kingdom: $109–$159

OPERATING HOURS Park hours vary and are influenced by special events. Check the calendar on the Disney World app or **disneyworld.com** for operating times, otherwise, you could find yourself expecting to stay all night when the park actually closes at 6pm for one of WDW's frequent separately ticketed evening events. EPCOT closes at 9pm, but otherwise, hours vary not only from park to park, but also from day to day. Near closing time, if you are permitted to get in line for something, you'll be able to stay until you ride, and shopping remains open for an hour after the posted closing time.

If you are a guest of a Disney-run hotel (or are staying at a hotel that explicitly offers the privilege), you may enter the park 30 minutes ahead of outsiders. That's not a lot of time and thousands of other people will use the same privilege, but you can get the jump on at least one ride.

TICKETS Tickets are priced by the day according to how busy the park is expected to be.

The first step is creating your Disney account. Find a link for creating one at the top of disneyworld.disney.go.com. You'll use your account with the official Disney World app to get into the parks, board rides, and order food (so don't forget to add a credit card). Without this account, you're sunk, so make sure you remember your login details. Everyone in your party must set up a unique profile. Then you must tell the system you're all traveling together by linking everyone. Do that by going to your profile (click "My Disney Experience" at the upper right), choosing "My Family & Friends" from the menu, and clicking "Add a Guest."

Go to disneyworld.disney.go.com/admission/tickets for the ticket pricing calendar. The least you can pay (outside of limited-time deals) for a 1-day ticket is $109 adult, $104 child (and at Disney, you're only a child from age 3–9). This lowest rate isn't valid most of the time, but it does appear in August and September after kids go back to school. On most days of the year, you'll actually wind up with a base price in the $120s to $150s for an adult, and a child's ticket is only about $5 less. The highest a day ticket for one park will ever go (so far) is $189 adult/$184 child during the peak December holidays. During heavy vacation periods like spring break and Thanksgiving, tickets are in the mid-$160s. When you start adding more days to that visit, it costs the same per day to get into any of the parks, and the per-day price drops ever so slightly for every day you add.

You also need to decide if you want to add the **Park Hopper** option. Without it, you can only visit one theme park per day. But if you buy it, you can enter multiple parks on the same day. This is a flexibility that is worth the expense when buying for the week. The price of the Park Hopper option is different by the day, but the cost is amortized across days for longer stays. If you're staying a full week, you might be essentially spending another $13 a day for the right to park-hop, whereas if you add Park Hopper to a ticket for just a single day, you could be paying an extra $60 to $85, which wouldn't make much sense. Take this example of how it may be worthwhile: With it, you can do the early-morning safari at Animal Kingdom, take a nap at your hotel, and then switch to Magic Kingdom for the fireworks.

Other possible add-ons: **Water Park and Sports Option** ($70, covers your entire stay, and you can visit the water parks as many times as you wish). This won't allow park-hopping (that's only for dry theme parks), but it does add entry to the two water parks (of which *only one is open* on any given day), the miniature golf courses that open at 4pm daily, and greens fees at Disney's Oak Trail Golf Course. It's not a good buy because you'll never use all of it. You can buy tickets

what is LIGHTNING LANE?

Simply put, it's a secondary entry line for an attraction that moves much faster than the walk-up "Standby" line. In past years, a similar but free program was known as Fast-Pass—but now it's a service you must pay for. There are two ways to get into the Lightning Lane.

The first way: Buy **Lightning Lane Multi Pass** (previously known as Genie+) for the day via the Disney World app. Although many attractions have Lightning Lane, it's only feasible to make timed reservations on three of them at once by choosing them from a preset list, which opens 3 days ahead of your visit, or 7 days if you're staying at a Disney resort. When you use a reservation, you may add another. If a ride breaks down during your booking time, you'll get a digital voucher that allows you to book another Lightning Lane instead. Cost: $15 to $39 per day, depending on crowds.

The second way: Pay per ride. One or two rides in each park are so popular that they don't let you use their Lightning Lanes through a daily Multi Pass subscription. This upper echelon only accepts **Lightning Lane Single Pass.** For these rides, the only way into the Lightning Lane is to pay separately via the app. You may only buy two Individual Lightning Lanes a day. They don't have to be in the same park, but they can't be the same ride. If a ride breaks down during your booking time, you'll be allowed to return once it reopens; if you are unable to wait, you'll have to go to Guest Relations to get your money back. If the ride remains closed all day, you'll get an automatic refund. Cost: up to $22 per person per ride.

For a much more in-depth look at Lightning Lane and how to maximize it, visit Frommers.com.

to all of those things independently as you go (waterslide parks cost $64–$69 adults, $58–$63 kids 3–9). Likewise avoid the **Park Hopper Plus Option,** which merely adds a park hopper option to Water Park and Sports. You'll never be able to do it all unless you're staying at least a week.

You don't have to use all your Disney tickets on consecutive days. You can take the day off and go do something else in Orlando, but Disney only gives you a couple of extra days of slack to do it.

MagicBands & MagicMobile

MagicBand is a waterproof, removable, *and entirely optional* bracelet that facilitates your stay at Walt Disney World. Each band contains two types of embedded radio frequency transmitters that enable both short-range and long-range tracking. Once linked with a guest's MDX profile via the Disney World app (download via Google Play or iPhone), it can do all sorts of things:

- Stores ticket info. Touch it to a lollipop-like scanner for entry.
- Records and redeems reservations such as dining. (The expanded capability is technically called MyMagic+.)
- Validates PhotoPass details. Scan it with photographers and tap it to post-ride photo kiosks to add new images to your photo portfolio, which is activated if you buy the **Memory Maker** photo access package (disneyworld.com/photopass; $210; $185 if you buy at least 3 days ahead of arrival).
- Allows Disney resort guests to make purchases (with a PIN; day visitors cannot) and opens hotel room doors and gates. They also tell tollkeepers if you have a parking pass.
- Allows Disney Parks to track your movements. That can be fun: You might open the photos on your Disney World app and discover a shot of you on Slinky Dog Dash or a video of yourself on the Seven Dwarfs Mine Train (available for purchase, of course).
- Furnishes a beautiful tan line.

But don't feel pressured to buy a MagicBand ($35–$65), because a smartphone can perform the same duties. **MagicMobile** turns eligible iPhones, Apple Watches, and Google Pay–enabled Android phones into *de facto* MagicBands. Once MagicMobile is added to your digital wallet through the Disney World app, you don't even have to unlock your phone to scan it.

If you have privacy concerns, you may forego both MagicBand and MagicMobile; you will be given a plastic card that only contains a passive radio transmitter chip that's used to tap for entry but cannot trace your movements.

MAGIC KINGDOM

The Magic Kingdom, opened in 1971, is the most enchanting and most popular of all the Disney parks. Taking center stage is Cinderella Castle, the best-known symbol of Disney. The park's "lands" encircle the Castle.

Main Street, U.S.A.

The gateway to the Kingdom, Main Street resembles an idealized version of a turn-of-the-20th-century American small town that never really existed. It has shops, restaurants, and sometimes street entertainment. Main Street, however, is best left for the end of the day when you're heading back to your hotel. There are no big rides or shows on Main Street, just the park's best souvenir shops—call it Purchaseland.

As soon as you arrive at Main Street, you can board the **Walt Disney World Railroad,** an authentic 1928 steam-powered train, for a 20-minute trip around the perimeter of the park. It's a good way to travel if your tired feet are headed to Fantasyland or back to the park entrance.

Adventureland

As you enter Adventureland from the Plaza, notice how the music gradually changes from the perky pluck of Main Street to the rhythms of Adventureland. Even the grade of the ground changes slightly to give the imperceptible sensation of travel. Such shifts in drama are integral to the Disney original method of park design.

On the 10-minute **Jungle Cruise,** take a G-rated, narrated river excursion through a wilderness inhabited by trademark Disney robotic figures and cornball humor. This is the ride where over a dozen Indian elephants wash together in a pool, one of the essential spectacles of any Disney visit.

The **Magic Carpets of Aladdin** ★ is a less-crowded alternative to Fantasyland's iconic spinner Dumbo, but unlike on Dumbo, a family of four can ride—there are two rows of seats on each "carpet."

Pirates of the Caribbean ★★ may be the quintessential Disney ride, although this version is shorter than Disneyland's. This indoor boat float glides past 65 Audio-Animatronic figures on lifelike sets. You'll see a few scenes that are now iconic to American culture, including a slapstick sacking of an island port, a cannonball fight, and much drunken chicanery from ruddy-cheeked buccaneers, but nothing scary or too loud. There's a short, pitch-black slope drop near the beginning, but you don't really get wet. The shop at Pirates' exit is one of the better ones because it's big on buccaneer booty.

At the adorable **Walt Disney's Enchanted Tiki Room** indoor show, which takes 10 minutes, robotic birds sing the catchy "In the Tiki Tiki Tiki Tiki Room" and wow 'em with creaky dad jokes. You can't help but feel the tingle of 1960s nostalgia.

Tiana's Bayou Adventure.

Frontierland

Kids today find it bizarre to learn that when Frontierland was conceived, cowboy stories were mainstream pop culture. Now there are rumors that this area, currently wearing the guise of a Western town, is on the cusp of a re-theming.

Big Thunder Mountain Railroad ★★: Here we have another Disney thrill mountain, a 2½-acre "runaway" train roller coaster that rambles joltingly through steaming, rusty Old West sets. Your train careens through caves and canyons, under waterfalls, past geysers and mud pots, and over a volcanic pool. Seats in the back give a slightly wilder ride.

The just-refurbished and updated **Country Bear Jamboree** ★, here since opening day in 1971, is a hoot. It's a 10-minute show featuring Audio-Animatronic forest creatures warbling a few bars and crooning plaintive love songs. It's a great place to cool off, too. You'll be seated.

It's hard to tire of the log flume **Tiana's Bayou Adventure** ★★★ because this 11-minute journey (until 2023, known as Splash Mountain) is packed with room after room of color, 47 marvelous Audio-Animatronic figures, seven giddy drops large and small, and a route that takes you indoors and out. Note the 40-inch minimum height requirement and that the line can as much as double when the weather gets steamy.

Liberty Square

Step back into 18th-century America, but with fleets of strollers. Thirteen lanterns, symbolizing the colonies, hang from the Liberty Tree, an immense live oak in the center of the courtyard.

Every U.S. president is represented by a lifelike Audio-Animatronic figure in the **Hall of Presidents** ★. The show begins with a film, and then the curtain rises on America's leaders. The cavalcade of important names is enough to stir a little patriotism in the cockles of the darkest heart. Figures were created with historical accuracy; if a president didn't live in an era of machine-made clothing, for example, he wears a hand-stitched suit.

Once you're inside the **Haunted Mansion** ★★★, darkness, spooky music, howling, and screams enhance the ambience. But as spook houses go, the 8-minute trip, conducted in a creepingly slowly gliding seat, is decidedly merry. All the ghosts (which are mostly cartoonish Audio-Animatronic figures) want to do is party. Kids 6 and under must ride with someone 14 or older.

Fantasyland

Fantasyland is the heart of Walt Disney World—it contains many of the characters that make the brand beloved. For shorter waits, race here first thing in the morning or arrive after dinner, when little ones start tiring out. Little would-be princesses should not miss **Sir Mickey's,** behind the Castle, where every major princess outfit is sold ($65 is typical) with optional slippers and accessories.

Nice to see a prince get a little recognition around here! **Prince Charming Regal Carrousel** ★★ was handmade in 1917 for a Detroit amusement park, and it spent nearly 4 decades in Maplewood, New Jersey, before Imagineers rescued it. Cinderella's personal steed has a golden ribbon tied to its tail.

Go round and round in one of 16 aerodynamic pachyderms of **Dumbo the Flying Elephant** ★, whose elevation kids can control with a joystick. Each car fits

VIRTUAL QUEUES: the ride lottery

Disney Parks' shift to digital solutions has introduced a new task to your preparations: joining Virtual Queues. The Virtual Queue system is typically for the newest, most popular rides and, when in force, that ride will not have a regular Standby line. If you don't sign up for the Virtual Queue for a ride that's using it, the only other way to get on is to purchase an expensive individual Lightning Lane booking (p. 369) for each person in your party.

If your trip is pre-planned, Disney may send you emails and push notifications to warn you which rides (and occasionally shows) will require Virtual Queue during your visit. The Virtual Queues option in the app shows what is using the system.

Drawings happen at 7am sharp on the day of your visit, when you vie for your spot at the attraction with your smartphone from wherever you are. (At 1pm, there's a second and usually final daily drawing for which you must be inside the same park as your target ride.) Well before 7am, prepare to enter by making sure your ticket is in order and ensuring your entire party has been linked to you using the "Family & Friends" section of the Disney World app.

A few minutes before 7am, navigate to the Virtual Queue section. Keep refreshing by dragging downward or tapping the button. When the clock strikes 7, if you're lucky, you'll get a "Boarding Group" (not a time). Click to join. It will all be over in a few seconds.

If you obtain a Boarding Group, track the ride's progress via the app. You'll be able to check which group is boarding at any time, and you'll also get a push notification when it's your turn. You may then check in for the ride (officially, you'll have an hour's grace period to do so) using your phone, MagicBand, or ticket, but there still may be a wait in the attraction's real queue of up to an hour.

---

only two adults across, or an adult and two small kids. There are two identical copies running to keep those toddlers flyin'.

Originally conceived for the 1964 New York World's Fair, **"it's a small world"** ★★★, slow and sweet as treacle, floats you past some 300 dancing-doll children from around the world. The ride's distinctive look came from Mary Blair, a rare early female Imagineer, and the music from the Sherman Brothers.

The conceit of **Mad Tea Party** ★—spinning teacups on a platter of concentric turntables—has given the name to an entire genre of carnival "teacup" rides. Get your twirl on within the 90 seconds allotted.

Mickey's PhilharMagic ★, a 12-minute computer-animated film that runs continuously, is honest Disney in the *Fantasia* mold: Classic characters, prominently Donald Duck, collide to a lush (and loud) soundtrack of Disney songs while pleasant extrasensory effects such as scents and breezes blow to further convince you that what you're seeing is real.

On **Peter Pan's Flight** ★★★, pirate-ship vehicles (maximum capacity: three adults with a child lap-sitter) hang from the ceiling, swooping gently up, down, and around obstacles, while the scenes below are executed in forced perspective to make it feel like you're high in the air. The effect is charming, but it has a low rider capacity, and the lines are long as a result.

The Many Adventures of Winnie the Pooh ★★ makes for a joyous 4-minute kiddie attraction with vibrant colors, plenty of peppy pictures, and a buoyant segment when Tigger asks you to bounce with him and in response, your "Hunny Pot" car gently bucks as it rolls. Adorable!

The mine cart roller coaster **Seven Dwarfs Mine Train** ★★★ provides a joyful little romp that pretty much always has a solid wait. This 2½-minute rambler is family-friendly, with plenty of S-curves and humps but no loops or major daredevil drops. People love it.

At **Enchanted Tales with Belle** ★★, our heroine (in the flesh) retells the same story you've seen in two film versions now—you encounter a thrillingly lifelike talking armoire, a fantastic Lumière figure, and, best of all, a trick with a miraculously transforming mirror that must be seen to be believed. There's no Beast (so we're safe, kids).

As you travel in slow-moving shell vehicles for 6 gentle minutes on **Under the Sea—Journey of the Little Mermaid** ★, retrace a truncated jukebox version of the film's plot. Nearby, kids get autographs from the underwater princess herself at **Ariel's Grotto,** and yes, there's a separate wait for that, so go ahead—make your choice.

Tomorrowland

In 2023's thrilling **Tron Lightcycle/Run** ★★★ coaster, the most monumental ride addition to Magic Kingdom in 30 years, we have a Grade A rush, pleasing on all levels, from its novel seating system (use the size tester out front first) to the elegant arcs of its curves, but without any inversions. From departure to completion, it's not even 2 minutes long, but its memorability exceeds its duration.

On the 3-minute **Buzz Lightyear's Space Ranger Spin** ★★, passengers are equipped with laser guns and the means to rotate their vehicles, and it's their mission to blast as many targets as they can. That's easier said than done, since the aliens are spinning, bouncing, and turning, and your laser sight appears only intermittently as a blinking red light.

The cosmic coaster **Space Mountain** ★ is a relatively tame indoor toboggan steel coaster (the top speed is barely 29 mph, and its biggest drop just 26 feet), but the near-total darkness and tight turns give your 2½-minute go-round a panache that makes it one of the park's hotter and more atmospheric tickets.

The immersive **Monsters, Inc., Laugh Floor** ★★ is a "Living Character" screen show, about 15 minutes long, in which computer-animated characters interact live, in the moment, with a theater full of people, singling humans out with a hidden camera for extremely gentle ribbing.

Younger kids love **Tomorrowland Speedway** ★, especially if their adult companion lets them drive (kids shorter than 54 inches can't go alone). Teens are less enthused—these are go-karts with no juice.

The novel twist of **Walt Disney's Carousel of Progress** ★★, created in 1964 and moved here, is that the stage remains stationary, but the auditorium rotates on a ring past six rooms (four "acts" and one each for loading and unloading) of Audio-Animatronic scenes that idealize the rise of electrical tools in the home.

Beloved by many, the tramlike second-story route of **Tomorrowland Transit Authority PeopleMover** ★★★ uses pollution-free "linear induction" magnetic technology to take a story-free scenic overview of Tomorrowland's attractions.

Parades, Fireworks & More

For up-to-the-moment schedules, which can be affected by wind and rain, tap the Today's Showtimes button in the Hours section of the Disney World app.

One of the tent poles of a day at the Magic Kingdom is the parade. When you see lines of masking tape appear on the ground, it's time to heed the crowd-control orders of the show's heralds. Each parade (there may be different versions in daytime, after dark, and for holiday parties) is a memorable production, with dozens of dancers and characters and up to a dozen lavish floats. Day parades generally start at 2 or 3pm while night parades, when they happen, tend to start just after dusk (sometimes twice); times for the evening parades vary, and they last for less than 15 minutes.

Although the evening sky shows are technically at least partially visible from anywhere, the most symmetrical view is from the Castle's front and Main Street, U.S.A. Roughly 18 minutes long, the show is quite a slick spectacle—lights dim everywhere, even at the ferry dock, and you can hear the soundtrack wherever you are. Areas around and behind the Castle are roped off to protect guests from falling cinders, and wide portions of the park's center are set aside for premium-paying guests, so arrive at least 30 minutes ahead or you may get shunted elsewhere by aggressive cast members. (Special dessert parties are offered for a steep upcharge, but the quality of the desserts has fallen in recent years.) Offseason, rides begin closing as soon as the fireworks start, and people start heading home; in summer, there are still hours left to play.

EPCOT

More than any other Disney park, EPCOT changes its personality, decorations, and kiosk menus by the season through passing themed events.

The 260-acre park has two distinct sections: **Future World** (divided into World Celebration, World Nature, and World Discovery) and **World Showcase** (broken into 11 pavilions connected by a 1.3-mile footpath—get ready to walk!).

Future World

Future World is centered on EPCOT's icon, a giant geosphere known as **Spaceship Earth** ★★. No mere golf ball, Spaceship Earth houses an eponymous ride using the OmniMover system of slow-moving vehicles linked together like an endless snake. Packed with classic Disney Audio-Animatronics, it cheerleads the history of communications, from Greek theater to the telegraph. Lines are shorter late in the day.

The fantastically fast and swervy **Guardians of the Galaxy: Cosmic Rewind** ★★★ is a roller coaster with a literal twist: Each car in the train rotates to gently turn you in one direction or another, usually so you can face projections that go fleeting past. That creates sensations that can be intense, but even people with an aversion to spinny rides tend to love it. There are no big drops or loops intended to terrify. Many call it Disney's best thrill ride.

Mission: SPACE ★★ uses a motion-controlled cockpit on a giant centrifuge to skillfully trick the mind that you're an astronaut being launched into space.

If you're uneasy about that, use the Green lane, which omits the spinning, and if you hate tight spaces, do neither.

Cars thunder enticingly around the bend of an outdoor motorway at 65 mph on **Test Track** ★★★, a long-running popular indoor/outdoor ride. It was closed for refurbishment as we went to press, so check its status before heading over.

The Land pavilion takes up 6 acres, more than all of Tomorrowland, and **Soarin'** ★★★ is why. In it, you're seated on benches and "flown," hang glider–like, in front of a movie that flies over 13 world landmarks while scents (grass, roses) waft, hair blows, and the seats gently rock in tandem with the motions of the flight. Soarin' is highly repeatable and deeply pleasurable for all ages. The Land's other ride is **Living with the Land** ★, a 14-minute (wonderfully air-conditioned) boat trip that skims over the realm of farming technologies and is still rooted endearingly in bygone 1980s EPCOT style.

At **The Seas with Nemo & Friends** ★★, explore one of the world's largest saltwater aquariums:

Journey of Water—Inspired by Moana, in EPCOT's World Nature, is a cool walk-through diversion for scorching Florida days.

It's 27 feet deep, 203 feet across, and holds 5.7 million gallons, and you can spend as long as you like watching the swimming creatures from two levels. A visit begins with a 5-minute, slow-moving ride in "clamobiles" through a simulated undersea world to find Nemo, who's lost yet again. In the continuous **Turtle Talk with Crush** ★★, the animated turtle from *Finding Nemo* and *Finding Dory* engages kids in a real-time conversation right from his movie-screen tank.

The fountains outside the **Imagination** ★★ pavilion are magical—but not so much with **Journey into Imagination with Figment** ★, a slow, track-based ride inside that purports to be an open house of the Imagination Institute but is assailed by even fervent Disney die-hards as cheap and dull-witted.

World Showcase

Eleven miniaturized nations surround the nearly 40-acre lagoon at the north end of the park, each one re-created with meticulous detail and featuring evocative architecture, landscaping, shops, and many, *many* chances to eat and drink. There is more stuff to do in World Showcase than the map lets on: The Disney World app posts times for unexpected musical and dance performances (which usually wrap up by dinnertime). Seeing them makes a day richer and squeezes value from your ticket. Rush and you'll miss a lot.

The landscape in **Canada** ★★ ranges from a mansard-roofed replica of Ottawa's 19th-century, French-style Château Laurier (here called Hôtel du

Canada) to Butchart Gardens–inspired plantings. But the highlight is ***Canada Far and Wide*** ★, a 12-minute, 360° Circle-Vision film that lavishes you with Canada's scenic splendor. Viewing requires standing (you can lean on railings).

United Kingdom ★★, a wild mix of architectural references, has no rides or shows, and it's popular chiefly for its English-style pub, the indoor Rose & Crown Pub & Dining Room, and its boutiques selling football (soccer) jerseys, Beatles merchandise, and overpriced British candy.

France ★★, done up to look like a typical Parisian neighborhood with a one-tenth replica of the upper stretch of the Eiffel Tower in the simulated distance (you can't go up it), is home to perfumeries, the **Les Halles Boulangerie-Pâtisserie** bakery, and **Remy's Ratatouille Adventure** ★★★. This family-friendly trackless indoor ride scoots you over rooftops, through sculleries, around kitchens, and across dining rooms just like the rodent gourmands in *Ratatouille*.

The pavilion for **Morocco** ★★ began in 1984 with high aspirations: The country's king took an active interest in its construction as a diplomatic endeavor, dispatching some 21 top craftsmen for the job. Currently it's in flux, with its formerly glorious restaurant and market in a semi-abandoned state.

Japan ★★★ has no giant attractions (a show building was erected but never filled with its intended ride), but its shopping is by far the best in EPCOT. The **Mitsukoshi Department Store,** named for the 300-year-old Japanese original, is the most fun to roam of all the World Showcase boutiques. It's stocked like a real store, not a theme park shop.

The **U.S.A.** ★★★ pavilion takes pride of place in an area that's supposed to celebrate other countries. Inside, attend the half-hour Audio-Animatronic show **The American Adventure** ★★★, a Disney-style jukebox, performed by those marvelous Disney robot figures, re-enacting moments of national mythology for Americans. You'll be impressed. Before the show, at times listed on the app, you'll hear **Voices of Liberty,** an a cappella act that is renowned among performers for the impeccable prowess of the vocalists it casts.

The tiny pavilion for **Italy** ★ lacks an attraction—the gondolas never leave the dock—so content yourself with the miniature, drive-thru versions of Venice's Doge's Palace and St. Mark's bell tower. An appealing, if incongruous, attraction that's not on the maps is the highly detailed **model train** display just between this pavilion and Germany.

EPCOT After Dark

EPCOT may not have any parades, but at 9pm, a pulse-pounding spectacular takes place over World Showcase Lagoon. Disney has had a hard time developing a show that clicks with modern audiences. As of press time, the current effort (and its third try since 2019) is **Luminous: The Symphony of Us** (fireworks, choreographed fountains, a sweeping symphonic Disney medley). The visuals are so huge that any view of the center of the lake is generally fine. Although it's a very good show, people don't claim good viewing spots hours in advance the way they used to, but take care to be upwind or you may be engulfed by smoke. Food kiosks close with the first downbeat of the show and people scram for their cars when it's over.

In EPCOT's World Showcase, the statue of St. George fighting a dragon pays homage to a similar one in the medieval town of Rothenburg in Bavaria, Germany.

Lacking a true attraction (a water ride based on the Rhine was planned but never completed), **Germany** ★★ is popular for its food. The connected candy-and-wine shop, **Weinkeller,** is worth a gander, and so is the Werther's Original **Karamell-Küche** shop for all sorts of caramel delights—its warm, hand-tossed caramel popcorn is a top treat on the lagoon.

This area between Germany and China was once slated to contain a pavilion canvassing equatorial Africa, but that fell through for political reasons, so instead, we get **Outpost** ★, a mushy catch-all for all things African. Several days a week, a craftsman is on hand, whittling and carving wares—Kenyan-born Andrew Matiso has run this concession at EPCOT since 1999.

Enter **China** ★★ through the remarkable replica of Beijing's Temple of Heaven for ***Reflections of China*** ★, a ravishing 14-minute movie filmed entirely in Circle-Vision 360, with nine projectors filling a wrap-around screen with images from all sides. Upon exiting the film, cross the hangarlike shop and enter House of Good Fortune, a particularly good store (photo op: a huge sculpture of Buddha).

Get yer *Frozen* merch here! **Norway** ★★★, the youngest pavilion (built 1988), is home to one of the few rides in World Showcase, **Frozen Ever After** ★★★, an abbreviated 5-minute float-along/sing-along with easy forward and backward motion with some pretty Audio-Animatronics of Elsa, Anna, Olaf,

Kristoff, Sven, and characters from the *Frozen* series. Nearby in the **Royal Sommerhus** cabin, kids can meet the princesses in the flesh.

Nearly everything to see in **Mexico ★★★** is inside the faux temple, which contains the *zócalo* of Plaza de los Amigos and a faux volcano, a faux night sky strung with lanterns, and a faux river for the **Gran Fiesta Tour Starring the Three Caballeros ★★**. As you pass movie screens, jiggling dolls, and dancing Day of the Dead skeletons on this inoffensive, 8-minute boat float, you quickly realize you're enjoying the product of Mexican tourist board input. The experience is sweet, and it's a worthy siesta break. Outside near the lagoon, check for performance times for the sublime musicians of **Mariachi Cobre,** who have been staples at EPCOT since the park opened in 1982.

DISNEY'S HOLLYWOOD STUDIOS

After Disney got rid of the working movie studio that once distinguished and defined **Disney's Hollywood Studios ★**, the company has worked for years to add more excitement to the 154-acre park. The kiddie rides of Toy Story Land (opened 2018) and Star Wars: Galaxy's Edge (2019) helped bring people back in, but apart from those two improvements, the rest lags.

Major Attractions & Shows

The slow-moving, sorta-1930s-styled kaleidoscope of **Mickey & Minnie's Runaway Railway ★★★** is visually dazzling, with lurid colors powered by a mysterious and hypnotic technology, a trackless ride system that shuffles vehicles mid-adventure, some strategic puffs of wind, appearances by Goofy and Daisy and a few more friends, and wacky multi-scene hijinks so ridiculous (but tame) that even small children will enjoy themselves.

The 30-minute, bone-rattling tour de force of **Indiana Jones Epic Stunt Spectacular ★★** is a stadium-seating demonstration of hair-raising daredevilry—rolling-boulder dodging, trucks flipping over and exploding. The acrobats and gymnasts are skilled, and the production values are among the highest of any show at a Disney park. It's mounted about five times daily, listed on the app.

In 5 minutes of **Star Tours—The Adventures Continue ★★**, a classic screen-based motion simulator ride, you manage to lose control, go into hyperdrive, dodge asteroids, navigate a comet field, evade a Star Destroyer, get caught in a tractor beam, and join an assault on the Death Star—or another combination of perils, since there are more than four dozen storylines.

The 30-minute, self-explanatory musical torture chamber **For the First Time in Forever: A Frozen Sing-Along Celebration ★** features live actors telling the history of Arendelle 6 to 10 times daily, generally hourly, as well as an opportunity for you to endure "Let It Go" for one more white-knuckled, motherloving time. This show usually finishes performing by evening.

The tallest ride at Disney World (199 ft.), **The Twilight Zone Tower of Terror ★★★**, is one of the smartest, most exciting experiences at the parks. After many pregnant moments of tension, you and a group of fellow seated riders are sent into what seems to be a free fall (in reality, you're being pulled faster than the speed of gravity) and a series of invigorating up-and-down leaps.

On **Rock 'n' Roller Coaster Starring Aerosmith ★★**, one of DHS's two coasters, 24-passenger "limousine" trains launch from 0 to 57 mph in under 3

CIRQUE DU SOLEIL does disney

Cirque du Soleil: Drawn to Life ★★★ The best live performance on Disney property is by the famous Canadian acrobatic troupe, which has a permanent home in its own arena at Disney Springs. *Drawn to Life*, a mostly wordless acrobats-and-clowns revue that's spectacular and entirely family-friendly, uses feats of the human body to make beautiful symbolic statements about the craft of animation, loss, and the healing power of art. There's not a bad seat in the house. West Side, Disney Springs, 4200 Conroy Rd., Orlando. cirquedusoleil.com/drawn-to-life. **877/773-6470.** $85–$185 (adults) or $64–$185 (kids 3–9), depending on date and seating; Wed–Sun 5:30pm and 8 or 8:30pm. 90 min., no intermission. Free parking; no theme park admission required.

Cirque du Soleil: Drawn to Life.

seconds, sending them through a 92-second indoor rampage through smooth corkscrews and turns that are intensified by fluorescent symbols of Los Angeles.

The 10-minute **Lightning McQueen's Racing Academy** ★ consists of a lone, full-size Lightning McQueen racecar, whom we find stuck on a dais, testing his skills using a simulator. He's so perfectly done that it's disappointing that other *Cars* characters like Mater, Cruz Ramirez, and Chick Hicks appear only on a wraparound screen.

The kid-friendly, 30-minute **Beauty and the Beast—Live on Stage** ★ is advertised as "Broadway-style," but it's really not. It's theme park–style, simplified with the most popular songs from the movie. Arrive 20 minutes early so you don't end up in the back where afternoon sun can seep in. No night shows. **The Little Mermaid—A Musical Adventure** ★★, new in 2024, gives a similar treatment to Ariel and friends, only indoors and with puppets and digital effects.

Star Wars: Galaxy's Edge

Disney's Star Wars is its own creation, a unique destination called Black Spire Outpost on the planet of Batuu, which had never been seen in films before. Designed with meticulous input from Lucasfilm to ensure every light saber burn mark fits in with the franchise's universe (literally), Galaxy's Edge is like the set of a play that no one has seen yet. The souvenirs sold here cannot be found elsewhere, and a few food items are signatures: the delicious Ronto Wrap (roasted pork, grilled sausage, tangy slaw, and peppercorn sauce) sold over the counter at **Ronto Roasters** and Green Milk or Blue Milk (vaguely floral and citrusy frozen slush) at the **Milk Stand.**

Star Wars: Rise of the Resistance ★★★ is the most ambitious and complex ride you've ever set foot on, unfolding over 20 minutes and evoking a sense of science fiction reality as if you're truly racing from scene to scene in a Star Wars movie, hounded by Stormtroopers and Kylo Ren. There are some big, bouncy dropping movements up and down, some light jostling simulator motion, and lasers aplenty—and it's probably the one unmissable ride at Walt Disney World.

Six guests drive a perfect mockup of the cockpit of Han Solo's battered but trusty ship on **Millennium Falcon: Smugglers Run** ★★, a non-nauseating motion simulator. And each passenger has something to control—like a group video game, the ride responds to your inputs. Do well for a high score; crash into everything to annoy the narrator.

At **Savi's Workshop,** you build your own light saber in a mystical 10-minute ritual. Reservations are essential, so go to disneyworld.com/savisworkshop (opens 60 days ahead) to see how Disney wants you to do it. You must pay $220 for the saber up front. **Oga's Cantina** is a grizzled and whimsical galaxy speakeasy to drink bizarre concoctions, but not eat meals. You need reservations for that, too, unless they're accepting walk-ins.

Toy Story Land

Toy Story Land is a tough zone on hot days because the trees are still too young to provide much shade and only one of the three rides (Toy Story Mania!) has an indoor queue.

Quick accelerations, banked turns, and humps with genuine air time make **Slinky Dog Dash** ★★★ more exuberant than it appears to be, yet for all its

Fantasmic! is a nighttime spectacle that can be tricky to snag a seat for, but worth the effort.

expansive sensations, its 2 minutes remain rambunctiously family-friendly. The line for this very popular ride gets shockingly hot on summer days, and the queue is exposed to the elements, so head here early or use Lightning Lane.

On **Toy Story Mania!** ★★★, a fun and highly repeatable attraction, you shoot your way through a series of six animated indoor midway games (themed as Woody's suction-cup shooting game, a Little Green Men ring toss, and the like) that you progressively ride past. Both accuracy and intensity count for points!

Alien Swirling Saucers ★ is essentially a covered variant of the tried-and-true Whip carnival thrill but with a Little Green Men theme. It's easy on kids (who must be at least 32 in.).

Fantasmic! ★★★ is the super-popular, 25-minute evening pyrotechnics show (a 59-foot man-made mountain, water jets, flaming water, character-laden showboats, pyrotechnics, and lots of projections on a massive water curtain—you know, your typical understated eye-popping spectacle). It takes place in the 6,500-seat waterfront Hollywood Hills Amphitheatre. People start arriving at the theater as much as 2 hours before showtime, and just like a ball game, there are snack stands to keep them pumped up. Although it's a strong event by dint of its uniqueness, it doesn't always play nightly, but when there are two shows, the second one is less crowded.

DISNEY'S ANIMAL KINGDOM

At the 500-acre Animal Kingdom, most of the real estate is devoted to a menagerie of exotic animals, who live in paddocks rimmed with trenches cleverly concealed by landscaping. Because animals retire to shade as the Florida heat builds, a visit here most times of year should begin as soon as the gates open, usually around 8am. Check the weather, because if it's excessively hot or wet, you will be miserable: Only six major attractions take place in air-conditioning. If you're lucky enough to come on a day when it's open past dark, seize the chance, because that's when the Pandora section glows with nocturnal colors.

Disney is preparing a new land to replace the dinosaur-themed Dinoland U.S.A. area, so the southeast quadrant of the park may not be open for your visit.

Discovery Island

Instead of a castle or a geosphere, the centerpiece here is the 14-story **Tree of Life** ★★, Discovery Island's central landmark. The tree (built on the skeleton of an oil rig) has 8,000 limbs, 102,000 leaves, and is covered with hundreds of animal carvings made to appear, at a distance, like the pattern of bark. There are also some animal habitats around the tree, so it's worth a walk around its roots on the way to see *It's Tough to Be a Bug!* ★★, a cleverly rigged cinema showing a 10-minute 3D movie based on the animated film *A Bug's Life*. Little kids who can't distinguish fantasy from reality may be scared by the marvelously realized Hopper figure in the show.

Pandora—The World of Avatar

An evocation of the fantastical planet and tribal people from the 2009 film *Avatar,* Pandora is dominated by a vine-covered cascade of "floating mountains"—an impressive sight that's hard to photograph. Simply wandering is the best way to experience it, taking in the sumptuous floral creations and listening for weird alien animal calls coming from the foliage. At night (if the park is open then), vegetation and walkways are illuminated with fluorescent light (Disney likes to call it "bioluminescent"), and that spectacle necessitates a second visit after dark.

The 4½-minute ride **Avatar Flight of Passage** ★★★ is very popular for its pleasant intensity even though it's basically just guests straddling bike-like motion simulators (it secures them by gripping the legs and bracing the back) in front of a very big movie screen; a breeze and water spritzes keep everyone from becoming nauseated. People beeline here when the park opens.

Na'vi River Journey ★★, a glowing alien variation on the old-fashioned Tunnel of Love, is a 4½-minute boat float through a dark but colorful Pandoran bog, and it's mesmerizingly mellow going.

Africa

Due to its star attraction, Africa is mobbed in the morning; in the afternoon, it's a popular place to eat. **Dawa Bar,** at the entrance to Tusker House, is a nice place to people-watch with a cocktail. Enter through **Harambe,** a simulation of an African coastal village at the edge of the 21st century.

The 20-minute excursion **Kilimanjaro Safaris** ★★★, easily the bumpiest ride at Disney World, is the crown jewel of Animal Kingdom. Climb into a super-size, 32-passenger jeep-like vehicle—an actual one with wheels, not a tracked cart—and be swept into what feels like a real safari through the African veldt. Considering the quality and quantity of animals on display—and the cleverness of

Kilimanjaro Safaris may be Disney's most persuasive illusion: an African-style safari on American soil.

the enclosure design, as there are never bars between you and them—it's easily the best animal attraction of the park. Ride twice if you want—the free will of the animals means it's never the same trip again.

Hippos, tapirs, ever-active mole rats, and other critters are often on the **Gorilla Falls Exploration Trail** ★★★ for your viewing. The pathway takes about a half-hour, but you can spend as long as you want. The gorillas come near the end, so budget your time. The trail closes before dusk.

Most visitors enjoy **Festival of the Lion King** ★★★, one of the resort's most lavish, colorful, and longest-running spectacles. Audiences sit indoors on benches (front rows are good for engaging with performers) to watch a warm-hearted revue of singers, acrobats, and dancers. Showtimes for the 40-minute performances are posted on the app but tend to wind down by about 5pm; they can fill up, so arrive 30 minutes early.

Rafiki's Planet Watch ★: On the 7-minute trip on **Wildlife Express Train,** you'll get glimpses of plain backstage work areas. You arrive at **The Affection Section,** a petting zoo hosting your typical petting-zoo denizens—domesticated farm animals, mostly—and Conservation Station, where you learn about the park's veterinary services.

Asia

Asia's decor (rat-trap wiring, fraying prayer flags) evokes Nepal or northern India. Don't miss the white-cheeked gibbons who live on the ruined temple at the exit of Kali River Rapids.

The 12-passenger round bumper boat **Kali River Rapids** ★ shoots a course of rapids, and sometimes you can get soaked—it depends on your bad luck—but it's generally milder than similar rides. Your feet, for sure, will get wet. To be safe, there are free 120-minute lockers available ($10/hour if you go over; $4 for a large one).

Too few people enjoy **Maharajah Jungle Trek** ★★, a self-guided, South Asian–themed walking trail featuring some gorgeous tigers (rescued from a circus breeding program), flying foxes, Komodo dragons, and a few birds frolicking among fake ruins.

The lavishly themed **Expedition Everest** ★★★ coaster is loaded with powerful set pieces: both backward and forward motion, pitch-black sections, and a fleeting encounter with a 22-foot Abominable Snowman, or Yeti. As with all Disney rides, the most dramatic drop (80 ft.) is visible from the sidewalk out front, so if you think you can stomach that, you can do the rest.

Feathered Friends in Flight! ★ is a classic and enjoyable presentation about exotic birds that affords the host an excuse to introduce you to some gorgeous creatures—parrots, toucans, bald eagles, peacocks, African birds of prey—who swoop around the semi-enclosed arena, barely clearing heads. Showtimes are on the app.

One of the better shows at Disney is **Finding Nemo—The Big Blue... and Beyond!** ★, a fast-forwarded indoor retelling of the *Nemo* movie. This winning and tuneful 25-minute show isn't as elaborate as the 40-minute version that ran before the pandemic, but it's still a good choice for taking a load off in the air-conditioning while enjoying some very talented entertainers. The final performance of the day happens in the late afternoon.

OTHER WDW ATTRACTIONS

Disney runs two water parks, **Blizzard Beach** ★★★ and **Typhoon Lagoon** ★★. Of the two, Blizzard Beach has a few more thrilling rides and Typhoon Lagoon has slightly more for smaller visitors. Not that you'll have a choice of which one to visit. Since the pandemic, Disney has only opened one of its waterslide parks at a time; they take turns being closed for months at a time.

One-day tickets to Disney water parks cost $64–$69 adults and $58–$63 kids 3–9; they can also be added to theme park tickets using Water Park and Sports options. There's free parking at the water parks. Hours vary, from 10am–5pm up to 9am–8pm in peak season. Private shaded cabanas are also available for a surcharge via the app or from ✆ **407/939-7529.**

At Disney Springs, a huge, round helium balloon (known as **Aerophile Balloon Ride** ★★) rises from a pier, lingers 400 feet up for a spell, and then descends back to earth within about 10 minutes. If you're adventurous, the trip is good fun, and of course, the view rocks. It's known to summarily shut down for breezes over 22 mph or if lightning is detected within 30 miles, so if it's flying and you want to go, don't assume it will still be open later.

Disney World also offers some backstage tours that show you how the "magic" is made. The superlative **Walt Disney World Park Tours** ★★★ (disneyworld.com/tours; ✆ **407/939-8687**) require tons of walking, and the quality depends on the ability of the guide, but they're also well organized, with coach

The waves at Typhoon Lagoon's surf pool can reach up to 5 feet and so can pack quite the punch.

transport, snacks, plenty of comfort breaks, and sometimes, a special pin souvenir. Not all of them go daily, so you have to check the Disney site for what's running when you visit. Fantastic choices have included **Up Close with Rhinos** at Kilimanjaro Safaris ($50), the **Dolphins in Depth** ($209) shallow-water animal interaction at EPCOT's The Seas, the 5-hour **Disney's Keys to the Kingdom** ($129–$149) that takes you briefly into the famous Utilidor tunnels under Magic Kingdom, and **Wild Africa Trek** ($219), which brings you on an adventure including a rope bridge in the safari area of Disney's Animal Kingdom.

BEYOND DISNEY: UNIVERSAL ORLANDO & SEAWORLD

There are so many other attractions in Orlando that Disney is less than half the story. Universal Orlando is booming; its two Orlando theme parks (**Universal Studios Florida** and **Islands of Adventure**) already entice some 21.8 million combined visits each year, more than Disney's Magic Kingdom, and a third park, **Universal Epic Universe,** will open in 2025 to global hype.

Universal Orlando

Universal operates best (but not exclusively) on the resort model—stay here, play here—and its campus is vastly easier to roam than Disney's. It's walkable or traversed by quick, free ferries or buses, so you can park your car and forget about it for days.

UNIVERSAL EPIC UNIVERSE: it all changes in 2025

As we go to press, Universal is hard at work constructing a fresh new theme park, **Universal Epic Universe,** which you can clearly see rising northeast of Orlando's Convention Center for an opening in summer 2025. For many amusement fans, its arrival will be the event of a generation—it's Orlando's first fully new theme park since 1999.

Epic Universe, a single park with 11 new rides and many themed lands, will live up to its name. We expect the largest **Super Nintendo World** area on the planet, with two rides plus another Orlando-only **Donkey Kong coaster;** a third **Wizarding World of Harry Potter** area, this one with a Parisian setting from *Fantastic Beasts* and featuring a Ministry of Magic ride; a **Dark Universe** area with a family coaster and a complex indoor ride based on Universal Pictures' classic monsters; **Stardust Racers,** a duo of dueling roller coasters with peaks you can see from miles away; and a **How to Train Your Dragon**–based land with another richly themed family boat ride and a multi-launch coaster, **Hiccup's Wing Gliders.** And much more besides that.

Although the new park will be about 2 miles south of Universal's original campus, it will have three giant resort hotels of its own, one of them fronted by an enormous performing fountain. And there's more space to expand as the years go on. Disney's days of dominance in O-Town are over.

If you want to see both Wizarding World of Harry Potter areas, you must purchase a ticket to *both* of its parks, but unless crowds are insanely nutty, such as before Halloween Horror Nights (p. 26) or during Christmas week, the two main parks take about 2 days to see adequately. Most of the time, lines are nowhere near as long as they are at Disney. With a two-park pass and a willingness to bypass lesser attractions, for now you can see the highlights in a marathon day, provided at least one of the parks stays open until 9 or 10pm. (If you want to see Volcano Bay, described on p. 392, you need an additional day.) In any event, bopping between the two theme parks is quick and easy, since their entrances are a 5-minute stroll apart, or a quick ride on the incredible Hogwarts Express connecting train.

TICKET PRICES Tickets for both parks cost the same, and you must specify the day you're going. Like Disney, Universal charges more on busy days. But Universal also gives you a $20 discount if you buy multi-day tickets online, so it's crucial you do so.

To enter both parks on the same day and to ride the Hogwarts Express train that links the two parks, you must have a **park-to-park** ticket, which allows unlimited entries of both parks each day. If you buy a limited, one-park ticket and change your mind midway through the day, don't worry. There are ticket upgrade kiosks at the Hogwarts Express train stations and the front gates that simply charge you the difference in price for a park-to-park ticket, and you can be on your way again.

Expect rates similar to these:

- **1-day ticket for one park:** $109–$159 adults, $104–$154 kids 3–9 (Make any 1-day ticket **park-to-park** for $55 more)
- **2 days, one park daily:** $273–$351 adults, $263–$341 kids 3–9 (Make any 2-day ticket **park-to-park** for $60 more)
- **3 days, one park daily:** $233–$316 adults, $223–$306 kids 3–9
- **3 days, two parks daily:** $327–$376 adults, $317–$366 kids 3–9

PARKING $30 (free after 6pm), $50–$60 for closer "prime" spaces, $65–$75 for all-day valet.

UNIVERSAL STUDIOS ATTRACTIONS

For in-depth coverage of Universal Orlando, pick up *Frommer's Disney World, Universal & Orlando.*

Despicable Me Minion Mayhem ★★ is a rigged movie cinema in which your seat moves a little, giving the little guys ample opportunity for some cartoon violence and giggly gags. Across the path, **Illumination's Villain-Con Minion Blast** ★★ is a wry upgraded version of a classic shooting gallery; you shoot from a meandering moving sidewalk.

Transformers: The Ride—3D ★★ repeats the technology and basic vehicle design of the gentler Adventures of Spider-Man next door at Islands of Adventure. Its roofless motion-simulator cars travel among sense-tricking rooms with 3D projections.

The 17-story vertical climb and inverted loop of **Hollywood Rip Ride Rockit** ★★, although exciting, are probably not long for the park; the coaster is bumpy and expensive to maintain, so the word is it's on its way out.

This grandma-appropriate theater-based **Race Through New York Starring Jimmy Fallon** was born more out of synergy than originality—*The Tonight Show* airs on NBC, Universal Orlando's corporate cousin. The 4-minute adventure hammers you with the show's running characters and jiggles your bench in motion simulation, but your life wouldn't be diminished by missing it.

The brilliant indoor coaster **Revenge of the Mummy** ★★★, one of the best rides in this park, goes backward and forward, twists on a turntable, and is full of surprises. (It doesn't go upside down.)

Fast & Furious—Supercharged uses underwhelming motion simulator technology and crisp lateral projections to simulate a car chase even though you're sitting safely on a tram with no seat belt. It's *meh* at best.

The best of the park is inside **The Wizarding World of Harry Potter—Diagon Alley** ★★★, a pitch-perfect re-creation of what you saw growing up in the Potter movies, complete with bespoke souvenirs you can only find here. Most guests spend a few hours exploring it. **Harry Potter and the Escape from Gringotts** ★★★ is part roller coaster, part motion simulator amid dominating 3D high-def screens, and the queue is deeply atmospheric. Separate from Diagon Alley, through the vaulted brick interior of a cunningly accurate King's Cross Station, you board **Hogwarts Express** ★★★, the hissing, steaming, and, to all appearances, vintage steam train to Hogsmeade, the other Harry Potter land in Islands of Adventure. Out the window, scenes of England and Scotland scroll by as you travel.

For **Men in Black: Alien Attack** ★★, you board six-person cars equipped with individual laser guns. As you pass from room to room—expect lots of herky-jerky motions, but nothing

Transformers: The Ride—3D.

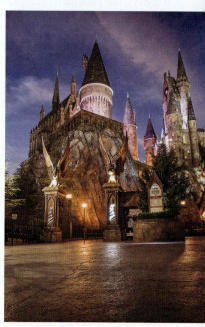

Hogwarts Castle by night.

sickening—your task is to fire upon any alien that pops out from around doorways, behind trash cans, and so on.

In the area that tributes *The Simpsons* with a life-size **Moe's Tavern** and **Kwik-E-Mart,** the motion-simulating "Thrilltacular Upsy-Downsy Spins-Aroundsy Teen-Operated Thrill Ride" **The Simpsons Ride** ★★ takes place in front of an 80-foot-tall screen. The premise, dense and ironic enough to please any Simpsons fan, parodies Orlando itself. At Universal's Dumbo ride, **Kang & Kodos' Twirl 'n' Hurl** ★, silly slobbering aliens trick you into boarding a Day-Glo flying saucer (fitting two adults or one adult and two kids).

A troupe of trained dogs, cats, birds, and the occasional horse anchor the charming and long-running 20-minute show **Animal Actors on Location!** ★★★ (times noted on the sign and app, but they tend to wrap by 5pm).

DreamWorks Land, new in 2024, is where most of the kiddie diversions are stashed, including the pint-size **Trolls Trollercoaster** ★; **Po Live!** ★, a video meet-and-greet with Po from *Kung Fu Panda*; and a meeting spot for Shrek, Fiona, and Donkey from the *Shrek* series. On **E.T. Adventure** ★★, the sole surviving ride from the park's opening day in 1990, you ride a flock of bikes that sweep and scoop across the moonrise and then through gardens on E.T.'s home planet (remember, he was a botanist), where a menagerie of goofy-looking aliens and creepy E.T. babies swing on vines. It's as endearingly weird as it sounds.

The Bourne Stuntacular ★★ is a 30-minute stunt show that doubles down on deeply impressive technology and Swiss-watch timing to supply the sensation of a filmic, moving panorama. The illusions work better the farther you sit from the stage.

This park's only homage to the B-movie origins of the Universal name, **Universal Horror Make-Up Show** ★★ is a 25-minute tongue-in-cheek exposé of horror-movie makeup effects. On paper, that seems like the kind of thing you might otherwise skip, but in truth park regulars love its wit and playful edge. For ribald ad-libbing and gross-out humor, the park suggests parental guidance, but I find most kids have heard it all before.

Islands of Adventure

Probably the best choice in Orlando in pound-for-pound thrills, Universal's second theme park has better theming and more intense rides than its older brother, Universal Studios Florida. IOA's 101 acres are laid out much like EPCOT's World Showcase: individually themed areas (here called "islands," although they're not) arranged around a lagoon. We'll take them clockwise, although many visitors head straight to Hogsmeade and VelociCoaster:

ISLANDS OF ADVENTURE ATTRACTIONS

Universal snapped up the Marvel characters for Orlando theme park use in long-term licensing deals ages ago, before Disney bought the brand, which is why the looks of the characters in **Marvel Super-Hero Island** are locked in the '90s. Every minute or so, a new **Incredible Hulk Coaster** ★★★ train blasts out of the 150-foot tunnel, over the avenue, and across the lakefront into a series of loopy inversions. The ride is quick—a little over 2 minutes—but it's invigorating. **The Amazing Adventures of Spider-Man** ★★★ fires on all cylinders, and the whole family can do it without fear. Mild open-air motion simulation, computer-generated animation, and cunning sense trickery (bursts of flame, water droplets, blasts of hot air) collaborate to impart the mind-blowing illusion of being drafted into Spidey's battles against a "Sinister Syndicate" of supervillains including Doctor Octopus and the Green Goblin, who have disassembled the Statue of Liberty with an anti-gravity gun. The twin 200-foot towers **Dr. Doom's Fearfall** ★★ rocket riders 150 feet up at a force of 4Gs, where they feel an intense tickling in their tummies, briefly soak up a terrific view of the park, and bounce (safely) back down to Earth. The low-priority **Storm Force Accelatron** ★ is a classic 90-second spinning-tub ride, like Disney's teacups.

The next zone clockwise, **Toon Lagoon,** harbors two water rides that will unquestionably drench you. The winding 5-minute journey of **Dudley Do-Right's Ripsaw Falls** ★★★—ups, downs, indoor, outdoor, surprise backsplashes, chunky robotic characters—climaxes in a stomach-juggling double-dip drop that hurtles, unexpectedly, through a humped underground gully. Although the 75-foot drop starts out at 45 degrees, it steepens to 50 degrees, creating a weightless sensation. Seats are tight, but it helps if you straighten your legs as you get in and out. **Popeye & Bluto's Bilge-Rat Barges** ★★★ is probably the most delightfully diabolical flume in the world. Twelve-passenger, circular bumper boats float freely and unpredictably down an outlandish white-water obstacle course—beneath waterfalls, through cartoonish tunnels, over angry rapids, and past features designed to mercilessly saturate you. It's like playing Russian roulette with water, and everyone loses.

As you enter the Jurassic Park land, the terrifying stone facade of **Skull Island: Reign of Kong** ★★ warns wimps away, but despite gargantuan appearances, it's mostly a screen-based motion-simulator ride, albeit one that uses a tram-like vehicle and requires 3D goggles. The hanging carts of **Pteranodon Flyers** ★ gently glide on the nifty-looking track over Camp Jurassic for a very short (about 75 sec.) clacking route through the trees. No adult may ride without a child. In that family-friendly Orlando tradition, the worst drop of **Jurassic Park River Adventure** ★★ is clearly warned; gauge the 85-foot descent from behind the Thunder Falls Terrace restaurant, where river boats kick up quite a spray as they hit the water at 30 mph. Before reaching that messy climax, boats embark on what's meant to be a benign tour of the mythical dinosaur park from the movie, only to be bumped off course and run afoul of spitting raptors and an eye-poppingly realistic T. rex that lunges for the kill. **Jurassic World VelociCoaster** ★★★ is steel coaster perfection. The towering 155-foot "top hat" vertical hill that can be seen for miles around is just a small segment of this wild adventure of sudden launches and rollover inversions that seem to emulate being thrashed in the jaws of a predator dinosaur. This is one of the best American roller coasters to be built in recent years.

It's as if the film set for Hogsmeade Village (the only British village for non-Muggles) and Hogwarts Castle have been transported to Florida for **The Wizarding World of Harry Potter—Hogsmeade,** and indeed, it was designed by the same team. You don't have to know the books or the movies to enjoy the astounding level of detail. Grab the signature treat, Butterbeer, from the cart in the middle. If you want to experience state-of-the-art ride tech, hop on **Hagrid's Magical Creatures Motorbike Adventure** ★★★ and hold tight. This $300-million roller coaster is one of the best rides in Orlando—or anywhere. There are lots of complex surprises that would be wrong to expose here, so I will just assure you that there are no stomach-grabbing sheer drops, no loops, you won't get dizzy, and

Real British fare (plus Butterbeer) at Harry Potter's Three Broomsticks at Universal.

nearly all the motion is satisfyingly swoopy and swervy, even as you repeatedly vault to 55 mph in a second or two. Doing this one after dark takes the excitement to an even higher level. There's a line for single riders that could cut the posted wait by two-thirds. On **Harry Potter and the Forbidden Journey** ★★★, an epic combination of motion-simulator movie segments and awe-inducing physical encounters greet you as you travel on a jolting, four-person bench that has been enchanted by Hermione to transport you around the grounds of Hogwarts Castle, which you also get to tour in one of the best queues ever. Try the test seat out front if you're a larger guest—many people are not able to ride. For little kids, you'll find **Flight of the Hippogriff** ★, a standard training roller coaster (basically a 1-min. figure eight) that offers a glimpse of Hagrid's Hut from the queue. The long-legged should cross their ankles to fit more comfortably. The film tavern **Three Broomsticks** ★★★ was gorgeously re-created, up to its wonky cathedral ceiling and down to the graffiti scratched in the timbers, as the only restaurant in this island (it serves barbecue and British dishes), and the filmmakers reportedly liked the design so much they featured the set more prominently in later movies. The realistic **Hogwarts Express** ★★★ train takes people to the Wizarding World inside Universal Studios, next door, every 5 minutes or so and requires a park-to-park ticket.

The quality of the meals in the cavelike **Mythos Restaurant** ★★★ (reservations strongly recommended; ⓒ 407/224-4534; main courses $22–$35) is many rungs higher than what most theme parks do. Expect pad Thai, beef medallions, a seasonal risotto, souvlaki couscous bowls, lamb loin, and more, plus a healthy slate of sandwiches and salads.

The 10-acre **Seuss Landing** area replicates the good Doctor's two-dimensional storybook bluster with three-dimensional exactitude. Just try to find a straight line. **The Cat in the Hat** ★★★ takes a nonthreatening 3½-minute excursion through the plot of the famous picture book as viewed from slow-moving mobile "couches" (really a typical flat-ride car). **One Fish, Two Fish, Red Fish, Blue Fish** ★★ is another iteration (albeit a good one) of Disney's enduring tot bait, Dumbo. Riders (two passengers per car normally, three if one of them loves the Wiggles) go around, up, and down by their own controls while a gauntlet of spitting fish pegs them from the sides. The bobbing menagerie of otherworldly critters on **Caro-Seuss-el** ★★ actually reacts to being ridden—ears wiggle, heads turn, snouts rise—making it delightfully over-the-top and appealing to kids who sniff at kiddie carousels. The railway threading overhead is **High in the Sky Seuss Trolley Train Ride!** ★★, a cheerful family-friendly glide, narrated in verse. The purple line surveys more of the area than the green line, which dawdles above the Circus McGurkus Cafe.

Volcano Bay

Universal Orlando's custom-built water park, the tiki-tastic, 28-acre **Volcano Bay** ★★★ (universalorlando.com; © **407/363-8000;** $80–$90 adults, $75–$85 kids 3–9; towel rental $6), is number seven in the world's most-attended water parks. This slippery playpen is a beaut: The centerpiece, a 200-foot volcano gushing with waterfalls and steaming with mist, is now a landmark beside I-4. Its systems are just as audacious. Guests borrow a sensor wristband, called TapuTapu, that they use to make purchases (if they've linked their credit card to the Universal app first) and trigger spray tricks and photo stations. Tap the band to the talisman posted at flume entrances to reserve a place in a virtual line for later. TapuTapu counts down your wait time while you do other things, and when it's time to ride, the wristband notifies you to head to the attraction.

SeaWorld Orlando

The second theme park chain to set up shop in town, after Disney, was **SeaWorld Orlando** ★★★. The park, which began in San Diego in 1964, staked a claim in Orlando in 1973, when societal attitudes toward animal attractions were much different. Many people no longer care to visit a park that is principally about looking at seagoing creatures in tanks. In 2009, before its troubles began with the documentary *Blackfish,* SeaWorld Orlando was the 12th most popular theme park in the entire world. Now it's not even in the top 25, but it is in 10th place in North America (4.45 million visits in 2022).

So, is it ethical to go? The park has not captured wild whales for decades, and the orcas that still live there, SeaWorld promises, will be the last generation to do so and will not be bred. The park also says it has rescued more than 30,000 animals to date—park visitors will see a lot of information about its conservation efforts—and it promotes its ongoing efforts to rescue animals in distress. SeaWorld survives because it's replacing many of its old animal-based amusements with new thrill rides (it has built four new roller coasters since 2016) and mounting special events like summer concerts and food festivals, but you will notice that its staffing levels and energy are not as high as at the other Orlando theme parks.

TICKET PRICES SeaWorld admission costs $58 to $110 for everyone aged 3 and up, depending on how busy it is; discounts are available online for some days. If you plan to go to Aquatica, its waterslide park, or Busch Gardens Tampa Bay, you can get a minor discount.

PARKING Parking is $30 for cars, light trucks, and vans. You can pay more for preferred parking, but it won't give you a significant location advantage.

SEAWORLD'S ANIMAL DIVERSIONS

SeaWorld is a mix of animal shows and rides. Open the SeaWorld app and click **View Park Schedule** (or look for the show schedule that's posted in the entry area) and build your day around what you want to catch. If rain halts the rides and cuts your day short, stop by the Guest Services Counter for the Sunny Day Guarantee, which grants you free entry on another day for up to a year.

Dolphin Adventures ★★ is the kind of dolphin show that has been a tourist standard for decades: Trainers in wetsuits recite from a cheerful script about the animals, which leap, flip, and frolic for your applause along to quasi-inspirational songs that sound like old soft drink commercials. SeaWorld promises that dolphins that aren't in the mood to perform are not forced to do it.

While orcas still live out their days at SeaWorld, the **Orca Encounter** ★★ show, which used to be known as Shamu's show, gives them something to do. When the killer whales start to fly, the crowd comes alive. Closed-circuit TV cameras capture and display the spectacle on a big screen as the animals thunder dauntingly through the water's surface, pointedly deluging seating sections in 52°F (14°C) water. The 25-minute plotless show occurs on such a scale as to make it required viewing. SeaWorld's long-running **Sea Lion & Otter Spotlight** ★★ is a goofy, try-not-to-smile spectacle. Expect everything you'd want from a sea lion and otter act conducted by a fake scientist in a white lab coat: cheesy tricks (animals doing double takes, sliding, waving), surprise splashes of water for the front rows, lots of interaction from kids, and much slapstick from the humans, who spend a lot of the time educating you.

> **Hook the Trainers**
>
> To get the most out of a visit, try to be in the same place as the animal trainers. Ask questions. Get involved. They may even allow you to feed or stroke the animals (set aside another $30 or so for fish food). These zoologists love sharing information about the animals they have devoted their lives to. Feeding times are usually posted outside each pavilion's entrance.

Pacific Point Preserve ★★★ is an open-air, rocky habitat that encourages feedings, but here the residents are incessantly barking California sea lions and a few demure seals. There's a narrow moat between the tank and the walkway, but you're encouraged to lean over and toss the doglike animals fresh fish; $8 for a few. You can find other places to feed animals by hand at **Stingray Lagoon & Feeding** ★ and **Shark Encounter** ★★★ for tarpon and shrimp.

At **Manatee Rescue and Rehabilitation** ★★, a circuitous entrance ramp brings you to an air-conditioned underwater viewing area for 1,500 Caribbean fish and sea turtles the size of coffee tables—worth the detour. Much attention is paid to the manatee's status as one of America's most adorable animals, and, in fact, the sluggish creatures on display here were all rescued from the wild.

Walk through at your own pace at **Wild Arctic Encounter** ★ for first a surface view and then an underwater look at Pacific walruses and the park's utterly beautiful white beluga whales, which look like swimming porcelain.

SEAWORLD'S RIDES AND ATTRACTIONS

Mako ★★★ ("*MAY*-ko") takes the crown as Orlando's longest (nearly a mile of track), fastest (73 mph), and tallest (200 ft.) coaster. It's billed as a "hypercoaster" with "relentless air time," which means there are lots of humps and drops, including several over water, which—combined with its deceptively loose restraint system—can make you feel weightless.

Rising above the center of the park is **Manta** ★★★, SeaWorld's "flying coaster" ridden face-down and head-first in a horizontal position (claustrophobics, breathe). You board sitting upright, and after your shoulders and ankles are secured, you're tipped forward and the train is dispatched over curious pedestrians for the swooping 2½-minute adventure.

Take a 2-minute dose of adrenaline on **Kraken** ★★. After you settle into your pedestal-like seat, the floor is retracted, leaving your legs to dangle (you may go barefoot) while you undergo seven upside-down "inversions" of one sort or another. The coaster, which hits 65 mph and drops 144 feet, is breath-stealing.

The mild launch coaster **Penguin Trek** ★★, new for 2024, takes families on a peppy indoor/outdoor course at top speeds of 43 miles per hour, culminating in an exit through the park's fantastically frigid penguin habitat for Antarctican life.

The 80-second coaster **Ice Breaker** ★★★ is a lot wilder than it looks from the ground. You're launched up a 93-foot-tall "top hat" hill, but you fail to crest it. That sends you backwards, peaking at 100° on a 93-foot spike. Then another speed boost successfully launches you over the hill—that's right: straight up and straight down—and into a tough tangle of rails. That's a lot of fun for a single coaster on a small footprint of lakeside land.

The 5-minute round-raft flume **Infinity Falls** ★★★ has you bouncing aggressively between waterfalls and soaking fountains operated by sadistic fellow guests, but that's nothing: You're also raised on a vertical elevator and dropped 40 feet along a steep ramp to a messy splashdown. Boats do not have compartments in which to keep things dry, so use the lockers.

On the 6-minute flume-slash-coaster ride **Journey to Atlantis** ★★ (you can't see the brief coaster section from the front), getting drenched is unavoidable, as the 60-foot drop should warn.

Pipeline: The Surf Coaster ★ is ridden standing up; saddle-like support stems slot between passengers' legs and move up and down through the zero-to-60 mph launch and steeply banked swooping inversions. Support yourself additionally with your legs (if you can) when the coaster valleys, and you'll suffer fewer effects on your future family line.

Jutting above the lagoon—and topped to still-greater heights by a colossal American flag—is the 400-foot, old-fashioned "Wheel-o-vater" **Sky Tower** ★★ which rotates as it climbs 300 feet for a panorama. If the park is busy, adults pay $5 to ride, but it's free otherwise, and always free for kids.

In 2023, SeaWorld brought the standing roller coaster to Orlando with Pipeline.

Behind Orca Stadium, kids have their own richly imagined area in **Sesame Street at SeaWorld Orlando ★★★**, a beautifully realized product of a partnership with Sesame Workshop. Children can romp among re-created sets of Mr. Hooper's store, Abby Cadabby's garden, and the 123 stoop. There's so much to discover by ringing doorbells, peeking through mail slots, buzzing apartment intercoms—even annoying Oscar by pounding on his trash can.

DINING AT SEAWORLD

In case you were wondering, SeaWorld serves only sustainable seafood, available mostly at counter-service locations. Prices are in line with everyone else's: $13 to $16 a meal, before a drink. **All-Day Dining Deals** (one entree, one side or dessert, one nonalcoholic drink each time through the line, once an hour) cost $50 for adults and $25 for kids; rare is the person who will stay (or eat) long enough to make it pay off.

The special meal event is **Dine with Orcas ★★**, during which you eat alongside the orca pools with the narration of trainers. Prices fluctuate by the day, but expect $40 to $60 for adults and $25 to $30 for kids.

Discovery Cove and Aquatica

It would be wonderful if more people could afford to enjoy Discovery Cove (discoverycove.com; © **407/513-4600**), Orlando's most civilized and relaxing theme park. Prices change with the seasons, but range from $140 to $337 for everyone aged 3+ and come with unlimited admission to SeaWorld and Aquatica for 2 weeks. The most expensive park in town (prices shift by the season) is a chill, all-inclusive experience called a "Day Resort Pass." Only around 1,000 people a day are admitted, guaranteeing this faux tropical idyll is not marred by a single queue (except maybe for the high-quality catered lunch). Admission lanyards include breakfast, equipment rental, sunscreen, beer if you're of age, and unlimited lunch—a good one, too, with options such as fresh grilled tilapia. Wade from perfect white sand into **Serenity Bay,** feed fresh fruit to the houseguests at the **Explorer's Aviary** for tropical birds, snorkel with barbless rays over the trenches of **The Grand Reef,** swim to habitats for monkeys in the **Freshwater Oasis,** or float down the slow-floating **Wind-Away River,** which passes through waterfalls into the aviary, preventing the birds from escaping. When it's your turn—if you've paid extra—head to the **Dolphin Lagoon,** where small groups of

A waterslide at Aquatica.

about eight (ages 6 and up) wade into the chilly water and meet one of the pod. Like humans, dolphins have distinct personalities and must be paired to people the trainers think they'll enjoy being with—but many of these dolphins are docile and friendly, having dwelled at SeaWorld for decades. The dolphins don't participate if they don't want to. Naturally, a photographer is on hand so if you want images or video, you'll pay for that, too, pushing a day to over $400.

Aquatica ★ (www.aquatica.com/orlando; ✆ **888/800-5447**), SeaWorld's waterslide park, is across International Drive from its parent park (a free, 3-min. van ride links it). Entry is $43 to $60, depending on the day, with online discounts available, and you can buy tickets that also include SeaWorld. It opens at 9 or 10am, closing time varies per day (closed Mon–Fri outside of summer season). On hot days, it can be busier than SeaWorld itself. There are nearly two dozen slides, making it a perfectly nice park, and it's favored somewhat by locals because it's less gimmicky than the others in town, but it's not the most cutting-edge park.

WORTHY AREA ATTRACTIONS

Don't neglect **Kennedy Space Center** (p. 431), which can be reached in less than hour by car on the eastern Space Coast.

Charles Hosmer Morse Museum of American Art ★★★
MUSEUM   The best museum in the Orlando area, and perhaps the finest in the state, presents an unparalleled cache of works by genius designer Louis Comfort Tiffany, from stained glass to vases to lamps, and even the lavishly decorated Daffodil Terrace and Reception Hall of his lost Long Island mansion, Laurelton Hall, and the bespoke fountains that ran through it. Set aside an hour or more, though it's easy to combine a visit with a stroll through Winter Park's boutiques, because it sits among them.

445 N. Park Ave., Winter Park. morsemuseum.org. ✆ **407/645-5311.** $6 adults, $5 seniors 60+, $1 students, free for kids 11 and under. Tues–Sat 9:30am–4pm; Sun 1–4pm.

Gatorland ★★★ ANIMAL PARK
Back in 1949, the reassuringly hokey Gatorland became Orlando's very first mass attraction, featuring Seminole Indians wrestling the animals for tourists. It's easy to get the highlights in 2 or 3 hours, but don't miss the **Jumparoo** (Mon–Fri at 10:45am), when gators get their exercise by eagerly leaping out of the water for suspended chunks of chicken. Bring a fistful of extra cash if you'd like to partake in the extras such as a **wading bird rookery,** a **petting zoo,** a **capybara,** a miniature **train,** a **climbing wall,** and a five-stage **zipline** over gator ponds. And save a few bills for one of Gatorland's 1960s-era Mold-a-Matic vending machines, which press a toy out of injected hot wax right before your eyes. They're perfect metaphors that capture the delightful throwback charm of Gatorland.

14501 S. Orange Blossom Trail, Orlando. gatorland.com. ✆ **407/855-5496** or 407/855-5496. $33 adults, $32 seniors 60+, $23 kids 3–12; $3 cheaper online. Free parking. Daily 10am–5pm; summer daily 10am–6pm.

King's Landing ★★★ NATURE RESERVE
Melt into some of Florida's most soothing wilderness as you float downstream on more than 8 miles of a perfectly clear, slow-moving shaded river. Paddle on your own with otters and turtles (you can rent a kayak here and staff will shuttle you back at the end of the route) or hire someone to do it for you and keep your eyes peeled for gators. King's

Landing accepts reservations (mornings are best), which keeps crowds small. Located about 25 miles north of downtown. For more excursions in Central Florida's pristine freshwater wilderness to paddle a boat in, visit the 18,000-acre **De Leon Springs State Park** ★★★ (601 Ponce de Leon Blvd., Deland; floridastateparks.org; © **386/985-4212**; $6 per carload; daily 8am–sundown) and the 2,600-acre **Blue Spring State Park** ★★ (2100 W. French Ave., Orange City; floridastateparks.org; © **386/775-3663**; $6 per car; daily 8am–sundown).

5722 Baptist Camp Rd., Apopka. kingslandingfl.com. © **407/886-0859.** $15 adults, $10 kids 4–17. Must be 3 or older to go onto the water. Daily 8am–5pm.

Legoland Florida ★★★ This extremely kid-friendly, soothingly mellow 150-acre lakeside park, located 45 minutes south of Disney World, is a godsend for parents who crave a slow-paced breather from the mechanical and authoritarian environment of Disney World. No other Florida park feels so spacious and caters so directly to kids aged 2 to 12. Everything is designed for little ones, from easy-to-tackle versions of adult rides to a large selection of things to do. For a break from the excitement, a healthy portion of the carefully tended **Cypress Gardens Historic Botanical Garden** (closes 30 min. before the park) was preserved, complete with Spanish moss, cypress knees jutting from tannic water, old-growth banyans (protected in the winter by hidden gas heaters), and signs warning of alligators, which live in the lake. It's attached to the separately ticketed, 5-acre **Peppa**

Legoland Florida's imaginative creations are whimsical reflections of the outside world.

Pig Theme Park ★★ (gate price: $59; daily 9 or 10am to 5pm, depending on the day), whose six bubbly rides and activities in cartoonish color dazzle and delight its target demographic: toddlers.

1 Legoland Way/6000 Cypress Gardens Blvd., Winter Haven. florida.legoland.com. **877/350-5346.** Gate price: $119 ages 3 and up (advance purchase $15–$20 cheaper), ticket bundles with Peppa Pig Theme Park available. Parking $30, preferred parking $50. Daily 10am to 5–9pm, depending on the day.

Orange County Regional History Center ★★★ MUSEUM

People who think Central Florida history began with Walt will have their eyes opened in this underrated museum, where the timeline starts 12,000 years in the past. Highlights: a Timacuan dugout canoe from around A.D. 1000, mastodon teeth, saddles used by the forgotten Florida cowmen; artifacts from the steamship tourist trade (in the 1870s, the St. John's River system was America's busiest one south of the Hudson); and the "Building a Kingdom" exhibition about the arrival of the theme parks. It was created without Disney funding so it could have the freedom to be frank.

65 E. Central Blvd., Orlando. thehistorycenter.org. **407/836-8500.** $8 adults, $7 seniors 55+, $6 kids 5–12, incl. audio tour. Free admission 3rd Thurs of month 5–8pm. Mon–Sat 10am–5pm; Sun noon–5pm.

The Orlando Eye ★ OBSERVATION WHEEL

You board 15-passenger climate-controlled pods for your slightly quivering circuit on the U.S. East Coast's tallest (400 ft.) observation wheel, which is constantly moving for an 18-minute rotation. You're too far away to see into the Disney parks, but you do see Universal Orlando, 2 miles north.

ICON Orlando 360, 8375 International Dr., Orlando. iconparkorlando.com. **407/601-7907.** $35 adults, $30 children 3–12 including digital photos; discounted pkgs. available with Madame Tussauds and SeaLife Aquarium; frequent discounts online. Free parking. Mon–Thurs 1–10pm; Fri 1–11pm; Sat noon–11pm; Sun noon–10pm; hours may be extended. Generally closed in early Feb for maintenance. Cannot stop wheel's motion to accommodate mobility scooters.

Scenic Boat Tour ★★★ TOUR

A true local institution. They've been showing visitors glorious lakeside mansions in Winter Park this way since 1938. Three of Winter Park's seven smooth cypress-lined lakes, which are connected by narrow hand-dug canals, are explored in a 1-hour, 12-mile tour narrated by neighborhood old timers. The lakes are flat and relaxing, with plenty of bird life and 250-year-old live oaks. You'll find this charmer 3 blocks east of the shops on Park Avenue. Bring sunscreen: The pontoons are exposed.

312 E. Morse Blvd., Winter Park. scenicboattours.com. **407/644-4056.** $16 adults, $8 kids 2–11. No credit cards. Hourly departures 10am–4pm daily.

WHERE TO STAY

In 2024, Orlando had around 133,000 hotel rooms—37,000 of them combined at Disney and Universal alone. As you can imagine, competition can be fierce, yet at properties with heavy turnover, quality can nevertheless be lax. Orlando's resorts rarely achieve true opulence, and even many hotels that pass themselves off as "deluxe" are actually just mid-level in their features. Often, when you pay too much for a fine Orlando hotel, you're paying for either proximity or mood. The lowest rates are usually available September through the first 2 weeks of December (excluding the week of Thanksgiving) and January through April (excluding the weeks of spring break). Unfortunately, a majority of area hotels impose some kind of daily fee, like a "resort fee," which can add substantially to your tab at the last minute. It's not legal in other countries, but the hotel lobby protects the practice here.

We've included a good selection of some of our favorite Disney resorts (reservations: © **407/934-1936**) below, but for a complete listing, as well as even more area hotels that may be less expensive, check out Frommer's *Disney World, Universal, & Orlando*. Walt Disney World's hotel rates are fixed by a calendar based on how many people are expected to be there. That calendar is not released publicly, but it's reflected in prices that change daily. Roughly speaking, rates break into six categories. They are, in descending order of expense: **Holiday, Peak, Summer, Regular, Fall,** and **Value,** and even those are parsed into levels, so you could easily pay several different nightly rates during the same stay. The major price spikes are around spring break, Easter, and the late December holidays—put simply, when more people can travel to Disney World. Likewise, there are three categories of Disney hotels: **Deluxe, Moderate,** and **Value,** and Disney marks them as such. Ergo, for the cheapest room, book a Value room in a Value period.

Resorts on Disney Property

All Disney hotels, regardless of class, have free parking for overnight guests both at the hotel and at the parks, big pools and shallow kiddie pools, free Wi-Fi, coin laundries, and playgrounds. Staying at one of these grants **early entry** into the theme parks 30 minutes before the general public (not much time, really). You'll probably be surprised by how utilitarian Disney's room designs are getting these days, even at the so-called Deluxe hotels. You won't find a minibar, robes, or even carpeting in most rooms. Disney hotels have **no resort fees**—but that doesn't matter since they cost a third or more than similar hotels outside the resort.

EXPENSIVE

Disney's Animal Kingdom Lodge ★★★ No grander lodge ever existed on the African veldt, and the higher tariff returns to you in the form of a 24-hour safari and lots of themed activities. The main part of the hotel, Jambo House, is where the hotel rooms are (Kidani House is for Disney Vacation Club units). If you've got a Savannah view (they start around $500—careful that you don't accidentally book a Standard one overlooking the parking lot or pool), when you look out of your window, you'll hopefully see whatever genial African animal is loping by at that moment, be it a giraffe, an ostrich, a zebra, or a warthog. (Packing binoculars will help.) Anyone can visit, even if they're not staying here; there's even a public animal viewing area straight out the back of the awe-inspiring vaulted lobby. The Lodge's principal drawback is its distance from everything except for Animal Kingdom; all connections are by road, which might have you wishing you'd stayed on the monorail instead. Standard room: 344 square feet.

2901 Osceola Pkwy., Bay Lake. disneyworld.com. © **407/934-7639** or 407/938-3000. 1,293 units. $487–$1,195 non-club standard. 2-adult maximum. Standard room: max. 4 people; deluxe room: max. 5 people. Extra person $35. Children 17 and younger stay free in parent's room. Parking free (self), $33/day (valet). **Amenities:** 2 restaurants; cafe; Club Level rooms; health club and limited spa; heated outdoor pool; kids' pool; room service; free Wi-Fi.

Disney's Beach Club/Disney's Yacht Club ★★★ Both excellent choices with 381-square-foot rooms, these adjoining sisters are on a pond across from the BoardWalk entertainment area (you'll need it, because the hotels are short on decent choices for cheap food) and a short stroll away from the International Gateway exit of EPCOT's World Showcase, which brings the fun close to your room, although you can't watch EPCOT's evening show from it. Their shared 3-acre pool area, Stormalong Bay, has sandy shores and the crazy Flying Jib waterslide that forms a straightaway shooting off the mast of a pirate ship. (It's easily the best pool on Disney property, and it's restricted to guests.) The difference between the two is nearly negligible—they're connected and many guests think they're one giant hotel. Both of them have layouts that confuse kids.

1800 EPCOT Resorts Blvd., Lake Buena Vista. disneyworld.com. ✆ **407/934-7639** or 407/934-8000. Beach: 583 units. Yacht: 630 units. $569–$1,252 non-club standard. Standard room: max. 5 people. Extra person $35. Children 17 and younger stay free in parent's room. Parking free (self), $33/day (valet). **Amenities:** 2 restaurants; grill; 3 bars; Club Level rooms; character meals; health club and small spa; 3-acre pool and play area; 2 outdoor heated pools; kids' pool; room service; 2 lighted tennis courts; boat rental; free Wi-Fi.

Disney's BoardWalk Inn ★★

The theme here, in a property split between Disney Vacation Club owners and nightly trade, is ostensibly turn-of-the-20th-century Atlantic City (not tatty, present-day Atlantic City), not that the theming is very apparent anymore. Rooms have been recently renovated and are a fair 371 square feet. The Luna Pool's 200-foot slide evokes a wooden roller coaster, but we prefer the quieter, tucked-away pool near Building 1 on the east side of the property. Really, you stay here because the side door to EPCOT is a 10-minute lakefront stroll away.

1800 EPCOT Resorts Blvd., Lake Buena Vista. disneyworld.com. ✆ **407/934-7639** or 407/934-8000. 379 units. $641–$1,199 non-club standard. Standard room: max. 5 people. Extra person $25. Children 17 and younger stay free in parent's room. Parking free (self), $33/day (valet). **Amenities:** Restaurant; bar; lounge; Club Level rooms; health club and small spa; 3-acre pool and play area; 3 outdoor heated pools; kids' pool; whirlpool; room service; boat rental; bike rental; free Wi-Fi.

Disney's Contemporary Resort ★★★

Pay ultra-high rates to stay a 5-minute walk from Magic Kingdom. Nothing says, "I'm at Disney World" more than the awesome sight of that monorail sweeping dramatically through the Contemporary's glassy Grand Canyon Concourse, which it does every few minutes on its way to and from Magic Kingdom. The hotel, one of the first two to open in 1971, is a midcentury architectural treasure. The current look of rooms: white and modern, with the bland whiff of IKEA, following a 2021 renovation. Best ones (422 sq. ft., among the largest standard rooms at Disney) are high up in the coveted A-framed Contemporary Tower, but there are stylish low-level Garden Rooms along Bay Lake, too, near the surprisingly blah pool, that are about $150 cheaper. Rooms on the west of the tower face Magic Kingdom itself (and an intervening parking lot)—the ninth floor has the *ne plus ultra* of Disney views—and every water-view room takes in the nightly parade that floats after dark. Drop by via monorail to see the 90-ft.-tall mosaics of children by the visionary Imagineer Mary Blair, which encapsulate the late 1960s futurist optimism out of which the resort was born.

4600 N. World Dr., Lake Buena Vista. disneyworld.com. ✆ **407/939-6244** or 407/824-1000. 1,008 units. $572–$1,423 non-club room. Standard room: max. 5 people. Garden View room: max. 4 people. Extra person $35. Children 17 and younger stay free in parent's room. Parking free (self), $33/day (valet). **Amenities:** 3 restaurants; grill; 4 lounges; Club Level rooms; character meals; small health club and spa; 2 outdoor heated pools; kids' pool; watersports rental; free Wi-Fi.

Disney's Grand Floridian Resort & Spa ★★

It's strange to spend $900 a night on a hotel room only to have a room with laminate flooring and to have to walk outside in the rain to reach the building it's in, but that's the situation here. The Grand Floridian's public spaces are encrusted with upper-class affectation and can't help but strum your imagination of what a true Victorian grande dame hotel might have felt like, even if you're paying insane rates for what amounts to a basic corporate room. There *are* vacation-making pluses I'd unreservedly celebrate here if money were no object, such as next-door access to Magic Kingdom by foot, ferry, or monorail; gourmet restaurants; careful staff; and an atmosphere more romantic than at any other Disney hotel—in fact, you'll probably have to dodge a few wedding parties. Typical standard rooms are 440 square feet, although rooms with dormer windows are smaller.

4401 Floridian Way, Lake Buena Vista. disneyworld.com. **407/934-7639** or 407/824-3000. 867 units. $824–$1,721 non-club doubles. Standard room: max. 5 people. Extra person $35. Children 17 and younger stay free in parent's room. Parking free (self), $33/day (valet). **Amenities:** 5 restaurants; grill; character meals; Club Level rooms; health club and spa; heated outdoor pool; kids' pool; room service; 2 lighted tennis courts; watersports rental; free Wi-Fi.

Disney's Polynesian Village Resort ★★★

The 25-acre longhouse-style complex remains one of the most transporting of the Disney resorts. Only the most expensive rooms have a view of the Magic Kingdom across the Seven Seas Lagoon (swimming in it is not allowed, but the pool area is huge and lush), but most have greenery views. The Polynesian is a notch above for families as the monorail to Magic Kingdom is steps away and rooms are on the big side, sleeping five. An easy favorite. The downside is availability: Several buildings have been allocated as Disney Vacation Club member units, reducing the standard room count by several hundred, so it's harder than ever to enjoy this hotel now. This is the hotel with **Trader Sam's Grog Grotto,** one of the country's most popular tiki cocktail bars.

1600 Seven Seas Dr., Lake Buena Vista. disneyworld.com. **407/939-6244** or 407/824-2000. 484 standard units, 360 studios. $691–$1,645 non-club doubles. Standard room: max. 5 people. Extra person $35. Children 17 and younger stay free in parent's room. Parking free (self), $33/day (valet). **Amenities:** 3 restaurants; cafe; tiki bar; Club Level rooms; nearby health club and spa (at Grand Floridian); 2 heated outdoor pools; kids' pool; character meals; room service; watersports rental; gas grills; free 7:30pm marshmallow roast; free 9pm outdoor movie; free Wi-Fi.

Disney's Wilderness Lodge ★★

This effective riff on Yellowstone's woody Old Faithful Lodge, swaddled by oaks and pines, is picturesque and the least expensive of the Deluxe category. The Magic Kingdom, 10 minutes away by ferry, is the only thing easy to reach if you don't have your own car (the other parks involve a laborious bus trek). Most of its tricks are in its dramatic atrium lobby: giant stone hearth, springs that flow to a thronged pool area out back—a geyser nearby spouts water 120 ft. high on the half-hour from 7am to 10pm. Because of surrounding woods, rooms (340 sq. ft.) are dark, but evocative.

901 W. Timberline Dr., Lake Buena Vista. disneyworld.com. **407/934-7639** or 407/938-4300. 909 units. $524–$1,216 non-club standard. Children 17 and younger stay free in parent's room. Standard room: max. 4 people. Extra person $35. Parking free (self), $33/day (valet). **Amenities:** 3 restaurants; Club Level rooms; health club and limited spa; 2 spa tubs; 2 heated outdoor pools; jogging trail; boat rental; kids' pool; room service; free Wi-Fi.

MODERATE

Disney's All-Star Resorts (Movies/Music/Sports) ★
The setup of all three is identical—an expanse of concrete-block buildings at the edge of the property studded with enormous emblems, as if a giant had spilled the Legos in his toy box. But these motel-style rooms are older (they opened in the 1990s) and there's no enlivening central pond, so they are the last-choice Values. You get (noisy) laminate flooring, a mini-cooler, and a table that doubles as a drop-down Murphy bed holding your second queen mattress, so families must choose whether to sleep or use the table. Of the three, I prefer Movies, because its exterior is laden with Disney-specific iconography while its sisters stick to dull musical and sports-equipment icons. Music is the only property with suites fitting six people. Meals are available at a food court in the main building of each, which may be far from your room.

Buena Vista Dr., Lake Buena Vista. disneyworld.com. ✆ **407/934-1936.** 1,920 units each. Standard rooms $118–$254, family suites $300–$581, 3rd and 4th adult $15. For preferred, add about $20. Standard room: max. 4 people plus 1 child 2 and under in crib. Children 17 and younger stay free in parent's room. **Amenities:** Food court; arcade; babysitting; 2 outdoor heated pools; kids' pool; free Wi-Fi.

Disney's Art of Animation Resort ★★★
This attractive 2012 addition benefits from theming more lavish than at other Values, including a spot-on Radiator Springs pool area. Family Suites have two bathrooms, convertible couches, and demi-kitchens (no stove). Standard *Little Mermaid* rooms are gorgeously and whimsically themed, too—better than at other Values. Suites draw on *Finding Nemo* (where there's the Big Blue pool, WDW's largest; these suites cost more than the others here) and *The Lion King*. Unfortunately, six-person suites cost three times more than basic four-person Value rooms, which is hard to justify. This is Disney's only pet-friendly Value resort. It also connects to Disney's Hollywood Studios and EPCOT via the free Skyliner gondola; it shares a busy station with the Pop Century.

1850 Century Dr., Lake Buena Vista. disneyworld.com. ✆ **407/938-7000.** 1,120 suites, 864 standard units. Standard rooms (*The Little Mermaid*) $209–$413, 6-person family suites (*Cars*, *The Lion King*, *Finding Nemo*) $478–$963. Standard room: max. 4 people plus 1 child 2 and under in crib. Extra person $15/night (standard rooms only). **Amenities:** 3 pools; food court; kids' pools; arcade; free Wi-Fi.

Disney's Caribbean Beach Resort ★
This resort sprawls around a central pond—1½ miles around, encircled by its own bus route. As you might expect, there's a loose island theme. Rooms (mostly full beds) feel vaguely Polynesian and are the Moderate category's largest (by a little), but water-view rooms don't have balconies. The main Old Port Royale pool area emulates a waterfront Spanish fort and has a giant tippy bucket, so you can see why families favor this property. The resort's principal downsides are a lack of elevators, bland food, and a risk of being placed very far from the lobby and pool (preferred rooms cost a little more to put you closer). But this is the best hotel in the Disney Skyliner gondola system, which goes straight to Disney's Hollywood Studios and EPCOT for free in minutes. (For everything else, you need wheels or take Disney's buses, also free.)

900 Cayman Way, Lake Buena Vista. disneyworld.com. ✆ **407/934-7639** or 407/934-3400. 2,112 units. $268–$552 standard doubles. Standard room: max. 5 people plus 1 child 2 and under in crib. Extra person $25. Children 17 and younger stay free in parent's room. **Amenities:** Restaurant; food court; arcade; heated pool; 6 smaller pools in the villages; kids' pool; free Wi-Fi.

Disney's Coronado Springs Resort ★

Built to attract convention crowds with a vibe to match, it nonetheless has fans for its subdued tone. The well-planted grounds, done in a hacienda style around a pond, are far-flung (some rooms are a 15-min. hike from the lobby, which gets old fast and bewilders many; or take the hotel shuttle bus around the perimeter), and rooms, with kings (for two) or queens (for four), have a single sink, as at the Values. The food court is above average, though, as is the pool area (with a 123-ft. slide), themed after a Mayan pyramid, and an inviting alfresco cocktail bar, Three Bridges, hovers in the center of the lagoon. The hotel is 10 minutes' drive from any parks.

1000 Buena Vista Dr., Lake Buena Vista. disneyworld.com. ✆ **407/934-7639** or 407/939-1000. 1,921 units. $260–$664 doubles. Standard room: max. 4 people plus 1 child 2 and under in crib. Extra person $25. Children 17 and younger stay free in parent's room. **Amenities:** Restaurant; grill/food court; arcade; health club and limited spa; 4 outdoor heated pools; kids' pool; free Wi-Fi.

Disney's Pop Century Resort ★★

The largest Value resort (opened in 2002) is a fair choice, with smallish (260 sq. ft.) rooms—one king bed or two queens—with cubbies instead of closets, one sink, and one mirror, and for dining, a heaving central food court with quality akin to the average mall. A renovation converted rooms' second queen bed into a Murphy bed that doubles as a table (so unless you're a couple, you have to choose whether to sleep or use the table). As if to counteract such dormlike austerity, the boxy sprawl of T-shaped buildings, some of which face a pleasant lake across from the Art of Animation Resort, is festooned with outsized icons of the late-20th-century: gigantic bowling pins, yo-yos, and Rubik's Cubes—which kids think is pretty cool. Pop Century is preferable to the All-Stars, where rooms are nearly the same, because it connects to Disney's Hollywood Studios and EPCOT via the Skyliner gondola, and that makes life easier.

1050 Century Dr., Lake Buena Vista. disneyworld.com. ✆ **407/938-4000**. 2,880 units. Standard rooms $183–$429. For pool view, add $7–$13. For preferred, add $12–$20. Standard room: max. 4 people plus 1 child 2 and under in crib. **Amenities:** Food court; 3 pools; kids' pools; arcade; jogging trail; free Wi-Fi.

Disney's Port Orleans Riverside and French Quarter ★★

An unwieldy name for an unwieldy property. It's actually two resorts, both built on a canal and awkwardly fused together. The **French Quarter** (1,000 rooms), built along right angles on simulated streets, purports to sort of imitate the real one in New Orleans. **Riverside** (2,048 rooms) is the nicer of the two: Its buildings are more successful pastiches, modeled on magnolia-trimmed Mississippi-style homes. Riverside also has more water for rooms to face (though the privilege will cost you another $30 a night) and is the locale for most activities for the two resorts. Not all buildings have elevators, so if you need one, make sure you request a room on the first floor when you check in. Riverside has five pools to French Quarter's one, but the main pool at Riverside is less elaborate than the French Quarter's, and Riverside's room windows all face an exterior corridor.

2201 Orleans Dr., Lake Buena Vista. disneyworld.com. ✆ **407/934-7639** or 407/934-5000. 3,048 units. $289–$533 doubles. Standard room: max. 5 people plus 1 child 2 and under in crib. Extra person $25. Children 17 and younger stay free in parent's room. **Amenities:** 2 restaurants; grill/food court; 6 heated outdoor pools; 2 kids' pools; arcade; free Wi-Fi.

Four Seasons Resort Orlando at Walt Disney World Resort ★★★

Orlando's most genuinely luxurious resort is a stunner in both looks and service: Quiet, 500-square-foot (46-sq.-m) rooms come with furnished balconies, walk-in closets, concierge e-tablets, and marble bathrooms. The par-71 golf course is also a bird sanctuary, and the landscaped 5-acre pool complex (with free sunscreen and valets bearing refreshments) goes on and on—adults-only pool, zero-entry family pool, lazy river with waterfalls that you could spend all day in, two waterslides in a faux fort. To see the fireworks just 2 miles away from your balcony, you can spring for a "Park View Room," which cost as much as $300 more than a "Lake View Room" on the lower floors. Daytime babysitting for kids 4 to 12 is free, and kids 5 and under eat free. Its Goofy breakfast is one of the best character meals because it's less crowded and you get lots of photo time with him.

10100 Dream Tree Blvd., Golden Oak. fourseasons.com/orlando. **407/313-6868** or 407/313-7777. 443 units. From $645 for a standard double. Valet parking $30 (no self-parking), parking for restaurants $5 with validation. No resort fee. **Amenities:** 3 restaurants; 3 bars; 3 pools; splash zone and waterslides; lazy river; spa; tennis courts; 24-hr. fitness center; 3 boutiques; character breakfast; free kids' club; kids 5 and under eat free; free Disney parks shuttle; free Wi-Fi.

Walt Disney World Swan and Dolphin ★ Redeeming rewards points is a big draw at the Starwood-run Swan and Dolphin, which are linked by a footbridge over the lake they share. Former Disney CEO Michael Eisner controversially allowed outside corporations to intrude on resort property, and the result was these dated 1989 exteriors—but given how boring Disney hotel construction has been since, we can't regret those 56-foot-tall dolphin statues. Staff is distracted, but the properties are stuffed with amenities and the location never quits—you can walk or ferry to EPCOT's side door in 15 minutes and Hollywood Studios in 20, avoiding the bus. They lack the tonal fantasy at Disney-run hotels, and there's no access to the Dining Plan, and no ability to make park purchases by room key or MagicBand. Staying here does, however, qualify you for 30-minute Early Theme Park Entry. Unlike Disney-run hotels, these often make discounted appearances on hotel booking sites.

1500 EPCOT Resorts Blvd., Lake Buena Vista. swandolphin.com. **407/934-4000.** Swan: 756 units, $290–$545 non-club standard. Dolphin: 1,509 units, $175–$334 non-club doubles. Extra person $25. Children 17 and younger stay free in parent's room. Parking $34/night (self), $44/night (valet). Resort fee $40/night. **Amenities:** 12 restaurants; cafe; character meals; 5 heated outdoor pools; game room; health club and spa; kids' program (2 hr. free if parents eat in one of its restaurants); room service; babysitting; free domestic phone calls; free Wi-Fi.

> ### The "Good Neighbor" Hotels
>
> Scattered throughout town are more than three dozen properties that brag Disney has certified them as "Good Neighbor" (wdwgoodneighborhotels.com). The appellation is mostly meaningless. It means that hotel will have shuttles, can sell park tickets, and screens a mesmerizing 24-hour channel touting all things Disney. Only the Good Neighbor properties on the west side of Apopka Vineland Road (mostly on Hotel Plaza Blvd.) enjoy half-hourly shuttles; the rest don't. So don't select a hotel just because it's a Good Neighbor hotel. Choose it because it's the right hotel for you.

Walt Disney World Swan Reserve ★★ Quieter and less packed with amenities than its chaotic sisters the Swan and Dolphin across the road (guests can use the amenities at those properties; there's a crosswalk with a signal), this 2021 hotel is set apart in a calmer space that is more attuned to adults than to children, even though it's kid-friendly. Staying here, you get all the benefits that you'd normally get at the Swan and Dolphin, including free buses to the Disney theme parks and entry to the Disney theme parks 30 minutes before they open to the general public. Nearly 150 of its 349 units are suites, so this is a good place to spread out.

1255 EPCOT Resorts Blvd., Lake Buena Vista. swandolphin.com. **800/227-1500**. 349 units. Typically $237–$458 doubles. Extra person $25. Children 17 and younger stay free in parent's room. Parking $34/night (self), $44/night (valet). Resort fee $40/night. **Amenities:** Restaurant; bar; pool; tennis courts; fitness center; sundries shop; free Disney shuttle; free Wi-Fi.

ROUGHING IT, DISNEY-STYLE

Disney's Fort Wilderness Resort & Campground ★★ Not to be confused with the Wilderness Lodge, an imitation of Yellowstone's Old Faithful Lodge, this 780-acre wooded enclave near Magic Kingdom consists of campsites and, as of 2024, modern, not-at-all-rustic mobile-home-style cabins with decks that sleep six on a mix of beds, pullouts, and bunks. Camping and RV parking under the thick pines are far and away the cheapest and most distinctive way to sleep on property, but it's twice the market rate, and without equipment (tents are $45, cots $6, if a group hasn't booked them first). The nightly marshmallow roast and outdoor Disney film screenings are perennial hits.

3520 N. Fort Wilderness Trail, Lake Buena Vista. disneyworld.com. **407/934-7639** or 407/824-2900. 784 campsites, 408 wilderness cabins. $99–$255 campsite/RV doubles, $466–$920 wilderness cabin doubles. Standard cabin: max. 6 people plus 1 child 2 and under in crib. Children 17 and younger stay free with parent. **Amenities:** Restaurant; grill; extensive outdoor activities (archery; fishing; horseback, pony, carriage, and hay rides; campfire programs; boat rental; and more); 2 outdoor heated pools; kids' pool; character dining; 2 lighted tennis courts; free Wi-Fi.

> ### WDW Occupancy Limits
>
> Disney room rates are quoted for two people. For more people, add $15 to $35 a night (depending on the resort category) for each person up to the room's stated maximum capacity, so a $179 Value room will actually be $209 if four people stay in it. (One child age 2 and under can stay without being counted toward the occupancy limit.) Value and Moderate resorts cap occupancy at four (not including a babe in a crib) and Deluxe cap at five. Families larger than four must rent two units, doubling the expense, but if you have seven or more people to accommodate, the tab gets ugly fast.

Lake Buena Vista Hotels

"Official" Disney hotels, though not owned and operated by Disney, line Hotel Plaza Boulevard, on the east side of Disney property and adjacent to Disney Springs. Guests can enjoy some of the perks of staying in a WDW resort (like free transportation to the Disney parks, but not the ability to charge park purchases to your room) while staying in a location close to I-4 and the rest of Orlando's offerings.

MODERATE

In terms of room quality, hotels in this category are usually a step above the "Moderate" resorts inside WDW, but they're farther from the parks with less frequent free shuttles.

Drury Plaza Hotel Orlando—Disney Springs Area ★★★

A super strong value. Built in 2021 out of the gut-renovated bones of a 1971-era Best Western tower, the Drury Plaza is packed with extras: free cooked breakfast including you-grill-them Mickey waffles, free evening "kickback" mixer with three free drinks (including wine) and snacks, free popcorn and soda in the evening, free parking, and all the benefits of a Good Neighbor hotel, including early entry privileges, free hourly shuttle service to Magic Kingdom, and service that's nearly as frequent to the other Disney parks (reservations 2 hr. ahead requested). Disney Springs is a 15-minute walk away on a safe sidewalk. The rooms, unfussy with comfortable beds and fat pillows, are just as good as in the more expensive business-class hotels. *Tip:* Rooms in the Palm tower have small balconies, while ones in Cypress don't. Also, even rooms that are said to have fireworks views won't if they're below the seventh floor.

2000 Hotel Plaza Blvd., Lake Buena Vista. druryhotels.com. **407/560-6111.** 604 units. Typically $130–$200 doubles. No resort fee. Parking $25/night (self), $29/night (valet). **Amenities:** Outdoor pool and spa tub with bar and grill; free cooked breakfast; free evening cocktails and snacks; free evening popcorn and soda; laundry machines; arcade; lobby Pizza Hut kiosk; grab-and-go sundries shop; fitness center; free Disney shuttles; free Wi-Fi.

Renaissance Orlando Resort & Spa ★★

The onetime B Resort, a 17-story tower from 1972 convenient to both I-4 and Disney Springs, is now a vaguely Miami-flavored corporate resort for families on a budget. It feels a bit airier than the usual tired pillow mills around here. King rooms are much larger than double-queen ones, but all are sizable with a mini-cooler, and higher-floor rooms claim views. Rooms ringing the zero-entry pool come with bunk beds. The Renaissance holds its own in Disney Springs for providing a grown-up stay that's still family-friendly. If you stay here, you're allowed into the Disney theme parks 30 minutes early.

1905 Hotel Plaza Blvd., Lake Buena Vista. marriott.com. **407/828-2828.** 394 units. Typically $109–$315 doubles, 2- or 3-night min. stay during peak periods. Parking $25/night (self), $35/night (valet). Resort fee $45/night. **Amenities:** Restaurant; heated pool; pool restaurant and bar; tennis courts; spa; 24-hr. fitness center; sundries shop; on-site Enterprise Rent-a-Car; free Disney shuttle; free Wi-Fi.

Signia by Hilton Orlando Bonnet Creek ★

Linked to the Waldorf Astoria by a convention hall and set in 482 mostly unbuilt acres, the hotel has rooms that lack balconies, which is a real bummer, but it's on Disney turf, which counts for a lot. Kids eat free for breakfast and dinner, which is fortunate considering how expensive the restaurants are. The 3-acre pool area is done in contemporary stonework—a bit like riding a lazy river in a hotel bathroom—and is abuzz with cocktails and activities. Overall, it's a fine place to disappear but it's too large and corporate to be romantic, although it does qualify for early entry to the Disney parks. And that resort fee! Park a car and you're paying $100 more a night on top of the room rate.

14100 Bonnet Creek Resort Lane, Orlando. hiltonbonnetcreek.com. **407/597-3600.** 1,001 units. $169–$380 standard king. Parking $38/night (self), $54/night (valet). Resort fee $50/night plus tax. **Amenities:** 6 restaurants; coffee bar; pool bar; heated pool w/activities; Disney shop; golf course; business center; fitness club; spa (at neighboring Waldorf Astoria); game room; free meals for kids 11 and under at Harvest Bistro w/adult purchase; free Disney shuttles; free golf club rental after 2pm; 2 bottles of water daily; free local and toll-free calls; free Wi-Fi.

Other Hotels Near Disney

The hotels in this section are within a few minutes' drive of the WDW parks, offering the location but not privileges of a stay at an "official" hotel. If you're more in the market for a vacation rental unit experience that feels like a resort, **Evermore Orlando** (evermoreresort.com; ✆ **855/341-9627**), a range of luxury 2- to 11-bedroom luxury rentals (houses, villas, apartments, plus central restaurant and supplies store), opened in 2024 alongside a swimming lake at the 1,100-acre just east of Magic Kingdom.

EXPENSIVE

Gaylord Palms ★ The Gaylord, situated away from the worst of Kissimmee, is geared to captive audiences attending meetings, so although its scenery is extravagant, so are its incidental charges. Still, it impresses: Beneath its mighty glass atrium is a 4½-acre Florida-themed ecosystem of gator habitats, caves, indoor ponds, sand sculptures, restaurants, and a full-size sailboat. All of that makes for an attraction unto itself, and to face it, you'll pay extra. Rooms have a decor with no particular point of view, but they sleep five and sport unusually nice granite-lined bathrooms. If Disney weren't right outside, you might never leave, what with the on-site Cypress Springs mini-waterpark (which would be elaborate enough to please a small town and is free to guests), main pool, and the Relâche Spa & Salon. It also schedules family activities and an annual holiday ICE! extravaganza.

6000 W. Osceola Pkwy., Kissimmee. gaylordhotels.com. ✆ **407/586-0000.** 1,718 units. $273–$469 king or double-queen rooms. Parking $38 (self), $50 (valet). Resort fee $45/night. **Amenities:** 5 restaurants; sports bar; 2 pools with splash zone; waterslide park; fitness center; spa; game room; car rental desk; free yoga class; free local phone calls; scheduled park shuttles (Disney free, others charged); free bottled water; Wi-Fi (free; fast $22/day).

Hyatt Regency Grand Cypress Resort ★★★ Probably the most complete resort for a reasonable price near Disney, the stepped tower packs every conceivable amenity into a lush 1,500-acre campus located practically inside Walt Disney World. There's an unforgettable 800,000-gallon waterfall-and-cavern-studded lagoon pool system (for our money, it's the best pool of any Orlando resort), lush trails wrapping around a private lake, horses, and top-floor views of the fireworks at EPCOT and Magic Kingdom. With so many extras (kayaks, paddleboats, minigolf), it feels like what resorts used to be.

1 Grand Cypress Blvd., Lake Buena Vista. grandcypress.hyatt.com. ✆ **800/233-1234** or 407/239-1234. 779 units. $175–$410 king or double queen. Self-parking $36/night; valet parking $51/night. Resort fee $49/night plus tax. **Amenities:** 2 restaurants; 3 cocktail bars; coffee bar; pool; babysitting; golf course; spa; kids' club; business center; gift shop; game room; tennis courts; golf course; biking; trails; rock climbing wall; 24-hr. fitness center; salon; beach; free park shuttles; free local and toll-free calls; free throttled Wi-Fi (full-speed $5/day).

MODERATE

Margaritaville Resort Orlando ★ This sprawling 300-acre resort on the southern fringe of the tourist zone mostly comprises cute Key West–style timeshare cottages from one to eight bedrooms—you can rent one but they're highly individual—but there's a hotel amid the spaciousness. Every room (and they're pretty big: 470 sq. ft., with giant, delightful bathrooms) has a shady porch with a view of the pool and beyond that, of a pond and nearly no other buildings. It's hardly a non-stop party—the last bar still closes by midnight—maybe 184 hotel rooms isn't quite enough to support all those amenities. Weirdly, there's no Margaritaville restaurant (that's at CityWalk), but the Promenade at Sunset Walk dining-and-entertainment strip mall area on the grounds offers a decent number of upscale bars and restaurants. There's also a minor waterslide park (Island H2O Water Park), that's separately ticketed. Between the resort fee and valet, the price is $75 higher than it looks.

8000 Fins Up Circle, Kissimmee. margaritavilleresortorlando.com. **855/995-9099** or 407/479-0950. 184 units. Standard rooms $175–$282. Self-parking free; valet parking $35/night. Resort fee $40/night plus tax. **Amenities:** Restaurant with bar; quick-service restaurant; pool; pool bar; spa; fitness center (off-site); free local and toll-free calls; kids' club; free transportation to Disney, Universal, and SeaWorld; free Wi-Fi.

INEXPENSIVE

AC Hotel Orlando Lake Buena Vista ★ If your plans involve lots of theme parks and you won't be in your room much by day, you're likely to find some excellent deals here right now—new highway ramps are being constructed near its northern side, which may scare some guests (even though rooms are well soundproofed). The AC, a by-the-book but modern-feeling roadside corporate hotel, was just renovated in 2022, so it's fresh and new. You can't walk to much from its lobby except the Waffle House in the parking lot (which, honestly, is a boon). It's also right beside an I-4 exit and just a 2-minute drive to Disney Springs, so you can hardly do better on proximity.

12799 Apopka Vineland Rd., Orlando. marriott.com. **407/597-3400.** 394 units. Typically $95–$159 double queen. Parking $18/night. No resort fee. **Amenities:** Bar/restaurant; outdoor pool; fitness center; laundry; sundries shop; free Disney shuttle; free Wi-Fi.

Aloft Orlando Lake Buena Vista ★★ From the outside, it looks like another six-floor cookie-cutter chain hotel building, but on the inside, this newly constructed addition (opened in 2021) emulates loft-style quarters—are all those exposed pipes and wires in the lobby real or just an interior designer's fulfilled fantasy? Rooms lead with contemporary 'tude—multicolored rugs and not carpets, bathroom sinks behind the bed by a demi-wall and WC hidden behind a slider door, plush sink-into-them beds, and TVs that can stream your Netflix account during your stay. Overall, it's easy to like because rooms don't feel like every other brand's, and it's midway between Disney and SeaWorld. We just wish that blah concrete swimming pool had a quarter of the design panache you see indoors. And why is parking so much?

7950 Palm Pkwy., Orlando. marriott.com. **407/778-7600.** 141 units. $74–$154 doubles, rollaway bed $15/night. Self-parking $26. No resort fee. **Amenities:** Pool; cocktail bar; 24-hr. fitness center; free Wi-Fi.

Comfort Suites Maingate East ★★ Thanks to attentive management, the Comfort Suites is now my only recommendation on this stretch of U.S. 192 east of Disney. You'll find it tucked a distance off the main drag, with the honky-tonk amusements of Fun Spot and Old Town steps from the door—but not so near that the nightly noise is truly annoying. The best rates are for "standard rooms" with either a king or queen bed, but you can get a "deluxe" two-bedroom for about

$30 more, and all rooms are on the large side with minifridges, pullout couches (to up your occupancy, if needed), and microwaves for basic meal preparation. The elevators can be overwhelmed when it's at capacity, but that's common in Orlando hotels across the board.

2775 Florida Plaza Blvd., Kissimmee. comfortsuitesfl.com. ⓒ **407/397-7848.** 198 units. $98–$169 1-room suites. Free parking. No resort fee. **Amenities:** Pool with poolside bar; 24-hr. fitness center; sundries shop; game room; business center; free park shuttles; free hot breakfast buffet; free Wi-Fi.

Destiny Palms Hotel ★   A safe option at the extreme low end. The decor and its motel bones are dated, but fortunately, so is the price. If you only have $80 to spend, this rambling, '70s-era building on U.S. 192 west of Disney holds up its end of the bargain—good management has kept it among our most affordable recommendations for years. The staff keep things spotless, and that's what you want. Rooms come stocked with a toaster oven and minifridge; you also get a continental breakfast upgraded with eggs, oatmeal, pancakes, and waffles. Outlets are in short supply. King rooms face the north parking lot and are on the small side; double queen rooms look south on some pleasing old-growth Florida woods. The east-facing pool (it, too, is motel-simple) also faces the trees, which keeps this place from feeling hemmed in.

8536 W. Irlo Bronson Memorial Hwy./U.S. 192, Kissimmee. destinypalmsmaingate.com. ⓒ **407/396-1600.** 104 units. From $70 doubles. Free parking. Resort fee $4.50/night. **Amenities:** Pool; free continental breakfast; free local calls; free Wi-Fi.

International Drive Area

I-Drive is a sensible place to stay if you don't have a car because it's full of places to eat. It's also the only hotel zone with a semblance of street life. If you stay on I-Drive, you'll be in the thick of the family-friendly come-ons, midway rides, souvenir hawkers, minigolf, and theme bars. You'll need wheels to reach Disney (most hotels offer shuttles, but not always to Disney, and not always free), although Universal is just across I-4 to the north and the dirt-cheap I-Ride Trolley (p. 365) links you with SeaWorld.

EXPENSIVE

Ritz-Carlton Grande Lakes Orlando ★★★ / JW Marriott Orlando, Grande Lakes ★★   The two towers form a busy city unto themselves in a 500-acre plot a few miles east of SeaWorld. If you stay in one of them, you can use the main amenities of the other, a 10-minute walk away. This JW's 24,000-square-foot pool area, landscaped with fake rocks, jungle greens, and a ¼-mile lazy river, is deservedly jammed on hot days, while the Ritz's water area is formal and refined. The JW's rooms are more palatial than the norm in town (and have bathtubs) and were renovated in 2023. Meanwhile, the Ritz's rooms completed a renovation in 2021 that filled them with soothing greys, putty colors, and dark woods, and the pampering and quality here are a notch higher than at the JW. The 40,000-square-foot Ritz-Carlton spa is one of the city's best. It's a resort that has it all and seduces you into sticking around, but the remote location means you'll have to drive somewhere every time your stomach rumbles if you want to escape high-priced food (even though the Ritz's Knife & Spoon, p. 424, is a knockout and the JW's Primo is a long-running pleaser). Rates fluctuate wildly if there's a conference.

4040 Central Florida Pkwy., Orlando. grandelakes.com. ✆ **888/707-9325** or 407/206-2400 for the Ritz; ✆ **800/433-5402** or 407/206-2300 for the JW Marriott. JW: 1,010 units, $228–$548 doubles. Ritz: 584 units, $391–$744 doubles. Minifridge $20. Parking $38 (self), $54 (valet; mandatory for Ritz guests). Resort fee $53/night. **Amenities:** 6 restaurants; 2 cafes; 2 outdoor heated pools with lazy river and tower with 3 waterslides; kids' pool; spa; health club; golf course (normally membership-only); 3 tennis courts; kayaking; Club Level rooms; Starbucks; babysitting; 1 daily hr. of kids' club (Ritz only); free local calls; free park shuttles (with 24 hr. notice); free Wi-Fi.

MODERATE

Home2 Suites by Hilton Orlando Near Universal ★★

A non-fussy option for families on a budget, the large rooms come with a kitchen (there's a microwave, but you have to borrow hot plates from the front desk), a living area, a big sleeping area, and lots of counter and desk space. You won't get a tub (it's a standing shower), but who cares? Yes, it's a characterless box hotel on a small plot with a breakfast area that feels like a classroom, but it's in a strong location with strong features for a low price, with a big pool that's never crowded. You can walk to lots of places to eat. A second in this brand (one about 3 years older) is **Home2 Suites by Hilton Orlando/International Drive South** at 12107 Regency Village, across from Orlando Premium Outlets and 5 minutes from Disney Springs (from $124).

5910 American Way, Orlando. home2suites.hilton.com. ✆ **855/618-4702** or 407/519-3151. 122 units. $132–$188 for suites sleeping up to 6. Free parking. No resort fee. **Amenities:** Pool; 24-hr. free coffee kiosk; spin cycle fitness center; free scheduled shuttle to Universal and SeaWorld; free Wi-Fi.

Hyatt House Across from Universal Orlando Resort ★★

It's not technically across from it—more like a 30-second drive around a bend—but at eight stories tall, west-facing rooms here have a good peek at some of Universal's rooftops, and it is somewhat fresh, having opened midway through 2018 (many neighbors opened 40 years ago). Hyatt House, if you don't know, is the hotel giant's "extended stay" product, which means it's ideal for families who like to be able to cook for themselves. Rooms and suites come with a microwave and cube fridge, and most suites have fully equipped kitchens and a living room. Studios have a floating divider but not an actual wall (easier for keeping an eye on little kids); bump up $20 or so if you want a bedroom door that shuts. But even studios can sleep six. (Den rooms are like standard hotel rooms.) It hits the value buttons.

5940 Caravan Ct., Orlando. acrossfromuniversalorlando.house.hyatt.com. ✆ **407/352-5660.** 168 units. Rooms $123–$259 with 2 double beds, $20 more for king bed. Parking $18/night. No resort fee. **Amenities:** Heated pool; bar; sundries shop; 24-hr. fitness center; free Universal shuttle; free breakfast buffet; free Wi-Fi.

Universal Orlando Resorts

Eight hotels are on Universal property, all operated by the Loews hotel group, totaling 9,000 rooms. The higher-priced ones come with strong advantages. First, most Universal hotels are within 15 minutes' walk or free transportation to the parks, and five are connected by a free boat that runs continuously into the wee hours. Guests at the top-tier hotels (Hard Rock, Portofino Bay, Royal Pacific) can use their room keys to join the Express line at the two parks' best attractions—that perk has the effect of freeing up a vacation schedule. Guests can also drink and dine all night at CityWalk next door without having to drive or wait for a bus (unless you're staying at Endless Summer, which requires a shuttle). Use the hotels' website to find Hot Deals, which grants discounts of 20% to 30% on specified nights; the website also posts floor plans of all room types. At Easter and during the December holidays, rates are, of course, higher. But there are *no resort fees!*

In 2025, Universal opens three new hotels near its new Universal Epic Universe theme park. They are **Universal Stella Nova Resort** and **Universal Terra Luna Resort,** each with 750 rooms, and the **Universal Helios Grand Resort,** where the best of its 500 rooms will overlook the park. Starting rates for the first two are around $150 for a double queen bed room; Helios Grand starting prices are usually over $200 and zoom upward when it's busy. (*Reservations for the new hotels:* universalorlando.com or ✆ **888/273-1311.**)

EXPENSIVE

Hard Rock Hotel ★   Besides being the city's most convenient hotel for any theme park—the two main Universal parks are both a 10-minute walk away—the Hard Rock has more perks for the money than most of the city's similarly priced hotels. Rooms have genuinely funky furniture, tons of mirrors, two sinks (one in and one out of the bathroom), two big beds, and music systems. The ginormous pool imitates a beach gently descending to depth and is one of the better ones in town.

5000 Universal Blvd., Orlando. hardrockhotels.com/orlando. ✆ **888/430-4999** or 407/503-2000. 650 units. Rooms $519–$680 doubles, $40 per extra adult per night. Max. of 5 people (w/ rollaway). Parking $33/night (self), $42/night (valet). **Amenities:** Universal Express Unlimited ride access; 3 restaurants; cocktail lounge; ice-cream shop; pool with activities and bar; free babysitting; supervised children's program; Club Level rooms; fitness center; free Wi-Fi.

Loews Portofino Bay Hotel ★★★   Universal's priciest and most romantic option faithfully re-creates the famous Italian fishing village, down to the angle of the boat docks and the bolted-down Vespas along the waterfront. Beyond that spectacular gimmick (said to have been Steven Spielberg's idea, like much at 1990s Universal), rooms are of a particularly high standard—standard ones are a generous 450 square feet and have top-end beds. Because the resort is the farthest on property from the parks (but still only about 5 min. by quick-loading boat or 15 min. by foot), it tends to appeal to couples. Choose from two enormous pools—one with a sand beach, zero entry, and waterslides, the other with palm trees, bocce, and a Mediterranean vibe—or a small third option for a cool break in your day.

5601 Universal Blvd., Orlando. loewshotels.com/portofino-bay-hotel. ✆ **888/430-4999** or 407/503-1000. 750 units. Double queen or king rooms $555–$824, $40 per extra adult per night. Parking $33/night (self), $42/night (valet). **Amenities:** Universal Express Unlimited ride access; 3 restaurants; ice-cream shop; Starbucks; 3 pools with activities and bar; fitness center; Mandara Spa; supervised children's programs; Club Level rooms; nightly opera show; free Wi-Fi.

Loews Royal Pacific Resort ★★★   The least expensive luxury option at Universal does an apt impression of South Seas style in the 1930s, with muted cream colors dominated by giant flowers on the walls. It's more luxurious yet cheaper than the Disney Polynesian, with a lush, green pool area (sandy beach, winding garden paths, interactive water play area) and a sophisticated, wood-and-antiquities look. The standard is high: very soft robes, cushy beds with fat pillows, and marble-top chests. You can walk to the two main Universal parks in 10 minutes or catch a free ferry.

6300 Hollywood Way, Orlando. loewshotels.com/royal-pacific-resort. ⓒ **888/430-4999** or 407/503-3000. 1,000 units. Doubles $460–$758, $40 per extra adult per night. Parking $33/night (self), $42/night (valet). **Amenities:** Universal Express Unlimited ride access; 2 restaurants; sushi bar; cocktail lounge; pool with activities and bars; free Wi-Fi.

MODERATE

Loews Sapphire Falls Resort ★★★

The Modern Caribbean–inspired Sapphire Falls is clean and understated. Service is strong, parking is sheltered, the energy is easygoing, and you can take ferries or walks to the parks (the more crowded Cabana Bay only has buses). Most rooms have either a king or two queens (321 sq. ft.), but for $100 more you can have a King Suite with a separate sitting area (595 sq. ft.), and for $200 more there are Kids Suites with a separate double-twin bedroom for children. Quick-service food options are lacking, but the 16,000-square-foot pool area, which catches sun until sunset, is a world unto itself. A stay does not come with Universal Express, but there is a free ferry to the parks.

6601 Adventure Way, Orlando. loewshotels.com/sapphire-falls-resort. ⓒ **888/884-7922** or 407/503-5000. 1,000 units. Double queen or king rooms $279–$359, $20 per extra adult per night. Parking $33/night (self), $42/night (valet). **Amenities:** 2 restaurants; 2 bars; fitness center; pool w/activities and bar; Avis car rental desk; free standard-speed Wi-Fi (full-speed $15/day).

Universal's Aventura Hotel ★★

When you need a hotel that's a little more urbane and less kid-clogged, come here. The most adult-feeling theme park hotel in Orlando is a 16-story tower with that polished-concrete-and-white-wall modern Miami aesthetic. Tucked down by Sapphire Falls (you'll access its ferry after a 5-min. walk), its signature destination is Bar 17 Bistro, an open-air rooftop bar and grill with fantastic views, truly adult cocktails, and a happy hour that starts at 10pm. Standard two-queen rooms are on lower floors and are 314 square feet; Skyline rooms are the same size, but are high enough for city views or to spot Disney's fireworks in the far distance (you'll want to be on floor 8 or above for that), and are $25 more; standard king rooms are smaller (238 sq. ft.) and come with a pullout couch. Instead of a restaurant, a food court does

Loews Sapphire Falls Resort has a massive, westward-facing pool area.

surprisingly good and quick global cuisine (sushi, stir-fry, burgers). Guests won't receive Express privileges, and they'll have to link with the parks by bus, but they will be allowed early park entry in the mornings.

6725 Adventure Way, Orlando. loewshotels.com/universals-aventura-hotel. ✆ **888/273-1311** or 407/503-6000. 600 units. Double queen or king rooms start at $194–$279, w/discounts for longer stays, $20 per extra adult per night. Max. of 4 people per room. Self-parking $23/night. **Amenities:** Food court; 2 bars; fitness center; pool w/bar; virtual reality game room; Avis car rental desk; free Wi-Fi (high-speed $15/day).

Universal's Cabana Bay Beach Resort ★★

Cabana Bay plays the role of a family vacation escape by kitsching it up as a retro 1950s beach hotel. Geometric midcentury fabrics, teals and lemons, swooping Space Age architecture, a Jack LaLanne–branded gym, and a 10-lane bowling alley all wink at the midcentury era. Things may *look* old but they're decidedly modern, down to the ample outlets in the bedrooms, gated parking, and air-conditioning that's whisper quiet. The music never stops in the two ginormous pool areas, which have Universal's only lazy river, and guests get a special side entrance to Volcano Bay next door. But there's a trade-off: no Express Pass privilege (you do get into the parks early), no room service, and to reach the action, you'll have to take a shuttle to CityWalk—there is no water taxi to this hotel. (Sapphire Falls, priced a notch higher, has that.)

6550 Adventure Way, Orlando. loewshotels.com/cabana-bay-hotel. ✆ **888/430-4999** or 407/503-4000. 2,200 units. Standard rooms from $194–$324, family suites from $244, w/discounts for longer stays, $20 per extra adult per night. Self-parking $23/night. **Amenities:** Food court; 10-lane bowling alley w/food; 2 pools; 2 pool bars; waterslide; lazy river; splash pad; ice-cream shop; fitness center; free standard-speed Wi-Fi for up to 4 devices (full-speed $15/day).

INEXPENSIVE

Universal's Endless Summer Resort ★★★

The beach-themed Endless Summer complex is actually two hotels (Surfside Inn and Suites and Dockside Inn and Suites) across the street from each other. Here, a two-bedroom family suite with a kitchenette and table costs less than Disney's most basic single motel-style room in low season—it also fits two additional people comfortably *and,* unlike Disney's options, it has two big windows and kids won't lose their way to the pool. The price undercutting is intentional: Universal wants families on tight budgets to stay with *them* for a change and commute for their Disney days (an UberX from here to Magic Kingdom usually costs under $30). At these prices, and with Disney's costs spiraling heavenward, that's finally a reasonable idea, and Endless Summer is so well executed we could recommend it at a higher price. Its free shuttle buses take all of 4 minutes (I time it on regular occasions) to deliver you to the rest of the resort. Endless Summer's hotels won't give you room service, but they do have two bars (pool and lobby), pizza delivery, a Starbucks, and early entry to the theme parks. Both pools are massive, but Dockside's faces the sun for longer in the late afternoon, and Dockside towers higher than Surfside, which makes it the busier of the two but the better choice for Orlando views.

7000 Universal Blvd., Orlando. loewshotels.com/surfside-inn-and-suites and loewshotels.com/dockside-inn-and-suites. ✆ **888/430-4999** or 407/503-7000. 2,800 units. Standard double queen rooms $139–$219; pool view adds $15/night. Two-bedroom suites $219–$239; pool view adds $20/night. Add $15 per extra adult per night; max. of 4 people/room for standard room, 6 for suite. Self-parking $19/night. **Amenities for both hotels:** Outdoor pool; pool bar and restaurant; food court; complimentary cribs (no rollaway beds available); Starbucks; fitness center; game room; free Wi-Fi.

WHERE TO DINE

You don't need this guidebook to find a chain restaurant—Orlando is crawling with those, and most of them serve variations on the same American menu of burgers, ribs, pizzas, and salads topped with meat. No, where you could use help is in locating independent, unusual, and family-run small businesses. Following the theme park options below, we list worthy restaurant discoveries in town that you might not otherwise have noticed among the corporate clamor.

Reservations at Disney Restaurants

Reservations are a necessity for all of Disney's table-service restaurants, both inside and outside of theme parks. Walk-ins are usually accepted, but with a wait. Bookings open 60 days in advance at 6am Florida time (if you have a booking at a Disney hotel, you can book for the whole length of your stay starting 60 days ahead of your first day) via disneyworld.disney.go.com/dining or the **Disney World app** (navigate to the restaurant's page) or at 7am by telephone (✆ **407/939-3463** [DINE]). Families throw themselves into grabbing seats like alligators at feeding time. Disney slaps you with a $10 to $25 per person fee if you fail to show up for your reservation even though every restaurant has a line in front of it. The deadline is 2 hours before the reservation. This could be considered greedy, but there's a side benefit: Restaurants that seemed impossible a few days ago may suddenly have space when people dump bookings to avoid penalty. In fact, there's a paid service, **Unlocked Magic** (unlockedmagic.com; $6/month) that will scout cancellations for you.

All **Disney-run restaurants** (disneyworld.disney.go.com/dining; ✆ **407/939-3463** [DINE]) can be booked by phone (expect a wait), online, or using the My Disney Experience app. **Tenant-run restaurants** (like the ones at Disney Springs) can be booked on the app, directly, or on OpenTable. All restaurants also maintain **walk-up wait lists** (sometimes, you can join via the app if you're a reasonable distance away), but those lists can close without notice.

Inside the Walt Disney World Theme Parks

Disney controls everything inside the parks except for Starbucks (each park has one). That doesn't do much for the quality of the food—the Magic Kingdom can evoke childhood memories, but some of them will be of your grade-school cafeteria. At least the math is easy. The **cheapest combo meals** are always from counter-service restaurants (called Quick Service in Disney-speak), where adults usually pay $11 to $17, including a side but not a drink (sodas are $4.50–$5.30)—the combo is called a "meal." Most outlets also post one or two special menu items that are slightly more interesting than the core menu but are only offered for a few months. Kids' meals (a main dish; milk, juice, water, or soda; and a choice of two items including grapes, carrot sticks, applesauce, a cookie, or fries) always cost $7 to $9 at Quick Service locations. If you want to sit down for a waiter-service meal—character meals are always in "table-service" restaurants—adults usually pay over $22 a plate, before gratuity or drinks, and kids' meals are about half as much. The Disney World app lists restaurant menus with prices; find the restaurant on the map or using the search function (magnifying glass icon).

No longer can you simply stroll into any restaurant that catches your eye and enjoy a meal. **For table-service meals, *always* make an advance dining**

saving money DINING AT WDW

If you plan to buy all your food at the park, sticking strictly to counter-service meals is the cheapest way to go. But considering you'll pay $10 to $15 each for a counter-service sandwich, plus at least $4.50 for a medium-size soft drink—the going rate in the Orlando parks—even that way, a family of four can easily spend $80 on every meal! Save money! Besides eating off premises, here's how:

- **Subtract unwanted combo items.** Although counter-service restaurants make the menu appear like it's mostly combo meals, sometimes you may eliminate unwanted items from adult selections and save money. Dropping fries or other bundled side dishes can save about $3. For carrot sticks!

- **Pack a little food of your own.** Park security usually looks the other way if you bring a soft lunch-bag-size cooler (hard-sided ones will be rejected). Or just tote sandwiches in plastic bags. If your lodging has a freezer, keep juice boxes in there; they'll be thawed by lunch.

- **Skip table-service meals or plan them strategically.** They can chomp as much as 90 minutes out of your touring time. Do that twice and you've lost a third of your day.

- **Adults may order cheaper and smaller kids' meals.** No one will stop them.

- **Snack on fruit.** Each park has at least one fruit stand ($3/piece).

- **Seek out the turkey legs.** This vanishing species is giant (1½ pounds, from 45-pound turkeys), salty, and costs around $15. They taste like ham because they're injected with brine before cooking for 6 hours.

- **Order drinks without ice.** Fountain soda is dispensed cold anyway.

reservation (✆ 407/939-3463)—you'll hear them called "ADRs"—starting 60 days out, or you're likely to be turned away or face waits.

MAGIC KINGDOM

In addition to the restaurants listed below, there are plenty of counter-service outlets throughout the park, of which **Cosmic Ray's Starlight Cafe** (fairly dull burgers, hot dogs, and chicken, serenaded by an alien robot crooner), and the **Columbia Harbour House** (fried shrimp, grilled salmon, lobster rolls, chicken strips, chowder) are your best choices. You may find that a quiet, sit-down meal is an essential, if brief, break from the activities of the day. Combo meals generally cost $10 to $18 at quick-service spots.

FANTASYLAND Atop the winding stone staircase inside Cinderella Castle is the Holy Grail of character meals: **Cinderella's Royal Table ★**, starring your favorite princesses. mock medieval vaulted ceilings, a royal red carpet, stained glass, and stylized crest shields adorning the walls. Meals aren't all-you-can-eat, but they're schmancy prix-fixe. Bookings open 180 days ahead at 7am Orlando time by phone or 6am via the Disney app (and must be prepaid by credit card) and are snapped up in moments. Breakfast $69 adults, $42 kids; lunch and dinner $84 adults and $49 kids. More for champagne flights with a good place to watch fireworks with a dessert.

The Crystal Palace ★★, named for its airy Victorian-style skylight canopy, is a favorite with families because of its all-you-can-eat character buffets (attended by Pooh and friends). Breakfast, lunch, and dinner buffets $30 to $40 kids and $48 to $61 adults.

Be Our Guest Restaurant ★: In this delightful mock-up of the Beast's castle (the room with the enchanted red rose is our favorite), the food is French-ish (filet mignon, trout amandine, French onion soup). If they prefer, kids can have chicken, mac and cheese, or beef. In all honesty, if this food was served in France, the locals would form a posse to detain the chef responsible, not the Beast. Dinner sometimes offers a chance to meet the Beast, who can only be met here and nowhere else in the park. Lunch and dinner: $70 adults, $41 kids.

EPCOT
World Showcase

World Showcase has the best range of dining options inside the WDW theme parks. Alcohol is served everywhere.

The restaurants below are arranged geographically, beginning at the Canada pavilion and proceeding counterclockwise around the World Showcase Lagoon. Since these pavilions host the most notable outlets, not everything is listed; the U.S.A. pavilion has a barbecue-style counter-service eatery, for example.

CANADA Le Cellier Steakhouse's ★★★ vaulted archways, stone walls, and lanterns create a cozy atmosphere, much like that of a centuries-old wine cellar. An all-American menu of filet mignon, rib-eye steak, and USDA Prime New York strip steak, plus Canadian flourishes like bison strip loin and sides such as *poutine* fries (topped with cheddar, truffle salt, and red-wine reduction). Main courses $34 to $62.

UNITED KINGDOM The Tudor-beamed **Rose & Crown ★★** is an English pub where folk music and saucy servers entertain as you dine. The short menu has British favorites, including fish and chips, bangers and mash, cottage pie, and warm bread pudding. Its patio, if you can somehow get a seat on it, is one of the best places to see the nightly lagoon spectacular. The attached pub is a place to *be* spectacular. Main courses $23 to $27.

FRANCE **Chefs de France ★★**: In a glassed-in dining room recalling a typical French bistro, dine on quiche and crepes or prototypical French food such as duck breast, beef bourguignon, escargot casserole, and filet de boeuf (lunch and dinner). There's also a $55 prix-fixe, three-course meal with one glass of wine. Main courses $26 to $43. In a contemporary dining room at France's back end near the Remy ride, **La Crêperie de Paris ★★** serves full-meal savory *galette* buckwheat crepes (meats or veggies) and sweet crepes (fruit or hazelnut chocolate spread), plus alcoholic ciders, salad, and soup of the day. There's also a take-away counter. Crepes $11 to $19. The finest table in France is **Monsieur Paul ★★★**, which is special-occasion dining, with both a fish course and a meat course and plenty of *bouche* amusing in between: lobster salad, snapper with scales made of roasted potato slices, plus all the amuse-bouches and long preparation explanations you'd expect of a fine establishment. Full meal prix fixe: $195.

JAPAN At **Teppan Edo ★**, a chef-slash-swordsmith slices, dices, and cooks at the teppanyaki griddle built into your table. The culinary acrobatics are a sight to see; the cuisine is average. Main courses $26 to $65, sushi $14 to $20 per order. **Tokyo Dining ★** does a menu offering both tempura/grills, donburi/noodles, and sushi in modest portions. Entrees $21 to $36, sushi $12 to $24 per order. **Takumi-Tei** ★ (no lagoon views) is decidedly pricey: Wagyu beef and premium sake, with sushi starters and a dress code of golf casual or business casual—no flip-flops or T-shirts allowed. Prix-fixe menus $150 to $250 adults, $100 kids. **Katsura Grill** ★★, a small bamboo-roofed teahouse, features such fare as Japanese udon, ramen, sushi ($9–$12 for four pieces), and chicken or beef teriyaki.

ITALY **Tutto Italia Ristorante** ★ is proclaimed authentic mostly by people who have never been to Italy, but this dusky environment of chandeliers and murals nonetheless packs 'em in for low-caliber pasta. Main courses $26 to $46. **Via Napoli Ristorante e Pizzeria** ★★ is the more enjoyable of Italy's two table-service restaurants and features lots of light, three-story vaulted ceilings, and three amusing wood-fired ovens shaped like the open mouths of giant mustachioed men named after volcanoes. Full pizzas $25 to $55, individual pizzas $21, kids' pizzas $12, pastas $27 to $30.

GERMANY The **Biergarten Restaurant** ★★ feels like a Bavarian village at Oktoberfest. Toddlers lurch forward to polka, dads dive into mugs of Radeberger pilsner, and strangers make friends with their neighbors at this rowdy, carb-loaded party, an all-you-can-eat stuffer featuring schnitzel, spaetzle, rotisserie chicken, sauerbraten (at dinner), and an oompah band for about 20 minutes at a time. Buffet $49 adults, $27 kids.

NORWAY **Akershus Royal Banquet Hall** ★★ is EPCOT's meet-the-princesses extravaganza for all three "feasts" daily, in a Norwegian castle-like setting of vaulted ceilings and banners. Someone always stops by, be it Belle, Aurora, Snow White, Cinderella, or Ariel, who must not have heard that Norwegians love devouring raw fish. This is the only character dining in World Showcase. Breakfast is the livelier time, and it lets you into World Showcase before the other guests arrive. Breakfast $35 kids, $55 adults; lunch and dinner $43 kids, $67 adults.

MEXICO It's always night at the **San Angel Inn Restaurante** ★, where amid the marketplace and by an indoor boat ride, tables and booths set a mood under a faux star-lit sky. Reasonably authentic food, including the *mole poblano* (chicken simmered in spices, ground tortillas, and a hint of cocoa), is on the menu. Main courses $18 to $54. **La Cava del Tequila** ★★, a tequila bar serving 200-plus types of tequila, is inside the pavilion. Outside, **La Cantina de San Angel** ★★, a quick-service counter, offers beef, fish, chicken tacos, cheese empanadas, nachos, and margaritas (from $11). That's outside, but on the water. Combo meal $11 to $16. Adjacent to the Cantina is **La Hacienda de San Angel** ★★. By day, it's a sunny place to get your tequila on. By night, this villa-themed restaurant (vaulted ceilings, hanging lanterns) is a fair place to sit for the nighttime show, but only if you're lucky enough to score a window seat. Get flavors such as ancho agave-marinated steak, chicken with poblano cream sauce, or fish of the day. Entrees $28 to $54.

World Celebration, World Nature, World Discovery

Inside the Seas with Nemo & Friends pavilion, the **Coral Reef Restaurant** ★ features tables scattered around a 5.6-million-gallon aquarium. Turns out fish are both friends *and* food: Through windows into the 27-foot-deep tank, admire the luckier buddies of the fish on your plate. Only about half the menu selections are fish, and the rest are things like prime rib or harissa chicken. It's about the cool view, not the cuisine. Main courses $26 to $36.

Garden Grill ★★, an upscale food court in The Land, is a slowly rotating, two-tiered circular restaurant serving all-you-can-eat, family-style "Chip 'n' Dale's Harvest Feast" platters of meats and vegetables, some of which were allegedly grown in the greenhouses downstairs. This is the only character meal in Future World, but it's a good choice because it's mellow and small enough so that the merry rodents can spend quality time with you. Breakfast $30 kids, $47 adults; lunch and dinner $40 kids, $62 adults.

Beside Mission: SPACE, the fun gimmick at **Space 220 Restaurant** ★★★ is you're dining (and wining—the wine list reaches for the stars) 220 miles above the ground aboard a space station. It's a lot like the Coral Reef Restaurant, but in a vacuum: A 250-foot-long digital screen wrapping outside a semicircle of windows completes the illusion. Two-course prix fixe $55 (lunch) or $79 (dinner). It's a tough reservation to nab, so you may have to queue up and wait.

In view of Spaceship Earth in the central plaza, **Connections Eatery** ★★★ does double pizza slices (the Five-Cheese is the best), burgers piled with things like bacon, brie, or corn-chipotle salsa, and fun, sweet, seasonal cocktails. You fill your own sodas here, so it's a good place for multiple free refills during a meal. Lunch and dinner $12 to $16.

AT DISNEY'S HOLLYWOOD STUDIOS

The real **Hollywood Brown Derby** ★ was a haunt for Hollywood's Golden Age that invented the Cobb salad. This high-priced imitation looks the part (caricatures of Tinseltown's most famous celebrities line the walls), even if the food is past its prime. Expect fillet of beef, chicken a la King, salmon, and cioppino, and a $29 mushroom risotto. The grapefruit cake ($13) is a specialty—they'll give you the recipe. Entrees $20 to $49.

At **50's Prime Time Café** ★★★, you dine atop Formica in detailed reproductions of Cleaver-era kitchens while TVs play black-and-white shows from the era. Waitresses sling attitude and blue-plate specials—meatloaf, pot roast, fried chicken, and other mom-like dishes—but the favorite here is the peanut butter and jelly milkshake ($10). Attached is the first-come, first served **Tune-In Lounge,** a standing-only TV room for adults serving beer and proper cocktails "from Dad's liquor cabinet" like Long Island iced teas. Main courses $18 to $27.

Roundup Rodeo BBQ ★★ in Toy Story Land is a jumping joint serving family-style meals (cheddar biscuits, salads, house-smoked meats, four sides) for a set price, themed as if you're in a cardboard rodeo arena for Andy's toys from *Toy Story*. Vegetarian versions available. When Andy sounds like he's coming, the entire restaurant freezes in place until he's gone. It's fun. Set price $45 adults, $25 kids.

Sci-Fi Dine-In Theater Restaurant ★★★: One of Disney World's most novel places to eat arranges mock-ups of 1950s automobiles before a silver screen showing a loop of B-movie clips and trailers. Couples sit side-by-side, like at a real drive-in movie, stars twinkle in the "sky." It's a brilliant idea. Dishes include fried pickle chips, burgers, salmon or chicken pasta, turkey sandwiches, and wedge salads. Main courses $19 to $25.

DISNEY'S ANIMAL KINGDOM

You'll find only a few meal options in the Animal Kingdom, and most of those are of the grab-and-go variety (of these, the **Flame Tree BBQ** ★★ combo meal for

$12–$18 is the best). These are our favorite spots where you can sit yourself down for a spell:

Satu'li Canteen ★★★ in Pandora is counter-service, not waiter-service, but has lots of indoor seating. Dishes are cooked with a kooky spin to make them appear alien: Sliced beef is served with yogurt boba balls, and the cheeseburgers are (deliciously) rethought as spongy steamed bao "pod" dumplings. The chili-garlic shrimp bowl isn't half bad. You'll want the Blueberry Cream Cheese Mousse for its Instagram factor alone. Combo meal $14 to $18.

At the thatched-roof **Tusker House** ★★, in the Africa section, under multi-colored banners in an ancient souklike environment, Donald, Daisy, Mickey, and Goofy greet families in safari garb for **Donald's Safari Breakfast** and **Donald's Dining Safari** for lunch and dinner all-you-can eat buffets. The buffet dares more than most of Disney's do, featuring spit-roasted chicken, curries, peri-peri roasted salmon on banana leaf, and other pleasingly aromatic choices. It also has good vegetarian options. It's near **Dawa Bar,** a relaxing spot mimicking a fortress on the water serving cocktails ($8–$16); though the bar only has 10 seats, more are under a bamboo shelter (it usually closes well before the park does). Breakfast and lunch $47 adults, $30 kids 3–9.

Yak & Yeti ★★, themed like a Nepalese mansion stocked with souvenirs from across Southeast Asia, has a menu just as geographically varied, serving Kobe beef burgers, lo mein, ahi tuna, fried honey chicken, and even roasted half duckling. The quick-service counter outside offers a shorter but similar menu for less, but at Animal Kingdom, sitting indoors in air-conditioning is the most delicious treat. It also has an outdoor counter-service window, **Yak & Yeti Local Food Cafes** ★★ (combo meal $12–$16). Main courses $23 to $38.

The most upscale place to eat in Animal Kingdom is **Tiffins Restaurant** ★★★. Its gently international menu is along the lines of shrimp and grits, surf-and-turf (tenderloin with scallops), and tamarind-braised short ribs, plus a flavorsome bread sampler. The casual **Nomad Lounge** (small plates $10–$17), attached, is an air-conditioned space on a delightful terrace over the water for small plates (poke, poutine, *saté*), cocktails, and bespoke beer including the Kungaloosh Spiced Excursion Ale, made just for here by Miami's Concrete Beach Brewery. Tiffins entrees $30 to $68.

In the Walt Disney World Hotels

These Disney hotel restaurants cost more than what you'd pay for a similar meal elsewhere, but the food generally is a few notches higher than what you find inside the theme parks. Reservations are a must. Most of them aren't open for lunch.

EXPENSIVE

Boma—Flavors of Africa ★★ AFRICAN   Make a reservation here and you get a bonus: a fine excuse to visit Disney's Animal Kingdom Lodge and pay a visit to the animals in its backyard paddocks, floodlit after dark—think of the high price as an admission fee for that. Dinner is a good time, too: a 60-item buffet menu, served in a dramatically vaulted dining room of thatching and bamboo. The food is not all African: It runs the gamut from roast chicken and beef to a very few African-themed delights such as watermelon rind salad and *bobotie* (a moussaka-like pie of ground beef from South Africa).

Disney's Animal Kingdom Lodge, 2901 Osceola Pkwy., Bay Lake. disneyworld.com. **407/939-3463.** Adults $37–$56, kids $22–$33. Daily 7:30–11:30am and 5–9:30pm.

California Grill ★★★ AMERICAN   For a blowout night with a view, the best choice is this beloved space on the 15th floor of the Contemporary Resort. The wine list is elaborate and excellent, and the menu is bright and seasonal but hearty—black truffle pizza, fire-roasted venison, black sea bass, saffron risotto—and sushi rolls are a popular sideline. Book as soon as you can—the maximum is 60 days before—and get a window seat for the **fireworks.** If you have a reservation that doesn't coincide with the show, you can still come that night to watch. The music for the show is even piped into the outdoor viewing platforms, which are practically on top of Tomorrowland. A dinner here is a fantastic excuse to stroll through the atrium of this iconic hotel. The self-explanatory **Steakhouse 71** (main dishes $24–$39) is also good, but it's off the lobby and has no view.

Disney's Contemporary Resort, 4600 N. World Dr., Lake Buena Vista. disneyworld.com. **407/939-3463.** 3-course meal: Adults $89, kids 3–9 $39. Daily 5–10pm.

Todd English's bluezoo ★ SEAFOOD   Although it's not the showplace it once was, bluezoo has kept its standards higher than most other resort restaurants, particularly at the Dolphin, and its flavors remain memorably rich. The menu is mainly seafood (choose your fish and then choose a sauce or sub in a lobster claw), but adds a few detours to beef, flatbreads, and pasta to make it kid-friendly. Eaten among Jeffrey Beers' decor of colored-glass baubles that suggest being underwater, the menu changes regularly to reflect seasons and what's freshest that day. Also consider upscale Mexican spot **Rosa Mexicano** in the same hotel.

Walt Disney World Dolphin Hotel, 1500 EPCOT Resorts Blvd., Lake Buena Vista. swandolphin.com/dining/todd-englishs-bluezoo. **407/934-1111.** Main courses $30–$57. Daily 5–11pm. Reserve on OpenTable.com.

Victoria & Albert's ★★★ FRENCH   Walt Disney World's most celebrated restaurant is the ultimate destination for anniversaries, proposals, and gourmands—and it's considered one of the finest places to eat in the state. The adults-only, 65-seater lays on its indulgent, prix-fixe multi-course menu (think amuse-bouches, Imperial caviar, Kobe-style beef with bone marrow pain perdu, New Zealand elk tenderloin, 500+ wines), revealed to you from under cloches like a parade of debutantes. It's like the Very Fancy Restaurant where a character might take a date on a sitcom, harpist and all, which adds to the theater. The resort's most exclusive reservation: the eight-person **Queen Victoria's Room,** where a private 10-course meal is served behind closed doors for $375 per person before wine. Not exquisite enough for you? The **Chef's Table** (4–6 people) is $425. Every seat in this place sells out, and fast, when reservations open 60 days ahead.

Disney's Grand Floridian Resort & Spa, 4401 Floridian Way, Lake Buena Vista. victoria-alberts.com. **407/939-3862,** answered Tues–Sat 10am–4pm. 10-course prix-fixe from $295, Chef's Table prix-fixe (bookable only by phone) from $425, wine pairings from $155 (non-alcoholic pairings $115). $100 cancellation fee within 5 days of reservation, 100% penalty for cancellation within 24 hr. 1 nightly seating 5:30–8:05pm. Dress code: semi-formal or formal; jacket required for men (loaners available), no children 9 and under permitted.

Disney Springs

Parking at Disney Springs is free in one of three covered structures. You'll find a lot more food options than these—such as **STK Steakhouse, Terralina Crafted Italian,** a **Rainforest Grill,** and the last surviving **Planet Hollywood** locations. These are our favorites, though, and unlike the best restaurants in Disney hotels, these are also open for lunch.

EXPENSIVE

The Boathouse ★★★ AMERICAN This convivial loftlike waterfront complex with three bars is elbow-to-elbow with people making a boozy evening out of its cocktails, craft beers, steaks, seafood, chops, and raw bar. Towering slices of baked Alaska are more daunting than the peak of Mt. Denali, and on weekends, there are musical brunches. The nautical theme (there are rare boats affixed overhead) isn't superficial.

The Landing, Disney Springs. theboathouseorlando.com. ✆ **407/939-2628.** Main courses $19–$65. Mon–Thurs 11am–11pm; Fri 11am–11:30pm; Sat 10am–11:30pm; Sun 10am–11pm. Reservations recommended. Reserve on OpenTable.com. Lime parking garage.

Chef Art Smith's Homecomin' ★★★ AMERICAN This is a hot property, so book ahead. Oprah's onetime personal chef, Art Smith, oversees a casual choice for tip-top Southern American comfort food: fried chicken in several forms, "Church Lady" deviled eggs, plus slaw, pimento cheese, and biscuits galore. Just to prove their barbecue is cooked perfectly, they won't give you a steak knife. The bar specializes in infused moonshine cocktails that will kick your butt all the way to Georgia, and a pineapple-banana Hummingbird Cake that will fly you back. On weekends, it does brunch (short rib hash, hush puppy Benedict, and so on).

Town Center, Disney Springs. homecominkitchen.com. ✆ **407/560-0100**, reservations 407/939-5277. Main courses $16–$30. Mon–Thurs 11am–11pm; Fri 11am–11:30pm; Sat 9am–11:30pm; Sun 9am–11pm. Reservations recommended. Lime parking garage.

Jaleo by José Andrés ★★★ SPANISH TAPAS Go to the massive multi-level Jaleo for a presentational evening of truly sensational Spanish tapas as interpreted though the futuristic cooking techniques of celeb chef José Andrés, a real-life hero who uses his fortune and expertise to feed victims of major international emergencies. Do not miss the *ibérico* ham that has been imported from Spain by a special arrangement and is sliced tissue-thin at your table, or the *aceitunas modernas y clásicas,* the miraculous "liquid olives" achieved through molecular gastronomy techniques. By far the most interesting and economical way to go is the 15-course ¡Eat LikeJosé! tasting menu ($150), which loads you up with a range of high-end delights you wouldn't have discovered otherwise. Here, it costs far more to buy dishes individually than to order a set menu.

Disney Springs West Side. jaleo.com. ✆ **321/348-3211.** Items $8–$42, tasting menu $100–$150. Sun–Thurs 11:30am–11pm; Fri–Sat 11:30am–11:30pm. Reservations recommended. Reserve via jaleo.com. Orange parking garage.

Morimoto Asia ★★★ ASIAN Iron Chef Masaharu Morimoto, known for innovative feats of kitchen derring-do, oversees this sweeping loftlike space (one of the grandest on Disney property). You can order approachable dishes like dim sum, bao, and sushi, but dare to delve into specialties like whole house-roasted Peking duck, the "buri-bop" twist on hot-pot *bibimbap* with seared yellowtail, the unbelievably flavorful sweet-and-sour deboned sea bass (don't neglect the flaky cheeks), and rock shrimp tempura coated in a spicy Korean *gochujang* aioli. There's also a sushi bar, open for dinner. Outside, its Street Food window (noon–8pm; $10–14) is where you'll find the mass-appeal grub, like ramen and egg rolls, they won't serve inside.

Town Center, Disney Springs. morimotoasia.com. ✆ **407/939-6686.** Main courses $19–$72, sushi set menus $60–$130 per person. Sun–Thurs 11:30am–11pm; Fri–Sat 11:30am–11:30pm; daily break 3:30–4:30pm. Reservations recommended. Reserve on OpenTable.com. Lime parking garage.

Raglan Road Irish Pub and Entertainment ★★ IRISH
Irish staples are turned into sprightly new visions, including glazed loin of bacon with cabbage, beef stew infused with Guinness, and good old fish and chips. Although the massive dining area is styled after an Irish pub, it's 20 times noisier. There's free live music most evenings. If you only want fish and chips, get it (plus beer) for less (about $16) on the south side of the building at the counter-service hole-in-the-wall **Cookes of Dublin** ★, run by the same people.

Town Center, Disney Springs. raglanroad.com. ☎ **407/938-0300.** Main courses $23–$38. Mon–Sat 11am–11:30pm; Sun 10am–11:30pm; Cookes of Dublin until 11pm. Reserve on OpenTable.com. Lime parking garage.

MODERATE

T-REX ★ AMERICAN If *The Simpsons* were to spoof Orlando theme dining, this would be its family-fun creation: life-size robotic dinosaurs braying above your table. Every so often, the ceiling (at least, the one outside the simulated ice cave) lights up with a projected meteor shower and, for your amusement, the destruction of all prehistoric life forms is delightfully simulated for hordes of families as they chow down. You can predict the fare: Bronto Burgers (*not made from actual brontos), Tar Pit fried shrimp, and to end it all, the Chocolate Extinction, a fudge cake sundae for four people.

Town Center, Disney Springs. trexcafe.com. ☎ **407/828-8739.** Main courses $20–$44. Sun–Thurs 11am–11pm; Fri–Sat 11am–11:30pm. Lime parking garage.

Wine Bar George ★★ WINE BAR
A welcome escape to adulthood within stroller-clogged Disneydom, WBG is run by a master sommelier who makes more than 100 choices available by the ounce, glass, or bottle. The acclaimed wine selection is obviously the point; liquor and beer selections are only standard. Prices are high across the (cheese) board; charcuterie-and-cheese boards clock in between $27 and $62. You can also order small plates (burrata, meatballs) or family-style plates that will satisfy most average people as a light meal, but this is generally a restaurant for enjoying fine flavors, not for stuffing yourself. Don't sit downstairs. Go upstairs, away from the din, where there's more space, more comfortable seating, and another bar. This concept and menu are more sophisticated than most places around here, which for foodie visitors will make for a refreshing change.

The Landing, Disney Springs, 1610 E. Buena Vista Dr., Lake Buena Vista. winebargeorge.com. ☎ **407/490-1800.** Small plates $9–$18. Mon–Thurs noon–11pm; Fri noon–11:30pm; Sat 10:30am–11:30pm; Sun 10:30am–11pm; brunch Sat–Sun 10:30am–2pm. Reserve on OpenTable.com. Lime parking garage.

INEXPENSIVE

Polite Pig ★★★ BARBECUE The Polite Pig is the inexpensive eatery we recommend above the others at Disney Springs. If you can't get up to Winter Park to eat at the long-running and influential gastropub the Ravenous Pig, the people behind it opened this smashing counter-service 'cue joint here. Along with pints of craft beer, find excellent gustatory ideas (brisket BBQ meatballs, smoked chicken salad, burnt ends chili) plus plates of meat from the smoker and fun twists on side dishes such as crispy whiskey-caramel Brussels sprouts and smoked corn with chipotle aioli.

Disney Springs Marketplace. politepig.com. ☎ **407/938-7444.** Sandwiches $13–$15, smoker meat plates $15–$26. Mon–Thurs 11am–11pm; Fri–Sat 11am–11:30pm; Sun 11am–11pm. No reservations accepted, but advance orders accepted online. Lime parking garage.

Universal Orlando

Universal's hotels have a few upscale restaurants (**Bice Ristorante** at Portofino Bay, **The Palm** steakhouse at the Hard Rock), but the **CityWalk** (universal orlando.com; free parking after 6pm) zone, located between the resort's parking garages and the entrances to the parks, attracts more diners who have no intention of proceeding to any rides. Among the established restaurant brands here you surely already know about: **Hard Rock Cafe Orlando, Pat O'Brien's** (New Orleans jazz), and **Jimmy Buffett's Margaritaville.**

EXPENSIVE

Bigfire ★★ AMERICAN   At first glance, Bigfire looks like standard grilled-meat stuff—a huge open-grill kitchen dominates the space—but on closer inspection, you're pleased to note that it imbues its all-American menu with an urban panache not usually seen in Themeparkland. Even so, its ingredients don't stray too far from the usual crowd-pleasers: its mac and cheese has accents of smoked pork, the Cobb salad is laden with meats and honey mustard dressing, smoked brook trout is spiked with tarragon tartar sauce, and the short rib pasta is flavored with sherry cream sauce. It's classic American comfort food, but smarter.

CityWalk. universalorlando.com. ✆ **407/224-3663.** Main courses $19–$60. Mon–Thurs 4–11pm; Fri–Sat 4pm–midnight; Sun 4–11pm. Reservations recommended.

MODERATE

The Cowfish ★★★ BURGERS/SUSHI   You'll find burgers. You'll find sushi. And you'll find sushi made with burger components (called Burgushi—it's a good time on rice). This offbeat concept is rendered with a cocktail bar and some interactive screens to pass the time. If there's a wait, head to the second floor for about 30 first-come, first-served bar seats; eight more are on the third floor. It's a refreshing idea, so it gets busy.

CityWalk. thecowfish.com. ✆ **407/224-3663.** Rolls $13–$22, main courses $18–$37. Mon–Thurs 4–11pm; Fri–Sat 4pm–midnight; Sun 4–11pm. Reservations recommended.

Toothsome Chocolate Emporium & Savory Feast Kitchen ★★

AMERICAN   The wild-looking, steampunk-style faux chocolate factory and restaurant is the current star at CityWalk, promising the Orlando usual (so-so steak, pasta, burgers, salads, flatbreads, plus all-day brunch, all average), but done as over-the-top, towering, and teetering constructions, and with themed characters walking around and interacting with diners. What it really does best is its major desserts—there's a separate line for a counter cranking out whimsical and expensive milkshakes ($15–$17) mixed in Mason jars.

CityWalk. universalorlando.com. ✆ **407/224-3663.** Main courses $17–$37. Daily 11am–11pm. Reservations recommended.

Outside the Resorts

Orlando's booming visitor culture attracts internationally trained chefs as well as first-generation immigrants from a variety of nations including Vietnam, Venezuela, and Cuba. Their contributions to the community support sensational places to eat that theme park-goers sadly miss.

Also, just north of Orlando's downtown around Colonial and Mills avenues, a thriving district for Vietnamese dining (variously called Little Vietnam, ViMi, and **Mills 50**) flourishes with multiple options for affordable meals true to Vietnam's reputation for nuanced flavors.

Please note that Tampa's wonderfully authentic Cuban eatery **Columbia Restaurant** ★★★ (see p. 316 for our full review) has an offshoot here about 10 minutes from Disney World at 649 Front St., Celebration.

EXPENSIVE

Knife & Spoon ★★★ AMERICAN The fine-dining anchor at the Ritz-Carlton Grande Lakes serves primarily house-aged steak and seafood, but it's far more than meets the eye, and it's laden with culinary awards for it. Dishes and cocktails that might appear standard when printed on the menu are in fact rendered unforgettably delectable by hidden scientific technique. So when something described as "Whole Fish" hits your tongue, you taste a buttery, perfectly soft masterpiece of *sous vide* preparation that only an expert team could manage. The selection changes based on local seasonality (inventions such as kimchi creamed spinach tend to remain on it), but behind the scenes, chefs are mastering flourishes of molecular gastronomy, bespoke fermentation projects, and advanced approaches.

4012 Central Florida Pkwy., Orlando. knifeandspoonrc.com. **407/206-2400.** Reservations recommended. Main courses $29–$78. Dress code: resort casual. Daily 5:30–11pm.

Norman's ★★★ AMERICAN Chef and cookbook author Norman Van Aken has won every conceivable award for his work, and to some Floridians, he is an icon of local cuisine. His eponymous restaurant is an Orlando institution. Among his beloved signature dishes: The shrimp and mussel chowder unveils a new profile of saffron and coconut with every sip (you'll wish you could have a gallon); the yellowtail sings with its citrusy glaze over garlic mash; the crab meat beignets are somehow fluffy and airy without losing meaty flavor. The Art Deco–inflected space is elegant and perhaps a little heady in a way luxury restaurants used to be—how lovely to be able to hear your dining companion moan softly in gustatory delight—as is the refined wine list and professional staff, many of whom have been associated with Norman for years. After all this time, coming to Norman's still feels like a special occasion.

7924 Via Dellagio Way, Orlando. normans.com. **321/754-1025.** Reservations recommended. Main courses $34–$52. Dress code: business casual. Tues–Sat 6–10pm.

MODERATE

El Tenampa ★★★ MEXICAN On a bleary stretch of U.S. 192 that'll have you wondering if you missed it, you discover a family-friendly hideaway of slotted-pot lanterns, hand-carved thrones, and an outdoor patio for fine-weather meals. Because Hispanic families show up in droves, you also know the food is authentic and good. The fresh *aguas frescas* (rejuvenating fruit-infused water drinks, flavors ranging from tamarind to lime) flow freely, and portions are big and reliable. Start with free salsa and delicate corn chips that are still shiny and hot from the fryer, but don't fill up, because main courses are huge and cheap. This is *not* the identically named location on Orange Blossom Trail.

4563 W. Irlo Bronson Memorial Hwy./U.S. 192, Kissimmee. eltenampakissimmee.com. **407/397-1981.** Main courses $13–$20. Sun–Thurs 9am–9pm; Fri–Sat 10am–10pm.

Maxine's on Shine ★★ INTERNATIONAL Hidden in a residential neighborhood (blink and you've passed it), Maxine's is a labor of love by its owners, Maxine and Kirt Earhart, who frequently emerge from the kitchen to party with guests and regularly win awards for what they've built. There's a good wine list plus a tiny stage hosting a roster of entertainment ('70s karaoke one night, classical piano the next). Two signature dishes stand out: fried green tomatoes with crab cakes and, as a main dish, pan-seared diced chicken with shallots, mushrooms, a Marsala wine cream sauce, and penne pasta (wow). On weekends, the restaurant brings in chill live music, which is popular with locals, so reservations are recommended then, particularly for its "Rejuicination Brunch" (Fri–Sun 10am–3pm).

337 N. Shine Ave., Orlando. maxinesonshine.com. ✆ **407/743-4227.** Main courses $19–$36. Wed–Sat 5–9pm; brunch Fri–Sun 10am–3pm. No kids 7 and under after 7pm Fri–Sat. Reservations recommended.

Q'Kenan ★★ VENEZUELAN   The strip mall location about 10 minutes east of Disney may not contain even a dozen tables—but the food is made with unbounded generosity, there is a full bar, and (sometimes) live music. A row of stews and meats lines the bar, from which meals are piled so high on plates. Suggestions: empanadas, overstuffed *arepa* (griddled corn flatbread), and *cachapas* (corn pancakes) filled with creamy aged cheese and sauces of every kind, or mixed plates like the *parrilla tepui,* with several kinds of meats, salad, yucca, and an *arepa,* and fresh juices. The timid eaters in your party can choose from burgers and chicken.

8117 Vineland Ave., Orlando. qkenan.com. ✆ **407/238-0014.** Main courses $13–$27. Tues–Sun 10am–9pm.

INEXPENSIVE

Bubbalou's Bodacious Bar-B-Que ★★ BARBECUE   Real barbecue done the way it oughta be, from cornbread to fall-off-the-bone ribs that'll stain shirts. There's no pretense at this tidied-up dive: Order at the counter and eat at picnic-style tables stocked with paper towel rolls and squirt bottles of sauce going from "sweet" to "killer." Get the standards: Texas brisket, pulled pork, half chicken, fried catfish, Brunswick stew, even gizzards. Sandwiches come with two sides, or order them by the pint, quart, or gallon. You can always pick up a gallon of Brunswick stew and bring it back to the gang.

5818 Conroy Rd., Orlando. kirkman.bubbalous.com. ✆ **407/295-1212.** Main courses $16–$21. Daily 10am–9pm.

Ethos Vegan Kitchen ★★★ VEGAN   As one of the only fully vegan restaurants in Central Florida (and one of the best anywhere), Ethos has garnered a loyal following since 2007. That's because when vegan cuisine is all that you do (even the cheese qualifies), you have to be skilled. Among the favorites are the coconut curry wrap, the lasagna, Cajun tempeh, and 10-inch pizzas. Kelly and Laina Shockley, who raised their kids through this place, are assiduous about ingredient sourcing and proudly pay their servers a living wage. Specials change according to seasonal crops, and there's always a soup of the day. About a third of the menu is gluten-free.

601-B New York Ave., Winter Park. ethosvegankitchen.com. ✆ **407/228-3898** or 407/228-3898. Main courses $13–$19. Mon–Fri 11am–11pm; Sat–Sun noon–11pm. Brunch Sat–Sun 9am-3pm.

Only in Orlando: Dining with Characters

A character meal is a rite of passage. Usually all-you-can-eat and mostly buffet, it guarantees face-to-fur time with beloved costumed characters who circulate as you dine. Always, *always book ahead*—bookings open 60 days out at 6am Orlando time (disneyworld.com/dining; ✆ **407/939-1947**). Each event hosts different characters, so if your heart is set on a particular one, ask if they're appearing. If you can't find a slot, check in the days before, when people whose plans have changed cancel before the no-show penalty. Expect prices in the $30s for kids 3–9 and in the $50s for adults.

At Disney (disneyworld.com/dining; *©* **407/939-1947**), character meals are usually offered for either breakfast or dinner at **Cape May Café** (in Disney's Beach Club Resort), **Chef Mickey's** (at Disney's Contemporary Resort), **Artist Point** (at Disney's Wilderness Lodge), **1900 Park Fare** (at Disney's Grand Floridian Resort & Spa), **'Ohana** (at Disney's Polynesian Village Resort), and **Ravello** (at Four Seasons Resort Orlando at Walt Disney World), plus a few others that come and go. The most popular meals are inside the parks, where an entry ticket is also required: **Cinderella's Royal Table** (in Cinderella Castle, Magic Kingdom), **Crystal Palace Buffet** (at the Crystal Palace, Magic Kingdom), **Donald's Safari Breakfast at the Tusker House** (in Africa, Animal Kingdom), **Garden Grill** (in The Land pavilion, EPCOT), **Akershus Royal Banquet Hall** (in EPCOT's Norway pavilion), and **Hollywood & Vine** (at Disney's Hollywood Studios).

Universal offers some seasonal options for its characters (not Harry Potter, who never appears), but they're ever-changing, so ask ahead: universalorlando.com; *©* **407/224-3663.**

NORTHEAST FLORIDA

by Lesley Abravanel

11

11

NORTHEAST FLORIDA

When driving through the elongated state of Florida, many people make the grave mistake of speeding through the Northeast without as much as a single stop beyond the Cracker Barrels, Waffle Houses, Buc-ee's, and gas stations lining the highways. Thankfully, Juan Ponce de León made the *fortunate* mistake of discovering just how magnificent the northeast part of the state is. You would do well to follow in his footsteps.

Northeast Florida traces its Western roots back to 1513, when the wandering de León, who later undertook a misguided quest for the Fountain of Youth, landed somewhere between present-day Jacksonville and Cape Canaveral. (He was a bit off course—he meant to land in what is now Bimini—but who can blame a guy who didn't have GPS?) Observing the land's lush foliage, he named it *La Florida,* or "the flowery land."

In 1565, the Spanish established a colony at St. Augustine, the country's oldest continuously inhabited European settlement. Not much, if anything at all, has changed in St. Augustine (in a wonderful way). The streets of the restored Old City look much as they did in Spanish times.

Not everything in Northeast Florida is antiquated, however. To the south, there's the "Space Coast," where rockets blast off from Cape Canaveral. In Cocoa Beach, you can watch surfers riding the rather sizable waves. In Daytona, brace yourself for the deafening roar of the stock cars and motorbikes that make this beach town the "World Center of Racing."

Going north along the coast, you'll come to a place that's a far cry from being populated with spring breakers on a budget: the moneyed haven of Ponte Vedra Beach, where golf takes precedence over manual labor. In Jacksonville, Florida's largest metropolis and a thriving port city and naval base, you can get a taste of city life before retreating to the beach.

Up near the state line, cross a bridge to Amelia Island, where you'll discover exclusive resorts that take advantage of 13 miles of beautiful beaches. Amelia's Victorian-era town, Fernandina Beach, is another throwback to the past, helping to further render the northeast region a fascinating juxtaposition of the old, the new, and somewhere in between.

THE SPACE COAST

46 miles SE of Orlando; 186 miles N of Miami; 65 miles S of Daytona

The "Space Coast," the area around Cape Canaveral, was once a sleepy place where city dwellers escaped the urban centers of Miami and Jacksonville. But then came NASA. Today the region produces and accommodates its own crowds, including the hordes who come to visit the Kennedy Space Center and enjoy the

---

PREVIOUS PAGE: Statue from the Bridge of Lions in St. Augustine.

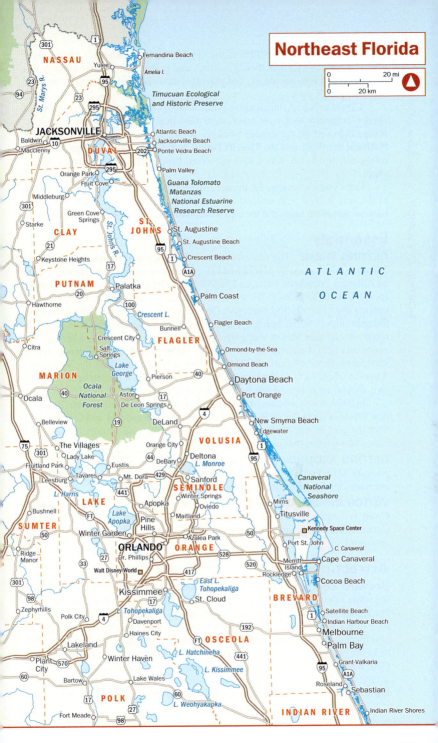

area's 72 miles of beaches (this is the closest beach to Orlando's mega-attractions), as well as excellent fishing, surfing, and golfing. And thanks to antsy billionaires bored with private jets and playing with rocket fuel, the area has ramped up with SpaceX fans.

Thanks to NASA, this is also a prime destination for nature lovers. The space agency originally took over much more land than it needed to launch rockets. Rather than sell off the unused portions, it turned them over to the **Canaveral National Seashore** and the **Merritt Island National Wildlife Refuge** (fws.gov/refuge/merritt-island), which have preserved these areas in their pristine natural states.

Port Canaveral is now the busiest cruise port in all of Florida. The south side of the port is lined with seafood restaurants and marinas, which serve as home base for gambling ships and the area's deep-sea charter and group fishing boats.

Essentials

GETTING THERE The nearest airport is **Melbourne Orlando International Airport** (mlbair.com; © **321/723-6227**), 22 miles south of Cocoa Beach, served by Allegiant, American, Delta, and Sun Country. **Orlando International Airport** (p. 360), about 35 miles to the west, is a much larger hub with many more flight options and generally less expensive fares. It's an easy 45-minute drive from the Orlando airport to the beaches via the Bee Line Expressway (Fla. 528, a toll road)—it can take almost that long from the Melbourne Airport, where all the major car rental companies have desks. The **Melbourne Airport Express** (shuttle serviceinmelbournefl.com; © **321/724-1600**) will take you from the Melbourne Airport to most local destinations from $75. Uber and Lyft tend to be less expensive, though surge pricing means that's not always true.

In 2024, it was announced that a new **Brightline** (gobrightline.com) train station would open in Cocoa Beach, located near State Road 528 and U.S. Route 1 with the goal of improving connectivity for residents and visitors to the Space Coast. Completion was expected sometime in 2025.

GETTING AROUND A car is essential in this area. **321 Transit** (321transit.com; © **321/633-1878**) operates buses ($1.50 adults, 75¢ seniors and students), but routes tend to be circuitous and extremely time-consuming.

VISITOR INFORMATION For information on the area, contact **Visit Space Coast** (visitspacecoast.com; © **321/617-1011**). The visitor center is at 267 W. Cocoa Beach Causeway, Cocoa Beach. They also have a helpful app you can download.

Attractions

Brevard Zoo ★★ This midsize zoo houses more than 900 animals, including white rhinos, red kangaroos, cheetahs, alligators and crocodiles, siamang gibbons, giant anteaters, emu, impala, howler monkeys, bald eagles, red wolves, and river otters. It also has a number of ways to get active, from its Treetop Trek (an adventure course around the zoo in which visitors zipline or climb above animals) to kayak tours around an animal exhibit or through 22 acres of restored wetlands ($6). It's also possible to hand-feed gentle giraffes and lorikeets in a free-flight aviary; and kids can get friendly with the wildlife at the Paws On play area, featuring a 22,000-gallon aquarium, water play, and petting zoo. A private tour of the

A family does the Treetop Trek at the Brevard Zoo.

zoo is only $15 extra per person and very much worth it.

8225 N. Wickham Rd., Melbourne (just east of I-95 exit 73/Wickham Rd.). brevardzoo.org. **321/254-9453.** Admission $34.95 adults, $29.95 seniors, $23.95 children 3–11, free for children 2 and under. Prices cheaper on their website. Daily 9:30am–5pm (last admission 3:30pm).

Kennedy Space Center Visitor Complex ★★★

In the late 1960s, Central Florida was the most exciting place on Earth, thanks to the moon. Kennedy Space Center was established on Cape Canaveral in 1958; boosted by a star-studded lineup of heroic astronauts, its visitor center ruled the tourist circuit alongside Disney in the 1970s. Today, KSC is still worth the trip to see the launchpads where it happened, though it doesn't get quite the crowds it once did, and we wish it did a better job educationally (more on that below).

For optimal touring, start at opening time. There may be a **Chat with an Astronaut** going on (that's an hour-long presentation in which an actual astronaut talks about their experiences and answers questions; they're announced on kennedyspacecenter.com/events; 9:45am and 2pm except Sun; another $50 adult, $35 child). Or a free **Astronaut Autograph Signing,** and a free **Mission Status Briefing** (both are listed on the daily schedule), which fills visitors in on all the projects they're currently working on here. Otherwise, proceed instantly to the can't-miss **Bus Tour,** which leaves every 15 minutes from 9:30am until about 2:15pm, and takes most people around 3 hours. *Warning:* Catching the last buses of the day doesn't leave you enough time to browse, so go early and do the Visitor Complex, where you first parked, afterward.

Buses with live on-board narration zip you around NASA's tightly secured compound. Combined with the nature reserve around it, the area (which guides tell visitors is one-fifth the size of Rhode Island) is huge, but you'll be making one stop not too far away. You'll see the distant launch sites used by the shuttle and by the Apollo moon shots. You'll buzz past eagles' nests, alligator-rich canals, pads now leased by private contractors SpaceX and Boeing, and the confoundingly titanic **Vehicle Assembly Building,** or VAB, where the shuttle—which NASA folks call "the orbiter"—was readied. It's just one story tall, but it's a doozy: The Statue of Liberty could fit through those doors with 200 feet left over. The main bus stop, the **Apollo/Saturn V Center,** is themed "Race to the Moon" and begins with a mandatory 5-minute film and then a full-scale mock-up of the "firing room"

11

NORTHEAST FLORIDA | The Space Coast

431

in the throes of commanding Apollo 8's launch, in all its window-rattling, fire-lit drama—to skip that 30-minute show and get to the good stuff, pass through. The adjoining hangar contains a Saturn V rocket, which is larger than you can imagine (363 ft. long, or the equivalent of 30 stories)—our modern SLS rockets are even bigger. Don't overlook the chance to reach into a case to touch a small moon rock, which looks like polished metal. The compelling presentation in the **Lunar Theatre,** which recounts the big touchdown, includes a video appearance by the late, reclusive Neil Armstrong. There's a cafeteria here and a few places back at home base, but there is nowhere else to eat within a 15-minute drive. (You can bring your own food in small, soft-sided coolers.)

A spacesuit on display at the Kennedy Space Center.

After that, hasten back via the bus to the **Visitor Complex** for the grand finale: The $100-million home of the space shuttle **Atlantis.** The way in which it's revealed to you, which I won't spoil, is spine-tingling. Hanging 26 feet off the ground at an angle of 43.21 degrees (like the numbers in a launch countdown), it's still covered with space dust, and it now tips a wing at everyone who comes to learn about it on the many interactive displays that surround it. On that building's lower floor, don't miss the commemorative Forever Remembered. Alongside favorite mementos provided by 11 of the 14 families of their crews, you'll find respectful displays of

Kennedy Space Center Special Tours

Astronaut Training Experience—KSC dubs the program ATX, but you could call it Space Day Camp. Over 5 hours, you'll test simulators of planet rovers, spacewalks, or Mars explorations and try a mock-up of a launch. Nothing is as intense as what astronauts experience, but this session is still plenty rigorous for most terrestrials, and the facilitators can answer nearly any question you can launch at them. The most options are available on Saturday and Sunday only, but many weekdays, you can book one-off time slots on a single simulator (such as for microgravity training or walking on Mars) for $30. More info at kennedyspacecenter.com/landing-pages/atx or by calling © **866/737-5235.** Pricing is $175 age 10 and older, adult participant required for ages 10–17, includes admission to KSC, minimum age 10.

a section of the hull of the Challenger, lost in 1986, and a slab of cockpit windows of the Columbia (lost in 2003), still encrusted with grass and mud from where it fell to Earth. You can also try the **Shuttle Launch Experience,** in which 44-person motion-simulator pods mimic an 8-minute launch with surprising, bumpy, but not nauseating, sensations. The souvenir store across the plaza is out of this world.

Once you've completed the bus tour and Atlantis, it's up to you whether you want to plumb the other business at the Visitor's Complex (IMAX, a Peanuts-themed puppet show, a few other play-oriented diversions). Sad to say it, most young people simply aren't aware of the incredible things the space programs did and the sacrifices required to achieve them, and at KSC that baseline education about the historic timeline is lacking. Delaware North, a private vendor that normally operates food service at stadiums and airports, runs KSC (no tax dollars are used). That results in something far more like a tourist attraction than a museum, which is a disservice. Exhibitions are overproduced and mimic Hollywood tropes (way too much John Williams–style symphonic music is just one of the problems here).

At least take the time to check the 42-foot-high black granite slab of the **Astronaut Memorial,** and **Heroes & Legends,** which pays tribute to the 100-odd explorers in the **Astronaut Hall of Fame** and where you'll see the impossibly low-tech Mission Control for the Mercury missions (they used rotary telephones to put men in space!), plus a tiny Mercury capsule and some authentic era spacesuits. (Astoundingly, the actual Mercury command building was torn down in 2010.) **Gateway,** a 2022 addition, ostensibly about deep space, has four immersive films seen from gently moving chairs, but it's not particularly good and has a terrible, slow-moving line, so it can be skipped.

Despite KSC's increasing shortcomings, a visit still gives you a rare chance to see where miracles and tragedy unfolded, and you might glimpse today's geniuses working on tomorrow's explorations. Prepare by doing some advance reading before arriving and familiarize yourself with the various stages of NASA's progress from Mercury to Gemini to the space shuttle to today. Also download KSC's free app, which helps you weed out the nonsense with maps and a schedule of shows. You can also pay extra for **Fly with an Astronaut,** during which an astronaut actually conducts your tour of the complex where they once worked ($206 adults, $181 kids 3–9, including admission; 5 hr.).

Space Commerce Way. kennedyspacecenter.com. **855/433-4210.** Admission $75 adults, $70 seniors, $65 children 3–11, free for children 2 and under. Daily 9am. Closing times vary according to season.

The engines of the Saturn V space rocket.

WATCHING A launch AT KENNEDY SPACE CENTER

Although the space shuttle has flown into history, Cape Canaveral still launches unmanned rockets—SpaceX and NASA's Artemis program conduct spectacular liftoffs from pad 39A, where the Apollo missions launched. Because launches are often postponed, it would be dangerous to plan a trip here just to catch one, but then again, if there's one when you're in town, it would be a shame to miss it, even if it means waking up at 5am. Kennedy Space Center maintains an updated schedule online both on its Kennedy Space Center Official Guide smartphone app and at **kennedyspacecenter.com/events**, and sometimes it arranges VIP seating at a safe distance. The general public is not permitted to flood NASA turf during the actual events, but Titusville, a town at the eastern end of S.R. 50, is a good place to get a clear, free view, because you'll be across the wide Indian River from the pad. Night launches are the most spectacular.

Beaches & Wildlife Refuges

To the north of the Kennedy Space Center, **Canaveral National Seashore** ★★★ is a protected 13-mile stretch of barrier-island beach backed by cabbage palms, sea grapes, palmettos, marshes, and Mosquito Lagoon. It also happens to be the longest stretch of undeveloped coastline in Florida, which is a remarkable feat. This is a top area for watching herons, egrets, ibises, willets, sanderlings, turnstones, terns, and other birds. You might also glimpse dolphins and manatees in Mosquito Lagoon. Canoeists can paddle along a marked trail through the marshes of Shipyard Island, and backcountry camping is possible November through April (permits required; see below). It also happens to be the most popular spot for rocket launches.

The **Apollo Visitor Center** is at 7611 S. Atlantic Ave., New Smyrna Beach (www.nps.gov/cana; © **321/428-3384**), on Apollo Beach, at the north end of the island. The southern access gate to the island is 8 miles east of Titusville on Florida 402, just east of Florida 3. A paved road leads from the gate to undeveloped **Playalinda Beach** ★★★, one of Florida's most beautiful. Though illegal, nude sunbathing has long been a tradition here (at least for those willing to walk a few miles to the more deserted areas). The beach has toilets, but no running water or other amenities, so bring everything you'll need. There's also a turtle-watch program.

For those looking for a little more history, the **Eldora Statehouse** ★★ is a step back in time, a well-preserved example of earlier life along Mosquito Lagoon. It is in Canaveral National Seashore's Apollo district, and is open year-round. The seashore is open daily from 6am to 8pm during daylight saving time, daily from 6am to 6pm during standard time. Entry fees are $25 per car, $20 per motorcycle, and $15 per pedestrian for a 7-day visit. National Park Service passports are accepted. Backcountry camping permits cost $20 per night and must be obtained from the New Smyrna Beach visitor center (see above). They also rent canoes for $25.

Canaveral National Seashore's neighbor to the south and west is the 140,000-acre **Merritt Island National Wildlife Refuge ★★★**, home to hundreds of species of shorebirds, waterfowl, reptiles, alligators, and mammals, many of them endangered. It's also one of the most productive estuaries in the country. The refuge was established as an overlay of the National Aeronautics and Space Administration's John F. Kennedy Space Center. Pick up a map and other information at the visitor center, on Florida 402 about 4 miles east of Titusville (it's on the way to Playalinda Beach). The center has a quarter-mile boardwalk along the edge of the marsh. Displays show the animals you may spot from 6-mile Black Point Wildlife Drive or from one of the nature trails through the hammocks and marshes.

The visitor center is open Tuesday through Saturday from 8am to 4pm. A Refuge Pass is required to enter the Black Point Wildlife Drive and Bio Lab Road, and to launch a boat at Bair's Cove, Beacon 42, and Bio Lab boat ramps.

A variety of passes can be purchased in person at the visitor center. Daily passes are $10 and can be purchased at self-pay stations with exact change. They can also be purchased online at recreation.gov.

For more info and a schedule of programs and events, contact the refuge (fws.gov/refuge/merritt-island; ✆ **321/861-0667**).

Note: Parts of the national seashore near the Kennedy Space Center and all of the refuge close 4 days before a rocket launch and usually reopen the day after.

A roseate spoonbill at Merritt Island National Wildlife Refuge.

Another nice beach area is **Lori Wilson Park,** on Atlantic Avenue at Antigua Drive in Cocoa Beach (✆ **321/455-1380**), which preserves a stretch of sand backed by a forest of live oaks. The park is open daily from sunrise to sunset.

The beach at the **Westgate Cocoa Beach Pier ★★**, on Meade Avenue east of A1A (cocoabeachpier.com; ✆ **321/783-7549**), is a popular spot with surfers, who consider it the East Coast's surfing capital. The rustic pier was built in 1962 and has 842 feet of fishing, shopping, and dining overlooking a wide, sandy beach (see "Where to Dine," p. 438). Because this is not a public park, there are no restrooms other than the ones in restaurants on the pier.

Jetty Park ★★, 400 E. Jetty Rd., at the south entry to Port Canaveral (portcanaveral.com; ✆ **321/783-7111**), has lifeguards, a fishing pier with bait shop, a playground, a volleyball court, a horseshoe pit, picnic tables, a snack bar, a grocery store, restrooms, changing facilities, and the area's only campground. From here, you can watch the big cruise ships as they enter and leave the port's narrow passage. The park is open daily from 7:30am to dusk; the pier is open 24 hours for fishing. Admission is $15 per car for nonresidents of Brevard County. The 150 tent and RV campsites (some of them shady, most with hookups) cost $24 to $64 a night, depending on the location and time of year. There are also eight cabins, each with queen bed, twin bunk beds, half-bathroom, lighted porch, ceiling fan, mini-fridge, and charcoal grill. Rates are $140 a night. Properly immunized pets are allowed in some areas of the park.

Located right next to Jetty Park is **The Cove at Port Canaveral,** 520 Glen Cheek Dr., Cape Canaveral, where there are restaurants, shops, bars, and charter boats (p. 439).

Outdoor Activities

ECO-TOURS Wildside Tours ★★★ 499 Ramp Rd., Cocoa Beach (wildside-tours.com; © **321/799-5495**), offers a superb, 2-hour eco-tour through the Thousand Island nature preserve and the Banana Lagoon on a quiet motor catamaran where you'll see manatees, dolphins, birds, and more. They provide binoculars, soft drinks, and water. Tickets are $40 ages 13 to 59, $35 for seniors 60 and older, and $30 for kids 12 and under. **Space Coast Eco Tours** ★★ (spacecoastecotours.com; © **321/326-4326**) offer private guided and narrated tours of the Indian River lagoon, where you'll see manatees, ospreys, dolphins, and alligators. They also do sunset tours, and the very cool bioluminescence tours, all on a luxe pontoon complete with LED lighting, Bluetooth surround sound, and changing area. Prices range from $40 and up.

FISHING Head to Port Canaveral for catches such as snapper and grouper. **Jetty Park,** at the south entry to the port, has a fishing pier equipped with a bait shop (see "Beaches & Wildlife Refuges," above). The south bank of the port is lined with charter boats. Deep-sea fishing is available on *Canaveral Princess* (misscape.com; © **321/783-5274**), one of the party boats based here. All-day, 9-hour voyages departing daily at 8am cost $100 adults, $80 kids 15 and under; all trips include breakfast, lunch, soda, fishing gear and license, and parking.

Note: Visitors must possess a Florida-issued boating education certificate (see p. 29).

GOLF The municipal **Cocoa Beach Country Club** ★, 500 Tom Warringer Blvd. (cityofcocoabeach.com; © **321/868-3351**), has 27 holes of golf and 12 tennis courts—2 clay, 10 hard (8 lit)—set on acres of natural woodlands, rivers, and lakes. Greens fees (including cart) are $18 to $70 depending on the time and season.

On Merritt Island south of the Kennedy Space Center, **The Savannahs Golf Club** ★★, 3915 Savannahs Trail (savannahsgolf.com; © **321/848-0582**), has 18 holes over 6,450 yards bordered by hardwood forests, lakes, and savannas inhabited by a host of wildlife. You'll have to hit over a lake to reach the 7th hole. Fees with a cart are about $18 to $55 and free for juniors 15 and under with a paying adult.

The best nearby course is the Gary Player–designed **Baytree National Golf Club** ★★★, 8207 National Dr., a half-mile east of I-95 in Melbourne (baytreenational.com; © **321/259-9060**), where challenging marshy holes are flanked by towering palms. This par-72 course has 7,043 yards with a red-shale waste area. Fees are $35 to $69 depending on the time and season, including cart.

KAYAKING For those who want to see Merritt Island National Wildlife Refuge at night, **A Day Away Kayak Tours** ★★★ (adayawaykayaktours.com; ✆ 321/268-2655) offers guided bioluminescence trips—meaning besides the moon, the only light you'll see on this fabulous tour is that of tiny, illuminated creatures swirling beneath the surface of the water and providing a lanternlike pathway across the water—through the refuge, Thursday through Monday nights, June through September. There are two types of tours—one in a regular kayak and the other in a clear kayak, which is like a glass-bottom boat. Both last 90 minutes. Cost is $55 for the regular, $75 for the clear. Book early and don't forget the mosquito repellent!

SURFING Rip through some occasionally awesome waves (by Florida's standards, not California's or Hawaii's) at the **Cocoa Beach Pier** area or down south at **Sebastian Inlet.** Get outfitted at **Ron Jon Surf Shop,** 4151 N. Atlantic Ave. (ronjonsurfshop.com; ✆ 321/799-8888), and then learn how to hang five or ten with **Ron Jon Surf School** ★, 150 E. Columbia Lane (ronjonsurfschool.com; ✆ 321/868-1980). The school offers equipment and lessons for beginners and pros at area beaches. Be sure to bring along a towel, flip-flops, sunscreen, and a lot of nerve. Rates range from $65 to $90 per person for private lessons and $50 to $70 per person for group lessons.

Where to Stay

The hotels listed below are in Cocoa Beach, the closest resort area to the Kennedy Space Center, about a 30-minute drive to the north. (For pop-culture junkies, Cocoa Beach was where the TV show *I Dream of Jeannie* took place.) Available accommodations also include the usual chain motels and many rental condominiums and cottages. For the latter, lowest prices will likely be on Airbnb and Vrbo, but **King Rentals, Inc.** (kingrentals.com; ✆ 321/784-5046) is a top resource for those who want service and a local operation to call should anything go wrong. It has a large inventory and is highly reliable, having been in business since 1978.

Given the proximity to Orlando, the generally warm weather year-round, and the business travelers visiting the space complex, there is little, if any, seasonal fluctuation in room rates here. They are highest on weekends, holidays, and during special events, such as rocket launches.

Tent and RV camping are available at **Jetty Park,** in Port Canaveral (see "Beaches & Wildlife Refuges," above).

You'll pay a 5% hotel tax on top of the Florida 7% sales tax here.

> ### Price Categories
>
> We're listing double room rates only. Please assume that suites will be pricier. Also note that some hotels fall into one price range in high season and a different one in low, hence the hybrid categories below.
> **Inexpensive:** $199 and under
> **Moderate:** $200–$325
> **Expensive:** $326 and up

The Inn at Cocoa Beach ★★★

Despite having 50 units, this seaside inn has an intimate B&B ambience and is far and away the most romantic place in the area. In fact, it's known as "the quiet place," and is adults only. Owner Karen Simpler, a skilled interior decorator, has furnished each unit with an elegant mix of pine, tropical, and French-country pieces, including four-poster beds in some units. Rooms in the three- and four-story buildings are much more spacious and have better sea views from their balconies than the "standard" units in the original two-story motel wing (all but six units here have balconies or patios). Other units open onto a courtyard with a pool tucked behind the dunes. Guests are treated to a full breakfast, evening wine and cheese and delicious fresh baked cookies on weekends. There's hot and iced tea and coffee available all day in the lobby. There's also an honor bar with snacks, a fitness center, and resident parrots Tango and Tangee, who somehow remarkably manage to still maintain The Inn's reputation as "the quiet place."

4300 Ocean Beach Blvd., Cocoa Beach. theinnatcocoabeach.com. © **321/799-3460.** 50 units. $167–$219 double. Rates include breakfast and evening social hour. **Amenities:** Bar (guests only); outdoor pool; fitness center; sauna; free Wi-Fi.

Lost Inn Paradise ★★★   Though the guest bungalows here are tidy, spacious, and filled with everything a couple or family could need on vacation (full-size fridges, speedy Internet, coffee makers, sleepable mattresses, microwaves, dining tables), our favorite room is one shared by all the guests. It's a storeroom, filled with one- and two-person kayaks, beach chairs, beach toys, beach towels, and wagons to lug all that gear to the sands across the street—all available free to those who stay here. It shows a thoughtfulness that's quite rare, and that is also apparent in the genuine hospitality of owners Don and Joanne, who make every guest feel like a friend. The property also has a nice pool, a small dock with room for two boats (for those who arrive by water), a barbecue grill, and a number of ADA-compliant rooms. Did we mention that wild dolphins often are viewable from the property's deck? You won't want to leave.

2902 S. Atlantic Ave., Cocoa Beach. lostinnparadise.com. © **321/783-4765.** 12 units. $185–$225 double. **Amenities:** Pool; kayaks; barbecue grill; guest laundry machine; free Wi-Fi.

Where to Dine

As in many scenic places with restaurants, the beauty of the view is in inverse proportion to the quality of the food and service. So, if you decide to dine on the **Cocoa Beach Pier** (cocoabeachpier.com), at the beach end of Meade Avenue, you'll get a fine view but a mediocre meal at most of the eateries perched on the pier. The exception is **Pier 62 Oceanfront Restaurant and Bar** ★★ (cocoabeachpier.com/dining; © **321/783-7549**), which we think has fresher grub, and more professional service, than its competitors. At Jetty Park, there's the **Cove at Cape Canaveral,** another conglomeration of bars and restaurants with waterfront views. Our favorite here would be **Fishlips Waterfront Bar & Grill** ★★ (fishlipswaterfront.com; © **321/784-4533**).

> **Price Categories**
>
> Meal per person, not including drinks or tip:
> **Inexpensive:** $20 and under
> **Moderate:** $21–$40
> **Expensive:** $40 and above

Florida's Fresh Grill ★★ SEAFOOD/STEAK   Leave the beachwear and flip-flops for restaurants at the Cove and Pier and put on something decent—not fancy—for this strip mall spot. Owned by a husband-and-wife team with years of hospitality experience, Florida's Fresh Grill serves crowd-pleasing dishes like beer-battered tropical coconut shrimp and "sea to table" fish, locally caught, grilled, and topped with your choice of mango salsa, lemon butter, lemon caper butter, teriyaki glaze, or our fave, jalapeno bacon cream sauce. All are served with a choice of two sides. There are also steaks, burgers, pasta, salads, and what some say is the best Key lime pie in town. They also happen to have a lively locals' bar scene, especially during the daily happy hour from 4:30 to 6pm (serious food and drink specials).

2039 N. Atlantic Ave., Cocoa Beach. floridasfreshgrill.com. © **321/613-5649.** Main courses $23–$50. Daily 4:30–9:30pm.

Moon Hut ★ DINER   This circa-1958, 148-seat retro diner isn't lying when it says that it's "Where the astronauts eat." Decorated with memorabilia from all the space ages, TVs inside air NASA channels and launches. The diner food is, well, diner food that's branded after space travel, like the Meteor Smash Burger, and the Eggs-Traterrestrial Benedict. There's a full bar, as well as smoothies, juices, and milkshakes.

7802 N. Atlantic Ave., Cape Canaveral. moonhutrestaurant.com. © **321/613-3185.** Main courses $13–$28. Daily 6:30am–9pm.

The Space Coast After Dark

For a rundown of current performances and exhibits, contact the **Brevard Cultural Alliance's Arts Line** (artsbrevard.org; © 321/690-6817).

For live music, walk out on the **Cocoa Beach Pier** at the beach or **The Cove at Port Canaveral,** where many of the bars and restaurants there feature bands on weekends, including the always lively **Grills Seafood Deck & Tiki Bar** ★★, 500 Glen Cheek Dr. (grillsseafood.com; © 321/868-2226), which has some form of entertainment there daily, be it official or just people-watching.

The tap room at the **Carib Brewery** ★★, 200 Imperial Blvd. (caribbrewery usa.com; © 321/728-4114), is the place for suds; they have daily happy hours from 4 to 6pm and late-night happy hours from 9pm until closing. **Ellie Mae's Tiki Bar** ★★★, 116 Jackson Ave. (emtikibar.com; © 321/613-5870), is a Polynesian-themed, boozy backyard party. It kicks off Wednesdays through Sundays at 11am and continues into the night with lawn games and Adirondack chairs out back. Cocktails are half off on weekdays from 2 to 5pm, because day drinking on vacation is always a good idea. Head there Sundays for Biscuits and Bloody Marys from 11am to 1pm.

From Bloody Marys to Hail Marys, check out the Gothic-themed, stained-glassy **Preacher Bar** ★★★, 8699 Astronaut Blvd. (preacherbar.com; © **321/613-4629**), a *very* dimly lit place serving "soulful food and Abbey ales." It's open until 1am on the weekends and has fun happy hours.

DAYTONA BEACH

54 miles NE of Orlando; 251 miles N of Miami; 78 miles S of Jacksonville

Daytona Beach is a town with many personalities. It is at once the self-proclaimed "World's Most Famous Beach" and "World Center of Racing," a mecca for tattooed motorcyclists *and* the home of a surprisingly good art museum. Though the city and developers spent millions trying to redevelop the beachfront area, and famous Main Street Pier, there's still something bleak about Daytona's famous strip. Many of its '70s-style beachfront condos and hotels are badly in need of a facelift. Thank goodness for Ponce Inlet, a scenic fishing village that still charms visitors.

During Biketoberfest, Daytona is awash in motorcyclists.

Racing fans, however, don't care what the place looks like. Daytona Beach has been a destination for them since the early 1900s, when "horseless carriages" raced on the hard-packed sand beach. Recent debate over the environmental impact of unrestricted driving on the beach caused an uproar from citizens who couldn't imagine it any other way. As it worked out, they can still drive on the sand, but not everywhere, and especially not in sea turtle nesting areas.

Today, hundreds of thousands of race enthusiasts come to the home of the National Association for Stock Car Auto Racing (NASCAR) for the **Daytona 500, Coke Zero Sugar 400,** and other races throughout the year.

Be sure to check the "Calendar of Events" (p. 25) in chapter 2 to know when the town belongs to thousands of leather-clad motorcycle buffs during Bike Week (Mar) and Biketoberfest (Oct), or racing enthusiasts for big competitions. You won't be able to find a hotel room, drive the highways, or enjoy a peaceful vacation when they're in town.

Essentials

GETTING THERE **American** and **Delta** fly into the small, pleasant, and calm **Daytona Beach International Airport** (flydaytonafirst.com; © **386/248-8030**), 4 miles inland from the beach on International Speedway Boulevard (U.S. 92), but you can usually find less-expensive fares to **Orlando International Airport** (p. 360),

about an hour's drive away. **Groome Transportation** (groometransportation.com; ✆ **386/257-5411**) provides van transportation to and from Orlando International Airport. One-way fares are about $40 for adults, $21 for children ages 3 to 7. The service takes passengers to the company's terminal at 1034 N. Nova Rd., between 3rd and 4th streets, or to beach hotels for an additional fee.

The ride from the airport to most beach hotels via **Daytona Beach Taxi Cab** (daytonabeachtaxicab.com; ✆ **386/333-2222**) is between $16 and $20. Uber and Lyft should cost the same.

All the major car rental companies have booths at the airport. Or why not rent a Harley? This is Daytona, home of Biketoberfest, after all. Contact **Daytona Harley-Davidson at Destination Daytona,** 1637 N. U.S. Hwy. 1 (daytonaharleydavidson.com; ✆ **386/261-1330**). Rates start at around $169 a day.

Amtrak (amtrak.com; ✆ **800/872-7245**) trains stop at Deland, 15 miles southwest of Daytona Beach, with bus service from Deland to the Hilton Daytona Beach Oceanfront Resort.

GETTING AROUND Although Daytona is primarily a driver's town, Volusia County's public transit system, **VOTRAN** (votran.org; ✆ **386/761-7700**) runs reliable buses around town. Fares are $1.75 for adults, 85¢ for seniors and children ages 7 to 18, and free for kids ages 6 and under who are riding with an adult.

VISITOR INFORMATION The **Daytona Beach Area Convention & Visitors Bureau** (daytonabeach.com; ✆ **800/844-1234** or 386/255-0415) has an informative website, and people who actually answer phones if you call for info.

A Visit to the World Center of Racing

Daytona International Speedway/NASCAR Racing Experience ★★
You don't have to be a racing fan to enjoy a visit to the **Daytona International Speedway,** 4 miles west of the beach. Opened in 1959 with the first Daytona 500, this 480-acre complex is one of the key reasons for the city's fame. The track presents about nine weekends of major racing events annually, featuring stock cars, sports cars, motorcycles, and go-karts, and is used for automobile and motorbike testing and other events the rest of the year. Its grandstands can accommodate more than 146,000 fans.

The NASCAR Racing Experience lets speed chasers drive an actual NASCAR race car on the track, with no lead car to follow, no instructor riding with you. Yikes. Pass slower cars and speed to the finish line. The need for speed isn't cheap—a 5-minute ride costs $411 and it goes all the way up to a 48-minute ride, which will set you back $3,327. Scared of driving but want an experience? Riding shotgun with pro-racing instructors costs $194 for three laps around the track, and $387 for six. Buckle in and buckle down!

For those who would rather walk around the speedway, daily, 60-minute tours are given from 9:30am until 3pm for $26 for adults, $21 for kids 5 to 12 and include admission into the **Motorsports Hall of Fame of America** (mshf.com). A **VIP Tour** goes into the NASCAR Archives & Research Center and press box, the Axalta Injector, the speedway's infield, and the Motorsports Hall of Fame of America. Tickets are $56 for all ages. Both tours include a digital photo package.

1801 W. International Speedway Blvd. (U.S. 92, at Bill France Blvd.). daytonainternationalspeedway.com; nascarracingexperience.com. ✆ **800/748-7467** for race tickets, or 704/886-2400 for NASCAR Racing Experience. Tours daily 9:30am–3pm.

The Coke Zero 400 at the Daytona International Speedway.

Hitting the "World's Most Famous Beach"

The beautiful and hard-packed beach here runs for 24 miles along a skinny peninsula separated from the mainland by the Halifax River. The bustling hub of activity is at the end of Main Street, where you'll find the **Daytona Beach Boardwalk & Pier,** a 1,000-foot wooden pier that has been around since 1925, even after being pummeled by several hurricanes and tropical storms. In 2023, it got a $1.56-million makeover that will hopefully extend its life another hundred years. Beginning at the pier, the city's famous oceanside **Boardwalk** is lined with restaurants, bars, an old-school arcade, bait shop, and T-shirt shops, as are the 4 blocks of Main Street nearest the beach. The city's $400-million **Ocean Walk Shoppes** redevelopment project begins here and runs several blocks north, featuring a movie theater, boutiques, and restaurants.

Just north and across the street from the Boardwalk and Ocean Walk Shoppes, is the **Daytona Lagoon** waterpark, 601 Earl St. (daytonalagoon.com; ⓒ **386/254-5020**), with waterslides, go-karts, bumper carts, and all sorts of theme-parky activities. Admission ranges from $20 to $50. Just south of the Boardwalk on A1A, are some sky-high thrill rides at the aptly named **Screamer's Park,** where rides like the Slingshot (slingshotdaytonabeach.com), which propels you 365 feet into the air at 70 miles per hour, are open 7 days a week, 365 days a year. Have fun with that.

> **Driving on the Beach at Daytona**
>
> You can drive and park on sections of the sand along 18 miles of the beach from 1 hour after sunrise to 1 hour before sunset. During sea-turtle nesting season, May 1 to October 31, driving hours are from 8am to 7pm. Traffic lanes and speed limits are clearly marked at low tide, but watch for signs warning of nesting sea turtles. There's a $20-per-day, per-vehicle access fee and 10-mph speed limit. Windows must be down for safety. *Watch out for the tides.* If you park at low tide and lose track of time, your vehicle may become an artificial reef at high tide!

There's another busy beach area at the end of Seabreeze Boulevard, known as the **Seabreeze Historic District** or **Seabreeze Entertainment District,** which has a multitude of restaurants, bars, and shops.

Folks seeking privacy usually prefer the northern or southern extremities of the beach. **Ponce Inlet,** at the very southern tip of the peninsula, is especially peaceful, as there is little commerce or traffic to disturb the silence. **Lighthouse Point Park,** 500 S. Atlantic Ave., is the best beach, consisting of 52 acres of pristine beaches on the northern end of Ponce Inlet. It features fishing, nature trails, an observation deck and tower, swimming, and picnicking. Admission is $10 per vehicle.

Outdoor Activities

ECO-TOURS **Ponce Inlet Watersports,** 4958 S. Peninsula Dr. (ponceinletwatersports.com; © **386/405-3445**), provides a 90-minute water tour on a 32-passenger flat-bottom boat of the area's ecosystem on the Intracoastal Waterway between Daytona and New Smyrna Beach. The boat also anchors off islands along the water so you can get off, explore, go shelling or sunning. Rates start at $31.50 per person.

FISHING The best way to fish offshore for cobia, sea bass, sharks, king mackerel, grouper, red snapper, and more is with **Ponce Inlet Fishing Charters ★★★** (ponceinletcharters.com; © **386/290-9897**), led by expert angler Captain Billy Rotne, whose knowledge of Ponce Inlet, Mosquito Lagoon, and the surrounding areas, as well as history about NASA, flora, fauna, geology, and more is an added bonus to your angling. Rotne has three boats—Hell's Bay Glades Skiff, Hell's Bay Professional, and Yellowfin 24 Bay, considered the premiere bay boat—and they go out on six different trips with rates ranging from $750 for two anglers for a full 8 hours, to $650 for 4 hours.

Or save the cost of a boat by fishing with the locals on the **Sunglow Pier** at **Crabby Joe's Deck and Grill,** 3701 S. Atlantic Ave.

GOLF There are at least 20 courses within 30 minutes of the beach, and most hotels can arrange starting times for you.

Two of the nation's top-rated links are at the **LPGA International ★★★**, 1000 Championship Dr. (lpgainternational.com; © **386/274-5742**): the Champions course, designed by Rees Jones, and the Legends course, designed by Arthur Hills. Each boasts 18 outstanding holes. LPGA International is a center offering workshops and teaching programs for professional and amateur women golfers, and the pro shop carries a great selection of ladies' equipment and clothing. Greens

A golfer tries to sink a putt at the famed LPGA International.

fees with a cart are usually about $59 to $105, lower in summer. *Pssst:* They let guys play here, too!

The North Course at **The Club at Pelican Bay** ★★, 550 Sea Duck Dr. (clubpelicanbay.com/golf; ✆ **386/756-0040**), designed by Bill Amick, winds through waterways, loblolly pines, bayberry and white cedars, and features long, demanding holes. Fun fact: In 1984, Orville Moody made a famous chip-in in a sudden death playoff to beat the legendary Arnold Palmer. Fees are about $25 to $50.

The city's prime municipal course is the **Daytona Beach Golf Club** ★★, 600 Wilder Blvd. (daytonabeachgc.com; ✆ **386/671-3500**), which has 36 holes. Winter fees are about $20 to $35 to walk, $30 to $50 to share a cart. Rates drop in summer.

HORSEBACK RIDING **Shenandoah Stables,** 4510 Colony Rd, New Smyrna Beach (✆ **386/871-4334**) offers daily trail rides and lessons.

SPECTATOR SPORTS The **Daytona Tortugas** (milb.com/Daytona; ✆ **386/257-3172**), a Class A minor-league affiliate of the Cincinnati Reds, play April through August at **Jackie Robinson Ballpark,** on City Island downtown. A game here is a treat, as the park has been restored to its classic 1914 style by the designers of Baltimore's Camden Yards and Cleveland's Jacobs Field. Tickets are $11 to $21.

WATERSPORTS Watersports equipment, bicycles, beach buggies, and mopeds can be rented along the Boardwalk, at the ocean end of Main Street (see above), and in front of major beachfront hotels.

Museums & Attractions

Halifax Historical Museum ★
On Beach Street, Daytona's original riverfront commercial district on the mainland side of the Halifax River (see "Shopping," p. 448), this local museum is worth a look for the 1912 neoclassical architecture of its home, a former bank. A mural of Old Florida wildlife graces one wall, the stained-glass ceiling reflects sunlight, and across the room is an original teller's window. The eclectic collection includes tools and household items from the Spanish and British periods, thousands of historic photographs, possessions of past residents (even a ball gown worn at Lincoln's inauguration), and, of course, model cars. A race exhibit opens annually in mid-January as a stage setter for Race Week.

252 S. Beach St. (just north of Orange Ave.). halifaxhistorical.org. ⓒ **386/255-6976.** Admission $10 adults, free for children 12 and under. Tues–Sat 10am–4pm.

Lilian Place Heritage Center ★
This restored Victorian is the original home of one of the founding families of Daytona and the home where *Red Badge of Courage* author Stephen Crane recovered when his boat sank off the nearby coast in 1896. Locals say Crane makes all sorts of spirited visits to the home. Thirty-minute tours of Lilian Place are given Wednesday through Sunday from 1

Famous bottles at the Root Family Museum.

to 4pm. The museum's beekeeper (yes, there are hives here) does a talk on apiary maintenance every Sunday at 1pm.

111 Silver Beach, Daytona Beach (Beachside over the Orange Ave. bridge). lilianplacehc.org. ✆ **386/256-4810.** Admission $5. Wed–Sun 1–4pm.

Marine Science Center ★★ *Note: As we went to press, this facility was closed for renovations but expected to reopen in late 2025. Check before heading over.* This marine museum has interior displays (with exhibits on mangroves, mosquitoes, shells, artificial reefs, dune habitats, and pollution solutions), a 5,000-gallon aquarium, 1,400-gallon touch pool, and educational programs and activities. Though the exhibit area is small, there's more than enough information to keep a child engaged. Perhaps the most interesting part is the area reserved for the rehabilitation of endangered and threatened sea turtles and seabirds. You can watch them in any of eight turtle pools—look for the ones that need life jackets to stay afloat!

100 Lighthouse Dr., Ponce Inlet. marinesciencecenter.com. ✆ **386/304-5545.** Admission $8 ages 13–49; $7 ages 50 and up, $5 children 3–12. Tues–Sat 10am–4pm; Sun noon–4pm. See directions for Ponce de León Inlet Lighthouse & Museum (below).

Museum of Arts & Sciences ★★★ An exceptional institution for a town of Daytona's size, this humongous complex features several museums, including the **Cici and Hyatt Brown Museum of Art,** home to the largest collection of Florida art in the world; it has a rotating collection of 2,600 Florida-themed oil and watercolor paintings by such big names as Thomas Hart Benton, John James Audubon, and N.C. Wyeth. As important is the **Cuban Foundation Museum,** with paintings acquired in 1956, when Cuban dictator Fulgencio Batista donated his collection to the city. And for pop culture enthusiasts there's the **Root Family Museum** which has the collection of the late Chapman S. Root, founder of the Coca-Cola empire; among the memorabilia are the mold for the original Coke bottle and the Root family's two private railroad cars.

But wait, there's more! **The North Wing** features permanent collections of American, African, and Chinese art; international decorative arts; weaponry from around the planet; and (a favorite) the **Helene B. Roberson Visible Storage Building.** On the science side there's a planetarium which presents 30-minute shows of what the night sky will look like on the date of your visit. For the wee ones there's a hands-on **children's museum** explaining the natural world; and the skeleton of a 13-foot-tall and a 130,000-year-old giant ground sloth, among other wonders. MOAS just happens to be on a 90-acre **Tuscawilla Nature Preserve** that features over .5 mile of boardwalk nature trails and learning stations that was closed as of this writing for enhancements that would assure long-term sustainability. The museum also displays new temporary exhibits bimonthly. Whew!

352 S. Nova Rd. (btw. International Speedway Blvd. and Bellevue Ave.). moas.org. ✆ **386/255-0285.** Museum $19 adults, $17 seniors, $10 children 6-17, free for children 5 and under. Planetarium shows $7 adults, $5 children. Mon–Sat 10am–5pm; Sun 11am–5pm. Take International Speedway Blvd. west, make a left on Nova Rd. (Fla. 5A), and look for a sign on your right.

Ponce de León Inlet Lighthouse & Museum ★★ This 175-foot brick-and-granite structure is the second-tallest lighthouse in the United States. Built in the 1880s, the lighthouse and the graceful Victorian brick buildings surrounding it have been nicely restored. There are no guided tours, but you can walk through the 12 areas, which feature different exhibits (lighthouse lenses, historical artifacts, and a film of early car racing on the nearby beach), and stroll around the tugboat *F. D. Russell,* now sitting high and dry in the sand. There are 203 steps to the top of the lighthouse; it's a grinding ascent, but the view from up there is spectacular.

4931 S. Peninsula Dr., Ponce Inlet. ponceinlet.org. © **386/761-1821.** Admission $6.95 ages 12 and up, $1.95 children 3-11. Sept–May daily 10am–6pm; May–Sept 10am–9pm. Follow Atlantic Ave. south, turn right on Beach St., and follow the signs.

Shopping

On the mainland, Daytona Beach's main riverside drag, **Beach Street,** is one of the few areas in town where people actually stroll. The street is wide and inviting, with palms down its median, and decorative wrought-iron archways and fancy brickwork overlooking a branch of the Halifax River. Today the stretch of Beach Street between Bay Street and Orange Avenue offers antiques and collectibles shops, galleries, boutiques, an old-school record store, a magic shop, a historical museum (see "Museums & Attractions," above), and several good cafes. At 154 S. Beach St., you'll find the home of the **Angell & Phelps Chocolate Factory** ★★ (angellandphelps.com; © **386/252-6531**), which has been making candy since 1925—try the chocolate-covered bacon. Watch the goodies being made (and get a free sample)!

"Hog" riders will find several shops along Beach Street, north of International Speedway Boulevard and technically in Ormond Beach, including **Teddy Morse's Daytona Harley-Davidson,** 1637 N. U.S. Hwy 1 (daytonaharleydavidson.com; © **321/671-7100**), a 20,000-square-foot retail outlet and diner serving breakfast and lunch. It's one of the nation's largest Harley dealerships. In addition to hundreds of gleaming new and used Hogs, you'll find as much fringed leather as you've ever seen in one place. They also own **Destination Daytona,** 1635 N. U.S. Hwy. 1 (daytonaharleydavidson.com; © **866/642-3464**), a virtual Harley theme park with Hog-themed bars and restaurants.

Located directly across from the Daytona International Speedway, **ONE DAYTONA,** 1 Daytona Blvd. (onedaytona.com; © **386/227-0016**), is an outdoor complex featuring **Autograph Collection** (see below), restaurants, shops, bars, and a movie theater.

The **Daytona Flea and Farmers' Market** ★, 2987 Bellvue Ave. (daytonafleamarket.com; © **386/253-3330**), is huge, with 1,000 covered outdoor booths plus 100 antiques and collectibles vendors in an air-conditioned building. Most of the booths feature new (though not necessarily first-rate) wares along the lines of socks, sunglasses, luggage, handbags, jewelry, tools, and the like. It's open year-round Friday through Sunday from 9am to 5pm. Admission and parking are free.

Where to Stay

Room rates here are among the most affordable in Florida. Some lodgings have several rate periods during the year, but generally they are somewhat higher from the beginning of the races in February to Labor Day. Rates skyrocket during major events at the speedway, during bikers' gatherings, and during spring break (see the "Calendar of Events," beginning on p. 25). Even if you find a room, there's often a minimum-stay requirement.

Thousands of rental condominiums line the beach. You can either turn to Airbnb or Vrbo to book, or **Peck Realty** (peckrealty.com; © **800/447-3255** or 386/257-5000), which is a large, well-respected local agency.

In addition to the 6.5% state sales tax, Volusia County levies a 6% tax on hotel bills.

Bahama House ★★ An older, condo-style beach hotel, Bahama House is a family-owned, 10-story oceanfront stay on a quiet stretch of the Atlantic coastline. All rooms have been updated with new furniture, carpets, and very comfortable mattresses, and offer private balconies with ocean and Intracoastal Waterway views. In addition to complimentary deluxe continental breakfast served daily, there's also a nightly cocktail reception. A heated pool on a newly renovated pool deck and direct beach access make Bahama House an ideal place for families.

2001 S. Atlantic Ave., Daytona Beach Shores. daytonabahamahouse.com. © **800/571-2001.** 96 units. $149–$272 double. Rates include breakfast, evening cocktail reception and free parking. **Amenities:** Jacuzzi; heated pool; fitness center; free Wi-Fi.

The Daytona, Autograph Collection ★★★ Honk if you think this isn't your typical Marriott! Conveniently located across from the Speedway and in the ONE DAYTONA entertainment and dining complex, this higher-end-for-the-area hotel has historic cars in its lobby, a glamorous restaurant with a gleaming motorcycle as its centerpiece, and a very good gym. We really like its retro-fab bar which pays homage to hot rod culture. Rooms are a bit more standard, done up in soothing blues, with quality beds and balconies. A nice pool deck and terrace bar, plus location, make this the best stay in the area that's not on the beach.

1870 Victory Circle in ONE DAYTONA. marriott.com. © **386/323-9777.** 144 units. $195–$284 double. Valet parking $20. **Amenities:** 2 restaurants; 2 bars; heated pool; hot tub; fitness center; free Wi-Fi.

Hard Rock Hotel Daytona Beach ★★★ With front-row seats to the alleged "World's Most Famous Beach," Hard Rock brings some much-needed modernity to the salty strip. The 200 rooms have sweeping ocean views and pictures of everyone from Justin Bieber to James Brown. The oceanfront pool is a sauced-up party with lots of ol' time rock 'n' roll, hip-hop, pop, and EDM beats blaring, especially on Saturdays and Sundays from 11am to 3pm when a DJ spins the popular brunch. Speaking of soundtracks, because it is a Hard Rock, you can request a Fender guitar or a record player be brought to your room to play what you really want to hear. Hopefully you won't be playing that guitar at 3am, though don't be surprised if someone else is. This isn't the place for calm and quiet, obvs. A 24-hour fitness center is a popular spot, as is the spa. If you partied too much the night before, there's free yoga on weekend mornings. The Roxity Kids Club offers music-inspired diversions for those 5 to 15. Also outdoors is the Wave Terrace, featuring booze, fire pits, and a stage for live music. Kids receive free breakfast and free dinner in Sessions with paying adult.

918 N. Atlantic Ave., Daytona Beach Shores. hotel.hardrock.com/daytona-beach. © **386/947-7300.** 200 units. $215–$329 double. Valet parking $35; self-parking $25. Pet fee $150. **Amenities:** Restaurant; 2 bars; concierge; heated outdoor pool; fitness center; spa; free Wi-Fi.

Max Beach Resort ★★ Yet another product of overzealous developers who thought people would flock to Daytona Beach to purchase multi-million-dollar condos, the Max Beach Resort is their loss and the tourists' win. It's a 12-story oceanfront condo-turned-resort featuring 72 ginormous, swanky suites sleeping up to eight guests, all with full eat-in kitchens, private balconies, and laundry room. A 25-meter saltwater pool overlooks the ocean, yoga is done on the rooftop, there's a lounge with chess and board games, and people can work out in a fitness center with fabulous views. The resort also offers private surf lessons with pros starting at $150 a guest. A $32 nightly resort fee includes parking.

1901 S. Atlantic Ave., Daytona Beach Shores. maxdaytona.com. ✆ **386/999-2555.** 72 units. $240–$356 studio. **Amenities:** Restaurant; bar; outdoor pool; hot tub; fitness center; bike rentals; free Wi-Fi.

Shoreline All Suites Inn & Cabana Colony Cottages ★★

The Shoreline All Suites Inn has one- and two-bedroom suites that occupy two buildings separated by a walkway leading to the beach. Most have small bathrooms with scant vanity space and—shall we say—intimate shower stalls. But every unit has a full kitchen, and there are barbecue grills on the premises. The Shoreline's sister property, the **Cabana Colony Cottages,** consists of 12 cottages built in 1927 and since upgraded. They aren't much bigger than a motel room with a kitchen, but they're light, airy, and attractively furnished in HomeGoods-esque beachy decor. The cottages share a heated pool with the Shoreline.

2435 S. Atlantic Ave. (A1A, at Dundee Rd.), Daytona Beach Shores. daytonashoreline.com. ✆ **800/293-0653** or 386/252-1692. 30 units. $109–$158 double. Rates include continental breakfast. **Amenities:** Heated outdoor pool; free Wi-Fi.

Where to Dine

Mostly fast-food joints line the major thoroughfares of Daytona Beach, especially along Atlantic Avenue on the beach and International Speedway Boulevard (U.S. 92) near the racetrack. Elsewhere in town there are a few better options—a few at least.

One chain restaurant is worth a mention, since it's a born-in-Florida chain: **Stonewood Tavern & Grill** (stonewoodgrill.com; ✆ **386/671-1200**). It's at 100 S. Atlantic Ave., in Ormond Beach and at 2150 LPGA Blvd., in Daytona Beach (✆ **386/317-0097**). Both have a nice, if dark, mahogany interior, solid American food, and excellent service. They're open only for dinner and usually packed, so get advance reservations.

AT THE BEACHES

Down the Hatch ★★ SEAFOOD

Occupying a 1940s fish camp on the Halifax River, Down the Hatch serves big portions of fresh fish and seafood, much of which come from its own shrimp boat (it's often docked outside). Inexpensive burgers and sandwiches are available, too. Boats and shorebirds are visible through its picture windows. At night, arrive early to catch the sunset over the river, and also to beat the crowd to this very popular place. There's live music on weekend nights. In summer, light fare is served on a covered deck.

4894 Front St., Ponce Inlet. downthehatchseafood.com. ✆ **386/761-4831.** Main courses $13–$42. Sun–Thurs 11:30am–9pm; Fri–Sat 11:30am–10pm. Take Atlantic Ave. south, turn right on Beach St., and follow the signs.

Off the Hook at Inlet Harbor ★★ SEAFOOD

For swell waterfront views, outdoor and indoor dining, live music, and a view of the Ponce Inlet Lighthouse, Off the Hook reminds visitors of why they're here. In addition to the solid sea fare—peel-and-eat shrimp, pan-fried grouper, deep-water lobster tails—there's also Florida fresh gator tail, fried and served with a honey mustard sauce. Yup, it tastes like, well, you know (chicken). The restaurant also has charter captains on-site to take you out boating; and, if you get lucky out there, the restaurant will even cook your catch for you. There's often live music and a fun bar scene. They have another location on New Smyrna Beach, **Off the Hook Raw Bar & Grill,** at 747 E. 3rd Ave.

133 Inlet Harbor Rd., Ponce Inlet. offthehookatinletharbor.com. ✆ **386/202-4490.** Main courses $12–$30. Sun–Thurs 11:30am–9pm; Fri–Sat 11:30am–10pm. Take A1A S.; make a right on Inlet Harbor Rd.

Red Bud Cafe ★★★ GLOBAL   This charmer was created by a well-traveled mother and daughter to share the recipes they tried (or invented) when living in Australia, Italy, and Yugoslavia. It makes for an eclectic menu, with a number of savory or sweet crepes, along with all-day breakfast dishes, lunch pastries like spinach-and-cheese burek, and a range of heartier plates from steak Diane to seafood pasta with vodka sauce. It's all delish, and served in a whimsical room, where quotes from Alice in Wonderland are inscribed on the counter, and the works of local artists adorn the walls.

317 Seabreeze Blvd., Daytona Beach. theredbud.cafe. ✆ **386/888-1974.** Main courses $14–$34. Tues–Sun 8:30am–3pm.

ON THE MAINLAND

The Cellar ★★ ITALIAN   This fine-dining Italian eatery occupies the basement of a 1907 Victorian built as President Warren G. Harding's winter home, and it is listed on the National Register of Historic Places. Brick walls make for a cozy, un-Florida-like ambience. Chef/owner Sam Moggio is a graduate of the Culinary Institute, and boy does it show! All pastas are homemade, and there are outstanding entrees, like snapper filet sautéed with artichokes and braised lamb shanks with vegetable risotto. For dessert: a sinful, semisweet flourless chocolate torte.

220 Magnolia Ave. (btw. Palmetto and Ridgewood aves.). thecellarrestaurant.com. ✆ **386/258-0011.** Main courses $26–$51. Tues–Sat 5–10pm.

Taste of Maharaja ★★★ INDIAN   It's Bombay on the beach! Large portions of authentic, if not authentically fiery, Indian food are the draw here, as is a festive dining room with a pressed-tin ceiling, embroidered chairs, and lots of Indian art everywhere. Servers understand that this is many diners' first encounter with food from the subcontinent, and they kindly lead guests through the extensive menu. This is an especially good choice for vegetarians, as they'll have many options. And though it's none of these things, the restaurant was featured on the show *Diners, Drive Ins and Dives* on the Food Network.

144 Ridgewood Ave., Daytona Beach. maharajadaytona.com. ✆ **386/492-2355.** Main courses $12–$18. Wed–Mon 11:30am–3pm and 5–9pm.

Daytona Beach After Dark

Daytona Beach is a day drinking kind of place, but that doesn't mean things shut down early. The spring breakers may have stopped coming in droves, but there's still that spring breaky-vibe at night—especially at the beach bars. Check the Daytona Beach *News-Journal* website (news-journalonline.com) for its entertainment and event listings.

THE PERFORMING ARTS   The city-operated **Peabody Auditorium,** 600 Auditorium Blvd., between Noble Street and Wild Olive Avenue (peabodyauditorium.org; ✆ **386/671-3462**), is Daytona's major venue for serious art, including concerts by the Symphony Society (dbss.org; ✆ **386/253-2901**).

The **Oceanfront Bandshell** (daytonabandshell.com; ⓒ **386/671-3462**), on the Boardwalk, hosts a series of free big-name concerts every Sunday night in summer.

THE CLUB & BAR SCENE **Main Street** and **Seabreeze Boulevard** on the beach are happening areas where dozens of bars (and a few topless shows) and clubs cater to the party hearty sets. The **Boot Hill Saloon** ★, 310 Main St. (boothillsaloon.com; ⓒ **386/258-9506**), is a bluesy, brewsy honky-tonk, especially popular during race and bike weeks. **ONE DAYTONA** is another nightlife hotspot. A popular beachfront pub for more than 40 years, the **Ocean Deck Restaurant & Beach Bar** ★★, 127 S. Ocean Ave. (oceandeck.com; ⓒ **386/253-5224**), is packed with a mix of locals and tourists, young and old, who come for live music and cheap drinks. Bands and DJs play daily and nightly. And watching the sun set from **Crabby Joe's** ★ (crabbyjoesdaytona.com) on the pier, with a beer in your mitt, is a pretty unbeatable way to start the evening's festivities.

A view of Daytona's famous beach from a seat at Crabby Joe's.

Side Trips from Daytona Beach

Daytona is a superb jumping off point for seeing some of Florida's most unusual areas, from a town built around spiritualism, to a surfer paradise, to fishing villages, wildlife refuges, and more.

CASSADAGA

If you're in the Daytona Beach/Orlando area, you might have an intuition to make a pit stop in **Cassadaga** ★★★, the tiny 115-year-old community composed of psychics and mediums who will be happy to tell you your fortune or put you in touch with the deceased—for a price, of course.

Should you find the whole concept of psychics and talking to the dead a bit far-fetched, consider the history of Cassadaga, which is fascinating in its own right. The story goes that, as a young man from New York, George Colby was told during a séance that he would someday establish a spiritualist community in the South. In 1875, the prophecy came true when Colby was led through the wilderness of Central Florida by his spiritual guide to a 35-acre area that became the Cassadaga Spiritualist Camp.

Consisting of about 57 acres and 55 no-nonsense clapboard houses, Cassadaga caters to those who have chosen to share in a community of like-minded people who happen to believe in the otherworldly. Yes, the people are eccentric, to say the least, but they're all friendly. About 25 of the camp's residents are mediums who channel their skills from their homes. Designated a Historic District on the National Register of Historic Places, Cassadaga is one of the few remaining "spiritualist" communities, like Lily Dale in upstate New York.

When you get to town, head straight for the information center (see below for directions), where you can find out which psychics and mediums are working that day, and make an appointment for a session, which ranges from $45 to $150 and up. A general store, a restaurant, a hotel (hotelcassadaga.com), and a few shops selling crystals and potions of sorts will keep you occupied while you wait for your appointment. Whether you're a believer or not, an hour or two in Cassadaga will make for interesting cocktail conversation.

From Daytona, take I-4 exit 114. Turn right onto Highway 472 at the end of the exit ramp toward Orange City/Deland. At the traffic light, turn right onto Dr. Martin Luther King, Jr., Parkway. Turn right at the first light, which is Cassadaga Road. Continue 1½ miles to the intersection with Stevens Street. The information center is on the right. For more information call ✆ **386/228-3171** or go to www.cassadaga.org.

NEW SMYRNA BEACH

Just 24 miles south of Daytona Beach on A1A is **New Smyrna Beach** ★★★, a popular surf town known for its 17-mile white-sand beach with some of Florida's finest wave action, and wave breaks that attract both experts and novices. In January 2024, the tiny town was abuzz with excitement over Brad Pitt, there filming an Apple original movie about a retired Formula One driver. But beyond the brief brush with Hollywood, and beyond the beach, is the **Canal Street Historic District,** a pedestrian-friendly, charming, tree-lined neighborhood filled with shops, boutiques, art galleries, and a **history museum,** 120 Sams Ave. (nsbhistory.org; ✆ **386/478-0052**), detailing the area's heritage since its founding in 1768. The town also has two vibrant art hubs: the 5,000-square-foot gallery **Arts on Douglas** ★★ (123 Douglas St.; artsondouglas.net); and a small museum for changing exhibitions called **Atlantic Center for the Arts** (1414 Art Center Ave.; atlanticcenterforthearts.org). Both are free to visit.

A Florida fusion of New Hope, Pennsylvania, Key West, and even Brooklyn, highlights of New Smyrna Beach include breakfast hot spot **The Mermaid Café,** 113 Flagler Ave. (✆ **386/410-4033**)—try the Elvis waffle; **Crimson House,** 219 N. Orange St. (✆ **386/402-4697**), a wine bar and restaurant in a turn-of-the-20th-century house with a tree-canopied shaded backyard and live music; **Third Wave Café & Wine Bar,** 204 Flagler Ave. (thirdwavensb.com; ✆ **386/402-7864**), a funky garden cafe decked out with 1940s-era sofas, lit by Edison bulbs, and featuring a menu of locally sourced seafood, small plates, and pizzas. Stroll 5 blocks from the river to the ocean along **Flagler Avenue** to discover independently owned boutiques selling everything from local honey to handmade jewelry.

Though you are close to Daytona and Cocoa Beach, where larger hotels abound, NSB has some adorable B&Bs. The **Black Dolphin Inn** ★, 916 S. Riverside Dr. (blackdolphininn.com; ✆ **386/410-4868**), is a Spanish-style boutique inn overlooking the Indian River, named for the dolphins that can be seen from your balcony or the inn's docks. The **Inn on the Avenue** ★★, 309 Flagler Ave. (innontheave.com; ✆ **386/693-4808**), is a pretty, old French cottage with six rooms located right in the heart of town. The stellar **Anchor Inn Bed and Breakfast** ★★★, 312 Washington St. (anchorinnbnb.com; ✆ **386/428-3499**), has six ocean-themed rooms in a craftsman bungalow just a short walk to boutiques, restaurants, and the Intracoastal. Nearby is the **Night Swan Intracoastal Bed and Breakfast ★★★**, 512 S. Riverside Dr. (nightswan.com; *©* **386/423-4940**), a handsome 16-room lodging spread between two historic Victorian-style homes and a guest cottage. Last, but possibly the most grand, the **Victoria ★★★** at 1883 Waterfront Estate, 532 N. Riverside Dr. (victoria1883.com; *©* **386/478-6009**), is a magnificent estate with expansive gardens, themed rooms, water views, and a hidden speakeasy.

PAYNES PRAIRIE PRESERVE

Micanopy (micanopytown.com) is Florida's oldest inland settlement, full of antiques shops and home to the **Paynes Prairie Preserve State Park ★★★**, 100 Savannah Blvd. (floridastateparks.org; *©* **352/466-3397**), a bird-watcher's mecca, featuring more than 300 species, as well as alligators, deer, and bison. Exhibits and an audiovisual program at the visitor center explain the area's natural and cultural history. A 50-foot-high observation tower near the visitor center provides a panoramic view of the preserve. You'll see eight trails below for hiking, horseback riding, and bicycling. Ranger-led activities are offered on weekends, November through April. Admission is $6 per vehicle with up to eight people, $4 single-occupant vehicle, and $2 pedestrians. From I-75 South, take exit 374, the Micanopy exit, and turn right at the end of the exit ramp. You will then be traveling east on C.R. 234. Stay on this road 1¼ miles until it intersects with U.S. 441. Turn left onto 441 and go about ⅔ mile to Paynes Prairie Preserve State Park.

ST. AUGUSTINE: AMERICA'S FIRST CITY

105 miles NE of Orlando; 302 miles N of Miami; 39 miles S of Jacksonville

America's oldest permanent European settlement, St. Augustine draws history buffs and romantics to its Colonial Spanish Quarter and 18th-century buildings. With its coquina buildings and sprawling, moss-draped live oaks, visitors can do more than just museum hop. St. Augustine encourages guests to sit down for a while, and to drink in scenes from the past along with a chilled glass of sweet tea.

Things to Do Historic sites top the list in this 16th-century town. The premier attractions include the **Oldest House Museum Complex and Gardens,** the

In the Beginning . . .

In 1562, a group of French Huguenots settled near the mouth of the St. Johns River, in present-day Jacksonville. Three years later, a Spanish force under Pedro Menéndez de Avilés arrived, wiped out the Huguenot men (de Avilés spared their women and children), and established a settlement he named St. Augustín. The colony survived a succession of attacks by pirates, Indians, and the British over the next 2 centuries. The Treaty of Paris, ending the French and Indian War, ceded the town to Britain in 1763, but the British gave it back to Spain 20 years later. The United States took control when it acquired Florida from Spain in 1821.

St. Augustine is one of Florida's most handsome cities.

Oldest Wooden Schoolhouse from the earliest days of Florida, and the **Lightner Museum,** a Victorian-era mansion packed with all kinds of fascinating curios and memorabilia.

Shopping Spanish-influenced home decor and furniture fill the antique shops and galleries in the historic district. Glossy oak tables, Mediterranean-style tiles, and silver bric-a-brac fill display windows along **Aviles Street** and **St. George Street.**

Nightlife & Entertainment Old Town St. Augustine amps it up on weekends and it's five o'clock always at the beach bars of St. Augustine and Ponte Vedra Beach. Check out the **Mill Top Tavern and Listening Room,** a warm and rustic bar housed in a 19th-century mill building (the waterwheel is still outside), the **Tini Martini Bar** at the Casablanca Inn, and the very cool **Ice Plant Bar,** housed in a 1927 industrial warehouse.

Restaurants & Dining Spicy food lovers, St. Augustine has something special for you: the Datil, one of the hottest peppers you'll ever find. Restaurants across town add whole and ground Datils to their menus. **August Heat Co.** sells an assortment of Datil delicacies you can take home with you. The gaudy neon stripes covering its exterior are just the beginning at **Gypsy Cab Company,** where the inventive menu constantly changes.

RESTAURANTS
August Heat Co.'s Hot Stuff **20**
Brisky's **2**
Catch 27 **17**
Collage **13**
Columbia **14**
The Floridian **15**
GAS Full Service Restaurant **33**
Gypsy Cab Co. **34**
Prohibition Kitchen **18**
The Purple Olive Restaurant & Wine Lounge **38**
St. Augustine Fish Camp **32**

HOTELS
Bayfront Westcott House Bed & Breakfast Inn **28**
Best Western Bayfront **16**
Carriage Way Bed & Breakfast **12**
Casa de Solana Bed & Breakfast **25**
Casa Monica Resort & Spa, Autograph Collection **23**
The Collector Inn **30**
Devil's Elbow Fishing Resort **39**
Hyatt Place St. Augustine/ Vilano Beach **1**
The Kenwood Inn **27**
La Fiesta Ocean Inn & Suites **37**
Pirate Haus Inn **19**
Victorian House Bed & Breakfast

Tourism is St. Augustine's main industry these days. However, despite the number of visitors, it's an exceptionally charming town, with good restaurants, a small-town nightlife, and shopping bargains. Give yourself 2 days here to see the highlights, longer to savor this historic gem.

Essentials

GETTING THERE The **Daytona Beach International Airport** (p. 440) is about an hour's drive south of St. Augustine, but service is more frequent—and fares usually lower—at **Jacksonville International Airport** (p. 476), about the same distance north.

GETTING AROUND Once you've parked at the visitor center, you can walk or take one of the sightseeing trolleys, trains, or horse-drawn carriages around the historic district. See our section on guided tours on p. 465.

The **Sunshine Bus Company** (sunshinebus.net; ✆ **904/823-4816**) operates public bus routes Monday through Saturday from 6am to 7pm. The line runs between the St. Augustine Airport on U.S. 1 and the historic district via San Marco Avenue and the Greyhound bus terminal on Malaga Street. Rides cost $2 for adults, $1 for seniors. All-day tickets are $4, $2 for seniors. Children 6 and under ride free.

For a taxi, reach out to **Salty Sea** (saltyseatransportation.com; ✆ **904/788-0518**). Uber and Lyft are also options.

Solano Cycle, 61 San Marco Ave., at Locust Avenue, 2 blocks north of the visitor center (solanocycle.com; ✆ **904/825-6766**), rents bicycles and scooters. Beach cruisers cost $18 for 24 hours, while scooters are $75 for a single passenger and $80 for two. Open daily from 10am to 6pm.

VISITOR INFORMATION You'll find good info at the **Florida's Historic Coast** website (floridashistoriccoast.com), which covers St. Augustine and Ponte Vedra, and **Visit St. Augustine** (visitstaugustine.com).

The **St. Augustine Visitor Information Center** has three offices: at 10 S. Castillo Dr., at San Marco Avenue, 10 W. Castillo Dr. just off U.S. 1, and opposite the Castillo de San Marcos National Monument (citystaug.com/618/Visitor-Information-Center; ✆ **904/825-1000**). All three sell tickets for the sightseeing trains and trolleys, which include discounted admission to the attractions. The centers are open Monday through Saturday from 8:30am to 5:30pm.

Seeing the Top Historic Attractions

St. George Street, from King Street north to the Old City Gate (at Orange St.), is the heart of the historic district. Lined with restaurants and boutiques selling everything from T-shirts to antiques, these 4 blocks get the lion's share of the town's tourists. You'll have much less company if you poke around the narrow streets of the primarily residential neighborhood south of King Street. Most of the town's attractions do not have guided tours, but many do have docents on hand to answer questions.

Be sure to drive through the parking lot of the **Villa 1565** motel, at 137 San Marco Ave., to see a gorgeous and stately **live oak tree ★★** that is at least 650 years old; then continue east to **Magnolia Avenue ★★**, a spectacularly beautiful street with a lovely canopy of old magnolia trees.

A note on timing: Consider coming during the holiday season. St. Augustine's **Nights of Lights ★★★** is one of the country's most festive, hands-down top 10 holiday light displays with the entire historic district draped and bathed in lights from the sidewalks to the rooftops. There are all sorts of events, from tree lightings to caroling, taking place from the moment Thanksgiving is over until at least the end of January. For more information, go to floridashistoriccoast.com/blog/enjoy-special-events-during-nights-lights.

Castillo de San Marcos National Monument ★★
Should you ever wish to build an authentic fort, take notes at Castillo de San Marcos, America's oldest and best-preserved masonry fortification. The structure represents the quintessence of the "bastion system" of fortification. It took 23 years (1672–95) to build, and its design includes a double drawbridge entrance (the only way in or out) over a 40-foot dry moat. Diamond-shaped bastions in each corner, which enabled cannons to set up a deadly crossfire, contained sentry towers. The Castillo was never captured in battle, and its *coquina* (limestone made from broken seashells and corals) walls did not crumble when pounded by enemy artillery or violent storms over more than 300 years. Today the old bombproof storerooms surrounding the central plaza have exhibits about the history of the fort, a national monument since 1924. You can tour the vaulted powder magazine, a dank prison cell (supposedly haunted), the chapel, and guard rooms. Climb the stairs to get a great view of Matanzas Bay. A self-guided tour map and brochure are provided at the ticket booth. If available, the 20- to 30-minute ranger talks are well worth attending. They also do weapons demos. Popular torchlight tours of the fort are offered in winter.

If you like forts, you should also check out **Fort Matanzas,** built on an island in the 1740s to warn St. Augustine of enemy attacks from the south (which were

Reenactors fire cannons at Castillo de San Marcos National Monument.

out of reach of Castillo de San Marcos). For information, visit nps.gov/foma. Ferrys depart for Fort Matanzas Wednesdays through Monday from 9:30am to 3:30pm, and admission and the ferry ride to the island are free, but boarding passes are required and available at the Fort Matanzas Visitor Center, 8635 A1A South (© **904/471-0116**).

1 E. Castillo Dr. (at San Marco Ave.). nps.gov/casa. © **904/829-6506**. Admission $15 adults for 7-day pass, free for children 15 and under. Fort daily 8:45am–5pm. Park grounds 6am–midnight.

Colonial Quarter St. Augustine ★★★ This is Florida's Colonial Williamsburg, a place of costumed folks doing things they used to do back in the 1700s, and no, it doesn't feel hokey. You'll watch as blacksmiths, carpenters, leather workers, musket shooters, and homemakers demonstrate their skills, but surprisingly, the **DeMesa-Sanchez House** (ca. 1740–60) is the only authentic Colonial-era structure in the compound. The others are reproductions, but all of the architecture and landscape have been so expertly re-created most visitors have no idea the structures are new. Be sure to climb the 35-foot watchtower for a great view of **Castillo de San Marcos;** you can dine 18th-century style at the British **Bull and Crown Publick House** or the Spanish tapas-style **Taberna Del Caballo.** Tours are offered daily at 10:30am, noon, 1:30 and 3pm. *Tip:* It's hard to see everything in one fell swoop, even on the tours, so I recommend you break up your visit into 2 days, or concentrate on the sections you are most interested in. Or better yet, plan a return visit.

14 S. Castillo Dr. colonialquarter.com. © **904/599-2113**. Admission $14.99 adults, $11.99 seniors, $8.99 children 5–15, free for children 4 and under. Daily 10am–5pm.

Lightner Museum ★★★ Now *this* is a museum. Henry Flagler's opulent Gilded Age–era Spanish Renaissance–style Alcazar Hotel, built in 1889, closed during the Depression and stayed vacant until Chicago publishing magnate Otto C. Lightner bought the building in 1948 to house his vast collection of Victoriana. The building is an attraction in itself (the lobby looks exactly as it did back in the 1800s), centering on a palm-planted courtyard with an arched stone bridge spanning a fishpond. The first floor houses a Victorian village, with shop fronts representing emporiums selling period wares. The Victorian **Science and Industry Room** displays shells, rocks, and Native American artifacts in beautiful turn-of-the-20th-century cases. Other exhibits include stuffed birds, an Egyptian mummy, steam-engine models, shrunken heads, hair art, Russian baths, and a lion that belonged to Winston Churchill. Yes, it's a strange amalgamation for a museum, but there's sure to be

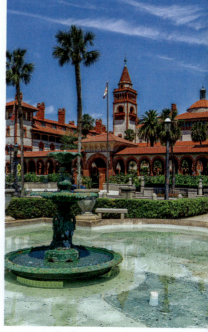

Flagler College.

something you're interested in here. Lightner aptly described it all as a "collection of collections." Plan to spend about 90 minutes exploring, and be sure to be here at 11am or 2pm, when a room of automated musical instruments erupts into concerts of period music. Check out the cafe too, housed in what used to be the hotel's pool (back in 1889 it was the world's largest).

The imposing building across King Street was Henry Flagler's rival resort, the Ponce de León Hotel. It now houses **Flagler College** (legacy.flagler.edu), which runs superb hourlong tours daily (at 10am and 2pm) from the rotunda at 74 King St. Visitors take in the building's magnificent Tiffany stained-glass windows, its ornate Spanish Renaissance architecture, and gold-leafed Maynard murals. Tours are $17 per person.

Across Cordova Street stands another beaut, the 1888 **Casa Monica Hotel** (p. 469).

75 King St. (at Granada St.). lightnermuseum.org. ⓒ **904/824-2874.** Admission $19 adults, $16 seniors and students, $12 youth 12–17, free for children 11 and under. Daily 9am–5pm (last tour 4pm).

The Oldest House Museum Complex ★★   Archaeological surveys indicate that a dwelling stood on this site as early as the beginning of the 17th century. What you see today, called the **Gonzáles-Alvarez House** (named for two of its prominent owners), evolved from a two-room coquina dwelling built between 1702 and 1727. The rooms are furnished to evoke various historical eras. Admission also entitles you to explore the adjacent **St. Augustine Surf Culture and History Museum,** an interactive museum with over 50 oral histories, hundreds of historical images, film, music, artifacts, memorabilia, trophies, articles, and historic surf boards. Allow about 45 minutes here.

14 St. Francis St. (at Charlotte St.). staughs.com. ⓒ **904/824-2872.** Admission $12.95 adults, $9.95 seniors 55 and over, $4.95 students and children 4–17, free for children 3 and under; $25.95 per family of 2 adults and children 17 and under. Daily 10am–5pm; tours depart every half-hour (last tour 4:30pm).

The Oldest Wooden Schoolhouse Historic Museum & Gardens ★★   Photo ops abound at this unique Minorcan homestead of Juan Genopoly, established in the late 1700s. One of three structures in town dating from the Spanish colonial period, this cedar-and-cypress structure is held together by wooden pegs and handmade nails, its hand-wrought beams still intact. The last class was held in 1864. Today the old-time classroom is re-created using animated pupils and a teacher, complete with a

The Oldest Wooden Schoolhouse Historic Museum.

dunce and below-stairs "dungeon" for unruly children, which will make your kids count their lucky stars that they weren't in school back then. Good news: All visitors here receive a diploma just for stopping by.

14 St. George St. (btw. Orange and Cuna sts.). oldestwoodenschoolhouse.com. ✆ **904/824-0192.** Admission $6.95 adults, $5.95 children 6–12, free for children 5 and under. Sun–Thurs 10am–6pm; Fri–Sat 10am–8pm.

Spanish Military Hospital Museum ★★

Hypochondriacs, doctors, and fans of medicine in general will love this place—but if you're squeamish in hospitals, this one isn't an exception. The clapboard building is a reconstruction of part of a hospital that stood here during the second Spanish colonial period, from 1784 to 1821. A 20-minute guided tour will show you what the apothecary, administrative offices, patients' ward, and herbarium probably looked like in 1791. The ward and a collection of actual surgical instruments of the period will enhance your appreciation of modern medicine. Daily 45-minute tours include, yikes, surgical demonstrations, and for some odd reason, the museum is pet friendly.

3 Aviles St. (south of King St.). smhmuseum.com. ✆ **904/342-7730.** Admission $14.95 adults, $12.95 seniors, $5.95 children 6–12. Daily 9am–5pm.

More Historic Attractions

Mission Nombre de Dios Museum ★★

This serene setting overlooking the Intracoastal Waterway is believed to be the site of the first permanent mission in the United States, founded in 1565. The mission is a popular destination of religious pilgrimages. Whatever your beliefs, it's a beautiful tree-shaded spot, ideal for quiet meditation.

101 San Marco Ave. missionandshrine.org. ✆ **904/824-2809.** Free admission; donations appreciated. Daily dawn to dusk.

Old Jail Museum ★

This 1891 jail was built by railroad magnate Henry Flagler and placed on the National Register of Historic Places in 1987. So yes, there's history here—the Old Jail served as the county jail until 1953—but there's also cheese, lots of it. Tour guides fronting as comedians are a turn-off to many people who just want to hear the cold, hard facts of old-world incarceration. At times during some of these tours, you, too, may feel incarcerated. If you can get past the tackiness, there's some truly fascinating history in here and, for fans of the paranormal, allegedly some ghostly jailbirds as well (there's an evening ghost tour). You'll visit "regular" cells, and a maximum-security cell where murderers and horse thieves were confined, a cell housing prisoners condemned to hang (they could see the gallows being constructed from their window), and a grim solitary-confinement cell with no windows or mattress. Tours last 30 minutes and depart every 20 minutes.

167 San Marco Ave. (at Williams St.). ✆ **904/829-3800.** Admission $18 adults, $9.50 children 4–12, free for children 3 and under. Rates cheaper online. Daily 9am–4:30pm.

Old St. Augustine History Museum ★

If you just haven't seen enough old stuff, you can always spend another 30 minutes wandering through this museum documenting 400 years of Florida's past, focusing on the life of Henry Flagler, the Civil War, and the Seminole Wars. Highlights are a collection of toys and dolls, mostly from the 1870s to the 1920s, and a replica of a Spanish galleon filled with weapons, pottery, and treasures, along with display cases filled with gold, silver, and jewelry recovered by treasure hunters. A typical wattle-and-daub hut of a Timucuan Indian in a forest setting illustrates the lifestyle of St. Augustine's first residents. If you're short on time (or cash), don't get FOMO over skipping this one.

167 San Marco Ave. © **904/829-93800.** Admission $8 but free with some tours. Daily 9am–4:30pm.

Peña-Peck House ★★ Built in the mid-1700s by order of the King of Spain as the residence of his royal Treasurer, Juan Esteban de Peña, this First Spanish Period home eventually became the property of Connecticut doctor Seth Peck, whose family lived here for 94 years. In 1892, the home became part of the Women's Exchange, which helped down-on-their-luck women get back on their feet. Today you can tour the place and see 18th-century American antiques and hear stories about what it was like to live in the Oldest City when, well, it wasn't so old.

143 St George St. penapeckhouse.com. © **904/829-5064.** Guided tours Wed–Sat noon–4pm.

Ponce De Leon's Fountain of Youth Archaeological Park Never mind that Juan Ponce de León never found the Fountain of Youth; this overrated archaeological park wrongly bills itself as North America's first historic site. Smithsonian Institution archaeological digs have established that a Timucuan Indian village existed here some 1,000 years ago, but there's no evidence that Ponce de León visited the spot during his 1513 voyage. You can wander the not-so-interesting grounds yourself, but you'll learn more on a 45-minute guided tour or at a planetarium show about 16th-century celestial navigation. ***Be warned:*** This place could define the phrase *"tourist trap"* (not to mention that the fountain's water smells and tastes *awful*). Nevertheless, the 15 waterfront acres and grounds are lovely and the non-fountain exhibits are okay.

11 Magnolia Ave. (at Williams St.). fountainofyouthflorida.com. © **904/829-3168.** Admission $19.95 adults, $17.95 seniors, $9.95 children 6–12, free for children 5 and under. Daily 9am–6pm (last entry at 5pm).

St. Augustine Lighthouse & Maritime Museum ★★ This 165-foot-tall structure, Florida's first official lighthouse, was built in 1875 to replace the old Spanish lighthouse that had stood at the inlet since 1565. The lightkeeper's cottage was destroyed by fire in 1970 but was meticulously restored to its Victorian splendor. The Victorian-style visitor center houses a museum explaining the history of the lighthouse and the area. Demos of lightkeeper duties, wooden boatbuilding, and underwater archaeology are especially interesting. There's also a play area, nature trails, and a World War II–themed restaurant. You should be in good condition (children must be at least 44 in. tall) to climb the 219 steps to the top of the lighthouse. The SyFy Network's popular show *Ghost Hunters* filmed an episode here and found that, after a thorough investigation, the lighthouse is, indeed, haunted; they offer ghost tours, including one inside the lighthouse at night, for $29.95.

81 Lighthouse Ave. (off A1A east of the Bridge of Lions). staugustinelighthouse.com. © **904/829-0745.** Admission to museum and tower $14.95 adults, $12.95 seniors, $12.95 children 7–11, free for children 6 and under and all active-duty and retired military personnel. Daily 9am–6pm. Follow A1A S. across the Bridge of Lions; take the last left before the turnoff to Anastasia State Park.

Villa Zorayda Museum ★★ The renovated and restored Gilded Age, castlelike winter home of architect Franklin Smith, inspired by Spain's Alhambra Palace, was built in 1883 and features a big collection of antiques. These include custom-made bone china, Oriental rugs, and exquisite Egyptian artifacts like the Sacred Cat Rug, a 2,400-year-old tapestry made from the hairs of ancient cats that roamed the Nile. Rumor has it there's a curse waiting for anyone who walks on it. Luckily, you won't be at risk, as the rug is hanging safely on a wall. The Villa is still owned by the family. Audio tours of the two-level home run between 45 and 60 minutes and detail the home's rich—literally—history, including details about its past as a casino, restaurant, and speakeasy. If you're in town around Christmas, do not miss the candlelight tours here—they're magical.

83 King St. villazorayda.com. **904/829-9887.** Admission $15.98 adults, $14.91 seniors, $11.72 students, $7.99 children 5–12. Mon–Sat 10am–5pm (last tour 4:30pm); Sun 11am–4pm.

Other Entertainment Attractions

Marineland Dolphin Adventure ★★ What once was a schlocky 7-acre tourist trap is now a world-class dolphin conservation center. This, the descendant of the former Marineland of Florida (home of Flippy, the first-ever trained dolphin) and Marine Studios (1938), is 15 minutes south of St. Augustine and is on the National Register of Historic Places. Today you can swim with dolphins in shallow- and deep-water programs, create one-of-a-kind paintings with dolphin artists, and experience what it's like to be a dolphin trainer from 1 to 3 full days. Dolphin encounters and experiences are very expensive and range from $100 to $350. The very young and those not inclined to participate may observe dolphins as they swim, play, and interact with guests, while more adventurous souls may take part in kayak tours exploring the estuaries of the Guana Tolomato Matanzas National Estuarine Research Reserve provided by Ripple Effect Ecotours for $55 adults, $45 kids 6 to 15. (*Note:* Swimming with dolphins has both its critics and its supporters. You may want to visit the Whale and Dolphin Conservation Society's website at cetaceanhabitat.org to read about both sides of this controversy.)

9600 Ocean Shore Blvd. marineland.net. **904/460-1275.** Admission $20. Free for kids 4 and under. Hours are seasonal. Call or visit the website for specific information.

St. Augustine Alligator Farm Zoological Park ★★ More than 2,700 alligators—including some rare white ones—live at this more-than-a-century-old attraction. It houses the world's only complete collection of all 24 species of crocodilians, a category that includes alligators, crocodiles, caimans, and gavials. In addition to an entire exhibit devoted to albino alligators, there are also rare ones including a small Chinese alligator, an Indian gharial, and Nile crocodile. But the most famous one in the park, the Taylor Swift, if you will, is the Australian, 5-foot-3-inch, 1,250-pound Maximo, the largest animal here. There are ponds and marshes filled with ducks, swans, herons, egrets, ibises, and other native wading birds. For a, uh, bird's-eye view of the park, there are two zipline courses over the entire park that will set you back an additional $40 a person. They also have lemurs, pythons, sloths, and more. Entertaining (and educational) 20-minute alligator and reptile shows take place hourly throughout the day, and you can often see narrated feedings spring through fall.

999 Anastasia Ave. (A1A), east of Bridge of Lions at Old Quarry Rd. alligatorfarm.com. **904/824-3337.** Admission $34.99 adults, $19.99 children 3–11, free for children 2 and under. Discounts available online. Daily 9am–5pm; summer 9am–6pm.

St. Augustine Pirate & Treasure Museum ★★ Pat Croce, former owner of the Philadelphia 76ers, is obsessed with pirates. And because he's rich enough to play into his passion, he opened this fantastic homage to all things swashbuckling. St. Augustine, it turns out, was a hotbed for pirates like Sir Francis Drake and Robert Searles. Among the 800 or so artifacts here are an original journal of Captain Kidd's last voyage, the oldest pirate wanted poster, and the world's only authentic pirate treasure chest. New and noteworthy at the museum is a rare burnt-wood remnant from one of two 16th-century ships attributed to Drake that Croce discovered with a team of explorers during an October 2011 expedition to Panama. Interactive exhibits and cheesy-but-amusing animatronics make for an engaging and entertaining visit. Depending on your level of pirate interest, you can spend anywhere from 30 minutes to over 2 hours here. Kids who are deep into their own pirate phases obviously flip over the place.

12 Castillo Dr., St. Augustine. thepiratemuseum.com. © **877/GO-PLUNDER** [467-5863]. Admission $18.99 adults, $15.99 seniors, $9.99 children 5–12. Daily 10am–7pm.

Guided Tours of St. Augustine

History is everywhere in St. Augustine, not just in its museums. So, taking a tour of the historic quarter can be a rewarding experience. But what flavor of tour is right for you? We have some advice.

TROLLEY & CARRIAGE TOURS

The sightseeing trolleys and trains follow 7-mile routes, stopping at the visitor center and at or near most attractions between 8:30am and 5pm daily. You can get off at any stop, visit the attraction, and step aboard the next vehicle that comes along about every 20 minutes. If you don't get off at any attractions, it takes about 1 hour and 10 minutes to complete the tour. The vehicles don't all go to the same sights, so speak with their agents at the visitor center in order to pick the right one for you. You can buy tickets, as well as discounted tickets to some attractions, at the visitor center or from the drivers.

Old Town Trolley Tours ★★ (trolleytours.com/st-augustine; © **844/388-6452**) takes visitors on an hour tour with more than 20 stops at the historic district and its most famous sites. You can hop on and off at your leisure all day, and the guides are, for the most part, talented storytellers. Tickets include admission to **St. Augustine History Museum,** and rides on a free beach shuttle which picks up and drops off passengers at various resorts and attractions around town. The tour costs $45 for adults, $24 for kids 4 to 12. Rates are cheaper online.

Ripley's Red Train Tours ★★, 19 San Marco Ave. (redtrains.com; © **904/824-1606**), is a fully narrated 7½-mile, 1-hour tour on red open-air trains that are small enough to go down more of the narrow historic-district streets. Guides tend to be a bit more humorous than on Old Town Trolley (though it will vary by who you get). Tickets are $23.99 for adults, $12.99 for kids 6 to 12 (rates are cheaper online). *Warning:* Ripley's packages steer you to attractions that aren't worth your time. Just go for the basic product.

You can also see the sights by horse-drawn carriage. **Country Carriages** ★★ (countrycarriages.net; © **904/669-8619**) offers slow-paced, entertaining, driver-narrated 45-minute rides past major landmarks and attractions from 8am to midnight. They have a spooky ghost ride from 6pm to closing every night. Carriage tours cost $35 for adults, $12 for kids 5 to 11.

WALKING TOURS, WITH & WITHOUT FOOD

Spyglass Travel and Tours ★★★ (spyglasstravel.org) was founded by historians Kevin and Angie Rose, both expert tale weavers, who run a number of walking tours of the city. These include walks through the historic district, as well as ghost tours, and tours about the seamy underside of St. Augustine. They also sell fun self-guided audio tours.

Tour Saint Augustine ★★ (tourstaug.com; ⓒ **904/825-0087**), the OG, in biz for 30 years and doing it all, from historic walking tours, to team building events, to food and wine experiences. *Inside Tip:* They offer a FREE tour every Sunday at 2pm: the **Mystery, Mayhem, and True Crime**, a 1-hour walking tour.

For a foodie tour of St. Augustine, **City Walks Food & Wine Tours** ★★★ (staugcitywalks.com; ⓒ **904/925-0087**) has a 3+-hour, all-inclusive walking, eating, and drinking tour exploring historical and cultural influences on St. Aug cuisine from tapas to desserts. The tour is limited to 10 guests per day and costs $149 per person, which includes alcoholic beverages, taxes, and tips.

Feast of St. Augustine ★★★ (feaststaugustine.com) is another excellent, and slightly less expensive, food/walking tour ($119, but alcohol is extra) which takes visitors to four top restaurants, and all around the historic district.

GHOST TOURS

For a paranormal investigation of the Old Jail after dark, **Ghosts & Gravestones** ★★, 108 Sea Grove Main St. (ghostsandgravestones.com; ⓒ **866/955-6101**), offers a very creepy 2½-hour tour with the latest in ghost-hunting equipment, limited to just 12 people. Children are not allowed on this tour. Cost is $101 per person.

Ghost Tours of St. Augustine ★★ is part of Tour St. Augustine (see above). It has guides in period dress leading visitors on 75-minute tours through the back alleys and off-the-beaten-path haunts of the historic district and the St. Augustine Lighthouse. Tickets are $25 per person. Their longer **Creepy Crawl Haunted Pub Tour and Paranormal Investigation** is a 2-hour jaunt that includes a welcome drink and uses EMF meters to detect paranormal activity. It is also $25 per person.

We'll note that pretty much all the tour companies listed under walking, trolley, and carriage tours, *also* do ghost tours (they're big biz in St. A), so if you have a good experience with one during the day, see what their options are for after dark.

Hitting the Beach

Sadly, erosion has almost swallowed the beach from the inlet as far south as Old Beach Road in St. Augustine Beach. The U.S. Army Corps of Engineers is reclaiming the sand (not without controversy as they are taking sand from the St. Augustine Inlet, which some say is harming the area's north beaches), but in the meantime, hotels and homes here have rock seawalls instead of sand bordering the sea.

Erosion has made a less noticeable impact on **Anastasia State Park** ★★, on Anastasia Boulevard (A1A) across the Bridge of Lions and just past the Alligator Farm, where the 4 miles of beach (on which you can drive and park) are still backed by picturesque dunes. On its river side, the area faces a lagoon. Amenities include shaded picnic areas with grills, restrooms, windsurfing, sailing and canoeing (on a saltwater lagoon), a nature trail, and saltwater fishing (for bluefish, pompano, redfish, and flounder; a license is required for nonresidents). In summer, you can rent chairs, beach umbrellas, and surfboards. There's good bird-watching here, especially in spring and fall; pick up a brochure at the entrance. The 139 wooded campsites are in high demand year-round; they come with picnic tables, grills, and electricity. Admission to the park is $8 per vehicle, $4 single-occupant vehicle, $2 per bicyclist or pedestrian. Campsites cost $28. For camping reservations, call ✆ **800/326-3521** or go to reserveamerica.com. The day-use area is open daily from 8am to sunset. You can bring your pets.

From Memorial Day to Labor Day, all St. Augustine beaches charge a fee of $3 per car at official access points; the rest of the year, you can park free, but there are no lifeguards on duty or restroom facilities on the beach.

Outdoor Activities

CRUISES **St. Augustine Scenic Cruises** ★ (scenic-cruise.com; ✆ **904/824-1806**) has been sailing on Matanzas Bay since the turn of the 20th century. They offer 75-minute narrated tours aboard the double-decker *Victory III*, departing from the Municipal Marina, 111 Avenida Menendez, just south of the Bridge of Lions. You can often spot dolphins, brown pelicans, cormorants, and kingfishers. Snacks, soft drinks, beer, and wine are sold onboard. Departures are at 11am and 1, 2:45, and 4:30pm daily except Christmas, with an additional tour at 6:45pm from April 1 to September 2 and sometimes in October. Call ahead—schedules can change during inclement weather. Fares are $24.50 for adults, $21 for seniors, $11 for children 4 to 12. If you're driving, allow time to find parking on the street.

Or hop the free ferry to Fort Matanzas on Rattlesnake Island. There are often dolphins in the water as you make the trip, and the fort is interesting. Ferries take off from 8635 Hwy. A1A (follow A1A S. out of St. Augustine for about 15 miles). Call ✆ **904/471-0116** or visit nps.gov/foma for more information.

ECO-TOURS **St. Augustine Eco Tours** ★★, 111 Avenida Menendez, (staugustineecotours.com; ✆ **904/377-7245**), offers several kayak and boat tours through St. Augustine's waterways, including Guana River and Lake, Moultrie Creek, Moses Creek, Washington Oaks, Faver-Dykes, and Six Mile Landing. Prices range from $25 to $65. They also have a 27-foot catamaran sailing into the remote backwaters, creeks, and estuaries for glimpses of manatees, sea turtles, dolphins, and birds. Cost is $65 for adults, $45 for kids 12 and under.

Ripple Effect Eco Tours ★★★ (rippleeffectecotours.com; ✆ **904/347-1565**) is a Marineland partner that offers excellent eco-educational walking tours, jet-boat tours, and lighted-firefly kayak sunset tours. Rates start at $60 per person.

For more adventurous types, **Game On Fishing Charters** ★ (gofcharters.com; ✆ **904/607-6399**) offers an alligator trapping tour led by a licensed trapper that takes you from swamps to golf course fairways on a mission to subdue and remove nuisance gators. Cost is $500 per person including license and equipment that will get you right into the middle of the action as you assist in the snaring, subduing, and taping of the gator's monster jaws. Good luck and, please, send us a picture.

FISHING You can fish to your heart's content at **Anastasia State Park** (see "Hitting the Beach," above). Or you can cast your line off **St. Johns County Ocean Pier,** at the north end of St. Augustine Beach (✆ **904/461-0119**). The pier is open 24 hours daily and has a bait shop with rental equipment that's open from 7am to 6pm. Admission is $6 (free for children 6 and under) for fishing, $2 for sightseeing.

For full-day, half-day, and overnight **deep-sea fishing** excursions (for snapper, grouper, porgy, amberjack, sea bass, and other species), contact **Sea Love Charters,** at Cat's Paw Marina, 220 Nix Boat Yard Rd. (sealovefishing.com; © **904/824-3328**). Full-day trips on the party boat *Sea Love II* cost about $120 for adults, $115 for seniors, and $110 for kids 14 and under; half-day trips $80 for adults, $75 for seniors, and $70 for kids 14 and under. No license is required, and rod, reel, bait, and tackle are supplied. Bring your own food and drink.

GOLF The area's best golf resorts are in Ponte Vedra Beach—a half-hour's drive north on A1A, closer to Jacksonville than St. Augustine and the home of PGA's global headquarters (see p. 483 for details).

The **Tournament Players Club (TPC) Sawgrass** ★★★ (tpc.com/sawgrass; © **904/273-3235**) offers the **Tour Player Experience** (tpc.com/sawgrass/tour-player-experience), where duffers will be treated like pros and have access to the exclusive wing of the 77,000-square-foot clubhouse where only actual pros, such as Vijay Singh and Jim Furyk, are allowed. You also get a personal caddy wearing a bib with your name on it. The experience also includes a stay at the Sawgrass Marriott Golf Resort and Spa, dinner, spa services, instruction at the Tour Academy, and a golf gift bag that includes balls, marker, and shirt. Rates start at $2,755 per person.

At World Golf Village, 12 miles north of St. Augustine, at exit 95A off I-95, the **Slammer & The Squire** and the **King & The Bear** (golfwgv.com; © **904/940-6088**) together offer 36 holes amid a wildlife preserve. Locals say they're not as challenging as their greens fees, which start at around $185 and go up, way up, from there. Specials, however, are available offseason and off times. For those not schooled in golf history, the "Slammer" is in honor of Sam Sneed, the "Squire" is for Gene Sarazen, the "King" is Arnold Palmer, and the "Bear" is Jack Nicklaus. Palmer and Nicklaus collaborated in designing their course.

Nicklaus also had a hand in the stunning course at the **Ocean Hammock Golf Club** ★★ at the Hammock Beach Golf Resort & Spa (hammockbeach.com; © **386/477-4600**), on A1A, in Palm Coast, about halfway between St. Augustine and Daytona Beach. With 6 of its holes skirting the beach, it is the first truly oceanside course built in Florida since the 1920s.

There are only a few courses in St. Augustine, including the **St. Augustine Shores Golf Club** ★★, 707 Shores Blvd., off U.S. 1 (capstonegolf.net; © **904/794-4653**), a par-70, 18-hole course with lots of water, a lighted driving range and putting green, and a restaurant and lounge. Greens fees are usually around $30ish, including cart.

WATERSPORTS Jet skis and equipment for surfing and windsurfing can be rented at **Surf Station,** 1020 Anastasia Blvd. (A1A), a block south of the Alligator Farm (surfstationstore.com; © **904/471-9463**); and at **Beaches Marina,** 250 Vilano Road St. (beachesmarina.com; © **904/429-9198**), which also rents Wave-Runners and pontoons, and offers water tours.

Shopping

The winding streets of the historic district are home to dozens of **antiques stores** and **galleries** stocked full of original paintings, sculptures, bric-a-brac, fine furnishings, china, and other treasures. Brick-lined **Aviles Street,** a block from the river, has an especially good mix of shops for browsing, as does **St. George Street** south of the visitor center, and the Uptown area on **San Marco Avenue** a few blocks north of the center. The **Alcazar Courtyard Shops,** at the Lightner Museum (✆ **904/824-2874;** p. 460), have a good selection of antiques. **Visit St. Augustine** has a helpful list of antiques shops at visitstaugustine.com/things-to-do/antiques.

For another type of treat, **Whetstone Chocolates ★★**, 139 King St. (whetstonechocolates.com; ✆ **904/825-1700**), has been making confections in St. Augustine since 1967. Chocolate-tasting tours are offered daily and are $10.95 for adults, $8.45 for children 5 to 17. Whetstone has a retail outlet at 42 St. George St., in the historic district, and another on Anastasia Island at 13 Anastasia Blvd.

Where to Stay

There are plenty of moderate and inexpensive motels and hotels in St. Augustine, including an exceptional Best Western (see below). A nice spot on the beach that's just 6 miles from Old Town is **La Fiesta Ocean Inn & Suites ★★**, 810 A1A Beach Blvd. (lafiestainn.com; ✆ **904/456-0942**). Each room or suite features a microwave and refrigerator. There's a heated pool and gardens. Best of all, guests enjoy a daily complimentary breakfast, delivered to their room. Rates range from $108 to $195. New on the beach in 2023 was the three-story, 120-room **Hyatt Place St. Augustine/Vilano Beach ★★**, 117 Vilano Rd. (hyatt.com; ✆ **904/295-1111**), located just steps from the sand and with a nice rooftop bar. Rates $136 to $352.

Once a ramshackle fishing camp, the **Devil's Elbow Fishing Resort ★★**, 7507 A1A S., St. Augustine (devilselbowfishingresort.com; ✆ **904/471-0398**), offers 10 homey waterfront rental cottages built in the classic Old Florida style with covered porches, tin roofs, roof-top cupolas, fully equipped kitchens, and hardwood floors. They also rent all kinds of boats, and offer slips to guests. Cottage from $300 to $600 daily.

If you're coming on a weekend, expect the higher end of the listed rates—almost all accommodations increase their prices on weekends, when the town is most crowded with visitors. Winter rates are also higher than summer. St. Johns County charges a 12.5% tax on hotel bills (6% bed tax plus 6.5% state tax).

HOTELS & MOTELS

Best Western Bayfront ★★ It's all about location, location, location, when it comes to this motel, formerly known as the Monterey Inn, overlooking the Matanzas Bay, right next to the Castillo de San Marcos National Monument and within walking distance of so many attractions of the Old City. Rooms are not especially spacious, but clean and almost stylish. The grounds are immaculate, especially the outdoor pool. There's no restaurant on-site, but there are restaurants within walking distance.

16 Av. Menendez (btw. Cuna and Hypolita sts.), St. Augustine. bestwestern.com. ✆ **904/824-4482.** 59 units. $179–$311 double. Parking $20. **Amenities:** Heated outdoor pool; free Wi-Fi.

Casa Monica Resort & Spa, Autograph Collection ★★★ If you're not a B&B kind of person, then Casa Monica is the place to stay in St. Augustine; it will still give you a feeling for the city's history, but with a bit more anonymity than you get at a B&B. Set in a Moorish Revival hotel built in 1888, it has an art

A SWASHBUCKLING budget inn

Families on a budget arrrrrrgh welcome at the **Pirate Haus Inn ★★**, 32 Treasury St., at Charlotte Street (piratehaus.com; *𝒞* **904/808-1999**), in the middle of the historic district. Done up in a pirate theme, this Spanish-style building has a communal kitchen, living room, and rooftop terrace plus five private rooms on the second floor (no elevator). The Jungle Room has a king bed and bunk beds; the Tree Room, Pirate Room, and Map Room sleep six with two sets of bunk beds; and if you choose the Mafia Room you'll sleep with the fishes (literally—there's fish decor). That last one has a king and futon. Room rates range from $128 to $199 and include Wi-Fi, board games, use of the house guitar if you play, the lodging's famous all-you-can-eat pancake breakfast (with "strong coffee approved by SpaceX as an alternate rocket fuel"), and "occasional free pirate beer." No bachelor/ette parties are allowed here because, as they say, "they ruin our beauty sleep."

---

gallery in the lobby, and lots of artistic touches throughout, like Moorish-style rouge carpet, elegantly appointed furnishings with gold accents, and sexy, plush red-velvet-tufted headboards. All units have big bathrooms equipped with high-end toiletries and either a large walk-in shower or a tub/shower combination. The five suites in the building's two tile-topped towers and fortresslike central turret are each uniquely decorated, and one is bi-level. A second-floor outdoor pool is nice, but better is the access to the **Serenata Beach Club** (serenataclub.com) less than 15 minutes away on South Ponte Vedra Beach. Do try to take advantage of that if you can. Service is tops.

95 Cordova St. (at King St.), St. Augustine. marriott.com. *𝒞* **904/827-1888.** 137 units. $220–$576 double. Valet parking $39. Pet fee $150 for first pet, $50 more for 2. **Amenities:** Restaurant; cafe; bar; babysitting; concierge; fitness center; Jacuzzi; heated outdoor pool; room service; free Wi-Fi.

The Collector Inn ★★★ Once the home of the Dow Museum of Historic Houses and built in 1906, this "carefully curated" adults-only 30-room hotel is a haven for those seeking history but with modern amenities. You won't smell the must of old times, but you will appreciate the bones that have been bolstered by bougie touches like triple-sheeted king-size beds, kitchenettes, rain showers, and a fabulous bar, **The Well,** open daily from 3 to 11pm. There's a beautiful, heated pool in a courtyard with fire pits. Included in the $35 daily amenity fee is an excellent European-style continental breakfast, a fascinating property history tour, outdoor movies, bikes, afternoon snacks, and valet parking.

149 Cordova St. thecollectorinn.com. *𝒞* **904209-5800.** 30 units. $206–$339 petite Queen room. **Amenities:** Bar; heated outdoor pool; bikes; free Wi-Fi.

BED & BREAKFASTS

St. Augustine has more than two dozen bed-and-breakfasts in restored historic homes—and one boat! They all provide free parking, breakfast, 24-hour refreshments, and plenty of atmosphere, but most don't accept children (check before booking). Those listed below are in the historic district. For more choices, go to **St.**

Augustine Historic Inns (staugustineinns.com), for descriptions of its member properties.

Bayfront Westcott House Bed & Breakfast Inn ★★★

Overlooking Matanzas Bay, this romantic, Key West–style wood-frame house offers uncluttered views from the porch, the second-story veranda, and a shady courtyard. The rooms—some with private balconies, two-person whirlpool tubs, and fireplaces—are exquisitely furnished. Yours might have authentic Victorian furniture including a brass bed made up with a white quilt and lace dust ruffle. Beds all have hypoallergenic, microfiber linens by The Comphy Company, which earns its name. A nightly social hour features wine, beer, sodas, and hors d'oeuvres, and the fabulous, full breakfasts are gourmet affairs. Children over the age of 12 are welcome.

146 Av. Menendez (btw. Bridge and Francis sts.), St. Augustine. westcotthouse.com. © **904/825-4602.** 16 units. $252–$439 double. Rates include parking, full breakfast, and social hour. **Amenities:** Concierge; free Wi-Fi.

Carriage Way Bed & Breakfast ★★

Primarily occupying an 1883 Victorian wood-frame house fronted by Mexican petunias and topiaries, this family-owned B&B is more comfortable and homey than fancy or formal. Books and games are provided in the parlor. Guest rooms in the main house are furnished with simple reproductions, including king and queen beds with pillow top mattresses and luxe sheets. One room retains its original fireplace. Two rooms can accommodate more than two people. For more privacy, two more rooms are down the street in the Cottage, a clapboard house built in 1885. The Cottage has a living room and kitchen, and both of its bedrooms have claw-foot tubs. The Amethyst and Gold rooms have two-person Jacuzzis, while the Silver Room has a private courtyard. Breakfasts are made to order. They also offer complimentary drinks, and cookies in the afternoon.

70 Cuna St. (btw. Cordova and Spanish sts.), St. Augustine. carriageway.com. © **904/829-2467.** 14 units. $202–$369 double. Rates include full breakfast, drinks, cookies, parking. **Amenities:** Concierge; Wi-Fi.

Casa de Solana Bed & Breakfast ★★★

Owned by an interior designer, this St. Augustine landmark has been beautifully restored with British colonial furnishings and accessories. It also happens to be the 7th oldest house on St. Augustine's oldest street. Just 1 block from the bayfront, the B&B offers a delicious breakfast (quiches, stuffed crepes, eggs Florentine, and more), evening wine in the inn's garden courtyard, loaner bikes, and more. Eight out of the 10 rooms have fireplaces and whirlpool tubs. One warning (that will be an enticement for some): This B&B is said to be haunted. The manager says that on occasion people have reported having their shoulders shaken in the middle of the night.

24 Aviles St., St. Augustine. casadesolana.com. © **904/824-3355.** 10 units. $183–$289 double. Rates include full breakfast and complimentary social hour and dessert. **Amenities:** Bikes; free Wi-Fi.

The Kenwood Inn ★★★

Built in 1865, the Kenwood Inn is the only remaining hotel structure of its size from St. Augustine's Gilded Age. In St. Augustine's most historic district, the Victorian-style inn boasts two living rooms, two dining rooms, and guest rooms and suites that are larger and more private than most other B&B accommodations in converted single-family homes. Some feature Jacuzzi tubs, and balconies with hammocks. Also unique to St. Augustine, it boasts a large outdoor saltwater pool and spacious sunning patio with chaise lounges. A gourmet buffet breakfast features hot entrees such as eggs Benedict, quiches, and waffles. Bloody Marys and champagne mimosas are offered on weekends. There's a nightly wine social and snacks, and the guest pantry is stocked with iced tea, lemonade, water, and coffee. Children are welcome, but a fee of $25 per child, per night pertains to kids 3 to 12.

38 Marine St. (at Bridge St.), St. Augustine. thekenwoodinn.com. © **904/824-2116.** 14 units. $219–$379 double. Pet fee $35–$50. Rates include breakfast, evening wine social, and parking. **Amenities:** Bikes; pool; Wi-Fi.

Victorian House Bed & Breakfast ★★

This 1897-vintage Victorian B&B has a wraparound porch and an adjoining old store, now dubbed the Carriage House. Victorian antiques adorn all units. All rooms—five in the main house, seven in the Carriage House—have private bathrooms, some with double Jacuzzi tubs. Some also have fireplaces, and private porches. Victorian House's location between the two oldest streets is an added perk for history buffs, but for those who relish privacy and quiet, its location away from the noise—with the exception of the clopping of a horse or two—is priceless. Breakfasts are abundant and delicious, as are the cookies offered all day long, much to many a dieter's dismay.

11 Cadiz St. (btw. Aviles and Charlotte sts.), St. Augustine. victorianhousebnb.com. © **904/824-5214.** 12 units. $227–$330 double. Rates include parking, full breakfast, and social hour. **Amenities:** Free Wi-Fi.

Where to Dine

In a town with as much tourist traffic as St. Augustine, there are, of course, a number of tourist trap restaurants. But on the whole, the food here, even at the popular eateries, is fairly priced and of good quality. And spicy! St. Augustine is the home of the Datil pepper, one of the hottest around. Lots of local restaurants have their own Datil pepper sauces and even "Datil Dust," which is used to heat up any dish. **August Heat Co.'s Hot Stuff,** in the historic shopping district at 34 Treasury St. (augustheatco.com; © 904/824-4944), features an assortment of hard-to-find sauces and sauces made exclusively with Datils in St. Augustine. Also check out datildoit.com.

The historic district has a branch of Tampa's famous **Columbia ★★**, 98 St. George St., at Hypolita Street (columbiarestaurant.com; © 904/824-3341). Like the original in Ybor City (p. 316), this one has Spanish architecture, including intricate tile work and courtyards with fountains. And if a barbecue hankering hits you, head directly to **Brisky's ★★**, 3009 N. Ponce de Leon Blvd. (© 904/907-2122), which slow cooks brisket to a T. For chili heads, the jalapeno popper burgers at **GAS Full Service Restaurant ★★**, 9 Anastasia Blvd. (gasrestaurant.com; © **904/217-0326**), are the bomb.

Catch 27 ★★ SEAFOOD

This place is named Catch for several reasons, one being the obvious—it's a seafood spot—and another because if you walk too fast, you may miss it. Then there's the Joseph Heller reference: Serving only fresh seafood bought locally on a daily basis, Catch 27 creates ordering dilemmas, offering on any given day temptations that range from a stellar Minorcan clam chowder in a smoky, spicy broth, to a simply seasoned blackened Florida triggerfish. Fish tacos with a side of black beans and rice are a favorite here, too, kicked up several notches with the local Datil pepper hot sauce. Non-fish eaters needn't steer clear, as they have several turf offerings, including a tender, red-wine-braised brisket. With just a few tables inside the clean-lined modern dining room, and on the cozy little patio outside, reservations are strongly recommended.

17 Hypolita St. catchtwentyseven.com. **904/217-8190.** Main courses $19–$38. Mon–Thurs 5–9pm; Fri 4–10pm; Sat 3–10pm; Sun 3–9pm.

Collage ★★★ NEW AMERICAN Quaint and romantic, in a tiny house reminiscent of something you'd find after getting lost on a cobblestoned European street, Collage is named for its multifaceted menu. If you want a "nice dinner" to celebrate a special occasion, this place would be it. The tablecloths, candles, and flowers certainly help set a romantic mood, and the food is first rate. Think: bison tenderloin, Asian-inspired duck, and a "Land and Sea Medaglioni" (egg noodle ravioli stuffed with braised short rib, squid ink ravioli stuffed with lobster mousse, all served in a roasted piquillo pepper sauce) that's superb. The wine list is impressive, and service is exceptional, thanks to a staff that genuinely seems to know and love food.

60 Hypolita St. (btw. Spanish and Cordova sts.). collagestaug.com. **904/829-0055.** Main courses $56–$70. Sun–Thurs 5–8:45pm; Fri–Sat 5–9:45pm.

The Floridian ★★★ SOUTHERN As hard as it is to find a native Floridian, it's even harder to find a restaurant that's wholly devoted to the cuisine and ingredients of the state. Enter the appropriately named The Floridian, which takes its moniker very seriously, right down to using purveyors that source from northeast and north-central Florida. Menus are seasonal and change often so a dinner might include local shrimp served with miso tomato aioli and Datil jam or maybe a "Florida Sunshine Salad," with your choice of blackened protein served over mixed greens with Florida strawberries, roasted sweet potatoes, candied pecans, house-pickled beets, local honey, and Sweet Grass Dairy's Asher blue cheese. Entrees include the Not Your Mama's Meatloaf Sandwich: Florida-grown, all-natural beef, baked with sweet onions, topped with spicy Datil ketchup. You can also go full Southern and add pimento cheese. Local and regional organic craft beers and biodynamic wines are also on the menu. And you gotta love the kooky, Floridian country-style decor, complete with a canoe hanging upside down from the ceiling. The no-reservations policy makes The Floridian a hot ticket, but if you call in advance you may be able to snag what they call "priority seating."

72 Spanish St. thefloridianstaug.com. **904/829-0655.** Main courses $12.50–$30. Wed–Mon 11am–close.

Gypsy Cab Co. ★★ NEW AMERICAN Billing itself as a temple of "urban cuisine," this high-energy establishment, with gaudy neon stripes outside and art-filled dining rooms inside, has a creative menu that changes often, though black-bean soup is a constant winner. The Chicken Buena Vista with pimentos, green onion, and Canadian bacon and the Cab burger (served until 4pm) are always on offer, and definite favorites. As a capper, I recommend peanut butter mousse or Key lime pie. Also of note is the house salad dressing, which is so good they sell it by the bottle. Tuesday is trivia night here and it's like *Jeopardy!* but with booze.

828 Anastasia Blvd. (A1A, at Ingram St., east of the Bridge of Lions). gypsycab.com. **904/824-8244.** Main courses $19–$28. Mon, Wed–Fri 11am–10pm; Tues 4:30–9pm; Sat–Sun 9am–10pm.

Prohibition Kitchen ★★★ GASTROPUB A 1920s-era-themed bar and restaurant with an industrial speakeasy style and the longest bar in town, this place is decked out in 400-year-old heart of pine ceiling boards that were also used to create the bar and booths. As vintage as it looks, the menu is thoroughly modern, showcasing local farmers, butchers, bakers, and fishermen, whose goods shine in dishes like the PK Poutine, where Canada takes a field trip to Historic St. Aug in the form of fries topped with smoked cheddar mornay, pork belly, sour cream, and chives; and the authentically spicy Datil chicken wings. A carb-heavy entrée we love: the flounder platter with mac and cheese *and* hushpuppies. Cocktails are killer, from the make-your-own Old Fashioned to cocktails on tap. Live music and a late-night menu bring in the party people.

119 St. George St. pkstaug.com. **904/209-5704.** Main courses $18–$32. Daily 11am–10pm; Fri–Sat late night menu 10pm–1am.

The Purple Olive Restaurant & Wine Lounge ★★ INTERNATIONAL An appealing and friendly bistro, the Purple Olive has a seasonal selection of small plates, flatbreads, and entrees by chef/owner Peter Kenney, whose menu takes you on a global tour of sorts. We're talking appetizers such as a delicious British Isles cheese plate or Mediterranean lamb meatballs; small plates like grilled stuffed eggplant or garlic shrimp; flatbreads with filet mignon and gorgonzola; and entrees such as their grilled Maple Leaf Farms duck breast. The chef will happily pair any of their very good wines with your meal.

4255 A1A S. purple-olive.com. **904/461-1250.** Main courses $18–$34. Wed–Sat 4–8pm.

St. Augustine Fish Camp ★★ SEAFOOD For a southern spin on your typical seafood fare, and eye-popping views, this is the pick. Oysters are fresh, peel-and-eat shrimp come in spicy or regular, the fried green tomatoes are crisp and tart, and for those who consider reptile to be seafood, there's fried gator tail with Datil pepper aioli. Stay simple with the fried fish sandwich with tartar sauce, or go for the iron skillet fried brook trout with arugula, bacon, crushed potatoes, and deviled egg sauce. Both are topnotch. There are three other locations: **Palm Valley Fish Camp,** 299 Roscoe Blvd. N., in Ponte Vedra Beach (**904/285-3200**), **Julington Creek Fish Camp,** 12760 San Jose Blvd., Jacksonville (**904/886-2267**), and **North Beach Fish Camp,** 100 First St., Neptune Beach (**904/249-3474**).

142 Riberia St. staugustinefishcamp.com. **904/827-7000.** Main courses $17–$44. Sun, Tues–Thurs 11am–9pm; Mon 4–9pm; Fri–Sat 11am–10pm.

St. Augustine After Dark

Especially on weekends, the Old Town is full of partiers making the rounds of dozens of bars, clubs, and restaurants. For up-to-date details on what's happening in town, check the local daily, the *St. Augustine Record* (staugustine.com), or the irreverent *Folio Weekly* (folioweekly.com). Another nighttime activity: taking one of the many ghost tours (p. 466).

And if you enjoy combining sightseeing with sipping, head to **San Sebastian Winery ★**, 157 King St. (sansebastianwinery.com; **904/826-1594**), in one of Henry Flagler's old East Coast Railway buildings a few blocks from downtown St. Augustine. The winery offers free guided tours and free (!) tastings of wines produced by their vineyards in Central Florida. Apparently, Florida's muscadine grapes are high in fiber and antioxidants, so drink up! The third floor of the winery,

Patrons enjoying cocktails at the Ice Plant's bar.

the **Cellar Upstairs Bar and Restaurant,** is a wine and jazz bar that serves appetizers, charcuterie, sandwiches, salads, wines, and beer.

For evening booze, locals' fave, **Ann O'Malley's ★★**, 23 Orange St., near the Old City Gate (annomalleys.com; © 904/825-4040), is St. Augustine's oldest Irish pub and is open until 2am on weekends. Besides the selection of ales, stouts, and drafts, it has live music, bingo, and trivia nights. **Barley Republic Pub & Culture ★★★**, 48 Spanish St. (© 904/547-2023), is open daily until 2am and features live music, small plates, and handcrafted cocktails.

Also popular with locals, **Mill Top Tavern ★★**, 19½ St. George St., at the Fort (milltoptavern.com; © 904/829-2329), is a warm and rustic tavern in a 19th-century mill building (the waterwheel is still outside). Weather permitting, it's an open-air space. There's music here every day from noon to midnight. For the oldest lounge in the oldest city, **Tradewinds Tropical Lounge ★★★**, 124 Charlotte St. (tradewindslounge.com; ©904/826-1590), is a fab, tiki-themed bar with live music, rich history, and strong drinks. Continuing with the topic of watering holes, the **Ice Plant ★★★**, 110 Riberia St. (iceplantbar.com; © 904/829-6553), is housed in a circa 1927 ice plant. The plant's original bridge crane sits on rails above the bar at this industrial-chic, cocktail den open until midnight on weekdays, 2am on Friday and Saturday.

Over at the Casablanca Inn, 24 Avenida Menendez, is the **Tini Martini ★★★** (casablancainn.com/martini-bar; © 904/829-0928), cozy inside and with a cool patio outside that sometimes hosts live music and movie screenings. It's open until at least midnight on weekdays, and 1am on Friday and Saturday. Another highly spirited speakeasy is the aptly named **Prohibition Kitchen** ★★★ (p. 474), with nightly live music, killer cocktails, and a late-night menu. Lastly, **Stogie's Jazz Club & Listening** ★★★, 36 Charlotte St. (© **904/826-4008**), is housed in an historic cottage and features craft beers, cocktails, and yes, excellent live music until at least 2am.

JACKSONVILLE

36 miles S of the Georgia border; 134 miles NE of Orlando; 340 miles N of Miami

Once infamous for its smelly paper mills, the sprawling metropolis of Jacksonville—residents call it "Jax," from its airport abbreviation—is now one of the South's insurance and banking capitals. Today it's awash in hotels, restaurants, attractions, and clubs, especially in suburban areas near the interstate highways. Aside from that, there are 20 miles of Atlantic Ocean beaches upon which to sun and swim, championship golf courses, and an abundance of beautiful and historic national and state parks to roam.

Spanning the broad, curving St. Johns River, downtown Jacksonville is a vibrant center of activity weekdays and on weekend afternoons and evenings. Besides downtown, locals head to the shops, restaurants, and bars in **San Marco,** a charming, walkable neighborhood south of downtown; **Riverside Avondale,** a historic district on the west bank of the St. Johns River; and Riverside's funky **Five Points,** built in the 1930s as Jacksonville's first shopping area outside of downtown.

Essentials

GETTING THERE **Jacksonville International Airport,** on the city's north side, about 12 miles from downtown (flyjacksonville.com; © **904/741-2000**), is served by Allegiant, American, Continental, Delta, Frontier, JetBlue, Southwest, Sun Country, and United.

The skyline of Jacksonville.

All of the major players have rental-car booths at the airport.

Airport shuttles and Ubers are available, but we recommend **ZTrip** (ztrip.com/jacksonville; © **904/222-222**), which is Jacksonville's own ride-sharing service, and has replaced the city's taxi companies (down to being hailable, if you don't want to call them on the phone or ping them online).

There's an **Amtrak** station in Jacksonville at 3570 Clifford Lane, off U.S. 1, just north of 45th Street (amtrak.com; © **800/USA-RAIL** [872-7245]).

GETTING AROUND In general, you're better off having a car if you want to explore this vast area. To get around downtown Jacksonville, however, you can take the **Skyway** (jtafla.com/ride-jta/skyway), a 2½-mile monorail system crossing the St. Johns River to Kings Avenue on the Southbank. The fully automated Skyway has eight stations, five in downtown, three on the Southbank. The Skyway operates Monday through Friday from 6am to 9pm, Saturday and Sunday for special events only. **JTA**'s buses connect to the Skyway. Fares are $1.75 and free for seniors 65 and over.

There's also **ZTrip** (see above), a local answer to Uber with fair pricing that can either be contacted over the phone, online, or by hailing a ride from the sidewalk.

Out at the beaches, the **St. Johns River Ferry** (ferry.jtafla.com) shuttles vehicles across the river between Mayport, an Old Florida fishing village on the south side, and Fort George Island, on the north shore. The boats run daily; times vary, so look at the website for the current schedule. One-way fare is $7 per two-axle private vehicle on weekdays, $8 on weekends, $1 per pedestrian or bicyclist. Even if you have to wait 30 minutes for the next ferry, the 5-minute ride greatly shortens the trip between the Jacksonville beaches and Amelia Island.

Bikers and hikers traveling along the 3,000-mile East Coast Greenway connecting major cities from Calais, Maine, to Key West can now take the "Blueway Bypass" thanks to the **Amelia River Cruises** (ameliarivercruises.com; © **904/26-9972**), which runs a minimum of three round-trips per day from Amelia Island, Florida, to Cumberland Island, Georgia, best known for the place where steel tycoon Andrew Carnegie had an estate, and where the late John F. Kennedy, Jr., married the late Carolyn Bessette. The trip takes approximately 1 hour and features live narration of the region's history, natural features, and wildlife. You'll also get to explore each of the cities. The trip costs $35 round-trip per adult, $33 for seniors, and $29 for kids.

VISITOR INFORMATION Visit **Jacksonville** (visitjacksonville.com; © **800/733-2668**) has a useful website.

Exploring the Area

Camp Milton Historic Preserve ★★
A key Confederate installation during the Civil War, Camp Milton served as a base for skirmishes between Union and Confederate soldiers. After years of neglect, the 124-acre park was preserved and is now a thriving nature preserve for pines, magnolias, blackberries, foxes, bobcats, armadillos, and hawks. A boardwalk leads into the woods where the remains of earthworks built by Confederate soldiers still stand. Reenactors dressed in period costumes talk about life in Jacksonville circa 1884, and for Civil War buffs, there are reenactors dressed in Union and Confederate regalia who tell the story of the not-so-bloody spats on the site back in the day. Every year the park holds a reenactment of events leading up to the Battle of Olustee, usually around

the last week in January. In addition to the historical markers throughout the park, there are bike paths, nature trails, and an interpretive center.

1175 Halsema Rd. timucuanparks.org. **904/824-1606.** Free admission. Daily 9am–5pm. Take I-10 west, exit 351; turn left onto Chaffee Rd. N; turn left onto Beaver St., U.S. 90; turn right on Halsema Rd.

Cummer Museum of Art & Gardens ★

Built on the grounds of a private Tudor mansion, this museum's permanent collection encompasses works from 2000 B.C. to the present. It's especially rich in American Impressionist paintings, 18th-century porcelain, and 18th-century Japanese woodblock prints. I find the art here a bit boring and too focused on landscapes, but that's my taste. Frankly—and art snobs may gasp at this statement—the landscaping of the museum is more spectacular. Don't miss the stunning Italian and English gardens set on the scenic St. Johns River. The museum hosts temporary and traveling exhibits, and sponsors a multitude of activities, so check the website to see what's happening.

829 Riverside Ave. (btw. Post and Fisk sts.). cummermuseum.org. **904/356-6857.** Admission $10 adults, $6 seniors 66 and over and military, $6 students and children 5 and under. Tues, Fri 11am–9pm; Wed–Thurs 11am–4pm; Sat 10am–4pm; Sun noon–4pm.

Jacksonville Zoo and Gardens ★★

Located between downtown and the airport, this environmentally sensitive zoo has become one of the Southeast's best. While the zoo's **Wild Florida** area presents 2¼ acres of local wildlife—including black bears, red wolves, Florida panthers, reptiles, birds, and alligators—the main exhibits (**The African Forest**) feature an extensive and growing collection of lions, rhinos, elephants, antelopes, cheetahs, western lowland gorillas, and other African wildlife. You'll enter the 120-acre park through an authentic thatched roof built by 24 Zulu craftsmen. Other highlights: the **Manatee Critical Care Center** rescues the lovable floating mammals and sends them back into the wild. The **Range of the Jaguar** exhibit focuses on a neotropical rainforest setting that can be found in Central or South America spotlighting jaguars, howler monkeys, golden lion tamarins, tapirs, capybaras, giant river otters, anteaters, and a variety of bird, amphibian, fish, and reptile species, including the anaconda. The **Asian Bamboo Garden** at the entry of the Asian animal exhibits has over 111 plant species and 29 varieties of bamboo, including the Parker's Hawaiian Giant, which can grow to 70-plus feet. Kids will especially love the 2½-acre **Play Park and Splash Ground** with mazes, a splash ground, a treehouse, and a rock-climbing area. Whether you go on foot or by train, allow at least 3 hours to tour this vast zoo.

370 Zoo Pkwy. jacksonvillezoo.org. **904/757-4462.** General admission $29.95 adults, $27.95 seniors, $24.95 children 3–12, free for children 2 and under. Tickets cheaper online and booked in advance. Daily 9am–5pm. Take I-95 N. to Heckscher Dr. (exit 358A) and follow the signs.

MOCA Jacksonville ★★

This museum of contemporary art is one of the Southeast's largest, housed in the renovated Western Union Telegraph Building. It also happens to be the second oldest contemporary art museum in the country, having turned 100 in 2024 (the Phillips Collection in Washington, D.C., is the oldest). Its permanent collection of over 1,000 works is like a Who's Who of contemporary art, and includes seminal pieces by Joan Mitchell, Frank Stella, Keith Haring, Jasper Johns, Richard Serra, Robert Mapplethorpe, and Nam June Paik,

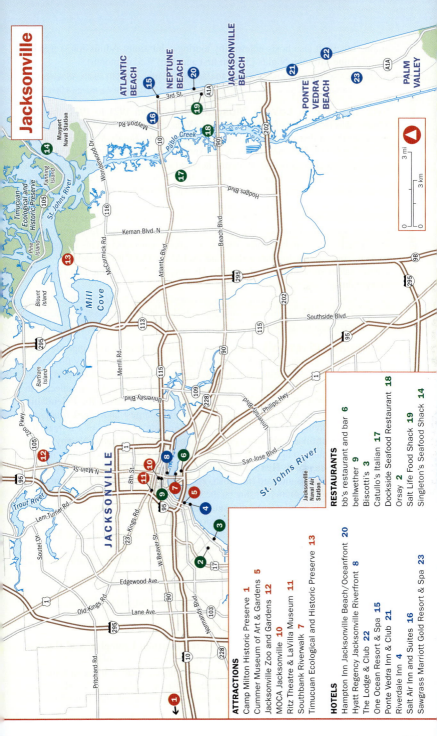

among others. It also hosts noteworthy touring exhibitions. Admission is free on Florida Blue Museum Nights (5–9pm first and third Wed of month).

333 N. Laura St. mocajacksonville.org. ✆ **904/366-6911**. Admission $10 adults; $6 seniors 60 and over, military, youth 6–17. Tues–Sun 11am–5pm; 1st and 3rd Wed of the month 11am–9pm.

Ritz Theatre & LaVilla Museum ★★   From 1921 to 1971, the Ritz Theatre was the center of cultural life in LaVilla, an African-American neighborhood so vibrant that it was known as the Harlem of the South. Many entertainers played the Ritz before moving on to the Apollo Theater in the real Harlem. Most of LaVilla's small clapboard "shotgun" houses (so called because you could fire a shotgun through the central hallway to the back room and not hit anything) have been torn down in anticipation of urban renewal, but the Ritz has been rebuilt and is once again a center of the city's cultural life. Only the northwest corner of the building, including the Ritz sign, is original, but the newer, 426-seat theater captures the spirit of vaudevillian times. Off the lobby, the LaVilla Museum recounts local Black history and exhibits artwork. Regularly scheduled events include free spoken-word nights, free art walks, and Puttin' on The Ritz, modeled after the famous talent show at Harlem's Apollo Theater, at 7:30pm on the first Friday of every month.

829 N. Davis St. (btw. State and Union sts.). ritzjacksonville.com. ✆ **904/632-5555**. Admission $8. Tues–Fri 10am–4pm. From downtown, take Main St. north, turn left (west) on State St. to theater and museum on Davis St.

Southbank Riverwalk ★★   Bordering the St. Johns River, opposite Jacksonville Landing, this 1.25-mile concrete zigzag boardwalk is usually filled with joggers, tourists, folks sitting on benches, and lovers walking hand-in-hand, all of them watching the riverboats, the shorebirds, and downtown's skyline reflected in the water. There's also a kayak launch. At 200 feet in diameter, the **Friendship Fountain,** near the west end, is one of the world's largest and tallest fountains, capable of spraying 17,000 gallons of water a minute to heights of 120 feet; it's especially beautiful at night when illuminated by 265 colored lights. Nearby, you'll pass military memorials, a small museum dedicated to the city's history, and the **Museum of Science & History of Jacksonville (MOSH)** ★★, at Museum Circle and San Marco Boulevard (themosh.org; ✆ **904/396-6674**). MOSH is an interactive children's museum focusing on the science and history of Northeast Florida. One of its stars is an allosaurus dinosaur skeleton. It also has a small planetarium, with shows included in museum admission: $19.50 for adults, $16.95 for seniors 55 and up, and $16.95 for children ages 3 to 12. The museum is open Monday through Friday from 10am to 5pm, Saturday from 10am to 6pm, and Sunday from noon to 5pm. The Riverwalk is the scene of special MOSH programs, seafood fests, parties, parades, and arts-and-crafts festivals.

On the south bank of St. Johns River, flanking Main St. Bridge, btw. San Marco Blvd. and Ferry St. ✆ **904/396-4900**. Take I-95 N. to Prudential Dr. exit, turn right, and follow the signs.

Timucuan National Park

Unusual for a national park, the 46,000-acre **Timucuan Ecological and Historic Preserve** ★★ (nps.gov/timu/index.htm) hasn't been hacked off from the rest of the community and drawn within arbitrary boundaries. Instead, it is a vast, intriguing system of sites (untouched wilderness, historic buildings, and informative exhibits on the area's natural history) joined by rural roads alongside tumbledown fish camps, trailer parks, strip malls, condominiums, and stately old homes. The park is named for the American Indians who inhabited central and north Florida some 1,000 years before European settlers arrived.

Entry to all park facilities is free (though donations are accepted). The **visitor centers** at Fort Caroline National Memorial and Zephaniah Kingsley Plantation (see below) are open daily from 9am to 5pm, except New Year's Day, Thanksgiving, and Christmas. The **Theodore Roosevelt Area** is open daily from 7am to 8pm during daylight saving time and daily from 7am to 5pm during standard time; closed for Christmas.

SOUTH OF THE RIVER

The preserve's prime attractions are 14 miles northeast of downtown on the south bank of the St. Johns River. Your starting point is the **Fort Caroline National Memorial** ★★, 12713 Ft. Caroline Rd. (nps.gov/timu/learn/historyculture/foca.htm; ⓒ **904/641-7155**), which serves as the preserve's visitor center. This was the site of the 16th-century French Huguenot settlement that was wiped out by the Spanish who landed at St. Augustine. This two-thirds-size replica shows you what the original was like. You can see archaeological artifacts and two well-produced half-hour videos highlighting the area as well.

The fort sits at the northwestern edge of the 600-acre **Theodore Roosevelt Area** ★★★, a beautiful woodland and marshland rich in history, which has been undisturbed since the Civil War. On a 2-mile hike along a centuries-old park trail, you'll see a wide variety of birds, wildflowers, and maritime hammock forest. Bring binoculars, because such birds as endangered wood storks, great and snowy egrets, ospreys, hawks, and painted buntings make their homes here in spring and summer. On the ground, you might catch sight of a gray fox or raccoon. You may also want to bring a picnic basket and blanket to spread beneath the ancient oak trees that shade the banks of the wide and winding St. Johns River. After the trail crosses Hammock Creek, you're in ancient Timucuan country, where their ancestors lived as far back as 500 B.C. Farther along is the site of a wilderness cabin that belonged to the reclusive brothers Willie and Saxon Browne, who lived without the modern conveniences of indoor plumbing or electricity until the last brother's death in 1960.

Fort Caroline.

If you're here on a weekend, take the fascinating 1½-hour guided tour of the fort and Theodore Roosevelt Area, offered every Saturday and Sunday (when weather and staffing permit). Contact the fort for details and schedules.

The **Ribault Monument,** on St. Johns Bluff about a half-mile east of the fort, was erected in 1924 to commemorate the arrival in 1562 of French Huguenot Jean Ribault, who died defending Fort Caroline from the Spanish. It's worth a stop for the dramatic view of the area.

To get here from downtown Jacksonville, take Atlantic Boulevard (Fla. 10) east, make a left on Monument Road, and turn right on Fort Caroline Road; the Theodore Roosevelt Area is entered from Mt. Pleasant Road, about 1 mile southeast of the fort (look for the trailhead parking sign and follow the narrow dirt road to the parking lot).

NORTH OF THE RIVER

On the north side of the river, history buffs will appreciate the **Kingsley Plantation** ★★★, at 11676 Palmetto Ave., on Fort George Island (nps.gov/timu; © **904/251-3537**). During the 18th and 19th centuries, many people came to Florida. Some, like Zephaniah Kingsley, sought to make their fortunes by obtaining land and establishing plantations. Others were forced to come to Florida to work on those plantations, their labor providing wealth to the people who owned them. Some of the enslaved would later become free landowners, struggling to keep their footing in a dangerous time of shifting alliances and politics.

A winding 2½-mile dirt road runs under a canopy of dense foliage to the remains of this 19th-century plantation. The National Park Service maintains the well-preserved two-story clapboard residence, kitchen house, barn/carriage house, and remnants of 23 slave cabins built of "tabby mortar"—oyster shell and sand. Exhibits in the main house and kitchen focus on slavery as it existed in the rice-growing areas of northern Florida, Georgia, and South Carolina. You can see it all on your own, but 40-minute ranger-guided tours are much more informative. They're usually given at 1pm Monday through Friday, and 1 and 3pm Saturday and Sunday; call to confirm. Allot time to explore the grounds. The well-stocked book-and-gift shop will keep you even longer. It's open Wednesday through Sunday 9:30am to 4:30pm.

To get here from I-95, take Heckscher Drive East (Fla. 105) and follow the signs. From Fort Caroline, take Florida 9A North over St. Johns River to Heckscher Drive East. The plantation is 12 miles east of Florida 9A, on the left. From the beaches, take A1A to the St. Johns River Ferry and ride it from Mayport to Fort George; the road to the plantation is a half-mile east of the ferry landing.

Hitting the Beach

You can fish, swim, snorkel, sail, sunbathe, or stroll on the sand dunes—at least from March to November, as winter can get downright chilly here. All these activities are just a 20- to 30-minute drive east of downtown at Jacksonville's four beach communities.

Atlantic Boulevard (Fla. 10) will take you to **Atlantic Beach** and **Neptune Beach.** The boulevard divides the two towns, and where it meets the ocean, you'll come to **Beaches Town Center** (beachestowncenter.com), a quaint community with shops, restaurants, pubs, and a few inns.

Beach Boulevard (U.S. 90) dead ends at **Jacksonville Beach,** where you'll find beach concessions, rental shops, and a fishing pier. This is also the most popular local surfing beach.

To the south, J. Turner Butler Boulevard (Fla. 202) leads from I-95 to the boundary between Jacksonville Beach and Ponte Vedra Beach. A right turn there will take you to **Ponte Vedra Beach** (pronounced here as *Pon*-ti *Vee*-dra). This ritzy, golf-oriented enclave is actually in St. Johns County (St. Augustine), but it's so much closer to Jacksonville that it's included in this section.

Outdoor Activities & Spectator Sports

CRUISES St. John's River Taxi & Tours (jaxrivertaxi.com; © **904/860-8294**) runs a water taxi that stops at 11 spots around the river, including Friendship Park and the Riverside Arts Market. The taxi runs noon to 9pm Wednesday, Thursday, and Sunday, and Friday and Saturday from noon to 10pm. An all-day pass costs $15. They also do various tours, including a downtown sunset cruise starting at $22 per person, a downtown sightseeing cruise for $18 adults and $15 children, a Jax Beach sunset cruise from $22 to $28 per person, a Jax Beach eco-cruise from $6 to $28, and a very popular, lively, downtown happy hour tour from $22 per person.

FISHING The least expensive way to fish for red snapper, grouper, sea bass, small sharks, amberjack, and more, 15 to 30 miles offshore in the Atlantic Ocean, is aboard the *Majesty,* a modern, 65-foot, air-conditioned deep-sea party boat that has a galley offering hot meals. The full-day trips depart at 7:30am daily from Monty's Marina, 4378 Ocean St. (A1A), a half-mile south of the Mayport Ferry landing (majestyfishing.com; © **904/220-6363**); they return at 4:30pm. The price is $120 per adult, $105 per child 6 to 14, including bait and tackle. Those who just want to sunbathe and watch the anglers pay $60. You don't need a license, but reservations are required.

GOLF The Jacksonville area has a big variety of golf courses, some of which are ranked among the top in the country. In Ponte Vedra Beach, the Sawgrass Marriott Resort sits on the most famous course, the Players Stadium Course at **TPC at Sawgrass** ★★★ (tpc.com/sawgrass), home of THE PLAYERS Championship in March. Ranked among the nation's top courses, its island hole is one of the most photographed in the world. Nearby are the **Ocean and Lagoon courses** ★★★ at the Ponte Vedra Inn & Club (p. 486).

Top courses open to the public include the **Bent Creek Golf Course** ★★★, 10440 Tournament Lane (golfbentcreek.com; © **904/779-0800**), an 18-hole championship course constantly hailed by *Golf Digest* as a top five "All Time Golf Value." It's a great bargain, with greens fees between $36 and $45. Lowest rates are online. The semiprivate **Cimarrone Golf Club** ★★, 2690 Cimarrone Blvd. (cimarronegolf.com; © **904/287-2000**), is a fast and watery semi-private course with greens fees ranging from $29 to $69. But the best public course in the city, hands down, is the 18-hole Mill Cove course at the **Blue Sky Golf Club** ★★★, 1700 Monument Rd. (golfbluesky.com; © **904/642-6140**), which features a par-71, 6,671-yard course with a slope rating of 129, designed by Arnold Palmer. Rates are exceptionally affordable at $29 to $68.

HORSEBACK RIDING For lessons or a scenic ride along the dunes or through Jennings State Forest, try **Diamond D Ranch,** located 3 miles west of Cecil Commerce Center and the Jacksonville Equestrian Center, off Normandy Boulevard (diamonddranchinc.com; © **904/289-9331**).

SPECTATOR SPORTS The 73,000-seat **EverBank Stadium,** 1 Stadium Place, at East Duval and Haines streets (everbankstadium.com; © **904/633-6100**), hosts the annual Florida–Georgia football game every October, and other college football games September through December. It's also the home field of the National

Football League's **Jacksonville Jaguars** (jaguars.com; ✆ 877/452-4784, or 904/633-2000 for ticket information).

The 15,000-seat **VyStar Veterans Memorial Arena,** 300 A. Phillip Randolph Blvd. (vystarveteransarena.com; ✆ **904/630-3900** for information, or 904/353-3309 for tickets), hosts National Hockey League exhibition games, college basketball games, ice-skating exhibitions, wrestling matches, and family shows.

Shopping

Jacksonville has plenty of shopping opportunities, including the upscale mall **The Avenues,** south of town at 10300 Southside Blvd.; **St. John's Town Center,** 4663 River City Dr.; and a number of flea markets. At **Beach Boulevard Flea Market** ★★, on Beach Boulevard/Florida 90 (jaxfleamarket.com; ✆ **904/930-4149**), more than 600 vendors show up Saturday and Sunday from 9am to 5pm to sell their wares in the partially covered facility. Some booths are open other days of the week as well.

San Marco Square, at San Marco and Atlantic boulevards, south of the river, is a quaint shopping district in the middle of a stunning residential area. Shops housed in meticulously refashioned Mediterranean Revival buildings sell antiques and home furnishings, in addition to clothing, books, and records.

Another worthwhile neighborhood to explore is the **Avondale/Riverside** historic district, southwest of downtown on St. Johns Avenue between Talbot Avenue and Boone Park, on the north bank of the river. More than 60 boutiques, antiques stores, art galleries, and cafes line the wide, tree-lined avenue. **The Riverside Arts Market** (riversideartsmarket.org; ✆ 904/554-6865), located under the Fuller Warren Bridge near downtown, is the largest free weekly arts and entertainment venue in the state and is open Saturdays from 10am to 3pm.

Nearby, the younger set hangs out at the historic **Five Points** (5pointsjax.com), on Park Street at Avondale Avenue, where used-record stores, vintage clothiers, coffee shops, and funky galleries stay open late.

Like St. Augustine, Jacksonville is a mecca for chocoholics. In 1983, Phyllis Lockwood Geiger opened her first chocolate shop in the San Marco neighborhood. Geiger's mission was to bring back the art of European chocolate making, and that she did. With 25 locations all over Florida now, **Peterbrooke Chocolatier** ★★ (peterbrooke.com; ✆ **904/398-2489**), has three locations in Jax, including one downtown at 110 W. Bay St.

Where to Stay

Because Jacksonville hasn't yet made it onto the hip list, there are no boutique hotels—yet. Instead, you get a mix of chains, B&Bs, and Airbnbs.

The accommodations listed below are arranged geographically, in and around downtown first, followed by beachy digs. The suburbs have dozens more options, especially along I-95. Many are clustered south of downtown in the **Southpoint** (exit 101, Turner Butler Blvd./Fla. 202) and **Baymeadows** (exit 101, Baymeadows Rd./Fla. 152) areas. These locales have a multitude of chain restaurants, and you can hop on the highways and zoom to the beach or downtown.

Rates in the downtown hotels are higher midweek, when rooms are in demand by business travelers. Beach accommodations are somewhat less expensive in the colder months from December to March.

Note: Hotel taxes in the area tack on an additional 15%.

IN JACKSONVILLE
Hyatt Regency Jacksonville Riverfront ★★ In the heart of downtown, this hotel is popular with the suit-and-tie crowd, but also with party people in town for concerts. Renovations to the hotel added a brand-new bar to the rooftop pool area, and sleek, if a bit faceless, decor in the guest rooms (they are very clean and comfortable, though). All have the Hyatt Grand Bed, 250-thread-count triple sheeting, down comforters, and very plush pillows.

225 E. Coast Line Dr., Jacksonville. hyatt.com. ✆ **904/588-1234.** 951 units. $180–$352 double. Valet parking $39, self-parking $29. Pet fee $200. **Amenities:** 3 restaurants; 2 bars; concierge; fitness center; pool; room service; free Wi-Fi.

Riverdale Inn ★★★ In turn-of-the-20th-century Jacksonville, more than 50 mansions lined Riverside Avenue in an area known as "the Row." Today, sadly, only two of these Victorian-style homes remain. The family-owned Riverdale Inn is one of them, and thank goodness for preservation. (The other is at 1541 Riverside Ave.) Riverdale is located within walking distance of restaurants and the Cummer Museum (p. 478). Eleven period guest rooms are available with antique rugs and furniture, some featuring canopy and four-poster beds and fireplaces, and all with Keurig machines and free Wi-Fi. Plush robes are found in all the bathrooms. Breakfast here is bountiful, with cooked-to-order dishes. A tearoom is open Monday through Saturday with advance reservations only, as it's a popular spot for ladies who lunch, serving traditional English tea and finger sandwiches. For a nightcap, there's an on-site honor bar, and a full bar (noon–midnight). There's a two-night minimum on weekends, and a two-person max occupancy per room, making it not a place for families.

1521 Riverside Ave., Jacksonville. riverdaleinn.com. ✆ **904/354-5080**. 11 units. $175–$244 double. Pet fee $35/day. Rates include full breakfast, parking. **Amenities:** Bar; free Wi-Fi.

AT THE BEACHES
A dozen modest hotels line Jacksonville Beach's First Street, along the Atlantic. The **Hampton Inn Jacksonville Beach/Oceanfront,** 1515 N. First St., 2 blocks east of A1A (hilton.com; ✆ **904/241-2311;** $149–$188 double), is one of best. Its clean rooms have balconies or screened patios, and guests can enjoy a large, heated lagoon-style pool with four rock waterfalls and a palm-fringed deck, a secluded grotto whirlpool, pool bar, and fitness center.

If you'd like to rent an old-fashioned cottage or a luxurious condominium in the affluent enclave of Ponte Vedra, contact **Ponte Vedra Club Realty** (pvclubrealty.com; ✆ **904/285-6927**). The company has more than 100 properties in its rental inventory, about 75% of them on the ocean. Its renters get a discount on use of facilities at the Lodge & Club at Ponte Vedra Beach, and at the Ponte Vedra Inn & Club (see below), and the agency's service is quite good. You can also, of course, look at **Airbnb** and **Vrbo** for these units and others in the vicinity.

The Lodge & Club ★★★ This posh, two-story Mediterranean-style beaut is right on the beach and features a number of different types of rooms and suites, all of which have a high level of luxury. Some are geared to romance, with two-person settees recessed in front of windows looking onto the beach, plus two-person tubs; others have gas fireplaces and ceiling fans hung from vaulted ceilings. Continuing the honeymoon theme, the beach has a couples-only pool and hot tub. But this is also a place for families, thanks to the rental kiosk on the beach for kayaks, paddleboards, beach cruisers, and more; and the zero-entry pool with splash park and waterslide. There's also a children's nursery and teen programming (photography and culinary activities). Guests here have access to all the facilities at sister resort **Ponte Vedra Inn & Club** (see below); a complimentary shuttle takes guests between the properties.

607 Ponte Vedra Beach Blvd. (at Corona Rd.), Ponte Vedra Beach. pontevedra.com. ⓒ **800/243-4304** or 904/273-9500. 66 units. $441–$701 double. **Amenities:** 2 restaurants; 2 bars; babysitting; bike rental; concierge; fitness center (w/lap pool); Jacuzzi; 2 heated outdoor pools; room service; watersports equipment/rentals; free Wi-Fi.

One Ocean Resort & Spa ★★

It's the gracious, efficient, friendly service that makes the return booking rate so high at this beachfront stalwart. Sure, it's not a brand-new resort, and could benefit from some updating. But all rooms and suites are spotless and have ocean views. Plus, you'll sleep well on their custom-designed, plush mattresses, and bathe well thanks to Molton Brown bath amenities. A fab spa and gourmet restaurant, not to mention a pristine stretch of sand and a great kids' club, make for a first-rate beach vacation.

1 Ocean Blvd. (at beach end of Atlantic Blvd.), Atlantic Beach. oneoceanresort.com. ⓒ **855/232-0453** or 904/247-9702. 193 units. $220–$390 double. Valet parking $55. **Amenities:** Restaurant; 2 bars; babysitting; outdoor pool; room service; spa; watersports equipment/rentals; free Wi-Fi.

Ponte Vedra Inn & Club ★★★

When was the last time you stayed at a hotel with its own coat of arms? At this historic (since 1928) resort, the symbols on it tell you about the resort's strengths. There's a tennis racket repping its excellent tennis center (with 15 Har-Tru clay courts); golf clubs tipping a hat to the Inn's two superb 18-hole courses; a runner representing the state-of-the-art, two-story gym, with four-lane Olympic pool; and a sailboat and two seahorses pointing to the breathtaking swatch of beach that fronts the 300-acre property. What they couldn't fit onto the coat of arms were the 28,000-square-foot spa (the largest in the area), four heated pools, a kids' playground and nursery (kids' activities Mon–Sat), and bike and watersports rentals. A Croquet Lawn & Bocce Court debuted in 2024. As for the guest rooms and suites, they're all darn nice, spacious, well appointed, and housed in 10 low-rise buildings. All have patios or balconies overlooking either the Atlantic Ocean or the golf course; but decor varies by building, ranging from preppy-chic rooms with pops of sky blue and yellow, to more historic-looking digs. Final selling point: Guests can use the resort facilities at the nearby Lodge & Club at Ponte Vedra Beach (see above); a complimentary shuttle zips them between properties. Service is stellar.

200 Ponte Vedra Blvd. (off A1A), Ponte Vedra Beach. pontevedra.com. ⓒ **888/839-9145** or 904/285-1111. 262 units. $474–$701 double. **Amenities:** 8 restaurants; 3 bars; market; babysitting; bike rental; children's programs; concierge; 2 golf courses; fitness center; indoor pool; room service; spa; 15 tennis courts; watersports equipment/rentals; free Wi-Fi.

Salt Air Inn and Suites ★★★

This cute motel gets top marks from us for its prime location (an easy stroll to both restaurants and the beach), its genuinely caring staff, and for the fun spin they've taken with beachy decor. Rooms have a retro-1950s vibe, are painted in chipper aquas and navy blues (some with a touch of fire-engine red), with captain's wheels on the wall, lots of pelicans and seahorses everywhere (on lamps, in paintings, and in cute sculptures), and wicker furnishings. And they all have kitchenettes—a real plus. The Sea Air Motel had been in business here since 1946. This iteration was the result of a gut reno in 2022, which added a swimming pool.

425 Atlantic Blvd., Beaches Town Center. visitsaltair.com. No phone. 12 units. $159–$215 double. **Amenities:** Pool; kitchenettes; loaner bikes; free Wi-Fi.

Sawgrass Marriott Golf Resort & Spa ★ One of the nation's largest golf resorts, the reason most stay here is to play on the Pete Dye–designed THE PLAYERS Stadium Course at TPC Sawgrass, home of the annual THE PLAYERS Championship. Overlooking the 13th hole, the seven-story hotel sits beside one of the lakes that make the course so challenging. On-site minigolf and lawn games are entertaining and less intense than the golf action. There are also 65 acres of Audubon-rated grounds, woodsy and very beautiful. So, should you stay here if you're not a golfer? Probably not. Rooms are dated, tired, and do not match their handsome surroundings. There are apartment-like villas, but they too could use a refurb.

1000 PGA Tour Blvd. (off A1A, btw. U.S. 210 and J. Turner Butler Blvd.), Ponte Vedra Beach. marriott.com. © **888/246-2437** or 904/285-0906. 514 units. $245–$527 double. Valet parking $35; self-parking $22. Pet fee $150. **Amenities:** 7 restaurants; 4 bars; babysitting; bike rental; children's programs; concierge; 8 golf courses; fitness center; Jacuzzi; 4 outdoor pools (2 heated); beach club (with free shuttle transportation); room service; watersports equipment/rentals; free Wi-Fi.

Where to Dine

We've concentrated here on restaurants in downtown Jacksonville and at the beaches.

DOWNTOWN JACKSONVILLE

Southbank Riverwalk (dtjax.com/poi/southbank-riverwalk) has several eating and drinking options. You'll also find a number of good cafes and restaurants in the San Marco Square, Springfield, and Avondale neighborhoods.

bb's restaurant and bar ★★ NEW AMERICAN South of the Southbank Riverwalk, this bistro son of Biscotti's (see below) is one of the city's hottest restaurants. That means the Art Deco dining room here can get very noisy (especially around the big marble-top bar), so don't come here for an intimate conversation. During the day, a small but inventive selection of sandwiches (the fried green tomato one is tops), salads, and pizzas is available. The nightly specials feature local seafood and run the gamut from scallops Rockefeller to wahoo etouffee. Saturday and Sunday brunch features fab Benedict-style crab cakes.

1019 Hendricks Ave. (btw. Prudential Dr. and Home St.). bbsrestaurant.com. © **904/306-0100.** Call for priority seating. Main courses $16–$36, more for steak. Mon–Thurs 11am–10:30pm; Fri 11am–midnight; Sat 10am–midnight (Sat brunch 10am–2pm); Sun 10am–9pm.

bellwether ★★★ FUSION We're not sure what the deal is with Jacksonville's eateries and their penchant for lowercase lettering. At any rate, bellwether is a downtown trendsetter, a sleekly contemporary restaurant (think: subway tile walls and black tables and chairs) with farm-to-table fare that veers between straight-forward (and tasty) Southern dishes like shrimp and grits, or cornmeal-dusted trout, to fusion offerings that are off-the-charts creative, but still very flavorful. In the latter category we recommend a tater tot variation, based around kimchi and cheese curds; and addictive chili pepper house-boiled peanuts. Dessert highlights are the deep-fried carrot cake bread pudding and s'mores cheesecake. There's an all-day happy hour every Friday from 11am until 7pm with all sorts of specials, and regular happy hour on all other days from 4 to 7pm. bellwether indeed and we'll forgive the lack of capitalization.

117 W. Forsyth St., downtown. bellwetherjax.com. © **904/802-7745.** Main courses $15–$38. Mon 11am–2pm; Tues–Thurs 11am–2pm and 4–9pm; Fri 11am–10pm; Sat 4–10pm. Closed Sun.

Biscotti's ★★ MEDITERRANEAN
This brick-walled gem in the Avondale neighborhood looks like it was airlifted from New York's East Village. Start your day here with a pastry and cup of joe. At lunch and dinner, daily specials are always fresh and handsomely presented, like duck and brie ravioli with roasted cherries and black truffle sauce, or pistachio and camembert tortellini with shaved speck, aged sherry, and pear *mostarda*. For something a bit less bougie, grilled pizzas are the go-to, especially the margarita pie. On warm days, grab a tiny sidewalk table and people-watch.

3556 St. Johns Ave. (btw. Talbot and Ingleside aves.), Avondale. biscottis.net. **904/387-2060.** Main courses $15–$47. Mon–Thurs 10:30am–10pm; Fri 10:30am–midnight; Sat 8am–midnight; Sun 8am–9pm.

Orsay ★★★ FRENCH/SOUTHERN
Don't take our word for it: Ask just about *anyone* in Jacksonville what the best restaurant in town is, and you'll be steered here. Serving classic French bistro food that has a Southern twang to it, Orsay delivers on all fronts. The service is grandmotherly in its kindness, and the food is *ooh la la*, from Southern-fried sweetbreads, to a bouillabaisse brimming with locally caught seafood (the restaurant is a proud leader of Tampa's slow-food movement). And if you're celebrating a birthday, an anniversary, or some other event—like half the tables are on most nights—the dessert tower with macarons and other petite fours is a wowza way to end the night. *Note:* Orsay also has a very long menu for vegans and vegetarians.

3630 Park St., Avondale. restaurantorsay.com. **904/381-0909.** Main courses $22–$44, more for steaks. Tues–Thurs 4–9pm; Fri 4–10pm; Sat 11am–10pm; Sun 11am–9pm.

AT THE BEACHES

In addition to the Ragtime Tavern (see "Jacksonville After Dark," below), you'll find several dining (and drinking) choices in the brick storefronts of **Beaches Town Center,** the old-time beach village at the end of Atlantic Boulevard.

Catullo's Italian ★★ ITALIAN
You no longer have to track where the food truck is to get Catullo's hugely popular pastas. Brothers Carl and Dave Catullo went from a mobile operation to a bricks-and-mortar one in 2023, opening two restaurants, where they hand roll pasta and simmer sauces from family recipes. Sometimes it's Mom working in the kitchen, but whoever's doing the cooking you can taste the love in every bite . . . and the spice, especially if you go with Pasta Calabrian, a fiery mix of sauteed Calabrian chili peppers, basil pesto, and goat cheese over pappardelle. They have a second restaurant in Ponte Vedra.

1650-2 San Pablo Rd. S. catullos-italian.club. **904/240-1252.** Main courses $16–$24. Mon–Thurs 5–9pm; Fri–Sat 5–10pm.

Dockside Seafood Restaurant ★★★ SEAFOOD
Perched on the east edge of the Jacksonville boat ramp, this modern seafood house has magnificent views and even better food. Choose from a number of freshly caught fish prepared fried, grilled, or blackened on a plate, on a roll, in a po' boy, or in a taco. Sides include hush puppies, bacon collard greens, fried okra, and bacon black-eyed peas. There's a lively bar, outdoor eating, and stellar service. The restaurant is related to **St. Augustine Fish Camp** and its sea-faring siblings (p. 474), so it's in good company, as will you be.

2510 2nd Ave. N., Jacksonville Beach. docksideseafoodrestaurant.com. **904/479-3474.** Main courses $12–$19. Daily 10:30am–9pm.

Salt Life Food Shack ★★ SEAFOOD As the *New York Times* put it: "First Salt Life was a tattoo. Then it became a logo. Now it's a lifestyle brand with plans to open stores from coast to coast." Let's add to that: it's also now a place to eat. Not content to just sell T-shirts, coolers, and other gear embossed with the name, the Floridian group behind this surfer brand is opening restaurants at a rapid clip. This is the flagship eatery, set 3 blocks off the sand and offering a menu that should fuel wave catching: hearty sandwiches, fresh rolled sushi, tacos, local fried shrimp, poke bowls, avocado fries, and our fave, a wood-grilled mahi sandwich. There's also beer, oysters, booze, and did we mention beer and booze? On Tuesdays from 4 to 7pm sushi and selected draft beer and wine are half off; Thursdays specials are on margaritas and oysters.

1018 3rd St. N., Jacksonville Beach. © **904/372-4456.** Main courses $13–$28. Daily 11am–10pm.

Singleton's Seafood Shack ★★ SEAFOOD This rustic fish camp, with the county's largest over-water deck, has been serving every imaginable kind of fresh-off-the-boat seafood since 1969. And rustic it is, constructed primarily of unpainted, well-weathered plywood nailed to two-by-fours. Unlike most other fish camps that tend to overwork the deep fryer, here the fried standbys (conch fritters, shrimp, clam strips, oysters, and squid) retain their seafood taste! Singleton's also offers other preparations such as blackened mahimahi and Cajun shrimp. Their broiled bacon pimento oysters are a must for anyone who's a fan of bacon with your brine. At dinner, your Styrofoam plate will come stacked with a choice of sides such as black beans and rice, marvelous horseradishy coleslaw, fries, and hush puppies. There's a selection of chicken dishes, too, but stick to the seafood. Great lunch specials weekdays, and some very good combo dinner platters, too.

4728 Ocean St. (A1A, at St. Johns River Ferry landing), Mayport. © **904/246-4442.** Main courses $9–$35. Sun–Mon, Wed–Thurs 11am–9pm; Fri–Sat 11am–10pm. Closed Tues.

Jacksonville After Dark

In addition to the spots recommended below, check the listings in the "Shorelines" and "Go" sections of Friday's *Florida Times-Union* (**jacksonville.com**) and *Folio-Weekly* (**folioweekly.com**), the free local alternative paper available all over town. Another source is **jaxevents.com**.

THE PERFORMING ARTS Jacksonville has plenty of seats for concerts, touring Broadway shows, dance companies, and big-name performers at the 15,000-seat **VyStar Veterans Memorial Arena,** 300 A. Phillip Randolph Blvd. (vystarveteransarena.com; © **904/630-3900**); the 4,400-seat **Jacksonville Center for the Performing Arts,** 300 Water St., between Hogan and Pearl streets (jacksonvillecenterfortheperformingarts.com; © **904/633-6110**); and the **Ritz Theatre** (p. 480; ritzjacksonville.com; © **904/807-2010**). A good website of event listings is **jaxevents.com**.

THE BAR AND LIVE MUSIC SCENE You won't go thirsty in JAX. Downtown has a fabulously old-school speakeasy, **The Volstead ★★★**, 115 W. Adams St. (thevolsteadjax.com; © **940/274-2832**), where, on some nights, there's swing dancing and live music. In San Marco, **Sidecar Jax,** 1406 Hendricks Ave. (© **940/527-8990**), an urban beer garden and cocktail lounge, lets you do some good while you tipple: Order the drink specials and part of the proceeds goes to local charities. **The Grape & Grain Exchange ★★**, 2000 San Marco Blvd. (grapeandgrainexchange.com; © **904/396-4455**), is a combination of three businesses: a wine store, a craft cocktails bar, and, past the secret door that everyone knows about, a speakeasy called **The Parlour**.

Out at **Beaches Town Center,** at the ocean end of Atlantic Boulevard, **Ragtime Tavern,** 207 Atlantic Blvd. (ragtimetavern.com; © **904/241-7877**), is a winner, a craft brewery with live jazz and blues Wednesdays through Sundays. Also there, **Poe's Tavern ★★** (poestavern.com; © **904/241-7637**), which pays homage not necessarily to the horrors of Edgar Allen Poe, but to the tavern culture of the Poe-era, with over 50 craft beers.

For ocean views, **The Lemon Bar ★★★**, 2 Lemon St., Neptune Beach (lemonbarjax.com; © **904/372-0487**), is a landmark beach bar that's almost always standing room only. A venerable dive bar from 1933, **Pete's Bar,** 117 1st St., Neptune Beach (petesbar.com; © **904/249-9158**), was the first bar to legally open in Duval County after Prohibition was repealed.

Rooftop bars are also especially popular, like **River & Post ★★**, 1000 Riverside Ave. (riverandpostjax.com; © **904/575-2366**), on the 9th floor in a prominent Riverside building; **Cowford Chop House ★★**, 101 E. Bay St. (cowfordchophouse.com; © **940/862-6464**), with an open-air rooftop bar and a surf-and-turf menu; the up high **Hoptinger Bier Garden & Sausage House ★★**, 1037 Park St. (hoptinger.com; © **904/903-4112**), in the Five Points area; and modern American **Coop 303 ★★** at Beaches Town Center (coop303.com; © **904/372-4507**). Lastly, the self-professed Jax-Mex minichain **Burrito Gallery ★★** has a rooftop bar at the Brooklyn Station location in Riverside (burritogallery.com; © **904/822-8035**).

AMELIA ISLAND

32 miles NE of Jacksonville; 192 miles NE of Orlando; 372 miles N of Miami

Paradise is found on the northernmost barrier island of Florida. With 13 beautiful miles of beach and a quaint Victorian town, Amelia Island is a charming getaway about a 45-minute drive northeast of downtown Jacksonville. This skinny barrier island, 18 miles long by 3 miles wide, has more in common with the Low Country of Georgia (across Cumberland Sound from here) and South Carolina. In fact, it's more like St. Simons Island in Georgia or Hilton Head Island in South Carolina than other beach resorts in Florida.

Amelia has five distinct personalities. First is its southern end, an exclusive real estate development built in a forest of twisted, moss-laden live oaks. Here you'll find world-class tennis and golfing at luxe resorts. Second is modest **American Beach,** founded in the 1930s so that African Americans would have access to the ocean in this then-segregated part of the country. Today it's a modest, predominantly Black community tucked away among all that south-end wealth. Third is the island's middle, a traditional beach community with a mix of affordable motels, cottages, condominiums, and a seaside inn. Fourth is the historic bayside town of **Fernandina Beach ★★★**, which boasts a 50-square-block area of gorgeous Victorian, Queen Anne, and Italianate homes listed on the National Register of Historic Places. And fifth is lovely **Fort Clinch State Park,** which keeps developers from turning the island's northern end into resorts.

The town of Fernandina Beach dates from the post–Civil War period, when Union soldiers who had occupied Fort Clinch began returning to the island. In the late 19th century, Amelia's timber, phosphate, and naval-stores industries boomed. Back then, the town was an active seaport, with 14 foreign consuls in residence.

You'll see (and occasionally smell) the paper mills that still stand near the small seaport here. The island experienced another economic explosion in the 1970s and 1980s, when real estate developers built condominiums, cottages, and two big resorts on the island's southern end. In recent years, Fernandina Beach saw its own boom in bed-and-breakfast establishments.

Essentials

GETTING THERE The island is served by **Jacksonville International Airport** (p. 476), 12 miles north of Jacksonville's downtown and 43 miles from the island. Skirting the Atlantic in places, the scenic drive here from downtown Jacksonville is via A1A and the St. Johns River Ferry. The fast, four-lane way is via I-95 North and the Buccaneer Trail East (A1A).

GETTING AROUND There's no public transportation on this 13-mile-long island, so you'll need a vehicle.

VISITOR INFORMATION For information, visit **Explore Amelia** (explore amelia.com) and the website of the **Amelia Island Welcome Center,** 102 Centre St., Fernandina Beach (ameliaisland.com; © **904/277-0727**), which is open daily from 10am to 4pm.

Hitting the Beach

Thanks to a reclamation project, the widest beaches on the island are at the exclusive enclave on the island's southern third. Even if you aren't staying at one of the swanky resorts, you can enjoy this section of beach at **Peters Point Beach Front Park ★★★**, on A1A, north of the Ritz-Carlton. The park has picnic shelters and restrooms. North of the resort, the beach has public-access points with free parking every quarter-mile or so. Like Daytona Beach, they allow driving on the sand here, but you must be a resident to do so. The center of activity is **Main Beach,** at the ocean end of Atlantic Avenue (A1A), with good swimming, restrooms, picnic shelters, showers, a food concession, a playground, and lots of free parking. This area is popular with families.

The beach at **Fort Clinch State Park ★★** (floridastateparks.org/fortclinch; © **904/277-7274**), which wraps around the island's heavily forested northern end, is backed by rolling dunes and is filled with shells and driftwood. It's popular for swimming and surfing, but visitors do so at their own risk, as the beach has no lifeguards. A jetty and pier jutting into Cumberland Sound are popular with anglers. There are showers and changing rooms at the pier. Elsewhere in the park, you might see an alligator—and certainly some of the 170 species of birds that live here—by hiking the Willow Pond nature trail, which is one of the first stops on the **Great Florida Birding and Wildlife Trail**. Rangers lead nature tours on the trail, usually beginning at 10:30am on Saturday. There are also 3.3 miles of paved roads for biking and 6 miles of off-road bike trails here. See p. 496 for information about the historic fort at the park. The park entrance is on Atlantic Avenue near the beach. Entrance fees are $6 per vehicle with up to eight occupants, $2 per pedestrian or bicyclist. The park is open daily from 8am to sunset.

There are three beaches at the **Talbot Islands State Parks ★★** (floridastate parks.org), the most photographable (if not necessarily swimmable) being Boneyard Beach on Big Talbott, thanks to its gnarled and sculptural looking trees. Little Talbot is where to head if you want to get into the surf. There's a $5 fee per vehicle. It's also open 8am through sunset.

Pets on leashes are allowed on all of the island's public beaches and in Fort Clinch State Park.

Outdoor Activities

BIKING **Riptide Amelia Island** ★★, 5 N. Fletcher Ave., Fernandina Beach (riptidewatersports.com; ⓒ **904/891-5687**), offers 2-hour bike tours of Amelia Island on which you'll pedal a beach cruiser under Victorian-home-lined canopy oak paths, through the historic downtown, and elsewhere. Cost is $60 for adults, $50 for children, including bike rental. The Amelia Island Culinary Academy's **Food & Bike Tour** ★★★ (ameliacooking.com; ⓒ **904/557-4035**) is a 3-hour jaunt that includes stops at some of the island's best restaurants and fruit stands. Tours include four tastings and bike rental for $150 per person.

BOATING, FISHING, SAILING, PADDLEBOARDING & KAYAKING **Amelia Angler Outfitters** ★ (ameliaangler.com; ⓒ **904/261-2870**), at Tiger Point Marina on 14th Street, north of the historic district (though the boats dock at Centre St.), can help arrange deep-sea fishing charters, party-boat excursions, and dolphin-watching and sightseeing cruises. Other charter boats also dock at Fernandina Harbor Marina, downtown at the foot of Centre Street.

Windward Sailing School ★, based at Fernandina Harbor Marina, 3977 First Ave. (windwardsailing.com; ⓒ **904/261-9125**), will teach you to skipper your boat; it also has charters and boat rentals.

You have to be careful in the currents, but the backwaters here are great for kayaking, whether you're a beginner or a pro. However, you'll have to travel just off the island to do it. Ray and Jody Hetchka's **Kayak Amelia** ★★ (kayakamelia.com; ⓒ **904/251-0016**) is based near Talbot Island State Park (technically in Jacksonville) and offers beginner and advanced-level trips on back bays, creeks, and marshes. Three-hour trips go for about $70 for adults, $60 kids 12 and under. Kayak, paddleboard, and canoe rentals go from $45 to $60.

Amelia River Cruises ★★ (ameliarivercruises.com; ⓒ **904/261-9972**) offers all sorts of tours (including a shrimping eco-tour—see below) to the area's salt marshes, wilderness beaches, and the historic riverbanks of Amelia, Fernandina Beach, and Cumberland Island, Georgia, where wild horses roam the beaches. Prices range from $27 to $35 for adults, $25 to $33 for seniors, and $21 to $29 for children 12 and under.

Note: To learn about getting a boating permit for Florida, see p. 29.

ECO-TOURS Fernandina Beach is known as the "Birthplace of the Modern Shrimping Industry," and **Amelia River Cruises** (see above) offers a shrimping eco-tour June through September on which you'll deploy an otter trawl net, retrieve it, and learn all about what you caught from an onboard marine biologist. Cost is $30 for adults and $20 for kids 12 and under.

Amelia Adventures ★, 432 S. 8th St., Fernandina Beach (ameliaadventures.com; ⓒ **904/500-TOUR** [8687]), offers many guided eco-tours of all sorts, including camps and retreats for those looking to really commune with nature. The company is owned by Thomas Oliver, a TV producer and photographer whose work has appeared on *Deadliest Catch* and *Coastguard Alaska,* and his wife Catherine, a former Outward Bound instructor.

GOLF The **Omni Amelia Island** (omnihotels.com; ⓒ **904/261-6161**), has a number of excellent options, including the Pete Dye–designed championship **Oak Marsh** ★★ golf course, and a Beau Welling–designed **Little Sandy** ★ short

course ($50 to play), where greens fees range from $89 to $155 per person depending on the time and season. If you are a hotel guest, the private Tom Fazio–designed **Long Point** course ★★★ is open to you, a mind-blowingly beautiful course with two par-3s in a row bordering the ocean. Fees are high, from $175 to well over $400 depending on the time and season. Or play the older and less expensive 27-hole **Fernandina Beach Golf Club** ★ (fernandinabeachgolfclub.com; © **904/277-7370**), where prices are $23 to $70.

HORSEBACK RIDING   You can go riding on the beach with **Amelia Horseback Riding** ★, 4600 Peters Point Rd., Fernandina Beach (ameliaislandhorsebackriding.com; © **904/753-1701**). They offer day rides, sunrise rides, sunset rides, and even wedding proposal rides. Rates range from $125 to $175.

TENNIS/PICKLEBALL   Ranked among the nation's top 50 by *Tennis* magazine, the **Omni Amelia Island**'s tennis program created by Cliff Drysdale, features 23 Har-Tru tennis courts (naturally shaded by a canopy of gorgeous trees), seven pickleball courts, and hosts many professional tournaments, and has seen the likes of Andre Agassi, Martina Navratilova, Chris Evert, Martina Hingis, Maria Sharapova, and the Williams sisters play on its courts. Lessons and clinics range from $25 to $145 per person. Amelia Island's **Central Park,** located at the intersection of South 13th Street and Atlantic Avenue, has six illuminated pickleball courts open to the public daily from 6am until 10pm. It's free, but it's first come, first serve. Heh.

An eagle's eye view of Fernandina Beach.

> ### Amelia Island's Black History
>
> There's a bit of Confederate history in these parts, but not taught in most Florida schools is the fact that during the Jim Crow era, there was a haven for Black people in this area called **American Beach,** most of which has been, sadly, razed by developers who put up pricey vacation homes. Founded by African-American businessman A.L. Lewis, the area was home to restaurants, hotels, night clubs, shops and more, and thrived until 1964, when Hurricane Dora devastated the area. **Coast One Tours** (coastonetoursllc.com; ✆ **904/635-9081**) conducts Black historical tours that will take you to the beach area where NaNa dune—the tallest in all of Florida—still exists, as well as to the **A.L. Lewis Museum** (see below) to learn more about the man who found triumph over segregation and disenfranchisement.

Exploring Amelia Island

An informative and entertaining way to tour the historic district is the 30-minute guided tours on an electric carriage with **Jeffers Carriages** (ameliaisland.com/partners/jeffers-carriages; ✆ **904738-1519**). Carriages pick up passengers at the corner of Front and Center streets in Fernandina Beach. Tours start at $40 per person.

A.L. Lewis Museum at American Beach, FLA ★★★

Opened in 2014, this fascinating museum was the dream of MaVynee Oshun Betsch, aka "The Beach Lady," who died in 2005, but happened to have been the great-granddaughter of A.L. Lewis, president of the Afro-American Life Insurance Company and a self-made millionaire, who created an oceanfront resort right here in Amelia Island where African Americans could enjoy "recreation and relaxation without humiliation" during the Jim Crow era. Betsch was an opera singer, historian, activist, and environmentalist who packed crates of documents, artifacts, books, and memorabilia from her great-grandfather's shuttered office and would invite locals over to peruse the memories—and they are fascinating. Now you can see them too at this fantastic museum that greets visitors with an 11-minute video of The Beach Lady herself, giving you her own up close and personal tour of her family's fabulous legacy. Expect to spend about an hour here.

1600 Julia St. allewismuseum.org. ✆ **904/510-7036.** Admission $10 adults, $8 seniors, $5 kids and students. Fri–Sat 10am–2pm; Sun 1–4pm.

Amelia Island Museum of History ★★

Housed in the old Nassau County jail, built of brick in 1878, this award-winning local museum explains Amelia Island's history, from Timucuan Indian times through its possession by France, Spain, Great Britain, the United States, and the Confederacy. Only an upstairs photo gallery is open for casual inspection, so plan to take the 1-hour docent-led tour (11am and 2pm Mon–Sat, 2pm Sun) telling the story of the eight flags that have flown over Amelia Island representing empires, pirates, scalawags, and entrepreneurs, offered.

The museum also offers excellent **walking tours** of historic Centre Street on Thursday and Friday from September to June. These last about an hour, cover 8 blocks, and cost $15 for adults, $10 for kids. We especially recommend the

Murder, Mystery, and Mayhem tour which is a 90-minute look into a mystery that has lasted over 2 centuries. Cost is $15 for adults, $10 for kids, though we don't recommend that one for the wee ones. The Gilded Age tour is an 8-block look at Fernandina's glorious north end, including the wealthy "Silk Stocking" District, site of some of the Historic District's most beautiful homes. Cost is $15 adults, $10 kids.

Leaving at 6pm every Friday from behind St. Peter's Episcopal Church is a ghost tour that takes you past some allegedly haunted buildings. Cost is $15 adults, $10 kids. A pub crawl takes place the first and third Wednesdays of the month during which you'll drink your way through four of the small town's most popular, notorious, or otherwise historic pubs and bars. Cost is $40 per person (age 21 and over only), and reservations for this one are a must.

233 S. 3rd St. (btw. Beech and Cedar sts.). ameliamuseum.org. **904/261-7378**. Admission $10 adults, $8 seniors, $5 students. Mon–Sat 10am–4pm; Sun 1-4pm.

Fort Clinch ★★ Construction on the remarkably well-preserved Fort Clinch began in 1847 on the northern tip of the island and was still underway when Union troops occupied it in 1862. The fort was abandoned shortly after the Civil War, except for a brief reactivation in 1898 during the Spanish-American War. Reenactors gather the first full weekend of each month to re-create how the Union soldiers lived in the fort in 1864 (including wearing their wool underwear, even in summer!). Rangers are on duty at the fort year-round, and they lead candlelight tours ($6/person) on Friday and Saturday evenings during summer, beginning about an hour after sunset. Entry into the Fort Clinch Museum is free with park

Cyclists in Fort Clinch State Park.

admission, but entry into the fort is $2.50 per person. You can arrange guided tours at other times for an extra fee.

2601 Atlantic Ave., Fernandina Beach. floridastateparks.org/fortclinch. ✆ **904/277-7274.** Entrance fees $6 per vehicle with up to 8 occupants, $2 per pedestrian or bicyclist. Admission to the fort $2, free for children 4 and under. The park is open daily 8am–sunset; the fort daily 9am–5pm. Museum daily 9am–4:30pm.

Where to Stay

More than two dozen of the town's charming Victorian and Queen Anne houses have been restored and turned into B&Bs. For vacation rentals not on Airbnb or Vrbo—and note that there are *plenty* of rentals on the island of all sorts—**ERA Fernandina Beach** (www.ameliavacations.com; ✆ **904/261-4011**) has been renting properties in the area for over 50 years, with over 150 well-maintained, well-located condos and 50 homes for rent.

Your best camping option here is **Fort Clinch State Park,** which has 69 campsites, some behind the dunes at the beach (no shade out there), most in a forest along the sound side. They cost $26 per night, plus tax, a $6.70 reservation fee, and $7 nightly utility fee for RVs. You can reserve a site up to 11 months in advance (a very good idea in summer) by calling ✆ **904/277-7274** or going to https://reserve.floridastateparks.org/Web/#!park/21.

Note: Rates are subject to a 12% hotel tax (7% sales tax, 5% bed tax).

Amelia Schoolhouse Inn ★★★ Built in 1886 as the island's first school, this evocative inn has many of its original details intact (heart pine floors, beautiful brickwork, original window designs), though today no elementary school age kids are allowed at this adults-only facility. Guest rooms pay homage to both the age of the building, and its history, which means the quality pillow top mattresses are swathed in colorful quilts, and rooms have classic round schoolhouse clocks on the wall, next to world maps, with old-timey globes on the desks. The "Principal's Office" is the cheeky name for the inn's bar; in the courtyard is a pool, putting green, and lots of seating. Staff get an A+ for service, and the inn is set in the heart of downtown Fernandina Beach.

914 Atlantic Ave., Fernandina Beach. ameliaschoolhouseinn.com. ✆ **904/310-6264.** 17 units. $145–$231 cozy queen room. **Amenities:** Bar; heated pool; loaner bikes; free Wi-Fi.

Beachside Motel ★★ There's truth in advertising at this friendly motel, the only one right on the beach on Amelia Island. Rooms won't win any design awards (the conch shell art on the walls is a bit goofy, and the furniture is mass produced), but they're spotlessly clean, all have ocean views, and all come with a fridge. Some have full and usable kitchens, though rates do include morning coffee and pastries, so if you're a light eater, your breakfast is taken care of. A very good value.

3172 S. Fletcher Ave., Fernandina Beach. beachsidemotel.com. ✆ **877/261-4236.** 14 units. $139–$184 efficiency. **Amenities:** Beach; pool; free parking; free Wi-Fi.

Elizabeth Pointe ★★ This three-story, Nantucket-style shingled beauty sits overlooking the beach on Amelia Island. Built in 1991, it has big-paned windows that look out from the comfy library (with stone fireplace) and a dining room to an expansive, wrap-around front porch and the surf beyond. Antiques, reproductions, and other smart touches lend the 20 oceanfront rooms in the main building a turn-of-the-20th-century cottage ambience. All have oversize tubs. The Ocean House Suites next door has four large guest rooms in a West Indies motif, and the two-bedroom, two-bathroom Miller Cottage is perfect for small groups. Rates include a Southern-style breakfast (the pecan pancakes are legendary), nightly beer, wine, hors d'oeuvres, beach chairs, and umbrellas.

98 S. Fletcher Ave. (just south of Atlantic Ave.), Fernandina Beach. elizabethpointeameliaisland.com. **800/772-3359.** 25 units, including 1 cottage. $302–$420 double. Rates include breakfast, parking, and wine hour. **Amenities:** Bike rentals; room service; on-site restaurant; beach; free Wi-Fi.

Fairbanks House ★★★

Boasting all the amenities, and almost as much privacy as a first-class hotel, this superbly refurbished, romantic 1885 Italianate home is the top B&B choice in the historic district. As gorgeous as it is, it used to be known as "Fairbanks's Folly," because of its ostentatious original decor, and because Mrs. Fairbanks, wife of a Confederate major turned Florida senator who built the place for her, hated it. Rooms here are each decorated differently, but they have one thing in common: They're very Victorian. Many rooms, and all of the cottages, offer private entrances for guests. The Captain's Room, originally Mrs. Fairbanks' bedroom, has a cedar closet, four-poster bed, fireplace, and Victorian claw-foot soaking tub. The Kitchen Suite, named for its original function in the home, is one of the finest units, with a private porch, and two-person Jacuzzi bathtub. The two-bedroom Grand Tower Suite, occupying the entire top floor, has plenty of room to spread out, plus 360-degree views and its own whirlpool tub. The manse rests on a lush acre of soaring oaks, swimming pool, Adirondack chairs, magnolias, fragrant jasmine arbors, and a butterfly garden (all landscaping meets eco-friendly standards). A gourmet, two-course breakfast is served in the formal dining room and on the breezy piazzas by the pool, there's also a daily social hour, and freshly baked cookies. Children 16 and over are welcome in the same room as their parents.

227 S. 7th St. (btw. Beech and Cedar sts.), Fernandina Beach. fairbankshouse.com. **904/277-0500.** 12 units, including 3 cottages. $265–$470 double. Rates include off-street parking, full breakfast, and evening social hour (beverages and hors d'oeuvres). **Amenities:** Free use of bikes; pool; free Wi-Fi.

Florida House Inn ★

Name droppers and history buffs love this place. Among those who have stayed here: Ulysses S. Grant, Henry Ford, Laurel & Hardy, Mary Pickford, José Martí, the Carnegies, and the Rockefellers. Florida House Inn is the state's oldest-operating hotel (it originated as a boardinghouse for workers), and is, in many ways, a charming throwback to simpler times. Each of the 17 rooms and suites offer varying color schemes and antiques but also have the modern comforts of good mattresses and Wi-Fi. **Leddy's,** the inn's dining room, serves lunch and dinner, and **The Mermaid Bar** often hosts live music. But that means that guest rooms can be quite loud. Some also have painfully small bathrooms, and decor that feels less historic than musty. (Hence our one-star review.) If you're a light sleeper, look elsewhere.

22 S. 3rd St. (btw. Centre and Ash sts.), Fernandina Beach. floridahouseinn.com. **800/258-3301** or 904/261-3300. 17 units. $137–$179 double. Rates include breakfast. **Amenities:** Restaurant; bar; free Wi-Fi.

The Ritz-Carlton, Amelia Island ★★

Sprawling over 13 acres of glamorous beachfront, the Ritz is where you go if you want a resort with many, many activities and amenities . . . and don't mind paying for that privilege, or sharing the space with conventioneers. The lobby was revamped in 2024 to reflect a more modern beachy aesthetic. The kids' program is tops, there's an eye-candy 18-hole championship golf course, extensive tennis facilities, and the oceanfront pool is large, but not as sprawling as the beachfront. The resort also offers all kinds of nature tours, activities, and events. As for the guest rooms, they're spacious and all have oceanfront or oceanview balconies or patios, and the types of top-quality beds, bathrooms, and decor you'd expect of a place in this price range. The resort's signature restaurant, **Salt ★★★** (saltameliaisland.com), is the longest-running AAA Five Diamond restaurant in Florida. An ocean view accompanies exceptional seafood; the restaurant is named after the 30-plus international salts the kitchen collects.

4750 Amelia Island Pkwy., Amelia Island. ritzcarlton.com. © **800/241-3333** or 904/277-1100. 446 units. $835–$1,063 double. Valet parking $40. Pet fee $150 plus $20/night. **Amenities:** 5 restaurants; 3 bars; babysitting; bike rental; children's programs; concierge; golf course; fitness center; heated indoor and outdoor pools; room service; spa; 9 tennis courts; watersports equipment/rentals; free Wi-Fi.

Where to Dine

Beyond the restaurants recommended below, don't forget **Salt ★★★** (see above), which is one of the top special occasion places in the area. For the truly indulgent, there's a private, seven-course Chef's Kitchen Table dinner paired with wines for around $275 per person.

If brunch is what you're seeking, **Florida House Inn's Leddy's Porch** (see above) serves a famous one Saturdays and Sundays from 9am to 2:30pm, featuring Southern specialties from biscuits and gravy to fried green tomatoes to grilled pimento cheese sandwiches, all with bottomless Bloody Marys.

When it comes to location, **Brett's Waterway Café**, 1 S. Front St. (at Centre St., on the water; © **904/261-2660;** daily 11:30am–8pm), wins as the only place in town where you can eat and drink while watching the boats come and go on the river and the sun set over the marshes. The food is as low country as it gets on Amelia Island, and we wish it were better quality, but for many, dining in front of that view is enough.

Burlingame ★★★ NEW AMERICAN   As you might be able to tell by the number of top-ranked restaurants in this section, Amelia Island has become something of a dining destination. Many folks first came to try the food at Salt (see above), but now they're sticking around to taste the food being created by the chef who earned his toque working in that kitchen. That would be chef Chad Livingston, who trained at the Culinary Institute of America before working at Salt. Now he's putting out top quality fare—Madagascar shrimp with grits, fish with lentils in a sweet vermouth sauce, crisp composed salads of all sorts—in several rooms of an atmospheric, 1940s home. Foodies are snapping up reservations weeks in advance. A top restaurant not just in Northeast Florida, but in the Northeast as a whole.

20 S. Fifth St., Fernandina Beach. burlingamerestaurant.com. © **904/432-7671.** Main courses $29–$57, more for steak. Mon–Fri 5:30–9pm; Sat 5:30–9:30pm.

First Love Brewing ★★★ PIZZA   Nothing is done halfway by owners Kevin and Jessie O'Brien. When they decided to serve pizza at their craft brewery, they traveled to Chicago to train with a master pizzaiolo. Under his tutelage, they learned the art of making a taste-forward, pliant pizza dough, and how to get the best ingredients for sauces and toppings (much is imported from Italy). The result: some of the best 'za south of Napoli (or maybe New York City), with both traditional and unusual add-ons like hot honey or blackened chicken with buffalo sauce. In addition, there are a number of toothsome apps (zucchini fries, gochujang wings), burgers, sandwiches, and some mighty tasty suds. Jessie is currently working toward her master's degree in brewing science, and has a number of apprenticeships under her belt already. Did we mention that dining here is also mighty fun?

22 S. 8th St. firstlovebrewing.com. **904/310-9721.** Pizza pies $16–$21. Wed–Fri 4–9pm; Sat noon–9pm; Sun noon–7pm.

Pogo's Kitchen ★★★ GOURMET AMERICAN Named for the 1940s cartoon possum who would create "speshul" meals for his fellow Florida swamp creatures, Pogo's appeal is that it is both homemade and high end. From the vinaigrettes to the pastas, everything is made in-house, and always from organic, local ingredients. (In fact, the chef has created a market as a side biz, so that home chefs can buy some of the produce, sauces, and other goods he creates and sources). As for the atmosphere, it's not as fancy as Salt (see above), but this isn't a place you should wander into in flip-flops. People come in tony resort wear to enjoy the sleekly woodsy decor, and Pogo's expertly executed she-crab soup, roasted duck with morels and farro, and seafood pasta (among other highlights of the menu).

1408 Lewis St., Fernandina Beach. pogoskitchen.com. **904/432-8483.** Main courses $16–$40. Tues–Sat 5–9pm; Sun 10am–2pm.

Timoti's Seafood Shak ★★★ SEAFOOD A counter-service seafood shack—er, shak—located a half-block off Main Street, Timoti's is hugely popular for the super fresh, and wild caught, seafood it serves. That can range from fried, blackened, or grilled shrimp or fish, to poke bowls, lobster rolls, and clam chowder. Their tacos rock, too. There's covered outdoor seating and a little playground so that kids can blow off steam while you dine. Another location is in Ponte Vedra at 152 Crosswater Pkwy. (**904/686-2431**). *Note:* There's often a line, but it moves quickly.

21 N. 3rd St., Fernandina Beach. timotis.com. **904/310-6550.** Main courses $11–$15. Mon–Sat 11am–8pm; Sun 11am-3pm.

After Dark

Palace Saloon ★★ AMERICAN The state's oldest continuously operating drinking establishment, you go to the Palace to drink in, well, the ambience of inlaid mosaic floors, embossed-tin ceilings, and murals depicting literary scenes from Shakespeare to Dickens. While the Saloon used to serve food, they now only cater to, as they say, "those on a liquid diet." Nightly entertainment from DJs to live bands is good, but not nearly as enthralling as the history of the place. It was originally constructed as a haberdashery in 1878 until 1903, when hats were replaced with booze, even on the very last night before Prohibition, when the Saloon was the last to close, staying open until midnight and grossing $60,000 in a single day. Incidentally, the Saloon was also the first hard liquor bar to begin serving Coca-Cola, around 1905.

117 Centre St. (at Front St.), Fernandina Beach. theaihg.com/the-palace-saloon. **904/502-7231.** Daily noon–2am.

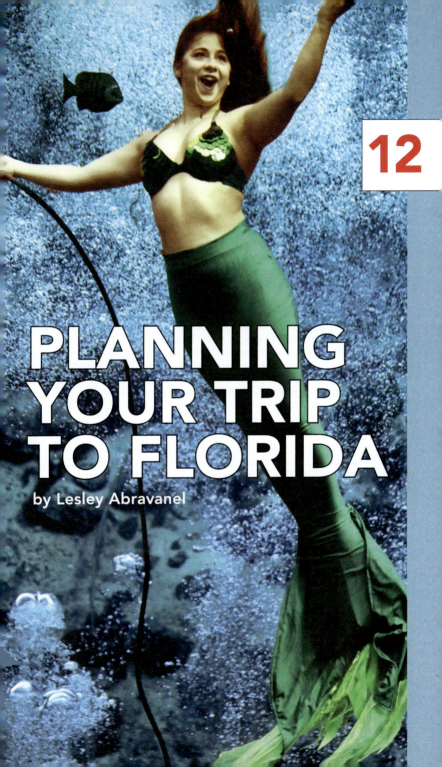

PLANNING YOUR TRIP TO FLORIDA

by Lesley Abravanel

12

Whether you plan to spend a weekend, a week, 2 weeks, or longer in the Sunshine State, you'll need to make many "where," "when," and "how" choices before you leave.

As for the where, well, that's a toughie. It depends on what sort of vacation you're looking for. There's relaxing, adventurous, kitschy, beachy, Mickey, Minnie, and, well, you get the picture . . .

How to get to Florida? We recommend almost every and any way except hitchhiking. And now to the when: That's the biggest question we get. As Florida shifts from a seasonal to a more year-round destination, there are many good times to visit. See chapter 2 for our full advice on weather and travel.

GETTING THERE

By Plane

You'll be hard-pressed to find airlines that *don't* fly to Florida. Most major domestic and even international airlines fly to and from many Florida cities.

Several so-called no-frills airlines—with low fares but few amenities—also fly to Florida. Some you may not have heard of include **Allegiant, Avelo, Breeze,** and **Frontier**. Be sure to factor in all of the costs (luggage, picking a seat, etc.) before booking with one of these, as the price can rise drastically.

By Bus

Greyhound (greyhound.com; © 800/231-2222) has more than 50 stops within the state of Florida and more than 2,400 service locations in North America. **GoToBus.com** is a good resource for other bus companies that head to Florida.

By Car

Florida is reached by **I-95** along the East Coast, **I-75** from the central states, and **I-10** from the west. The **Florida Turnpike,** a toll road, links Orlando, West Palm Beach, Fort Lauderdale, and Miami (it's a shortcut from Wildwood on I-75 north of Orlando to Miami). **I-4** cuts across the state from Cape Canaveral through Orlando to Tampa.

International visitors should note that insurance and taxes are almost never included in quoted rental car rates in the U.S. Be sure to ask your rental agency about additional fees for these. They can add a significant cost to your car rental.

Most car-rental companies in Florida require that you be 25, but if not, there's a hefty surcharge applied to renters 21 to 24 years old.

And because Florida isn't exactly known for stress-free driving, the Florida Department of Transportation has come out with the **Florida 511 Traveler Information** system (fl511.com), a free traffic and travel info system that offers advice on routes, airports, and even traffic to avoid. It's also a mobile app.

PREVIOUS PAGE: Say hello to mermaids at Weeki Wachee Springs State Park.

FINDING A good airfare

Book at the right time. It sounds odd, but you can often save a good amount by booking domestic airfare 28 to 35 days in advance of departure. That figure comes from a 2024 study of over 40 million airfare transactions by an industry group called the Airlines Reporting Corporation. Book earlier than that, and you won't have access to the lowest-priced seats, as the airlines only release them when they have an idea of how the plane is selling. Book too close to departure, and the airline knows they've "got you" and will charge more. That same study found that those who purchased their tickets on a Sunday spent 5% less statistically—not a huge amount, but still a savings (the savings are higher for international fares).

Fly when others don't. Those who fly Friday, Tuesday, or Wednesday, and who stay over a Saturday night, generally pay less than those who fly at more popular times, according to the study cited above.

Do a smart Web search. We did a study on Frommers.com and found the best prices, most consistently, on sister sites **Momondo.com** and **Skyscanner.com**. Both search all the discount sites as well as the airline sites directly, so that you get a broader and more impartial search. The only airline that won't come up is Southwest Airlines, so be sure to search it separately.

Be anonymous in your search. Clear your cookies and engage the privacy setting on your browser, or better yet, use a different browser or computer than you usually do when searching for airfares. The airlines and airfare booking sites do track users (though they deny it) and are getting increasingly expert in serving up fares tailored to customers' past buying history. To see the actual lowest rates, you have to cloak your identity.

By Train

Amtrak (amtrak.com; © 800/USA-RAIL [872-7245]) offers train service to Florida from both the East and West coasts. It takes some 26 hours from New York to Miami, and 68 hours from Los Angeles to Miami.

Amtrak's *Silver Meteor* and *Silver Star* both run twice daily between New York and either Miami or Tampa (only the *Silver Star* goes to Tampa), with intermediate stops along the East Coast and in Florida. The *Silver Meteor* gets to South Florida faster than the *Silver Star.* The West Palm Beach station is closest to the ocean, for those who care—a 7-minute car ride or 45-minute walk. Trains do not travel in the Panhandle.

Amtrak's **Auto Train** runs daily from Lorton, Virginia (12 miles south of Washington, D.C.), to Sanford, Florida (just northeast of Orlando). You ride in a coach while your car is secured in an enclosed vehicle carrier. Make your train reservations as far in advance as possible.

Once in Florida, you have **Brightline** (gobrightline.com), an inter-city, eco-friendly high-speed rail serving Miami, Aventura, Fort Lauderdale, Boca Raton, West Palm Beach, Stuart, and Orlando. Though the train has made headlines for several unfortunate pedestrian deaths, it has been well-received in the state—especially for travel between Miami and Orlando: 32 trains run daily with 16 daily departures from Miami and Orlando.

GETTING AROUND

Having a car is the best and easiest way to see most of Florida's sights. Public transportation is available only in the cities and larger towns, and even there, it may provide infrequent or inadequate service. Getting from one city to another, cars and planes are the way to go.

By Plane

The commuter arms of most major airlines, including Spirit and United, provide extensive service between Florida's major cities and towns. Fares for these short hops tend to be reasonable. See p. 503 for tips on air savings.

By Car

Jacksonville is about 350 miles north of Miami and 500 miles north of Key West, so don't underestimate how long it will take you to drive all the way down the state. The speed limit is either 65 mph or 70 mph on the rural interstate highways, so you can make good time between cities. Not so on U.S. 1, U.S. 17, U.S. 19, U.S. 41, or U.S. 301; although most have four lanes, these older highways tend to be heavily congested, especially in built-up areas.

Every major **car-rental company** is represented in Florida. State and local **taxes** will add as much as 20% to your final rental bill. You'll pay an additional $2 per day in statewide use tax, and local sales taxes will tack on at least 6% to the total, including the statewide use tax. Some airports add another few dollars to $10 a day "recovery" fees. You can avoid the recovery fee by picking up your car in town rather than at the airport. Competition is so fierce among Florida rental firms that many have now stopped charging **drop-off fees** if you pick up a car at one place and leave it at another (but do check).

To rent a car, most companies require you to be at least 25 years old. Some also set maximum ages and may deny cars to anyone with a bad driving record.

As for gas, prices were down at press time to less than $3 a gallon, though Florida, as usual, has some of the highest gas prices in the country. One U.S. gallon equals 3.8 liters or .85 imperial gallons. For an up-to-the-minute listing of gas prices at stations throughout Florida, go to **floridastategasprices.com**.

By Train

The high-speed, only in Florida railway **Brightline** (GoBrightline.com) is sometimes the speediest way to get around, when you factor in Florida's traffic. It operates 30 trains daily between Orlando and Miami, with 15 daily departures from each city. The first Orlando train leaves at 4:38am with the last one departing at 8:54pm. The first Miami train leaves at 6:41am and the last one departs at 9:41pm.

Total travel time between Miami and Orlando clocks in at around 3 hours and 25 minutes—a bit less than the amount of time it takes to drive between the two destinations without traffic, and a *lot* less during high traffic times.

The sleek, clean yellow trains run on biodiesel and have four or five cars; one of those is considered "Premium" class, which includes food and drink, while the rest of the cars are "Smart" class, which still have comfy seats with lots of leg room, free Wi-Fi, USB ports, and forward and rear-facing options. We think there's no need to upgrade, frankly. Both are quite nice.

Cost, however, is high for both classes, starting at $79 for one-way adult tickets and $39 for kids ages 2 to 12 in "Smart," and from $149 including checked luggage in "Premium" with kids starting at $79. Checked luggage in "Smart" class costs $10. Fares are much cheaper if you travel between West Palm Beach, Boca

Raton, Fort Lauderdale, and Miami. As well, you'll usually pay less online in advance than you will buying a ticket at the station.

Tri-Rail (tri-rail.com), the commuter rail line linking Miami, Fort Lauderdale, and West Palm Beach, is also a smart way to get around and can be paired with Brightline. Its relatively new 9-mile extension, known as the Tri-Rail Downtown Miami Link, runs from the Tri-Rail Metrorail Transfer Station, 2601 E. 11th Ave. in Hialeah, for the trip to downtown Miami on the same tracks as Brightline. Tri-Rail trains from Hialeah now stop at MiamiCentral station, 600 NW First Ave. in downtown Miami. Brightline trains run from that station, with stops in Aventura, Fort Lauderdale, Boca Raton, West Palm Beach, and Orlando. The downtown Miami station connects with Miami-Dade Transit buses, Metrorail, and Metromover.

By Bus

Greyhound (p. 502) connects a number of Floridian cities.

TIPS ON ACCOMMODATIONS

Florida accommodations are as varied in personality as the weather is in mid-July: motels, luxury hotels, historic B&Bs, high-rise condo rentals, tent sites, cabins, and more. But saving money at all of these types of lodgings has become trickier. Here are some strategies:

- **Choose your season carefully.** Room rates can vary dramatically—by hundreds of dollars in most cases—depending on what time of year you visit. See p. 24 for more info on when high season falls in different parts of the state.

- **Make a reservation you can cancel.** As the date of the stay approaches, hotels start to play "chicken" with one another, dropping the price a bit one day to try to lure customers away from a nearby competitor. So, search again the week you're traveling, and then within 48 hours of arrival. This strategy takes vigilance and persistence, but since your credit card won't usually be charged until 24 hours before check-in, little risk is involved and it's paying off more often than ever before, thanks to current conditions. The savings is *always* better than the "deals" you get from booking ahead.

- **Choose a chain.** Chains can be a good option, particularly if you have reward points or can access some type of corporate discount.

- **Book blind.** Extreme discounts are found on sites where you bid for lodgings without knowing which hotel you'll get. You'll find these on such sites as Priceline.com and Hotwire.com, and they can be money-savers, particularly if you're booking within a week of travel (that's when the hotels resort to deep discounts to get beds filled). As these companies use only major chains, you can rest assured that you won't be put up in a dump. For Priceline, you can install the browser extension **Hotel Canary** for free on your computer, and it will tell you the name of the hotel Priceline is trying to hide from you. There's not as easy a hack for Hotwire, but if you search for it on Frommers.com you'll find our four-step method for correctly guessing hotels.

- **Consider joining Room Steals, Travel + Leisure's Go, or one of the travel clubs associated with many professional organizations.** These clubs have access to the "fire sales" of the hotel industry: room rates that are slashed to a level hotels would never want to surface on a Google search. These clubs work best for frequent travelers, as there are initial membership fees. All these entities unlock wholesale prices that consistently shave 25% off the nightly rate at hotels, more for really pricey ones.

- **Use the right hotel search engine.** They're not all equal, as we at Frommers.com learned after putting the top 20 sites to the test in 20 cities around the globe. We discovered that HotelsCombined.com and Google/Hotels both listed the lowest rates for hotels in the city center 20 out of 20 times—the best record, by far, of all the sites we tested.

[FastFACTS] FLORIDA

Business Hours
"Normal" business hours are usually 9am to 5pm, but in certain parts of the state—Miami, especially—hours range from "whenever" to "whenever." Always look online for hours as they will vary.

Drinking Laws
The legal age for purchase and consumption of alcoholic beverages is 21; proof of age is required and often requested at bars, nightclubs, and restaurants, so it's always a good idea to bring ID when you go out. Do not carry open containers of alcohol in your car or any public area that isn't zoned for alcohol consumption. The police can fine you on the spot. Florida state law prohibits the sale of alcohol between 3 and 7am, unless the county chooses to change the operating hours later. For instance, Miami-Dade County liquor stores may operate 24 hours. Alcohol sales on Sundays vary by county; some, such as Palm Beach and Miami-Dade County, can start serving booze as early as 7am while other counties such as Monroe don't start popping corks until noon. Supermarkets and other licensed business establishments can sell only beer, low-alcohol liquors, and wine. The hard stuff must be sold in dedicated liquor stores, which may be in a separate part of a grocery or a drugstore. Beer must be sold in quantities of 32 ounces or less or greater than 1 gallon.

Don't even think about driving while intoxicated. Drivers suspected to be under the influence of alcohol or drugs must agree to breath, blood, or urine testing under "implied consent laws." Penalties for refusing testing can mean suspension of the driver's license for up to 1 year.

As for open container laws: Having open alcoholic containers on public property, including streets, sidewalks, or inside a vehicle, is prohibited.

Emergencies
To reach the police, ambulance, or fire department, dial 🕻 **911** from any phone.

Family Travel
Florida is a top family destination. Consequently, most Florida hotels and restaurants let children aged 17 and younger stay free in a parent's room (be sure to ask when you reserve). Most full-service beach resorts will have a children's activities program in high season and some will even mind the youngsters while the parents enjoy a night off! Even if they don't have a children's program of their own, most will arrange babysitting services.

Health
Florida doesn't present any unusual health hazards for most people. Folks with certain medical conditions, such as liver disease and diabetes, should avoid eating raw **oysters.** Cooking kills the bacteria, so if in doubt, order your oysters steamed, broiled, or fried.

Florida has millions of **mosquitoes** and invisible biting **sand flies** (known as no-see-ums), especially in the coastal and marshy areas. There have been cases of mosquitoes carrying malaria and West Nile virus, so it's wise to keep these pests at bay with a good insect repellent.

It's especially important to protect yourself against **sunburn.** Don't underestimate the strength of the sun's rays down here, even in winter. Use a sunscreen with a high protection factor and apply it liberally and often.

Internet & Wi-Fi   When it comes to Internet and Wi-Fi, Florida is pretty connected. Most major cities offer free Wi-Fi hot spots, and all hotels now offer free Wi-Fi to their guests. Also, most public libraries throughout the state offer free Internet access/Wi-Fi, as do Starbucks and other cafes.

Legal Aid   While driving, if you are pulled over for a minor infraction (such as speeding), never attempt to pay the fine to a police officer; this could be construed as attempted bribery, a much more serious crime. Pay fines by mail, or directly into the hands of the clerk of the court. If accused of a more serious offense, say and do nothing before consulting a lawyer. In the U.S., the burden is on the state to prove a person's guilt beyond a reasonable doubt, and everyone has the right to remain silent. Once arrested, a person can make one telephone call to a party of his or her choice. The international visitor should call his or her embassy or consulate.

LGBTQ Travelers   **Fort Lauderdale** wears the rainbow-colored crown as the most gay-friendly city in the state, followed closely by **Key West. South Beach** in **Miami** used to be a gay mecca but that has changed, and the Florida government has been putting pressure there, and elsewhere, on entities that host drag events. For travel warnings, events, and tips, go to **Equality Florida** at eqfl.org. Also, the **International Gay and Lesbian Travel Association (IGLTA;** iglta.org; 800/448-8550 or 954/776-2626) offers an online directory of gay- and lesbian-friendly travel businesses and tour operators.

Mail   At press time, domestic postage rates were 56¢ for a postcard and 73¢ for a letter. For international mail, a first-class letter of up to 1 ounce costs $1.65; a first-class postcard also costs $1.65. For more information go to **usps.com**.

Medical Requirements   Unless you're arriving from an area known to be suffering from an epidemic (particularly cholera or yellow fever), inoculations or vaccinations are not required for entry into the United States.

Mobile Phones   Someone without a cellphone in Florida is as rare as an albino crocodile. But it happens. Reception varies from excellent to spotty, depending on where you are. The Everglades used to be an abysmal place to use a mobile phone, but thanks to new cellphone towers, reliable service is almost as guaranteed as a gator sighting. Typically, however, the more remote in the state you are, the less chance your phone will work.

If you're not from the U.S., you'll be appalled at the poor reach of our **GSM (Global System for Mobile Communications) wireless network,** which is used by much of the rest of the world. Your phone will probably work in most major U.S. cities; it definitely won't work in many rural areas. And you may or may not be able to send SMS (text messaging) home.

THE VALUE OF THE U.S. DOLLAR VS. OTHER POPULAR CURRENCIES

US$	Aus$	Can$	Euro (€)	NZ$	UK£
1	1.44	1.35	0.90	1.57	0.75

Money & Costs   Frommer's lists exact prices in the local currency. The currency conversions quoted above were correct at press time. However, rates fluctuate, so before departing consult a currency-exchange website such as **oanda.com/currency/converter** to check up-to-the-minute rates.

Packing   Florida is typically a warm-weather state, but not always. Be sure to pack a sweater, long sleeves, and pants in case the weather cools or, more likely, you go into a place where the air-conditioning is arctic. Long sleeves and pants also come in handy during pesky mosquito season.

Safety While Florida is generally quite safe, it pays to use common sense when traveling throughout the state. When on beaches, keep close watch on your personal items; when in South Beach, Key West, Fort Lauderdale, and pretty much any other Sunshine State hot spot, watch your drinks and never leave them unattended. And while we completely encourage exploration, avoid areas not heavily trafficked. If you feel vulnerable someplace, trust your intuition and leave. Our biggest safety tip, however, is sunscreen. Use it generously. You'll still get a tan. Trust us.

Senior Travel With one of the largest retired populations of any state, Florida offers a wide array of activities and benefits for seniors. Don't be shy about asking for discounts, but always carry some kind of identification, such as a driver's license, which shows your date of birth. In most cities, people 60 and older qualify for reduced admission to theaters, museums, and other attractions, as well as discounted fares on public transportation.

The U.S. National Park Service offers a **Senior Annual Pass,** which gives seniors 62 years or older lifetime entrance to all properties administered by the National Park Service—national parks, monuments, historic sites, recreation areas, and national wildlife refuges—for a one-time processing fee of $20 or a lifetime pass for $80. The pass must be purchased in person at any NPS facility that charges an entrance fee. For more information, go to nps.gov/planyourvisit/senior-pass-changes.htm or call ✆ **888/467-2757.**

Smoking Smoking is prohibited in all enclosed indoor workplaces, which includes restaurants but not stand-alone bars. That means that establishments making more profit from food than from beverages must be smoke free, though some renegade bars and restaurants defy the law despite the hefty fines. Marijuana was not legal in Florida, except for medicinal uses, as we went to press.

Taxes The Florida state sales tax is 6%. Many municipalities add 1% or more to that, and most levy a special tax on hotel and restaurant bills. In general, expect at least 9% to be added to your final hotel bill. The United States has no value-added tax (VAT) or other indirect tax at the national level. Every state, county, and city may levy its own local tax on all purchases, including hotel and restaurant checks and airline tickets. These taxes will not appear on price tags.

Time The Florida peninsula observes **Eastern Standard Time,** but most of the Panhandle, west of the Apalachicola River, is on **Central Standard Time,** 1 hour behind the rest of the state.

Daylight saving time is in effect from 2am on the second Sunday in March to 2am on the first Sunday in November, except in Arizona, Hawaii, the U.S. Virgin Islands, and Puerto Rico. Daylight saving time moves the clock 1 hour ahead of standard time.

Tipping In hotels, tip **bellhops** at least $2 per bag ($3–$4 if you have a lot of luggage) and tip the **chamber staff** $1 to $5 per day (more if you've left a big mess for him or her to clean up). Tip the **doorman** or **concierge** only if he or she has provided you with some specific service (for example, calling a cab for you or obtaining difficult-to-get theater tickets). Tip the **valet-parking attendant** $5 every time you get your car.

In restaurants, bars, and nightclubs, tip **service staff** and **bartenders** 18% to 22% of the check, and tip **valet-parking attendants** $2 per vehicle. But keep an eye on your bill in tourist hot spots such as South Beach, where as much as an 18% to 20% auto gratuity could be already added to the total check.

As for other service personnel, tip **cab or rideshare drivers at least** 18% of the fare; tip **skycaps** at airports at least $2 per bag

WHAT THINGS COST IN FLORIDA — $

Taxi from the airport to major destination	30.00–70.00
Double room, moderate	230.00
Double room, inexpensive	150.00
Three-course dinner for one without wine, moderate	50.00–75.00
Bottle of beer	6.00
Cup of coffee	3.50
1 gallon of gas	3.38
Admission to most museums	Free–30.00
Admission to most national parks	5.00–35.00

($2–$3 if you have a lot of luggage); and tip **hairdressers** and **barbers at least** 15% to 20%.

Toilets You won't find public toilets or "restrooms" on the streets in most U.S. cities, but they can be found in hotel lobbies, bars, cafes, restaurants, museums, department stores, railway and bus stations, and service stations. Large hotels and fast-food restaurants are often the best bet for clean facilities. Restaurants and bars in resorts or heavily visited areas may reserve their restrooms for patrons.

Travelers with Disabilities Florida is exceptionally accommodating to those with special needs. In addition to special parking set aside at every establishment, out-of-state vehicles with disability parking permits from other states can park in these spots. Florida state law and the Americans with Disabilities Act (ADA) require that guide dogs be permitted in all establishments and attractions, although some ride restrictions do apply. For those who have hearing impairments, **TDD service** is available by dialing ⓒ **711** via the Florida Relay Service. There are several resources for people with disabilities who are traveling within Florida, including special wheelchairs with balloon tires provided free of charge at many Florida beaches. For more go to **visitflorida.com/things-to-do/accessible-travel**.

Index

See also Accommodations and Restaurants indexes, below.

A

The Abbey Brewing Co. (Miami), 147
Accessibility, 509
Accommodations. *See also* Accommodations index; Camping
 Amelia Island, 497–499
 best of, 14
 Biscayne National Park, 233
 Boca Raton & Delray Beach, 267–269
 Clearwater Beach, 336–338
 Cocoa Beach, 437–438
 Daytona Beach, 448–450
 Everglades National Park, 227–229
 Fort Lauderdale, 249–254
 Jacksonville, 484–487
 Key West, 199–204
 Lower Keys, 182–183
 Miami, 62–79
 Orlando, 398–413
 Palm Beach & West Palm Beach, 284–289
 Sarasota, 351–354
 saving money, 505–506
 St. Augustine, 469–472
 St. Pete Beach, 335–336
 St. Petersburg, 326–327
 Tampa, 310–312
 Upper & Middle Keys, 169–173
Actors' Playhouse at the Miracle Theatre (Miami), 144
Addresses, Miami, 54
Adrienne Arsht Center for the Performing Arts of Miami-Dade County, 146
Adventure Island (Tampa), 297–298
Aerophile Balloon Ride (WDW), 385
Air travel, 502–504
Airboats, 225–226
Airplane tours, Key West, 195
Alabama Jack's (Key Largo), 158
A.L. Lewis Museum at American Beach, FLA, 495
Alligator farms, 7–8
Alonzo's Oyster Bar (Key West), 209
Amelia Island, 42, 50, 490–500
 accommodations, 497–499
 arrival information, 491
 attractions, 495–497
 beaches, 491
 dining, 499–500
 nightlife, 500
 outdoor activities, 492–494
 transportation in, 491
 visitor information, 491
Amelia Island Museum of History, 495–496
American Beach (Amelia Island), 42, 495

American Sandsculpting Festival (Fort Myers Beach), 27
Anastasia State Park (St. Augustine), 466–467
Ancient Spanish Monastery (Miami), 121–122
Animal encounters, 162–165, 325, 392–393
Ann and Alfred G. Goldstein Marine Mammal Research and Rehabilitation Center (Sarasota), 350
Ann Norton Sculpture Gardens (West Palm Beach), 280
Anne's Beach (Florida Keys), 159–160
Apollo Visitor Center (Cape Canaveral), 434
Aquatica (Orlando), 396
Area codes, Miami, 61
Arrival information, 502–503
Art Basel Miami Beach, 27, 117
Art Center Sarasota, 347
Art Deco District (South Beach), 114–121
Arts on Douglas (New Smyrna Beach), 453
Asolo Theater (Sarasota), 349, 357–358
Atlantic Center for the Arts (New Smyrna Beach), 453
Audubon House & Tropical Gardens (Key West), 190
Authentic experiences, best of, 2–3
Auto racing, 10, 140, 442
Aventura Mall (Miami), 141

B

Babysitting services, 366
Bahia Honda State Park (Big Pine Key), 3, 179–180, 183
Ball and Chain (Miami), 152
Ballet Flamenco La Rosa (Miami), 146
Bar Nancy (Miami), 147
Barnacle State Historic Site (Miami), 128
Bars. *See* Nightlife
Baseball, Miami, 140
Basketball, Miami, 140
The Bass Museum of Art (Miami), 10, 36, 117
Bay of Pigs Brigade 2506 Museum (Miami), 125
Bayshore Boulevard (Tampa), 305
Beaches
 Amelia Island, 491
 best of, 3, 6
 Biscayne National Park, 233
 Boca Raton & Delray Beach, 262–263
 Daytona Beach, 443–444
 Fort Lauderdale, 240–242
 Jacksonville, 482–483
 Key West, 196–197
 in Miami, 111–114

 Palm Beach & West Palm Beach, 278
 Sarasota, 344–345
 Space Coast, 434–436
 St. Augustine, 466–467
 St. Pete & Clearwater Beaches, 331–333
The Berry Farm (Miami), 86
Berry picking, 86
Big Cypress National Preserve, 48, 218
Big Pine Key (Florida Keys), 36, 38, 178–185
Bike tours, Key West, 195
Bike Week (Daytona Beach), 25–26
Biketoberfest (Daytona Beach), 26
Biking, 28
 Amelia Island, 492
 Everglades National Park, 222–223
 Key West, 188–189, 197
 Lower Keys, 180
 Miami, 61, 137
 Palm Beach & West Palm Beach, 278–279
 Sarasota, 345
 St. Petersburg, 323
 Tampa, 305
Bill Baggs Cape Florida State Park (Key Biscayne), 3, 46, 122–123
Bird-watching, 28, 180–181, 213, 223
Biscayne Corridor (Miami), 57, 95–98, 142
Biscayne National Park, 49, 230–233
Bishop Museum of Science and Nature (Sarasota), 350
Blue Angels Homecoming Air Show (Pensacola), 27
Blue Spring State Park (Orlando), 397
Boat tours
 Everglades National Park, 225–227
 Jacksonville, 483
 Key West, 195
 Orlando, 398
 Sarasota, 345
 St. Augustine, 467
Boating, 28–29. *See also* Outdoor activities
Boca Chita Key (Biscayne National Park), 230, 232
Boca Raton & Delray Beach, 49, 260–275
 accommodations, 267–269
 arrival information, 262
 attractions, 264–266
 dining, 269–273
 nightlife, 273–275
 outdoor activities, 262–264
 shopping, 266–267
 transportation in, 262
 visitor information, 262

Boca Raton Museum of Art, 264
Bonnet House Museum & Gardens (Fort Lauderdale), 41, 245–246
Books & Books @ The Studios (Key West), 39, 199
Books & Books (Miami), 143
Books in/about Florida, 22–23
Boston's on the Beach (Delray Beach), 273
Bowling, Miami, 149
Boynton Beach, 274
Brevard Zoo (Cape Canaveral), 430–431
Broken Shaker (Miami), 147
Broward County, 238
Bus travel, 59–60, 188, 502, 505
Busch Gardens Tampa Bay, 9, 49, 298–300
Business hours, 61, 506
Butterfly World (Fort Lauderdale), 47, 246

C

Ca' d'Zan (Sarasota), 348
Café cubano, 104
Caladesi Island State Park (Dunedin/Clearwater Beach), 6, 331, 332
Calendar of events, 25–27
Calle Ocho Festival (Little Havana), 26
Camp Milton Historic Preserve (Jacksonville), 477–478
Camp Milton (Jacksonville), 43
Camping, 29
　Bahia Honda State Park, 183
　Biscayne National Park, 233
　Disney's Fort Wilderness Resort & Campground (Orlando), 405
　Everglades National Park, 227–228
　Fort Clinch State Park (Amelia Island), 497
　Fort DeSoto Park (St. Petersburg), 333
　Garden Key (Dry Tortugas), 214
　Jetty Park (Port Canaveral), 437
　John Pennekamp Coral Reef State Park (Key Largo), 173
　Sugarloaf Key/Key West KOA Resort, 183
　Sun Outdoors Sugarloaf Key, 183
Canaveral National Seashore (Cape Canaveral), 430, 434
Canoeing, 30. See also Outdoor activities
Cape Canaveral, 50. See also Space Coast
Capital One Orange Bowl (Miami), 27
Captain Tony's Saloon (Key West), 209–210
Car rental companies, 60, 442, 504
Carnival Center (Miami), 146
Casinos, Miami, 138
Cassadaga, 7, 452–453
Castillo de San Marcos National Monument (St. Augustine), 459–460
Character meals (Orlando), 425–426

Charles Hosmer Morse Museum of American Art (Orlando), 396
Chihuly Collection (St. Petersburg), 321
Christmas at Walt Disney World (Orlando), 27
Cici and Hyatt Brown Museum of Art (Daytona), 447
Cigars, 199, 307
Circus Museum (Sarasota), 349
Cirque du Soleil: Drawn to Life (WDW), 380
City Walks Food & Wine Tours (St. Augustine), 466
Classical music, Miami, 145
Clearwater Beach. See St. Pete & Clearwater Beaches
Clearwater Jazz Holiday, 26
Clearwater Marine Aquarium, 334
Club Space (Miami), 150
Cocoa Beach, 437–439
Coconut Grove (Miami), 58
　accommodations, 78–79
　attractions, 128–129
　dining, 103–105
　shopping, 142
Collins Park Cultural Center (Miami), 117
Colonial Quarter St. Augustine, 460
Colony Theatre (Miami), 146
Columbus Day Regatta (Biscayne Bay), 7
Conch Republic Independence Celebration (Key West), 26
Conch Tour Train (Key West), 38, 194
Coral Castle (Miami), 46, 132
Coral Gables (Miami), 46–47, 58
　accommodations, 75–78
　attractions, 126–128
　dining, 105–107
　shopping, 143
Coral Gables Museum (Miami), 126
The Corner (Miami), 147
Cosmo's (Boca Raton), 273
Costs, typical, 509
The Cove at Port Canaveral, 436
Cox Science Center & Aquarium (West Palm Beach), 280
Crane Point Hammock Museum & Nature Trails (Marathon), 161
Crazy Uncle Mike's (Boca Raton), 274
Cruises. See Boat tours
Cuban coffee, 104
Cuban Foundation Museum (Daytona), 447
Cummer Museum of Art & Gardens (Jacksonville), 478
Currency exchange, 507
Cypress Gardens Historic Botanical Garden (Orlando), 397

D

Dada (Delray Beach), 274
Daggerwing Nature Center (Boca Raton), 265
The Dalí (St. Petersburg), 10, 321

Dance clubs, Miami, 149–151
Dance performance, Miami, 146
Daytona Beach, 50, 439–454
　accommodations, 448–450
　arrival information, 440, 442
　attractions, 442, 446–448
　beach area, 443–444
　dining, 450–451
　nightlife, 451–452
　outdoor activities, 444–446
　shopping, 448
　side trips, 452–454
　spectator sports, 445
　transportation in, 442
　visitor information, 442
Daytona International Speedway, 10, 442
De Leon Springs State Park (Orlando), 397
De Soto National Memorial (Sarasota), 350
Delray Beach, 40–41, 49, 260–275
Dentists, 61, 366
Design District (Miami), 56
　accommodations, 75
　dining, 95–98
　shopping, 143
　walking tours, 133
Dining. See also Food & drink; Restaurants index
　Amelia Island, 499–500
　best of, 11–12
　Boca Raton & Delray Beach, 269–273
　Clearwater Beach, 340–342
　Daytona Beach, 450–451
　Everglades National Park, 229–230
　Fort Lauderdale, 254–260
　Indian Rocks Beach, 340
　Jacksonville, 487–489
　Key West, 205–209
　Lower Keys, 183–184
　Miami, 79–109
　Orlando, 414–426
　　character meals, 425–426
　　SeaWorld Orlando, 395
　　Universal Orlando, 423
　　Walt Disney World, 414–422
　Palm Beach & West Palm Beach, 289–293
　Sarasota, 354–357
　Space Coast, 438–439
　St. Augustine, 472–474
　St. Pete Beach, 339
　St. Petersburg, 327–329
　Tampa, 312–318
　Upper & Middle Keys, 173–177
Discovery Cove (Orlando), 395–396
Disney Springs, 46, 385, 420–422
Disney's Animal Kingdom, 45, 382–384, 418–419
Disney's Fort Wilderness Resort & Campground, 405
Disney's Hollywood Studios, 45, 46, 379–382, 418
Diving, 12–13, 31–32. See also Outdoor activities
Doctors, 61, 366
Dolphin Research Center (Marathon), 39, 162–163

511

INDEX

Dolphins, 8
Downtown Miami, 56
　accommodations, 72–75
　attractions, 123–125
　dining, 88–93
　shopping, 143
Downtown Orlando, 364
Dr. Von D. Mizell-Eula Johnson State Park (Fort Lauderdale), 3, 242
Drinking laws, 62, 506
Driving, 502, 504
　Daytona Beach, 444
　Gold Coast, 235
　the Keys, 157–158
　Miami, 60
　Orlando, 362
　Palm Beach & West Palm Beach, 276
Dry Tortugas National Park, 13, 212–214
Duck Tours South Beach (Miami), 133–134
Dunedin, 323
Duval Street (Key West), 39

E

Eco-Adventure Tours (Miami), 134
Eco-tourism, 27–28, 30
　Amelia Island, 492
　Daytona Beach, 444
　Everglades National Park, 226–227
　Sarasota, 346
　Space Coast, 436
　St. Augustine, 467
Eldora Statehouse (Cape Canaveral), 434
Ellie Schiller Homosassa Springs Wildlife State Park, 324–325
Elliott Key (Biscayne National Park), 230, 232
Emergencies, 61, 366, 506
EPCOT (WDW), 44–45, 46, 375–379, 416–418
Ernest Hemingway Home and Museum (Key West), 38, 190–191
Everglades City Seafood Festival, 25
Everglades National Park, 20, 40, 48–49, 216–230
　accommodations, 227–229
　attractions, 221–222
　camping, 227–228
　dining, 229–230
　entrances, 218–219
　fees & regulations, 219–220
　outdoor activities, 222–225
　ranger programs, 220
　safety, 220–221
　seasons, 220
　tours, 225–227
　visitor information, 219
Exchange rates, 507

F

Fairchild Tropical Garden (Miami), 126–127
Family-friendly activities, 8–10, 46–48, 506
Fantasy Fest (Key West), 7, 26–27
Feast of St. Augustine, 466
Fernandina Beach (Amelia Island), 42
Fillmore Miami Beach at Jackie Gleason Theater, 152
Films in Florida, 22–23
Fireworks shows, 375, 377
Fishing, 30. See also Outdoor activities
Flagler College (St. Augustine), 460–461
Flagler Museum (Palm Beach), 41, 281
Flamingos, 132
Florida
　best of, 2–14
　current context, 16
　fast facts, 506–509
　history of, 17–22
　itineraries, 35–48
　overrated experiences, 7–8
　in pop culture, 22–24
　regions in brief, 48–50
　when to visit, 24–25
The Florida Aquarium (Tampa), 302
Florida Grand Opera (Miami), 145
Florida Holocaust Museum (St. Petersburg), 322
Florida Keys. See The Keys
Florida Keys Aquarium Encounters (Marathon), 163–164
Florida Keys Eco-Discovery Center (Key West), 189
Florida Keys Food Tours, 173
Florida Keys National Wildlife Refuge, 180
Florida Keys Overseas Heritage Trail, 157
Florida Keys Shipwreck Trail, 13, 198
Florida Keys Wild Bird Center (Tavernier), 164
FloridaRAMA (St. Petersburg), 321–322
Food & drink. See also Dining
　Cuban coffee, 104
　fruit stands, 86
　mead, 178
　Miami Latin cuisine, 99
　orange juice, 8
Food Network South Beach Wine & Food Festival (Miami), 25
Food tours, 11, 93, 173
Football, Miami, 140
Fort Caroline National Memorial, 42
Fort Clinch State Park (Amelia Island), 491, 496–497
Fort DeSoto Park (St. Petersburg), 6, 331, 333
Fort East Martello Museum (Key West), 191
Fort Jefferson (Dry Tortugas), 212–213
Fort Lauderdale, 41, 47, 49, 237–260
　accommodations, 249–254
　arrival information, 238–240
　attractions, 245–248
　beaches, 240–242
　dining, 254–260
　nightlife, 260
　outdoor activities, 243–245
　shopping, 248–249
　spectator sports, 244–245
　transportation in, 240
　visitor information, 240
Fort Matanzas (St. Augustine), 459–460
Fort Zachary Taylor Historic State Park (Key West), 196–197
Fox's Lounge (Miami), 148
Friendship Fountain (Jacksonville), 480
Frost Science Museum (Miami), 9–10, 47, 123
Fruit and Spice Park (Miami), 47, 132
Fruit stands, 86, 132
The Funky Biscuit (Boca Raton), 274

G

GableStage (Miami), 144–145
Garden Key (Dry Tortugas), 214
Gato Village Pocket Park (Key West), 192
Gatorland (Orlando), 396
Gay and Lesbian Historic Trolley Tour (Key West), 196
Ghost Tours of St. Augustine, 466
Ghosts & Gravestones Frightseeing Tour (Key West), 195
Ghosts & Gravestones (St. Augustine), 466
Giraffe Ranch (Dade City), 303
Glazer Children's Museum (Tampa), 303
Gold Coast, 49, 235–294
　Boca Raton & Delray Beach, 260–275
　driving, 235
　Fort Lauderdale, 237–260
　Palm Beach & West Palm Beach, 275–294
Golf, 30–31. See also Outdoor activities
Gonzáles-Alvarez House (St. Augustine), 461
Gramp's (Miami), 148
The Green Parrot Bar (Key West), 210
Gumbo Limbo Nature Center (Boca Raton), 47, 265

H

Halifax Historical Museum (Daytona), 446
Hallandale Beach, 238
Halloween Horror Nights (Orlando), 26
Harry S. Truman Little White House (Key West), 39, 191
Health tips, 506–507
Henry B. Plant Museum (Tampa), 303
Hialeah Park Casino (Miami), 132
Hiking, 31, 181, 232, 323
Hillsboro Inlet Lighthouse (Fort Lauderdale), 246–247
History of Diving Museum (Islamorada), 161–162
History of Florida, 17–22
HistoryMiami Museum, 124, 133

Holidays, 25
Hollywood, 49, 238
Hollywood Beach, 241
Holocaust Memorial (Miami), 36, 117–118
Homestead (Miami), 107–109, 132
Horse racing, Miami, 140–141
Horseback riding, 346, 445, 483, 494
Hospitals, Orlando, 366
Hotels. *See* Accommodations; Accommodations index
Hugh Taylor Birch State Park (Fort Lauderdale), 242

I

Imagine Museum (St. Petersburg), 321
Indian Key (Florida Keys), 160
Indian Key Historic State Park (Florida Keys), 161
Indian Rocks Beach, 340
International Drive (I-Drive), 364, 365, 409–410
International Swimming Hall of Fame (ISHOF) (Fort Lauderdale), 41, 247
Internet service, 61, 507
Islamorada (Florida Keys), 158–178
 accommodations, 169–173
 animal encounters, 162–165
 arrival information, 159
 dining, 173–177
 nightlife, 177–178
 outdoor activities, 159–162
 visitor information, 159
 watersports, 167–169
Itineraries, 35–48
 Northern Florida in 1 week, 42–43
 Orlando's theme parks, 43–46
 South Florida, family-style, 46–48
 South Florida in 2 weeks, 35–42

J

Jacksonville, 43, 50, 476–490
 accommodations, 484–487
 arrival information, 476–477
 attractions, 477–480
 beaches, 482–483
 dining, 487–489
 nightlife, 489–490
 outdoor activities, 483–484
 shopping, 484
 spectator sports, 483–484
 Timucuan Ecological & Historic Preserve, 480–482
 transportation in, 477
 visitor information, 477
Jacksonville Zoo and Gardens, 478
Jeffers Carriages (Amelia Island), 495
Jetty Park (Port Canaveral), 435–436, 437
Jewish Museum of Florida (Miami), 36, 118–119
Jezebel (Miami), 148
John and Mable Ringling Museum of Art (Sarasota), 10, 348

John Pennekamp Coral Reef State Park (Key Largo), 13, 39, 165–167, 173
Johnnie Brown's (Delray Beach), 274
John's Pass Village and Boardwalk (St. Pete/Clearwater Beach), 334, 342
Judah P. Benjamin Confederate Memorial at Gamble Plantation State Park (Sarasota), 350–351
Julia & Henry's (Miami), 47
Jungle Island (Miami), 119–120
Jungle Queen Riverboat (Fort Lauderdale), 47, 247

K

Kayaking, 30. *See also* Outdoor activities
Kendall, 107–109
Kennedy Space Center Visitor Complex (Cape Canaveral), 8–9, 50, 431–434
Key Biscayne (Miami), 46, 55–56
 attractions, 122–123
 beach area, 114
 dining, 102–103
Key Largo, 48, 158–178
 accommodations, 169–173
 animal encounters, 162–165
 arrival information, 159
 dining, 173–177
 John Pennekamp Coral Reef State Park, 13, 39, 165–167
 nightlife, 177–178
 outdoor activities, 159–162
 visitor information, 159
 watersports, 167–169
Key West, 38–39, 48, 185–211
 accommodations, 199–204
 arrival information, 185, 188
 attractions, 189–194
 dining, 205–209
 nightlife, 209–211
 outdoor activities, 196–198
 shopping, 198–199
 tours, 194–196
 transportation in, 188–189
 visitor information, 189
Key West Aquarium, 191
Key West Butterfly & Nature Conservatory, 192
Key West Cemetery, 192
Key West Lighthouse & Keeper's Quarters Museum, 192
Key West Literary Seminar, 25
Key West Museum of Art and History at the Custom House, 192
Key West Shipwreck Treasure Museum, 192–193
The Keys, 48, 155–211. *See also* Islamorada; Key Largo; Key West; Marathon
 driving, 157–158
 itineraries, 36, 38–39
 Lower Keys, 178–185
 Upper & Middle Keys, 158–178
King's Landing (Orlando), 396–397
Kingsley Plantation, 42
Kissimmee, 364
Knaus Berry Farm (Miami), 86

L

Lake Buena Vista, 364, 405–406
Lake Worth Beach, 274
Latin clubs, Miami, 152–153
Latin cuisine (Miami), 99
Lauderdale-By-The-Sea, 256
Launches, viewing, 434
LaVilla Museum (Jacksonville), 43, 480
Legal aid, 507
Legoland Florida, 50
Legoland Florida (Orlando), 397–398
LGBTQIA+ travelers, 507
 Fort Lauderdale, 259
 Key West, 196, 210–211
 Miami, 151–152
Lightner Museum (St. Augustine), 460–461
Lightning Lane (WDW), 369
Lignumvitae Key Botanical State Park (Florida Keys), 160–161
Lilian Place Heritage Center (Daytona), 446–447
Limousines, Miami, 53
Lion Country Safari (Loxahatchee), 47, 281–282
Little Haiti (Miami), 95–98
Little Havana (Miami), 46, 57–58
 dining, 98–102
 shopping, 142
 walking tours, 134–135
Little Torch Key (Florida Keys), 36, 38
LIV (Miami), 151
Live music, Miami, 152–153
Long Key State Recreation Area (Florida Keys), 167
Looe Key National Marine Sanctuary (Florida Keys), 13, 181
Lori Wilson Park (Cocoa Beach), 435
Lost property, Miami, 62
Lowe Art Museum (Miami), 127
Lower Keys Underwater Music Fest, 26
Lummus Park (Miami), 3

M

Mac's Club Deuce (Miami), 148
Magic Kingdom (WDW), 43–44, 370–375, 415–416
MagicBands (WDW), 370
MagicMobile (WDW), 370
Mail, 507
Mallory Square (Key West), 38
Manatee Critical Care Center (Jacksonville), 43
Manatees, 2, 325
Mango's Tropical Café (Miami), 153
Mar-a-Lago (Palm Beach), 40, 280
Marathon (Florida Keys), 158–178
 accommodations, 169–173
 animal encounters, 162–165
 arrival information, 159
 dining, 173–177
 nightlife, 177–178
 outdoor activities, 159–162
 visitor information, 159
 watersports, 167–169

513

Marie Selby Botanical Gardens (Sarasota), 347
Marine Science Center (Daytona), 447
Marineland Dolphin Adventure (St. Augustine), 464
Marjory Stoneman Douglas Biscayne Nature Center (Key Biscayne), 46, 122
Matheson Hammock Park Beach (Miami), 47
Mead, 178
Medical requirements, 507
Mel Fisher Maritime Museum (Key West), 11, 38, 193
Merritt Island National Wildlife Refuge (Cape Canaveral), 430, 435
Miami, 35–36, 46–47, 48. See also South Beach
  accommodations, 62–79
  addresses, 54
  arrival information, 52–53
  attractions
    Art Deco District, 114–121
    Coconut Grove, 128–129
    Coral Gables, 126–128
    downtown Miami, 123–125
    Homestead, 132
    Key Biscayne, 122–123
    midtown Miami, 125–126
    north Miami, 121–122
    South Miami-Dade County, 130–131
    Wynwood, 129–130
  beaches, 111–114
  berry picking, 86
  dining, 79–109
  fast facts, 61–62
  Latin cuisine, 99
  neighborhoods in brief, 54–58
  nightlife, 144–153
  outdoor activities, 137–140
  public transportation, 59–60
  shopping, 141–143
  spectator sports, 140–141
  tours, 133–135
  visitor information, 53–54
  watersports, 135–136
Miami Beach, 54–55
  accommodations, 69–72
  beach area, 112–114
  dining, 83–85
Miami Beach Botanical Garden, 117
Miami Beach Regional Library, 117
Miami Book Fair International, 27
Miami Children's Museum, 9, 120
Miami City Ballet, 146
Miami Culinary Tours, 11, 93
Miami International Boat Show, 25
Miami Light Project, 144
Miami Music Week (MMW), 150
Mickey's Not-So-Scary Halloween Party (Orlando), 26
Midtown Miami, 56, 93–95, 125–126
Mission Nombre de Dios Museum (St. Augustine), 462
Mobile phones, 507
MOCA Jacksonville, 43, 478–480
Mode Downtown (Miami), 148

Monkey Jungle (Miami), 130–131
Morikami Museum and Japanese Gardens (Delray Beach), 40, 47, 265–266
MOSI (Museum of Science and Industry) (Tampa), 10, 304
Mote Marine Laboratory & Aquarium (Sarasota), 349–350
Mote Science Education Aquarium (Sarasota), 350
Motorsports Hall of Fame of America (Daytona), 442
Museum of Arts & Sciences (Daytona), 10, 447
Museum of Contemporary Art (MOCA) (Miami), 10, 122
Museum of Discovery & Science (Fort Lauderdale), 47, 248
Museum of Fine Arts (St. Petersburg), 322
Museum of Science & History of Jacksonville (MOSH), 480
Museum of Sex Miami, 124
Museum of the American Arts and Crafts Movement (St. Petersburg), 320
Museums, best of, 10–11
Music of Florida, 23–24

N

NASCAR Racing Experience (Daytona), 10, 442
National Key Deer Refuge (Big Pine Key), 38, 180
New Smyrna Beach, 453–454
New World Symphony (Miami), 145
Newspapers, Miami, 62
Nightlife
  Amelia Island, 500
  Boca Raton & Delray Beach, 273–275
  Daytona Beach, 451–452
  Fort Lauderdale, 260
  Jacksonville, 489–490
  Key West, 209–211
  Lower Keys, 184–185
  Miami, 144–153
  Palm Beach & West Palm Beach, 294
  Sarasota, 357–358
  Space Coast, 439
  St. Augustine, 474–476
  St. Pete & Clearwater Beaches, 342
  St. Petersburg, 329
  Tampa, 318–319
  Upper & Middle Keys, 177–178
Nights of Lights (St. Augustine), 27, 458
Nike Hercules Nuclear Missle Base (Everglades), 40, 222
Nikki Beach (Miami), 151
NKF Labor Day Pro-Am Surfing Festival (Cocoa Beach), 26
North Miami, 86–87, 121–122
Northeast Florida, 50, 428–500
  Amelia Island, 490–500
  Daytona Beach, 439–454
  Jacksonville, 476–490
  1-week itinerary, 42–43
  Space Coast, 428–439
  St. Augustine, 454–476

Norton Museum of Art (West Palm Beach), 41, 282
NSU Art Museum Fort Lauderdale, 41, 248

O

Offbeat experiences, best of, 6–7
Old Jail Museum (St. Augustine), 462
Old St. Augustine History Museum, 462–463
Oldest House Museum & Garden (Key West), 193
The Oldest House Museum Complex (St. Augustine), 461
The Oldest Wooden Schoolhouse Historic Museum & Gardens (St. Augustine), 461–462
Oleta River State Park (Miami), 121
Olympia Theater (Miami), 146
Opera, Miami, 145
Orange County Regional History Center (Orlando), 398
Orange juice, 8
Orlando, 50, 360–426
  accommodations, 398–413
  arrival information, 360–362
  attractions, 396–398
  city layout, 363
  dining, 414–426
  fast facts, 366–367
  neighborhoods in brief, 363–364
  package tours, 362
  theme park itinerary, 43–46
  theme parks
    Aquatica, 396
    Discovery Cove, 395–396
    Legoland Florida, 397–398
    SeaWorld Orlando, 392–395
    Universal Orlando, 386–392
    Walt Disney World, 367–386
  transportation in, 364–366
  visitor information, 362
The Orlando Eye, 398
Outdoor activities
  Amelia Island, 492–494
  Biscayne National Park, 232–233
  Boca Raton & Delray Beach, 262–264
  Daytona Beach, 444–446
  Dry Tortugas National Park, 213–214
  Everglades National Park, 222–225
  Fort Lauderdale, 243–245
  Jacksonville, 483–484
  Key West, 196–198
  Lower Keys, 180–182
  Miami, 137–140
  Palm Beach & West Palm Beach, 278–280
  Sarasota, 345–347
  Space Coast, 436–437
  St. Augustine, 467–468
  St. Pete & Clearwater Beaches, 333
  St. Petersburg, 323
  Tampa, 305–307
  Upper & Middle Keys, 159–162
Overrated experiences, 7–8

P

Packing tips, 507–508
Paddleboarding, 168, 232, 346, 492
Palace (Miami), 151
Palace Saloon (Amelia Island), 42, 500
Palm Beach, 40–41, 49, 275–294
  accommodations, 284–289
  arrival information, 276
  attractions, 280–283
  dining, 289–293
  nightlife, 294
  outdoor activities, 278–280
  shopping, 283–284
  transportation in, 276
  visitor information, 276
Palm Beach Zoo & Conservation Society, 283
Parades, Magic Kingdom (WDW), 375
Parking
  Key West, 189
  Miami, 60
  SeaWorld Orlando, 392
  Universal Orlando, 387
  Walt Disney World, 367
Pass-a-Grille Public Beach (St. Pete Beach), 331
Patricia and Phillip Frost Art Museum (Miami), 10, 130
Paynes Prairie Preserve State Park, 454
Peña-Peck House (St. Augustine), 463
Peppa Pig Theme Park (Orlando), 398
Pérez Art Museum Miami, 10, 36, 125
Performing arts. See Nightlife
Pet boarding, Orlando, 366–367
Peters Point Beach Front Park (Amelia Island), 491
Pharmacies, Orlando, 367
Pickleball. See Tennis/Pickleball
Pigeon Key (Marathon), 162
Pinecrest Gardens (Miami), 119
Pinellas Trail (St. Petersburg), 323
Police, Miami, 62
Polo, 278
Ponce de León Inlet Lighthouse & Museum (Daytona), 447–448
Ponce De Leon's Fountain of Youth Archaeological Park (St. Augustine), 463
Post offices, 62, 322, 367
Preston B. Bird and Mary Heinlein Fruit and Spice Park (Miami), 47, 132
Psychics, 7, 452–453
Public transportation
  Boca Raton & Delray Beach, 262
  Daytona Beach, 442
  Fort Lauderdale, 240
  Jacksonville, 477
  Miami, 53, 59–60
  Orlando, 364–366
  Palm Beach & West Palm Beach, 276
  Sarasota, 344
  Space Coast, 430
  St. Augustine, 458
  St. Pete & Clearwater Beaches, 331
  St. Petersburg, 320
  Tampa, 297

Q–R

R House Wynwood (Miami), 152
Rail travel. See Train travel
Rapids Water Park (West Palm Beach), 283
Raymond F. Kravis Center for the Performing Arts (West Palm Beach), 294
Redland Tropical Trail Tours (Miami), 86, 135
Reservations, Disney restaurants, 414
Responsible travel, 27–28. See also Eco-tourism
Restaurants. See Dining; Restaurants index
Richard and Pat Johnson Palm Beach County History Museum, 283
Ride-sharing services, 53, 60–61, 366
The Ringling Circus Museum (Sarasota), 10, 348–349
Ripley's Red Train Tours (St. Augustine), 465
Ritz Theatre (Jacksonville), 43, 480, 489
Riverside Avondale (Jacksonville), 43
Robbie's of Islamorada (Florida Keys), 161
Robbie's Pier (Islamorada), 38, 164–165
Robert Is Here (Homestead), 86
Robinson Preserve (Sarasota), 351
ROLEX 24 at Daytona, 25
Ron Jon Surf School (Cocoa Beach), 3
Root Family Museum (Daytona), 447
Rubell Museum (Miami), 10, 125–126

S

Safari Splash (Loxahatchee), 282
Safari Wilderness Ranch (Lakeland), 303
Safety, 508
  Everglades National Park, 220–221
  health tips, 506–507
  Miami, 62
Sailing, 28–29, 323, 346–347, 492
San Carlos Institute (Key West), 193–194
Sand Key Park (Clearwater Beach), 331
Sarasota, 49, 342–358
  accommodations, 351–354
  arrival information, 344
  attractions, 347–351
  beaches, 344–345
  dining, 354–357
  nightlife, 357–358
  outdoor activities, 345–347
  spectator sports, 347
  transportation in, 344
  visitor information, 344
Saving money
  accommodations, 505–506
  air travel, 503
  dining at Walt Disney World, 415
Scenic Boat Tour (Orlando), 398
Schnebly Redland's Winery (Miami), 86, 134
Schoolhouse Children's Museum (Boynton Beach), 274
Scuba diving. See Diving; Outdoor activities
Sea Life Safari (Clearwater Beach), 334
Sea turtles, 242
Seagrass Adventure (Miami), 9, 123
SeaWorld Orlando, 46, 50, 392–395
Security, Walt Disney World, 368
Segafredo l'Originale (Miami), 148
Seminole Hard Rock Hotel & Casino (Fort Lauderdale), 41, 238
Seminole-Hard Rock Winterfest Boat Parade (Fort Lauderdale), 27
Senior travel, 508
Seven Mile Bridge (Florida Keys), 38, 162
Shell shops, 7
Sheriff's Animal Farm (Florida Keys), 204
Shopping
  Boca Raton & Delray Beach, 266–267
  Daytona Beach, 448
  Fort Lauderdale, 248–249
  Jacksonville, 484
  Key West, 198–199
  Miami, 141–143
  Palm Beach & West Palm Beach, 283–284
  St. Augustine, 468–469
  Tampa, 307
Siesta Key Beach, 3
Sloppy Joe's (Key West), 38, 210
Smoking, 508
Snorkeling, 12–13, 31–32, 325. See also Outdoor activities
Soccer, Miami, 141
Solomon's Castle (Sarasota), 351
Sombrero Beach (Marathon), 156, 160
SoundScape Park (Miami), 145
South Beach, 8, 35–36, 54
  accommodations, 64–68
  Art Deco District, 114–121
  dining, 80–83
  shopping, 143
South Miami-Dade County, 58, 130–131
South Pointe Park (South Beach), 117
Southbank Riverwalk (Jacksonville), 480
Space Coast, 428–439
  accommodations, 437–438
  arrival information, 430
  attractions, 430–434

515

INDEX

beaches, 434–436
dining, 438–439
nightlife, 439
outdoor activities, 436–437
transportation in, 430
visitor information, 430
Spanish Military Hospital Museum (St. Augustine), 462
Special-interest trips, 28–33
Spectator sports
Daytona Beach, 445
Fort Lauderdale, 244–245
Jacksonville, 483–484
Miami, 140–141
Palm Beach & West Palm Beach, 279
Sarasota, 347
St. Petersburg, 323, 326
Tampa, 306–307
Speedweeks (Daytona), 25
Spyglass Travel and Tours (St. Augustine), 466
St. Augustine, 42, 50, 454–476
accommodations, 469–472
arrival information, 458
attractions, 458–465
beaches, 466–467
dining, 472–474
nightlife, 474–476
outdoor activities, 467–468
shopping, 468–469
tours, 465–466
transportation in, 458
visitor information, 458
St. Augustine Alligator Farm Zoological Park, 464
St. Augustine Lighthouse & Maritime Museum, 463
St. Augustine Pirate & Treasure Museum, 465
St. Augustine Surf Culture and History Museum, 461
St. Pete & Clearwater Beaches, 49, 330–342
accommodations, 335–338
attractions on land, 334
dining, 339–342
nightlife, 342
outdoor activities, 333
transportation in, 331
visitor information, 331
St. Pete Pier, 320
St. Petersburg, 49, 319–329
accommodations, 326–327
arrival information, 319
attractions, 320–322
dining, 327–329
nightlife, 329
outdoor activities, 323
spectator sports, 323, 326
transportation in, 320
visitor information, 320
Stock Island (Florida Keys), 204
Stonewall National Museum (Fort Lauderdale), 259
Stranahan House (Fort Lauderdale), 248
Sugarloaf Key (Florida Keys), 178–185
Sugarloaf Key/Key West KOA Resort, 183
Summerland Key (Florida Keys), 178–185

Sun Outdoors Sugarloaf Key, 183
Sunken Gardens (St. Petersburg), 322
Superblue Miami, 10, 35, 129–130
Surfing, 3, 26, 437
Swimming. *See* Beaches

T

Talbot Islands State Parks (Amelia Island), 491
Tampa, 49, 296–319
accommodations, 310–312
arrival information, 297
attractions, 297–305
dining, 312–318
nightlife, 318–319
outdoor activities, 305–307
shopping, 307
spectator sports, 306–307
transportation in, 297
visitor information, 297
Tampa Baseball Museum, 305
Tampa Bay, 49
Sarasota, 342–358
St. Pete & Clearwater Beaches, 330–342
St. Petersburg, 319–329
Tampa, 296–319
Tampa Bay History Center, 304
Tampa Museum of Art, 304
Tarpon Springs, 341
Taxes, 62, 367, 508
Taxis, 53, 60–61, 442
Tennessee Williams Museum (Key West), 39, 194
Tennis/Pickleball, 32–33, 279
Amelia Island, 494
Boca Raton & Delray Beach, 264
Fort Lauderdale, 245
Miami, 139–140
Sarasota, 347
St. Petersburg, 326
Tampa, 307
Theater. *See* Nightlife
Theater of the Sea (Islamorada), 165
Theme park itinerary, 43–46
Three Sisters Springs, 325
Tickets
SeaWorld Orlando, 392
Universal Orlando, 387
Walt Disney World, 368–370
Time zones, 62, 508
Timucuan Ecological & Historic Preserve (Jacksonville), 42, 480–482
Tipping, 367, 508–509
Toilet seat cut (Florida Keys), 6
Toilets, 62, 509
Tour Saint Augustine, 466
Tours. *See also* Boat tours; Eco-tourism; Walking tours
American Beach (Amelia Island), 495
Everglades National Park, 225–227
Kennedy Space Center, 432
Key West, 194–196
Miami, 133–135
Orlando, 362
St. Augustine, 465–466
Tampa, 302

Walt Disney World, 385–386
Ybor City, 305
Train travel, 503–505
Transit information, 62, 240, 504–505
Trolley tours, 194–195, 465
Turtle Hospital (Marathon), 38, 165
Turtles, 242
Tuscawilla Nature Preserve (Daytona), 447
Twist (Miami), 152

U

Ultra Music Festival (Miami), 150
Universal Orlando, 8, 44–45, 50, 386–392
accommodations, 410–413
character meals, 426
dining, 423

V

Venetian Pool (Miami), 47, 127–128
Villa Zorayda Museum (St. Augustine), 464
Vino Wine Bar & Kitchen (Boca Raton), 275
Virginia Key Beach Park (Key Biscayne), 114
Virtual Queues (WDW), 373
Vizcaya Museum and Gardens (Miami), 36, 128–129

W

Walking tours
Art Deco, 116
Key West, 195–196
Miami, 35, 36, 56, 133–135
St. Augustine, 466
Walt Disney World, 8, 21, 50, 363–364, 367–386
accommodations, 399–405
character meals, 425–426
dining, 414–422
Disney's Animal Kingdom, 382–384
Disney's Hollywood Studios, 379–382
EPCOT, 44–45, 375–379
fast facts, 366–367
hours of operation, 368
Magic Kingdom, 43–44, 370–375
tickets, 368–370
tours, 385–386
transportation in, 365
water parks, 385
when to visit, 368
Warehouse District (West Palm Beach), 292
Water parks, 385, 392
Water taxis, 41, 240
Weather, 24–25, 62, 367
Weedon Island Preserve (Tampa Bay), 325
Weeki Wachee Springs State Park, 8, 324
West Palm Beach. *See* Palm Beach
Westgate Cocoa Beach Pier, 435
Wet Bar at the W South Beach (Miami), 149
Wet Willie's (Miami), 149

Whetstone Chocolates (St. Augustine), 469
Wi-Fi, 61, 507
Wilton Manors (Fort Lauderdale), 259
Wilzig Erotic Art Museum (Miami), 120
Windsurfing, Miami, 136
Winter Music Conference (WMC) (Miami), 150
Winter Park, 364
Winter Party (Miami Beach), 26
The Wolfsonian (Miami), 10, 36, 120–121
Womenfest (Key West), 26
Wreck Bar (Fort Lauderdale), 41
Wynwood (Miami), 56–57
 accommodations, 75
 attractions, 129–130
 dining, 93–95
 shopping, 143
Wynwood Walls (Miami), 10, 35, 130

X–Y–Z

Ybor City, 304–305
Ybor City Museum State Park, 305

Zoo Miami, 47, 131
ZooTampa at Lowry Park, 302–303

Accommodations

1 Hotel South Beach (Miami), 64
The 1910 Inn (Tarpon Springs), 341
AC Hotel Orlando Lake Buena Vista, 408
AC Wynwood (Miami), 75
Acqualina Resort & Residences (Miami), 69
Aloft Orlando Lake Buena Vista, 408
Ambrosia Key West, 202
Amelia Schoolhouse Inn (Amelia Island), 497
Anchor Inn Bed and Breakfast (New Smyrna Beach), 453
Arlo Wynwood (Miami), 75
The Atlantic Hotel & Spa (Fort Lauderdale), 250
Avalon (St. Petersburg), 327
Bahama House (Daytona Beach), 449
Baker's Cay Resort Key Largo, Curio Collection by Hilton, 170
The Balfour Hotel (Miami), 67
Barefoot Bay Resort and Marina (Clearwater Beach), 338
Bay Palms (St. Pete Beach), 336
Bayfront Westcott House Bed & Breakfast Inn (St. Augustine), 471
Bayview Plaza (St. Pete Beach), 336
Beach Haven (St. Pete Beach), 336
Beachside Motel (Amelia Island), 497
Best Western Bayfront (St. Augustine), 469

The Best Western Gateway to the Keys (Everglades), 229
The Betsy Hotel (Miami), 66
Biltmore Hotel (Miami), 76
Black Dolphin Inn (New Smyrna Beach), 453
The Boca Raton, 267
Bougainvillea (Fort Lauderdale), 253
The Brazilian Court Palm Beach, 284–285
The Breakers Palm Beach, 14, 285–286
Cabana Colony Cottages (Daytona Beach), 450
The Capitana (Key West), 200
Captain's Table Hotel (Everglades), 228
Carillon Miami Wellness Resort, 69
Carriage Way Bed & Breakfast (St. Augustine), 471
Casa de Solana Bed & Breakfast (St. Augustine), 471
Casa Faena (Miami), 70
Casa Monica Resort & Spa, Autograph Collection (St. Augustine), 469–470
Casa Morada (Islamorada), 171
citizenM Miami Worldcenter, 74–75
The Collector Inn (St. Augustine), 470
The Colony (Palm Beach), 287–288
Colony Hotel & Cabana Club (Delray Beach), 268–269
Comfort Suites Maingate East (Orlando), 408–409
Conrad Fort Lauderdale, 249–250
Crane's Beach House Boutique Hotel & Luxury Villas (Delray Beach), 268
d Suites by Hilton Tampa USF Near Busch Gardens, 310
The Daytona, Autograph Collection (Daytona Beach), 449
Destiny Palms Hotel (Orlando), 409
Devil's Elbow Fishing Resort (St. Augustine), 469
Disney's All-Star Resorts (Movies/Music/Sports) (Orlando), 402
Disney's Animal Kingdom Lodge (Orlando), 399
Disney's Art of Animation Resort (Orlando), 402
Disney's Beach Club/Disney's Yacht Club (Orlando), 399–400
Disney's BoardWalk Inn (Orlando), 400
Disney's Caribbean Beach Resort (Orlando), 402
Disney's Contemporary Resort (Orlando), 400
Disney's Coronado Springs Resort (Orlando), 403
Disney's Fort Wilderness Resort & Campground (Orlando), 405
Disney's Grand Floridian Resort & Spa (Orlando), 401

Disney's Polynesian Village Resort (Orlando), 401
Disney's Pop Century Resort (Orlando), 403
Disney's Port Orleans Riverside and French Quarter (Orlando), 403
Disney's Wilderness Lodge (Orlando), 401
The Don CeSar (St. Pete Beach), 335
Dream South Beach (Miami), 68
Drury Plaza Hotel Orlando—Disney Springs Area, 406
Dua Miami Brickell, An Autograph Collection Hotel, 74
Eau Palm Beach Resort and Spa, 286
Elizabeth Pointe (Amelia Island), 497–498
The Elser Hotel (Miami), 72
Epicurean Hotel, Autograph Collection (Tampa), 310
Everglades Adventures Hotel Suites, 228
Everglades City Motel, 228
Faena Hotel Miami Beach, 14, 69–70
Fairbanks House (Amelia Island), 498
Fairfield Inn and Suites Marathon Florida Keys, 172–173
Flamingo Lodge and Restaurant (Everglades National Park), 227
Florida House Inn (Amelia Island), 498
Four Seasons at the Surf Club (Miami), 70–71
Four Seasons Hotel & Residences Fort Lauderdale, 250
Four Seasons Resort Orlando at Walt Disney World Resort (Orlando), 403–404
Four Seasons Resort Palm Beach, 286–287
Freehand Miami, 72
The Gardens Hotel (Key West), 14, 200
Gaylord Palms (Orlando), 407
the goodtime hotel, Miami Beach, A Tribute Portfolio Hotel, 68
The Grand Guesthouse (Key West), 202
Hampton Inn & Suites (Tampa), 310
Hampton Inn Jacksonville Beach/Oceanfront, 485
Hard Rock Hotel Daytona Beach, 449
Hard Rock Hotel (Orlando), 411
High Noon Beach Resort (Fort Lauderdale), 252–253
Hilton West Palm Beach, 288
Holiday Inn Express & Suites (Tampa), 310
The Hollander Hotel St. Petersburg Downtown, 327
Home2 Suites by Hilton Orlando Near Universal (Orlando), 410

517

ACCOMMODATIONS INDEX

Hoosville Hostel (Everglades), 229
Hotel Haya Ybor City, 310–311
Hotel St. Michel (Miami), 77–78
Hyatt House Across from Universal Orlando Resort, 410
Hyatt Place St. Augustine/Vilano Beach, 469
Hyatt Place Tampa/Busch Gardens, 310
Hyatt Regency Grand Cypress Resort (Orlando), 407
Hyatt Regency Jacksonville Riverfront, 485
The Inn at Cocoa Beach, 437–438
Inn on the Avenue (New Smyrna Beach), 453
The Inn on Third (St. Petersburg), 327
Innisbrook Golf Resort (Clearwater Beach), 338
InterContinental Miami, 74
Isla Bella Beach Resort (Marathon), 171
Island City House Hotel (Key West), 202–203
Ivey House Everglades Adventure Hotel, 228
Jules Undersea Lodge (Key Largo), 6, 170
JW Marriott Clearwater Beach Resort & Spa, 336–337
JW Marriott Orlando, Grande Lakes, 409–410
JW Marriott Tampa Water Street, 311
The Kenwood Inn (St. Augustine), 471–472
KeySea Houseboats (Key Largo), 170
Kimpton EPIC Hotel (Miami), 74
Kona Kai Resort, Gallery & Botanic Garden (Key Largo), 172
La Fiesta Ocean Inn & Suites (St. Augustine), 469
Lago Mar Beach Resort and Club (Fort Lauderdale), 251
Life House South of Fifth (Miami), 66–67
Lime Tree Bay Resort (Long Key), 172
Little Palm Island Resort & Spa (Little Torch Key), 14, 182
The Lodge & Club (Ponte Vedra Beach), 485–486
Loews Coral Gables (Miami), 77
Loews Portofino Bay Hotel (Orlando), 411
Loews Royal Pacific Resort (Orlando), 411–412
Loews Sapphire Falls Resort (Orlando), 412
Lost Inn Paradise (Cape Canaveral), 14, 438
Margaritaville Beach Resort Hollywood Beach (Fort Lauderdale), 250
Margaritaville Resort Orlando, 407–408
Marquesa 414 (Key West), 200
Marquesa Key West, 200
Max Beach Resort (Daytona Beach), 449–450

Mayfair House Hotel & Garden (Miami), 78
Miccosukee Casino & Resort (Everglades National Park), 227
Mondrian (Miami), 67
The Moorings Village (Islamorada), 14, 170–171
Mr. C Miami, 79
Napoli Belmar (Fort Lauderdale), 253
National Hotel Miami Beach, 67
Night Swan Intracoastal Bed and Breakfast (New Smyrna Beach), 454
Ocean Key Resort & Spa (Key West), 201
Ocean's Edge Resort & Marina (Stock Island), 204
Oleta River State Park (Miami), 121
One Ocean Resort & Spa (Jacksonville), 486
Opal Grand Resort (Delray Beach), 268
The Opal Sands (Clearwater Beach), 337
Palm Beach Historic Inn, 288
The Palms Hotel & Spa (Miami), 71–72
Parmer's Resort (Little Torch Key), 182
Pelican Grand Beach Resort (Fort Lauderdale), 251
Pelican Hotel (Miami), 67–68
Perry Hotel & Marina (Stock Island), 204
PGA National Resort (Palm Beach), 288–289
The Pillars Hotel & Club (Fort Lauderdale), 251
Pioneer Inn (Palm Beach), 289
Pirate Haus Inn (St. Augustine), 470
Plaza Beach Hotel Beachfront Resort (St. Pete Beach), 336
Ponte Vedra Inn & Club, 486
Ragged Edge Oceanfront Resort & Marina (Islamorada), 172
Ramada by Wyndham Sarasota Waterfront, 352
The Ray (Delray Beach), 268
Renaissance Orlando Resort & Spa, 406
The Residences on Siesta Key Beach, 353
The Resort at Longboat Key Club, 352
The Ritz-Carlton, Amelia Island, 498–499
Ritz-Carlton Grande Lakes Orlando, 409–410
Riverdale Inn (Jacksonville), 485
Riverside Hotel (Fort Lauderdale), 253
Rod & Gun Lodge (Everglades), 228
Salt Air Inn and Suites (Jacksonville), 486
Sandpearl Resort (Clearwater Beach), 337

The Sarasota Modern, a Tribute Portfolio Hotel, 352
Sawgrass Marriott Golf Resort & Spa (Ponte Vedra Beach), 487
Sea Downs (Fort Lauderdale), 253
Seascape Inn Bed & Breakfast (Key West), 203
Seashell Motel & Key West Hostel, 204
Seminole Hard Rock Hotel & Casino Hollywood (Fort Lauderdale), 252
Seminole Hard Rock Hotel & Casino Tampa, 311–312
The Setai (Miami), 66
Shamrock Coral Gables (Miami), 78
Shephard's Beach Resort (Clearwater Beach), 338
Sheraton Sand Key Resort (Clearwater Beach), 337–338
Shoreline All Suites Inn & Cabana Colony Cottages (Daytona Beach), 450
Siesta Key Beach Resort and Suites, 353–354
Signia by Hilton Orlando Bonnet Creek, 406
Silver Palms Inn (Key West), 203
Simonton Court Historic Inn & Cottages (Key West), 14, 201
Sirata Beach Resort (St. Pete Beach), 335
snooze (Fort Lauderdale), 253
Southernmost Beach Resort (Key West), 201
Southernmost Point Guest House By the Beach (Key West), 203
St. Pete Beach Suites, 336
St. Regis Longboat Key Resort, 352
Sugarloaf Key Hotel, 183
The Tampa EDITION, 312
Tampa Marriott Water Street, 312
THesis Hotel Miami, 78
The Tony (Miami), 68
Turtle Beach Resort & Inn (Siesta Key), 14, 354
Universal Helios Grand Resort (Orlando), 411
Universal Stella Nova Resort (Orlando), 411
Universal Terra Luna Resort (Orlando), 411
Universal's Aventura Hotel (Orlando), 412–413
Universal's Cabana Bay Beach Resort (Orlando), 413
Universal's Endless Summer Resort (Orlando), 413
Victoria (New Smyrna Beach), 454
Victorian House Bed & Breakfast (St. Augustine), 472
Vinoy Resort and Golf Club, Autograph Collection (St. Petersburg), 326
W South Beach (Miami), 66
Walt Disney World Swan and Dolphin (Orlando), 404
Walt Disney World Swan Reserve (Orlando), 404–405

Weatherstation Inn (Key West), 203–204
The Westin Tampa Waterside, 312
Wyndham Grand Clearwater Beach, 337

Restaurants

1-800-LUCKY (Miami), 95
7th & Grove (Tampa), 317
11th Street Diner (Miami), 82
50's Prime Time Café (WDW), 418
aba (Miami), 85
Akershus Royal Banquet Hall (WDW), 417
Alabama Jack's (Key Largo), 3
Andiamo! Brick Oven Pizza (Miami), 97
Anthony's Coal Fired Pizza (Fort Lauderdale), 254
Anthony's Runway 84 (Fort Lauderdale), 254
Antonia's (Key West), 205
Ariete (Miami), 103
Armature Works (Tampa), 317
Atlantic's Edge (Islamorada), 173–174
Baba (St. Petersburg), 328
Bachour (Miami), 105
Banana Café (Key West), 206
Barracuda Grill (Marathon), 175
bb's restaurant and bar (Jacksonville), 487
Be Our Guest Restaurant (WDW), 416
Bella's Italian Cafe (Tampa), 314–315
bellwether (Jacksonville), 487
Bern's Steak House (Tampa), 12, 313
Biergarten Restaurant (WDW), 417
Big Pink (Miami), 82
Bigfire (Universal Orlando), 423
Biscotti's (Jacksonville), 488
Blase Martini Bar/Pi Pizza 3.14 (Siesta Key), 356, 358
Blue Collar (Miami), 96
Blue Heaven (Key West), 12, 207
Boat House Bar & Grill at Turtle Kraals (Key West), 208
Boat in the Moat (Sarasota), 351
The Boathouse (WDW), 421
Bob Heilman's Beachcomber (Clearwater Beach), 340
Bobby's Bistro (Clearwater Beach), 340
Bodega on Central (St. Petersburg), 328
Boia de (Miami), 96
Boma—Flavors of Africa (WDW), 419
Boo's Ice House & Dog Bar (Sarasota), 354
BO's Fish Wagon (Key West), 207–208
Bouchon (Miami), 105
Brett's Waterway Café (Amelia Island), 499
Brisky's (St. Augustine), 472
Brulé Bistro (Delray Beach), 271
Bubbalou's Bodacious Bar-B-Que (Orlando), 425
Buccan (Palm Beach), 289–290

Bulla Gastrobar (Miami), 107
Bunbury (Miami), 89–90
Burlingame (Amelia Island), 499
The Butcher's Club (Palm Beach), 289
Butterfly Café (Marathon), 174
The Café at Books & Books (Miami), 107
Café La Trova (Miami), 11, 98
Cafe l'Europe (Palm Beach), 290
Café Marquesa (Key West), 205
Café Martorano (Fort Lauderdale), 255
Cafe Maxx (Fort Lauderdale), 255
Cafe Prima Pasta (Miami), 85
Café Quiquiriquí (Tampa), 311
Caffe Abbracci (Miami), 105
California Grill (WDW), 420
Camellia Street Grill (Everglades), 230
Capri Restaurant (Everglades), 229
Cap's Place Island Restaurant (Fort Lauderdale), 257
Captain Morgan's Seafood Grill (Everglades), 229
Caretta on the Gulf (Clearwater Beach), 337
Carmine's Seventh Avenue (Tampa), 318
Casa D'Angelo (Fort Lauderdale), 255
Catch 27 (St. Augustine), 472–473
Catullo's Italian (Jacksonville), 488
The Cellar (Daytona Beach), 451
Ceviche Tapas Bar & Restaurant (St. Petersburg), 327
Chef Art Smith's Homecomin' (WDW), 421
Chef Michael's (Islamorada), 174
Chefs de France (WDW), 416
Christy's (Miami), 106
Chug's Diner (Miami), 103
Cinderella's Royal Table (WDW), 415
City Cellar Wine Bar & Grill (Palm Beach), 290
City Oyster (Delray Beach), 269
Coconut's (Fort Lauderdale), 257
Coco's Kitchen (Big Pine Key), 184
Collage (St. Augustine), 473
Columbia Harbour House (WDW), 415
Columbia Restaurant (Orlando), 424
Columbia Restaurant (St. Augustine), 472
Columbia Restaurant (Tampa), 12, 316–317
Connections Eatery (WDW), 418
Coolinary and the Parched Pig (Palm Beach), 291
Coral Reef Restaurant (WDW), 417
Cosmic Ray's Starlight Cafe (WDW), 415
Counter Culture (Tampa), 314
The Cowfish (Universal Orlando), 423
Crabby Bill's Seafood (St. Pete Beach), 339
Crimson House (New Smyrna Beach), 453

The Crystal Palace (WDW), 416
Cut 432 (Delray Beach), 269
Dada (Delray Beach), 271–272
Dimitri's on the Water (Tarpon Springs), 341
Dining Room at Little Palm Island (Little Torch Key), 183
Dockside Seafood Restaurant (Jacksonville), 488
Dogma Grill (Miami), 97
Down the Hatch (Daytona Beach), 450
Dunedin Mix, 323
Eating House (Miami), 106
Ebbe–Chef's Counter (Tampa), 316
edison: food+drink lab (Tampa), 314
El Palacio de los Jugos (Miami), 11, 108–109
El Rey de Las Fritas (Miami), 100
El Tenampa (Orlando), 424
Ela Curry & Cocktails (Palm Beach), 292
Élevage (Tampa), 310
Elisabetta's (Delray Beach), 272
Enriquetta's Sandwich Shop (Miami), 95
Ethos Vegan Kitchen (Orlando), 425
Eva (Miami), 103
Even Keel Fish Shack (Fort Lauderdale), 256
Everglades Gator Grill, 229
Farmer's Table (Boca Raton), 272
Fern Street Wine Bar & Kitchen (Palm Beach), 291
Fiola (Miami), 107–108
First Love Brewing (Amelia Island), 499–500
First Watch (Sarasota), 354
Fishlips Waterfront Bar & Grill (Cape Canaveral), 438
Flame Tree BBQ (WDW), 418
Flor Fina (Tampa), 311
Florida Keys Brewing Company, 176
Florida's Fresh Grill (Cocoa Beach), 438–439
The Floridian (St. Augustine), 12, 473
Food@Science (Miami), 123
Food+Beer (Sarasota), 354
Fourth Street Shrimp Store (St. Petersburg), 328
Foxy Brown (Fort Lauderdale), 257
Frenchy's Original Cafe (Clearwater Beach), 341
Frenchy's Outpost Bar & Grill (Dunedin), 341
Frenchy's Rockaway Grill (Clearwater Beach), 341, 342
Frenchy's Salt Water Café (Clearwater Beach), 341
Frenchy's South Beach Café (Clearwater Beach), 341
Front Porch Café (Miami), 82
G&B Oyster Bar (Fort Lauderdale), 257
Garcia's Seafood Grille & Fish Market (Miami), 90
Garden Grill (WDW), 418

519

RESTAURANT INDEX

GAS Full Service Restaurant (St. Augustine), 472
Georgie's Alibi (Fort Lauderdale), 259
Ghee Indian Kitchen (Miami), 108
Gilbert's 17th St. Grill (Fort Lauderdale), 258
Glass & Vine (Miami), 47, 104
Grandview Public Market (Palm Beach), 292
Green Turtle Inn (Islamorada), 174
Green's Pharmacy (Palm Beach), 292–293
The Grove (Delray Beach), 269
The Grove (Fort Lauderdale), 242
Guppy's on the Beach (Indian Rocks Beach), 340
Gypsy Cab Co. (St. Augustine), 473
Hakkasan (Miami), 83
Havana Harrys (Miami), 105
Haven (Tampa), 314
Hiyakawa (Miami), 93
Hogfish Bar & Grill (Key West), 209
Hollywood Brown Derby (WDW), 418
Honeybelle (Palm Beach), 289
The Honor Bar (Palm Beach), 291
Hot Tin Roof (Key West), 205
Howley's (Palm Beach), 293
Hurricane Seafood Restaurant (St. Pete Beach), 339
Indigenous (Sarasota), 354–355
Islamorada Fish Company, 176
Island Dogs Bar (Key West), 209
Island Grill (Islamorada), 176
Island Way Grill (Clearwater Beach), 342
J&J's Seafood Bar & Grill (Delray Beach), 269
Jaleo by José Andrés (WDW), 421
Jaxon's Ice Cream Parlor & Restaurant (Fort Lauderdale), 258
JB's on the Beach (Fort Lauderdale), 256
Jimmy's Eastside Diner (Miami), 98
Joe's Stone Crab Restaurant (Miami), 80
Joey Aventura (Miami), 86–87
Josh's Deli (Miami), 85
Julia & Henry's (Miami), 90–91
Julington Creek Fish Camp (Jacksonville), 474
The Katherine (Fort Lauderdale), 258
Katsura Grill (WDW), 417
Key Largo Conch House Restaurant & Coffee Bar, 175
Keys Fisheries (Marathon), 175–176
Kiki's Sandbar Bar & Grille (Little Torch Key), 182, 184
Knife & Spoon (Orlando), 424
Kōsen (Tampa), 316
La Camaronera Seafood Joint (Miami), 101
La Cantina de San Angel (WDW), 417
La Cava del Tequila (WDW), 417
La Crêperie de Paris (WDW), 416
La Hacienda de San Angel (WDW), 417
La Mar by Gaston Acurio (Miami), 88
La Mexicana Taco Bar (Fort Lauderdale), 259
La Nouvelle Maison (Boca Raton), 270
La Sandwicherie (Miami), 82–83
La Spada's Original Hoagies (Fort Lauderdale), 258–259
La Terrazza (Miami), 108
La Trattoria (Key West), 206
Latitudes (Key West), 205–206
Lazy Days (Islamorada), 176
Le Bouchon du Grove (Miami), 104
Le Cellier Steakhouse (WDW), 416
Le Tub (Fort Lauderdale), 254
Leddy's (Amelia Island), 498, 499
Lester's Diner (Fort Lauderdale), 254
Libby's Neighborhood Brasserie (Sarasota), 356
The Library (St. Petersburg), 328
Lilac (Tampa), 312
The Limani (Tarpon Springs), 341
Los Fuegos by Francois Mallmann (Miami), 84
Lost Boy Dry Goods (Miami), 92
Louie's Backyard (Key West), 206
Luca Osteria (Miami), 106
Lucali (Miami), 83
Luff's Fish House (Boca Raton), 272
Lung Yai Thai Tapas (Miami), 98, 100
Maass by Chef Ryan Ratino (Fort Lauderdale), 250, 254
Macchialina (Miami), 81
Makoto (Miami), 84
Mandolin Aegean Bistro (Miami), 96
Mangrove Mama's Restaurant (Sugarloaf Key), 183–184
Maritana (St. Pete Beach), 335
Marker 88 (Islamorada), 174
MaryGold's Brasserie (Miami), 93
Maty's (Miami), 11, 94
Maxine's on Shine (Orlando), 424–425
Meat Market (Tampa), 313
Mel's Hot Dogs (Tampa), 313
The Mermaid Café (New Smyrna Beach), 453
Miami Slice, 93
Michael's Genuine Food & Drink (Miami), 97
Michael's on East (Sarasota), 355
Mignonette (Miami), 91
Mise en Place (Tampa), 315
Monsieur Paul (WDW), 416
Moody Tongue Omakase (Palm Beach), 287
Moon Hut (Cape Canaveral), 439
Morgans (Miami), 94
Morimoto Asia (WDW), 421
Morton's Gourmet Market (Sarasota), 356
Motek (Miami), 87
Mykonos (Tarpon Springs), 341
NAOE Miami, 88
Neverland Coffee Bar (Miami), 87
New York Prime (Boca Raton), 270
Nine One Five (Key West), 207
NIU Kitchen (Miami), 92
No Name Pub (Big Pine Key), 184
Nomad Lounge (WDW), 419
Norman's (Orlando), 424
North Beach Fish Camp (Neptune Beach), 474
Oceans 234 (Fort Lauderdale), 256
Off the Hook at Inlet Harbor (Daytona Beach), 450–451
Off the Hook Raw Bar & Grill (New Smyrna Beach), 451
Okeechobee Steakhouse (Palm Beach), 290
Old Key Lime House (Lantana), 273
Olivia (Tampa), 313
OMAKAI (Miami), 104
The Original Wolfie's & Rascal House (Sarasota), 354
Orsay (Jacksonville), 488
Oxford Exchange (Tampa), 315
Pacific Rim (Sarasota), 356
Palm Beach Grill, 291
Palm Valley Fish Camp (Ponte Vedra Beach), 474
Panther Coffee (Miami), 93
Pao by Paul Qui (Miami), 84
Paradise Grille (St. Pete Beach), 339
Pastis Miami, 94
PB Catch (Palm Beach), 291
The Pearl (Tampa), 317
Pepe's (Key West), 207
Pier 62 Oceanfront Restaurant and Bar (Cocoa Beach), 438
Pierre's (Islamorada), 11, 175
Pig Beach BBQ (Palm Beach), 293
Pit Bar-B-Q (Everglades), 229
Pogo's Kitchen (Amelia Island), 500
Polite Pig (WDW), 422
Porky's Bayside Restaurant & Marina (Key Largo), 176–177
Prohibition Kitchen (St. Augustine), 474, 476
Pub on the Drive (Fort Lauderdale), 259
Puerto Sagua (Miami), 83
The Purple Olive Restaurant & Wine Lounge (St. Augustine), 474
Q'Kenan (Orlando), 425
Queen Miami Beach, 80–81
Raglan Road Irish Pub and Entertainment (WDW), 422
Red Bud Cafe (Daytona Beach), 451
Red Mesa Cantina (St. Petersburg), 329
Red Rooster Overtown (Miami), 88–89
Regatta Grove (Miami), 105
The Restaurant (West Palm Beach), 282
Restaurant BT (Tampa), 314
Reunion Kitchn Bar (Miami), 87

Rhythm Café (Palm Beach), 291–292
The Ringling Grillroom (Sarasota), 349
The River Oyster Bar (Miami), 92
Rooster & The Till (Tampa), 317
Rosa Mexicano (WDW), 420
Rose & Crown (WDW), 416
Rosie's Bar & Grill (Fort Lauderdale), 259
Roundup Rodeo BBQ (WDW), 418
Rustic Inn Crabhouse (Fort Lauderdale), 255–256
Rusty Pelican (Miami), 102–103
Sal's Ballyhoo's (Key Largo), 177
Salt (Amelia Island), 499
Salt Life Food Shack (Jacksonville), 489
The Salt Rock Grill (Indian Rocks Beach), 340
San Angel Inn Restaurante (WDW), 417
Sanguich (Miami), 101
Sanpocho (Miami), 101
Satu'li Canteen (WDW), 419
Sci-Fi Dine-In Theater Restaurant (WDW), 418
Seaspice (Miami), 89
Seven Fish (Key West), 206
Seven Mile Grill (Marathon), 173
Singleton's Seafood Shack (Jacksonville), 12, 489
Sistrunk Marketplace (Fort Lauderdale), 259–260
SIX (Tampa), 311
SKOB (Siesta Key), 356, 358
Snapper's (Key Largo), 177
Space 220 Restaurant (WDW), 418
Springs Taproom (Tampa), 300
St. Augustine Fish Camp, 474
Stage (Palm Beach), 292
State Street Eating House + Cocktails (Sarasota), 355

Steak 954 (Fort Lauderdale), 256
Steakhouse 71 (WDW), 420
Stonewood Tavern & Grill (Daytona Beach), 450
Strachan's Ice Cream & Desserts (Dunedin), 323
Stubborn Seed (Miami), 81
The Studio Public House (St. Petersburg), 329
Sugarcane Raw Bar Grill (Miami), 94
Sun Garden Cafe (Siesta Key), 357
The Surf Club Restaurant (Miami), 84–85
Sweet Liberty Drinks & Supply Company (Miami), 81–82
Swifty's (Palm Beach), 288
Tablé by Bachour (Miami), 97
Takumi-Tei (WDW), 417
Tam Tam (Miami), 92
Tap Room Restaurant + Bar (St. Petersburg), 327
Taquiza Tacos (Miami), 85
Taste of Maharaja (Daytona Beach), 451
Ted Peters' Famous Smoked Fish (St. Pete Beach), 339
Teppan Edo (WDW), 416
Terras Rooftop (Miami), 101
Thai Me Up (Fort Lauderdale), 259
Third Wave Café & Wine Bar (New Smyrna Beach), 453
Tiffins Restaurant (WDW), 419
Timoti's Seafood Shak (Amelia Island), 500
The Tin Muffin Cafe (Boca Raton), 273
Todd English's bluezoo (WDW), 420
Tokyo Dining (WDW), 416
Toothsome Chocolate Emporium & Savory Feast Kitchen (Universal Orlando), 423
Tramonti (Delray Beach), 269
Trattoria Romana (Boca Raton), 270

T-REX (WDW), 422
Tropical Acres Steakhouse (Fort Lauderdale), 258
Tropical Chinese (Miami), 108
Tropical Smokehouse (Palm Beach), 293
Tune-In Lounge (WDW), 418
Turtle Club (Key Largo), 177
Tusker House (WDW), 419
Tutto Italia Ristorante (WDW), 417
Twenty Twenty Grille (Boca Raton), 270–271
Verde (Miami), 125
Versailles (Miami), 102
Via Napoli Ristorante e Pizzeria (WDW), 417
Victoria & Albert's (WDW), 420
The Village Grille & Pump (Fort Lauderdale), 256
Voo La Voo Café (Fort Lauderdale), 259
Walrus Rodeo (Miami), 96
The Whale's Rib (Fort Lauderdale), 256
Whiskey Creek Hideout (Fort Lauderdale), 242
Whiskey Joe's Bar & Grill (Tampa), 315–316
White Lion Cafe (Everglades), 229
White Lion Cafe (Miami), 109
Wine Bar George (WDW), 422
Wink Wink Food & Drink (Sarasota), 352
Wolfie's Box Office (Sarasota), 354
Yak & Yeti Local Food Cafes (WDW), 419
Yak & Yeti (WDW), 419
Yoder's Restaurant & Amish Village (Sarasota), 355
Zak the Baker (Miami), 95
Ziggie and Mad Dog's (Islamorada), 175
Zitz Sum (Miami), 106–107
Zuma (Miami), 89

PHOTO CREDITS

Front cover: © ondrejsustik / Shutterstock; p. i: © Karl Shakur / Visit Florida; p. iii: © Nancy Pauwels / Shutterstock; p. 1: © Thierry Eidenweil / Shutterstock; p. 3: © A. Emson / Shutterstock; p. 6: © Margaret.Wiktor / Shutterstock; p. 7: © Larry Blackburn; p. 8: © Timothy Holle / Shutterstock; p. 9, top: © L Galbraith / Shutterstock; p. 9, bottom: © Miami2youPhoto / Shutterstock; p. 11: © Michael Gordon / Shutterstock; p. 12: © Daniel Korzeniewski / Shutterstock; p. 13: © Durden Images / Shutterstock; p. 14: © Leonard Zhukovsky / Shutterstock; p. 15: © Dennis MacDonald / Shutterstock; p. 19: © Dennis MacDonald / Shutterstock; p. 20: © Everett Collection / Shutterstock; p. 26: © Chuck Wagner / Shutterstock; p. 32: © Peter W. Cross and Patrick Farrell / Visit Florida; p. 34: © Daytona Beach Area CVB; p. 36: © Peter W. Cross and Patrick Farrell / Visit Florida; p. 38: © Darryl Brooks / Shutterstock; p. 39: © Trevor Green / Visit Florida; p. 40: © Andy Lidstone / Shutterstock; p. 41: © Ceri Breeze / Shutterstock; p. 43: © Sean Pavone / Shutterstock; p. 44: © Universal Parks USA; p. 45: © VIAVAL TOURS / Shutterstock; p. 46: © Wirestock Creators / Shutterstock; p. 47: © travelview / Shutterstock; p. 48: © Hayk_Shalunts / Shutterstock; p. 49: © Leonard Zhukovsky / Shutterstock; p. 50: © Daytona International Speedway; p. 51: © Sergio TB / Shutterstock; p. 55: © fotomak / Shutterstock; p. 56: Courtesy of the Greater Miami Convention and Visitors Bureau, MiamiandBeaches.com; p. 57: Courtesy of the Greater Miami Convention and Visitors Bureau, MiamiandBeaches.com; p. 64: © Richard Petronio / Shutterstock; p. 70: © Wirestock Creators / Shutterstock; p. 76: © Felix Mizioznikov / Shutterstock; p. 82: Courtesy of the Greater Miami Convention and Visitors Bureau, MiamiandBeaches.com; p. 90: © Felix Mizioznikov / Shutterstock; p. 91: © Sebastian Bednarski / River

PHOTO CREDITS

Oyster Bar; p. 95: Courtesy of the Greater Miami Convention and Visitors Bureau, MiamiandBeaches.com; p. 100, top: Courtesy of the Greater Miami Convention and Visitors Bureau, MiamiandBeaches.com; p. 100, bottom: Courtesy of the Greater Miami Convention and Visitors Bureau, MiamiandBeaches.com; p. 102: Courtesy of the Greater Miami Convention and Visitors Bureau, MiamiandBeaches.com; p. 106: © Merge Studios / Visit Florida; p. 110: © EQRoy / Shutterstock; p. 112: © xbrchx / Shutterstock; p. 114: Courtesy of the Greater Miami Convention and Visitors Bureau, MiamiandBeaches.com; p. 117: Courtesy of the Greater Miami Convention and Visitors Bureau, MiamiandBeaches.com; p. 118: © godongphoto / Shutterstock; p. 119: Courtesy of the Greater Miami Convention and Visitors Bureau, MiamiandBeaches.com; p. 121: Courtesy of the Greater Miami Convention and Visitors Bureau, MiamiandBeaches.com; p. 122: © Peter W. Cross / Visit Florida; p. 124: Courtesy of the Greater Miami Convention and Visitors Bureau, MiamiandBeaches.com; p. 125: © Aleksandr Dyskin / Shutterstock; p. 127: © Feng Cheng / Shutterstock; p. 128: Courtesy of the Greater Miami Convention and Visitors Bureau, MiamiandBeaches.com; p. 129: © Erika Cristina Manno / Shutterstock; p. 131: Courtesy of the Greater Miami Convention and Visitors Bureau, MiamiandBeaches.com; p. 133: © JHVEPhoto / Shutterstock; p. 134: © Felix Mioznikov / Shutterstock; p. 136: © meunierd / Shutterstock; p. 139: © Celso Diniz / Shutterstock; p. 142: Courtesy of the Greater Miami Convention and Visitors Bureau, MiamiandBeaches.com; p. 145: Courtesy of the Greater Miami Convention and Visitors Bureau, MiamiandBeaches.com; p. 147: Courtesy of the Greater Miami Convention and Visitors Bureau, MiamiandBeaches.com; p. 151: Courtesy of the Greater Miami Convention and Visitors Bureau, MiamiandBeaches.com; p. 153: © MDV Edwards / Shutterstock; p. 154: © Connect Images - Curated / Shutterstock; p. 160: © Scott Barnette / Visit Florida; p. 163: © pisaphotography / Shutterstock; p. 164: © Maridav / Shutterstock; p. 166: © Off Axis Production / Shutterstock; p. 168: © Peter W. Cross and Patrick Farrell / Visit Florida; p. 169: © Emergent Media / Visit Florida; p. 179: © Jacqueline Faust / Shutterstock; p. 180: © moosehenderson / Shutterstock; p. 188: © travelview / Shutterstock; p. 189: © Chuck Wagner / Shutterstock; p. 190: © EWY Media / Shutterstock; p. 194: © Dennis MacDonald / Shutterstock; p. 196: © Steve Smith / Shutterstock; p. 202: © Fotoluminate LLC / Shutterstock; p. 208: © Elena Elisseeva / Shutterstock; p. 209: © Fotoluminate LLC / Shutterstock; p. 210: © Daniel Korzeniewski / Shutterstock; p. 211: © Terry Kelly / Shutterstock; p. 213: © Mia2you / Shutterstock; p. 215: © Charles Lillo / Shutterstock; p. 218: © Inga Locmele / Shutterstock; p. 219: © DnDavis / Shutterstock; p. 221: © Olivia Novak / Shutterstock; p. 222: Courtesy of the Greater Miami Convention and Visitors Bureau, MiamiandBeaches.com; p. 224: © Francisco Blanco / Shutterstock; p. 226: Courtesy of the Greater Miami Convention and Visitors Bureau, MiamiandBeaches.com; p. 229: Courtesy of Captain Morgan's Seafood Grill; p. 231: © Kelly vanDellen / Shutterstock; p. 234: © YES Market Media / Shutterstock; p. 237: © Scott Barnett / Visit Florida; p. 241: © Scott Barnett / Visit Florida; p. 243: © Steve Beaudet / Visit Florida; p. 244: © YES Market Media / Shutterstock; p. 245: © Brian Logan Photography / Shutterstock; p. 247: © Henryk Sadura / Shutterstock; p. 252: © Bilanol / Shutterstock; p. 256: © NPI Productions / Visit Florida; p. 257: © Visit Florida; p. 259: © YES Market Media / Shutterstock; p. 263: © Peter W. Cross / Visit Florida; p. 265: © Matthew Klingsberg / Shutterstock; p. 266: © Wagner Santos de Almeida / Shutterstock; p. 271: Courtesy of Subculture Group; p. 276: © Leonard Zhukovsky / Shutterstock; p. 281: © mariakray / Shutterstock; p. 282: © Leonard Zhukovsky / Shutterstock; p. 285: © Sean Pavone / Shutterstock; p. 287: © EQRoy / Shutterstock; p. 293: © Emergent / Visit Florida; p. 295: © 500PX / Visit Florida; p. 298: © Art_Gants / Shutterstock; p. 302: © Visit Tampa Bay; p. 307: © Keir Magoulas / Visit Tampa Bay; p. 311: © Noah Densmore / Shutterstock; p. 314: © Emergent Media / Visit Florida; p. 315: © Visit Florida; p. 318: © Visit Florida; p. 320: © Michael O'Keene / Shutterstock; p. 321: © Kevin McGeever / Visit Florida; p. 324: © Chase D'animulls / Shutterstock; p. 328: © Emergent Media / Visit Florida; p. 330: © Visit Florida; p. 332: © Spark / Visit Florida; p. 334: © Brenda Kean / Shutterstock; p. 345: © Visit Florida; p. 348: © Kevin McGeever / Visit Florida; p. 353: © Visit Sarasota County; p. 357: © Sean Pavone / Shutterstock; p. 359: Courtesy Disney; p. 363: Courtesy Disney; p. 365: Courtesy Disney; p. 371: Courtesy Disney; p. 376: © Jason Cochran; p. 378: © Jason Cochran; p. 380: Courtesy Disney; p. 381: Courtesy Disney; p. 383: Courtesy Disney; p. 385: Courtesy Disney; p. 388, top: © 2021 Universal Orlando. All Rights Reserved; p. 388, bottom: © 2021 Universal Orlando. All Rights Reserved; p. 391: © 2021 Universal Orlando. All Rights Reserved; p. 394: Courtesy of Seaworld Orlando; p. 395: © Mia2you / Shutterstock; p. 397: © Joseph M. Arseneau / Shutterstock; p. 412: © Anatoliy Tesouro / Shutterstock; p. 427: © Rob Wilson / Shutterstock; p. 431: © Emergent Media / Visit Florida; p. 432: © Mia2you / Shutterstock; p. 433: © Robert Hoetink / Shutterstock; p. 435: © Wilfred Marissen / Shutterstock; p. 440: © Daytona Beach Area CVB; p. 443: © Daytona International Speedway; p. 445: © Daytona Beach Area CVB; p. 446: © Museum of Arts & Sciences; p. 452: Courtesy of Crabby Joe's; p. 455: © Sean Pavone / Shutterstock; p. 459: © Anurak Pankham / Shutterstock; p. 460: © Kristi Blokhin / Shutterstock; p. 461: © Dennis MacDonald / Shutterstock; p. 475: © Vy Nguyen Films / Visit Florida; p. 476: © Red Lemon / Shutterstock; p. 481: © EWY Media / Shutterstock; p. 494: © Sean Pavone / Shutterstock; p. 496: © Joni Hanebutt / Shutterstock; p. 501: © John Athanason / Visit Florida; back cover: © Jose Luis Stephens / Shutterstock.